The Law of Torts

The Law of Torts

Eighth Edition

Margaret Brazier LLB, Barrister
Senior Lecturer in Law
at the University of Manchester

Butterworths
London, Edinburgh
1988

United Kingdom	Butterworth & Co (Publishers) Ltd, 88 Kingsway, LONDON WC2B 6AB and 61A North Castle Street, EDINBURGH EH2 3LJ
Australia	Butterworths Pty Ltd, SYDNEY, MELBOURNE, BRISBANE, ADELAIDE, PERTH, CANBERRA and HOBART
Canada	Butterworths. A division of Reed Inc., TORONTO and VANCOUVER
New Zealand	Butterworths of New Zealand Ltd, WELLINGTON and AUCKLAND
Singapore	Butterworth & Co (Asia) Pte Ltd, SINGAPORE
USA	Butterworths Legal Publishers, ST PAUL, Minnesota, SEATTLE, Washington, BOSTON, Massachusetts, AUSTIN, Texas and D & S Publishers, CLEARWATER, Florida

British Library Cataloguing in Publication Data
Brazier, Margaret, *1950–*
    The law of torts.–8th ed.
    1. England. Torts. Law
    I. Title II. Street, Harry, 1919–1984. Law
    of torts
    344.2063
    ISBN 0 406 66211 8 Hardcover
          0 406 66212 6 Softcover

Printed and bound in Great Britain by
Butler & Tanner Ltd, Frome and London

Preface

Harry Street's untimely death in 1984 deprived the present generation of law students of his inimitable and incisive analysis of the law of torts. Manchester University lost one of its most eminent scholars and the Faculty of Law his guidance and example. My own debt to him as a student and later a colleague is beyond repayment. I have been conscious in producing this new edition of *Street on Torts* of his abiding influence and I hope that despite the changes in the work the book retains the crisp and radical nature of Harry's original enterprise.

The expansion in negligence noted by Professor Street in the preface to the previous edition has come to a sharp halt since then. I doubt whether the new mood of judicial caution would win his commendation. The chapters on negligence have been largely rewritten to take account of current developments both in case law and academic literature. Parliament has also been active, and the Police and Criminal Evidence Act 1984, the Latent Damage Act 1986 and the Consumer Protection Act 1987 are fully dealt with. I have resisted the temptation to treat negligence as the tort *par excellence*. This new edition seeks to emphasise the continuing relevance of the intentional torts. To this end Part VI on intentional interference with economic interests has been substantially revised and becomes Part III of this edition.

My thanks are due to all my colleagues and students who have listened so patiently as I tested my ideas on them. I acknowledge, in particular, the help given to me by Jean McHale who did an invaluable task in researching materials for Part VIII on remedies and by Lesley Anderson, Richard Bragg and Hazel Carty who read and commented on a number of chapters in draft. I must also thank the secretaries in the Faculty of Law who coped with my handwriting with such skill.

March 1988   Margaret Brazier

Contents

CHAPTER 29   COMPENSATION FOR PERSONAL INJURIES 477

CHAPTER 30   EXTINCTION OF REMEDIES 500

Abbreviations

American Restatement	Restatement of the Law of Torts (American Law Institute).
Aus LJ	Australian Law Journal
Blackstone	Commentaries on the Laws of England, by Sir William Blackstone (1796).
Camb LJ	Cambridge Law Journal.
Can BR	Canadian Bar Review.
Clerk and Lindsell	Law of Torts by J F Clerk and W H B Lindsell (15th edn, 1982).
Comyns	Comyns' Digest of the Laws of England (5th edn, 1822).
Fleming	Law of Torts by J G Fleming (5th edn, 1977).
Gatley	Law and Practice of Libel and Slander by J C Gatley (8th edn, 1981).
Green	Judge and Jury by Leon Green (Kansas, 1930).
Halsbury	The Laws of England (4th edn, 1973–83).
Harper and James	Law of Torts by F V Harper and F James (1956).
Harv LR	Harvard Law Review.
HFI	History of English Law, by Sir William Holdsworth (1922–38).
Kenny	Outlines of Criminal Law (17th edn, 1958 by J W Turner).
LQR	Law Quarterly Review.
MLR	Modern Law Review.
Munkman	Employer's Liability at Common Law by J Munkman (9th edn, 1979).
Pollock	The Law of Torts by Sir F Pollock (15th edn, 1952, by P A Landon).
Porter Report	Report of the Committee on the Law of Defamation (Cmd 7636, 1948).
Prosser	Handbook of the Law of Torts by W L Prosser (3rd edn, 1964).
Report	Third Report of the Law Reform Committee (Occupiers, Liability to Invitees, Licensees and Trespassers) (Cmd 9305, 1954).
Russell	On Crime (12th edn, 1964, by J W C Turner).
Salmond & Heuston	Law of Torts by Sir John Salmond (19th edn, 1987, by R F V Heuston).
UTLJ	University of Toronto Law Journal.
Williams, *Animals*	Liability for Animals by Glanville L Williams (1939).
Williams, *Bankruptcy*	Law and Practice in Bankruptcy by Sir Roland Williams (18th edn by Muir Hunter, 1968).
Williams, *Joint Torts*	Joint Torts and Contributory Negligence by Glanville I Williams (1950).
Winfield & Jolowicz	Law of Tort by Sir Percy Winfield (12th edn, 1984).
Winfield, *Cases*	Cases on the Law of Tort by Sir Percy Winfield (4th edn, 1948).
Winfield, *Present Law*	Present Law of Abuse of Legal Procedure, by P H Winfield.
Winfield, *Province*	Province of the Law of Tort by P H Winfield (1931).

Table of statutes

References in this Table to *Statutes* are to Halsbury's Statutes of England (Fourth Edition) showing the volume and page at which the annotated text of an Act will be found.

List of cases

Pages on which cases are principally treated are indicated by the use of bold figures.

Part I

Introduction[1]

1 See Winfield *Province;* Glanville Williams 'The Foundations of Tortious Liability' (1939) 7 Camb LJ III; and 'The Aims of the Law of Tort (1951) Current Legal Problems 137; Seavey 'The Principles of Torts' (1942) 56 Harvard LR 72; Wright 'The Law of Torts; 1923–47' (1948) 28 Can BR 46; Prosser ch 1; G Williams and BA Hepple *Foundations of the Law of Tort* (2nd edn, 1984) Butterworths; J G Fleming *The Law of Torts* (6th edn).

CONTENTS

Chapter 1

General observations

SECTION 1. DIFFICULTY IN ARRIVING AT A DEFINITION OF TORTS

Much ink has been spilt in unsuccessful attempts to define a tort[1]. No further attempt will be made here, since, as Pollock said,[2]

> there is ... rather too much talk about definitions. A definition, strictly speaking, is nothing but an abbreviation in which the user of the term defined may please himself ...

It is the function and purpose of the law of torts that are of greater import, and these are matters which can be explained in comparatively simple terms.

The law of torts is concerned with those situations where the conduct of one party causes or threatens harm to the interests of other parties. One may define 'interest' in the context as

> a claim or want or desire of a human being or group of human beings which the human being or group of human beings seeks to satisfy, and of which, therefore, the ordering of human relations in civilised society must take account.[3]

It is accordingly the aim of the law of torts to define the obligations imposed on one member of society to his or her fellows, and to adjust, once it is decided that some adjustment is to be made, those losses which must inevitably result from the ever-increasing activities of those who live in a common society. This adjustment is made by providing compensation for the harm suffered by those whose interests have been invaded owing to the conduct of others.

It is true that the same circumstances may give rise both to an action in tort and one for breach of contract: for example, a medical practitioner who negligently treats his patient may have broken an implied term in his contract to take reasonable care, and at the same time his conduct will constitute an invasion of a tort-protected interest, viz, the interest in freedom from physical harm, for which an action in negligence will lie. Apart from the formal distinction that the contractual duty may be said to spring from agreement of the parties, whereas the tortious one is created by operation of law independently of the consent of the parties, there is a substantial difference in the respective aims of the two. The purpose of contract is always to protect the same single interest: the interest in the performance of promises by others, whereas, as will be seen in the list set out later in this chapter, the interests protected in tort are very diverse.

Certain types of conduct simultaneously constitute both a crime and a tort; thus the thief who steals my watch commits both the crime of theft and

---

1 For a detailed treatment, see Winfield *Province* ch 1.
2 Book review (1931) 47 LQR 588.
3 Pound *Selected Essays* 86.

the tort of conversion. The function of criminal law is to protect the interest of the public at large (or of the State)—whereas the primary aim of the law of torts is to protect the interests of individuals rather than to punish certain categories of wrongdoer.

The same circumstances may give rise to actions both in tort and in quasi-contract, as will be seen when the problem of election of remedies is later considered.[4] The underlying purpose of this group of fictitious contracts implied by law would seem to be the prevention of unjust enrichment of one man at the expense of another, and not to compensate a man for a loss which he has suffered in respect of a particular interest. Further, an action by the Crown for the recovery of a penalty under a statute is not a claim in tort: it is a public claim, not one for the protection of any individual's interest.[5]

SECTION 2. ISSUES COMMON TO ALL TORTS

In most branches of English law the effect of historical accidents and procedural requirements is to obstruct orderly and scientific exposition—this is especially true of branches such as the law of torts where the sources are to be found mainly in common law and not in statute law. The difficulties in tort are magnified by the fact that the situations where clashes of interests occur have been continually increasing and taking on new forms, with the result that the development and expansion of the law has been called for.

In the nineteenth century railways, and in the twentieth motor vehicles have had great impact on the law relating to accidents. Broadcasting and television have necessitated changes in the law of defamation, and in the future satellite broadcasting and cable television will no doubt occasion more. Pirating of tapes, both sound and video, is now posing new issues in economic torts. The complexities of modern industrial organisation—trade unions, company conglomerates—induce reactions in tort law from judges and Parliament alike. More involved methods of manufacture and marketing of goods have been factors influencing the introduction of strict liability for defective goods; relationships are infinitely more diverse than when the maker of goods customarily used to sell them directly to the person who used them.

In the light of these considerations it would not be surprising therefore if the law of torts has in some instances aims other than compensating for (or even preventing the recurrence of) harms sustained by private individuals. Occasionally, the effect of the law of torts is to aid the administration of the criminal law (as with the former rule that prosecutions for felony had to precede an action in tort on the same facts[6]) or to punish a wrongdoer (eg by the award of exemplary damages[7]). These deviations are, however, justifiable, or, at least, explicable on historical or other grounds. Thus they need not prevent our accepting that the primary aim of the law of torts is to compensate those who have suffered harm through the invasion of certain of their interests occasioned by the conduct of others.[8]

Three issues are common, then, to all cases in tort.

4 See p 472, post.
5 *A-G v Canter* [1939] 1 KB 318.
6 See 7th edn of this work at p 89.
7 See p 466, post.
8 For another view, see Glanville Williams 'The Aims of the Law of Tort, (1951) CLP 137.

1 What interests does the law of torts protect?
2 Against what general types of conduct, malicious, intentional, negligent, or accidental, are these several interests protected?
3 When will conduct of a defendant, which would normally be a tort in accordance with points 1 and 2 above, not subject him to liability because there is some special circumstance which requires an exception to the general rule? Thus, to arrest another is ordinarily a tort, but a policeman, or even a private person, may in certain circumstances be authorised to make an arrest, whereupon he will have a defence to an action in tort. Many defences are common to most and perhaps all torts—these are often styled general defences. Examples of these general defences are consent, statutory authority, judicial act. For convenience, these defences will be discussed in the Part of the book dealing with intentional interference with persons and property, but it must be firmly grasped that they are capable of being defences to torts other than those examined in that Part.

It is probably generally true that whereas in the development of some torts, eg interference with the right to vote, or defamation (interest in reputation), the emphasis has been on the nature of the interest violated, in many others, eg negligence, the stress has been on the character of the act of the defendant. Although it is usual to expound the law of torts by stressing the wrong of the defendant rather than the interest of the plaintiff, it has been found convenient in the present work to emphasise the interest of the plaintiff.

SECTION 3.   THE VARIOUS INTERESTS PROTECTED BY THE LAW OF TORTS

The interests which the law of torts protects will be examined in the following order.

A. INTENTIONAL INVASION OF PERSONAL AND PROPRIETARY INTERESTS

The protection of the person from deliberately inflicted physical harm and restriction on freedom of movement, and the protection of interests in tangible property, especially the right to non-interference with land and goods, were historically the most important concerns of the law of torts. Their importance will be recognised by dealing first with the invasion of these interests by intentional conduct: the relevant torts include interference with goods and trespass in its various forms.

B. INTERESTS IN ECONOMIC RELATIONS, BUSINESS AND TRADING INTERESTS

The extensive protection afforded to individuals' interests in freedom from physical harm and in their property is not mirrored by similar protection of interests in economic and business activities. The so-called 'economic torts' remain unclear in their scope and bedevilled by their relationship with ever-changing legislation on trade union immunities. Furthermore very real difficulties exist in reconciling protection of one individual's economic interests with the concept of free competition in a market economy. Torts in this area include deceit, passing off, interference with contractual relations, conspiracy and intimidation.

C. INTERESTS IN INTELLECTUAL PROPERTY

Interests in tangible property, in land and in goods are as we shall see well protected by the common law. Intellectual property in confidential information, in copyright, in patents, poses greater problems. Much of the law in this field is statutory and interests in intellectual property generally overlap with interests in economic relations. But this is not invariably so. For example, breach of confidence, as yet an embryonic and even disputed tort, protects a patient's right to confidentiality from his doctor as much as a multinational company's right to protection of their trade secrets.

D. NEGLIGENT INTERFERENCE WITH PERSONAL, PROPRIETARY AND ECONOMIC INTERESTS

Protection of persons and property limited to deliberately inflicted harm would be manifestly inadequate in our complex and overcrowded world. Since the landmark judgment of *Donoghue v Stevenson* in 1932 the courts have rapidly, albeit with occasional trepidation, developed the tort of negligence as it safeguards interests in physical safety and freedom from damage to tangible property. Just as protection of economic interests from deliberate harm has proved problematical so have the judges adopted a cautious and unpredictable approach to protecting economic interests from negligently inflicted harm.

E. FURTHER PROTECTION OF PERSONAL AND PROPRIETARY INTERESTS

Personal and proprietary interests rank so highly in the order of priority of interests protected by the law of torts that further torts have emerged offering protection for those interests against conduct which is not necessarily, or cannot be proved to be, either intentional or negligent. There are torts of ancient origin such as nuisance and the rule in *Rylands v Fletcher*. These highlight the importance vested by the common law in the landowner's interest in his enjoyment of his property. The action for breach of statutory duty represents the common law's response to Parliamentary intervention usually to improve standards of public health and personal safety. Most importantly and recently strict liability for injuries caused by defective and dangerous goods has been introduced into English law at the behest of the European Community.

F. REPUTATION

The law of torts has long protected individuals' interest in their reputation

via the torts of libel and slander. To some extent the embryonic tort of breach
of confidence also fulfils this function.

G. DUE PROCESS

A right to protection from malicious abuse of the judicial process is recognised
in the tort of malicious prosecution and its ancillary tort of abuse of process.
Now it seems that a tort to prevent abuse of the administrative process is in
its early infancy.

H. MISCELLANEOUS INTERESTS

This residual group includes the remaining and largely peripheral interests
protected by the law of torts.

SECTION 4.   SOME CONSEQUENCES OF THIS EMPHASIS ON THE INTERESTS PROTECTED

A. A LAW OF TORT OR A LAW OF TORTS?

A discussion of the question whether there is a law of tort or a law of torts
is thus rendered superfluous. It is inconsistent with the authorities to contend
that the infliction of unjustifiable harm is always a tort. On the other hand,
there is no fixed catalogue of circumstances which alone and for all time
mark the limit of what are torts. There is no problem peculiar to the law of
torts here. Certain situations have been held to be torts and will continue to
be so in the absence of statutory repeal (similarly, others have been held not
to be torts, and courts upon which those decisions are binding will follow
them). These fundamental points are also often camouflaged behind the Latin
maxims *damnum sine injuria* and *injuria sine damno*, which (not because of
their aid to understanding, but because the student may meet them elsewhere)
must be shortly explained. *Damnum sine injuria* merely means that a man
may have suffered damage and yet have no action in tort—in short, the
damage is not to an interest protected by the law of tort. *Injuria sine damno*
is a shorthand version of the rule that some interests are so important that
their violation is an actionable tort without proof of damage.

B. MALICE OR MOTIVE

Likewise it is unprofitable to dwell here on the importance of motive or
malice. It follows from what has been said that an act, even though it is
malicious, will not be a tort unless the interest which it violates is protected
by some tort. On the other hand, if the interest interfered with is rated so low
in the hierarchy of tort-protected interests that only malicious invasions are
forbidden, that will be a case where malice will be essential to liability: which
these are the reader will see for himself as he progresses through the book.

   The catalogue of torts is very much more extensive than it was, say, two
hundred years ago. This expansion is the work of the judges, in whose
handling of the precedents one may detect the same characteristics as are

found in other branches of the law: logic and the use of analogy, appropriate, though imprecise, reflection of contemporary social and economic attitudes, recognition of the guiding (and sometimes cramping) effects of history and the like. At the same time, it may be worth while to enumerate some general considerations which are a guide to an understanding of the law of torts, past, present and future.

SECTION 5.   'GHOSTS FROM THE PAST'

FORMS OF ACTION

Until the passing of the Common Law Procedure Act 1852 and the Judicature Act 1875 a plaintiff could only sue in tort if he brought his cause of action within a recognised form of action, ie one for which some particular writ of summons was available. Although the forms of action are now abolished, many old cases cannot be understood without some knowledge of forms of action.[9] Moreover, classifications of torts derive from the various writs, so that rules worked out under them have necessarily been the jumping-off place for any growth in the law of torts which has taken place since. Many seemingly arbitrary divisions between one tort and another to-day are explained only by reference to the forms of action. Thus, the writ of trespass lay only for direct injuries; the form of action known as action on the case developed separately for indirect injuries: it will be seen[10] that even now trespass is not committed where the injury is indirect.

A plaintiff does not have to *plead* a tort of negligence, trespass or whatever. In his pleading he merely sets out the relevant facts. Torts 'overlap' when on those facts he might have succeeded by contending at trial that they satisfied the requirements of either tort. To state, for example, that the plaintiff might have succeeded had he relied on nuisance rather than on negligence, means that if the plaintiff had argued that the facts proved satisfied all the requirements of the tort of nuisance he would have succeeded even though those facts did not contain all the elements of the tort of negligence. The plaintiff's error will be one of oral argument, not of pleading, except when he fails to plead an allegation of fact which, although not material in negligence, would have been requisite for nuisance. Strictly speaking, a judge could find for the plaintiff merely by holding that, on the facts proved, there was a tort. But, given the splitting up into compartments of the law of torts, he will ordinarily decide that the plaintiff wins because the defendant has committed some specific tort. The law does not say that intentionally and carelessly inflicted harm will be tortious in certain circumstances: it defines the limits of each tort, many of which overlap, eg the same facts could be negligence, nuisance and *Rylands v Fletcher*—and says to the plaintiff: 'You win if you establish facts which satisfy the definitions of any one of those torts.' With regard to any particular decided case, the student is then concerned to know, not only that the plaintiff has succeeded on certain facts, but also which tort has been committed, for he then learns the elements of that tort. Normally a court cannot be expected to find for a litigant on the basis of arguments which he has not advanced in court. If the facts pleaded constitute nuisance but not

---

9 Williams and Hepple *Foundations of the Law of Tort* ch 2, 'The Ghost Story'. See Sutton *Personal Actions at Common Law* (1929), and Bullen and Leake's *Pleadings* (3rd edn, 1868).
10 See p 24, post.

negligence he can hardly complain at losing when he fails to argue before the court that the tort of nuisance has been committed.

SECTION 6.   GENERAL ISSUES AND THE LAW OF TORTS

A. CONFLICT BETWEEN CERTAINTY AND JUSTICE

The conflict between the demands of certainty and justice is a recurrent theme in case law. The claims of certainty are less pressing in the case of the law of torts than in some other branches, eg the law of property. The purchaser of land must be assured that the law on the faith of which he acquires a good title is not liable to change; it is less important that the law should settle precisely and for all time, say, the limits of liability of area health authorities for harm caused to their patients. Yet, the development of some torts has been seriously affected by the judicial urge for that certainty which is believed by many to result from making rigid categories—the courts have, for example, thought fit to divide entrants on to land into three rigid categories: invitees, licensees and trespassers, in order to determine the duty of occupiers to them in respect of their personal safety—with the result that in 1957 the Occupiers' Liability Act had to be passed in order to clear up the confusion that this method had brought about.[11]

B. JUDICIAL CAUTION IN RESPECT OF NON-MATERIAL HARMS

Damages in many torts cannot be fixed with mathematical precision: the problem, say, of calculating damages in the tort of false imprisonment is different entirely from that of measuring damages in an action for breach of contract based on failure to perform a contract for the sale of goods. The courts have properly been on their guard to restrain gold-digging actions. Sometimes, they have perhaps been excessively wary, and later courts have had to overrule earlier decisions—for example, the courts at first refused to recognise nervous shock as a head of damage.[12]

C. THE JUDGES AND LAISSEZ-FAIRE

Much of the law relating to economic transactions is only understood if the implied judicial acceptance of *laissez-faire* is considered. This is merely one facet of the individualism of the law of torts, especially in the nineteenth century—an influence which still persists, although less pervasively,[13] in the face of the modern tendency towards collectivism.

---

11 See chapter 16, post.
12 See p 177, post.
13 For an evaluation of the influence of collectivism on recent development of the law of torts see Friedmann 'Social Insurance and the Principles of Tort Liability' (1949) 63 Harvard LR 241, substantially reproduced in his *Law and Social Change in Contemporary Britain* (1951) ch 4.

D. LIMITS OF THE EFFECTIVENESS OF THE LAW OF TORTS

The law of torts is essentially practical. Judges have little patience with trivial claims—for example, they may deny a remedy by way of trespass to the person for mere touching.[14] They recognise the limits of the wrongs which the law is capable of redressing, however morally reprehensible they may be—avarice, brutal words, ingratitude, for instance, are not dealt with by the law of torts. Along with this is a judicial dread of a flood of actions. For this reason the courts have so far been reluctant to allow claims for negligently inflicted foreseeable economic loss where the range of claimants as a result of one incident might be large.[15]

E. LOSS DISTRIBUTION

The traditional approach of the law of torts has been merely to ask whether a loss which B has suffered should be shifted to A. If A were at fault the answer would usually be to shift that loss from innocent B to wrongdoer A. Many judges, for instance Viscount Simonds twenty years ago and Lord Diplock today, say that this is indeed the one judicial function in the law of torts. There is, however, another view: by spreading the loss from an individual victim to many who benefit from an activity that has caused it, the loss is more easily borne. The employer whose workman is injured can spread the loss through raising the price of his product. The same argument applies where his product injures a consumer. This principle of loss distribution is seen in the firm acceptance of vicarious liability: that an employer is answerable for the torts committed by those who work for him. It is the reason why courts have rejected the argument that if a manufacturer has a contractual liability to X he cannot have a tortious liability to Y—the manufacturer is today answerable to the eventual user of his carelessly made defective goods.

This notion of loss distribution is reinforced by insurance. The employer or manufacturer or vehicle owner can readily insure (and indeed is often compelled) against the risk of his negligently inflicting harm on third parties. He pays the premium which can be reflected in the price mechanism or result in all those who are in the same class of insured persons paying premiums reflecting the damages which insurers have to meet. Some judges, notably Lord Denning, overtly acknowledged that judges are the readier to find negligence or to make high compensatory awards when they know that the damages will be paid by an insurance company. It must be said that other judges take notice of insurance in order to refuse an extension of tort boundaries. For example, law lords have refused to make car owners vicariously liable whenever members of their family negligently cause accidents, and other judges have refused to allow claims for widespread economic losses on the ground that insurance companies have fixed their premiums on the assumption that such liabilities did not exist and would therefore not be covered by their insurance policies.

14 See p 21, post.
15 See p 185, post.

F. ECONOMICS AND LAW

Much academic interest has been engendered in recent years by economic analysis of law.[16] The law is criticised and evaluated on the basis of criteria of economic efficiency. So in the context of torts the crucial issue becomes whether the operation of the particular tort is cost effective.[17] The principal objectives should be not to eliminate all damage but to deter conduct resulting in damage where the cost of accident prevention is less than the cost of the accident occurring. On such criteria any change from negligence based liability to strict liability would have to depend on proof that the total additional costs to the potential defendants, additional precautions, insurance and so on, did not exceed the total cost to individuals of the risk created by the enterprise. Concepts of fairness and justice can be relevant only if susceptible to being assigned economic value.

Economic analysis is a useful tool to attain understanding of the operation of certain torts, in particular negligence and product liability. It offers a measure by which our often confused system of compensation law may be judged and found wanting. Economic analysis can never be an all-embracing explanation of the objective of the law of torts, nor have English judges expressly relied on academic exposition of economic analysis when making law.[18] Economic efficiency is simply one of the several and sometimes contradictory objectives of tort.[19] The law is not the marketplace and efficiency must always be subordinated to justice to individuals.

G. THE FUTURE

The wide range of social security benefits and other state funds available for accident victims will be looked at briefly later. They do raise a fundamental question for later discussion. Is the law of torts the appropriate mechanism for accident compensation? Or should social security schemes take over exclusively? Or is there a case for the continuance of both tortious remedies and government-funded social security payments to victims? In so far as the case for social security to replace tort is made out, why should victims of accidents caused by third parties be better treated than those suffering accidents in the home or those who are merely sick from natural causes? As we shall see, a Royal Commission on Civil Liability and Compensation for

16 For a general introduction to economic analysis see P Burrows and C G Veljanowski *The Economic Approach to Law* (1981) and A I Ogus and C G Veljanowski *Readings in the Economics of Law and Regulation* (1984).

17 G Calabresi *The Cost of Accidents* (1970); R A Posner *The Economic Analysis of Law* (3rd edn, 1987); R A Posner *Tort Law—Cases and Economic Analysis* (1982) illustrates the application of economic analysis in case law in the USA.

18 Although they do take economic efficiency into account in determining the limits of liability for negligence. See post at pp 185–193 on the limits of liability for economic loss and then read W D Bishop 'Economic Loss in Tort' (1982) 2 Oxford J Legal Studies.

19 As economic analysis develops, more emphasis has been placed on the regulatory aims of torts. Could the desired result, minimising risk and damage, be more effectively and cheaply achieved by concentrating resources on regulations aimed at accident prevention? For example rather than imposing extra cost on the pharmaceutical industry via strict liability (see post at ch 18) should we use that money to enhance the operation of the Committee for Safety of Medicines which grants licences to market pharmaceuticals. On law and regulation generally see Ogus and Veljanowski op cit.

Personal Injury spent five years on this matter before reporting in 1978[20] with some compromise proposals which would have left the tort system substantially intact.[1] There is, however, little prospect of the Government enacting its proposals.

20 Cmnd 7054.
 1 See p 498, post.

Part II

Intentional invasions of interests in person and property

CONTENTS

Chapter 2

Intentional torts today

The examination of the rules of the various torts will begin with a discussion of those torts which effect an intentional interference with interests in the person and in property.

Most of the torts examined in this Part are forms of trespass: the separate tort of Negligence will be examined in Part IV. Before proceeding to a detailed consideration of these various torts, one may usefully consider three matters of general importance: the relationship of trespass to negligence; and the sense in which, the extent to which, in trespass an intentional act on the part of the defendant is required, and the context in which intentional torts, in particular trespass, remain relevant today.

SECTION 1. TRESPASS AND NEGLIGENCE[1]

Compensation for injuries to the person and to property was first given by the courts from at least the thirteenth century onwards. By this time writs of trespass were in common use. A suit in trespass could succeed only where the interference was 'direct'; the action on the case was developed for injuries not 'directly' inflicted. The Court of Appeal has held that it is still not enough to set out in the writ the facts and the relief or remedy sought—the writ must also state the cause of action.[2] An allegation of trespass will still fail if the act of the defendant is not direct,[3] although, of course, some other right of action in tort may lie.

Until 1965 one could confidently say that trespass and negligence overlapped in that both might be available where direct injuries were sustained as a result of non-accidental conduct. (The 1965 case of *Letang v Cooper* will be considered two pages later.) Nevertheless, one is justified in treating trespass under the heading of 'intentional invasions' because, in practice, the separate tort of negligence is almost always relied on if the conduct of the defendant is negligent, but not intentional. There are several explanations of this.[4]

1 A claim based on negligence is not affected by any doubt there may be whether the injury is direct.
2 The writ of trespass did not lie against a master for the torts of his servant.[5]

---

1 See Trindade (1971) 20 ICLQ 706.
2 *Sterman v E W Moore Ltd* [1970] 1 QB 596, [1970] 1 All ER 581, CA
3 For the meaning of 'direct' in the various forms of trespass, see pp 24, 65, post.
4 See Winfield and Goodhart (1933) 49 LQR 359.
5 *Sharrod v London and North Western Rly Co* (1894) 4 Exch 580. Nevertheless, under the old writ system an action on the case would have lain against the master even for the intentional wrongdoing of a servant: *Seymour v Greenwood* (1861) 7 H & N 355; *Bayley v Manchester, Sheffield and Lincolnshire Rly Co* (1873) LR 8 CP 148. Although then, LORD TUCKER accurately states in *Esso Petroleum Co Ltd v Southport Corporation* [1956] AC 218 at 244,

15

On the other hand, it is possible that trespass has one advantage over negligence where negligent conduct is complained of. Perhaps in trespass the plaintiff does not have to prove that the defendant owed him a duty of care—it may be enough if the defendant did not show towards the plaintiff the care of a reasonable man.[6] Although it is true that the judicial trend (and that of the Bar) is towards actions based on negligent conduct being treated as actions of negligence merely, the notion that trespass lies for negligent acts, for example, the direct application of force to the person (a battery[7]), seems too firmly rooted to be displaced now. In those instances where there was no duty in negligence though harm to the plaintiff was foreseeable, then, trespass, but not negligence, might lie. It is impossible to be sure of this, because the courts have usually stated in these cases that there must be 'negligence', without indicating whether they meant a negligent (ie careless) trespass or something which would give rise to an action of Negligence. For instance, it will be seen later[8] that a duty of care to trespassers is not owed merely because their presence is foreseeable: if A carelessly (even though not recklessly) shoots on his land and hits a trespasser of whose presence he was unaware but ought to have known, the trespasser may be able to recover in trespass to the person.[9]

The further question, whether an act of the defendant, which is in its nature careless and a breach of a duty owed to some third party but which is not careless with reference to the plaintiff, is also actionable in trespass (though it certainly is not in negligence), is more doubtful. A hits a golf ball without warning B, who is on the green a hundred yards ahead—no doubt B could sue A either in trespass or in negligence for this careless act if he were hit. But suppose C is sleeping in rough grass off the fairway and is hit by A's shot in circumstances where A could not have foreseen this consequence of his 'careless' act, although C's injury is the direct result of A's act—an action in negligence would fail, and it is thought unlikely that an action alleging trespass would succeed.[10]

[1955] 3 All ER 864 at 873, HL that *trespass* does not lie against the servant's master, this does not mean that the master can only be sued if the servant's conduct constitutes negligence—an action derived from the old action on the case will still lie against the master where an act committed by his servant in the course of his employment, although it does not constitute negligence, does constitute an intentional trespass. This distinction between trespass and negligence is therefore of little importance since the abolition of the forms of action eg *National Coal Board v J E Evans & Co (Cardiff) Ltd and Maberley Parker Ltd* [1951] 2 KB 861, [1951] 2 All ER 310, and see p 18, post. This same difference may give trespass an advantage over negligence. Suppose that a trespass is committed in circumstances which humiliate or insult the plaintiff but he suffers no other damage. No action in negligence would lie but under the rules about aggravated damages in trespass (p 466, post) that damage would be recoverable in trespass; see *Fogg v McKnight* [1968] NZLR 330.

There is at least another minor difference. Trespass is actionable *per se*; in negligence damage must be proved. If, therefore, there is an interval between the wrongful act and the occurrence of damage, an action of trespass may be time-barred before one of negligence; cf *Roberts v Read* (1812) 16 East 215.

6 The meanings of 'duty of care' and 'reasonable man' are examined in Part IV, post.
7 See p 21, post.
8 See p 270, post.
9 Unless, as in *National Coal Board v J E Evans & Co (Cardiff) Ltd and Maberley Parker Ltd* [1951] 2 KB 861, [1951] 2 All ER 310, the damage is held attributable to the plaintiff's own misconduct.
10 Goodhart would apparently find this a trespass on the basis that C's damage resulted directly from *A's act of intentionally hitting the ball*; see his criticism of the *American Restatement, Torts* (1st edn) § 18, illustration 3, in (1935) 83 U of Pennsylvania LR 411 at 417. And see

There is a similar problem in relation to remoteness of damage. We shall see that in negligence the defendant is liable for only that harm which materialises in a foreseeable way; if the defendant should have foreseen that he might damage the plaintiff's goods by impact he is not liable when his careless act sets fire to them.[11] It is undecided whether this rule extends to trespass.

All these examples are a heritage of the distinctions which were based on the forms of action. The judge's instinct will be that if a plaintiff is the victim of carelessness he should succeed on the tort of negligence or fail. He will strive to deny the continuance of different rules in trespass when the effect would be to give a remedy in trespass for careless conduct in circumstances where an action in negligence would fail. What remains uncertain is how far a judge will feel free to attain his objective when to do so entails ignoring the historical origins and basis of trespass.

Letang v Cooper shows how the judges approach this problem.[12]

> The defendant negligently drove his Jaguar on an hotel's grass car park over the legs of the plaintiff who was sunbathing. More than three years later the plaintiff sued the defendant. Actions for 'negligence, nuisance or breach of duty' are barred after three years and other tort actions are barred after six years. The plaintiff relied on trespass in an effort to prevent her action from being time-barred.

Naturally the Court of Appeal did not wish to reach the absurd conclusion that trespass would still lie, although negligence would not. Therefore they made good the draftsman's ambiguities by holding that 'breach of duty' covered trespass as well as negligence. LORD DENNING MR and DANCKWERTS LJ also held that the distinction between trespass and case is obsolete; that there is no overlap of trespass and negligence—if the act is intentional it is trespass and not negligence, if the act is negligent, it is negligence and not trespass. DIPLOCK LJ accepted that trespass could still be committed negligently, but expressly refrained from considering whether there were any substantive differences between negligent trespass and negligence. *Letang v Cooper* illustrates the current judicial tendency to avoid overlap of trespass and negligence. It is too soon to conclude that trespass has no relevance when negligent conduct is relied on.

SECTION 2.   INTENTION AND TRESPASS

The mental state of the doer of an act is often important in tort. It is essential to distinguish motive, intention, negligence, accident, and involuntariness. An act may be regarded as a muscular contraction or relaxation that is not effected under compulsion, either by acts or events. In order to determine

the discussion of the allied problem of 'transferred intent' with regard to intentional acts, p 22, post.

11 Page 225 et seq, post. Similarly, in *Williams v Humphrey* (1975) Times, 20 February, where the defendant pushed the plaintiff into a swimming pool, and the latter sustained a serious ankle injury, in trespass the injury was compensable merely on proof that the damage was direct, whereas in negligence the plaintiff also had to prove that the defendant's push created the foreseeable risk of the ankle injury.

12 [1965] 1 QB 232, [1964] 2 All ER 929, CA.

whether a tort has been committed intentionally, one must ask: what constitutes for the purpose of the particular tort an invasion of the interest of the plaintiff, and then whether the defendant, in doing this act, desired that invasion as a consequence. There is, however, one refinement of this which makes difficulties. If in the circumstances he had knowledge that his conduct was substantially certain to result in that act (not merely that he might have foreseen the result) his act would still be deemed to be intentional. Consequences ulterior to those consequences which constitute the tortious invasion of the interest of the plaintiff may be desired by the defendant. For example, a defendant may disable the plaintiff in order to prevent him from competing against him in a race; when, as in battery, the tort itself is concerned with the intentional striking, those desired consequences more remote than the striking itself may be called 'motive'. 'Motive' is also properly used to describe the emotion which prompts the defendant to commit the act; for example, rage, hatred or jealousy. An act is negligent when a reasonable man would have foreseen that it would lead to the particular invasion of the plaintiff's interest which constitutes that tort. There are some torts where there may be a liability for acts that are neither intentional nor negligent, ie for accidental acts. Yet, in such cases, although the doer neither intended nor ought to have foreseen the consequences he must have done the act—there must be a muscular reaction which is something more than a reflective one, one which is not effected under compulsion.

If a man throws a stone at a woman, his trespass to her person is intentional; that he threw it because she had jilted him would be immaterial in determining his liability in trespass—that would be his motive. If he did not throw the stone for the purpose of hitting her but ought to have foreseen that it was likely that the stone would hit her, his act would be unintentional but nevertheless negligent. If the stone hit her solely because it rebounded off a tree at which he had thrown it his conduct would be voluntary, ie the hit would be accidental. But, if, while he was holding the stone in his hand, a third party seized his arm and by twisting it compelled him to release his hold on it, whereupon it fell on the woman, his conduct would be involuntary and could never give rise to liability on his part.

That trespass (and the rules are the same whether it be trespass to person, land, or goods) can be committed either intentionally or negligently, and that it cannot be committed involuntarily[13] is plain—the difficulty concerns the non-negligent and unintentional act. The early common lawyers were not interested so much in the mental state of the defendant but were satisfied to ask whether the defendant by his act inflicted on the plaintiff the harm complained of.[14] With the development of the separate tort of negligence in the nineteenth century the problem of accidental trespass became important and was examined in a series of important cases.[15] The effect of these cases (however challengeable their interpretation of older cases may be[16]) is that in the absence of negligence a suit alleging trespass based on an unintentional act will not now succeed. Moreover, it was decided in *Fowler v Lanning* (1959)

---

13   *Weaver v Ward* (1616) Hob 134; *Gibbons v Pepper* (1695) 1 Ld Raym 38.
14   HEL vol viii 456–8.
15   *Holmes v Mather* (1875) LR 10 Exch 261; *Stanley v Powell* [1891] 1 QB 86; *Gayler and Pope Ltd v Davies (B) & Son Ltd* [1942] 2 KB 75; *Manton v Brocklebank* [1923] 2 KB 212, CA; *National Coal Board v Evans (J E) & Co (Cardiff) Ltd* [1951] 2 KB 861; cf *Morriss v Marsden* [1952] 1 All ER 925.
16   See *Pollock* 128 (Editor's Excursus B).

that the plaintiff in trespass has the burden of proving negligence on the part of the defendant.[17]

SECTION 3.   RELEVANCE OF TRESPASS TODAY

A glance at indices to the law reports will reveal several judgments in negligence and perhaps one or two judgments in trespass to the person, to goods or land. Does this evidence indicate either that these intentional torts are failing in their purpose, or that trespass should be regarded as of historic interest only? Certainly not. First the boundaries set by the trespass torts on intentional, deliberate interference with another's person or property are well understood in society generally. All sorts of grey areas exist in negligence, for example, the extent to which the law protects individuals against emotional distress,[18] or businesses against loss of profits.[19] Fewer such grey areas afflict trespass. That the civil law complements the criminal law in prohibiting one man from beating another, or seizing his goods, or invading his land, is clear beyond debate. As it is often grey areas of the law which generate contested litigation, a proliferation of trespass claims is not to be expected. The obligations imposed on each member of society to his or her fellows are in general defined with precision by the trespass torts.[20]

Secondly, good practical reasons can be seen to explain why even if many individuals did, or do, breach those obligations imposed on them by the trespass torts few victims would go to court to sue for compensation. The tort of trespass to the person overlaps to a considerable extent with crimes of assault. The rate of reported criminal assaults far exceeds that of writs issued for trespass to the person. This is because, of course, the perpetrator of the criminal assault is rarely worth suing. He has no funds from which compensation may be claimed. If the criminal has funds then he can and may well be pursued in the civil courts. In 1986 the press made a great hullabaloo over the award of just over £17,000 in damages to two women who had been viciously and sexually assaulted. They hailed it as a novel case of compensation for rape victims.[1] In law the women's claim was far from novel. There can scarcely be a clearer example of trespass to the person than rape. What was exceptional was that the rapist had earlier been awarded £45,000 compensation for injuries which he had suffered in a road accident. These injuries included brain damage resulting in a change of personality responsible for the aggressive and perverted sexual impulses motivating his attacks on the women.[2]

17 [1959] 1 QB 426, [1959] 1 All ER 290, which made generally applicable a rule which had not been extended hitherto beyond trespasses on or adjoining highways, as in *Holmes v Mather* supra, and in *dicta* of LORD BLACKBURN in *River Wear Commission v Adamson* (1877) 2 App Cas 743. *Ctra McHale v Watson* (1965) 111 CLR 384 (H Ct Australia).
18 See later at pp 177–181.
19 See later in ch 12.
20 But see *Wilson v Pringle* [1987] QB 237 post at p 21.
 1 *W v Meah, D v Meah* [1986] 1 All ER 935. The main interest of the case is that the women were awarded only £17,000. Was this sufficient compensation for their injuries and trauma?
 2 *Meah v McCreamer* [1985] 1 All ER 367; and see Meah's unsuccessful attempt to recover the £17,000 which he was ordered to pay *his* victims from insurers of the defendant in the road accident claim *Meah v McCreamer (No 2)* [1986] 1 All ER 943. Consider generally the circumstances in which victims of criminal assault can use the trespass torts. Parents of two of the young women murdered by Peter Sutcliffe, the 'Yorkshire Ripper', recovered for their

Finally, estimating the importance of litigation in the trespass torts from judgments cited in an index under the headings of assault and battery or trespass is misleading. There are several important judgments on police powers the essence of which are the limits the trespass torts place on the police in the execution of their duties.

First, the Police and Criminal Evidence Act 1984 authorises police officers to do a variety of acts which were they not justifiable as the exercise of statutory powers to arrest persons, or seize goods, or enter property, would constitute trespass. Where an officer exceeds those powers he commits a trespass and a civil action will lie against him and his Chief Constable. For example, an arresting officer may use reasonable force. For several officers to thrust an elderly man to the floor of a police van and sit on him exceeds any reasonable degree of force required.[3] In this and similar cases we shall see that the issue as it reaches law reports is not has there been a trespass; it is rather, was the behaviour of the police such an abuse of power that they ought to have to pay additional exemplary damages.[4]

Second, several recent cases explore the limits of police powers to take informal action to pursue their inquiries at the stage where officers are not yet ready to arrest or formally search a person. What steps may a policeman take to attract a citizen's attention, to encourage him to answer his questions? A tap on the shoulder to attract the man's attention is permissible. Grabbing and holding his elbow is not.[5] The policeman may not exceed the generally acceptable contacts we all impliedly agree to in our crowded society. His conduct may be judged in the light of the task which he has in hand. But he has no powers additional to those of the ordinary citizen save those expressly conferred on him by statute. Judgments on these vital issues of civil liberties arise generally not by means of the individual aggrieved suing the police but in a criminal prosecution for assaulting a police officer in the execution of his duty. The man touched by the police officer pushes him off. The question of whether he has criminally assaulted the officer depends on whether the prior act of the officer exceeded his lawful powers so making that act a trespass against the accused to which he could respond with reasonable force.

The intentional torts, and trespass in particular, are far from at death's door. They define the limits of acceptable conduct between citizen and citizen, and between individuals and the police. They have a crucial role to play in support of our right to individual autonomy and freedom from harassment. The foundation of civil liberties in England lies still in the trespass torts.

---

loss occasioned by the battery that led to their daughters' death after criminal bankruptcy proceedings against Sutcliffe resulted in funds being available for them to claim against.
3 *Allen v Metropolitan Police Comr* [1980] Crim LR 441.
4 See, for example, *Holden v Chief Constable of Lancashire* [1987] QB 380, [1986] 3 All ER 836; *George v Metropolitan Police Comr* (1984) Times, 31 March; and see generally *Clerk and Lindsell* para 14–79 and post at p 466.
5 See *Collins v Wilcock* [1984] 3 All ER 374, [1984] 1 WLR 1172; and see generally *Clerk and Lindsell* ch 26.

Chapter 3

Intentional torts to the person

SECTION 1.   BATTERY

The form of trespass to the person known as battery is any act of the defendant which directly and either intentionally or negligently causes some physical contact with the person of the plaintiff without the plaintiff's consent.

A. STATE OF MIND OF THE DEFENDANT

Today most suits for battery are likely to be based on an intentional act of the defendant. Where the act causing contact with the plaintiff results from the defendant's carelessness the claim will usually lie in negligence. *Letang v Cooper*[1] cannot be regarded as finally eliminating claims for negligent trespass, but the plaintiff will gain little or no advantage from so categorising his claim.

What is crucial then is to define what state of mind is required of the defendant to render him liable in battery. He must have intended a contact with the plaintiff. But is proof of a deliberate voluntary touching of the plaintiff sufficient? He need not have intended the plaintiff any harm. Battery is actionable per se without proof of any injury or damage to the plaintiff. He must have understood that his conduct was beyond the bounds of physical contact '... generally acceptable in the ordinary conduct of everyday life.'[2] The Court of Appeal held in *Wilson v Pringle*[3] that the plaintiff must show that the defendant's touching of the plaintiff was a 'hostile' touching. Hostility is not to be equated with ill-will or malevolence. It means an understanding by the defendant that he is doing something that the plaintiff may object to, that the plaintiff may regard as an unlawful intrusion on his rights to physical privacy and personal autonomy. Thus bare averments that one 13 year old boy jumped on another in the course of horseplay were insufficient of themselves to establish a battery. Further evidence of intent to injure or distress the plaintiff was called for. Had a grown man engaged in similar conduct the result might well have been different. Off the sportsfield mature adults do not generally regard it as acceptable conduct for their colleagues to leap at them and wrestle them to the ground.

Lack of hostility in the sense the term is used in *Wilson v Pringle* gives one explanation too of why the casualty surgeon operating in emergency on an unconscious patient does not commit a battery.[4] He is not acting with

1 [1965] 1 QB 232, [1964] 2 All ER 929 CA.
2 *Collins v Wilcock* [1984] 3 All ER 374 at 378, [1984] 1 WLR 1172 at 1178.
3 [1987] QB 237, [1986] 2 All ER 440; contrast the facts and decision of this case with *Williams v Humphrey* (1975) Times, 20 February (15-year-old schoolboy liable for prank of pushing another boy into swimming pool).
4 *Wilson v Pringle* supra at 447. Alternative explanations of why the surgeon is not liable in battery are (a) implied consent by the patient or (b) a defence of necessity in emergency.

'hostility' towards his patient. He does not act beyond the limits of what is generally acceptable in modern society. The term 'hostility' can be misleading though. A surgeon operating to sterilise a severely mentally handicapped woman may be motivated by what he perceives as her 'best interests'. Where she is incapable of giving a valid consent to surgery he may still commit a battery if he acts without the sanction of a court.[5] There is no lawful authority justifying his unpermitted contact with the woman, save where intervention to protect her health is immediately necessary.

Battery is both a tort and a crime and in many cases it is accordingly important to know to what extent criminal cases are relevant in tort. Perhaps the position is accurately stated in *Scott v Shepherd*:[6] 'And though criminal cases are no rule for civil ones, yet in trespass I think there is an analogy.' If A intends to hit B with a stone thrown by him in circumstances that would have amounted to the crime of battery were he to hit B but A hits C instead, although with regard to C the conduct of A is neither intentional nor negligent, A commits a crime.[7] The point is undecided in tort; it is difficult to forecast whether the courts would, like the American ones, follow the criminal analogy by having recourse to a fiction of 'transferred' intent.[8] It is arguable that such conduct should be branded as morally wrong, and thus deserving of criminal punishment, and yet that, unless the defendant could have foreseen harm to the plaintiff, there is insufficient relationship towards him to entitle him to a remedy in tort. Both motive and malice are irrelevant in determining liability for battery, though either may affect the amount of damages.

B. NO CONSENT BY THE PLAINTIFF

The absence of consent is so inherent in the notion of a tortious invasion of interests in the person that the absence of consent must be established by the plaintiff. So, it has been held that 'an assault must be an act against the will of the party assaulted: and therefore it cannot be said that a party has been assaulted by his own permission'.[9]

Any lingering doubt that the onus of proving absence of consent lies on the plaintiff was laid to rest in *Freeman v Home Office (No 2)* .[10] A prisoner alleged that he had been injected with powerful mood-changing drugs against his

---

5   *Re B (A Minor) (Wardship: Sterilisation)* [1987] 2 All ER 206, [1987] 2 WLR 1213 HL; *Re X* (1987) Times, 4 June; *Re T* (1987) 131 Sol Jo 1286 (the difficulty is whether even the court has any power to authorise treatment of incompetent adults).

6   (1773) 2 Wm Bl 892 at 899 (per DE GREY CJ); cf *Coward v Baddeley* (1859) 4 H & N 478 at 480 (per POLLOCK CB).

7   *R v Latimer* (1886) 17 QBD 359 (unlawful wounding).

8   *American Restatement, Torts* (2d). §32. Winfield, in a note at (1935) 83 U of Pennsylvania LR 416, n 15 accepted this doctrine of transferred intent in the English law of torts. Is an intention to cause an apprehension of harm enough? Eg A swings a golf club near B in order to alarm him; without negligence on his part, the head flies off and hits B. Can B sue A? In *Livingstone v Ministry of Defence* (1984) 15 NIJB, CA it was held that where the defendant fired a baton round injuring the plaintiff it mattered not whether he fired at P or another person; the defendant was guilty of battery unless he could prove lawful justification for his act.

9   *Christopherson v Bare* (1848) 11 QB 473 at 477 (per PATTESON J).

10   [1983] 3 All ER 589 at 594–5; affd by the Court of Appeal, [1984] QB 524, [1984] 1 All ER 1036.

will. The judge held that the essence of battery is a specific and unpermitted intrusion on the plaintiff's body. Unless the plaintiff can establish that the intrusion was unpermitted no battery is proved. A contrary result would have posed severe problems for all doctors, not just prison medical officers. Any contact with the patient, from surgery, through vaccinations to examining sore throats with a spatula would be prima facie a battery. The doctor would have to prove consent. Where minor procedures were in issue and no written consent had been obtained, or if records were lost, or the doctor had died,[11] this would pose acute difficulties for the defendant. On the other hand in the context of actions by suspects against the police, or prisoners against prison authorities, casting the burden of proving lack of consent on them, their word against those in power, against 'respectable' members of society, may make the action for battery a less effective weapon to enforce civil liberties for all.

C. THE CHARACTER OF THE ACT OF THE DEFENDANT

There is no battery unless there is an act by the defendant. Merely to obstruct entrance to a room by standing still is not of itself enough.[12] No battery is committed if there is an incident over which the defendant has no control; he is not liable where a frightened horse runs away with him and collides with the plaintiff.[13]

There can be no battery unless there is contact with the plaintiff. Is any contact, however slight, enough? It would be rational to say that this tort protects not merely the interest in freedom from bodily harm, but also that in freedom from insult. There does not, however, seem to be any express authority for the latter proposition. If there were such a rule, it would explain why spitting in the face is battery but touching another in a crowd is not. Further, the views of HOLT CJ, 'that the least touching of another in anger is battery' but that 'if two or more meet in a narrow passage, and without any violence or design of harm, the one touches the other gently, it is no battery'[14] may be reconciled as follows. The courts cannot, and should not be expected to, give protection against these unavoidable incidents of everyday life, and thus his second statement[15] can be classed as an example of a permitted contact, and for the reasons already given, not tortious. Battery, then, protects a person against all unpermitted contacts, irrespective of

---

11 As the prison doctor in *Freeman v Home Office* (No 2) had.
12 *Innes v Wylie* (1844) 1 Car & Kir 257 at 263 (per LORD DENMAN CJ). A motorist who accidentally drives his car on to a police constable's foot while parking his car commits no battery but does he if he then ignores the constable's plea to 'Get off my foot?'; *Fagan v Metropolitan Police Commissioner* [1969] 1 QB 439, [1968] 3 All ER 442.
13 *Gibbons v Pepper* (1695) 2 Salk 637; *Weaver v Ward* (1616) Hob 134; *Holmes v Mather* (1875) LR 10 Exch 261.
14 *Cole v Turner* (1704) 6 Mod Rep 149.
15 This explains, too, the *dictum* in *Tuberville v Savage* (1669) 1 Mod Rep 3, that striking another on the breast in discourse is not actionable. What if a police constable who knows that a passing pedestrian does not wish to answer his questions continues to tap him on the shoulder so that he will stop to be interrogated?; *Donnelly v Jackman* [1970] 1 All ER 987.

whether there is physical harm or insult. So, taking fingerprints,[16] spitting in one's face,[17] cutting one's hair against one's will[18] are all batteries.

As for all trespasses to the person, the act must be a 'direct' one; it is not enough that the act 'causes' the contact.[19] Contact must immediately follow from the act of the defendant;[20] it must be a continuation of his act.[1] For a ship to ram another may be a trespass despite the effect of the current,[2] but where A struck B's horse which ran off and threw B, who was trampled on by the horse of a third party, B could not recover damages from A in trespass.[3]

The contact must be with the person of the plaintiff. But, it is trespass to the person to throw over a carriage or chair in which the plaintiff is sitting.[4] If battery protected against insult generally and not merely against bodily harm, then contact with anything so closely attached to or associated with the person that it could be regarded as part thereof would be treated as a battery. The matter was investigated in *Pursell v Horn*[5] where it was decided that throwing water on to the clothes being worn by the plaintiff was not necessarily battery. This case suggests that contact with things attached to the person may be battery only if there is a transmission of force to the body of the plaintiff.[6] The protection from insult or indignity afforded by the tort of battery is limited to insult or indignity inflicted by touching another person, however trivial the touching may be.[7]

D. DAMAGES

Battery, like all suits in trespass, is actionable *per se*, ie without proof of damage. It seems also that, once the tort is proved, consequential loss in respect of goods, as well as the personal damage sustained, can be recovered.[8] Despite the doubt whether there is a battery when the contact injures merely feelings without causing physical contact, the courts can award additional

---

16 *Dumbell v Roberts* [1944] 1 All ER 326 at 330 (per SCOTT LJ); *Callis v Gunn* [1964] 1 QB 495, [1963] 3 All ER 677.
17 *R v Cotesworth* (1704) 6 Mod Rep 172.
18 *Forde v Skinner* (1830) 4 C & P 239; cf *Nash v Sheen* (1953) Times, 13 March (application to the plaintiff's hair of a 'tone-rinse', the dye in which caused a rash, by the defendant hairdresser, to whom the plaintiff went for a permanent wave, held to be actionable trespass).
19 See p 26, post.
20 *Leame v Bray* (1803) 3 East 593 at 603 (per LE BLANC J).
1 *Scott v Shepherd* (1773) 2 Wm Bl 892 at 899 (per DE GREY CJ).
2 *Covell v Laming* (1808) 1 Camp 497.
3 *Dodwell v Burford* (1670) 1 Mod Rep 24. Is it a battery if A pulls away B's chair as he is about to sit on it, whereupon B falls to the floor? If X cuts a rope to which Y is holding, or if X waggles it? Presumably to daub a towel with the intention that another should wipe his face on it, which he does, is too indirect for trespass. It is important to notice that there may be an action on the case even though trespass is not proved; pp 26 et seq, post. Cf *Sadler v South Staffs etc Tramways Co* (1889) 23 QBD 17.
4 *Hopper v Reeve* (1817) 7 Taunt 698.
5 (1838) 8 Ad & El 602.
6 LORD DENMAN CJ, at 604: 'It must imply personal violence.' PARKE B, held in *R v Day* (1845) 4 LT OS 493 that it was the crime of battery to slit with a knife the clothes which a man was wearing, and although the man's hand was cut this did not seem material because it was cut in reaching for the knife.
7 Is kissing a sleeping lady in the presence of her friends a battery? It is suggested that it is.
8 *Glover v London and South Western Rly Co* (1867) LR 3 QB 25; and pp 464 et seq, post.

damages on account of insult or injury to feelings for a battery which has also caused harm.[9]

SECTION 2.   ASSAULT

That type of trespass to the person known as assault is any act of the defendant which directly and either intentionally or negligently[10] causes the plaintiff immediately to apprehend a contact with his person.

It may seem surprising that the law of tort should protect an interest in freedom from one particular form of mental anxiety. The explanation must be that since assaults were likely to result in breaches of the peace trespass was invoked in order to enforce the criminal law. This association with criminal law, and the fact that the search for a rational basis for compensation in the form of the plaintiff's apprehension[11] is comparatively recent, explain the emphasis in the old cases on the intention of the defendant rather than on the effect produced on the plaintiff—there is therefore difficulty in reconciling some old and new cases.

A. THE CHARACTER OF THE DEFENDANT'S CONDUCT

The law of assault is substantially the same as that of battery except that apprehension of contact, not the contact itself, has to be established. Usually when there is a battery, there will also be an assault, but not, for instance, when a person is hit from behind. To point a loaded gun at the plaintiff, or to shake a fist under his nose, or to curse him in a threatening manner, or to aim a blow at him which is intercepted, or to surround him with a display of force,[12] is to assault him. Clearly, if the defendant by his act intends to commit a battery and the plaintiff apprehends it, it is an assault. What must be apprehended, however, is actual physical contact. Photographing a person against his will is an intrusion on his privacy but not an actionable assault.[13]

The effect of the origin of this tort on the present law is seen when one asks whether to brandish an unloaded pistol is an assault. In 1840 it was still being said that this was not assault because the defendant could not have intended a battery.[14] TINDAL CJ had said ten years previously that 'it is not every threat, when there is no actual physical violence, that constitutes an

---

9 *Loudon v Ryder* [1953] 2 QB 202, [1953] 1 All ER 741, CA. There is little in the way of authority on quantum of damages for battery in *W v Meah, D v Meah* [1986] 1 All ER 935 WOOLF J awarded Miss W £6,750 for a horrifying and degrading sexual assault and Mrs D £10,250 for a brutal rape.

10 It is in accordance with principle to include foreseeable though unintended harm, but decisions are lacking. E g if a defendant unintentionally brandishes a stick close to a lady, but without intending to hit or alarm her, it is submitted that his conduct is tortious if he could reasonably foresee that his act would have one of those effects. C A Wright (1957) 4 SPTLJ (NS) 29 would not require the harm to be foreseeable by the defendant, *sed quaere*.

11 Cf *Comyns*, II, 275.

12 *Read v Coker* (1853) 13 CB 850.

13 *Murray v Minister of Defence* [1985] 12 NIJB 12.

14 *Blake v Barnard* (1840) 9 C & P 626; *Winfield*, 53, regards this as the *ratio*, but it seems that the *ratio* of LORD ABINGER was that since the plaintiff in his declaration averred that a 'loaded' gun was pointed at him, and then sought a verdict at the trial on the basis that it was unloaded, there was no evidence to go to the jury on the facts set out in the declaration.

assault, there must, in all cases, be the means of carrying the threat into effect'.[15] These cases have not been overruled, but it is the *ratio* of one criminal case that to point an unloaded gun at the plaintiff is an assault.[16] An act which causes a reasonable person to apprehend a battery ought to constitute an assault. If it is clear to the plaintiff that the defendant has no present ability to carry out a battery, because he is too far away to commit it, there is no assault. On principle, it would seem that the test should be, not whether this plaintiff apprehends impact, but whether a reasonable person would so do (at least if the defendant does not know of this plaintiff's timidity).

Where the intervention of the police, or other protective measures, ensure that threats of violence and abuse cannot be carried out by the defendants, there is no assault committed. So where working miners were bussed into their collieries with police guards, the threats yelled at them by strikers were not assaults.[17] The plaintiffs knew, as reasonable men, that those threats could not be carried out there and then. The distress and emotional strain caused to them by the abuse was not the result of apprehension of an immediate battery. The tort of assault as a means of protecting freedom from mental anxiety can thus be seen as limited in scope.

It is usually stated (but on inadequate authority) that mere words without bodily movement do not constitute an assault.[18] But it would seem preferable to treat this statement as merely an illustration of the principle that the defendant must have caused the plaintiff to apprehend an immediate contact rather than to make it a separate rule. If the plaintiff turns a corner, to be confronted by a motionless robber who, with gun in hand, commands 'Hands up', why should this not be assault?[19] On the other hand, words accompanying an act may explain what might otherwise be an assault, as when the defendant with hand on sword said: 'If it were not assize-time, I would not take such language from you.'[20]

SECTION 3.   INTENTIONAL PHYSICAL HARM OTHER THAN TRESPASS TO PERSON

A wilful act (or statement) of the defendant, calculated to cause physical harm to the plaintiff and in fact causing physical harm to him, is a tort.

This was established by WRIGHT J, in *Wilkinson v Downton*:[1]

The plaintiff was told by the defendant, who knew it to be untrue, that her husband had been seriously injured in an accident. Believing this, she

---

15 *Stephens v Myers* (1830) 4 C & P 349 at 349–50. In *Osborn v Veitch* (1858) 1 F & F 317 it was held that to point a loaded gun at half-cock at the plaintiff was an assault but this was because there was '"a present ability" of doing the act threatened'.

16 *R v St George* (1840) 9 C & P 483.

17 *Thomas v NUM* [1985] 2 All ER 1 at 24.

18 A case of murder, *Meade and Belt's case* (1823), 1 Lewin 184, where it is said *obiter* (at 185 per HOLROYD J) that 'no words or singing are equivalent to an assault', is the one usually relied on.

19 Or words spoken from concealment. CF LORD GODDARD CJ, in *R v Wilson* [1955] 1 All ER 744 at 745: 'He called out "Get out your knives", which itself would be an assault', and *Fairclough v Whipp* [1951] 2 All ER 834. In *Barton v Armstrong* [1969] 2 NSWLR 451 (NSW Supt Ct) it was held that uttering threats on the telephone could be assault.

20 *Tuberville v Savage* (1669) 1 Mod Rep 3.

1 [1897] 2 QB 57, 66 LJQB 493 (the fullest report).

suffered nervous shock resulting in serious physical illness, and was held to have a cause of action.

The Court of Appeal upheld *Wilkinson v Downton* in *Janvier v Sweeney*:[2]

> The defendants, private detectives, told the plaintiff that unless she procured certain letters of her mistress for them, they would disclose to the authorities that her fiancé, an internee, was a traitor; they knew that they had no such evidence. She recovered damages for the physical illness brought on by nervous shock occasioned by the defendants' conduct.

Is this tort limited to nervous shock cases? There seems no reason why it should be. Because of the rule that intentional acts which indirectly cause harm are not trespasses, there are many situations where, but for this principle, there might be no action. Putting poison in another's tea, digging a pit into which it is intended that another shall fall, perhaps passing on an infectious disease—these are not trespasses, but should properly be regarded as intentional physical harms within the principle of *Wilkinson v Downton*. The old cases declaring that it is a tortious act deliberately to set spring guns or other mechanical devices with the intention of injuring trespassers seem to belong to this category—the acts are in each instance consequential and thus not trespasses.[3] It seems confusing to speak of negligence when the defendant has deliberately inflicted the harm.

It has been suggested that it is wrong to state that in this tort one must prove that the defendant intended to cause the harm, and that the cases decide that one need only prove an intention to do the act.[4] But WRIGHT J, said:[5] 'One question is whether the defendant's act was so plainly calculated to produce some effect of the kind which was produced that an intention to produce it ought to be imputed to the defendant.' Remembering that intention covers the case where a man must be presumed to have intended the natural consequences of his conduct, it seems clear that the defendant must be proved to have intended to violate the interest of the plaintiff in his freedom from physical harm—an intention to do an act the non-remote consequence of which is physical harm is not enough.[6] That a joke is the motive, as in *Wilkinson v Downton*, is irrelevant.

SECTION 4. FALSE IMPRISONMENT

The trespass rather inadequately known as false imprisonment[7] may be

---

2 [1919] 2 KB 316, CA.

3 *Deane v Clayton* (1817) 7 Taunt 489 (court equally divided whether it was actionable on the case to set iron spikes for dogs); *Bird v Holbrook* (1828) 4 Bing 628 (setter of spring gun liable in case to pursuer of stray fowl); cf *Townsend v Wathen* (1808) 9 East 277 and p 82, post.

4 Goodhart, Book Review (1944) 7 MLR 88.

5 At 59.

6 This interpretation of the case is supported by LUSH J, IN *Shapiro v La Morta* (1923) 130 LT 622 at 625. Cf *Bunyan v Jordon* (1937) 57 CLR 1 (H Ct Australia): D fired revolver into the air, thereby inflicting nervous shock resulting in physical illness; because D intended merely to frighten, ie a mere transient shock, not a nervous breakdown or other physical harm, held not liable. This tort is not committed unless there is actual illness with ascertainable objective physical consequences; anguish or fright is not enough.

7 'False' in the sense of 'false' step; the confinement need not be in 'prison'.

defined as *an act of the defendant which directly and intentionally or negligently causes the confinement of the plaintiff within an area delimited by the defendant*.

Usually when there is a false imprisonment there will also be an assault or battery, but not, for example, where A voluntarily enters a room and B then locks the door. This tort protects the interest in freedom from confinement, that is, in freedom of movement.

A. STATE OF MIND

Normally this tort must be intentional in the sense that the defendant must intend to do an act which is at least substantially certain to effect the confinement. Malice is irrelevant. On principle negligence ought to be enough. Accordingly, if a person locks a door, being negligently unaware of the presence of somebody in the room, or even if he negligently allows such a door to lock, this should be false imprisonment.

B. CHARACTER OF THE ACT

Like other trespasses, this tort is actionable *per se* but the courts have not thought that so great a protection ought to be afforded against any restraint of the person; so there must be a total restraint.[8] To prevent a man from crossing a bridge except by making a detour around part of the area of the bridge which has been closed off is not false imprisonment.[9] Nor, so it was held in an old case, was it false imprisonment if A were able to escape from his confinement by a nominal trespass on the land of a third party.[10]

> Every confinement of the person is an imprisonment, whether it be in a common prison or in a private house, or in the stocks, or even by forcibly detaining one in the public streets.[11]

One may be confined in a house,[12] in a prison,[13] in a mine,[14] or in a vehicle.[15] How large the area of confinement can be must obviously depend on the circumstances of each particular case—it could be tortious to restrict a man to a large country estate, or perhaps even to restrain him from leaving, say, the Isle of Man, yet if A prevented B from landing in England from the Continent that act could not be a false imprisonment.[16] The boundaries of

---

8 Partial restraints may be the subject of an action on the case, on proof of damage; *Wright v Wilson* (1699) 1 Ld Raym 739; *Bird v Jones* (1845) 7 QB 742 at 752 (per PATTESON J).
9 *Bird v Jones* supra.
10 *Wright v Wilson* supra; the court thought that a special action on the case would lie.
11 *Blackstone*, III, 127.
12 *Warner v Riddiford* (1858) 4 CB (NS) 180.
13 *Cobbett v Grey* (1850) 4 Exch 729.
14 *Herd v Weardale Steel, Coal and Coke Co Ltd* [1915] AC 67, HL.
15 *Burton v Davies* [1953] QSR 26 (Queensland), driving a car at such a speed as to prevent a passenger from alighting is false imprisonment.
16 But in *Kuchenmeister v Home Office* [1958] 1 QB 496, [1958] 1 All ER 485, it was held false imprisonment for immigration officers to prevent an alien from proceeding from an airport to an aircraft and from embarking on it, even though the Aliens Order, 1953, authorised them to prescribe limits within which he must remain.

the area of confinement must be fixed by the defendant. As COLERIDGE J, said in *Bird v Jones*:[17]

> Some confusion seems ... to arise from confounding imprisonment of the body with mere loss of freedom: ... imprisonment ... includes the notion of restraint within some limits defined by a will or power exterior to our own.

LORD DENMAN, in his dissenting judgment in the same case, said:[18]

> As long as I am prevented from doing what I have a right to do, of what importance is it that I am permitted to do something else? ... If I am locked in a room, am I not imprisoned because I might effect my escape through a window, or because I might find an exit dangerous or inconvenient to myself, as by wading through water ...?

Although this contention was rejected so far as the adequacy of a partial restraint is concerned, it is thought that, if a man can only escape at the risk of personal injury or if it is otherwise unreasonable[19] for him to escape, it constitutes the tort of false imprisonment.

The barriers need not be physical; when a Commissioner in Lunacy wrongfully used his authority to dissuade the plaintiff from leaving his office, he was liable in false imprisonment.[20] Restraint on movement in the street even by a mere threat of force which intimidates a man into compliance without laying hands on him is false imprisonment.[1] A restraint effected by an assertion of authority is enough—so those who seek compensation because they have been wrongfully arrested by policemen claim for false imprisonment, and need not establish that the policeman touched them.[2] The plaintiff need not risk violence by resisting his arrester.

Once a person is lawfully in police custody, or lawfully confined in a prison, can a change in his conditions of imprisonment render that imprisonment unlawful? Nineteenth century cases held it to be false imprisonment to move a person to a part of a prison where prisoners of his category should not be kept, for example, to move a debtor into the company of felons.[3] The Prison Act 1952 provides that a prisoner sentenced by the court may be confined in any prison. Prisoners are no longer sub-divided into categories subject to different regimes of imprisonment. Changes in an individual's conditions of custody, for example solitary confinement in the notorious control units, have been held not to render that imprisonment unlawful even though breach of Prison Rules may be established.[4] There is disagreement at present[5] as to whether conditions falling below even minimal standards of humane treat-

---

17 Supra at 744.
18 At 754–5.
19 If A removes B's bathing costume in a swimming pool and B does not leave the pool until he has found someone to lend him another costume, is he falsely imprisoned?
20 *Harnett v Bond* [1925] AC 669, HL.
 1 Can you imprison by telephone? Is a threat of force to a member of one's family sufficient?
 2 *Warner v Riddiford* (1858) 4 CB (NS) 180, especially at 204 (per WILLES J); *Chinn v Morris* (1826) 2 C & P 361; *Grainger v Hill* (1838) 4 Bing NC 212; *Wood v Lane* (1834) 6 C & P 774. What if a plaintiff is accused of shoplifting, but in order to avoid the embarrassment of a conversation in a crowded store he accompanies the store detective to the office; cf *Conn v David Spencer Ltd* [1930] 1 DLR 805?
 3 *Cobbett v Grey* (1849) 4 Exch 729; *Osborne v Milman* (1886) 17 QBD 514.
 4 *Williams v Home Office (No 2)* [1981] 1 All ER 1211.
 5 *R v Board of Visitors of Gartree Prison, ex p Sears* (1985) Times, 20 March (no modern authority that lawful detention may become unlawful if conditions of imprisonment changed).

ment, such as overcrowded insanitary police cells,[6] may constitute false imprisonment albeit the plaintiff's original detention was entirely lawful.

Presumably this trespass must be direct. So, it is not false imprisonment to cause a person to be temporarily detained in an asylum by making false statements to the authorities about his behaviour,[7] or to dig a pitfall into which the plaintiff falls.[8] However short the period of detention, an action for false imprisonment will lie, provided that the other requirements of the tort are satisfied.

A person who is held liable in false imprisonment will normally have performed some positive act. *Herd v Weardale Steel, Coke and Coal Co*[9] posed the problem of whether there might be liability in respect of a mere omission:[10]

> The plaintiff, a miner employed by the defendants, descended their mine in pursuance of his contract of employment. During his shift the plaintiff requested the defendants to carry him to the surface in their cage. In refusing this request the defendants committed no breach of contract: their contractual obligation was to transport him to the surface at the end of his shift. The action in false imprisonment failed.[11]

This case is authority for the proposition that failure to provide a means of egress from premises is not a tort where there is no duty to provide it: thus, if A falls down the mine of B while trespassing it is not false imprisonment should B refuse to bring him to the surface in his lift.[12] What it does not decide is whether the failure to carry out a duty, whether contractual or otherwise, may constitute a false imprisonment even though there is no positive act on the part of the defendant. The House of Lords did not consider this point, but the two judges who constituted the majority in the Court of Appeal held that the omission to perform a contractual duty was not a false imprisonment.[13]

C. KNOWLEDGE OF THE PLAINTIFF

A controversial point is whether the plaintiff must know that the defendant is committing an act which restrains his freedom. On principle, knowledge

---

6 See *Middleweek v Chief Constable of Merseyside* (1985) Times, 1 August, CA.

7 But an action on the case lay against a medical practitioner, who negligently certified that the plaintiff was insane, whereupon she was detained in a mental hospital; *De Freville v Dill* (1927) 96 LJKB 1056.

8 It may be the tort of intentionally causing physical harm; ch 3, section 3, ante. Is it false imprisonment to deflate the tyres of the invalid chair in which a cripple is travelling, or to take away the ladder of a tiler who is on the roof?

9 [1913] 3 KB 771, CA; affd [1915] AC 67, HL.

10 Because both are acts of commission, not of omission, *Winfield*, 58, is not justified in treating his two examples of the student forbidden to leave the lecture room until the end of the lecture, and the conductor who will not allow one who has boarded the wrong bus to alight without paying his fare, as similar to *Herd v Weardale etc Co* supra.

11 Cf *Robinson v Balmain New Ferry Co Ltd* [1910] AC 295 at 299, PC: 'There is no law requiring the defendants to make the exit from their premises gratuitous to people who come there upon a definite contract which involves their leaving the wharf by another way; ...'

12 And if B's refusal caused A to die of starvation?

13 Buckley and Hamilton LJJ [1913] 3 KB 771, CA. *Winfield*, 59, wrongly states that the House of Lords held that omission to perform a contractual duty might be the tort of false imprisonment.

of confinement ought to be required, because the interest protected seems a mental one, as in assault. In *Herring v Boyle*[14] it was held that a schoolmaster who detained a boy at school during the holidays, because his parent had not paid the fees, was not liable when the child did not know of any act of detention and, in any event, there was no evidence of actual restraint. In *Meering v Graham-White Aviation Co*[15] the facts were:

> At the request of, and accompanied by, two works policemen, the plaintiff went to the works office voluntarily to answer questions about certain thefts. Unaware that he was suspected, he remained in the office for a considerable time during which the works policemen stayed outside the room without his knowledge. The jury said 'Yes' in answer to the question: 'Was the plaintiff detained?' and by a majority of two to one the Court of Appeal held that there was evidence on which the jury could so answer.

WARRINGTON LJ, did not in that case consider the question of knowledge nor is it clear whether it was argued, but he found evidence that the plaintiff was no longer a free man. DUKE LJ, dissenting, held that the plaintiff's lack of knowledge was conclusive of the fact that there was no evidence for the jury, but the *ratio decidendi* of ATKIN LJ, in a judgment which did not refer to *Herring v Boyle* was that knowledge was irrelevant. His view was that the tort protects freedom of movement as such, not the mental effects of being knowingly confined which would merely be relevant in fixing the amount of damages.[16] Whether *Herring v Boyle* is to be preferred to the *Meering* case raises fundamental issues of the function of the law of torts. Is it solely a means of adjusting losses between individuals in which case the former decision must be preferred as the plaintiff unaware of his imprisonment may suffer no injury? Or does tort properly have a deterrent function to prevent wrongful behaviour and reinforce civil liberties? It would seem that, if the plaintiff reasonably but mistakenly believes himself to be confined and the defendant has intentionally placed him in that position, there is false imprisonment. It is still open to the courts to hold that in some instances there is a non-contractual duty to release from confinement and that mere omission to perform that duty is false imprisonment.[17]

D. WHO IS LIABLE, THE POLICEMAN OR THE AGGRIEVED DEFENDANT WHO CALLS IN THE POLICEMAN

The usual question to be asked when deciding who can be sued for false imprisonment is: Who was 'active in promoting and causing' the con-

---

14 (1834) 1 Cr M & R 377.

15 (1919) 122 LT 44.

16 His illustration, that the arresters may inform others of his detention, seems to postulate that this tort protects reputation; *sed quaere*. Prosser (1955) 55 Columbia LR 847 contends that ATKIN LJ's rule is necessary in order to protect the plaintiff in such situations as these: A locks B, a 2-year-old child, in a vault; 2 days elapse before the vault is opened, and B's health is impaired. But would not such cases fall within section 3 of this chapter, *ante*?

17 Eg not letting out a prisoner after serving his sentence. Is one who has accidentally confined another under such a duty once he knows: the library assistant who locks up the library when a student is still in, or the attendant who will not release the lady locked in the public lavatory (and see *Sayers v Harlow Urban District Council* [1958] 2 All ER 342)?

finement?[18] It is often necessary to determine who can be sued when a person is detained and charged for an offence where the arrest is unjustified by law.[19] (The separate question of when lawful arrest is a defence will be examined later.)[20] In particular, if the defendant signs the charge sheet at the police station, does that make him answerable for the detention? In itself, signing the charge sheet is not evidence of a detention by the signatory,[1] but if the defendant also states that he 'did give him in charge' it may be.[2] Where, however, the defendant sent for a policeman, who, having made independent inquiries, then arrested the plaintiff on his own authority, and, after having accompanied the policeman and the plaintiff to the police station, was directed to sign the charge sheet, the defendant was held not to be liable for false imprisonment.[3] If the policeman had refused to take the plaintiff into custody unless the defendant charged him, then the defendant would be answerable.[4] If a citizen, in reply to the inquiry of a policeman, merely identifies the plaintiff as the suspected criminal, he is not liable.[5]

If the defendant wrongfully gives the plaintiff into custody and then the magistrate remands the plaintiff the defendant is answerable in false imprisonment for damages only up to the time of the judicial remand. Once a judicial act interposes, liability for false imprisonment ceases.[6] It becomes important at this stage to distinguish false imprisonment from malicious prosecution, a tort concerned with the abuse of the judicial process, and which, unlike false imprisonment, calls for proof of malice and of absence of reasonable cause.[7] Therefore, if A wrongfully prefers a complaint against B before a magistrate who then issues a warrant or tries him forthwith or remands him, A has not committed the tort of false imprisonment,[8] even if the magistrate has no jurisdiction.[9]

E. DAMAGES

False imprisonment is actionable without proof of damage. In addition to damages for loss of liberty the court may compensate for injury to feelings and loss of reputation.[10] Damages are at large and may be aggravated by the

---

18 *Aitken v Bedwell* (1827) Mood & M 68. In *Ansell v Thomas* [1974] Crim LR 31, managing director left factory early only because two policemen summoned by his co-directors threatened to eject him forcibly if he did not leave; the co-directors held liable in trespass. A person may be liable in false imprisonment either because he himself effected the arrest or, in line with the general principle that he who instigates another to commit a tort is a joint tortfeasor (p 526, post), because he actively promoted the arrest by another.
19 See *Pike v Waldrum & P & O Navigation Co* [1952] 1 Lloyd's Rep 431 on the liability of naval authorities and a ship's captain for the arrest of a seaman.
20 See p 87, post.
 1 *Sewell v National Telephone Co Ltd* [1907] 1 KB 557, CA.
 2 *Clubb v Wimpey & Co Ltd* [1936] 1 All ER 69; new trial ordered by the Court of Appeal, [1936] 3 All ER 148, who neither approved nor expressly disapproved the decision of the court below on this point.
 3 *Grinham v Willey* (1859) 4 H & N 496.
 4 *Hopkins v Crowe* (1836) 4 Ad & El 774; *Austin v Dowling* (1870) LR 5 CP 534.
 5 *Godsen v Elphick* (1849) 4 Exch 445.
 6 *Lock v Ashton* (1848) 12 QB 871.
 7 See ch 26, post.
 8 *Brown v Chapman* (1848) 6 CB 365.
 9 *West v Smallwood* (1838) 3 M & W 418.
10 *Hook v Cunard Steamship Co Ltd* [1953] 1 All ER 1021.

circumstances.[11] Exemplary damages may be awarded against a policeman or other official who falsely imprisons the plaintiff.[12]

SECTION 5.   OTHER FORMS OF COMPENSATION

Many of the torts discussed in this chapter will also be crimes. A court which has convicted a person of an offence (other than a road traffic offence) may require him to compensate the victim for any personal injury, loss or damage resulting.[13]

Claims for ex gratia repayments of compensation may also be made by victims of crimes of violence to the Criminal Injuries Compensation Board.[14]

11 *Childs v Lewis* (1924) 40 TLR 870; *Walter v Alltools Ltd* (1944) 171 LT 371, CA.
12 See pp 466–68, post. The award for exemplary damages need not be for a specific sum separate from the other general damages; *AG of St Christopher, Nevis and Anguilla v Reynolds* [1980] AC 637, [1979] 3 All ER 129, PC. An award of exemplary damages should not be made automatically against policemen; *O'Connor v Hewitson* [1979] Crim LR 46. But it need not be proved that the officers act maliciously or violently. An erroneous belief in a power of arrest will not excuse the 'unconstitutional' conduct justifying the award of exemplary damages; *Holden v Chief Constable of Lancashire* [1987] QB 380, [1986] 3 All ER 836. In *White v Metropolitan Police Commissioner* (1982) Times, 24 April, 2 plaintiffs were each awarded £20,000 exemplary damages in addition to aggravated and special damages.
13 Sections 35 to 38 of the Powers of Criminal Courts Act 1973, as amended by s 60 of the Criminal Law Act 1977. The maximum award by a magistrates' court is £1,000.
14 The 1979 scheme is set out in full in Hepple and Matthews *Tort Cases and Materials* (3rd edn) p 800 et seq.

Chapter 4

Goods

SECTION 1. INTRODUCTION

The law might be expected to protect persons whose title to, or possession
of, goods is interfered with, or whose goods are damaged by intentional
conduct. Broadly speaking, English law does this but not in any systematic
way. As SIR JOHN SALMOND said:[1]

> ... we are still called upon to observe distinctions and subtleties that have no
> substance or justification in them, but are nothing more than an evil inheritance
> from the days when forms of action and of pleading held the legal system in their
> clutches. In no branch of the law is this more obvious than in that which relates
> to the different classes of wrongs which may be committed with respect to goods.
> In particular the law of trover and conversion is a region still darkened with the
> mists of legal formalism, through which no man will find his way by the light of
> nature or with any other guide save the old learning of writs and forms of action
> and the mysteries of pleading.

Unfortunately Salmond's criticism of the law of torts as it protects
interests in goods is as pertinent today as it was in 1903. This is so despite a
systematic review by the Law Reform Committee[2] of the several and ancient
torts concerning goods which are often collectively referred to as the chattel
torts. Their proposal that all those torts relating to intentional interference
with goods should be replaced by a single tort of 'wrongful interference with
chattels' was, as we shall see, only implemented to a very limited extent by
Parliament in the Torts (Interference with Goods) Act 1977.[3] Hence students
must still attempt to understand the historical development of the various
chattel torts.

The action for *trespass to goods*, trespass *de bonis asportatis*, affords a
remedy where there has been a direct interference with goods in the plaintiff's
possession at the time of the trespass, whether that be by taking the goods
from him or damaging the goods without removing them. It is of no help
where the relevant interference with the goods is indirect, nor, generally, is
trespass available where the goods are not in the possession of the plaintiff.
Thus if student A lends this book overnight to student B, who gives it or sells
it to C, trespass may not lie against C.

The oldest of the chattel torts, the writ of *detinue*, developed to provide a
remedy for wrongful detention of goods. A person with a right to immediate
possession of goods could, by way of an action in detinue, recover the goods

---

1 21 (1903) LQR 43.
2 See the 18th Report of the Law Reform Committee (Conversion and Detinue) (1971) Cmnd
4774.
3 See Palmer 'The Application of the Torts (Interference with Goods) Act 1977 to Actions in
Bailment' (1978) 41 MLR 629 and 'The Abolition of Detinue' [1981] Conv 62, and see
Thorneley [1977] CLJ 248.

themselves or payment of their value *and* consequential damages for their detention upon evidence that the defendant had wrongfully refused to deliver up the goods on demand. The loss or destruction of the goods where the defendant owed the plaintiff a duty to take care of those goods (as a bailee)[4] was no justification for failing to redeliver the goods. In many instances the facts which gave rise to a remedy in detinue simultaneously created a cause of action in conversion, the latest of the major chattel torts to evolve. Detinue is abolished by the Torts (Interference with Goods) Act 1977. The one clear instance of detinue (loss or destruction of goods in breach of duty by a bailee) which did not constitute conversion at common law is 'converted' into a statutory conversion by section 2(2) of that Act.[5]

The action for *conversion* (originally called *trover*) developed upon a legal fiction.[6] The original form of the pleadings alleged that the defendant had found the plaintiff's chattels (hence the name 'trover') and had wrongfully converted them to his own use. The allegation of finding (trover) could not be traversed and the essence of the tort became the wrongful conversion of the goods to the use of the defendant. Once refusal to deliver up the goods was treated as evidence of conversion,[7] conversion and detinue became largely concurrent torts. As seizing goods and carrying them away is quite clearly a wrongful conversion of goods conversion is also often available concurrently with trespass. But merely moving or damaging goods without converting them to the defendant's own use remains remediable in trespass alone.[8] The action for conversion lies not only where the plaintiff has actual possession of the relevant goods but also where he has a right to immediate possession of the goods. Consider again the earlier example of the aggrieved student A. Should B refuse to return the book to him he commits conversion. Should B have sold the book to C who also refuses to deliver the book back to its true owner A both B and C may be sued for conversion.

The major extant chattel torts of trespass and conversion protect interests in possession. *Residual torts* derived from the action on the case protect the rights of owners not in possession in certain cases. Trespass and conversion deal with intentional interference with goods. Where goods are lost or damaged as a result of the defendant's breach of a duty of care an action may lie in *negligence*.

The archaic nature of the chattel torts adds to the intrinsic difficulty of the subject of interference with goods. That intrinsic difficulty is unavoidable in that, as the essence of trespass or conversion is very often whether the defendant wrongfully and unlawfully dealt with the plaintiff's goods, the

---

4 When goods are entrusted by one person (the *bailor*) to another (the *bailee*) a *bailment* is created which imposes on the bailee duties towards the bailor in respect of those goods. The nature of the bailment whether it is gratuitous or for reward, voluntary or involuntary, will determine the scope of the duty owed by the bailee. Bailments may be for a fixed term (hire of a car for one week) or at will. This will be relevant to determine the relevant rights to sue in conversion of bailor and bailee. See N E Palmer *Bailment*.

5 See *Palmer* (supra) who argues that there are other instances of detinue in relation to breach of bailment not now actionable as conversion. The issue is discussed but not decided in *Howard E Perry v British Railways Board* [1980] 2 All ER 579, [1980] 1 WLR 1375.

6 For details of the history of detinue and conversion and the interplay between the historic chattel torts, see Ames *Select Essays on Anglo-American History* (1907) vol 3 417; Milsom 'Not Doing is No Trespass' [1954] CLJ 105; Simpson 'The Introduction of the Action on the Case for Conversion' (1959) 75 LQR 364.

7 See *Alexander v Southey* (1821) 5 B & Ald 247.

8 *Bushel v Miller* (1718) 1 Stra 128; *Fouldes v Willoughby* (1841) 8 M & W 540.

basic question of law in issue may be one of contract or personal property. For example, A enters into a conditional sale agreement with B to purchase a car. Before A has completed all the payments on the car he sells it to C. When B seeks to recover the car or its value from C via an action for conversion the court will have to consider the authority (if any) of A to sell the car to B. That will depend on:

1 the terms of the contract between A and B; and
2 the relevant rules of the law of personal property on title to goods.

What the Law Reform Committee had hoped to do was at least to simplify the tortious remedies available to plaintiffs. One statutory tort of 'wrongful interference with chattels' was recommended which would lie wherever goods were intentionally interfered with without lawful justification. Negligent interference would remain actionable, if at all, only under the existing law of negligence.

The Torts (Interference with Goods) Act 1977 introduces a collective description 'wrongful interference with goods'[9] to cover conversion, trespass to goods, negligence resulting in damage to goods or to an interest in goods and any other tort insofar as it results in damages to goods or an interest in goods. This is done to facilitate common treatment of all chattel torts in respect to remedies and procedure. The Act neither redefines nor replaces the existing substantive rules on trespass, conversion, or the residual chattel torts. The substantive impact of the Act is extremely limited. Detinue is abolished[10] and the one clear instance of detinue which did not constitute conversion at common law (wrongful loss or destruction of goods by a bailee) is declared to be conversion by section 2(2). New provision is made for bailees to dispose of uncollected goods.[11]

The main impact of the 1977 Act is as we shall see to simplify and rationalise the remedies and procedures relating to chattel torts. The intricacies of conversion and its relationship to trespass must still be explored. As conversion is in practical terms the pre-eminent chattel tort it is dealt with first.

SECTION 2.   CONVERSION

Conversion may be defined as an intentional[12] dealing with goods which is seriously inconsistent with the possession or right to immediate possession of another person.

The tort protects the plaintiff's interest in the dominion and control of his goods; it does not protect his interest in its physical condition. It follows, therefore, that the tort is much concerned with problems of title to personal property. Indeed, many cases on conversion are in essence disputes on title

---

9 Section 1.
10 Section 2.
11 Without statutory authority to do so bailees (eg drycleaners) disposing of uncollected goods would be liable for conversion for so doing. Sections 12, 13 and Sch 1 repeal and replace the earlier and unsatisfactory. Disposal of Uncollected Goods Act 1952.
12 At common law an act of conversion had to be a *voluntary* act; hence once detinue was abolished the need to make the wrongful loss or destruction of goods by a bailee in breach of duty a statutory conversion; see post at p 51.

which often involve complex rules of commercial law.[13] Consequently, this subject is one of the most difficult in the law of torts.

A. INTEREST OF THE PLAINTIFF

The plaintiff must have either possession or the right to immediate possession.[14] English law in this respect favours possession at the expense of ownership.[15] Thus in *Roberts v Wyatt*:[16]

> The defendant, the attorney of the vendor of certain land, delivered the abstract of title to the attorney of the plaintiff purchaser. This attorney took counsel's opinion on the title; this took the form of pencilled comments on the abstract. The abstract was left with the defendant for him to answer. Being unable to answer the queries raised by counsel, he refused to return the abstract, and was held liable in conversion to the plaintiff, who was entitled to the temporary possession of it.

(1) BAILMENT

A bailee of goods can sue third parties in conversion.[17] If the bailment is at will then the bailor may also sue because he is then deemed to have an immediate right to possession.[18]

A bailment which originally gave to the bailor no immediate right to possess may become a bailment at will. *Manders v Williams*[19] is illustrative:

> The plaintiff brewer supplied porter in casks to a publican on condition that he was to return empty casks within six months; it was held that the plaintiff could sue a sheriff who seized (within six months of their being supplied) some empty casks in execution for a debt of the publican, because, once the casks were empty, the effect of the contract was to make the publican a bailee at will, whereupon the plaintiff was entitled to immediate possession.

Similarly, if a bailee does a wrongful act which may be deemed to terminate the bailment the bailor may sue. Sale of the goods by the bailee will ordinarily

---

13 For a typical illustration of how conversion is linked with problems of title under the law of personal property, see *Jerome v Bentley* [1952] 2 All ER 114. The tort appears to be actionable without proof of special damage; *Hiort v London and North Western Rly Co* (1879) 4 Ex D 188.

14 *Gordon v Harper* (1796) 7 Term Rep 9; *Farrant v Thompson* (1822) 5 B & Ald 826. An equitable title is no disqualification where the person entitled has a right to possess; *International Factors Ltd v Rodriguez* [1979] QB 351, [1979] 1 All ER 17, CA.

15 For the rights of an owner not entitled to immediate possession, see p 63, et seq, post.

16 (1810) 2 Taunt 268. In *City Motors (1933) Properties Ltd v Southern Aerial Service* (1961) 106 CLR 477, H Ct Australia, the owner was liable for dispossessing his bailee during the subsistence of the bailment, which was not one terminable at will.

17 The bailment gives him the right to possession of the goods for the period of the bailment. In *The Winkfield* [1902] P 42, the Postmaster-General, as bailee, could recover the full value of mails lost through the wrongdoing of the defendant. For the changes with regard to damages in such cases see p 52, post.

18 As the bailment can be terminated at will, the owner retains the right to demand the goods back instantly ie the right to immediate possession. *Nicolls v Bastard* (1835) 2 Cr M & R 659; *Kahler v Midland Bank Ltd* [1950] AC 24 at 56 (per LORD RADCLIFFE), [1949] 2 All ER 621 at 641.

19 (1849) 4 Exch 339.

terminate the bailment and the bailor can then sue either the bailee or the third party.[20] Destruction of the goods[1] or dealing with them in a manner wholly inconsistent with the terms of the bailment,[2] will have the same result. It will be a difficult matter of interpretation of contract to decide whether a particular act of the bailee determines the bailment, or, at least, makes it determinable at will. This is especially true and important in the case of hire-purchase agreements.[3] These normally prohibit the hirer from selling or otherwise disposing of the goods,[4] and empower the owner to terminate the agreement if the prohibition is disregarded; if the agreement dispenses with notice to the hirer of termination, the owner can sue a party who purchases from the hirer in unwitting contravention of such a prohibition.[5] In *Whiteley v Hilt*:[6]

> The hire-purchase agreement empowered the hirer to purchase a piano after payment of the final instalment. It did not prohibit her from transferring the piano during the hiring period. It was held that the owners had no cause of action against the transferee who had paid all the instalments remaining owing.

With this may be compared *Belsize Motor Supply Co v Cox*:[7]

> The owners were authorised to determine the agreement if the hirers parted with possession of the hired goods. It was held that the owners could recover from a pledgee of the hirer only the instalments which were still owing and that the agreement continued in force despite the transfer of the goods.

In effect, the courts treat hire-purchase agreements as *sui generis* in that they are regarded as creating a proprietary interest separate from the mere contract of bailment.[8]

(2) LIEN AND PLEDGE[9]

The holder of a lien, too, may sue in conversion,[10] but if he wrongfully parts

20 *Cooper v Willomatt* (1845) 1 CB 672; of course, at the conclusion of the purported act of sale the bailee's interest is forfeited and the bailor is entitled to immediate possession, but if the sale is one of those, eg in market overt, which passes a title to the third party, at what moment of time can the bailor be said to have an immediate right to possess and thus a right to sue the bailee in conversion?
1 *Bryant v Wardell* (1848) 2 Exch 479 at 482.
2 *Plasycoed Collieries Co Ltd v Partridge, Jones & Co Ltd* [1912] 2 KB 345 at 351 (per HAMILTON J); but not presumably a mere excess of permitted user.
3 And see now Consumer Credit Act 1974, Parts VII and IX.
4 It is standard practice in hire-purchase agreements, by express terms, to make the benefits of the hirer's option to purchase unassignable; *Helstan Securities Ltd v Hertfordshire County Council* [1978] 3 All ER 262.
5 *North Central Wagon and Finance Co Ltd v Graham* [1950] 2 KB 7, [1950] 1 All ER 780 (sale by bailee made hiring determinable at will of bailor: as explained in *Reliance Car Facilities Ltd v Roding Motors* [1952] 2 QB 844, [1952] 1 All ER 1355) CA; *Union Transport Finance Ltd v British Car Auctions Ltd* [1978] 2 All ER 385, CA (damages recovered from auctioneer who sold car on instructions of a hire-purchaser).
6 [1918] 2 KB 808, CA.
7 [1914] 1 KB 244; *Wickham Holdings Ltd v Brooke House Motors Ltd* [1967] 1 All ER 117.
8 Cf *Karflex Ltd v Poole* [1933] 2 KB 251 at 263–4, [1933] All ER Rep 46 at 50, 51 (per GODDARD J).
9 And see now Consumer Credit Act 1974, ss 114–22.
10 In *Lord v Price* (1874) LR 9 Exch 54, the buyer of goods in possession of the seller, who had a lien for the price, could not sue a third party. Is it desirable to prevent the owner from suing a third party if a carrier has a lien?

with the possession of the goods he loses his lien, and his act is a conversion which ends the bailment and entitles the owner to sue him.[11] A pledge, however, confers something more than the personal right of retention given by a lien—for there is, in addition, a power to sell in default of payment on the agreed date. So, in *Donald v Suckling*[12] it was held that a repledge by the pledgee did not end the pledge and the original pledgor could not sue the second pledgee without tendering the sum owing. Similarly the assignee of a pledgor cannot sue the pledgee who sells the goods because, until the sum owing is tendered, there is no immediate right to possession.[13]

(3) SALE

It is often difficult to discover which of the parties to a contract for the sale of goods have an interest sufficient to support an action in conversion. The crucial question is whether at the date of the alleged conversion the buyer has a sufficient right to immediate possession of the goods. In *Empresa Exportadora de Azucar v IANSA*:[14] the plaintiffs had contracted to buy, and had paid for, two cargoes of sugar to be shipped to them in Chile by the defendants from Cuba. On the orders of the Cuban government, after a military takeover in Chile, the ship discharging the first cargo sailed away with the cargo only partially unloaded and the second ship was diverted back to Cuba part way through its voyage. The buyers were held to have an immediate right to possession of both the partially unloaded cargo and the diverted cargo and succeeded in their action for conversion against the sellers. Sales on credit terms pose rather more difficulties. In *Bloxam v Sanders*[15] it was held that, where goods were sold on credit, the buyer could ordinarily sue the seller in conversion if he wrongfully sold them to a third party, but, that if the seller exercised his right of stoppage *in transitu* upon the buyer's becoming insolvent, the buyer could no longer sue. In the absence of credit terms, the court further declared, the buyer, although he may have the property in the goods, has no right to immediate possession until he tenders or pays the price. In *Chinery v Viall*[16] the seller of goods on credit terms had resold them to a third party. Stating that their decision did not turn on the fact that the original contract was a sale on credit, the court held that 'where there has been no default by the buyer' the buyer may sue the seller. It is thought that *Bloxam v Sanders* is to be preferred, and that a buyer to whom property has passed, but who has not been given credit terms, has no immediate right to possess until he tenders the price. *Wood v Bell*[17] illustrates how problems of conversion can often be solved only by application of the general law of personal property:

A was building a ship for B and, before its completion, A's assignees in

---

11 *Mulliner v Florence* (1878) 3 QBD 484.
12 (1866) LR 1 QB 585. A mere equitable pledge may be sufficient; *Maynegrain Pty Ltd v Compafina Bank* [1984] 1 NSWLR 258.
13 *Halliday v Holgate* (1868) LR 3 Exch 299. Cf *Bradley v Copley* (1845) 1 CB 685. The assignee of a bill of sale which authorises the borrower to remain in possession of the goods cannot sue in conversion for a wrongful seizure of the goods by a sheriff, because, until the assignee has demanded payment and been refused, or the borrower has otherwise defaulted in payment, he has no immediate right to possession.
14 [1983] 2 Lloyd's Rep 171, CA (a defence of 'act of state' was rejected).
15 (1825) 4 B & C 941.
16 (1860) 5 H & N 288.
17 (1856) 5 E & B 772.

bankruptcy seized it. It was held that supervision by B of the construction, and the punching of his name on the keel evidenced the intention of the parties to pass the property to B as the work progressed, so that he could successfully sue the assignees in conversion.

(4) LICENSEE

Sometimes a licensee may be able to sue in conversion. In *Northam v Bowden*[18] the plaintiff had a licence to prospect certain land for tin, and the defendant, without permission, carted away some of the soil on this land. It was held that 'if the plaintiff had a right to the gravel and soil for the purpose of getting any mineral that could be found in it, he had such a possession of the whole as entitled him to maintain an action for its conversion against a wrongdoer'.[19] Apart from such cases of *profits à prendre*, licensees of goods are bailees and call for no separate treatment.

(5) FINDER

The rules regarding finding have been authoritatively settled in *Parker v British Airways Board*[20] although their application to particular facts is often difficult:

> The finder of a chattel acquires no rights over it unless it has been abandoned or lost and he takes it into his care and control. He acquires a right to keep it against all but the true owner or one who can assert a prior right to keep the chattel which was subsisting at the time when the finder took the chattel into his care and control.

In the classic case of *Armory v Delamirie*:[1]

> A chimney sweeper's boy found a jewel and handed it to an apprentice of a goldsmith to be valued. He removed the jewel from its setting and handed back the setting to the boy and offered him $1\frac{1}{2}$d. for the jewel. The boy refused the offer for the jewel whereupon the goldsmith declined to return the jewel to him. The court found for the boy against the goldsmith in trover.

Any servant or agent who finds goods in the course of his employment does so on behalf of his employer who acquires a finder's rights. Anyone with finder's rights has an obligation to take reasonable steps to trace the true owner.

An occupier of land or a building has rights superior to those of a finder over goods in or attached to that land or building. Thus, rings in the mud at the bottom of a pool,[2] and a prehistoric boat embedded in the soil six feet below the surface,[3] belong to the landowner. Similar rules apply to ships, vehicles and aircraft. An occupier of premises has rights superior to those of a finder over goods upon or in, but not attached to, the premises only if,

---

18 (1855) 11 Exch 70.
19 At 73 (per MARTIN B).
20 [1982] QB 1004, [1982] 1 All ER 834, CA. See especially the judgment of DONALDSON LJ.
 1 (1722) 1 Stra 505.
 2 *South Staffordshire Water Co v Sharman* [1896] 2 QB 44.
 3 *Elwes v Briggs Gas Co* (1886) 33 Ch D 562.

before the finding, he has manifested an intention to exercise control over the building and the things which may be upon it or in it.

This last rule is difficult to apply, as the cases show. In *Parker v British Airways Board*:[4]

> The plaintiff was in the defendants' first class lounge at Heathrow Airport awaiting his flight. He found a gold bracelet on the floor and handed it to the defendants' employee with his name and address and a request that it be returned to him if unclaimed. Nobody claimed it and the defendants failed to return it and sold it. The Court of Appeal held that the proceeds belonged to the plaintiff.

The defendants had shown no intention beforehand to exercise such control over the lounge as to displace the plaintiff's rights as a finder. In *Bridges v Hawkesworth*[5] the finder of a packet of bank notes lying on the floor in the public part of a shop was held to be entitled to them as against the owner of the shop. A soldier billeted in a house who found a brooch loose in a crevice on top of a window frame there was held entitled as against the non-occupying owner to the brooch.[6] Owners of premises were entitled, as against demolition workmen-finders, to bank notes found by the latter in a box in the wall safe of an old cellar.[7] An occupier with a superior claim to a finder must also take reasonable steps to trace the true owner.

(6) JUS TERTII (THIRD PARTY RIGHTS)

Under the unamended common law a plaintiff often succeeded in conversion even though the defendant could show that a third party had a better title than the plaintiff. As it was said, the defendant could not plead *jus tertii*. A most significant procedural reform implemented by the 1977 Act, a reform of procedure which in effect also amends substantive law, is the abolition of the common law rules on *jus tertii*.[8]

The defendant in an action of conversion or other wrongful interference is now entitled to prove that a third party has a better right than the plaintiff with respect to all or any part of the interest claimed by the plaintiff. The aims of this reform were to avoid multiplicity of actions by allowing interested third parties to apply to be joined in actions, to protect defendants against the risk of being liable to two different claimants in respect of the same interference, and to limit the plaintiff's damages to his actual loss.

The Act empowered the making of Rules of Court to implement this change.[9] Under those rules, the plaintiff in an action for conversion is required to give particulars of his title and to identify any person who, to his knowledge, has or claims an interest in the goods.[10] The defendant is authorised to apply for directions as to whether any person should be joined with a view to establishing whether he has a better right than the plaintiff, or has a claim as a result of which the defendant might be doubly liable.[11] The relevant date

---

4 [1982] QB 1004, [1982] 1 All ER 834, CA.
5 (1851) 21 LJQB 75.
6 *Hannah v Peel* [1945] KB 509, [1945] 2 All ER 288.
7 *London Corporation v Appleyard* [1963] 2 All ER 834.
8 Section 8(1).
9 Section 8(2).
10 RSC Ord 15 r 10A(1). Would it be sufficient for P to plead that D stole the car from X (unknown) and therefore X has the better title?
11 RSC Ord 15 r 11A(2).

for ascertaining the interest of the third party is the date of the alleged conversion.[12] Where a party fails to appear at the hearing or to comply with a direction the court may by order deprive him of any right of action against the defendant for the wrong, either unconditionally or subject to such terms and conditions as might be specified.[13]

These rules abolish the former principle that a possessor of goods could recover for the full amount of their value although he was not the owner, and even though he was not personally liable to the owner to that extent.[14] The same rules abolish the principle that a bailee was estopped from denying his bailor's title: the bailee when sued by his bailor can now have a named third party joined in.

B. THE SUBJECT MATTER

Any goods can be the subject-matter of conversion. Although cheques are of value only as choses in action, the courts have satisfied the demands of commercial convenience by allowing the full value represented by them to be recovered in actions for conversion. So, where a banker has not handled actual cash or notes but has merely made the appropriate entries by way of credit or debit balances, the courts will treat the conversion as being of the goods, ie of the piece of paper, the cheque, under which the money was transferred, and the value of the goods converted as being the sum represented by the cheque.[15] This doctrine, which is certainly applicable to all negotiable instruments, makes substantial inroads on any possible rule, traceable to the former fiction of losing and finding, that conversion does not lie in respect of rights in intangible property. But this is not the limit of the doctrine; in *Bavins Junr and Sims v London and South Western Bank*[16] all the judges in the Court of Appeal thought that the full value of a non-negotiable document evidencing a debt could be recovered in an action for conversion. It would seem that whenever a particular intangible right is represented in the ordinary course of business by a special written instrument, even though not negotiable, the value of the right is recoverable in an action for conversion of the instrument; so, a life insurance policy[17] or a guarantee[18] may be converted.

These rules are unaffected by the 1977 Act. That Act provides that unless the context otherwise requires 'goods' includes all goods personal other than things in action and money.[19] That retains the common-law rule that money as currency (though not as coins[20]) does not fall within the ambit of conver-

---

12 *De Franco v Metropolitan Police Comr* (1987) Times, 8 May, CA.
13 RSC Ord 15 r 10A(4).
14 Eg *Glenwood Lumber Co v Phillips* [1904] AC 405. Decisions like *The Winkfield* [1902] P 42 are affected. There the Postmaster-General, as bailee, was able to recover the full value of mail lost through the defendant's wrongdoing even though he was not accountable to the bailors for the loss. Now the Post Office would have to identify the bailors, whereupon the defendant could join them in the proceedings and the damages would be apportioned as between bailors and bailee.
15 *Lloyds Bank v Chartered Bank of India, Australia and China* [1929] 1 KB 40, CA, at 55–6 (per SCRUTTON LJ).
16 [1900] 1 QB 270.
17 *Wills v Wells* (1818) 2 Moore CP 247; *Watson v McLean* (1858) EB & E 79.
18 *M'Leod v M'Ghie* (1841) 2 Man & G 326.
19 Section 14(1).
20 Eg Money in a bag: *Taylor v Plumer* (1815) 3 M & S 562.

sion. The rule that a document evidencing a thing in action, although not the thing in action itself, can be converted, is also unaffected.

C. STATE OF MIND OF THE DEFENDANT

Save for the statutory conversion created by section 2(2) of the 1977 Act there can only be a conversion if there is *intentional conduct* resulting in an interference with the goods of the plaintiff.

In *Ashby v Tolhurst*:[1]

> A third party had driven away the plaintiff's car which he had left in the car park of the defendants. At the trial the plaintiff gave evidence that the attendant told him that he had 'given' the car to the third party. His case in conversion rested on the assertion that this word 'imports that the attendant took some active step to place this thief in possession of the motor-car'[2] but it was found 'impossible to collect that meaning out of the words'. There was therefore no conversion, quite apart from the fact that the conditions on the ticket were also deemed to exclude liability.

If the defendant intends that dealing with the goods which, in fact, interferes with the control of the plaintiff, that act will be conversion

> though the doer may not know of or intend to challenge the property or possession of the true owner.[3]

Mistake and good faith are irrelevant:

> the liability ... is founded upon what has been regarded as a salutary rule for the protection of property, namely, that persons deal with the property in chattels or exercise acts of ownership over them at their peril.[4]

So, as against the true owner, it is no defence for an auctioneer, after selling goods on behalf of a client, honestly delivering them to the buyer, and paying the proceeds of sale to his client, to say that he was unaware that his client did not own the goods.[5] And bailiffs seizing and selling a cash register at auction were liable to the plaintiff who had sold the cash register under an HP agreement whereby he retained property in the register until all payments were made, albeit the bailiffs had no reason to believe possession of the goods vested in any person other than the company against whom the seizure order was made and in whom physical possession of the register vested.[6]

---

1 [1937] 2 KB 242, [1937] 2 All ER 837, CA.
2 Ibid, at 251, 841, respectively (per Sir WILFRED GREENE MR).
3 *Caxton Publishing Co Ltd v Sutherland Publishing Co* [1939] AC 178 at 202, [1938] 4 All ER 389 at 404 (per LORD PORTER); *Douglas Valley Finance Co Ltd v S Hughes (Hirers) Ltd* [1969] 1 QB 738, [1966] 3 All ER 214 (ratio).
4 *Fowler v Hollins* (1872) LR 7 QB 616 at 639 (per CLEASBY B); affd sub nom *Hollins v Fowler* (1875) LR 7 HL 757; followed in *Union Transport Finance Ltd v British Car Auctions Ltd* [1978] 2 All ER 385, CA and *R H Willis & Son v British Car Auctions Ltd* [1978] 2 All ER 392, CA.
5 *Consolidated Co v Curtis & Son* [1892] 1 QB 495. In *Moorgate Mercantile Co Ltd v Finch and Read* [1962] 1 QB 701, [1962] 2 All ER 467, CA, the borrower of a car had it confiscated upon conviction for carrying in it uncustomed watches. This was rightly held to be a conversion, for the confiscation was the result of his intentional act of carrying the watches in the car.
6 *Chubb Cash Ltd v John Crilley & Son* [1983] 2 All ER 294, [1983] 1 WLR 599.

D. ACTS OF CONVERSION

In some of the acts of conversion now to be enumerated, especially those involving a sale of the goods, it is unchallengeably clear that the act is sufficiently inconsistent with the rights of the true owner to be a conversion. In many of the other ways of committing conversion, the courts have a discretion whether they will treat the act as sufficiently inconsistent with the right of the true owner to be a conversion—this is especially true in the case of physical damage to the goods and breach of bailment.

The courts have not freely spelt out the factors which go to the exercise of their discretion: the most important probably are the extent and duration of the control or dominion exercised over the goods, the intention and motive of the defendant, the amount of harm caused to the goods, and the expense and inconvenience suffered by the owner.

(1) TAKING GOODS OR DISPOSSESSING

To take goods out of the possession of another may be to convert them. To steal, or to seize under legal process without justification,[7] is a conversion. If, after lopping off the branches of his neighbour's apple tree when they overhang his land, a householder appropriates the fruit, he commits conversion.[8] Merely to remove goods from one place to another is not conversion;[9] where a porter moved goods of another in order to reach his own, and negligently failed to replace them, he was not liable in conversion for their subsequent loss.[10] It may be, however, that if they are moved to an unreasonable place with a consequent risk of loss, this is conversion; in *Forsdick v Collins*,[11] for instance, the defendant came into possession of land on which the plaintiff had a block of Portland stone and the removal of the Portland stone by the defendant 'to a distance' was held to be a conversion. A deprivation of the goods which is more than a mere moving of the goods, but in reality deprives the plaintiffs of the use of the goods for however short a time, will generally constitute conversion.[12] To make the plaintiff hand over goods under duress is conversion.[13]

(2) DESTROYING OR ALTERING

To destroy goods is to convert them, if done intentionally.[14] The *quantum* of harm constituting a destruction for this purpose is clearly a question of degree, but damage as such is not a conversion.[15] A change of identity not amounting to destruction is enough; for example, to draw out part of a vessel

---

7 *Tinkler v Poole* (1770) 5 Burr 2657; *Burton v Hughes* (1824) 2 Bing 173; *Chubb Cash Ltd v John Crilley (a firm)* (supra).
8 *Mills v Brooker* [1919] 1 KB 555.
9 *Fouldes v Willoughby* (1841) 8 M & W 540, where the defendant removed the plaintiff's horses from a ferry boat on to the shore because he did not wish the plaintiff to travel in the boat.
10 *Bushel v Miller* (1718) 1 Stra 128.
11 (1816) 1 Stark 173; cf *Sanderson v Marsden and Jones* (1922) 10 Ll L Rep 467, CA (defendant removing timber from quay to his premises not a conversion).
12 *Empresa Exportadora de Azura v IANSA* [1983] 2 Lloyd's Rep 171, CA; but see to the contrary *384238 Ontario Ltd v The Queen in the Right of Canada* (1983) 8 DLR (4th) 676.
13 *Grainger v Hill* (1838) 4 Bing NC 212.
14 Accidental destruction is not conversion: *Simmons v Lillystone* (1853) 8 Exch 431.
15 *Fouldes v Willoughby*, supra, at 549 (per ALDERSON B).

of liquor and fill it up with water is conversion,[16] but perhaps merely to cut a log in two is not.[17] If goods are applied for a purpose which eliminates their utility as goods in their original form, for instance, the making of wine from grapes, or of clothing from cloth, this is conversion,[18] but not to bottle another's wine in order to preserve it.[19]

(3) USING

'If a man takes my horse and rides it and then redelivers it to me nevertheless I may have an action against him, for this is a conversion . . .'[20] To use goods as your own is ordinarily to convert them; it was thus conversion for a person, to whom carbolic acid drums were delivered by mistake, to deal with them as his own by pouring the contents into his tank.[1] 'The wearing of a pearl is a conversion.'[2] In *Mulgrave v Ogden*[3] it was said:

> no law compelleth him that finds a thing to keep it safely; as if a man finds a garment, and suffers it to be moth-eaten; or if one find a horse, and giveth it no sustenance: but if a man find a thing and useth it, he is answerable, for it is conversion: so if he of purpose misuseth it; as if one finds paper, and puts it into the water, etc., but for negligent keeping no law punisheth him.

The claim of the plaintiff 'would not be defeated by the fact that the defendant whom he sues for the misuse of his temporary dominion of the property claims to be an agent for someone else'.[4] In a Scottish case a vendor who, without negligence, used a boat sold by him has been held liable in conversion to the buyer to whom property had passed.[5]

A mere misuse by a bailee, unaccompanied by any denial of title, is not a conversion although it might be some other tort.[6]

(4) RECEIVING

Voluntarily[7] to receive goods in consummation of a transaction which is intended by the parties to give to the recipient some proprietary rights in the goods may be a conversion actionable by the owner.[8] It has been held a

---

16 *Richardson v Atkinson* (1723) 1 Stra 576.
17 *Dictum* of PARKE B, in *Simmons v Lillystone* supra at 442.
18 Cf *Hollins v Fowler* (1875) LR 7 HL 757 at 764, 768 (*dictum* of BLACKBURN J, that a miller innocently grinding another's corn commits conversion).
19 *Philpott v Kelley* (1835) 3 Ad & El 106.
20 Rolle, *Abridgement*, tit. Action sur Case, 5.
 1 *Lancashire and Yorkshire Rly Co v MacNicoll* (1918) 88 LJKB 601.
 2 *Petre (Lord) v Hemeage* (1701) 12 Mod Rep 519 at 520 (per HOLT CJ).
 3 (1591) Cro Eliz 219.
 4 *Morison v London County and Westminster Bank Ltd* [1914] 3 KB 356, CA, at 386 (per PHILLIMORE LJ, *obiter*).
 5 *Knight v Wilson* 1949 SLT 26.
 6 *Lee v Atkinson and Brooks* (1609) Yelv 172 (when hirer of horse deviates, action on case lies) approved in *Donald v Suckling* (1866) LR 1 QB 585 at 615, by BLACKBURN J, who said that if the act is repugnant to the bailment, it is conversion, but 'where the act, though unauthorised, is not so repugnant to the contract as to show a disclaimer' it is case. *Penfolds Wines Proprietary Ltd v Elliott* (1946) 74 CLR 204; Paton, *Bailment*, 149, 303–4, 370; Palmer, *Bailment*, (1979) 754.
 7 Receipt by an involuntary bailee is not conversion, p 49, post.
 8 Cf *M'Combie v Davies* (1805) 6 East 538 at 540 (per LORD ELLENBOROUGH CJ): 'Certainly a man is guilty of a conversion who takes my property by assignment from another who has no authority to dispose of it; for what is that but assisting that other in carrying his wrongful act into effect?'

conversion for a purchaser so to receive goods,[9] or for a banker to receive a cheque from a person who has no title to it and to credit the proceeds to his account.[10] If the defendant in good faith receives the goods as a ware-houseman then he does not commit conversion;[11] this principle will extend to all who receive goods for transportation or safe keeping, because it is not the main purpose of such transactions to pass interests in the goods, although the law may collaterally attach interests by way of lien. Receipt of goods by way of pledge is conversion if the delivery of the goods is conversion.[12]

Exceptions to the principle that receiving is conversion

There are, however, many instances where the demands of commercial convenience have been thought to outweigh the need to protect owners of goods: indeed, the courts have in certain circumstances gone so far as to hold that receivers of goods from persons with no title commit no conversion, and sometimes that they even acquire a good title to them. Just some examples are given here.

(i) Where goods are sold in market overt, according to the usage of the market, the buyer acquires a good title to the goods and commits no conversion, provided that he buys them in good faith, and without any notice of any defect of title on the part of the seller.[13]

(ii) A true owner of goods may be precluded by his conduct from denying the seller's authority to sell, whereupon the buyer will acquire a good title.[14] Where a mercantile agent having authority in the ordinary course of his business to dispose of goods is in possession of such goods with the consent of the owner, any disposition of them made by him in the course of the business of a mercantile agent to a bona fide purchaser for value is as valid as if he had the authority of the owner.[15]

In recent times this provision has been most frequently invoked with reference to motor cars; for example, in *Pearson v Rose and Young Ltd*:[16]

> The plaintiff left his car with a mercantile agent who was not given instructions to sell but who was asked to see what offers would be made for it. The agent received it, intending to sell it and pocket the proceeds. To further this purpose he tricked the plaintiff into leaving the registration book in his office in circumstances clearly showing that the plaintiff never intended to leave it with him. The agent did sell the car and the plaintiff sought to recover it from a subsequent purchaser. The three judges in the Court of Appeal agreed that the plaintiff succeeded because the sale was

---

9　*Farrant v —— (1822) 3 Stark 130.
10　*Fine Arts Society v Union Bank of London* (1886) 17 QBD 705; *Underwood (AL) Ltd v Bank of Liverpool* [1924] 1 KB 775, CA; *Lloyds Bank v Chartered Bank of India, Australia and China* [1929] 1 KB 40, CA.
11　Per BLACKBURN J, in *Hollins v Fowler* (1875) LR 7 HL 757 at 767; cf *Sheridan v New Quay Co* (1858) 4 CB (NS) 618 (carrier).
12　Sale of Goods Act 1979, s 11(2).
13　Sale of Goods Act 1979, s 29. The judgment of DENNING J, in *Bishopgate Motor Finance Corporation Ltd v Transport Brakes Ltd* [1949] 1 KB 322 at 337–8, [1949] 1 All ER 37 at 46, 47, illustrates particularly clearly the way in which, when there is a sale in market overt, the clash between the principle of protecting property and that of protecting commercial transactions is resolved in favour of the latter.
14　Sale of Goods Act 1979, s 21.
15　Factors Act 1889, ss 1(1), 2(1).
16　[1951] 1 KB 275, [1950] 2 All ER 1027, CA.

outside the Factors Act, 1889, s 2(1); they agreed that the car, itself obtained by the agent by means of larceny by a trick, was none the less in his possession 'with the consent of the owner' within the meaning of the section. SOMERVELL LJ, and VAISEY J, held that a sale of a car is only 'in the ordinary course of business' if it is sold with the car's registration book to the possession of which by the agent the owner has consented, and that the plaintiff had not here consented. DENNING LJ agreed that the crucial point was that the plaintiff never consented to the agent's having possession of the registration book and said that the sale was outside the Act because, 'in the case of a car, "goods" in the Act means the car together with the registration book'.[17]

(iii) The receipt in good faith of goods or documents of title under a disposition by a person, (or his mercantile agent) who, having sold the goods, continues in possession of the goods or of the documents of title to the goods, is not a conversion.[18] Conversely, if a buyer transfers goods which have not yet vested in him, by himself or his mercantile agent delivering the goods or documents of title to a person receiving them in good faith, and if the buyer was in possession with the consent of the seller, there is no conversion by the recipient who may acquire a valid title.[19]

(iv) If a bona fide purchaser acquires a good title to a negotiable instrument upon delivery by a person without title his receipt of it on transfer is not a conversion.[20]

(v) If a seller or pledgor has a voidable title to the goods, and his title has not been avoided at the time of sale or pledge, a buyer or pledgee from him in good faith and without notice of the defect in his title will acquire a good title and will commit no conversion.[1] A voidable[2] title will arise, for example, under a contract induced by fraud, undue influence or duress.

(5) DISPOSITION WITHOUT DELIVERY

A person who agrees to sell goods to which he has no title and who does not transfer possession of them does not thereby ordinarily commit conversion, for the bargain and sale is void if the seller has no rights in the goods.[3] If,

---

17 *Pearson v Rose and Young Ltd* [1951] 1 KB 275 at 290 and 1033, 1034, respectively. In *Stadium Finance Ltd v Robbins* [1962] 2 QB 664, [1962] 2 All ER 633, CA, the owner left the car (but not the ignition key) with a dealer; the owner accidentally left the log book in the locked glove compartment. The owner left the car in order that the dealer could report any offers to buy it. Held that a sale by the dealer without the owner's actual authority was not in the ordinary course of business of a mercantile agent within the meaning of s 2(1). And see *Beverley Acceptances Ltd v Oakley* [1982] RTR 417, CA. (A car log book is not a document of title within s 2(1) of the Factors Act 1889.)

18 Factors Act 1889, s 8; Sale of Goods Act 1979, ss 24, 25: for its effect on hire-purchase transactions, and especially on the meaning of 'continues … in possession' see *Worcester Works Finance Ltd v Cooden Engineering Co Ltd* [1972] 1 QB 210, [1971] 3 All ER 708, CA.

19 Factors Act 1889, s 9; Sale of Goods Act 1979, s 25(1). And see *Newtons of Wembley Ltd v Williams* [1965] 1 QB 560, [1964] 3 All ER 532.

20 Sometimes now statutory, eg ss 29, 38, of the Bills of Exchange Act 1882, extended to cheques (s 73) and promissory notes (s 89). There are special, detailed and complex rules relating to cheques, see the Cheques Act 1957, s 4(3) and the Banking Act 1979, s 47.

1 Section 23, of the Sale of Goods Act 1979; *King's Norton Metal Co Ltd v Eldridge, Merrett & Co* (1897) 14 TLR 98, CA.

2 Of course, this is not so if the contract is void; hence the importance of the distinction between mistake nullifying consent and fraud.

3 *Lancashire Waggon Co v Fitzhugh* (1861) 6 H & N 502; he may, however, be liable for injurious falsehood; see ch 8, post.

however, the agreement of sale is made in market overt, the agreement passes the property in the goods, and will amount to a conversion by the seller even though the goods are never delivered to the buyer.[4]

(6) DISPOSITION AND DELIVERY

Ordinarily a person who without lawful authority disposes of goods with the intention of transferring the title or some other right in the goods, and who delivers the goods, thereby commits a conversion. A sale and a pledge[5] may each constitute such a disposition. In *Syeds v Hay*[6] the rule applied to a sea-captain who delivered goods to a wharfinger in the wrong belief that the wharfinger had a lien on them.

The main difficulty arises where the defendant is an innocent transferor. Innocence of itself is no defence; so the auctioneer who sells in good faith goods which do not belong to his client commits conversion by handing them over to the buyer.[7] Yet it is felt that this need to support the validity of commercial dealings must, in the interests of innocent defendants, have some limits.

In *Hollins v Fowler*[8] LORD BLACKBURN said:

> one who deals with goods at the request of the person who has the actual custody of them, in the *bona fide* belief that the custodier is the true owner, or has the authority of the true owner, should be excused for what he does if the act is of such a nature as would be excused if done by the authority of the person in possession, if he was a finder of the goods or intrusted with their custody.

This did not exclude from liability the defendants in the instant case, who were acting as cotton brokers, buying, not as agents on account of a certain customer as principal, but in expectation of finding a customer. The principle seems to be this: if the defendant has himself negotiated the transaction and then disposes of the goods in pursuance of it, he is liable; if, on the other hand, someone else has effected the transaction, and the defendant acting on his behalf merely delivers in consummation of that transaction, it is not conversion by the defendant. Therefore, a packer shipping goods on the order of his principal does not commit conversion;[9] nor in similar circumstances do mere carriers[10] or warehousemen.[11] *National Mercantile Bank v Rymill*[12] marks the furthest limit of this exception and is distinguishable from *Consolidated Co v Curtis* only in that the auctioneer did not negotiate the sale.

---

4 Section 22 of the Sale of Goods Act 1979.

5 *Parker v Godin* (1728) 2 Stra 813.

6 (1791) 4 Term Rep 260. But if one man entrusts another with a chattel to be used by him, the bailor impliedly authorises the bailee to allow a lien for the cost of necessary repairs to be created over it: *Green v All Motors Ltd* [1917] 1 KB 625, CA; *Tappenden v Artus* [1964] 2 QB 185, [1963] 3 All ER 213, CA.

7 *Consolidated Co v Curtis & Son* [1892] 1 QB 495; *Barker v Furlong* [1891] 2 Ch 172 at 181.

8 (1875) LR 7 HL 757 at 766–7; in *Re Samuel* (No 2) [1945] Ch 408, [1945] 2 All ER 437, n, a solicitor who received jewellery from the agent of his bankrupt client and handed it to another agent on his client's instructions knowing of the intention to sell it, was held to be acting ministerially and not liable in conversion.

9 *Greenway v Fisher* (1824) 1 C & P 190.

10 *Sheridan v New Quay Co* (1858) 4 CB NS 618.

11 *Glyn Mills v E & W India Dock Co* (1880) 6 QBD 475 at 491 (per BRAMWELL B), affd (1882) 7 App Cas 591, HL.

12 (1881) 44 LT 767.

Goods were deposited with the defendant auctioneer to sell; the seller eventually sold them himself, and, on his instructions, the defendant handed them to the buyer and in so doing was held not liable in conversion to the true owner.

In *R H Willis & Son v British Car Auctions Ltd* Lord Denning treated the *Rymill* case as a departure from *Hollins v Fowler* by a court anxious to protect the auctioneer, and decided that an auctioneer is liable in conversion to the true owner where goods are sold by his intervention, under the hammer or as the result of a provisional bid.[13]

If an involuntary bailee, acting reasonably, delivers goods to one who is not entitled to them he does not commit conversion. Thus, where, upon goods being refused at the consignee's late place of business, the carrier took them back to his store and notified the consignee, and then handed them to a former employee of the consignee (being unaware that this man had left the consignee's employment), this was no conversion.[14] If the defendant is not placed in the dilemma of the involuntary bailee and none the less makes himself a party to an unauthorised transfer he commits conversion. In *Hiort v Bott*,[15] for example,

> an invoice and delivery order were mistakenly sent by the plaintiffs to the defendant. Thinking that he was thereby correcting the error, on his own initiative the defendant indorsed the delivery order over to the plaintiff's agent, who thereby obtained the goods for himself. This was conversion.[16]

In the case of cheques and some other negotiable instruments there is a limited statutory exemption from liability. A banker paying a cheque (even though not indorsed or irregularly indorsed) in good faith and in the ordinary course of business to the collecting banker is in the same position as if he had paid it to the true owner.[17]

(7) MISDELIVERY BY CARRIER

A carrier[18] or warehouseman[19] who by mistake delivers goods to the wrong person, commits a conversion whether or not his mistake was innocent.[20] But failure to deliver because the goods have been lost or destroyed by accident

---

13 [1978] 2 All ER 392, CA where the police seized a gig from A, and, when he was later found not guilty of stealing it, after demand by the true owner for possession, handed it back to A, this was a conversion by the police actionable by the true owner; *Winter v Bancks* (1901) 84 LT 504.

14 *Heugh v London and North Western Rly Co* (1870) LR 5 Exch 51; cf *Elvin and Powell Ltd v Plummer Roddis Ltd* (1933) 50 TLR 158, where plaintiff's counsel conceded that the defendant did not intend to deny the title of the plaintiff.

15 (1874) LR 9 Exch 86.

16 Contra, if as in *Elvin and Powell v Plummer Roddis* supra, the goods themselves had been delivered to the defendant and handed by him to the third party.

17 Section 80 of the Bills of Exchange Act 1882, as amended by s 1 of the Cheques Act 1957.

18 *Youl v Harbottle* (1791) Peake 68, NP.

19 *Devereux v Barclay* (1819) 2 B & Ald 702.

20 If the carrier delivers in accordance with the seller's instructions (or even as a carrier would interpret his instructions according to the usual course of business although he in fact delivered them to a person to whom the seller did not intend delivery to be made) this is not a misdelivery—*McKean v McIvor* (1870) LR 6 Exch 36. It is conversion by a carrier to deliver goods to another carrier by whom they are misappropriated, unless the defendant carrier is authorised to make a sub-contract; *Garnham, Harris and Elton v Alfred W Ellis (Transport) Ltd* [1967] 2 All ER 940.

or carelessness is not conversion.[1] Nor is it conversion for a bailee[2] or pledgee[3] without notice of the claim of the true owner to return goods to the person from whom he received them.

(8) REFUSAL TO SURRENDER ON DEMAND

A refusal to surrender goods upon lawful and reasonable demand is a conversion.[4] In particular, this covers the situation where the possession of the defendant was originally lawful; it may be invoked, for example, where the receiving is not itself actionable.

Many of the cases on wrongful detention were actions of detinue. With the abolition of detinue, conversion will now apparently lie in every case in which detinue would formerly have lain. The most important case since the 1977 Act is *Howard E Perry & Co Ltd v British Railways Board*.[5]

> The defendants admitted that the plaintiffs owned and were entitled to immediate possession of steel held by them as carriers in their depots. There was a national steelworkers' strike, and their union had sought the support of railway unions. The defendants feared sympathetic industrial action by their employees if they allowed the plaintiffs to collect the steel. Their refusal to allow the plaintiffs to enter the depots and collect the steel was held wrongful.

There is a large amount of case-law on this topic, but the principles are quite simple. Even if the defendant no longer has possession at the time of the demand and refusal it is no defence for him to prove that prior to the accrual of the plaintiff's title he wrongfully parted with them.[6] If the defendant refuses to surrender in circumstances where it would be unreasonable for him to do so immediately on demand, this is not conversion. The defendant may postpone surrender until after he has had a reasonable time in which to confirm the title of the claimant, or, if he is a servant, to consult his master.[7] This reasonableness is a question of fact; many factors may be relevant—the time of the demand, the expense and inconvenience of immediate compliance, the knowledge on the part of the defendant of the claimant's title, and of his identity, and whether the defendant has adequately conveyed to the plaintiff the grounds for his temporary refusal. The doctrine of estoppel may sometimes operate to prevent the defendant from setting up facts which would otherwise have justified a refusal.[8]

---

1 *Owen v Lewyn* (1672) 1 Vent 223; *The Arpad* [1934] P 189 at 232, CA (per MAUGHAM LJ).
2 *Hollins v Fowler* (1875) LR 7 HL 757 at 767 (per BLACKBURN J). Otherwise the bailee would be in an impossible position, for if he retained he could not plead a title paramount of which he was unaware.
3 *Union Credit Bank Ltd v Mersey Docks and Harbour Board* [1899] 2 QB 205.
4 *Eason v Newman* (1596) Cro Eliz 495; *Isaack v Clark* (1615) 2 Bulst 306 at 310 (per DODDERIDGE J); *Baldwin v Cole* (1704) 6 Mod Rep 212.
5 [1980] 2 All ER 579.
6 *Bristol and West of England Bank v Midland Rly Co* [1891] 2 QB 653, CA.
7 *Alexander v Southey* (1821) 5 B & Ald 247.
8 *Seton, Laing & Co v Lafone* (1887) 19 QBD 68; *Henderson & Co v Williams* [1895] 1 QB 521, CA.

(9) GOODS LOST OR DESTROYED

At common law there could be no conversion where there was no voluntary act. Section 2 of the Torts (Interference with Goods) Act 1977 which abolishes detinue therefore further provides in section 2(2):

'An action lies in conversion for loss or destruction of goods which a bailee has allowed to happen in breach of his duty to his bailor (that is to say it lies in a case which is not otherwise conversion, but would have been detinue before detinue was abolished)'.[9]

Denial of title is not of itself conversion.[10] There may, however, be conversion of goods although the defendant has not physically dealt with them,[11] or been in physical possession of them,[12] if his acts deprive the plaintiff of his right to possession or amount to a substantial interference with that right.[13] But a mere threat to prevent an owner in possession from removing his goods will not of itself amount to conversion.[14]

Where goods are left on land, and the occupier refuses to allow the owner of the goods to enter the land and retrieve them, the refusal is not necessarily conversion.[15] It may become conversion, however, if the occupier sets up in himself any right in respect of the goods,[16] or denies the plaintiff most of the rights of ownership, including the right to possession, for a period which is plainly indefinite.[17]

(10) RESIDUAL ACTS AMOUNTING TO A CONVERSION

It must be emphasised again that the above are not exhaustive categories of acts of conversion. There are other acts which are not capable of being readily classified and which may yet fall within the definition of conversion.[18] In these residual cases the judicial discretion whether to treat the act as sufficiently inconsistent with the true owner's rights for a conversion is especially important.

9 A bailee will ordinarily be liable unless he disproves fault; *Houghland v R R Low (Luxury Coaches) Ltd* [1962] 1 QB 694, [1962] 2 All ER 159, CA. An involuntary bailee is not liable for failure to return merely because he has lost it; *Howard v Harris* (1884) 1 Cab & El 253, but he is liable if he destroys or damages the goods. If the bailee is unaware that the goods on his premises are not his property, ie an 'unconscious bailee', he is under a duty to exercise reasonable care to ascertain that they were his own before he destroys them; *AVX Ltd v EGM Solders Ltd* (1982) Times, 7 July.
10 Torts (Interference with Goods) Act, 1977, s 11(3). Cf *Oakley v Lyster* [1931] 1 KB 148, CA.
11 *Van Oppen & Co Ltd v Tredegars Ltd* (1921) 37 TLR 504.
12 Eg *Oakley v Lyster* [1931] 1 KB 148, CA (conversion of hardcore on another's land by taking possession of part thereof and total denial and repudiation of owner's right to remainder); and see *Halsbury* para 1427.
13 *Oakley v Lyster* [1931] 1 KB 148, CA; *Lancashire and Yorkshire Rly Co, London and North Western Rly Co and Graeser Ltd v MacNicoll* (1918) 88 LJ KB 601.
14 *England v Cowley* (1873) LR 8 Exch 126 (landlord wishing to distrain stated that he would not permit holder of bill of sale to remove goods unless rent was paid).
15 *Wilde v Waters* (1855) 24 LJ CP 193 at 195, MAULE J; *British Economical Lamp Co Ltd v Empire Mile End Ltd* (1913) 29 TLR 386.
16 *Walker v Clyde* (1861) 10 CB (NS) 381; *H E Dibble Ltd v Moore* [1970] 2 QB 181, [1969] 3 All ER 1465, CA.
17 *Howard E Perry & Co Ltd v British Railways Board* [1980] 2 All ER 579 at 583, per SIR ROBERT MEGARRY VC; *Bryanston Leasings Ltd v Principality Finance Ltd* [1977] RTR 45.
18 Binding together infringing sheets of a book is conversion under the Copyright Act—*Caxton Publishing Co Ltd v Sutherland Publishing Co* [1939] AC 178, [1938] 4 All ER 389, HL.

E. CONVERSION AS BETWEEN CO-OWNERS

Co-ownership does not afford a defence to certain proceedings in conversion. Section 10(1)(a) of the 1977 Act provides that co-ownership is no defence to an action founded on conversion where the defendant, without the authority of the other co-owner, destroys the goods, or disposes of them in a way giving a good title to the entire property in the goods, or otherwise does anything equivalent to the destruction of the other interest in the goods. This principle was well established at common law,[19] and section 10(1)(a) is declared to be by way of restatement of existing law.[20] Thus a partner who paid cheques into a third person's bank account was, by excluding his co-owner's right to enjoy the proceeds, liable for conversion.[1] A co-owner cannot, however, be sued for conversion if he merely makes use of the common property in a reasonable way.[2] Nor was there necessarily a conversion where the co-owner took and kept the goods.[3] The law required (and still does) a destruction of the goods or something equivalent to it.[4]

The 1977 Act, however, does alter the common law by further providing in section 10(1)(b) that it is also no defence to an action founded on conversion where the defendant, without the authority of the other co-owner, purports to dispose of the goods in such a way as would give a good title to the entire property in the goods if he were acting with the authority of all co-owners of the goods. At common law a sale and delivery by a co-owner which did not pass title was not a conversion because it was not akin to destruction of the plaintiff's property.

The foregoing rules do not affect the law concerning execution or enforcement of judgments, or concerning any form of distress.[5]

F. REMEDIES: DAMAGES

The major effect of the 1977 Act is to rationalise the remedies available to plaintiffs suing in conversion both in relation to the damages which may be awarded and in making provision for specific return of the goods by way of orders for delivery.

(1) At common law a plaintiff with a limited interest in the goods could normally recover their full value from a third party. Under section 8 of the 1977 Act and rules of court the plaintiff now has to identify any other person whom he knows to have an interest in the goods and any such interested party may be joined, whereupon the damages may be apportioned amongst

---

19 *Jacobs v Seward* (1872) LR 5 HL 464.
20 Torts (Interference with Goods) Act 1977, s 10(3).
 1 *Baker v Barclay's Bank Ltd* [1955] 2 All ER 571.
 2 As, for instance, by cutting grass and making hay in the common field (*Jacobs v Seward* (1872) LR 5 HL 464) or extracting the oil and the other valuable parts of a dead whale which is owned in common (*Fennings v Lord Grenville* (1808) 1 Taunt 241).
 3 The bailee of common property from one co-owner is not guilty of conversion if he refuses to deliver the property on the demand of another co-owner (*Atwood v Ernest* (1853) 13 CB 881; *Harper v Godsell* (1870) LR 5 QB 422) unless the latter has a special property in the entire chattel (*Nyberg v Handelaar* [1892] 2 QB 202, CA).
 4 *Morgan v Marquis* (1854) 9 Exch 145; *Baker v Barclay's Bank Ltd* [1955] 2 All ER 571.
 5 Torts (Interference with Goods) Act 1977, s 11(2). The rules apply equally to intentional trespass to goods as they apply to conversion.

the interested parties in proportion to their respective interests.[6] Where the other interested party is not traced, as in cases of finding, or a missing bailor, the plaintiff in possession can recover the full value of the goods, but is liable to account to the true owner.[7]

Where the defendant has an interest in the goods, then the plaintiff's damages in respect of the interference with his interest are limited to the value of that interest.[8] An unpaid seller who sold to a third party has been held liable to the original buyer, to whom he had not delivered the goods,[9] who was not in default, only for the value of the goods less the contract price owing to him; the policy behind this is lucidly explained by BRAMWELL B:[10]

> a man cannot by merely changing the form of action[11] entitle himself to recover damages greater than the amount to which he is in law entitled, according to the true facts of the case and the real nature of the transaction.

(2) The plaintiff in conversion is entitled to be compensated to the extent of the value to him of the goods of which he has been deprived. This will often appropriately be the market value of the goods. Where goods are of a kind which can be readily bought in the market the actual market value[12] will be the appropriate measure; otherwise the replacement value in a comparable state[13] or the original cost minus depreciation will be the standard. Where the actual value of the plaintiff's interest in the goods is less than the market value he may be awarded the value of that interest and not the higher market value.[14] In *Wickham Holdings Ltd v Brooke House Motors*[15] the hirer of a car sold the car in breach of his hire purchase agreement. The finance company, who owned the car, were held able to recover from the ultimate purchaser of the vehicle only the value of the outstanding hire purchase instalments due, and not the higher value of the car itself. In *Chubb Cash Ltd v John Crilley (a firm)*[16] the plaintiff sold a cash register on hire purchase terms. He then assigned the instalments due under the agreement to a credit company in return for a loan agreeing to pay all instalments due should the purchaser of the register default on the hire purchase company. In his action for conversion against bailiffs who had seized the cash register the plaintiff was awarded only the market value of the goods and not the higher amount due under his agreement with the credit company. That consequential loss was held to be irrecoverable.

Where a negotiable instrument or other document ordinarily representing a chose in action is converted, the value which the document represents, and

---

6   Section 7(2) and p 41, ante.
7   *Wilson v Lombank Ltd* [1963] 1 All ER 740.
8   *Johnson v Stear* (1863) 15 CB (NS) 330 (owner suing pledgee); *Belsize Motor Supply Co v Cox* [1914] 1 KB 244 (owner suing assignee of hirer).
9   If an unpaid seller takes goods out of the buyer's possession he is liable in conversion for the full value of the goods without deduction for the unpaid price: *Healing (Sales) Pty Ltd v Inglis Electrix Ltd* (1968) 42 AJLR 280, H Ct Australia, following *Gillard v Britton* (1841) 8 M & W 575.
10 *Chinery v Viall* (1860) 5 H & N 288.
11 Ie from breach of contract to conversion.
12 Including, where applicable, purchase tax. *Martin v London County Council* [1947] KB 628.
13 *Hall (J & E) Ltd v Barclay* [1937] 3 All ER 620, CA.
14 But see *Edmondson v Nuttall* (2864) 17 CB (NS) 280; and *Wilson v Lombank Ltd* [1963] 1 All ER 740 (a case in trespass).
15 [1967] 1 All ER 117, CA.
16 [1983] 2 All ER 294.

not merely its value as a piece of paper, is the basis of the *quantum* of damages. Where there is an infringement of copyright in part of a book the damages are based on the proportion of the value of the whole book, less the cost of binding, which the infringing matter bears to the whole of the book.[17] In *Ash v Dickie*[18] an article in the defendant's newspaper infringed the plaintiff's copyright, and it was held that the damages were to be based, not on the pulp value by weight, but upon the selling price of the newspaper and the proportion which the infringing article bore to the whole issue.

(3) The time at which the value of the goods is to be determined is, ordinarily, the date of the conversion. Once a claim for conversion has accrued to the plaintiff it is not open to him to delay the issue of his writ and thereby base his action on a subsequent demand and refusal—the duty to mitigate damages operates.[19]

If the goods decrease in value between the date of the conversion and the date of judgment the plaintiff may still recover the value at the date of conversion.[20] In *Solloway v McLaughlin*[1]

> The defendant broker fraudulently and contrary to his instructions sold shares of the plaintiff deposited with him. By the time of the trial the defendants had bought in replacement an equivalent number of the shares at a greatly reduced market value. Although the net result was to put the plaintiff in a better position than if his instructions had been obeyed, he was held entitled to recover the differences between the value of the shares at the time of the conversion and the value of the shares since bought in replacement.

Nevertheless, the market value (even where ascertainable) at conversion will not necessarily mark the top limit of damages recoverable in conversion in the following instances:

(i) Evidence comes in later to show what was the value at conversion.[2]

(ii) The market value of the goods rises between the date of the cause of action and trial. If the act of conversion relied on by the plaintiff is a sale, and by the time when the plaintiff knows or ought to know of the sale the value has increased, the plaintiff can recover that higher value.[3] There is some authority also for the view that the plaintiff may recover from a broker who has sold his stock its increased value within a reasonable time for buying replacement stock,[4] ie the court estimates the value of the chance of a profit.[5] In *Greening v Wilkinson*:[6]

> The defendant refused to hand over to the plaintiff the plaintiff's

---

17 *Caxton Publishing Co Ltd v Sutherland Publishing Co* [1939] AC 178, HL.
18 [1936] Ch 655, [1936] 2 All ER 71, CA.
19 *Empresa Exportadora de Azucar v IANSA* [1983] 2 Lloyd's Rep 171, CA.
20 *Rhodes v Moules* [1895] 1 Ch 236; the defendants converted the plaintiff's bearer shares, the market price of which dropped after the conversion, and the Court of Appeal refused to allow the defendant to satisfy the judgment against him by purchasing the same number of shares for the plaintiff.
1 [1938] AC 247, [1937] 4 All ER 328, PC.
2 *Caxton Publishing Co Ltd v Sutherland Publishing Co* [1939] AC 178 at 203, HL (per LORD PORTER).
3 *Sachs v Miklos* [1948] 2 KB 23, [1948] 1 All ER 67, CA.
4 *Samuel and Escombe v Rowe* (1892) 8 TLR 488.
5 *Aiken v Gardiner* (1956) 4 DLR (2d) 119 (Ontario HC).
6 (1825) 1 C & P 625.

warrants for cotton and relying on this demand and refusal the warrants were worth 6d. per lb. and at trial 10½d. The jury awarded
damages on the basis of 10½d. per lb. in accordance with ABBOTT CJ's
ruling that they 'may give the value at the time of the conversion, or
at any subsequent time, at their discretion, because the plaintiff might
have had a good opportunity of selling the goods if they had not been
detained'.[7]

(iii) If the defendant converts the plaintiff's goods and he then increases their
value the plaintiff cannot ordinarily recover that increased value.[8] Thus
where the defendant converted a partially built ship which he then
completed at his own expense the court's view was that the plaintiff was
entitled to recover the market value of the completed ship less the expense
incurred by the defendant in completing it.[9] Where the act of conversion
relied on takes place after the improvement made to the goods, section
6(1) of the Act is applicable now. If the defendant has improved the
goods in the mistaken but honest belief that he had a good title to them
an allowance is made for the extent to which at the time at which the
goods fall to be valued in assessing damages, the value of the goods is
attributable to the improvement. If, for example, the improver is sued
for later selling the goods, the statutory allowance applies.[10] A similar
allowance is enjoyed by purported purchasers of goods improved by
another, provided again that the purchaser acted in good faith.[11] Subsequent purchasers enjoy the same protection.[12] Thus an eventual buyer
in good faith of a stolen car when sued by the true owner will have the
damages reduced to reflect any improvements made on it since the
theft. The Act leaves it uncertain whether the common law rule that an
improver who did not act in good faith was entitled to a deduction still
survives, or whether the statutory requirement of good faith must be
taken to supersede the common law. At common law special rules
applied to goods severed from the land such as coal and other minerals,[13]
and timber:[14] if, for instance, the defendant innocently severed the plaintiff's coal he was liable only for the value of the coal in the seam, but if
his act was wilful, he was liable for its value immediately after severance.[15]
These rules may be unaffected by the Act.[16]

(iv) If the plaintiff incurs pecuniary loss as a direct consequence of the
conversion he may recover this as special damage in addition to the

---

7 LORD PORTER left open the soundness of this judgment in *Caxton Publishing Co Ltd v
Sutherland Publishing Co* [1939] AC 178 at 203, HL.
8 *Caxton Publishing Co Ltd v Sutherland Publishing Co* supra; *Greenwood v Bennett* [1973] 1
QB 195, [1972] 3 All ER 586.
9 *Reid v Fairbanks* (1853), 13 CB 692 (the parties settled the size of the damages awarded).
10 And see *Munro v Willmott* [1949] 1 KB 295, [1948] 2 All ER 983 at common law (where
plaintiff relied on a demand and refusal rather than an earlier conversion the plaintiff could
not recover the value as increased by the defendant's improvement).
11 Section 6(2).
12 Section 6(3).
13 The English cases have concerned coal; the rule was applied to shale in *Blenheim Borough
and Wairau River Board v British Pavements (Canterbury) Ltd*, [1940] NZLR 564.
14 *Burmah Trading Corpn v Mirza Mahomed Allay Sherazee and Burmah Co Ltd* (1875) LR 5
Ind App 130; *Union Bank of Canada v Rideau Lumber Co* (1902) 4 OLR 721; *Greer v Faulkner*
(1908) 40 SCR 399 (Canada).
15 *Wood v Morewood* (1841) 3 QB 440n.
16 The Act applies only where the defendant improves goods; it seems doubtful whether severing
minerals to make them saleable is to 'improve' them.

market value of the goods. A workman deprived of his tools recovered loss of wages;[17] the owner of a converted pony could claim the cost of hiring another.[18]

In *Strand Electric and Engineering Co Ltd v Brisford Entertainments Ltd*[19] (an action in detinue):

> In the course of their business the plaintiffs hired to the defendants some switchboards. The plaintiffs claimed the return of the goods and damages for their detention. Besides ordering the return of the goods the court awarded damages on the basis of a reasonable hiring charge for the entire period of detention until judgment. Nor were the damages to be limited to the loss of profit of the plaintiff; the fact that for some of the period during which the defendant detained the equipment the plaintiff would not have been able to find another hirer was irrelevant.

Although detinue is abolished by section 2(1) of the 1977 Act, section 3 of the Act, in effect, preserves the remedies for what would previously have constituted detinue by making such remedies available in conversion.[20] Where the defendant has possession of the goods at the time that proceedings are begun, he cannot, by disposing of the goods, reduce his liability for loss occasioned by detention of a profit earning chattel to the market value thereof.[1]

(v) The effect as between the parties to a satisfied judgment for damages in conversion is to transfer the title to the defendant.[2] It follows that the court will not award damages for loss of use as well as the value of the goods where the effect would be doubly to compensate the plaintiff: the capacity for profitable use is part of the value of the goods. Thus where the defendant converted certain manufacturing plant of the plaintiff, he was liable for the value of the plant when converted but not for loss of use between that date and trial.[3] On the other hand, if the defendant wrongfully detained goods and later sold them it seems that the plaintiff could recover in addition to their value the loss of use from the date of the unlawful detention until sale,[4] and indeed until the plaintiff had a reasonable opportunity to buy a replacement after learning of that sale,[5] but not for loss of use until trial.

(vi) It is doubtful in what circumstances a buyer who does not recover his goods can claim a loss of re-sale profit,[6] where the action of conversion

---

17 *Bodley v Reynolds* (1846) 8 QB 779.
18 *Davis v Oswell* (1837) 7 C & P 804.
19 [1952] 2 QB 246, [1952] 1 All ER 796, CA. Where a defendant converted a Rolls Royce on hire from the plaintiffs and then put it out of his power to return it, he remained liable for the hiring charge until it was returned, namely over £13,000, although its value when converted was only £7,500. *Hillesden Securities Ltd v Ryjak Ltd* [1983] 2 All ER 184, [1983] 1 WLR 959.
20 *Hillesden Securities Ltd v Ryjak Ltd* [1983] 2 All ER 184, [1983] 1 WLR 959.
 1 Ibid.
 2 *Ellis v John Stenning & Son* [1932] 2 Ch 81, [1932] All ER Rep 597.
 3 *Re Simms, Ex parte Trustee* [1934] Ch 1, [1933] All ER 302, CA.
 4 *Strand Electric and Engineering Co Ltd v Brisford Entertainments Ltd* [1952] 2 QB 246, [1952] All ER 796, CA, at 255 and 801 respectively (per DENNING LJ).
 5 *Re Simms, Ex parte Trustee* supra, at 30 (per ROMER LJ).
 6 This loss was recovered in *France v Gaudet* (1871) LR 6 QB 199.

based on non-delivery is an alternative to an action in contract and the seller is unaware of the re-sale contract, this loss of profit is not recoverable as such in conversion, although where there is no market in the goods the re-sale price may be evidence of value.[7]

The courts will, if the defendant returns the goods before trial, reduce the damages in conversion by the amount of its value at that time:[8] in short, the court will not enforce a sale on the defendant, and 'subject to the payment of costs and special damages (if there are any) an action for damages for conversion can always be stayed if the defendant offers to hand over the property in dispute'.[9] The value of the goods when returned is set off against the damages calculated as set out in the preceding paragraphs. Where goods acquired by the plaintiff for use in a manufacturing process have been wrongfully detained and later returned to him, the plaintiff must show that a loss of profit or other pecuniary loss has resulted from the detention.[10] If he fails to prove that he would have used the goods at any time before their return he cannot recover the fall in their market value over the period of their detention and may receive only nominal damages.[11] It will be otherwise where he has purchased the goods for re-sale during the period of detention.[12]

G. REMEDIES: OTHER FORMS OF RELIEF

The 1977 Act introduces common remedies for all forms of 'wrongful interferences with goods'. Section 3 provides that in proceedings for conversion, or for any other chattel tort, against a person in possession or control of goods,[13] the following relief may be given, as far as is appropriate:[14] an order for delivery and for payment of any consequential damages;[15] an order for delivery of the goods, but giving the defendant the alternative of paying

---

7 *The Arpad* [1934] P 189, CA. Conversely, a buyer still recovers the market value from a seller not delivering to him, although the loss of the buyer on his contract of re-sale is less than this sum; *D. Joseph Ltd v Ralph Wood & Co Ltd* [1951] WN 224.

8 *Fisher v Prince* (1762) 3 Burr 1363; *Solloway v McLaughlin* [1938] AC 247 at 258–9, [1937] 4 All ER 328 at 332, 333, PC.

9 *USA and Republic of France v Dollfus Mieg et Compagnie SA and Bank of England* [1952] AC 582 at 619, [1952] 1 All ER 572 at 590 (per LORD RADCLIFFE).

10 *Brandeis Goldschmidt & Co Ltd v Western Transport Ltd* [1981] QB 864 at 870, [1982] 1 All ER 28 at 31, CA per BRANDON LJ; *Williams v The Peel River Land and Mineral Co Ltd* (1886) 55 LT 689 at 692–693, CA per BOWEN LJ. See also *Williams v Archer* (1847) 5 CB 318; *Barrow v Arnaud* (1846) 8 QB 595.

11 *Williams v Peel River Land and Mineral Co Ltd* (1886) 55 LT 689 at 692–693, CA per BOWEN LJ; *Bryanston Leasings Ltd v Principality Finance Ltd* [1977] RTR 45; *Brandeis Goldschmidt & Co Ltd v Western Transport Ltd* [1981] QB 864 at 871, [1982] 1 All ER 28 at 32, CA per BRANDON LJ.

12 *Brandeis Goldschmidt & Co Ltd v Western Transport Ltd* [1981] QB 864 at 873, [1982] 1 All ER 28 at 34, CA per BRANDON LJ.

13 Even though the defendant is no longer in possession at the date of judgment, the liability in damages for what was formerly detinue remains under section 3; *Hillesden Securities Ltd v Ryjack Ltd* [1983] 2 All ER 184.

14 Torts (Interference with Goods) Act 1977, s 3(1). See *Secretary of State for Defence v Guardian Newspapers Ltd* [1985] AC 339, [1984] 3 All ER 601 (the plaintiff sought delivery up of a photostatic copy of a secret ministerial memorandum).

15 Section 3(2)(a). Cf *Howard E Perry & Co Ltd v British Railways Board* [1980] 2 All ER 579.

damages by reference to the value of the goods, together in either alternative with payment of any consequential damages;[16] or damages.[17]

If it is shown to the court's satisfaction that an order for delivery and payment of any consequential damages has not been complied with, the court may revoke the order (or the relevant part of it)[18] and make an order for payment of damages by reference to the value of the goods.[19]

Where an order is made for delivery but giving the defendant the alternative of paying damages,[20] the defendant may satisfy the order by returning the goods at any time before execution of judgment, but without prejudice to liability to pay any consequential damages.[1]

Where goods are not detained (as where they are lost or destroyed) the normal form of judgment is for damages.

H. LIMITATION OF ACTIONS

The Limitation Act 1980 provides that once the period of limitation has expired, the plaintiff's title to the goods is extinguished.[2] The Act further provides that where there are successive conversions in respect of the same goods, whether by the same person or not, the cause of action is extinguished after six years from the first conversion.[3] If the action is based on fraud or if the right of action is concealed by fraud the period of limitation (normally six years under the Act)[4] does not begin to run until the plaintiff discovers or ought to have discovered the fraud.[5] The first part of this has no application to conversion which is not an action based on fraud, but if the circumstances of the commission of a conversion are such that a plaintiff could not reasonably be expected to know that the conversion was taking place, this is a concealment of the right of action within the Act.[6]

The Limitation Act 1980 also has complex provisions designed to enable owners from whom goods are stolen to sue the thief without limit of time.[7]

---

16 Section 3(2)(b). Cf *Howard E Perry & Co Ltd v British Railways Board* supra.
17 Torts (Interference with Goods) Act 1977, s 3(2)(c).
18 Section 3(4)(a).
19 Section 3(4)(b).
20 Ie under Torts (Interference with Goods) Act 1977, s 3(2)(b). An order for delivery of the goods under s 3(2)(a) or 3(2)(b) of the Act may impose such conditions as may be determined by the court, or pursuant to rules of court, and in particular, where damages by reference to the value of the goods would not be the whole of the value of the goods, may require an allowance to be made by the claimant to reflect the difference: s 3(2)(b). For example, a bailor's action against the bailee may be one in which the measure of damages is not the full value of the goods. Then, the court may order delivery of the goods, but require the bailor to pay the bailee a sum reflecting the difference: ibid. Where an allowance is to be made under s 6(1) or 6(2) of the Act in respect of an improvement of the goods and an order is made under s 3(2)(a) or 3(2)(b) of the Act, the court may assess the allowance to be made in respect of the improvement and by the order require, as a condition for delivery of the goods, that allowance to be made by the claimant.
1 Section 3(5).
2 Section 2(3)(2). *R B Policies at Lloyd's v Butler* [1950] 1 KB 76, [1949] 2 All ER 226.
3 Section 3(1).
4 See p 510, post.
5 Section 32. The section adds that a subsequent bona fide purchaser is not prejudiced by these provisions should the owner seek to recover the property from him; and see *Eddis v Chichester Constable* [1969] 2 Ch 345, [1969] 2 All ER 912, CA.
6 *Beaman v ARTS Ltd* [1949] 1 KB 550, [1949] 1 All ER 465.
7 Section 40.

SECTION 3.   TRESPASS TO GOODS

An intentional or negligent interference with goods in the possession of the plaintiff is a trespass provided that the interference is direct.

This tort protects several interests. First, it protects the plaintiff's interest in the retention of possession of his goods (though the tort of conversion also protects this interest and is more often relied on for this purpose than is trespass). Secondly, trespass protects his interest in the physical condition of his goods, and thirdly his interest in the inviolability of his goods; ie protection against intermeddling.

A. FORMS OF TRESPASS

It follows that trespass to goods assumes various forms. Taking goods out of the possession of another,[8] moving them from one place to another,[9] or even bringing one's person into contact with them,[10] or directing a missile at them[11] have all been held to be trespasses.

B. CHARACTER OF THE ACT OF THE DEFENDANT

There cannot be a trespass if the interference is indirect.[12] Thus, to lock the room in which the plaintiff has his goods is not a trespass to them.[13] Although he who mixes a drug with the feed of a racehorse commits a trespass *quoad* the feed, his act does not become a trespass to the racehorse when the stable boy later gives this feed to it.[14] Nor is it clear whether it is trespass to cause the goods of a plaintiff to come into harmful contact with some other object; for example, to drive sheep over the edge of a cliff into the sea below.[15]

It is trespass to goods to cut and take away trees,[16] to beat a dog[17] or to shoot racing pigeons[18] (whether or not the goods were capable of being stolen is irrelevant[19]).

In order to decide whether a mere touching of goods is a trespass one must ask whether trespass to goods is actionable *per se*. A *dictum* of LORD BLANESBURGH in *Leitch & Co Ltd v Leydon*[20] is often cited[1] to support the

---

8 *Brewer v Dew* (1843) 11 M & W 625.
9 *Kirk v Gregory* (1876) 1 ExD 55; *Fouldes v Willoughby* (1841) 8 M & W 540 at 544–5 (per LORD ABINGER).
10 *Fouldes v Willoughby* (1841) 8 M & W 540 at 549 (per ALDERSON B *obiter*): 'Scratching the panel of a carriage would be a trespass.'
11 *Hamps v Darby* [1948] 2 KB 311, [1948] 2 All ER 474, CA.
12 *Covell v Laming* (1808) 1 Camp 497.
13 *Hartley v Moxham* (1842) 3 QB 701.
14 Unless the poison goes from the hand of the defendant directly into the mouth of the animal. *Hutchins v Maughan* [1947] VLR 131 (Victoria Sup Ct) carries the point in the text.
15 It is not trespass merely because one's animal inflicts direct injury on goods; *Manton v Brocklebank* [1923] 2 KB 212, CA, especially per ATKIN LJ at 229.
16 *Heyden v Smith* (1610) 2 Brownl 328.
17 *Wright v Ramscot* (1665) 1 Wms Saund 183.
18 *Hamps v Darby* [1948] 2 KB 311, [1948] 2 All ER 474, CA.
19 Ibid, at 322, 478, respectively (per EVERSHED LJ).
20 [1931] AC 90 at 106 (SC).
1 Eg *Salmond* 89.

view that it is always actionable *per se*. There in fact it was left undecided whether the proprietor of a soda fountain committed a trespass by filling with soda water, for his customers, bottles which he knew to belong to the plaintiffs, mineral water manufacturers. The *dictum* of LORD BLANESBURGH is only a summary of the argument of counsel for the appellant which the noble lord expressly stated must not be taken to be his own view. Some, on the other hand, state that there is clear authority for the proposition that trespass is actionable *per se*, but only where there is a dispossession of the plaintiff.[2] Yet in *Kirk v Gregory*[3] a woman, who moved rings belonging to a man who had just died from one room in his house to another, was held liable in nominal damages for this asportation, ie for this carrying away of the goods from one place to another. This case has been treated as consistent with this latter view by saying of it that 'there was a complete asportation while the intermeddling lasted'.[4] But an asportation or moving of the goods is not necessarily a dispossession:[5] If in gently reversing my car I touch the bumper of another car, the brake of which has not been applied, and, without damaging it, cause it to move a few feet, I have not dispossessed the owner, though I have asported it. There are good reasons for making trespass to goods always actionable *per se*, and it is thought that it is both consistent with the authorities and in accordance with the general principle of trespass so to hold. Otherwise, persons could touch museum exhibits with impunity; the law would leave remediless the perhaps not oversensitive person who declined to use his toothbrush any more after another had used it without his consent. Perhaps the correct question is not whether trespass to goods is alienable *per se*. It should be. But was this relevant touching 'hostile'.[6] Moving a fellow hotel guest's toothbrush out of my way is not an act I would expect him to object to. Using his toothbrush clearly is!

C. STATE OF MIND OF THE DEFENDANT

The problem of whether there is liability for trespasses which are neither intentional nor negligent has been examined already. In *National Coal Board v Evans (J E) & Co Cardiff Ltd*[7] the Court of Appeal held that a contractor whose servant, while excavating, damaged the cable of the plaintiff and whose act was neither intentional nor negligent,[8] was not liable in trespass to goods. There is, then, no liability for an accidental trespass to goods.[9] But, if the

---

2 Eg *Pollock* 264.

3 (1876) 1 ExD 55.

4 *Pollock* 265n36.

5 Cf CHANNELL B, in *Burroughes v Bayne* (1860) 5 H & N 296 at 305–6.

6 On analogy with trespass to the person; see *Wilson v Pringle* [1987] QB 237, [1980] 2 All ER 440 discussed supra at pp 21–22.

7 [1951] 2 KB 861, [1951] 2 All ER 310. Although the *ratio* probably is that the injury was caused by the conduct of the plaintiff (see especially COHEN LJ at 875) all three judges gave considered judgments to the effect that there was no liability for accidental trespass to goods.

8 He willed the operation of the machine was excavating the earth, but he neither desired nor ought to have foreseen that damage to the cable which constituted the tortious invasion of the plaintiff's interest—his act, therefore, was neither intentional nor negligent.

9 In *Manton v Brocklebank* [1923] 2 KB 212 at 229, CA, ATKIN LJ, held that 'whether a horse directly injures goods, or a dog accomplishes an *"asportavit"* of a golf ball, he does not involve his owner in liability for trespass to goods, at any rate unless the owner has intentionally caused the act complained of'. Why negligence should not be enough for trespass here is not clear, and it is relevant that a finding of no negligence was made.

defendant intended to interfere, his trespass is intentional even though he did not know that his act amounted to a trespass;[10] if, for example, he believed that the goods interfered with were his own.

D. THE INTEREST OF THE PLAINTIFF

The plaintiff must be in possession of the goods at the time of the interference. Possession connotes both the power (*factum*) of exercising physical control and the intention (*animus*) to exercise such control on his own behalf. Whether the plaintiff is the owner is immaterial. So if A intends to catch a butterfly, which is in his garden, and before he can do so it flies on to the highway where B catches it A has no possession—there is *animus* but not *factum*. On the other hand, he has possession of the butterfly specimens in his natural history collection. LORD ESHER has said:

> The plaintiff in an action of trespass must at the time of the trespass have the present possession of the goods, either actual or constructive, or a legal right to the immediate possession.[11]

Thus, a cyclist who parks his cycle outside a shop remains in possession of it, but if a thief rides away on it the thief then has the possession although he obtained it wrongfully.

Therefore, if A took B's gun and handed it to C, B could not sue C in trespass (unless he showed that C authorised or ratified A's act), because B would have had no possession at the time when C received possession from A.[12] If a lodger holds goods on sale or return from a shopkeeper, and those goods are seized in pursuance of a lawful execution on the landlord's goods, this has been held to be a trespass to the lodger.[13] If X and Y both claim the right to goods which neither has previously possessed, and in a scuffle for them X snatches them from Y's hand Y has not possession to found a suit in trespass.[14] A bailee, even a gratuitous one,[15] can sue in trespass. The Crown may therefore sue in respect of the loss of Post Office mails.[16] Where a landlord demised land to the plaintiff for 21 years, with liberty to dig a half acre of brick-earth annually, and to dig in excess of that at an agreed price, the plaintiff could sue a third party who took away brick-earth from the land.[17] A bailor does not have possession and therefore cannot ordinarily sue in trespass for an act done to the goods bailed.[18] If, however, the bailor has

---

10 HEL vol viii, 466, seems confused on this. He thinks that because of cases such as *Kirk v Gregory*, the rule for trespass to goods is more strict than for trespass to persons. This is not so; for instance, if a father hits a child through mistakenly identifying her as his daughter in circumstances that would have afforded him a defence but for his error, he would be liable for battery.

11 *Johnson v Diprose* [1893] 1 QB 512 at 515.

12 *Wilson v Barker* (1833) 4 B & Ad. 614; cf *Badkin v Powell* (1776) 2 Cowp 476. And see *Wilson v Lombank Ltd* [1963] 1 All ER 740.

13 *Colwill v Reeves* (1811) 2 Camp 575; contra 'If a man puts corn into my bag ... because it is impossible to distinguish what was mine from what was his.' (Per LORD ELLENBOROUGH *obiter* at 576.)

14 *Peachey v Wing* (1826) 5 LJ OS KB 55.

15 *Rooth v Wilson* (1817) 1 B & Ald 59.

16 *The Winkfield* [1902] P 42, CA. For the present law with regard to damages in such cases, see p 52, ante.

17 *Attersoll v Stevens* (1808) 1 Taunt 183.

18 *Gordon v Harper* (1796) 7 Term Rep 9; *Ward v Macauley* (1791) 4 Term Rep 489 but see LORD PORTER in *USA v Dollfus Mieg et Compagnie SA* [1952] AC 582 at 611, [1952] 1 All ER 572.

an immediate right to possession as in the case of a bailment at will, he may then sue.[19]

Want of possession precluded success in the following cases; against a police commissioner who, while in possession of the certificate of character of the plaintiff, wrote across it: 'Dismissed the police service';[20] by the assignees of a bankrupt against a sheriff who seized goods when unaware of a secret act of bankruptcy by the bankrupt.[1] For the same reason a telephone subscriber would have no action in trespass if the police tapped his telephone line. There are three apparent exceptions to the rule that possession is essential:

1 In *White v Morris*[2] it was held that, where goods were assigned as security for a loan upon trust to permit the assignor to remain in possession until default in repayment, the assignee could sue in trespass while the goods were still in the assignor's possession. It may be assumed, despite lack of authority for such a general proposition, that all trustees may sue for trespass to goods in the hands of the beneficiary on the basis that they share possession with him.[3]
2 The title of executors or administrators relates back to the death of the deceased, and this entitles them to sue for a trespass committed between the date of the death and that of the grant.[4]
3 The owner of a franchise in wrecks has been deemed to have constructive possession of a wreck so as to enable him to sue in trespass a person who seized a cask of whisky before he could do so.[5]

'Trespass to goods' is expressly included within the definition of a wrongful interference with goods' in the 1977 Act.[6] Therefore the defence of *jus tertii* is no longer available,[7] and the statutory rules regarding co-ownership also apply, as in an appropriate case are all forms of relief provided for by that Act.[8]

E. DAMAGES

(1) MEASURE

Where the plaintiff has been deprived of the goods, he is entitled to their value by way of damages. This rule applies to suits by bailees against third parties, but when the assignee under a bill of sale wrongfully seized from the assignor goods comprised in the bill, the damages awarded to the assignor were limited to the value of his interest in them.[9] A plaintiff may recover

---

19 *Lotan v Cross* (1810) 2 Camp 464; *Penfolds Wines Pty Ltd v Elliott* (1946) 74 CLR 204 at 226–8 (per DIXON J).
20 *Taylor v Rowan* (1835) 7 C & P 70; cf *Wennhak v Morgan* (1888) 20 QBD 635.
 1 *Balme v Hutton* (1833) 9 Bing 471.
 2 (1852) 11 CB 1015.
 3 See *Barker v Furlong* [1891] 2 Ch 172 (conversion).
 4 *Tharpe v Stallwood* (1843) 5 Man & G 760.
 5 *Dunwich Corporation v Sterry* (1831) 1 B & Ad 831.
 6 Section 1(b).
 7 Section 8(1). Section 11(1) excludes contributory negligence as a defence in proceedings based on intentional trespass.
 8 Section 10(1) and p 52, ante.
 9 *Brierly v Kendall* (1852) 17 QB 937.

general damages for loss of use of goods (as distinct from special damages for loss of profits from the goods) although he would not have been using them during the period within which he has been deprived of their use.[10] The provisions of the Act of 1977 relating to damages apply to actions for trespass to goods.[11]

(2) TRESPASS AB INITIO[12]

Where any person having by authority of law[13] entered on land or seized goods, or arrested a person, subsequently commits a trespass his original act will in certain circumstances be deemed itself to be a trespass.[14]

The doctrine has little practical relevance today. Its importance is mainly limited[15] to the fact that, presumably, damages may be assessed on the basis that the entire conduct of the defendant and not merely his subsequent wrongful act is tortious.[16]

SECTION 4.   RESIDUAL TORTS

There are many circumstances where the violation of interests in goods is not protected by trespass, conversion or even the tort of negligence. The action analogous to the old action on the case has proved very fruitful in filling these gaps; and what now follows is to be treated as illustrative of this wider right of action and not as exhaustively defining the circumstances in which it may be held available in the future. These torts are forms of 'wrongful interference with goods' so that, where relevant, the provisions of the Act of 1977 apply.

Trespass and conversion are especially restrictive in that they are not available to a plaintiff who neither possesses nor has an immediate right to possess the goods. The leading case of *Mears v London & South Western Rly Co*[17] has firmly established that if goods are destroyed or damaged, the owner may sue without having possession or an immediate right to possess. The rule benefits, for example, a bailor, a purchaser where the vendor has a lien for unpaid purchase money, and a mortgagee. He must prove damage to his interest—taking the goods from the possessor without affecting title is insufficient. Presumably, the act complained of must be wrongful in the sense that it is one which, had the plaintiff had possession or the immediate right to it, would have grounded a suit in trespass, or conversion. So, where the employer of the plaintiff, a conductor of a public transport vehicle, endorsed

10 *The Mediana* [1900] AC 113 at 117–8 (per EARL OF HALSBURY LC).
11 P 52, ante.
12 See *Clerk and Lindsell* at 22–29 and the seventh edition of this work at p. 56.
13 Authority of *law*, as distinct from permission of another—for example, it covers one who enters an inn, but not the buyer of a ticket for a seat at a theatre.
14 The Distress for Rent Act 1737, s 19, abolished this rule in the case of distress for rent.
15 It may also matter where the entrant sues the occupier of the land. If the entrant becomes a trespasser *ab initio* the occupier will be able to use reasonable force to eject him, whereas the mere commission of a misfeasance after lawful entry would not justify forcible ejection from the land. It might also affect the duty owed to him by an occupier in respect of the state of the premises and acts done therein; ch 16, post.
16 *Shorland v Govett* (1826) 5 B & C 485, *obiter*.
17 (1862) 11 CB (NS) 850.

on the plaintiff's licence (which was in the employer's possession) 'discharged for being 1s. 4d. short' he was liable in case for defacing it.[18]

Credit agreements present interesting problems in this respect. If a car which is the subject of a credit agreement is seriously damaged, can the owner sue in case? If the hirer exercises his option to buy, what does the owner lose? And, yet, if (as is likely in such an event), the hirer does not exercise it, the owner is left without effective remedy other than in case. It seems that, until the hirer opts, the owner is to be regarded as the reversioner and can sue.

It will be recalled, too, that a bailee disregarding the terms of his bailment may sometimes be liable in case, though not in conversion[19] and that to deny the plaintiff access to his goods or to interfere with his freedom of using them is also actionable on the case.[20] Further, to place baited traps on one's land near the highway so as to attract dogs into the traps, and in consequence of which dogs are so trapped, is a tort of this category.[1]

---

18 *Rogers v Macnamara* (1853) 14 CB 27; cf *Hurrell v Ellis* (1845) 2 CB 295 (recovered damages for loss of employment where libel did not lie).
19 See p 38, ante.
20 See pp 59, et seq, ante.
 1 *Townsend v Wathen* (1808) 9 East 277.

Chapter 5

Land

SECTION 1. TRESPASS

Intentionally or negligently entering or remaining on, or directly causing any physical matter to come into contact with, land in the possession of another is a trespass (trespass quare clausum fregit).

This tort protects the interest of the bailiff in having his land free from physical intrusion. Because of this emphasis on physical interference with possession, it follows that it is not the function of the tort to protect ownership as such. None the less, because the owner is often in possession, the purpose of many a suit in trespass is not the recovery of damages but the settlement of disputed rights over land, and a judgment may be backed by the sanction of an injunction if the action succeeds. The use of this action in tort as a means of resolving disputes on title has been facilitated by the rule that trespass is actionable *per se*.[1]

A. TYPES OF ACTS

As with all forms of trespass, the immediate act must constitute the trespass complained of; it is not trespass if the invasion of the plaintiff's land is merely consequential upon the act of the defendant. So, a plaintiff landowner who complains that the defendant has erected a spout to drain away water from the eaves of the house of the defendant, as a result of which water has dripped on to the plaintiff's adjoining land, can sue only in case, not in trespass.[2] How difficult it is to draw the line between 'direct' and 'consequential' is shown by *Gregory v Piper*[3], which held that it was trespass where rubbish,

---

1 *Bush v Smith*, (1953) 162 Estates Gazette 430, CA. The growing awareness of the scope of the declaratory judgment could lead to a declining use of trespass for this purpose; cf *Loudon v Ryder (No 2)* [1953] Ch 423, [1953] 1 All ER 1005; *Acton Corporation v Morris* [1953] 2 All ER 932, CA. (The defendant locked the door of his house, thereby denying the plaintiff access to his upper flat. Though the court doubted whether this was trespass, it held that the plaintiff could have a declaration of his right of access). The action for recovery of land is also important in this connection, p 73, post. A plaintiff who does not mention trespass to land in his pleadings is not restricted to his alternative claim for breach of contract, and so can claim exemplary damages for the trespass. *Drane v Evangelou* [1978] 2 All ER 437, CA and see p 466 post.
2 *Reynolds v Clarke* (1725), 2 Ld. Raym 1399, cf *Lemmon v Webb*, [1894] 3 Ch 1, at 24 (per KAY LJ), (and [1895] AC 1) that the encroachment of boughs and roots of trees is not trespass.
3 (1829) 9 B & C 591. This, it seems, cannot be reconciled with the decision of DENNING LJ in *Southport Corporation v Esso Petroleum Co Ltd*, [1954] 2 QB 182 at 195–6, [1954] 2 All ER 561 at 570, CA supported by LORDS RADCLIFFE and TUCKER, [1956] AC at 242, 244, HL, respectively (discharge of oil from ship, which, when carried by tide on to plaintiff's foreshore, held not to constitute a trespass, because that was consequential, not direct). See also *Covell v Laming* (1808) 1 Camp 497 (defendant at the helm guided his ship in a certain direction.

which was placed near the plaintiff's land, on drying, rolled on to it, because this was the result of natural forces.

To enter another's land is a trespass.[4] Of course, such an entry may be an assertion of title, and then the suit in trespass will, in effect, determine who has title.[5]

To cause some foreign matter[6] to enter or come into physical contact with the land of the plaintiff is a trespass. Firing a gun into the soil,[7] placing a ladder against,[8] or driving nails into,[9] the wall of the plaintiff, encouraging a dog to run to his land,[10] removing the doors and windows,[11] and throwing a person on to another's land,[12] are all trespasses. But in all cases the intrusion on the plaintiff's land must result from some act or omission on the part of the defendant, or persons for whom he is responsible. The intrusion on the plaintiff's deer sanctuary by a pack of hounds does not of itself impose liability for trespass on the Master of hounds.[13] Liability for trespass to land is not absolute.

To remain on land after a trespassory entry thereon is in itself also a trespass, a 'continuing trespass' as it is commonly styled. So, if A places goods on B's land and is successfully sued by B in trespass for this act, he is liable, if he fails thereafter to remove them, to further actions in trespass for the continued presence of the goods on the land.[14] If, on the other hand, he merely commits an act such as digging a hole, or removing goods, ie he does not wrongfully allow *anything to remain* on the land, the fact that the harm thus occasioned continues is not enough to make it a continuing trespass; damage can be recovered once only for such a trespass.[15] There is a continuing trespass only when that which continued after the first action is itself a

---

The wind and waves were only instrumental in carrying along the ship in the direction in which he guided it. Upon the ship's colliding with the plaintiff's ship, held to be a trespass). And see *Home Brewery Co Ltd v William Davis & Co (Leicester) Ltd* [1987] QB 339, [1987] 1 All ER 637 (water squeezed out from osier bed filled in by defendants flooding the plaintiff's higher land *quaere* trespass or nuisance).

4 A squatter, i e 'one who, without any colour of right, enters on an unoccupied house or land, intending to stay there as long as he can', is a trespasser: *per* LORD DENNING, at 456 in *McPhail v Parsons, Names Unknown* [1973] Ch 447 [1973] 3 All ER 393, CA.

5 If the defendant has not entered, it will normally be impossible, then, to use an action in trespass as a means of settling a dispute in title.

6 Perhaps anything having size or mass, including gases, flame, beams from searchlights and mirrors, but not vibrations.

7 *Pickering v Rudd* (1815) 4 Camp 219 at 220 (*per* LORD ELLENBOROUGH).

8 *Westripp v Baldock* [1938] 2 All ER 779, affd, [1939] 1 All ER 279, CA.

9 *Simpson v Weber* (1925) 133 LT 46.

10 *Beckwith v Shordike* (1767) 4 Burr 2092.

11 *Lavender v Betts* [1942] 2 All ER 72. But not the defendant's turning off the gas and electricity at the meter in his cellar, for the purpose of evicting the tenant of rooms on an upper floor, because the consequence is indirect, *Perara v Vandiyar* [1953] 1 All ER 1109, CA, [1953] 1 WLR 672. This is now a criminal offence under s 1 of the Protection from Eviction Act 1977, but no action for breach of statutory duty lies: *McCall v Abelesz* [1976] QB 585.

12 *Smith v Stone* (1647) Sty 65.

13 *League against Cruel Sports Ltd v Scott* [1986] QB 240, [1985] 2 All ER 489.

14 If the plaintiff seeks an injunction, the court has a discretion to award damages in lieu of such injunction which also take into account the likely future damage. This, in effect, settles the price which the defendant must pay for the right to commit the trespass in the future, and no subsequent action will lie in respect thereof: *Leeds Industrial Co-operative Society v Slack* [1924] AC 851, HL. Nevertheless prima facie the landowner is entitled to his injunction even where the acts complained of cause no harm; *Patel v (WH) Smith (Eziot)* (1987) Times, 16 February, CA.

15 *Clegg v Dearden* (1848) 12 QB 576 at 601.

trespass, hence, for a person to remain or leave goods[16] there is such a trespass. A person who is on land with the permission of the possessor has been held a trespasser if he remains there for an unreasonable time after the termination of the permission.[17] 'When a householder lives in a dwelling-house to which there is a garden in front and does not lock the gate of the garden, it gives an implied licence to any member of the public who has lawful reason for doing so to proceed from the gate to the front door or back door, and to inquire whether he may be admitted and to conduct his lawful business.'[18] If the licence is withdrawn he is also not a trespasser during the reasonable time which he takes to leave the premises.[19] In *Konskier v Goodman (B) Ltd*[20] the facts were as follows:

The defendant builder had permission from the possessor of a building to leave rubbish there while demolishing part of it. During the currency of this licence, the plaintiff became tenant of the building and was held entitled to recover in trespass from the builder when the latter did not remove the rubbish after the expiry of the licence.

If a tenant, with the consent of the landlord, holds over at the expiration of his term, so that he thereby becomes a tenant, either from year to year or at his will, his remaining is not an act of trespass so long as the tenancy has not been properly determined.[1] If, however, he is a mere tenant at sufferance (thus remaining without permission of the landlord) the landlord may enter and demand possession and sue in trespass.[2] *Watson v Murray & Co* provides an illustration (if not an extension[3]) of the types of acts which may constitute trespass to land.[4]

The defendants who were sheriff's officers, seized goods in the plaintiff's shop under writs of execution. It was held that each of the following acts amounted to trespass: locking the plaintiff's premises so as to exclude her therefrom when they had lotted the goods for the purpose of a sale; opening her premises for a public viewing of the goods; affixing posters on her premises.

16 *Holmes v Wilson* (1839) 10 Ad & El 503.
17 *Minister of Health v Bellotti* [1944] KB 298, [1944] 1 All ER 238; cf the conflicting *obiter dicta* of LORD ELLENBOROUGH and BAYLEY, J in *Winterbourne v Morgan* (1809) 11 East 395 at 402, 405 respectively.
18 *Robson v Hallett* [1967] 2 QB 939 at 953–4, per DIPLOCK, LJ, [1967] 2 All ER 407. In *Brunner v Williams* (1975) 73 LGR 266, a weights and measures inspector was held to have no implied licence to enter a plaintiff's garden to see whether a coal dealer was infringing the Weights and Measures Act 1963; all he may do is go to the plaintiff's door and ask permission; *Winfield* 199 wrongly reaches the opposite conclusion on this case.
19 *Robson v Hallet* [1967] 2 QB 939 at 953–4, per DIPLOCK, LJ, [1967] 2 All ER 407.
20 [1928] 1 KB 421, CA. Presumably, the defendant's successor in title to the chattels would also be liable in trespass for knowingly allowing them to remain on the plaintiff's land.
1 *Dougal v McCarthy* [1893] 1 QB 736 at 739–40 (*per* LORD ESHER); *Meye v Electric Transmission Ltd* [1942] Ch 290.
2 Foa *Landlord and Tenant* (8th edn) p 711 if the deceased tenant's widow remains there after his death, she too, can be sued in trespass, *Thompson v Earthy* [1951] 2 KB 596, [1951] 2 All ER 235. The common-law position as set out above is much modified where the Rent Acts apply.
3 Were all the acts here held to be trespasses sufficiently direct? See *Acton Corporation v Morris*, [1953] 2 All ER 932, CA, not cited in the present case.
4 [1955] 2 QB 1, [1955] 1 All ER 350.

B. SUBJECT MATTER

The tort is trespass to land; obviously, then, to walk on the surface of the plaintiff's land is enough to constitute the tort of trespass. Anything attached to the soil, and capable of being separately possessed, may be the subject matter of trespass *quare clausum fregit*: damage to grass[5] or turnips,[6] or a *profit à prendre* such as a fishery.[7]

Possession of land may be separated as it were, horizontally so that, for instance, A may possess the pasturage, B the surface and subsoil, and C the minerals below; each of them may sue if the subject matter of his possession is invaded. Highway authorities, for example, often have the surface of streets vested in them by statute: and so they (not the owners of the adjoining land[8]) may sue for surface trespasses, such as breaking up the street,[9] or erecting structures on the highway.[10] It may be trespass to tunnel beneath the surface of land, to mine there, to use a cave beneath it or to drive building foundations through the soil; in the absence of specific provision to the contrary, the owner of the surface is presumed to own that which is underground.

It is trespass to invade that portion of the air-space which is requisite for the ordinary use of the land and the structures upon it.[11] An aircraft does not infringe any of the plaintiff's rights to airspace by being flown over his land for the purpose of photographing it.[12]

Apart from the position at common law, the Civil Aviation Act 1982[13] provides that, with the exception of aircraft belonging to or exclusively employed in the service of Her Majesty,[14] no action shall lie in respect of trespass or nuisance by reason only of the flight of an aircraft over any property at a height above the ground, which, having regard to weather and other circumstances of the case, is reasonable.[15] Subject to the same exception, the owner of an aircraft is liable for all material loss or damage to persons

---

5 *Richards v Davies* [1921] 1 Ch 90 at 94–5 (per PO LAWRENCE J).
6 *Wellaway v Courtier* [1918] 1 KB 200.
7 Cf. *Hill v Tupper* (1863) 2 H & C 121 at 127 (per POLLOCK CB): *Mason v Clarke,* [1955] AC 788, HL (right to take rabbits). But not an easement; *Paine & Co v St Neots Gas and Coke Co* [1939] 3 All ER 812, CA.
8 In *Hubbard v Pitt* [1976] QB 142, [1975] 1 All ER 1056, CA LORD DENNING held that where the surface of a pavement was vested in the local highway authority the adjoining owner could not sue for trespass to the pavement. In *Randall v Tarrant* [1955] 1 All ER 600, CA, a motorist who parked his car on the highway and then trespassed on the adjoining field was held not to be a trespasser on the highway.
9 *Hyde Corporation v Oldham Ashton and Hyde Electric Tramway, Ltd* (1900) 64 JP 596, CA.
10 *Sewai Jaipur v Arjun Lal* [1937] 4 All ER 5, PC; they are not thereby authorised to build lavatories underneath; *Tunbridge Wells Corporation v Baird* [1896] AC 434, HL. See also *Cox v Glue* (1848) 5 CB 533.
11 *Kelsen v Imperial Tobacco Co (of Great Britain and Ireland) Ltd* [1957] 2 QB 334, [1957] 2 All ER 343 (defendant's advertising sign projecting into airspace above plaintiff's shop held a trespass); *Anchor Brewhouse Developments v Berkley House (Docklands) Development* (1987) 284 Estates Gazette 625, (crane passing over land without permission).
12 *Bernstein of Leigh (Baron) v Skyviews and General Ltd* [1978] QB 479, [1977] 2 All ER 902.
13 Section 76.
14 Section 49(3), 76(1).
15 Section 76(1). The section applies to all flights which are at a reasonable height and comply with statutory requirements, but the ordinary liabilities in trespass or nuisance would arise for any other wrongful activity carried on by or from the aircraft, such as deliberate emission of vast quantities of smoke that polluted the plaintiff's land; *Bernstein of Leigh (Baron) v Skyviews and General Ltd* [1978] QB 479 at 489, [1977] 2 All ER 902 at 906, (per Griffiths J).

or property caused by that aircraft, whether in flight, taking off[16] or landing, or by a person in it or articles falling from it, without proof of negligence or intention or other cause of action.[17]

A highway is land in the possession and ownership of a person (who, except for any rights in respect of the surface enjoyed by a highway authority is presumed to be the owner of the adjoining land) subject to a public right of way. If a person uses a highway for purposes other than those 'reasonably incident to its user'[18] as a highway his act is a trespass. The purpose need not be unlawful in itself; interrupting a grouse shoot[19] obtaining information on the speed and performance of race-horses on the adjoining land of the owner of the highway soil,[20] have been held trespasses.

C. STATE OF MIND OF THE DEFENDANT

The rules here seem to be essentially similar to those for other forms of trespass. If the defendant intended to enter the land on which he in fact is, then he trespassed, whether or not he intended to invade the plaintiff's interest in his own exclusive possession. Mistake, as such, is no defence in trespass; it will not avail the defendant that he thought that he was on his own land.[1] As with all torts, there is no liability if there is no voluntary act on the part of the defendant; a person thrown on to the land by a third party is not liable in trespass.[2] *Letang v Cooper* notwithstanding, it must be assumed for the time being that a negligent unintentional act of trespass is enough; for example, if A intentionally throws a stone on to C's land and, as he should have foreseen, it ricochets on to B's land, this is trespass to B's land as well as C's. On the other hand, it is thought that an unintentional non-negligent act is not trespass.[3]

In *League Against Cruel Sports Ltd v Scott*[4] the plaintiffs owned land which they maintained as a deer sanctuary and on which hunting was prohibited. Hounds from a local hunt intruded on the sanctuary and disturbed the deer. PARK J held that the master of the hounds could not be liable in trespass unless it could be proved that he (or some person for whom he was responsible) either deliberately encouraged the dogs to enter the plaintiffs' land, or by negligence failed to prevent them intruding on the sanctuary.

D. THE INTEREST OF THE PLAINTIFF IN THE LAND

If the plaintiff has a legal estate and exclusive possession then he may sue in trespass. The tenant (not the landlord) can sue if a third party trespasses on

---

16 The ordinary common law applies to accidents caused by the aircraft, while taxi-ing to the take-off point: *Blankley v Godley* [1952] 1 All ER 436n.
17 Section 76 (2).
18 *Liddle v Yorkshire (North Riding) County Council* [1934] 2 KB 101 at 127, [1934] All ER Rep 222 at 235 (per SLESSER LJ), CA.
19 *Harrison v Duke of Rutland* [1893] 1 QB 142, CA.
20 *Hickman v Maisey* [1900] 1 QB 752, CA.
 1 *Basely v Clarkson* (1681) 3 Lev 37.
 2 [1965] 1 QB 232, [1964] 2 All ER 929, CA.
 3 *Contra dicta* (perhaps not *ratio*) of the *Case of Thorns* (1466) YB 6 Edw 4 fo, 7 pl 18.
 4 [1985] 2 All ER 489.

the land demised.[5] So, too, the owner of an equitable interest with possession can sue.[6] A statutory possession will found an action of trespass.[7]

The Court of Appeal has held that 'a person may have such a right of exclusive possession of property as will entitle him to bring an action for trespass against the owner of that property but which confers no interest whatever in the land',[8] for example, a statutory tenant under the Rent Acts. Those whose interests fall short of those of a lessee may nonetheless be able to sue in trespass if in fact they have exclusive occupation. Whether a lodger can sue in trespass would rest on whether on the facts he had exclusive occupation—it would be relevant whether he had an outdoor key and whether he could bar access to the rooms.[9]

In *National Provincial Bank Ltd v Ainsworth*[10] the House of Lords unanimously held that a deserted wife has no proprietary interest in the matrimonial home, but only a personal right. Nonetheless LORD UPJOHN stated that she had exclusive occupation and could therefore bring proceedings against trespassers. In *Hill v Tupper*:[11]

> X Co leased certain land, which adjoined their canal, to the plaintiff. He was also given 'the sole and exclusive rights' to let out on hire pleasure boats for use on the canal. Subsequently, the defendant set up a rival concern, whereupon he was sued in trespass by the plaintiff. The latter conceded that X Co could sue the defendant in trespass but at the same time he argued that he himself could do so.

---

5 *Cooper v Crabtree* (1882) 20 ChD 589, CA. A plaintiff with an *interesse termini* could not sue if he never took possession; *Wallis v Hands* [1893] 2 Ch 75.

6 *Mason v Clarke* [1955] AC 778, HL. Another example is *Loudon v Ryder* [1953] 2 QB 202, [1953] 1 All ER 741, CA, where the plaintiff was entitled to the premises under a declaration of trust merely (and see *Re Lewis's Trusts* (1953) Times, 26 March) and yet recovered damages for trespass to the land. A beneficiary under a trust for sale may also sue; *Bull v Bull* [1955] 1 All ER 253 at 255 (per DENNING, LJ., obiter).

7 *Cruise v Terrell* [1922] 1 KB 664, CA; *Lewisham Borough Council v Maloney* [1948] 1 KB 50, [1947] 2 All ER 36. Whether a landlord of a tenant at will can sue third parties in trespass is undecided: *Attersoll v Stevens* (1808), 1 Taunt 183: *Shrewsbury's (Countess) Case* (1600), 5 Co Rep 13b.

8 *Marcroft Wagons Ltd v Smith* [1951] 2 KB 496 at 501, [1951] 2 All ER 271 at 274, CA (per EVERSHED, MR). *Brown v Brash and Ambrose* [1948] 2 KB 247, [1948] 1 All ER 922, CA and *Thompson v Ward* [1953] 2 QB 153, [1953] 1 All ER 1169, CA, show that a statutory tenant who leaves his premises even for a period of five to ten years with the intention of eventually returning there and who 'clothes his inward intention with some formal, outward and visible sign of it' (per ASQUITH LJ, at 254, in *Brown v Brash and Ambrose*) by installing someone as licensee, or maybe by leaving furniture there, has the right to sue in trespass anyone who occupies the premises, eg the landlord.

9 *Lane v Dixon* (1847) 3 CB 776; *Monks v Dykes* (1839) 4 M & W 567; *Helman v Horsham and Worthing Assessment Committee* [1949] 2 KB 355, [1949] 1 All ER 776 (per EVERSHED LJ), at 347, 783 respectively; *R v St George's Union* (1871) LR 7 QB 90. Similarly, a plaintiff who could not rely on possession under his lease from the Crown because it was void for non-compliance with a statute was held to have 'actual possession ... sufficient to entitle the party possessing it to maintain trespass against persons who have no title at all, and are mere wrongdoers'. *Harper v Charlesworth* (1825) 4 B & C 574 at 591 (per BAYLEY, J). The House of Lords in *Street v Mountford* [1985] AC 809, [1985] 2 All ER 289 recently held that where the intention evidenced by the agreement between the parties was to grant exclusive possession for a return at a rent there will normally be found to be a tenancy in any case.

10 [1965] AC 1175, [1965] 2 All ER 472, HL. Although the Matrimonial Homes Act 1967 has affected the ratio of this case it does not alter the effect of LORD UPJOHN's dictum cited in the text.

11 (1863) 2 H & C 121.

Since the plaintiff's concession was tantamount to an admission that he did not have exclusive occupation, it is not surprising that the court dismissed the action. It did, however, add that only if he could prove that his interest was a new species of property could he succeed,[12] and that it was the policy of the law not to allow the creation of new rights in land. On balance it is thought that *Hill v Tupper* notwithstanding the weight of House of Lords and Court of Appeal authority sustains the proposition that a person who has exclusive occupation may sue in trespass although he has no legal estate or other right in the land.[13]

It is no defence to a wrongdoer that the possession of the plaintiff is unlawful; the fact of possession is enough.[14] But as against the true owner, the rule is different; in *Delaney v T P Smith Ltd*[15] the plaintiff entered property held under a lease which was unenforceable because it did not comply with the requirements of section 40 of the Law of Property Act 1925 relating to a memorandum in writing, and it was held that he was unable to sue his landlord in trespass for ejecting him. Two other *dicta* are important here:

A mere trespasser cannot, by the very act of trespass, immediately and without acquiescence, give himself what the law understands by possession against the person whom he ejects, and drive him to produce his title, if he can, without delay, reinstate himself in his former possession.[16]

If there are two persons in a field, each asserting that the field is his, and each doing some act in the assertion of the right of possession, and if the question is, which of those two is in actual possession, I answer, the person who has the title is in actual possession, and the other is a trespasser.[17]

If a plaintiff has a right to immediate possession of the land, he can, once he has entered upon it, sue for trespasses committed by third parties between the date of accrual of his right and his entry:[18] this is often called trespass by relation.[19]

---

12 It will be recalled that interference with a *profit à prendre* may be trespass; p 68, ante.

13 'In recent years it has been established that a person who has no more than a licence may yet have possession of the land.' per MEGARRY J in *Hounslow London Borough Council v Twickenham Garden Developments Ltd* [1971] Ch 233 at 257, [1970] 3 All ER 326. But see *Street v Mountford* (supra) on the distinction between tenancies and occupational licences.

14 *Graham v Peat* (1801), 1 East 244. In *Mason v Clarke* [1955] AC 778, [1955] 1 All ER 914, HL, VISCOUNT SIMONDS and LORD OAKSEY (CONTRA, LORD KEITH) held that the bare possession of a *profit à prendre* was enough to found an action in trespass. This was *obiter* because the successful plaintiff had in fact an equitable title to the profit. CF *Bristow v Cormican* (1878) 3 App Cas 641, HL.

15 [1946] KB 393, CA.

16 *Browne v Dawson* (1840) 12 Ad & El 624 at 629. In *Portland Managements Ltd v Harté* [1977] QB 306, [1976] 1 All ER 225, CA, it was held that if the plaintiff proves ownership and his intention to resume possession the onus is on the defendant to prove that he is not a trespasser.

17 *Jones v Chapman* (1849) 2 Exch 803 at 821 (MAULE J), approved *Lows v Telford* (1876) 1 App Cas 414 at 426, HL (per LORD SELBORNE).

18 *Barnett v Guildford (Earl)* (1855) 11 Exch 19.

19 Suppose that the effect of a proviso for forfeiture in a lease is that the lease subsists until proceedings for forfeiture are brought; this doctrine of trespass by relation would not then allow a lessor, who is entitled by the terms of the lease to forfeit it, to claim damages for the period between the act giving ground for forfeiture and the issue of the writ; *Elliott v Boynton* [1924] 1 Ch 236, CA.

The *ratio decidendi* of the House of Lords in *Jacobs v Seward* was:[20]

... unless there be an actual ouster of one tenant in common by another, trespass will not lie by the one against the other so far as the land is concerned.

E. DAMAGES

The plaintiff is entitled to full restitution for his loss. Generally, the depreciation in selling value will be an adequate measure for destruction of or damage to land and buildings, though sometimes the plaintiff can also recover special damages, for example, business profits.[1] However, where the cost of reinstatement or repair exceed the diminution in value of the property, those costs may be awarded as damages providing expenditure on such reinstatement and repair is reasonable.[2] And the cost of repair will always be important evidence of the plaintiff's loss, especially where there is no market in which the value of the property may be ascertained or the plaintiff can prove that it was reasonable to have the property restored.[3] All tests such as market value or replacement cost are subordinate to the over-riding principle of restoring the plaintiff to the same position as before the tort was committed.[4]

The measure of damages for wrongful occupancy of land is the reasonable rental value of the land during the time of the defendant's occupancy. For example, if the defendant uses part of the land for tipping, the plaintiff is not limited to the diminution in sale value of the land; he can recover the reasonable value of that particular use of that part of the land made by the defendant together with the diminution in value of the rest of the land.[5]

Where goods such as coal or other minerals or trees are severed from the land the measure of damages depends upon whether the act is wilful or innocent.[6] If his severance is innocent the defendant can deduct his cost of

---

20 (1872) LR 5 HL 464 at 472; and holding that it was not an ouster for a tenant in common to put a lock on the gate to a field and make hay there, cf *Bull v Bull* [1955] 1 QB 234, [1955] 1 All ER 253, CA.
 1 *Watson v Murray & Co* [1955] 2 QB 1, [1955] 1 All ER 350; cf *Dunn v Large* (1783) 3 Doug KB 335 (when defendant ejected plaintiff from inn, closed it down and sent custom elsewhere, plaintiff refused loss of sale value, but only because he did not specially plead it).
 2 *Heath v Keys* [1984] CLY 3568; measure of damages based on the cost of repair is only available when the plaintiff does in fact intend to carry out repairs, *Perry v Sidney Phillips & Son* [1982] 3 All ER 705, [1982] 1 WLR 1297, CA.
 3 For a lucid statement, see *Hutchinson v Davidson*, 1945 SC 395.
 4 In *Bisney v Swanston* (1972) 225 *Estates Gazette* 2299, CA, D put a trailer on P's transport café ground so as to interfere with P's business as much as possible. As well as damages for loss of business, £250 aggravated damages were awarded against D for intending to interfere with malice and spite.
 5 *Whitwham v Westminster Brymbo Coal and Coke Co* [1896] 1 Ch 894; affd, [1896] 2 Ch 538, CA. In *E. Marsden (Woodwork Productions) v Colnbrook Trading Co* (1954) Times, 6 March, damages for deprivation of use were awarded to the plaintiffs in trespass when the defendants failed to remove vehicles from the plaintiff's land upon the expiry of a licence. Cf *Strand Electric and Engineering Co Ltd v Brisford Entertainments Ltd* [1952] 2 QB 246, [1952] 1 All ER 796, CA, p 56, *ante*. In *Swordheath Properties Ltd v Tabet* [1979] 1 All ER 240, CA a defendant who occupied residential premises as a trespasser was liable for damages calculated by reference to the full letting value of the premises although no evidence was adduced that the plaintiff could or would have let them.
 6 'Wilful' includes 'fraudulent'; whether it includes 'negligent' is doubtful: *Wood v Morewood* (1841), 3 QB 440n; *Re United Merthyr Collieries Co* (1872) LR 15 Eq 46; FRY J said *obiter* in *Trotter v Maclean* (1879) 13 Ch D 574 at 587 that the burden of proving wilfulness is on the plaintiff.

severance from the value of the goods.[7] If the act is wilful the defendant cannot deduct his expenses of severing, although he can deduct subsequent expenses such as hauling coal to the surface.[8] Whether in either case the defendant can also deduct an additional sum by way of profit for his work, or whether the plaintiff is entitled to the value of the severed goods less only the defendant's actual expenses, is not settled.[9]

A tenant who is unlawfully evicted by his landlord may recover exemplary damages in trespass—to teach the landlord that tort does not pay.[10]

SECTION 2.   ACTIONS BY REVERSIONERS

Although trespass is not available to those without possession whose interests in land are violated, they are not remediless. A landlord will ordinarily have contractual rights against tenants who damage his interest, for example, by allowing premises to fall into disrepair, and that branch of the law of property known as waste will also afford a remedy of a tortious nature to a landlord who establishes that his tenant has damaged the reversionary interest.[11]

If a non-possessory interest in land is violated by a third party, an action derived from the old action on the case may lie. The plaintiff must prove 'such permanent injury as would be necessarily prejudicial to the reversioner';[12] it was not enough to prove that the defendant's cart wheels had made an impression on the surface of the land.[13]

---

7 *Jegon v Vivian* (1871) 6 Ch App 742.
8 *Martin v Porter* (1839) 5 M & W 351; *Morgan v Powell* (1842) 3 QB 278. If the plaintiff could not himself reach the seam in order to extract the mineral, his damages are based on what a third party would pay him by way of royalty for permission to extract: *Livingstone v Rawyards Coal Co* (1880) 5 App Cas 25.
9 *Jegon v Vivian, supra* and *A-G v Tomline* (1880) 14 Ch D 58 would allow the innocent defendant his profit; contra *Re United Merthyr Collieries Co* (1872) LR 15 Eq 46. *Tai Te Wheta v Scandlyn* [1952] NZLR 30, held that even an innocent trespasser could not set off the value of improvements done by him to the land; see also *Lord Cawdor v Lewis* (1835) 1 Y & C Ex 427.
10 *Drane v Evengelou* [1978] 2 All ER 437. Surprisingly, however, *Devonshire v Jenkins* (1979) 129 NLJ 849 held that exemplary damages were not recoverable if in fact the evicting landlord did not obtain that profit which he sought by his attempted unlawful eviction.
11 Landlord-tenant relationships of this kind are customarily, and appropriately treated in text-books of real property, and not in those on torts.
12 *Baxter v Taylor* (1832) 4 B & Ad 72 at 75 (per TAUNTON, J.).
13 Ibid. For a lessee to deny access to a reversioner entitled to enter and view is also actionable on the case: *Hunt v Dowman* (1618) Cro Jac 478.

Chapter 6

Defences to intentional torts to the person and property

In this chapter will be discussed all the important defences which may be available in respect of the torts so far described. It must not, however, be thought that these defences apply only to these torts. Many of them, eg consent, statutory authority, are general defences, and are capable of being defences to almost any tort.

SECTION 1. MISTAKE AND INEVITABLE ACCIDENT

A. MISTAKE AS SUCH IS NO DEFENCE

It has been shown[1] that mistake is no defence to intentional torts. If the defendant intended to drive his tractor on to that land on to which it in fact went, then his reasonable mistake that the land was his will be no defence.[2] Mistake must, however, be distinguished from inevitable accident. If the defendant shows that the tractor went on to that land solely because of a defect in the steering which no amount of care could have prevented, he will not be liable; for in such a case he neither intended to do that which he has done (ie enter the land which in fact belongs to the plaintiff), nor could he have avoided doing so by taking every care.

Although mistake is no defence in tort, it may be relevant, in deciding if some other defence is open to the defendant, to know whether he was mistaken as to some fact. If a policeman arrests without warrant someone who in fact has not committed an arrestable offence, and whom he had no grounds for believing to have committed one, this is false imprisonment; if, on the other hand, he mistakenly believed on reasonable grounds that the plaintiff had committed an arrestable offence the defence of lawful arrest is open to him.[3]

B. INEVITABLE ACCIDENT

It used to be asserted that the defendant was liable in trespass unless he discharged the burden of proving that his conduct was neither intentional nor negligent, ie, unless he sustained a plea of 'inevitable accident'. Then it became clearly established that if the act of trespass took place in the course of ordinary use of a highway, then, even though the ensuing damage was only to the plaintiff's land or chattels adjoining the highway, the plaintiff

---

1 See p 69, ante.
2 Similarly, where there is liability for negligent acts, if, though his act is not intentional, he foresees the consequences, mistake about the surrounding circumstances will not afford him a defence.
3 See p 88 et seq, post.

could only succeed if he discharged the burden of proving that the defendant harmed him through not taking reasonable care.

Then in 1959 there was decided *Fowler v Lanning*:[4]

> In an action based on trespass to the person the plaintiff's statement of claim alleged simply that on a certain date and at a certain place 'the defendant shot the plaintiff', and that by reason thereof the plaintiff sustained personal injuries, particulars of which were given. The defendant by his defence traversed the allegations of fact and objected that the statement disclosed no cause of action on the ground that the plaintiff did not allege that the shooting was intentional or negligent.

It was held that the basic law of evidence that he who affirms must prove applied. Thus the onus of proving negligence lay upon the plaintiff; because he had not pleaded negligence, his statement of claim disclosed no cause of action: in trespass there is no 'defence' of 'inevitable accident'.

SECTION 2.   CONSENT

A. DISTINGUISHED FROM ASSUMPTION OF RISK

It is, of course, a general policy of the common law and consistent with its individualism that one who has freely assented to conduct by another cannot sue that other for damages resulting from that conduct: *volenti non fit injuria*. Consent may take two forms, either where the plaintiff consents to an invasion of his interest which would otherwise be a tort (this form is conveniently called consent), or a willingness on the part of the plaintiff to run the risk of injury from a particular source of danger (often called assumption of risk). Consent is particularly important with regard to the torts already dealt with, whereas assumption of risk is especially important in negligence. The first type will therefore be dealt with here, and the other in the Part on negligence, but it must be understood that consent in the first sense is not a defence merely to the above intentional torts, and that assumption of risk also is not restricted to negligence.[5]

B. WHAT CONSTITUTES CONSENT

It is convenient to treat consent as a defence although it will be recalled that it is now clear that in trespass to the person, but not in trespass to land, the burden of proving want of consent is on the plaintiff.[6] Consent may be given expressly by words or be inferred from conduct. A boxer cannot complain if

---

4 [1959] 1 QB 426, [1959] 1 All ER 290.

5 So, if a spectator at a cricket match were hit by the ball and sued the batsman in trespass, assumption of risk might be pleaded. Yet, consent would be a defence to a defendant who had been invited by the plaintiff to publish a statement defamatory of him.

6 See p 22, ante; *Freeman v Home Office (No 2)* [1984] QB 524, [1983] 3 All ER 589 at 594–5; affd [1984] 1 All ER 1036, CA. On one interpretation, LORD BLANESBURGH in *William Leitch & Co Ltd v Leydon* [1931] AC 90 at 109, [1930] All ER Rep. 754 at 762, HL, could be applying the rule relating to assault to trespass to goods. In *Jolliffe v Willmett & Co* [1971] 1 All ER 478, a wife living apart from her husband authorised an inquiry agent to enter her husband's flat; the inquiry agent's defence of leave and licence failed when the husband sued him for trespass to land.

his opponent hits him with a straight left to the nose. Obviously, there are difficult questions of fact here. Can a schoolboy sue another who has hidden his book by way of a practical joke? If perhaps consent may be reasonably inferred there, what if one Sandhurst cadet does the same with another's webbing immediately before an important parade? A footballer consents to those tackles which the rules permit, and, it is thought, to those tackles contravening the rules where the rule infringed is framed to maintain the skill of the game; but otherwise if his opponent gouges out an eye or perhaps even tackles against the rules and dangerously.[7] Similarly, it may be a defence to trespass to land by a child if the plaintiff has habitually allowed children to play on that land.

Consent must be to the act complained of. The lessee may have consented to the lessor's entering the land to examine the repairs but not to his assaulting him. The courts say that consent obtained by fraud going to the quality of the conduct and being not merely collateral is no consent: therefore, consent to intercourse with another on the representation of that other that he is free from syphilis was held to be still consent,[8] but there seems no logical way of deciding when a mistake is collateral.[9] Consent obtained by duress[10] is no consent. An important question is the effect of consent obtained by a show of authority—for example, the policeman, who, without formally arresting or charging a suspect, asks him to accompany him to the police station, has no defence if the plaintiff goes because of an assertion of authority by him: consent obtained by show of authority is no consent.[11] If the plaintiff is drunk or otherwise incapable of giving consent, then there is no defence.[12]

The over-riding interest of the state in maintaining order and punishing wrongdoers is such that it is not necessarily a defence in criminal law that the victim has consented to the criminal act. No considerations of policy prevent the courts from holding that consent to a crime is a valid defence in tort, and it may be assumed that the courts will hold that consent may be a defence in tort in such circumstances.[13]

---

7 See *R v Billinghurst* [1978] Crim LR 553; *Affutu-Nartoy v Clarke* (1984) Times, 9 February. As to duty of care owed by one competitor to another see *Condon v Basi* [1985] 2 All ER 453, [1985] 1 WLR 866.

8 *Hegarty v Shine* (1878) 14 Cox CC 124. Do you think that *Hegarty v Shine* would be decided the same way today in a different moral climate? Would consent to intercourse defeat a claim in trespass where the plaintiff had been infected with A.I.D.S.?

9 What if the defendant impersonates the plaintiff's husband, or a bigamist 'marries' the innocent plaintiff and has intercourse (held actionable in *Graham v Saville* [1945] 2 DLR 489, Ontario CA), or the singing teacher convinces his pupil that intercourse will improve her voice? To what does the plaintiff consent? Is it intercourse, marital intercourse, intercourse free from venereal disease, any penetration? Should the test be whether the mistake induced relates to that which is harmful or offensive in the act?

10 Yet in *Latter v Braddell* (1881) 50 LJQB 448, a servant who complied, reluctantly, crying and under protest, with an order of her mistress that she be medically examined to check whether she was pregnant, was held to have consented.

11 *Warner v Riddiford* (1858) 4 CB(NS) 180. Submissions in *Freeman v Home Office* (supra) that the relationship between prisoner and prison doctor was such that the former could *never* freely consent to treatment by the latter failed. But the judge at first instance made it clear that in looking at the reality of a prisoner's consent to medical treatment the doctor's power to affect the prisoner's situation must be borne in mind.

12 Must the plaintiff's consent be manifested to the defendant? Is it enough if the defendant reasonably believes that the plaintiff has consented?

13 *Barnes v Nayer* (1986) Times, 19 December; *Murphy v Culhane* [1977] QB 94; [1976] 3 All ER 533 where the Court of Appeal held that the defence of consent might be available in respect of a crime, and at the same time also held that a plea of *ex turpi causa* might also be open to the defendant. (See p 97, post).

C. CONSENT TO MEDICAL TREATMENT

Any physical contact with a patient without his consent to that contact is *prima facie* a battery.[14] Consent need not be written and in practice will often be implied from conduct, for example, holding out your arm to receive an injection. Where surgery or more serious invasive treatment is contemplated patients will usually be asked to sign a standard consent form agreeing to the operation or other treatment 'the effect and nature of which have been explained to me'. Such a consent is ineffective unless an adequate explanation of the broad nature of what is to be done to the patient is given to him.[15] But a failure to warn the patient of the risks or side-effects of the treatment proposed will not vitiate the patient's consent.[16] It may be a breach of the doctor's duty to give the patient proper and skilled advice, but as such it will be actionable only in negligence[17] and not in battery.

The Family Law Reform Act 1969, section 8, provides that a minor over 16 may effectively consent to surgical, medical or dental treatment. In the case of children under 16 that Act preserves the common law that providing the individual child is mature enough to make his or her own decision on the treatment proposed, the child herself can give an effective consent to treatment.[18] Thus Mrs Gillick's attempt to ensure that no girl under 16 could lawfully be prescribed the Pill without parental agreement failed. By a majority the House of Lords held that a doctor faced with a request by a young girl for contraceptive treatment (or an abortion) should always try to persuade his patient to consult her family. But should she refuse to do so he might lawfully treat her provided that he was satisfied that she had a sufficient understanding of what was involved in the treatment and its implications for her. In the case of younger children parental consent to treatment will be effective to authorise treatment beneficial to the child.[19] No battery is committed by a doctor who with parental consent vaccinates a protesting four year old against measles.

Where treatment proposed is not clearly and unequivocally beneficial to the child parental consent alone may be insufficient to authorise that treatment. Several cases have been heard lately relating to the sterilisation of mentally handicapped girls. Where the surgery is proposed, not to deal with some immediate physical problem, such as a hysterectomy to remove a cancerous uterus, the authorisation of the court must be sought before such serious and generally irreversible surgery is performed or the surgeon may risk liability for battery and prosecution for criminal assault.[20] When the patient is under 18, authorisation can be sought by means of making her a ward of court.[1]

---

14 *Re T* (1987) The Independent, 14 July; and see Brazier *Medicine, Patients and the Law* (1987) ch 4.

15 *Chatterton v Gerson* [1981] QB 432 at 443 (per Bristow J).

16 *Chatterton v Gerson* (supra) at 444; *Freeman v Home Office* (No 2) (supra); *Hills v Potts* [1983] QB 493. The bringing of actions in battery where the essence of the complaint is inadequate advice was deplored by their Lordships in *Sidaway v Governors of Bethlem Royal Hospital and the Maudsley Hospital* [1985] 2 WLR 480 at 489.

17 See *Sidaway v Governors of Bethlem Royal Hospital* (supra) discussed post at p 213.

18 Section 8(3); *Gillick v West Norfolk and Wisbech Area Health Authority* [1986] AC 112, [1985] 3 All ER 402.

19 *Re D* [1976] Fam 185, [1976] 1 All ER 326 and see *Re B* [1981] 1 WLR 1421.

20 *Re B (a minor) (wardship: sterilisation)* [1987] 2 All ER 206 at 214.

 1 Ibid.

Where a patient is over 18 but is incapable by reason of mental handicap of making a rational decision to consent to surgery the law is at present in a state of confusion. In one case a mentally handicapped woman had become pregnant. Doctors caring for her wished to perform an abortion and to sterilise her. WOOD J[2] regretted the apparent absence of general *parens patriae* jurisdiction enabling the courts to authorise medical treatment of mentally incompetent adults. Exceptionally, he held, where no valid consent could be obtained from a patient or anyone else doctors might operate without consent when good medical practice indicated that this was the correct course of action. This is the basis on which much routine medical and dental treatment of mentally handicapped persons is already performed. Is it satisfactory where such drastic and controversial procedures as sterilisation or abortion are in issue? In one case specific provision for treatment of the mentally ill is made. The Mental Health Act 1983, Part IV dispenses with the consent of patients detained under that Act (not informal patients) to treatment given to treat the mental disorder in respect of which they are detained. Elaborate safeguards for the rights of such patients are built into the Act.

When an otherwise competent patient is temporarily incapable of agreeing to treatment because he is unconscious, perhaps he has been rushed into casualty after a road accident, the surgeon carrying out immediately necessary surgery commits no battery. He does no 'hostile' act in relation to the patient. His course of action is one sanctioned in everyday life to which he would expect the reasonable patient to agree.[3] Alternatively he may invoke the defence of necessity.[4]

D. REVOCATION OF LICENCES[5]

A controversial and important problem of English law, which is of only indirect relevance in the law of torts, is when a licence to enter particular land or to do some other act there may be revoked. In *Hurst v Picture Theatres Ltd*[6]

> The plaintiff paid for his admission to the defendant's theatre. The defendant, believing that he had obtained admission without payment, after asking him to leave his seat (which he refused to do), ejected him forcibly. The plaintiff won his action for assault and false imprisonment.

The issue was whether the defendant could revoke his permission to the plaintiff to enter the cinema, ie whether, after being asked to leave, the plaintiff could be deemed to be a trespasser on the defendant's land. This turns on complex problems of the law of property and contracts namely, whether these licences create proprietary interests, or in any event are protected in equity by injunction—these matters are outside the scope of the law of torts: their relevance in the law of torts is solely in deciding whether there is a consent by one person to what would otherwise be a tortious act on the part of the other.

---

2 *Re T* (1987) 131 Sol Jo 1286.
3 *Wilson v Pringle* [1987] QB 237, [1986] 2 All ER 440.
4 See post at p 83.
5 For a fuller treatment of this problem in its tortious setting, see *Salmond*, 74 *et seq*.
6 [1915] 1 KB 1 CA; disapproved in *Cowell v Rosehill Race Course Co Ltd* (1937) 56 CLR 605 (H Ct Australia); see also *Wood v Leadbitter* (1845) 13 M & W 838.

SECTION 3.   CONTRIBUTORY NEGLIGENCE

This defence will be examined in what is obviously its most appropriate place, in negligence.[7] Contributory negligence is no defence to proceedings founded on conversion or intentional trespass to goods.[8] The defence is available in battery.[9]

SECTION 4.   SELF-DEFENCE

If A hits B or damages his clothes, then *prima facie* he commits trespass to the person or to goods. If A should prove that he did so to defend himself against B he may have the justification of self-defence to an action in battery or trespass to goods brought against him by B.[10] The defendant must prove that in the circumstances it was reasonable that he should defend himself and that the force used by him was reasonable. So, in *Cockcroft v Smith*.[11]

> The clerk of a court sued an attorney for biting off his forefinger in a scuffle in court. HOLT CJ, held that in itself it was no defence that the plaintiff had first run his fingers towards the defendant's eyes, for a man must not 'in case of a small assault, give a violent or an unreasonable return'.

One may likewise resist an unlawful arrest.[12]

What is reasonable force is a question of fact in each case.[13] It will be material to consider whether the plaintiff could have escaped, whether he resisted with the most reasonable means available, whether the act of the defendant went beyond the limits of defence to mere revenge, whether the defendant continued to use violence after the danger had passed, and whether the plaintiff's attack was, or was reasonably expected to be, violent. It has been said[14] that, even though the force used is no greater than is requisite for protection, it is still no defence unless the defendant also proves that the force used was not disproportionate to the nature of the evil sought to be avoided, but the cases relied on do not establish such a legal rule.[15] It is suggested that

---

7 See pp 144 et seq, post.

8 Section 11(1) Torts (Interference with Goods) Act 1977, except that the defence is open to a collecting banker sued for conversion of a cheque; Banking Act 1979, s 47.

9 *Murphy v Culhane* [1977] QB 94, [1976] 3 All ER 533. CA. *Barnes v Nayer* (supra).

10 Even though the provocation by the plaintiff may not on the facts justify the battery, it may be a ground for reducing damages; *Fraser v Berkeley* (1836) 7 C & P 621 at 624 (per LORD ABINGER). See also s 3 of the Criminal Law Act 1967, p 83 post.

11 (1705) 2 Salk 642. In fact the plaintiff failed on a finding that his act did endanger the defendant's eye.

12 *Codd v Cabe* (1876) 1 Ex D 352.

13 Cf HOLMES J, in *Holmes-Laski Letters*, v. 1, 335, on the supposed duty in *law* to retreat to the wall before killing assailant: 'I think it an instance of an early statement ossifying by repetition into an absolute principle when rationally it is only one of the circumstances to be considered with the rest in deciding whether the defendant exceeds the reasonable limits'. The notion of any duty to retreat was expressly condemned by the Court of Appeal in *R v Bird* [1985] 2 All ER 513, [1985] 1 WLR 816. As to force exerted where the danger was miscalculated but the intervention based on a reasonable mistake, see *Albert v Lavin* [1982] AC 546 DC. The point was not considered in affirming the decision in the House of Lords [1982] AC at 516.

14 *Salmond* p 120.

15 Ie *Cook v Beal* (1697) 1 Ld Raym 176; *Cockroft v Smith*, supra; Dale v Wood (1822) 7 Moore CP 33. In each case the force used was unnecessary for self-defence.

the relation between the harm threatened by the plaintiff and the means of defence used is one element of fact to be considered in deciding the general question of reasonableness.[16] Suppose that A pins Miss B against a wall and repeatedly kisses her against her will, and the only means whereby Miss B can compel A to desist is by lacerating his wrists with scissors—it surely cannot be a proposition of law that she has no defence to an action of trespass brought by A; on the contrary, it is suggested that it is open to the court to declare this reasonable self-defence.

SECTION 5.   DEFENCE OF THE PERSON OF ANOTHER

A servant may justify a battery in defence of his master[17] and a master may lawfully strike someone in defence of his servant.[18] A wife may defend her husband and there is no doubt that a man may defend any member of his household.[19] It may be that the defence extends to the protection of other persons, although authority is lacking; for instance, that a guard could defend railway passengers. It is submitted that the question ought always to be: 'Was it reasonable for the defendant to protect the other person in this way?'

As with self-defence, the conduct of the defendant must be reasonable in all the circumstances, and it is conceivable that one relevant factor may be the relationship between the defendant and the person whom he defended, ie that one may use greater force in defence of a close relative than of a stranger; at least, the facts must probably[20] be such as to have justified the third person in defending himself. If the defendant acted in order to prevent the plaintiff from perpetrating a felony jeopardising the life of a third party, that was in itself a defence[1] on the authority of *Handcock v Baker,* and a *dictum* there suggested that 'it is lawful for a private person to do anything to prevent the perpetration of a felony'.[2] Felonies were abolished by the Criminal Law Act 1967 and it is suggested that any general right to intervene to prevent a criminal attack on another is now provided for solely by section 3 of that 1967 Act. If the defendant goes beyond merely protecting another and chastises the attacker, then, unless he has the defence of discipline,[3] he is liable for that act of chastisement.

SECTION 6.   DEFENCE OF ONE'S PROPERTY

One may use reasonable force to defend land or chattels in one's possession

---

16 Cf *Turner v Metro-Goldwyn-Meyer Pictures Ltd* [1950] 1 All ER 449 at 471, HL (per LORD OAKSEY *obiter*): 'If you are attacked by a prize-fighter you are not bound to adhere to the Queensberry rules in your defence.'

17 *Barfoot v Reynolds* (1734) 2 Stra 953.

18 *Seaman v Cuppledick* (1615) Owen 150; *Tickell v Read* (1773) Lofft 215; contra *Leward v Basely* (1695) 1 Ld Raym 62.

19 *A-G's Reference* ((No2) of 1983) [1984] QB 456, [1984] 1 All ER 988; *Leward v Basely*, supra.

20 There is one doubtful case; when the defendant reasonably but mistakenly believes that the third party had, in the cirumstances, the privilege to defend himself.

1 A bystander may also use force to arrest another committing a breach of the peace in his presence, p 89, post.

2 (1800) 2 Bos & P 260 at 265 (per CHAMBRE J). See also *Coupey v Henley* (1797) 2 Esp 539.

3 See pp 85–87, post.

against any person threatening to commit or committing a trespass to the property.

The defendant must have such possession as would enable him to sue the plaintiff in trespass. Thus the captain of a cricket club who removed the plaintiff from the field could not plead that he had ejected a trespasser, because the captain had not possession of the field.[4] Similarly, in *Scott v Matthew Brown & Co Ltd:*[5]

> The defendant was on the land merely as a result of ejecting the plaintiff by an act of trespass whereupon the plaintiff, the true owner, at once re-entered. The defendant forcibly removed him, and was held not to have sufficient possession to sue in trespass, and therefore to have no defence against the action of battery by the plaintiff.

If the defendant has a mere right to possess, but not possession, he may have some other defence, re-entry in the case of land, or recaption in the case of chattels, but he cannot successfully plead that he was defending his property.[6]

To remain on land after permission has expired is trespass: therefore the defence is available to a defendant who ejects such a person.[7] A threatened intrusion is also sufficient: if the plaintiff has taken the key of the defendant's car and is about to enter the car, the defendant may resist this potential trespass to his chattel.

As with defence of the person, if the defendant has a reasonable belief that force is essential to end the trespass, he may use it although he is mistaken in thinking it to be necessary, but if he mistakenly believes that the plaintiff is a trespasser, he has no defence. What is reasonable force depends here also on the facts, though guidance may be sought from decided cases:[8]

> If a person enters another's house with force and violence, the owner of the house may justify turning him out (using no more force than is necessary), without a previous request to depart; but if the person enters quietly, the other party cannot justify turning him out, without a previous request to depart.

As the law does not value interests in property quite so highly as those in the person, the use of force in defence of the former is, then, harder to justify than in the case of self-defence. Thus, it has been held unjustified to pull away a ladder on which the plaintiff was standing, although he was a trespasser on the land of the defendant.[9] A publican had no privilege to wound a man who merely refused to leave a public house on request after creating a disturbance,[10] yet a house-holder was justified in defying, with a clothes prop and spade, a sanitary inspector who sought to enter land to do drainage repairs without having given the statutory notice.[11] If a tramp jumps on a goods train he certainly trespasses on a chattel, but the guard may not throw him off when the train is travelling at 30 m.p.h. Indeed, unless the plaintiff resists his expulsion so as to bring the rules of self-defence into play, force likely to

---

4 *Holmes v Bagge* (1853) 1 E & B 782; *Dean v Hogg* (1834) 10 Bing 345.
5 (1884) 51 LT 746.
6 *Roberts v Tayler* (1845) 1 CB 117 at 126–7 (per TINDAL CJ).
7 *Green v Bartram* (1830) 4 C & P 308; *Moriarty v Brooks* (1834) 6 C & P 684.
8 *Tullay v Reed* (1823) 1 C & P 6 (per PARK J); cf *Green v Goddard* (1702) 2 Salk 641; *Polkinhorn v Wright* (1845) 8 QB 197.
9 *Collins v Renison* (1754) Say 138.
10 *Moriarty v Brooks* (1834) 6 C & P 684.
11 *Stroud v Bradbury* [1952] 2 All ER 76.

cause death or serious bodily harm will not be justifiable in defence of property. A man may justify shooting his neighbour's tame pigeons found damaging the crops if there were no other practicable means of driving them off.[12]

The courts have often had to consider the extent to which a defendant could use mechanical devices or other methods to protect his property. No principle is set out explicitly in the series of cases, but the test here is also one of reasonableness. To deter trespassers by barbed wire or spiked railings on the confines of one's land is reasonable, and there is no liability if another is injured by them;[13] but deliberately and without notice to set spring guns or any device calculated to kill or cause grievous bodily harm is not reasonable.[14]

Under the Animals Act 1971 a person is not liable under those provisions of that Act to impose strict liability[15] 'for any damage caused by an animal kept on any premises or structure to a person trespassing there, if it is proved either (*a*) that the animal was not kept there for the protection of persons or property; or (*b*) (if the animal was kept there for the protection of persons or property) that keeping it there for that purpose was not unreasonable.'[16]

Section 9 of the Animals Act creates a special statutory defence for the killing of or injury to dogs worrying livestock. The defence is available only if (or the defendant reasonably believed it to be so) the dog is worrying or is about to worry the livestock and there are no reasonable means of ending or preventing the worrying; or the dog has been worrying livestock, has not left the vicinity and is not under the control of any person and there are no practicable means of ascertaining to whom it belongs. The defendant must also be entitled to protect the livestock; that is, the livestock or the land on which it is belongs to him or to any person under whose authority he is acting, and the livestock was not killed on land to which it had strayed by a dog for which the occupier of that land was responsible.[17] The defendant must further notify the police within 48 hours of the killing or injury.

SECTION 7.   DEFENCE OF THE PROPERTY OF ANOTHER

Blackstone states that it is a defence to protect the property of other members of one's household,[18] and although one might expect the courts to confine this defence within narrow limits, by analogy with defence of the person of another it may be assumed to exist.

---

12 *Hamps v Darby* [1948] 2 KB 311, [1948] 2 All ER 474, CA.
13 See *Deane v Clayton* (1817) 7 Taunt 489.
14 *Bird v Holbrook* (1828) 4 Bing 628, distinguished in *Jordin v Crump* (1841) 8 M & W 782 (setting with notice dog spears for the purpose of protecting game against dogs held lawful); see now Offences against the Person Act 1861, s 31. In *A-G Reference (No 2 of 1983)* (supra) the accused had armed himself with petrol bombs to repel rioters who had earlier smashed into his shop. The Court of Appeal held he was entitled to acquittal if his object was to protect his family or his property from imminent attack and the force employed was reasonable. As to an occupier's duty of care to a trespasser see now the Occupiers' Liability Act 1984 discussed post at p 270.
15 Ch 21, post.
16 Section 5(3).
17 There was a substantially similar defence at common law, eg *Cresswell v Sirl* [1948] 1 KB 241, [1947] 2 All ER 730, CA, except that the police need not be notified. Section 9 does not repeal the common-law defence expressly—perhaps it is still available although the police were not notified.
18 Book III, 3; no modern cases have been traced.

SECTION 8.   PREVENTING CRIME

The above discussion relates to the right given to individuals at common law to defend themselves, their property and other closely related persons. Section 3 of the Criminal Law Act 1967 confers a public right to use 'such force as is reasonable in the prevention of crime'. Very often where a man uses force to defend himself or his child from attack it matters not whether his defence is categorised as self-defence at common law or invokes the authority to use force to prevent crime bestowed on every citizen by section 3. The private and the public rights to use force defensively must be distinguished in at least two instances. It is unclear whether at common law any private right justifies the use of force to repel an attack on a stranger. Section 3 clearly does where that attack is criminal. But in a second instance the right to use force conferred by section 3 is clearly inferior to the private right of self-defence conferred at common law. Should your attacker be insane, or a child under ten, no crime may be committed. Can section 3 be invoked to authorise force against what is reasonably believed to be, but in fact is not, and could not be, a criminal offence?

SECTION 9.   NECESSITY

A. DISTINGUISHED FROM DEFENCE OF PROPERTY

As a justification for a trespass, defence of property is sometimes difficult to distinguish from necessity. Confusion is all the more likely because, in deciding whether defence of property or self-defence is available, one may have to consider whether the act of the defendant was reasonably necessary for that defence. The difference is that self-defence or defence of property presupposes that the plaintiff is *prima facie* a wrongdoer: the defence of necessity contemplates the infliction of harm on an innocent plaintiff. When, for instance, the defendant barricades his land against flood-water and, in consequence, the plaintiff's land is flooded, the defence of necessity may lie against the plaintiff who is not responsible for creating the threat of danger. Obviously, then, the law may here be expected to attach a greater importance to the plaintiff's interest, and, accordingly, to restrict the scope of the defence.

B. SCOPE

(1) PRIVATE NECESSITY

One may lawfully[19] protect one's person and property[20] (and that of another[1])

---

19 There is no English authority (contra in USA *Vincent v Lake Erie Transportation Co* (1910) 109 Minn 456) that the privilege is incomplete in the sense that he must compensate the plaintiff for the actual loss sustained by him: an *obiter dictum* of TINDAL CJ in *Anthony v Haney* (1832) 8 Bing 186 at 193 sometimes cited as such authority is solely on reception.

20 *Cope v Sharp (No 2)* [1912] 1 KB 496, CA (defendant justified in burning heather on plaintiff's land in order to prevent fire on plaintiff's land spreading to land on which defendant's master had shooting rights).

1 *Proudman v Allen* [1954] SASR 336 (defendant, believing that plaintiff's unoccupied car was about to run into another vehicle, jumped into the driving seat with the result that the car ran into the sea and sank—held no trespass).

against the threat of harm even though the consequence is that an innocent person suffers a loss.

Perhaps the most remarkable illustration in this century of the scope of this defence is *Leigh v Gladstone*:[2]

> A suffragette prisoner who was fasting was forcibly fed through the mouth and nose by prison officers; she sued them for battery. It was held to be a good defence that the forcible feeding was necessary to save her life.

Could a doctor today then invoke the defence of necessity to justify treatment carried out on a patient without her consent? First, suicide ceased to be a crime in 1961 so refusing further medical treatment or even declining to eat is no longer an unlawful act by the patient himself. Second, it must be understood that by not enforcing treatment, even when the doctor knows it to be necessary, the doctor is not negligent. His duty is to offer adequate and skilled treatment. The law protects the competent patient's right of self-determination to choose whether or not to accept treatment offered. Thus any defence of necessity invoked today against a NHS or private patient in the community who expressly refuses treatment is likely to fail, and will probably fail in most circumstances too against a prisoner patient as well.[3] The proper function of the defence of necessity in the context of medical treatment is to justify emergency procedures carried out on a patient incapable at the time of giving any consent. Some latitude by the courts in defining incapacity, perhaps to disregard a hysterical refusal of treatment by a feverish or acutely ill patient, may well be expected.

The removal of the goods of a lately deceased person is justified only if necessary for their safety.[4] One may do what is necessary to protect one's own property against a threatened flood,[5] even though flooding of one's neighbour's land ensues, and it has been held to be justifiable to divert locusts from one's land although the result is that they damage the crops of one's neighbour instead.[6] Homeless persons who enter empty houses of a local authority which are awaiting development to provide housing do not have the defence of necessity for their trespass; the Court of Appeal restricted the application of the defence to an urgent situation of imminent peril.[7]

(2) PUBLIC NECESSITY

It used to be accepted that a citizen might lawfully enter another's land to

---

2 (1909) 26 TLR 139. But would the decision have been the same if the plaintiff had neither been a suffragette, nor in prison? Does the decision rest on the statutory duty of prison officers to preserve the life of prisoners? See Zellick 'The Forcible Feeding of Prisoners: An Examination of the Legality of Enforced Therapy' [1976] P.L. 15'.

3 See Zellick (ibid); M. Brazier 'Prison Doctors and their Involuntary Patients' [1982] P.L.

4 *Kirk v Gregory* (1876) 1 ExD 55.

5 *Nield v London and North Western Ry Co* (1874) LR 10 Exch 4 at 7 (per BRAMWELL B); *Maxey Drainage Board v Great Northern Ry Co* (1912) 106 LT 429 at 430 (per LUSH J) Div Ct; *Gerrard v Crowe* [1921] 1 AC 395, PC. If the defendant's land is *already* flooded he may not divert that flood water on to the plaintiff's land: *Whalley v Lancashire Ry Co* (1884) 13 QBD 131.

6 *Greyvensteyn v Hattingh* [1911] AC 355, PC (the defendant entered land of a third party while diverting them).

7 *Southwark London Borough v Williams* [1971] Ch 734, [1971] 2 All ER 175, CA.

erect fortifications for the defence of the realm[8] or to fight fires.[9] Public necessity also justifies throwing cargo overboard in order to save the lives of the ship's passengers.[10] Whether compensation is payable to the victims of acts committed because of public necessity is obscure.[11]

In order to raise the defence of either public or private necessity there must be both an actual (or what to a reasonable man seems to be) danger, and the steps taken must in the light of the facts be reasonable.[12] If the plaintiff relies on an allegedly negligent act the defence of necessity need not be considered, for the same standard is then applied to determine the issues of both necessity and negligence, viz, the reasonable man.[13]

Thus in *Rigby v Chief Constable of Northampton*[14] the police were held liable for firing a CS gas canister into the plaintiff's shop to flush out a dangerous psychopath without having adequate firefighting equipment available. The shop was burned out. The judge held that necessity was a good defence to trespass in such an emergency, but that the police were liable in negligence for their failure to ensure that they had sufficient fire-fighting back-up when the canister was released onto the plaintiff's property.

SECTION 10.   DISCIPLINE

Where force is used neither in self-defence nor in the prevention of crime, but rather to punish the offender, the trespass against him, be it a battery or a false imprisonment, must now generally be justified by statutory authority, for example, the Prison Act 1952 or the legislation governing the control of mentally disordered persons. The sanction given by the common law to those in authority disciplining those subject to their authority is virtually a matter of legal history alone now. It is nearly a century ago that it was finally determined that a husband has no right to discipline his wife whether by beating her or imprisoning her. Exercise of disciplinary powers remains a defence to an action in tort only in relation to children and in the bizarre case of passengers on ships.

---

8 YB 8 Ed 4 f 23 Mich pl. 41 (per counsel); YB 21 H 7, 27 (*dictum* of KINGSMILL J—the point was taken on demurrer but no judgment given on it); *The Case of the King's Prerogative in Saltpetre* (1606) 12 Co Rep 12 (*obiter dictum* in resolution of judges).
9 *Dewey v White* (1827) Mood & M 56 (defendant justified in throwing down plaintiff's chimney because of fire risk that it would otherwise fall on highway below); per KINGSMILL J., supra, and *Case of Saltpetre*, supra (justified in destroying buildings); fire brigades now have statutory authority dating from Metropolitan Fire Brigade Act 1865, s 12 to commit such trespasses—Viner, *Abr* Trespass K a pl 3 (justified in taking to safety goods in burning house).
10 *Mouse's Case* (1608) 12 Co Rep 63; cf *Southport Corporation v Esso Petroleum Co Ltd* [1954] 2 QB 182, [1954] 2 All ER 561; rvd [1956] AC 218, [1955] 3 All ER 864 HL; cf also the restricted common law right to deviate from a foundrous highway at least where it is public, and the land entered belongs to a person responsible for the highway's foundrous state (*Stacy v Sherrin* (1913) 29 TLR 555).
11 No: Bohlen 39 HLR 370; Glanville Williams *Current Legal Problems* vol 6, 216. Yes: Scott and Hildesley *Case of Requisition* p 136 *et passim*; BULLER J (*obiter*) in *British Cast Plate Manufacturers (Governor & Co) v Meredith* (1794) 4 Term Rep 794 at 797; Ambiguous; *dicta* in *Case of Saltpetre*, supra. Inconclusive; *obiter dicta* in *Burmah Oil Co Ltd v Lord Advocate* [1965] AC 75, [1964] 2 All ER 348, HL.
12 *Cope v Sharp (No 2)* p 83 ante, illustrates both these requirements.
13 *Southport Corporation v Esso Petroleum Co Ltd* supra.
14 [1985] 2 All ER 985, [1985] 1 WLR 1242.

A. CHILDREN

(1) BY PARENTS

Save in the case of injuries inflicted before birth where children are expressly excluded from suing their mothers, children are not prevented from suing their parents even while they remain minors.[15] It is presumed, however, that parents can justify an assault and battery by way of chastisement provided reasonable force by way of correction is used.[16] And similarly parents may be able to justify detention of their children by way of punishment as a defence to an action of false imprisonment. It is suggested, however, that there is only a right to detain where it is reasonable in the circumstances; and that whereas a parent, who locked up his twelve-year-old daughter at night to prevent her from associating with Hell's Angels, might have a defence to an action of false imprisonment, a parent, who detained a seventeen-year-old daughter whereby she was prevented from sitting a university examination, would have no defence.

(2) BY SCHOOLTEACHERS AND OTHERS RESPONSIBLE FOR THEIR TRAINING AND EDUCATION

At common law head and assistant teachers, both at boarding and day schools, and in the maintained and the independent sector, had the right to use reasonable force to correct the children under their tutelage.[17] Section 47 of the Education (No 2) Act 1987 prohibits corporal punishment in maintained schools and for state funded pupils in independent schools. Use of force to punish a child as opposed to limited force needed to protect a child from harming himself or others will be no defence to an action for assault and battery. The defence of exercise of disciplinary powers will remain available to teachers in independent schools against fee paying pupils, and the defence of disciplinary powers will remain available to all teachers in respect of acts not involving beating the child where available at common law, for example to justify detention after school or confiscating the child's property. A pretty serious breach of discipline would have to be shown to justify detaining or in particular locking up a child.[18] Disciplinary powers may afford a defence to trespass to goods as where a master removed from a boy a pocket book, which, he thought, would identify the ringleaders in a school conspiracy to disturb order.[19]

In independent schools where corporal punishment is not yet prohibited correction may be administered (even at a day school) for acts done outside school affecting school discipline.[20] The force used must be reasonable in the

---

15 In *Ash v Lady Ash* (1696) Comb 357 a daughter was able to sue her mother in trespass to the person; in *Roberts v Roberts* (1657) Hard 96, an infant obtained an injunction against her father to prevent waste and in the Scottish case of *Young v Rankin* 1934 SC 499, a child passenger in a car driven by his father was held to be able to sue his father for injuries received consequent upon his father's negligent driving.

16 Children and Young Persons Act 1933, s 1(7), takes this to be the common law.

17 *Fitzgerald v Northcote* (1865) 4 F & F 656 (headmaster, boarding school); *Ryan v Fildes* [1938] 3 All ER 517 (assistant mistress, day school).

18 Ibid.

19 Ibid.

20 *Cleary v Booth* [1893] 1 QB 465; (fighting on the way to school); *R v Newport (Salop) Justices, Ex parte Wright* [1929] 2 KB 416. Div Ct (smoking in street after school).

circumstances—presumably the offence, the age and physique of the child, his past behaviour, the punishment, the injury inflicted, are all material. It may be that, consistent with the change of public opinion on the matter, the lawful limits of this disciplinary power are narrower than hitherto—a moderate box on the ear of an unruly ten-year-old causing deafness has been held unjustifiable.[1] Probably, not only must the teacher use force which is objectively reasonable, but he also himself must have thought it reasonably necessary in the circumstances.[2]

The basis of the defence is the need to maintain order in the particular organisation responsible for the training of the child, and that, at most, school rules and parental instructions are factors to be taken into consideration when deciding what is reasonable.[3]

B. PASSENGERS IN PUBLIC TRANSPORT

The captain of a ship may use reasonable force against anyone on his ship who commits 'some act calculated in the apprehension of a reasonable man to interfere with the safety of the ship or the due prosecution of the voyage',[4] provided also, it seems, that he believes it necessary for the purpose.[5] A captain was not therefore justified in detaining a passenger in his cabin for a week because the passenger put his hand to his nose to the captain and did not apologise.[6]

The cases traced have only been concerned with ships, but the same defence may be available to captains of aircraft, and, though perhaps in a restricted class of events, to those in charge of rail and road transport.

SECTION 11.   ARREST, SEARCH AND SEIZURE

The powers of arrest, search and seizure conferred on police officers, and to a limited extent on private citizens, by the Police and Criminal Evidence Act 1984 are perhaps in practice the most important of all the defences discussed in this chapter. Lawful arrest, search or seizure may constitute a defence to false imprisonment, battery or interference with goods. Unlawful arrest may justify action which would otherwise be a battery by the person resisting arrest. The 1984 Act to some degree codifies earlier case-law and legislation on police powers as well as conferring new powers and duties on the police. Nevertheless a fair amount of pre-1984 Act case-law remains relevant to the definition of police powers.

1 *Ryan v Fildes* [1938] 3 All ER 517; there is a significant reference to Tucker J: 'in these days', at 520.
2 See *Hook v Cunard SS Co Ltd,* [1953] 1 All ER 1021, on the somewhat analogous case of powers of a ship's captain to place a seaman under arrest in the interest of ship's discipline.
3 And see *Craig v Frost* (1936) 30 QJP 140 (Queensland): defendant teacher ordered child not to gallop horse to and from school, whereas father permitted galloping. Held since the order was reasonable in the interests of the child's safety, teacher's disciplinary powers overrode parental instructions.
4 *Aldworth v Stewart* (1866) 4 F & F 957 at 961 (per Channell B).
5 *Hook v Cunard SS Co Ltd* [1953] 1 All ER 1021.
6 *Aldworth v Stewart* supra.

A. ARREST

(1) BY A POLICEMAN WITH A WARRANT

A policeman who arrests a person under a warrant acts lawfully and commits no trespass. Even if there is a 'defect of jurisdiction' in the magistrate who issued the warrant, a constable is statutorily exempt from liability if he acts in obedience to the warrant.[7] Thus it has been held that this section protects a constable obeying an 'invalid or unlawful warrant'.[8] But even if the warrant is good the constable is protected only if he acts in obedience to it: he is liable if he arrests the wrong person, or acts outside his jurisdiction.[9] And he must produce the warrant on demand and will be liable if he fails to do so. The arrested person having sight of the warrant may then be able to sue the magistrate if the warrant itself is defective.

(2) ARREST WITHOUT WARRANT

Section 24 of the Police and Criminal Evidence Act 1984 provides for a category of 'arrestable offences'. These are criminal offences (1) for which the sentence is fixed by law, (2) for which a statute authorises imprisonment for five years, (3) a list of specific offences in sub-section (2), and (4) inciting, conspiring or attempting to commit any of the above offences. Any person, constable or private citizen, may arrest without warrant anyone who is or whom, with reasonable cause, he suspects to be, in the act of committing an arrestable offence.[10] Any person may further arrest anyone whom he has reasonable cause to believe has committed an arrestable offence provided that that arrestable offence has in fact been committed.[11] Private citizens act at their peril. If despite appearances no crime has been committed at all they may be liable for false imprisonment consequent on the unlawful arrest.[12] Constables enjoy greater powers. Even though no arrestable offence has been committed, a constable may, if he reasonably suspects that such an offence has been committed, arrest any person, whom he, with reasonable cause, suspects to be guilty of that offence.[13] And he may arrest any person who is, or whom he, with reasonable cause, suspects to be, about to commit an arrestable offence.[14] Section 117 of the 1984 Act expressly authorises constables to use reasonable force in the exercise of any of their powers under the Act including effecting an arrest. Private citizens arresting a person under the 1984 Act must rely on section 3 of the Criminal Law Act 1967 which authorises the use of reasonable force by anyone in the prevention of crime.

So far the powers of arrest conferred on private citizens and constables can be seen to be little changed from those embodied in earlier legislation,

---

7 Constables Protection Act 1750, s 6; see generally *Clerk and Lindsell* paras 26–118–26–120.
8 *Horsfield v Brown* [1932] 1 KB 355 at 369; *quaere* whether a constable is protected if the warrant is irregular in form eg it is not signed by a qualified magistrate or does not specify the cause of arrest.
9 As to constables' jurisdiction see now the Magistrates' Courts Act 1980, s 125(2).
10 Section 24(4).
11 Section 24(5).
12 Thus retaining the common law rule; see *Walters v WH Smith & Sons Ltd* [1914] 1 KB 595. The defendant arrested the plaintiffs on reasonable suspicion that he had stolen a book. Other books, but not that book, had been stolen. The arrest was unlawful and the plaintiff's detention false imprisonment.
13 Section 24(6).
14 Section 24(7).

the Criminal Law Act 1967. Section 25 of the Police and Criminal Evidence Act provides a significant extension to police powers of arrest, a power of general arrest, not limited to arrestable offences. Constables who have reasonable cause to believe that *any* offence is being or has been committed may arrest any person reasonably suspected of that offence if it appears to the constable that the service of a summons is impracticable or inappropriate because any of the general arrest conditions is satisfied. The general arrest conditions are wide in scope. They include (*inter alia*) that the constable believes that the suspected person has given a false name, or refuses to give a satisfactory address for service of a summons, or that he may, unless arrested, injure himself or another, or cause damage to property, or commit an offence against public decency. And, it must not be overlooked that in addition to police powers of arrest in respect of arrestable offences and the novel general arrest power under the 1984 Act, that statute expressly preserves a number of specific arrest powers under earlier Acts,[15] and new legislation post 1984 annually confers further arrest powers on the police.[16] Finally common law powers to intervene to prevent breaches of the peace are unaffected by the 1984 Act. Constables and private citizens may arrest without warrant a person committing a breach of the peace, or who, having committed such a breach, is reasonably believed to be about to renew it,[17] or where an imminent breach is reasonably apprehended.[18] Exceptionally a person may be detained without a formal arrest in order to prevent, or stop, a breach of the peace.[19]

B. REASONABLE CAUSE

Powers of arrest, and the police's complementary crime prevention powers of search and seizure, are generally dependent on reasonable cause for relevant suspicion. The adjustment of the conflict between the citizen's interest in personal freedom and the public interest in efficient enforcement of the criminal law is a delicate one. Traditionally the common law has dictated that the courts show no tendency to attach excessive weight to the second, to the detriment of the first factor. So the burden of proving reasonable cause, of justifying the arrest lies on the defendant,[20] albeit that in malicious prosecution it is on the plaintiff.[1] Jury trial is still available in actions for false imprisonment. The jury must find the facts on which the matter depends, but what amounts to reasonable cause is a question of law for the judge.[2] Mere suspicion, a policeman's hunch, is insufficient, but suspicion is a lesser state of mind than knowledge of guilt.[3] Some evidence, some information from

---

15 Section 26 and section 2. Various other statutes confer a variety of powers on private citizens too.
16 For example, the Public Order Act 1986.
17 *Timothy v Simpson* (1835) 1 Cr M & R 757. Police are not entitled to arrest for obstruction of an officer in the execution of his duty unless the disturbance caused or was likely to cause a breach of the peace *Wershof v Metropolitan Police Comr* [1978] 3 All ER 540, CA.
18 *R v Howell* [1982] QB 416, [1981] 3 All ER 383.
19 *Albert v Lavin* [1982] AC 546, [1981] 3 All ER 878, HL.
20 *Holtham v Metropolitan Police Comr* (1987) Times, 8 January; *Allen v Wright* (1838) 8 C & P 522.
1 See post p 433.
2 *Lister v Perryman* (1870) LR 4 HL 521.
3 *Hussien v Chong Fook Kam* [1970] AC 942, [1969] 3 All ER 1626, PC.

witnesses, affording objective grounds for suspicion must be established.[4] Once reasonable cause for suspicion is established, the constable need not generally prove that arrest was necessary. Constables are endowed with a discretion to arrest; they are rarely under a duty to do so. The House of Lords in *Holgate-Mohammed v Duke*[5] held that the constable's discretion to arrest could be challenged only if he could be proved to have acted on some immaterial or irrelevant consideration. Arrest of a woman in the belief that once in police custody she would more readily confess was held to be not unreasonable. An arrest for the purpose of using the period in custody to dispel or confirm suspicion by questioning the suspect or seeking further evidence was well within the discretion of a constable. Taking advantage of suspicion of crime to arrest your wife's lover and incarcerate him for a few hours would be clearly unlawful!

C. MANNER OF ARREST

Section 28 of the Police and Criminal Evidence Act sets out the basic rules governing the manner of a lawful arrest.[6] An arrested person must be told as soon as is practicable both:

(1) that he is under lawful arrest; and (2) what are the grounds for the arrest.

That information must be volunteered by the arrestor regardless of whether the fact of, or the ground for, the arrest, appear obvious.[7] Only escape before the arrestor can practicably explain the arrest and its grounds can now excuse a failure to impart the relevant information.[8] But the dual requirement of section 28 is very basic and earlier case-law elaborating the criteria for valid arrest remain relevant. For example, an arrested person must be told why he is being detained in plain simple English and given enough details to enable him to understand fully why he is being arrested.[9] It is not enough to tell him that he has been arrested 'for burglary'. He has to be told in general terms when and where he is suspected of having committed burglary.[10] Should an arrested person be deaf or unable to understand English, if the arrestor should have been aware of the problem he must take reasonable steps to try to communicate with his suspect. But the arrest will not be invalid because the arrestor cannot immediately summon an interpreter to his side.[11] And arrest by words alone will generally not be sufficient unless the arrested person submits to arrest. Some physical contact is required to bring the arrested person, nominally at least, under the arrestor's control.[12]

One novel problem concerning the manner of arrest arises from the intro-

---

4 *Davis v Russell* (1829) 5 Bing 354.
5 [1984] AC 437, [1984] 1 All ER 1054.
6 Section 28 largely enacts the common law rules derived from the classic judgment in *Christie v Leachinsky* [1947] AC 573, [1947] 1 All ER 567. Compare the judgment of Viscount Simon at 587 with the provision now made by s 28.
7 Section 28(2), (4).
8 Section 28(5).
9 *Christie v Leachinsky* (supra) per Viscount Simon at 587.
10 *R v Telfer* [1976] Crim LR 562.
11 *John Lewis & Co Ltd v Tims* [1952] AC 676 at 681; *Wheatley v Lodge* [1971] 1 WLR 29 at 34.
12 *Hart v Chief Constable of Kent* [1983] RTR 484 DC.

duction of the general arrest power in section 25 of the 1984 Act. Will it be sufficient for a constable to inform a suspect of the offence constituting the ground of the arrest? Or must he further explain why he is invoking the general arrest power? On principle the latter should be the correct approach. Rules governing the manner of arrest are designed to enable arrested persons to become aware that their liberty has been lawfully curtailed: that they cannot lawfully resist detention.[13] The general arrest power, which theoretically permits arrest for any offence, even a parking offence, must require that the constable tell the arrested person what exceptional circumstance justifies arrest.

Private citizens effecting an arrest must, as soon as is reasonable, hand the arrested person over to the police. They cannot imprison suspects on their own premises, or launch their own investigations. But that does not always mean the police must be summoned instantly. In *Lewis v Tims*[14] the plaintiff was arrested by the defendants' store detectives. She was held for some twenty to sixty minutes while the manager decided whether to call the police. The House of Lords found that in the circumstances the delay and its purpose was reasonable.

Police officers have rather wider powers after an arrest. The provisions of the 1984 Act largely preserve the common law rules. Generally a constable arresting a person must take him as soon as is practicable to a police station.[15] However, he may delay taking him there immediately where '. . . the presence of that person elsewhere is necessary in order to carry out such investigations as it is reasonable to carry out immediately.'[16] So he may where appropriate take the arrested person to his home or place of employment to, for example, check out an alibi claim, or establish evidence of identity or to look for stolen property.[17] The 1984 Act further provides detailed rules that are intended to ensure that, normally, arrested persons are taken only to designated police stations properly equipped to receive and hold arrested persons.

Occasionally suspects may be taken by police to the police station without arrest in order 'to help the police with their inquiries'. The police can then decide after questioning the suspect whether to charge him. There is no power to hold suspects without arrest for 'questioning'.[18]

In a case where a deaf mute had been detained without arrest for three nights in a police station before being charged, DEVLIN J told the jury[19] 'You may sometimes read in novels and detective stories, perhaps written by people not familiar with police procedure, that persons are sometimes taken into custody for questioning. There is no such power in this country. A man cannot be detained unless he is arrested.'

Only if the evidence establishes that the plaintiff freely agreed to go to and remain in the police station can liability for false imprisonment in such a case be rebutted.[20] The unlawful practice of detention without arrest must be

---

13 See *Christie v Leachinsky* (supra) per Viscount Simon at 587.
14 [1952] AC 676, [1952] 1 All ER 1203.
15 Section 30(1).
16 Section 30(10).
17 See *Dallison v Caffery* [1965] 1 QB 348, [1964] 2 All ER 610, CA.
18 Save by virtue of the exceptional provision made by the Prevention of Terrorism (Temporary Provisions) Act 1984.
19 *R v Roberts* (1953) as reported in the *Manchester Guardian*, 25 March.
20 See *Warner v Riddiford* (1858) 4 CBNS 180 (show of authority may negate apparent consent: on whom would the burden of proving absence of consent fall?)

distinguished from another more common practice. A person is arrested on a minor charge while further inquiries about a more serious matter are pursued. Providing lawful grounds exist for the first arrest the decision to exercise the discretion to arrest the person on that charge can be challenged only if it can be proved to have been effected in bad faith or for some irrelevant or improper purpose.[1]

D. ENTRY, SEARCH AND SEIZURE

The Police and Criminal Evidence Act confers on constables powers to enter premises, search persons and property and to seize evidence which are far greater in extent than the uncertain and ill-defined powers enjoyed by the police at common law. Exercise of powers of entry, search and seizure will in an appropriate case provide a good defence to actions for trespass whether to land, person, or goods, and to actions for conversion.

Detailed exposition of the powers provided for by the 1984 Act is beyond the scope of a work on torts.[2] Police powers include power to stop and search persons in public places for stolen or prohibited articles.[3] Powers of entry to effect an arrest for an arrestable offence are conferred by section 17 as is a surprisingly new power[4] to enter premises to save life or lives or prevent serious damage to property. Arrested persons may be personally searched for items with which they may injure themselves or others, or effect an escape, or which may constitute evidence relating to an offence.[5] But the extent of a body search in such circumstances is strictly limited[6] and detailed conditions are laid down for the conduct and authorisation of an intimate search.[7] Premises may be entered and searched where the occupier has been arrested for an arrestable offence for evidence concerning that or any related offence.[8] Any premises on which a person is arrested for any offence may be searched.[9] All these powers are additional to the power to seek a search warrant from magistrates.[10]

This list is by no means conclusive. Three major questions relating to the ambit of police powers of search and seizure as defences to intentional torts await an answer:

1 The protection for the citizen against unjust infringement of his liberty under the Act lies in the immensely detailed rules laid down in the Act for the execution of such powers, including rules as to making comprehensive records of searches undertaken. Will the courts enforce these rules to the letter holding any infringement however minor fatal to a defence based on the Act?

2 Will earlier case-law requiring that police explain the grounds for any

---

1 See *Mohammed-Holgate v Duke* (supra).
2 See *Clerk and Lindsell* ch 26; Robilliard and McEwan *Police Powers and the Individual* (1986).
3 Section 1.
4 No such power existed at common law. And see *Kynaston v DPP* (1987) Times, 4 November
5 Section 32.
6 See s 1(9), s 32(4), s 54(7).
7 Section 55.
8 Section 18.
9 Section 18.
10 Section 8.

search of a person as they would be required to explain an arrest still hold good?

3 And most importantly what is the exact scope of section 19 of the Act? For section 19 appears to provide that whenever police are lawfully on premises they may seize anything reasonably believed to be evidence of or the fruits of any crime, thus evading other provisions of the Act such as section 18 which limit police powers of entry to seizure of evidence relating to the crime for which the arrested person has been arrested or a related offence.

SECTION 12.   EXECUTION OF PROCESS

It may be a defence to false imprisonment, trespass or conversion, that the act was done in the execution of judicial process.

A sheriff or other officer of the court, acting on a warrant issued by a superior court of record, is protected although the judgment on which the warrant is issued is invalid.[11] So, a sheriff, who effects the dispossession of the tenant of rent-controlled premises and is then sued in trespass by the tenant, will have a defence if he produces the authority of the court to effect dispossession, although it may be that in the circumstances the tenant is lawfully entitled to possession.[12] Nor is he affected if the judgment is subsequently set aside.[13] But this does not mean that a sheriff is protected if the warrant itself is invalid; ie where the judgment is valid but there is no legal authority to issue the particular warrant.[14] Certainly, if the warrant is not signed and marked in the required manner[15] and probably, whenever the warrant does not bear on its face the accepted characteristics of a valid warrant, and possibly, whenever the warrant, as distinct from the judgment on which it is based, is void and not merely voidable, the sheriff has no protection.[16]

Where the process is not issued out of a superior court of record, the officer acting under it is protected if the subject matter of the suit is within the general jurisdiction of the court and the warrant is regularly issued, even though the judgment itself is not sustainable.[17] If the officer knows of an excess of jurisdiction,[18] or if the warrant is bad in form[19] then the officer who executes it has no defence.

If a private person irregularly obtains a warrant he is not protected in executing it.[20] If the warrant is void, then he has no defence.[1] If it is voidable the private individual is protected unless 'the process has been set aside by reason of some misconduct, or at least some irregularity, on the part of the person suing it out'[2]. 'The plaintiff is liable to an action for executing the

---

11 *Brown v Watson* (1871) 23 LT 745.
12 *Williams v Williams and Nathan* [1937] 2 All ER 559, CA.
13 *Ives v Lucas* (1823) 1 C & P 7.
14 *Andrews v Marris* (1841) 1 QB 3 at 17 (per DENMAN CJ).
15 *Hooper v Lane* (1847) 10 QB 546 at 560–1 (*obiter*).
16 See the judgments in the last two cases cited, and *Demer v Cook* (1903) 88 LT 629.
17 *Andrews v Marris* (1841) 1 QB 3.
18 *London Corporation v Cox* (1867) LR 2 HL 239 at 263 (per WILLES J *obiter*); *Watson v Bodell* (1845) 14 M & W 57 at 70 (per PARKE B, *ratio*).
19 *Carratt v Morley* (1841) 1 QB 18.
20 *Painter v Liverpool Oil Gas Light Co* (1836), 3 Ad & El 433; *Codrington v Lloyd* (1838) 8 Ad & El 449.
 1 *Brooks v Hodgkinson* (1859) 4 H & N 712.
 2 *Williams v Smith* (1863) 14 CBNS 596 at 624 (per WILLES J).

process of an inferior court in a matter beyond its jurisdiction, and cannot justify under such process, whether he be aware of the defect or not.'[3]

Of course, if the defendant, whether he be an official or private individual, does not act in accordance with the process, as by acting after it has expired,[4] seizing a person or goods not named in the writ, or, having properly seized goods, by disposing of them in an unauthorised way,[5] he is liable.

In general, these rules seem to strike a fair balance between the necessary protection of private rights and the proper security which bailiffs and policemen require in performing their duties.[6]

SECTION 13.   STATUTORY AUTHORITY

Public bodies and officials may only do acts which would be unlawful in others if they are authorised to do them by statute. Of course, as government has become increasingly regulatory and far-reaching in its effects, more and more such powers have been given. The question before the courts in tort cases of this type is whether the Act in question authorised the official to commit the tort complained of.[7]

Certain guiding principles have been worked out by the courts in order to answer this question. Either a *duty* or a *power* to do the act will afford a defence.[8] The defendant must prove that the tort would be an inevitable result of performing the act authorised: if, for instance, a local authority built an efficient electricity generating station, the fumes from which damaged crops of the plaintiff, they would only have a defence if they proved not merely that an efficient station had been built, but also that they had used all reasonable care[9] in the light of current technical and scientific skill to prevent the commission of a tort; however, they have an absolute defence, regardless of proving these precautions, if they can discharge the very heavy burden of proving that the Act authorised them to disregard these matters.[10]

In determining whether Parliament intended to deprive the plaintiff of a right to sue, the presence of some alternative special provision in the Act for compensating those injured by the statutory activity may be material, and sometimes even decisive. It is also important to look at the nature of the power. Powers to execute some particular work or carry on some particular undertaking, such as building a reservoir or a gasworks, 'are, in the absence of clear provision to the contrary in the Act, limited to the doing of the particular things authorised without infringement of the rights of others, except in so far as any such infringement may be a demonstrably necessary

---

3 *London Corporation v Cox* (1867) LR 2 HL 239 at 263 HL (per WILLES J) *obiter*.
4 *Watson v Bodell* (1845) 14 M & W 57.
5 *Jelks v Hayward* [1905] 2 KB 460. See *Neumann v Bakeaway Ltd* [1983] 2 All ER 935; *Observer v Gordon* [1983] 2 All ER 945, [1983] 1 WLR 1008; (protection afforded by common law and statute to sheriffs).
6 For the power of a policeman to search premises and seize property there, see now the Police and Criminal Evidence Act 1984 discussed above at pp 92–93.
7 *IRC v Rossminster Ltd* [1980] AC 952 [1980] 1 All ER 80 HL is a recent example of the difficult problems of statutory construction which may arise.
8 *Hammersmith and City Ry Co v Brand* (1869) LR 4 HL 171.
9 *Tate and Lyle Industries Ltd v Greater London Council* [1983] 2 AC 509, [1983] 1 All ER 1159.
10 *Manchester Corporation v Farnworth* [1930] AC 171, HL; *Geddis v Bann Reservoir Proprietors* (1878) 3 App Cas 430, HL.

consequence of doing what is authorised to be done'.[11] If, however, a public body is authorised to execute a variety of works at its discretion (many of which are likely to affect private rights) then the body will rarely be prevented from infringing those rights, for that would prevent it from doing the very task which it was set up to perform.[12]

SECTION 14.   JUDICIAL ACTS

A judge in a superior court of record is not liable to tort for any judicial act performed by him within his jurisdiction, even though he be malicious.[13] The Court of Appeal in *Sirros v Moore*[14] extended this rule by holding that such a judge is not liable for acts in excess of his jurisdiction if he acts in good faith.

LORD DENNING in *Sirros v Moore* sought to extend the immunity afforded to judges of superior courts in respect of acts done in excess of jurisdiction to their brethren in the lower courts, including magistrates. In *Re McC*[15] the House of Lords unanimously held that he was wrong and however anomalous it might seem judges of inferior courts of limited jurisdiction remain liable for acts done in good faith. Magistrates who sentenced a boy to a custodial sentence when they had no power so to do were liable to the boy for false imprisonment. Special provision is made regarding the liability of magistrates in the Justices of the Peace Act 1979. Other persons, for example, members of tribunals,[16] may share in the limited immunity of judges[17] of inferior courts and in their related immunity from proceedings for libel and slander.[18]

SECTION 15.   ACTS CONNECTED WITH PARLIAMENTARY PROCEEDINGS

It is a defence that the act complained of took place in the course of parliamentary business and as part thereof[19] for each House of Parliament has a parliamentary privilege to regulate its own concerns.[20] Whether this extends

---

11 *Marriage v East Norfolk Rivers Catchment Board* [1950] 1 KB 284 at 307 (per JENKINS LJ); [1949] 2 All ER 1021, CA; cf *Metropolitan Asylum District v Hill* (1881) 6 App Cas 193, HL.

12 Ibid at 307–8. The cases on this defence of statutory authority are very numerous but since they turn on the interpretation of the particular statutes and merely illustrate the general principle set out in the text, it seems unprofitable to discuss them here.

13 *Fray v Blackburn* (1863) 3 B & S 576; *Anderson v Gorrie* [1895] 1 QB 668, CA.

14 [1975] QB 118, [1974] 3 All ER 776, CA.

15 [1985] AC 528, [1984] 3 WLR 1227.

16 See M Brazier 'Judicial Immunity and the Independence of the Judiciary' [1976] PL.

17 Some judicial or quasi judicial function must be conferred on the individual by statute. Simply because a professional duty includes acting fairly will not confer any immunity from suit *Sutcliffe v Thackrah* [1974] AC 727, [1974] 1 All ER 859, HL (no immunity for architect certifying amount of building work done). *Arenson v Casson, Beckman, Rutley & Co* [1977] AC 405, [1975] 3 All ER 901 (defence possibly available to arbitrators but not valuers).

18 *Ackerley v Parkinson* (1815) 3 M & S 411; *Everett v Griffiths* [1921] 1 AC 631 and see post at pp 408–9.

19 *Report of Select Committee on Official Secrets Acts* HG 101 of 1939.

20 *Bradlaugh v Gossett* (1884) 12 QBD 271; *R v Graham-Campbell, Ex parte Herbert* [1935] 1 KB 594.

to an assault committed within the Chamber on the Speaker was expressly left open in *Eliot's Case*.[1]

SECTION 16.   EXECUTIVE ACTS

In general, it is no defence that the act complained of is an act of the Executive.[2] To this there are two exceptions.

A. ACT OF STATE

Neither the official responsible nor the Crown can be sued for injuries tortiously inflicted outside the territorial jurisdiction of the Crown upon aliens by authority or subsequent ratification of the Crown.[3] If the act is committed in British territory, the defence is available only where the plaintiff is an enemy alien,[4] or, possibly, a friendly alien resident in British territory who has broken his duty of temporary local allegiance to the Crown.[5]

B. PREROGATIVE

The Crown still retains a few prerogative powers to interfere with the rights of the citizen. If it takes property under prerogative powers it ordinarily has to pay compensation.[6] If, however, the power is exercised during or in contemplation of war there is no entitlement to compensation in respect of damage to or destruction of property.[7]

SECTION 17.   AN ACT WHICH IS ALSO A CRIME

A. ASSAULT AND BATTERY

The ordinary principle of *res judicata* applies to suits in tort, with the result that it is a defence to subsequent proceedings that the same issue has previously been litigated between the same parties. It is, however, no defence

1 (1629) 3 State Tr 293.
2 *Leach v Money* (1765) 19 State Tr 1001.
3 *Buron v Denman* (1848) 2 Exch 167; *Walker v Baird* [1892] AC 491. In *A-G v Nisson* [1970] AC 179, [1969] 1 All ER 629, the House of Lords left undecided whether in any circumstances Act of State could ever be pleaded against British subjects in respect of acts outside the realm.
4 *R v Bottrill, Ex parte Kuechenmeister* [1947] KB 41 at 57 (per ASQUITH LJ), CA; *Netz v Chuter Ede* [1946] Ch 224, [1946] 1 All ER 628.
5 *Johnstone v Pedlar* [1921] 2 AC 262, HL. It may be, however, that the Crown must indicate that it has withdrawn its protection of the alien before the defence becomes available (per LORD ATKINSON at 285).
6 *A-G v Nissan*, supra.
7 Section 1(1) War Damage Act 1965 reversing *Burmah Oil Co Ltd v Lord Advocate* [1965] AC 75, [1964] 2 All ER 348, HL.

that the act is also a crime for which the defendant has been convicted or acquitted.[8] To this rule section 45 of the Offences against the Person Act 1861 furnishes an exception. If the defendant has been charged with common assault, or with aggravated assault on a female or a male child by or on behalf of the party aggrieved, and the justices convict him and he serves his imprisonment or pays his fine, or the justices make out a certificate that they have dismissed the complaint on the ground that the assault was not proved, or was justified, or was too trivial to merit punishment, 'he shall be released from all further or other proceedings, civil or criminal, from the same cause'. A man who suffered business loss consequent upon an assault which had been dealt with by the justices,[9] and a husband whose wife was the victim of such an assault, have been held to be barred by the Act,[10] but the master of the convicted person remains vicariously liable.[11]

SECTION 18.   PLAINTIFF A WRONGDOER

If the plaintiff's success in tort depends on his establishing a contract and that contract is tainted by illegality, his action in tort will fail: *ex turpi causa oritur non actio*. So in *Taylor v Chester*[12] the plaintiff deposited with the defendant half of a £50 note as a pledge to secure the defendant's charges for the use by the plaintiff of her brothel for an orgy, and could not sue in detinue for its return because he could deny the validity of the pledge only by showing its immoral purposes. Take also the High Court of Australia decision in *Thomas Brown & Sons v Fazal Deen:*[13]

> P had deposited gold with D in breach of exchange control laws. When P sought to recover the gold from D it transpired that D had parted with the gold so long ago that a cause of action based on his conversion was time-barred. He therefore sued in detinue, and failed because he then had to found his action on the illegal contract of bailment.

If on the other hand, although the goods came into the possession of the defendant under an illegal contract between the parties, the plaintiff does not have to rely on that contract, he may sue in conversion.[14]

Where the facts fall outside these rules but the harm complained of arises out of and in the course of carrying out an unlawful act, the courts have a discretion whether to bar the claim on the ground that the plaintiff is a

---

8 But see *McIlKenny v Chief Constable of the West Midlands* [1980] QB 283, [1980] 2 All ER 227.

9 *Solomon v Frinigan* (1866) 30 JP Jo 756.

10 *Masper v Brown* (1876) 1 CPD 97.

11 *Dyer v Munday* [1895] 1 QB 742.

12 (1869) LR 4 QB 309.

13 (1962) 108 CLR 391.

14 *Bowmakers Ltd v Barnet Instruments Ltd* [1945] KB 65, [1944] 2 All ER 579, CA. The case was followed in *Singh v Ali* [1960] AC 167, [1960] 1 All ER 269, PC, and in *Belvoir Finance Co Ltd v Stapleton* [1971] 1 QB 210, [1970] 3 All ER 664, CA. Similarly where a landlord had made an illegal lease the Judicial Committee of the Privy Council held that he could sue the tenant for recovery of the land because his title depended on a valid registration, not on the illegal agreement, *Mistry Amar Singh v Kulubya* [1964] AC 142, [1963] 3 All ER 499.

wrongdoer; they say that it is a matter of public policy[15] but do not ordinarily define the factors which govern their decision. In *Meah v McCreamer (No 2)*[16] a rapist was ordered to pay substantial damages in battery to his victims. His attempt to recover that sum from insurers of the motorist responsible for the brain damage which resulted in the change of personality, which triggered his violent behaviour, failed. WOOLF J held that as a matter of policy criminals should not be indemnified against their own criminal acts. In 1868 it was held that a woman who contracts venereal disease as a result of extra-marital intercourse cannot sue in trespass, even if the defendant had misrepresented his condition.[17] Similarly, if the defendant has induced the plaintiff to be his mistress by representing that he is entitled to a decree for nullity and will marry her when he obtains it, her being a party to the immoral association prevents her suing in deceit.[18] The defence has been held not to be available to an employer sued by his workman for breach of statutory duty where the workman was guilty of abetting the offence by having misplaced the guard to certain machinery, because to hold otherwise would run counter to the purpose of the legislation.[19] During a quarrel a 64-year-old man attempts to strike another 40 years younger and the latter then grievously assaults him. The old man will not be defeated by *ex turpi causa*—each case must be looked at on its own facts to decide whether the plaintiff is incriminated in an illegal venture.[20] When one of three drunken burglars was injured through the careless driving of one of them, as they were making their getaway in a car owned by one of them, no duty of care was owed on grounds of public policy.[1] It would appear that one factor which influences the courts is whether the tortious act is committed not merely after the unlawful enterprise has been agreed on but during the period of its execution.[2]

SECTION 19.   SELF-HELP REMEDIES

In addition to the defences so far discussed the law sanctions a number of

---

15 *Hardy v Motor Insurers' Bureau* [1964] 2 QB 745, [1964] 2 All ER 742, CA; *Burns v Edman* [1970] 2 QB 541, [1970] 1 All ER 886, wife's loss of support from death of her burglar and robber husband cannot sustain a claim under the Fatal Accidents Act where the moneys he received were only from the proceeds of his crime. The decision in respect of the wife can be justified because she knew he was a burglar but it is difficult to justify the rejection of the infant dependants' claims in *ex turpi causa*; *Ashmore, Benson, Pease & Co Ltd v A V Dawson* [1973] 2 All ER 856, CA, (P's employees knew their load on D's lorry to be excessive and illegal; P barred in negligence action for D's overturning lorry and damaging load). In *Shelley v Paddock* [1980] QB 348, [1980] 1 All ER 1009, CA; the plaintiff's breach of exchange control regulations in buying a house abroad did not prevent her from suing in deceit for a fraudulent representation about the house. And see *Thackwell v Barclays Bank plc* [1986] 1 All ER 676; *Saunders v Edwards* [1987] 2 All ER 651, [1987] 1 WLR 1116.
16 [1986] 1 All ER 943; and see *Gray v Barr* [1971] 2 QB 554, [1971] 2 All ER 949.
17 *Hegarty v Shine* (1878) 14 Cox CC 145.
18 *Siveyer v Allison* [1935] 2 KB 403.
19 *Cakebread v Hopping Brothers (Whitestone) Ltd* [1947] KB 641 at 654 (per COHEN LJ, *ratio decidendi*), [1947] 1 All ER 389, CA, approved in *National Coal Board v England* [1954] AC 403 at 419, [1954] 1 All ER 546 at 552, HL (per LORD PORTER).
20 *Lane v Holloway* [1968] 1 QB 379, [1967] 3 All ER 129, CA, distinguished in *Murphy v Culhane* [1977] QB 94, [1976] 3 All ER 533, CA, deceased's involvement in a criminal affray in which he was killed could be *ex turpi causa* when his wife and daughter sued under the Fatal Accidents Act.
1 *Ashton v Turner* [1981] QB 137, [1980] 3 All ER 870.
2 *National Coal Board v England* supra at 428–9 (per LORD ASQUITH).

'self-help' remedies enabling a person against whom some prior tort has been committed to take action to remedy the damage done which would otherwise itself be tortuous. These include retaking chattels wrongly withheld from the plaintiff,[3] abatement of nuisance,[4] distress damage feasant[5] and replevin.[6] They are fully dealt with in the seventh edition of this work[7] and will not be discussed further here. In general self-help remedies are now looked on by the courts with disfavour and are strictly construed.[8]

3 This defence known as recaption of chattels can therefore be used where a trespass to or conversion of the plaintiff's goods has taken place. See *Blades v Higgs* (1861) 10 CBNS 713, (1865) 11 HL Cas 621; *Patrick v Colerick* (1838) 3 M & W 483; *Anthony v Haney* (1832) 8 Bing 186.

4 Eg chopping off branches of overhanging trees; see *Lemmon v Webb* [1895] AC 1.

5 Seizing a chattel unlawfully on your land as 'security' until compensation is paid (eg until the bus company pays for the damage done to your rosebed by a bus which has veered off the road and into your garden). Distress damage feasant may no longer be utilised to seize animals: s 7(1) Animals Act 1971. For a fuller account of legitimate self-redress see *Clerk and Lindsell* paras 21–128 et seq.

6 An action to reclaim goods taken under some wrongful judicial process; see *Clerk and Lindsell* paras 21–128 et seq.

7 At pp 75–78.

8 See *Lagan Navigation Co v Lambeg Bleaching Dyeing and Finishing Co* [1927] AC 226 at 244 (abatement of nuisance) is 'a remedy which the law does not favour'.

Part III

Intentional interference with economic interests

CONTENTS

Chapter 7

Interference with economic interests

SECTION I. 'RIGHTS' AND ECONOMIC INTERESTS

The law of torts affords every member of society comprehensive protection from deliberately inflicted harm to his person, his goods and his land by means of the torts discussed in the previous Part. Protection of legitimate interests in a person's livelihood, in his business and trading interests, is significantly less comprehensive. Should my, and my family's economic prosperity, be diminished because I have been physically attacked and can no longer work, my attacker must compensate us for our loss of income. Where the defendant claims some justification or authority for what he did to me, the onus lies on him to establish lawful grounds for interfering with my right to bodily security. If one workman take the tools of the trade of another he does so at his peril. A misguided belief that the tools were his own will not avail him. Yet if a businessman motivated by pure spite against another mounts a campaign to destroy the other's business, to seduce away from him his customers, to dissuade other traders from dealing with him, the injured party may have no remedy in tort for the loss of his livelihood.

In *Keeble v Hickeringill*[1] HOLT CJ, in 1706, enunciated a wide principle of liability for intentional harm to economic and trading interests. He held that 'he who hinders another in his trade or livelihood is liable to an action for so hindering him'. But that principle never took root in English law. In *Allen v Flood*[2] in 1896, the House of Lords, by a majority, stifled the growth of any general principle of liability in tort for intentional and malicious interference with economic and business interests. Flood and Taylor were shipwrights taken on for the day by the Glengall Iron Company to work on the woodwork of a ship. During the day other employees of the company, who were boilermakers working on the ironwork of the ship, discovered that the respondents had previously been employed by another firm working on ironwork. The boilermakers belonged to a union which objected strongly to shipwrights being employed to do ironwork. Allen, an official of the union, sought an interview with an officer of the Glengall Iron Company and told him that unless the respondents were dismissed all the boilermakers would 'knock off work'. Flood and Taylor were told at the end of the day that their services would be no longer required. They brought an action against Allen for maliciously inducing the company not to employ them on subsequent occasions, for intentionally interfering with their livelihood.

The case for the respondents depended largely on their establishing a positive right to protection of their economic interests. Expressing the minority opinion, who held that such a right did exist, HAWKINS J described it thus:[3]

1 (1706) 11 East 574n.
2 [1898] AC 1, HL.
3 At 14.

... the legal right which each of the plaintiffs, in common with every man in this country, has to pursue freely and without hindrance, interruption or molestation that profession, trade or calling which he has adopted for his livelihood.

The majority in *Allen v Flood* refused to recognise such a right, akin to rights to bodily security, property or reputation. All the law recognises is a person's freedom to pursue his livelihood or business. Allen in seeking to persuade the company not to re-engage the respondents was equally exercising his freedom to arrange affairs, as he saw it, in the interests of the members of his union. The House of Lords, having found nothing intentionally unlawful in what Allen did, further rejected the contention that his motive, to 'punish' the respondents for their earlier breach of the boilermakers' desired 'monopoly' of ironwork, transformed an otherwise lawful act into an unlawful act actionable in tort.

The absence of any right to protection of economic interests in English law has several consequences. First and obviously, it restricts the scope of the law of torts in guarding plaintiffs against unfair practices by others. An English plaintiff in the equivalent circumstances of the American plaintiff in *Tuttle v Buck*[4] would be left remediless. The defendant, a rich banker, set up a rival barber's shop with the sole intention of driving the plaintiff out of business by undercutting his prices. In Minnesota the plaintiff recovered for his losses.[5]

Secondly, development of the economic torts became haphazard.[6] The prior existence of specific torts of inducing breach of contract and conspiracy was confirmed in *Allen v Flood*. The next eighty years or so saw the extension of that first tort to interference with subsisting contracts and the development of the tort of intimidation and other innominate torts of unlawful interference. Now LORD DIPLOCK has suggested that there is a common principle linking the economic torts. There is a 'genus' tort of *unlawful* interference with the trade or business of another of which the traditional economic torts are 'species'.[7]

Thirdly, the restricted development of liability for deliberately inflicted harm to economic interests has necessarily had an effect on the development of negligence in relation to damage to economic interests. Can a rational system of law refuse a remedy to a businessman who suffers financial losses because of the deliberate and spiteful conduct of a rival, and grant a remedy where identical losses result from some third party's negligence? Consider this illustration. A firm of cattle auctioneers lose business because a rival firm undercut their fees and offer inducements to farmers to send cattle only to them. The firm's loss is irrecoverable. But what if that same firm suffer an identical loss of business because a neighbouring research institute *negligently* allows foot and mouth disease to spread to local cattle, and government

---

4   107 Min 145 (1909).
5   On the development of rights in economic interests in the USA generally, see J D Heydon *Economic Torts* (2nd edn).
6   See LORD WEDDERBURN's comment that the economic torts have been at best 'a ramshackle construction for decades' (1984) 46 MLR 224 at 229. And see P Elias and R Ewing 'Economic Torts and Labour Law: Old Principles and New Liabilities' [1982] CLJ 321.
7   *Merkur Island Shipping Corpn v Laughton* [1983] 2 AC 570. For an analysis of the implication of such a 'genus' tort and consideration of the role of tort in this area see H Carty 'Intentional Violation of Economic Interests: The Limits of Common Law Liability' (1988) 104 LQR. (forth coming)

restrictions on the movement of cattle stop all cattle auctions for a period of months?[8] We shall suggest a little later that it is not in fact inconsistent to make the latter liable for his negligence while the former remains free of legal responsibility for his deliberate actions.

SECTION 2. FREE COMPETITION; UNFAIR COMPETITION[9]

What must next be considered is *why* the English courts rejected a general rule of economic interests. The clearest explanation is to be found in a *dictum* of ATKIN LJ in *Ware and de Freville Ltd v Motor Trade Association*[10]

> The truth is that the right of the individual to carry on his trade or profession or execute his own activities, whatever they may be, without interruption, so long as he refrains from tort or crime, afford an unsatisfactory basis for determining what is actionable, in as much as the right is conditioned by precisely similar right in the rest of his fellow men. Such co-existing rights do in a world of competition necessarily impinge upon one another ... The true question is, was the power of the plaintiff to carry on his trade etc, interrupted by an act which the law deems wrongful.

English law embraced a fundamental doctrine of free competition, which was manifestly inconsistent with any assumption that the interest in pursuing a livelihood or a trade was entitled to absolute legal protection. Acts of competitors, or others, damaging a person in his business were to be tortious only if the act causing the damage was in itself 'unlawful'. That of course is a rather circular statement. For it begs the question of what constitutes an 'unlawful' act in the context of damaging another's trade or business.

'Unlawful' acts resulting in liability for violation of economic interests may be divided into three categories. The first, which is relatively uncontroversial, comprises those specific torts concerned with false representations. Free competition does not validate the use of lies and fraud to do down your competitors. Thus the tort of deceit imposes liability for false representations in reliance on which the plaintiff suffers damage. Passing off prevents one trader falsely cashing in on the reputation of another by seeking to mislead customers by representing his goods as another's or by some other 'fraudulent' trade practice. And injurious falsehood 'punishes' the trader who falsely disparages his competitors. All these torts are in a very real sense 'unfair competition' torts, and are fully discussed in the next chapter.

Secondly, there are the classic economic torts of inducing breach of contract, conspiracy, intimidation and so on. These are the torts which LORD DIPLOCK has now suggested belong to one 'genus' of unlawful acts interfering with trade or business. These torts although equally capable of being utilised as 'unfair competition' torts have suffered over the past eighty years from their embroilment in the controversy over trade union rights. They have come to be seen, and often to be taught, as almost exclusively labour law torts of little interest to the tort student as such. Thirdly and finally, there is a growing group of torts concerned with the protection of intellectual property. Many

---

8 See *Weller & Co v Foot and Mouth Disease Research Institute* [1966] 1 QB 569 discussed post at p 190.
9 See R Whish *Competition Law* (1985) chs 1 and 2.
10 [1921] 3 KB 40 at 79, CA. For the origins of the doctrine of free competition within the common law, see the *Case of Gloucester Grammar School* (1410) YB 11 Hen 4 fo 47 pl 21.

are largely statutory, for example, actions for breach of copyright and infringement of patents, but at present the action for breach of confidence remains subject to development by the common law alone.

The categories of torts concerned with economic interests will be dealt with in the order outlined above. No attempt will be made to outline or consider in any detail the immunities of trade unions in respect of torts in the second category. The emphasis will be placed on this broad function of the torts (or tort) in the context of fair competition, and the civil rights of employers and workers. Detailed examination of statutory provision for breach of copyright or infringements of patents is beyond the scope of this work. The chapter on the third category of intellectual property torts will thus be short and intended simply to complete the picture of liability in respect of interference with economic interests. What has to be assessed overall is to what extent the law of torts now imposes liability for unfair competitive practices.

SECTION 3. ECONOMIC LOSS AND NEGLIGENCE

An attempt must now be made to answer the question posed earlier of whether the common law can rationally impose liability for negligent violation of economic interests while intentional violations remain non-actionable. Two primary issues need to be considered. Do the reasons for not imposing liability in respect of intentional violations apply with equal force to negligence? If it is now correct to explain the basic principle of liability for intentional interference with economic interests in terms of a 'genus' tort of liability for any unlawful act violating economic interests, can negligence be regarded as a further 'species' of unlawful act? The rationale for regarding the 'right' to pursue a trade or livelihood as a freedom, a power, to carry on that trade or livelihood, as opposed to a right accorded the same status as the right to bodily security, derives from the judicial perception of the demands of free competition. Just as I am free to set up in business as a greengrocer, to choose to whom I will sell and from whom I will buy my produce, so is my neighbour free to do the same. And to promote his business he may adopt any lawful strategy. To put it crudely if that drives me out of business, tough. I have proved to be insufficiently hardy and skilled at the trade. The market economy encourages success and depends on the 'best' man winning. But if my business suffers because of another's negligence, for example, a negligent contractor fractures a gas main and the road leading to my shop is blocked off for several days while repairs are carried out, there is no harm done to the doctrine of free competition in penalising the negligent actor. Indeed rather the opposite, a competitive economy requires that each enterprise should maximise its skill and so enhance its own profitability and offer the optimum service. The careless or unskilled should be penalised.

So, the second question becomes that if there is no reason derived from the principle of free and fair competition that negligent interference with economic interests should not be actionable, can negligence properly be regarded as a 'species' of unlawful act resulting in liability for invasion of economic interests? Carelessness as such can no more constitute a tort in relation to economic interests than malice or spite on their own. A negligently caused explosion in South Manchester which because of the vagaries of the city's ancient sewage system results in part of the city centre being blocked to traffic for several hours will not and should not result in liability for all the consequent business losses. But where the relationship of the plaintiff and the defendant is sufficiently close to induce or require the plaintiff to rely and depend on the care and skill of the defendant to safeguard his economic interests then a failure to do so, a breach of duty, can properly be regarded as an unlawful act creating liability for the ensuing loss subject to two *caveats*.

The first concerns the respective roles of contract and tort.[11] Any business-man relying on another to provide goods or services is free to contract for those goods or services. If they fail to meet contract standards the supplier will be liable in breach of contract. If there is no contract it is argued the law of torts should not rush in and impose liability.[12] Nor, similarly it is argued, should tort liability be imposed where the plaintiff relies on a contract to which he is not a party. That it is said would breach the rules on privity of contract. Hence in many instances where it is alleged that negligent conduct causing economic loss is tortious no tort can be committed because any relevant duty can arise in contract alone. The second *caveat* relates to the implications of liability for negligently inflicted economic loss. Where would the limits of liability be drawn to avoid the spectre of liability 'in an inde-terminable amount for an indefinite time to an indeterminate class'.[13] Both illustrated the very real problems of defining the scope of any duty to avoid negligently inflicted economic loss. Neither problem constitutes an unanswerable case that such loss should never be recoverable in tort.

SECTION 4. ECONOMIC TORTS AND ECONOMIC REGULATION

The discussion so far in this chapter has ignored two important elements in the debate on the role of the economic torts. The doctrine of free competition may be called into doubt. And even those who accept the basic premise of a competitive economy may come to wonder how much of the original doctrine had survived recent developments. Increasingly Parliament has legislated to regulate the economy, to eliminate unfair practices. And the judiciary has responded[14] taking account of the emphasis now placed on free competition being fair competition. These developments must be noted as we examine the scope of the economic torts in 1988.

---

11 See further post at p 171.
12 See P Cane 'Contract, Tort and Economic Loss' in *The Law of Tort* ed by M Furmston (1986).
13 *Ultramares Corpn v Touché* 255 NY 170 (1931).
14 See, for example, '... increasing recognition by Parliament of the need for more rigorous standards of commercial honesty is a factor which should not be overlooked by a judge confronted by the choice whether or not to extend by analogy to circumstances in which it has not previously been applied a principle which has been applied in previous cases whether the circumstances although different had some features in common with those of the case which he has to decide' per LORD DIPLOCK in *Erven Warninck BV v J Townend & Sons (Hull) Ltd* [1979] 2 All ER 927 at 933.

Chapter 8

False representations

SECTION 1. DECEIT

The use of deliberately false representations on which the plaintiff is induced to, and does, rely to his detriment has for nearly two hundred years been actionable by means of the tort of deceit.[1] Judicial recognition that fraud never constituted fair competition has a much longer history[2] but whether earlier authorities are founded in contract, equity or tort is a matter for the legal historian. What is still of crucial importance to the law student is that the law relating to misrepresentations cannot be fully understood by considering tort alone. A misrepresentation may concurrently create rights of action in tort and for breach of contract. A misrepresentation not actionable in tort may give rise to a right to rescind a contract and misrepresentations unconcerned with contract may create an estoppel. The interrelation of common law and equity in respect of remedies for misrepresentation further complicate the picture.[3]

The development of the separate tort of deceit, with which we are concerned in this chapter, dates from the judgment in *Pasley v Freeman*.[4]

The defendant falsely misrepresented to the plaintiff that X was a person to whom the plaintiff might safely sell goods on credit. The plaintiff suffered loss through relying on this representaton and was held to have an action on the case for deceit.

The tort may be defined as:

a false representation made by the defendant knowingly, or without belief in its truth or recklessly, careless whether it be true or false, with the intention that the plaintiff should act in reliance upon the representation, which causes damage to the plaintiff in consequence of his reliance upon it.

A. FALSE REPRESENTATION

Usually the representation will consist of written or spoken words, but it may be assumed that any conduct calculated to mislead will be sufficient[5]—for example, to turn back the mileage indicator on the odometer of a motor car when negotiating its sale. 'Where the defendant has manifestly approved and adopted a representation made by some third person' he may himself commit

1 *Pasley v Freeman* (1789) 3 Term Rep 51.
2 From 1201 there has been a writ of deceit.
3 See Cheshire, Fifoot and Furmston's *Law of Contract* (11th edn) pp 255–296.
4 (1789) 3 Term Rep 51.
5 Cf *R v Barnard* (1837), 7 C & P 784.

the tort.[6] Where a statement is capable of bearing at once a true and a false interpretation and the defendant knows of the falsity there is a false representation for the present purpose.[7]

Active concealment of the truth whereby the plaintiff is prevented from getting information which he otherwise would have got is sufficient misrepresentation although no positive misstatement is made.[8] Although mere non-disclosure is not enough, a statement which is misleading because it is incomplete may be actionable. Thus LORD CAIRNS held in the House of Lords case of *Peek v Gurney*[9] that 'there must ... be some active misstatement of fact, or, at all events, such a partial and fragmentary statement of fact, as that the withholding of that which is not stated makes that which is stated absolutely false'.

Where a statement by the defendant was accurate when made, but owing to a change of circumstances of which the defendant has become aware, it ceases to be true, there is an actionable misrepresentation if the defendant, by remaining silent, induces the plaintiff to act on the basis of the original statement, as *Incledon v Watson* illustrates:[10]

> In an advertisement for the sale of his school the defendant stated the number of scholars at that time. That statement was not proved to be inaccurate. During the course of negotiations, the number decreased. The plaintiff, who bought on the faith of the representation, and who was not informed of the reduction, was held to have an action in deceit for damages.

This case illustrates the rule that what counts is whether the statement is false at the time when the plaintiff acts upon it.[11] There is some,[12] though inconclusive, support for the view that an action lies if the defendant, though believing the statement to be true when he made it, later learns of its falsity but does not disclose this to the plaintiff who subsequently relies on that statement. There are contracts in which, because one party alone can know the material facts, eg contracts of insurance, that party has a legal duty to disclose material information; upon breach of this duty the contract is voidable: whether that failure to disclose amounts to the tort of deceit is undecided.

B. KNOWLEDGE OF FALSITY

Derry v Peek[13] establishes that, in order to make the defendant liable, he must have made the statement 'knowingly, or without belief in its truth, or recklessly, careless whether it be true or false'. In short, the plaintiff must

---

6 Per LORD MAUGHAM in *Bradford Third Equitable Benefit Building Society v Borders* [1941] 2 All ER 205, at 211, HL.
7 Per LORD BLACKBURN in *Smith v Chadwick* (1884) 9 App Cas 187, at 201, HL. If the court construes documents as false, but is not satisfied that the defendant intended to give them that false meaning, he is not liable in deceit: *Gross v Lewis Hillman Ltd* [1970] Ch 445, [1969] 3 All ER 1476, CA.
8 Cf *Schneider v Heath* (1813) 3 Camp 506 (buyer of ship obtained rescission of a contract induced by seller's taking ship from slipway into water, thereby concealing its rotten timbers).
9 (1873) LR 6 HL 377, at 403.
10 (1862) 2 F & F 841. *Jones v Dumbrell* [1981] VR 199.
11 Cf *Briess v Woolley* [1954] AC 333, [1954] 1 All ER 909, HL.
12 Per LORD BLACKBURN (*obiter*) in *Brownlie v Campbell* (1880) 5 App Cas 925 at 950, HL.
13 (1889) 14 App Cas 337 at 374 (per LORD HERSCHELL), HL.

prove[14] that the defendant did not honestly believe it to be true; it is not deceit merely because he has no reasonable grounds for believing it. The facts of the case show how onerous this burden may be:

> A company was empowered by private Act to run trams by animal power, or, if the consent of the Board of Trade was obtained, by steam power. The directors, believing that the Board of Trade would give this consent as a matter of course, since the Board of Trade had raised no objection when the plans were laid before them, issued a prospectus saying that the company had the power to run trams by steam power. Relying on this prospectus, the respondent took up shares from the company. The Board of Trade eventually refused their consent, and later the company was wound up.

The House of Lords held that an action of deceit against the directors failed because no want of honest belief on the part of any director was established by the respondent.[15] However negligent a defendant may be, that is not ordinarily sufficient to make him liable for the tort of deceit.

C. INTENTION TO DECEIVE

The plaintiff must prove that the statement was 'made with the intention that it should be acted upon by the plaintiff, or by a class of persons which will include the plaintiff'.[16] Thus, an action in deceit may be based on an advertisement in a newspaper if the plaintiff shows that he was one of the class of persons at whom the advertisement was directed.[17] LORD CAIRNS in *Peek v Gurney*[18] might be taken as saying that the plaintiff must prove that the defendant 'intended' in the sense that he 'desired' or 'had the purpose' that the plaintiff should act on the statement. 'Intention' is, however, best interpreted in the way in which it is normally interpreted in torts: ie, if the misrepresentation is calculated, or if its natural and necessary consequence is, to induce the plaintiff, then the defendant's conduct is 'intentional'.[19]

A misrepresentation need not be communicated to the plaintiff by the defendant, provided that the defendant intended that it be communicated to him and that he rely thereon. In *Pilmore v Hood*:[20]

> A, who was negotiating the sale of a public house to B, made certain false statements to B concerning the takings of the public house. The transaction fell through: to A's knowledge B passed on to C these false statements. A

---

14 Although the plaintiff need not shoulder a criminal standard of proof, his burden of proving fraud is stricter than that of the ordinary civil standard: *Hornal v Neuberger Products Ltd*, [1957] 1 QB 247, [1956] 3 All ER 970, CA.

15 But see now the Companies Act 1985, ss 67–69 (statutory liability for false prospectuses).

16 Per LORD MAUGHAM in *Bradford Third Equitable Benefit Building Society v Borders* [1941] 2 All ER 205, at 211, HL.

17 *Richardson v Silvester* (1873) LR 9 QB 34 (plaintiff misled by false advertisement in Press that a farm was for sale).

18 (1873) LR 6 HL 377.

19 *Polhill v Walter* (1832) 3 B & Ad 114; *Richardson v Silvester*, supra, and *dicta* of LORD CHELMSFORD (at 399) and of LORD COLONSAY (at 401) in *Peek v Gurney*, supra, lend support to this view.

20 (1838) 5 Bing NC 97, and see *Langridge v Levy* (1837) 2 M & W 519.

then sold to C without correcting these statements and was held liable to him in deceit.

The plaintiff must also have been influenced in the manner intended. If, therefore, company promoters issued a prospectus to the plaintiff, who bought shares, not by subscribing to this issue, but subsequently on the market, and the prospectus was not calculated to influence market dealings, no action would lie.[1] The motive of the defendant is irrelevant; it is no excuse that the defendant who made a false statement about shares of some company genuinely believed that investment in that company would be advantageous to the plaintiff,[2] and still less that the defendant did not intend the plaintiff to suffer any loss in consequence of the misrepresentation.[3]

D. RELIANCE OF THE PLAINTIFF

The plaintiff must prove that the misrepresentation of the defendant did cause him to act to his own prejudice as he did.[4] The action lies if the misrepresentation was only one of several factors acting upon the mind of the plaintiff; if the court is satisfied that the false statement was 'actively present to his mind' when he acted, it will not readily hold that the plaintiff might, even if the false statement had not been made, nevertheless have acted as he did.[5] The courts sometimes say that the misrepresentation must be material; they mean that if the plaintiff acted in a way that a person was likely to act in reliance on the statement of the defendant, this would be *prima facie* evidence that he did so rely on it.[6]

It is sometimes doubted whether a misrepresentation of an opinion is actionable. Of course, there is an area of privilege to lie without liability in deceit: for example, the seller who puffs his house as highly desirable and commodious—such sales talk does not constitute actionable misrepresentation. Further, if both parties have equal access to information about goods, and one falsely describes them as first class, no action lies. When, however, the opinion purports to impart information to another who is not on an equal footing; for example, if a dealer states to a customer that a new machine of the type sold by him can lift 5,000 lbs, or if an opinion purports to be expert and accordingly derived from a background of knowledge not possessed by the plaintiff, an action will lie for such misrepresentations.[7]

The same general principles govern statements of law.[8] If the rep-

---

1 *Peek v Gurney*, supra, had similar facts; cf *Andrews v Mockford* [1896] 1 QB 372, CA. The Stock Exchange now makes a public advertisement of an issue a condition precedent to the grant of a market quotation, and intention to induce marketing dealings will presumably now be imputed.
2 LORD BLACKBURN in *Smith v Chadwick* (1884) 9 App Cas 187 at 201, HL.
3 *Brown, Jenkinson & Co Ltd v Percy Dalton (London) Ltd* [1957] 2 QB 621, [1957] 2 All ER 844, CA.
4 *Smith v Chadwick* (1884) 9 App Cas 187, HL; *Macleay v Tait* [1906] AC 24, HL. There must be some conduct of the plaintiff in reliance on the representation. Harmful effects produced directly on the plaintiff (eg if the false statement causes him to be ill) are not the subject of a claim for this tort even though the plaintiff does recover in the same action for loss suffered through acts performed in reliance: *Wilkinson v Downton* [1897] 2 QB 57, p 26, ante.
5 *Edgington v Fitzmaurice* (1885), 29 ChD 459, CA.
6 *Arnison v Smith* (1889) 41 ChD 348 at 369 (per LORD HALSBURY, LC).
7 Cf *Brown v Raphael* [1958] Ch 636, [1958] 2 All ER 79, CA.
8 *West London Commercial Bank v Kitson* (1884) 13 QBD 360, CA.

resentations refer to legal principles as distinct from the facts on which these principles operate, and the parties are on equal footing, those representations are only expressions of belief and of the same effect as expressions of opinion between parties on an equal footing. In other cases where the defendant professes legal information beyond that of the plaintiff the ordinary rules of liability for deceit apply.

It is equally confusing to state that a misrepresentation of intention is never actionable deceit. Certainly, if a defendant promises to do something and fails to carry out his promise the plaintiff must ordinarily look to the law of contract for his remedy. If, however, the defendant at the time of his statement lacks either the will or the power to carry out the promise, there is a misrepresentation capable of giving rise to proceedings for deceit; the diner who orders and consumes his meal without intending to pay for it is liable in deceit. Similarly, it has been held to be actionable to state, in an invitation to the public to subscribe to an issue of debentures by a company, that the loan was being floated in order to improve buildings, when the real purpose was to discharge existing liabilities.[9]

Contributory negligence has been held to be no defence in an action for deceit. A plaintiff who relied on the statement made by the defendant about the turnover of a public house which was to be sold was successful in an action in deceit although, had he availed himself of the opportunity afforded to him by the defendant of examining the accounts, he would have discovered the error.[10] On the other hand, a plaintiff who is aware of the falsity,[11] and, perhaps, one who is misled by any patent defect,[12] cannot recover.

E. DAMAGE

There is no cause of action unless the plaintiff proves that he has sustained damage.[13] Ordinarily, the damages will be for pecuniary loss, but damages for personal injuries,[14] and for loss of property,[15] are recoverable.

The plaintiff is entitled to recover all the actual damage directly flowing from the fraud, even though not foreseeable. If he is induced by fraud to buy business property he can claim not only the difference between the price and

---

9 *Edgington v Fitzmaurice* (1885), 29 ChD 459, CA.
10 *Dobell v Stevens* (1825) 3 B & C 623.
11 He is not taken to know of facts coming to the knowledge of his agent where that agent did not acquire that knowledge in his capacity as agent for this plaintiff; *Wells v Smith* [1914] 3 KB 722.
12 Cf *Horsfall v Thomas* (1882) 1 H & C 90.
13 Damage need not be proved in order to obtain rescission: per SARGANT LJ in *Goldrei Foucard & Son v Sinclair and Russian Chamber of Commerce in London* [1918] 1 KB 180 at 192, CA; *Lemprière v Lang* (1879) 12 ChD 675 (infant on becoming tenant made false representation—landlord could rescind although he could not recover damages for value of use and occupation).
14 *Langridge v Levy* (1837) 2 M & W 519, see p 110, ante; *Graham v Saville*, [1945] 2 DLR 489 (CA Ontario), (a plaintiff who was induced to 'marry' the defendant by his fraudulent misrepresentation that he was a bachelor, and who became pregnant by him, recovered damages in deceit for physical injuries consequent on the pregnancy and for reduced matrimonial prospects).
15 *Mullett v Mason* (1866) LR 1 CP 559: fraudulent misrepresentation that a cow was free from disease; the loss of five other infected cows was held recoverable in deceit.

market value, but also, for example, expenses reasonably incurred in trying to run the business fraudulently sold to him,[16] and interest on loans entered into to facilitate the purchase of the property.[17]

It is unclear whether exemplary (punitive) damages can be awarded in deceit in order to teach the defendant that tort does not pay.[18] The availability of exemplary damages in this tort depends on whether LORD DEVLIN's judgment in *Rookes v Barnard*[19] restricting exemplary damages to three classes of conduct concurrently extended the range of torts in which awards of exemplary damages may exceptionally be made. Aggravated damages to compensate the plaintiff for the injury to his feelings and dignity will be awarded in deceit.[20]

F. AGENCY

Agency is a concept of little relevance generally in the law of torts. Deceit is an exception to the rule. As well as being vicariously liable for false statements made by agents who are servants (employees), a principal may also be liable for representations, made on his behalf by independent persons acting for him in relation to a particular transaction, for example, estate agents or brokers.

A principal who expressly authorises a statement which he and the agent know to be untrue is liable with the agent as a joint tortfeasor. He is vicariously liable for statements known to be untrue by the agent and will further be liable where one agent passes on to another information which he knows to be false in order that the second 'innocent' agent may pass it onto the plaintiff who then acts on it to his detriment.[1] It is unclear whether, if an agent makes a statement without knowing it to be untrue and without authority to make that statement, the principal is liable in deceit if *he* would have known of the falsity of the statement.[2]

The key question in relation to liability for deceit by agents is generally whether the false representation was made within the scope of the agent's actual or ostensible authority. Was it a representation which the agent was actually authorised to make, or which the principal's conduct of affairs

---

16 *Doyle v Olby (Ironmongers) Ltd* [1969] 2 QB 158, [1969] 2 All ER 119, CA. Opinion is divided on whether the plaintiff can also recover for loss of bargain, ie, that profit he would have made if the representation had been true. Yes—*Jewson & Sons Ltd v Arcos Ltd* (1933) 47 Ll Rep 93, CA; *Kitchen v Fordham* [1955] 2 Ll Rep 705; *Watts v Spence* [1975] 2 All ER 528. No—Mayne and McGregor, *Damages*, § 1359, Treitel, *Contract* (6th edn, 1983) p 279 and cases cited by them.

17 *Archer v Brown* [1985] QB 401, [1984] 2 All ER 267 (that the loss resulted from the plaintiff's impecuniosity did not prevent its recovery).

18 *Mafo v Adams* [1970] 1 QB 548, [1969] 3 All ER 1404; *Archer v Brown* (supra); *Metall und Rohstoff AG v ACLI Metals (London) Ltd* [1984] 1 Lloyds Rep 598.

19 [1964] AC 1129, [1964] 1 All ER 367. On exemplary damages generally see post at p 466.

20 *Archer v Brown* (supra); *Shelley v Paddock* [1980] QB 348, [1980] 1 All ER 1009; *Saunders v Edwards* [1987] 2 All ER 651, [1987] 1 WLR 1116.

 1 *London County Freehold and Leasehold Properties Ltd v Berkeley Property and Investment Co Ltd* [1936] 2 All ER 1039, CA, as explained in *Anglo-Scottish Beet Sugar Corpn Ltd v Spalding UDC* [1937] 2 KB 607, [1937] 3 All ER 335.

 2 *Armstrong v Strain* [1952] 1 KB 232, [1952] 1 All ER 139 (held not to be tortious); but was this judgment *per incuriam* see *Woyka & Co v London and Northern Trading Co* (1922) 10 HL Rep 110, CA.

allowed him to appear to be authorised to make?[3] At any rate where the agent is also a servant[4] the fact that he sets out to deceive his employer as well as the plaintiff, and intends to benefit himself alone, will not relieve the principal from liability for the agent's deceit.[5] But the false representation must be one which the agent had ostensible authority to make. The employer-principal will not be liable simply because the agent is his servant. For the purposes of the tort of deceit the servant's course of employment is delimited by the scope of his authority.[6] LORD KEITH explained the rationale of the rule governing a principal's vicarious liability for deceit thus:[7]

> In the end of the day the question is whether the circumstances under which a servant has made a fraudulent representation which has caused loss to an innocent party contracting with him are such as to make it just for the employer to bear the loss. Such circumstances exist where the employer by words or conduct has induced the injured party to believe that the servant was acting in the lawful course of the employer's business. They do not exist where such belief, although it is present, has been brought about through misguided reliance on the servant himself, when the servant is not authorised to do what he was purporting to do, when what he is purporting to do is not within the class of acts that an employee in his position is usually authorised to do and when the employer has done nothing to represent that he is authorised to do it.

A principal whose agent has been bribed to induce him to enter into a transaction on the principal's behalf has a claim in tort against the briber for damages.[8] He cannot, however, receive double compensation by pursuing both his equitable remedy to recover the bribe from the agent and his tort action against the briber. He must elect between these two remedies. Where an agent offers a bribe acting within the scope of his actual or ostensible authority, the principal will be liable for that fraud as much as for any other act of deceit.[9]

G. STATUTE OF FRAUDS AMENDMENT ACT 1828

By section 6 of this statute:

> No action shall be brought whereby to charge any person upon or by reason of any representation or assurance made or given concerning or relating to the character, conduct, credit, ability, trade, or dealings of any other person, to the

---

3 In *Kooragang Investments Pty Ltd v Richardson and Wrench Ltd* [1982] AC 462, [1981] 3 All ER 65, the fraudulent agent had been expressly prohibited from preparing valuations relating to companies in which he had an interest. Nevertheless he prepared valuations in reliance on which the plaintiffs lent money to the companies. The defendant's corporate name did not appear on the valuations. It was held that the plaintiffs did not rely on any apparent authority granted to the agent by his employers. His authority was thus delimited by the scope of his actual authority.
4 When the agent is not a servant and the fraud is initially aimed at the principal there will be no vicarious liability to other victims of the fraud; see *Kwei Tek Chao v British Traders and Shippers Ltd* [1954] 2 QB 459, [1954] 1 All ER 779.
5 *Lloyd v Grace Smith & Co Ltd* [1912] AC 716 discussed fully post at 462.
6 *Armagas Ltd v Mundogas SA, 'The Ocean Frost'* [1986] AC 717, [1986] 2 All ER 385, HL; see post at p 448.
7 Ibid at 781.
8 *Mahesan s/o Thambiah v Malaysian Government Officers' Co-operative Housing Society Ltd* [1979] AC 374, [1978] 2 All ER 405.
9 *Armagas Ltd v Mundogas SA* [1985] 3 All ER 795, CA.

intent or purpose that such other person may obtain credit, money, or goods upon, [*sic*] unless such representation or assurance be made in writing signed by the party to be charged therewith.

The section prevents evasion of the Statute of Frauds (which requires guarantees to be in writing) by suing in tort instead of contract, and, in interpreting it, the courts have consistently taken heed of this legislative purpose.[10]

The Act does not apply to actions for breach of contract, and in all probability is confined to 'actions upon representations as such'.[11] The signature of an agent does not satisfy the requirements of the section.[12] Even though the defendant has induced the plaintiff to give credit in order to secure a pecuniary gain for himself, it seems that the Act applies.[13]

H. MISREPRESENTATION ACT 1967

Section 2 (1) enacts:

Where a person has entered into a contract after a misrepresentation has been made to him by another party thereto and as a result thereof he has suffered loss, then, if the person making the misrepresentation would be liable to damages in respect thereof had the misrepresentation been made fraudulently, that person shall be so liable notwithstanding that the misrepresentation was not made fraudulently, unless he proves that he had reasonable ground to believe and did believe up to the time the contract was made that the facts represented were true.

Its very important effect is that where the misrepresentation by a party induces the plaintiff to enter into a contract with him the plaintiff can recover damages for resulting loss without proving fraud. If all the other requirements of the tort of deceit are satisfied he will then have an action unless the defendant proves that he believed on reasonable grounds that his statement was true. A plaintiff may succeed under this Act although he fails in negligence because no duty of care in making the statement was owed to him.[14] The other rules about the tort of deceit discussed in this chapter will continue to apply in respect of these misrepresentations to persons entering into contracts. The Act does not extend the scope of the tort of negligence. It extends the separate tort of deceit, and the rules of deceit not negligence will govern such issues as damages.[15] Where the representation falls outside the Act, as for instance where it is made by a person who is not a party to the contract, the victim of negligence will still have to rely on the tort of negligence. The 1967 Act does not impose liability on the agent personally if he makes false

10 *Lyde v Barnard* (1836) 1 M & W, 101; *Banbury v Bank of Montreal* [1918] AC 626, HL.
11 *Banbury v Bank of Montreal*, supra.
12 *Swift v Jewsbury and Goddard* (1874) LR 9 QB 301 (Ct Ex Ch). Signature on behalf of a company by its duly authorised agent is for the purposes of s 6 the signature of the company; *UBAF Ltd v European American Banking Corpn* [1984] QB 713, [1984] 2 All ER 226, CA.
13 So held by the House of Lords when interpreting the analogous provisions of a Scottish statute in *Clydesdale Bank v Paton* [1896] AC 381, HL (Sc).
14 *Howard Marine & Dredging Co Ltd v Ogden & Sons (Excavations) Ltd* [1978] QB 574, [1978] 2 All ER 1134, CA.
15 In *Watts v Spence* [1976] Ch 165, [1975] 2 All ER 528, damages awarded for innocent misrepresentation under the Act included compensation for loss of bargain. And see *André & Cie SA v Ets Michel Blanc et Fils* [1977] 2 Lloyds Rep 166 at 181, [1979] 2 Lloyds Rep 427, CA.

representations to induce the making of a contract. His liability too remains to be established in deceit or negligence.[16]

Prior to the 1967 Act there were circumstances in which the victim of an innocent misrepresentation could seek rescission of a contract although he could not have sued for deceit. Secton 2 (2) of the Act provides that the court may, if of the opinion that it would be equitable to do so, having regard to the nature of the misrepresentation and the loss that would be caused by it if the contract were upheld, as well as to the loss that rescission would cause to the other party, declare the contract subsisting and award damages in lieu of rescission. In effect, then, the court has a discretion to require the victim of an innocent misrepresentation to accept damages in lieu of rescission. Rescission can be obtained although damage is not proved;[17] presumably the court could award damages in lieu of rescission to a person who had not proved damage.

SECTION 2. PASSING OFF—UNFAIR TRADING

The action for deceit affords a remedy to businessmen who are the direct target of fraudulent misrepresentation. The tort of passing off protects traders against misrepresentations aimed at their customers which are calculated to damage the trader's business or goodwill. The classic tort of passing off was limited to the use, in connection with his own goods, of the trade name or trade mark of a rival intended to induce that rival's customers to believe that the goods were produced by the rival trader and so cash in on his goodwill. The House of Lords in 1915 laid the foundation for a more all-embracing tort of unfair trading practice, and in 1979 confirmed that this tort, for the sake of convenience still entitled passing-off, has a broad role to play in controlling dishonest competitive practices. In *A G Spalding & Bros v A W Gamage Ltd*[18] LORD PARKER OF WADDINGTON described the right which is protected by this tort as the 'property in the business or goodwill likely to be injured by the misrepresentation'.[19]

The extent of the broader tort was tested in *Erven Warnink BV v J Townend & Sons (Hull) Ltd.*[20]

> The plaintiffs were Dutch traders who manufactured an alcoholic drink known as 'advocaat'. Its principal ingredients were eggs and spirits with an admixture of wine. The defendants had for several years manufactured another alcoholic egg drink composed of egg and fortified wine known as 'egg flip' and up to 1974 marketed by them under that name. Because of the vagaries of the excise law which imposes higher duties on spirits than fortified wine 'egg flip' retailed at a lower price than 'advocaat'. In 1974 the defendants began to market their alcoholic egg drink as 'Keeling's Old English Advocaat' and captured an appreciable share of the English market in 'advocaat'.

> The House of Lords held that no-one was likely to be deceived into

16 *Resolute Maritime Inc v Nippon Kaiji Kyokai* [1983] 2 All ER 1, [1983] 1 WLR 857.
17 P 108, ante,
18 (1915) 84 LJ Ch 449.
19 At 284.
20 [1979] AC 731, [1979] 2 All ER 927, HL.

believing that the defendant's drink was Dutch 'advocaat' (ie that they were buying the plaintiffs' product), and so no cause of action for passing off in its classic form arose. Nevertheless the name 'advocaat' was generally understood to denote a distinct species of drink by virtue of which the plaintiffs had built up their reputation and goodwill, and the defendants' misrepresentation had induced the public to believe they were buying 'advocaat' causing damage to the plaintiffs' business and goodwill. On these findings a cause of action in tort arose.

LORD DIPLOCK identified five characteristics[1] necessary to found an action for passing off in its wider form. There must be:

(A) a misrepresentation;
(B) made by a trader in the course of trade;
(C) to prospective customers of his or ultimate consumers of goods and services supplied by him;
(D) which is calculated to injure the business or goodwill of another trader (in the sense that it is a reasonably foreseeable consequence); and
(E) which causes actual damage to the business or goodwill of the trader by whom the action is brought or will probably do so.

A. THE MISREPRESENTATION

The misrepresentation may take any of the following forms:[2]

(1) MARKETING A PRODUCT AS THAT OF THE PLAINTIFF

A defendant must not market a commodity with a statement that it is the product of the plaintiff when this is not so.[3]

(2) USING A PLAINTIFF'S NAME

To engage in the same line of business as the plaintiff and to use a similar name may be passing off.[4] If the defendant carries on business in his own name (or one which he has assumed for some time[5]) then he does not commit this tort unless there are further special circumstances showing dishonesty[6]:

1 At 472 and 932 respectively; see the slightly more restrictive definition given by LORD FRASER OF TULLYBELTON at 482 and 943 respectively. Both judgments are considered in *Anheuser-Busch Inc v Budejovicky Budvar NP* [1984] FSR 413.
2 The list in the text is not necessarily exhaustive: eg in *Francis Day and Hunter Ltd v Twentieth Century Fox Corporation Ltd* [1939] 4 All ER 192 at 199, PC LORD WRIGHT thought it would be this tort where persons went to a performance of the defendant's work under the impression that they were going to witness the plaintiff's work.
3 *Byron (Lord) v Johnston* (1816) 2 Mer 29 (defendant publisher advertised poems as Byron's when they were written by some other person of a different name); *C G Volkes Ltd v F J Evans and Marble Arch Motor Supplies Ltd* (1931) 49 RPC 140, CA: CE Ltd were sub-contractors for the plaintiff. *Held* P could restrain D, who acquired these wipers direct from CE, Ltd, from passing them off as P's wipers—because P normally inspected the wipers D was deemed to have represented that P had done so in this instance.
4 *Tussaud v Tussaud* (1890) 44 ChD 678. *Boswell-Wilkie Circus (Pty) Ltd v Brian Boswell Circus (Pty) Ltd* [1985] FSR 434.
5 *Jay's Ltd v Jacobi* [1933] Ch 411, [1933] All ER Rep 690.
6 *Sykes v Sykes* (1824) 3 B & C 541; cf *Croft v Day* (1843) 7 Beav 84. In *Wright, Layman and Umney Ltd v Wright* (1949) 66 RPC 149, CA, the defendant could use his own name, but committed passing off once he traded as 'Wright's Chemical Co'.

he is entitled knowingly to take advantage of the benefits which may accrue to him from the trade use of his own name.[7] But if he confusingly describes his goods by his own name it is no defence that his user is bona fide.[8] A company does not, however, acquire and incorporate the individual rights of its promoters to carry on business under their own names.[9]

(3) USING A PLAINTIFF'S TRADE NAME

To use the plaintiff's trade name, ie the designation adopted by the plaintiff to identify goods which he markets or services which he renders, may constitute the tort. The following are examples:

> To describe and sell sauce as 'Yorkshire Relish' was to commit a tort against the original manufacturer of sauce under that name.[10]
>
> At the request of the defendant, the plaintiff used the name, 'Dr Crock and his Crackpots' when broadcasting with his band in the defendant's programme, 'Ignorance is Bliss'. When the plaintiff had left this programme, he was entitled to restrain the defendant from putting another band in the programme with the title 'Dr Crock and his Crackpots'.[11]

If the trade name merely describes the goods or their characteristics then ordinarily the plaintiff cannot prevent others from using it: eg vacuum cleaner,[12] gripe water,[13] 'cellular' textiles,[14] nourishing stout,[15] shredded wheat.[16] A very heavy burden of proof is cast on the plaintiff who seeks to establish that a name which is merely descriptive of the product has acquired a technical secondary meaning so exclusively associated with the plaintiff's own products that its use by others is calculated to deceive purchasers. This burden was discharged by the makers of 'Camel Hair Belting' in the leading case of *Reddaway v Banham*.[17] The task is a little easier where the descriptive words connect the product with the place of its manufacture: the manufacturers of 'Glenfield Starch',[18] 'Stone Ales'[19] and 'Chartreuse' liqueurs,[20] have, for instance, succeeded in passing off actions.

The courts are much more willing to protect the use of a fanciful name, ie

---

7 *John Brinsmead Ltd v Brinsmead and Waddington & Sons Ltd* (1913) 29 TLR 237, on appeal (1913) 29 TLR 706; *Burgess v Burgess* (1853), 3 De GM & G 896. There is no similar protection for a nickname: *Biba Group v Biba Boutique* [1980] RPC 413.

8 *Parker-Knoll, Ltd v Knoll International Ltd* [1962] RPC 265, HL; *WH Allen & Co v Brown Watson Ltd* [1965] RPC 191 (P published a very successful unexpurgated edition of Frank Harris's *My Life and Loves*; D committed passing off when he then bought the rights of, and published, an expurgated abridged edition under the same title).

9 *Tussaud v Tussaud* (1890) 44 ChD 678; nor has a foreign company a right to set up in England in competitive business with the plaintiff company of the same name; *Sturtevant Engineering Co Ltd v Sturtevant Mill Co of USA Ltd* [1936] 3 All ER 137.

10 *Powell v Birmingham Vinegar Brewery Co* [1896] 2 Ch 54 CA.

11 *Hines v Winnick* [1947] Ch 708; cf *Forbes v Kemsley Newspapers, Ltd* [1951] 2 TLR 656 (*Sunday Times* could not publish articles under name of Mary Delane, unless they were writtten by plaintiff, its former correspondent of that name).

12 *British Vacuum Cleaner Co Ltd v New Vacuum Cleaner Co Ltd* [1907] 2 Ch 312.

13 *Re Woodward's Trade Mark, Woodward Ltd v Boulton Macro Ltd* (1915) 85 LJ Ch 27.

14 *Cellular Clothing Co v Maxton and Murray* [1899] AC 326, HL.

15 *Raggett v Findlater* (1873) LR 17 Eq 29.

16 *Canadian Shredded Wheat Co v Kellogg Co of Canada Ltd* [1938] 1 All ER 618, PC.

17 [1896] AC 199, HL.

18 *Wotherspoon v Currie* (1872) LR 5 HL 508.

19 *Montgomery v Thompson* [1891] AC 217, HL.

20 *Rey v Lecouturier* [1908] 2 Ch 715; affd sub nom *Lecouturier v Rey* [1910] AC 262, HL.

one that does not describe the quality of the goods, for example, 'Apollinaris'.[1] It has been suggested that a person originally entitled to protection for a fanciful name may lose his right if the name later becomes a mere description of that type of product rather than a word associated with goods of the plaintiff;[2] this may well be so, but no case deciding it has been traced.[3] The attempt failed in *Havana Cigar and Tobacco Factories Ltd v Oddenino*:[4]

> The plaintiffs were the original manufacturers of Corona cigars; the defendants supplied other cigars as Corona cigars. The plaintiffs successfully sued in passing off, the court rejecting the argument of the defendants that the word no longer described a brand of cigar, but only a particular size of cigar.

(4) USING PLAINTIFF'S TRADE MARK

It may be tortious to use the plaintiff's trade mark, ie a design, picture or other arrangement affixed by him to goods which he markets so as to identify them with him.[5]

Section 2 of the Trade Marks Act 1938 expressly saves the common-law action of passing off in respect of trade marks. If, for instance, the plaintiff fails to prove registration, or if the registration does not extend to the goods in question, or is invalid, the statutory action for infringement of trade mark will fail and it will be necessary to resort to the common-law action.

(5) IMITATING APPEARANCE OF PLAINTIFF'S GOODS

To imitate the appearance of the plaintiff's goods (and especially where this is accompanied by other sources of confusion, such as a not dissimilar name[6]) may be passing off.

If the appearance complained of is dictated by functional considerations, for example, the purpose or performance of the goods, or simplicity in handling or processing them, the courts will be reluctant to interfere: an action to prevent the use by the defendant of the normal shape of shaving

---

1 *The Apollinaris Co Ltd v Norrish* (1875) 33 LT 242.
2 Eg *Ford v Foster* (1872) 7 Ch App 611 (*obiter*).
3 The ones usually said to cover the point are *Liebig's Extract of Meat Co Ltd v Hanbury* (1867) 17 LT 298 (but there, before the plaintiffs ever manufactured the product, the inventor had freely given his recipe to the world, and various persons had made it under that name) and *Lazenby v White* (1871) 41 LJ Ch 354n (a shorthand writer's note merely, presumably not a citable authority in court, 'It being assumed at the hearing that "Harris's Sauce" was the name of an article which was open to anybody in the world to manufacture as a sauce by that name.'). One further case not cited in the text-books is, however, much more nearly in point: *G H Gledhill & Sons Ltd v British Perforated Toilet Paper Co* (1911) 28 RPC 429, 714, CA. The trial judge did hold that the plaintiffs could not restrain the defendants from styling the paper supplied by them for the plaintiffs' 'Gledhill cash tills' as 'Gledhill Cash-Till Rolls' because by 1907 the words were *publici juris*, although they were not so in 1901. Affirming his decision, the Court of Appeal proceeded on a slightly different ground: that the plaintiffs' interest was in the tills, and that they had therefore no monopoly in the provision of suitable paper for the tills. For a case where the plaintiffs lost the protection of a trade name in a magazine, 'Today', seven years after it had amalgamated with another magazine, see *Norman Kark Ltd v Odhams Press Ltd* [1962] 1 All ER 636.
4 [1924] 1 Ch 179, CA.
5 *Millington v Fox* (1838) 3 My & Cr 338; *Singer Machine Manufacturers v Wilson* (1877) 3 App Cas 376, especially at 391–2 (per LORD CAIRNS LC), HL.
6 *Massam v Thorley's Cattle Food Co* (1880) 14 ChD 748, CA.

stick container accordingly failed.[7] Yet the manufacturer of laundry blue which had a knobbed stick through the middle of the container was able to prevent the defendant from marketing a product similar in appearance, since he satisfied the court that this appearance was more than merely functional—the defendant was at liberty to have a stick in his product, but not one of the same get up as the plaintiff's.[8] Protection will not be afforded where the defendant's product is merely similar to that of the plaintiff's in particulars which are common to all types of that manufactured product.[9]

(6) SELLING INFERIOR GOODS OF PLAINTIFF, THEREBY MISLEADING PURCHASER

A defendant must not sell goods which are in fact, and which are described as, the goods of the plantiff, but which are of a quality inferior to that of the normal new and current product of the plaintiff, in such a way as to cause prospective purchasers to believe that the goods are the normal new and current product of the plaintiff.

Thus the manufacturers of Gillette razor blades obtained an injunction restraning the defendant from selling used Gillette blades as 'genuine' ones.[10] On the other hand, a general dealer in a working-class area who advertised in his shop: 'All types of electric lamps and fittings at cut prices' was held not liable in passing off to the manufacturers of Osram lamps for selling old Osram lamps, because it was not established that his acts were calculated to deceive the public into thinking that new lamps were being offered for sale.[11] Judicial reluctance to settle the respective merits of various products[12] led to a denial of a remedy in *Harris v Warren and Phillips*:[13]

> The publishers of a song-writer, who had recently attained fame, were unable to restrain the defendants from passing off the writer's early work (in which the defendants had the copyright, and which, it was contended, was of greatly inferior quality to her latest work) as new work—the court held that it could draw no sharp dividing line between the quality of her early songs and that of her recent ones.

(7) FALSE ADVERTISING

Two cases will illustrate when false advertising may amount to passing off. The first is *Cadbury Schweppes Pty Ltd v Pub Squash Co Pty Ltd*:[14]

---

7 *J B Williams Co v H Bronnley & Co Ltd* (1909) 26 RPC 765 CA.
8 *William Edge & Sons Ltd v William Niccolls & Sons Ltd* [1911] AC 693, HL.
9 *Jamieson & Co v Jamieson* (1898) 14 TLR 160, CA.
10 *Gillette Safety Razor Co and Gillette Safety Razor Ltd v Franks* (1924) 40 TLR 606; cf *Spalding & Brothers v Gamage (A W), Ltd* (1915) 84 LJ Ch 449, HL (defendants restrained from selling plaintiffs' footballs with false inference that they were of the type currently marketed by the plaintiffs). *Wilts United Dairies Ltd v Thomas Robinson Sons & Co, Ltd* [1958] RPC 94, CA (defendants sold canned milk under the plaintiffs' trade name without revealing that the contents were appreciably older than those habitually marketed by the plaintiffs). *Morris Motors Ltd v Lilley* [1959] 3 All ER 737: defendant dealer sold a car as a 'new Morris' when he had bought it from a retail customer who had taken delivery of it as a new car immediately before; the defendant was representing himself as a dealer authorised by the plaintiffs, the car manufacturers, and that passing off therefore injured the goodwill of the plaintiffs.
11 *General Electric Co and British Thomson-Houston Co v Pryce's Stores* (1933), 50 RPC 232.
12 Cf *White v Mellin* [1895] AC 154, HL.
13 (1918) 87 LJ Ch 491.
14 [1981] 1 All ER 213, PC.

The plaintiffs successfully launched a new canned lemon drink with a big television and radio advertising campaign. Next year the defendants launched a similar drink with a television and radio campaign in which they imitated the slogans and visual images of the plaintiff's advertising. It was held that such advertising could be passing off, but the action failed because the plaintiffs did not prove that there had been confusing misrepresentation.

Secondly, *Masson Seely & Co Ltd v Embossotype Manufacturing Co:*[15]

The defendants deliberately created a market for their goods by copying the plaintiffs' catalogue in such a way as to induce the public to believe that goods offered by the defendants were those of the plaintiffs—customers of the plaintiffs normally ordered goods by reference to certain coined key-words in the catalogue, and the defendants used the same artificial words in their catalogue; the defendants' goods were inferior to those sold by the plaintiffs. This was held to be passing off.

(8) CASHING IN ON GOODWILL

The examples so far given of misrepresentations constituting passing off all, in the main, concern attempts to induce consumers to believe that they are purchasing the plaintiffs' products. Passing off is no longer restricted to such misrepresentations alone. The process of extending the tort to more general forms of unfair trade practice gained momentum first from the famous 'Champagne' case. In *J Bollinger v Costa Brava Wine Co.*[16]

The defendants marketed 'Spanish Champagne', a Spanish wine. The plaintiffs were one of several manufacturers of champagne in Champagne, France. The court found that members of the public bought the defendants' wine in the mistaken belief that they were buying champagne from the vineyards of Champagne. It was held that the defendants committed the tort of passing off.

DANCKWERTS J held that the description 'champagne' was part of the plaintiffs' goodwill and a right of property. A group of persons producing goods in a certain locality and naming those goods by reference to that locality were entitled to protection against competititors who sought to cash in on their goodwill and reputation by attaching that name to a product originating from a different locality and with which the competing product has no rational association. The limitation of goods produced in a certain locality was considered immaterial in *Erven Warnink BV v J Townend & Sons (Hull) Ltd.*[17] The Dutch traders recovered for the loss in their business resulting from the defendants misleading appropriation of the name 'advo-caat' for their different and cheaper alcoholic egg drink. The crucial issue was

---

15 (1924) 41 RPC 160; cf *Purefoy Engineering Co Ltd v Sykes Boxall & Co Ltd* (1955) 72 RPC 89, CA.

16 [1960] Ch 262; subsequent proceedings [1961] 1 All ER 561, [1961] 1 WLR 277; following in *Vine Products Ltd v Mackenzie & Co Ltd* [1969] RPC 1 ('Sherry' used alone restricted to products from Jerez district of Spain) and in *John Walker & Sons Ltd v Henry Ost & Co Ltd* [1970] 2 All ER 106, [1970] 1 WLR 917 (injunction granted to one whisky blender to restrain defendant from passing off as 'Scotch Whisky' whisky mixed with cane spirit).

17 [1979] AC 731, [1979] 2 All ER 927, HL. And see ante at p 116.

1 whether there was a 'distinctive class of goods'; and
2 that those goods were marketed in England by a class of persons whose product was genuinely indicated by the use of the name 'advocaat'.

An earlier judgment not confined to goods or services as such further illustrates the protection afforded by this tort to reputation and goodwill. In *Illustrated Newspapers Ltd v Publicity Services (London) Ltd.*[18]

The plaintiffs owned certain illustrated periodicals. The defendants supplied hotels with folders (bearing the name of the appropriate periodical) for them, and without the plaintiffs' permission inserted a four-page advertisement in the middle, headed 'Supplement'. The defendants justified their conduct on the ground that nobody was induced to deal with them in the mistaken belief that he was dealing with the plaintiffs. Nonetheless the plaintiffs were held to have a cause of action for the injury thus caused to their goodwill in their advertising media by the defendants' misrepresentation.

B. IN THE COURSE OF TRADE

The representation must be made in the course of a trade. Trade is liberally defined and includes pursuit of a profession[19] and a person's interest in his literary and performance rights.[20] The tort is not available to protect the name of a political party. In 1982 an attempt to prevent the defendant calling his party the Social Democrat Party failed.[1]

C. A REPRESENTATION TO CUSTOMERS OR ULTIMATE CUSTOMERS

The representation must be made either to prospective customers of the plaintiff or to ultimate consumers of goods or services supplied by him.[2] If the parties have no common field of activity, that in itself does not defeat an action, provided that injury to goodwill from confusion is established. A bank was held able to restrain a moneylender from setting up in trade under the same name on the ground that it would endanger its reputation if it were thought also to be a moneylender;[3] *The Times* newspaper obtained an injunction against the defendant who represented it to be his principal or business associate in his cycle dealer business.[4] On the other hand Granada

---

18 [1938] Ch 414, [1938] 1 All ER 321.
19 *Society of Incorporated Accountants v Vincent* (1954) 71 RPC 325.
20 See *Byron (Lord) v Johnston* (1816) 2 Mer 29; *Hines v Winnick* [1947] Ch 708, [1947] 2 All ER 517; *Illustrated Newspapers Ltd v Publicity Services Ltd* [1938] Ch 414, [1938] 1 All ER 321.
1 *Kean v McGivan* [1982] FSR 119.
2 *Erven Warnink BV v J Townend & Sons (Hull) Ltd* [1979] AC 731 at 742, [1979] 2 All ER 927 at 932–3 (per LORD DIPLOCK), HL. A foreign based company must establish that it has customers in England (per LORD FRASER at 943–944). The action failed for this reason in *Athletics Foot Marketing Associates Inc v Cobra Sports Co* [1980] RPC 343. On the other hand Maxim's, the famous Paris restaurant, succeeded in preventing a Norfolk restaurant from trading under that name; *Maxim's Ltd v Dye* [1977] FSR 364.
3 *Harrods Ltd v R Harrod Ltd* (1923) 40 TLR 195, CA.
4 *Walter v Ashton* [1902] 2 Ch 282.

TV could not prevent Ford from calling a new model Granada, for there was neither a connection or association between the two activities nor any proved confusion of the public.[5] A well-known children's broadcaster who used the pseudonym Uncle Mac could not prevent the defendants from marketing 'Uncle Mac's Puffed Wheat' because he failed to prove such confusion as would lead to damage to his goodwill.[6] Nor could the originator of *The Wombles* prevent the defendants from marketing Wombles Skips.[7]

Where the misrepresentation relates to a product produced by a group of traders, rather than one single plaintiff, the group must establish that they constitute a distinctive class of traders who have built up goodwill by the use of a particular name or description of goods. Thus the French producers of champagne succeeded by establishing they all operated from a particular geographical area: Champagne in France.[8] And the Dutch manufacturers of 'advocaat' proved that their product was generally recognised to share a particular and distinctive composition, eggs and spirits.[9]

D. CALCULATED TO INJURE GOODWILL

Proof of intention to deceive is not essential in contrast to the tort of deceit.[10] The test is rather whether a false representation has in fact been made, fraudulently or otherwise, which will foreseeably result in misleading consumers.[11] It is unnecessary (though desirable, where possible) to prove that any members of the public were deceived; thus, where the defendant had done no more than sell to middlemen, who were not themselves deceived, the action was held still to lie where it was to be expected that in due course the act of the defendant would be calculated to cause confusion in the minds of the purchasing public.[12] It is not essential that the person deceived should know the name of the plaintiff: it is enough 'if a person minded to obtain goods which are identified in his mind with a certain definite commercial source is led by false statements to accept goods coming from a different commercial source'.[13] If the public will not be confused, there is no tort.[14]

5 *Granada Group Ltd v Ford Motor Co Ltd* [1973] RPC 49.
6 *McCulloch v Lewis A May (Produce Distributors) Ltd* [1947] 2 All ER 845.
7 *Wombles Ltd v Wombles Skips Ltd* [1977] RPC 99; contra *Annabel's (Berkeley Square) Ltd v G Schock* [1972] RPC 838, CA (Annabel's Club and Annabel's Escort Agency).
8 *J Bollinger v Costa Brava Wine Co* (supra).
9 *Erven Warnink BV v J Townend & Sons (Hull) Ltd* (supra).
10 *Baume & Co Ltd v A H Moore Ltd* [1958] Ch 907, [1958] 2 All ER 113; and see *Clerk and Lindsell* para 29–29.
11 *Spalding & Brothers v Gamage (A W) Ltd* (1915) 84 LJ Ch 449, HL, at 452 (per LORD PARKER). For cases where there was held to be no confusion, see *Grand Hotel Co of Caledonia Springs v Wilson* [1904] AC 103, PC (plaintiff's 'Caledonian waters'—defendant found a new spring in Caledonia and marketed its product as 'from our springs at Caledonia'); *Office Cleaning Services Ltd v Westminster Office Cleaning Association* (1944), 61 RPC 133, CA, affirmed (1946) 63 RPC, 39 HL (rival firms of office cleaners trading under the above names respectively).
12 *Draper v Trist* [1939] 3 All ER 513, CA.
13 Per LORD GREENE in *Plomien Fuel Economiser Co Ltd v National School of Salesmanship, Ltd* (1943) 60 RPC 209 at 214, CA and even though the drug passed off by imitating get-up was sold on prescription only so that the public had no choice of supplier, *F Hoffman-La Roche & Co AG v DDSA Pharmaceuticals, Ltd* [1969] FSR 410.
14 Recent examples of failure for this reason are: *Cadbury Schweppes Pty Ltd v Pub Squash Co Pty Ltd* [1981] 1 All ER 213, PC and *Newsweek Inc v BBC* [1979] RPC 441, CA (the owners of the magazine 'Newsweek' could not prevent the BBC from calling a new current affairs

In determining whether the representation is confusing, one must take into account the experience and perceptiveness of those likely to buy the goods, as well as the purpose of the defendants: where the defendant put a design of two elephants on yarn tickets of material to be sold in rural districts of India, the fact that his design was different from that of the two elephants pictured on the plaintiff's yarn tickets did not prevent the House of Lords from finding for the plaintiff.[15] Similarly, although the ordinary standard to be applied is that of the unwary member of the public, if the particular trade is exclusively with experts, the test must be whether such an expert is likely to be deceived.[16]

E. PROOF OF DAMAGE

The action lies even though no damage is proved;[17] probability of damage is enough.[18]

F. DEFENCES

None of the general defences to torts which might apply calls for special attention: perhaps consent is the most important.[19]

G. REMEDIES

(1) INJUNCTION

This remedy is often the most important to the plaintiff. As always, it is in the discretion of the court whether to grant it, and the actual form of the injunction is often one of the most contested points in this class of litigation.[20] If the defendant's conduct is calculated to divert customers even though no sale has occurred, then in accordance with general principles an injunction will lie to prevent the apprehended wrong.[1]

programme, 'Newsweek', for nobody would confuse that programme with the magazine, even though that descriptive word was its title); *Stringfellow v McCain Foods (GB) Ltd.*

15 *Johnston v Orr-Ewing* (1882) 7 App Cas 219, HL; cf *William Edge & Sons Ltd v William Niccolls & Sons Ltd* [1911] AC 693, HL; *Lee Kar Choo v Lee Lian Choon* [1967] 1 AC 602; [1966] 3 All ER 1000, PC.

16 *Singer Manufacturing Co v Loog* (1882) 8 App Cas 15, HL.

17 *Draper v Trist* [1939] 3 All ER 513, CA; *Procea Products Ltd v Evans & Sons Ltd* (1951), 68 RPC 210.

18 *Bulmer (HP) Ltd and Showerings Ltd v J Bollinger SA*, [1978] RPC 79, CA. Only want of damage prevented an action for this tort from being available in *McCulloch v Lewis A May (Produce Distributors) Ltd* [1947] 2 All ER 845, p 123, ante. Other cases where the action failed for this reason are *A-G and General Council of Medical Education of United Kingdom Registration v Barrett Proprietaries Ltd* (1932), 50 RPC 45 (publishers of British Pharmacopoea could not recover against defendants who used letters 'BP' on cartons of drugs made by them).

19 *Ex turpi causa* is a defence; *Lee v Haley* (1869) 5 Ch App 155; *Ford v Foster* (1872) 7 Ch App 611 at 630–1 (per MELLISH LJ).

20 In the absence of a threat to continue the acts complained of, the courts may grant a declaration, but not an injunction (though giving liberty to apply for an injunction, eg if the defendant does continue); *Treasure Cot Co Ltd v Hamley Brothers* (1950), 67 RPC 89.

1 *Reddaway v Bentham Hemp Spinning Co* [1892] 2 QB 639 at 648, CA per A L SMITH LJ.

(2) DAMAGES

The plaintiff recovers damages for the loss of profits which he has sustained in consequence of customers' being diverted from him to the defendant: in addition he may recover for loss of business reputation[2] and goodwill.[3] The alternative to the common-law inquiry into damages is the equitable remedy of an account of the profits actually made by the defendant in consequence of the passing off.[4] There are *dicta* to the effect that an account of profits will not be directed for such period as the defendant's action was innocent:[5] it is uncertain whether more than nominal damages may be awarded when the defendant neither knew nor ought to know[6] that he was passing off.[7]

H. UNFAIR TRADING AND PASSING OFF

The landmark judgment of the House of Lords in *Erven Warnink BV v Townend & Sons (Hull) Ltd* extending, as we have seen, the classic tort of passing off to a wider class of misrepresentations resulting in damage to a rival's goodwill leaves open the limits of the tort as a means of controlling unfair trading practices. LORD DIPLOCK[8] recognised that Parliament has progressively intervened to impose on traders higher standards of commercial candour. He clearly indicated that the steady trend in legislation reflecting the legislative view of what is today acceptable conduct in the market place should be matched by the development of the common law. Consequently earlier judgments that misleading trade practices were not on their facts tortious as the classic tort of passing off must be treated with some caution. Consider the following two cases. Would either or both now fall within the wider principle enunciated in the *Warnink* judgment?

In *Cambridge University Press v University Tutorial Press*[9] the plaintiff's book was the one prescribed for a matriculation examination. The defendants' conduct in deceiving the public that their book was the one prescribed afforded the plaintiffs no cause of action.

In *Sales Affiliates Ltd v Le Jean Ltd*[10] the plaintiffs marketed appliances and materials for 'Jamal' permanent waves. The defendants in business as hairdressers, when asked by their customers for 'Jamal' treatment, used materials other than those of the plaintiffs, and by misrepresenting their own process as being one associated with the name and goodwill of the plaintiffs,

---

2 *Spalding (A G) and Brothers v Gamage (A W), Ltd* (1918) 35 RPC 101; *Treasure Cot Co Ltd v Hamley Brothers,* supra.
3 *Aktiebolaget Manus v R J Fullwood and Bland Ltd* (1954) 71 RPC 243.
4 In computing this profit, sales by the defendant to middlemen can be considered, although the middlemen were not deceived, and have not yet passed the goods on to the public; *Lever v Goodwin* (1887) 36 ChD 1, CA.
5 *Edelsten v Edelsten* (1863) 1 De G J & Sm 185 at 199 (per LORD WESTBURY).
6 *Edward Young & Co Ltd v Holt* (1947) 65 RPC 25, held that 'innocent' bears this meaning.
7 *Draper v Trist,* p 124, ante; *Marengo v Daily Sketch and Sunday Graphic Ltd* (1948) 65 RPC 242 at 251, HL, per LORD SIMONDS.
8 [1979] 2 All ER 927 at 933; see ante at p 107.
9 (1928) 45 RPC 335.
10 [1947] Ch 295, [1947] 1 All ER 287. And consider *Rima Electric Ltd v Rolls Razor Ltd* [1965] RPC 4 (was there in this case any damage to the plaintiffs as opposed to misleading the customers and inducing them to spend money which they would otherwise have spent elsewhere?).

thereby caused damage to the plaintiffs. There seems no reason of public policy to prevent that unfair trading from now being held to be passing off.

SECTION 3. INJURIOUS FALSEHOOD

The tort of injurious falsehood also operates to protect interests in goodwill and economic reputation. Passing off prevents competitors from using false representations to cash in on the plaintiff's goodwill. Injurious falsehood affords a remedy where business reputation is maliciously disparaged even though no aspersion is made against the character of an individual sufficient to give rise to a cause of action in defamation.

The Court of Appeal has defined this tort as follows:[11]

> That an action will lie for written or oral falsehoods ... where they are maliciously published, where they are calculated in the ordinary course of things to produce, and where they do produce, actual damage ...

A. INTERESTS PROTECTED[12]

Originally this tort protected persons against unwarranted attacks on their title to land, by virtue of which they might be hampered in the disposal of that land; hence, it was called 'slander of title'.[13] Later it was held equally applicable to goods, in which case the tort was usually called 'slander of goods'.[14] By 1874 it was established that disparagements of the quality of property, as well as aspersions on title to it, were tortious.[15] Before the end of the century, *Ratcliffe v Evans*[16] had decided that the tort could be committed whenever damaging lies about a business were uttered; since then, the tort has been comprehensively styled 'injurious falsehood'.

Any type of interest in land, whether vested in possession or not,[17] is protected. Trade marks,[18] patents,[19] trade names,[20] copyright,[1] company shares,[2] may all be the subject of actionable disparagements. The following random illustrations of circumstances treated by the courts as being within the scope of the tort will demonstrate its extent; an untrue statement by the defendant to a customer that the plaintiff, a commercial traveller with whom the customer had formerly dealt, was now in the employment of the defendant's firm;[3] failure to delete the name of the plaintiff, a musical accompanist,

---

11 *Ratcliffe v Evans* [1892] 2 QB 524 at 527, CA.
12 And see Newark, 'Malice in Actions on the Case for Words' (1944) 60 LQR 366.
13 Eg *Gerard v Dickenson* (1590) Cro Eliz 196.
14 *Malachy v Soper* (1836) 3 Bing NC 371; cf *Green v Button* (1835) 2 Cr M & R 707 (defendant told person who had contracted with plaintiff to sell him timber that he, the defendant, had a lien on it, and thereby prevented plaintiff from obtaining delivery).
15 *Western Counties Manure Co v Lawes Chemical Manure Co* (1874) LR 9 Exch 218.
16 Supra.
17 *Vaughan v Ellis* (1608) Cro Jac 213.
18 *Greers, Ltd v Pearman and Corder Ltd* (1922) 39 RPC 406, CA.
19 *Wren v Weild* (1869) LR 4 QB 730.
20 *Royal Baking Powder Co v Wright, Crossley & Co* (1900) 18 RPC 95, HL.
 1 *Dicks v Brooks* (1880) 15 ChD 22.
 2 *Malachy v Soper* (1836) 3 Bing NC 371.
 3 *Balden v Shorter* [1933] Ch 427, [1933] All ER Rep 249. The action failed for another reason.

from the programme of a concert series in which she was no longer to appear (because, as a result of this, others might not offer her engagements for the period covered by the advertised programme);[4] a false statement in the defendant's newspaper that the plaintiff had ceased to carry on business;[5] an erroneous statement that the plaintiff's wife who helped the plaintiff in his drapery business, had committed adultery in the shop with the parson newly appointed to the parish.[6] *Joyce v Motor Surveys Ltd*, is an example of a successful action in injurious falsehood:[7]

> The plaintiff became tenant of one of defendants' lock-up garages in order to have premises at which he could be registered as a tyre dealer. The defendants subsequently wished to evict the plaintiff in order to sell the entire property with vacant possession. They therefore told the Post Office not to forward any more mail to him at that address, and told the tyre manufacturers' association that he was no longer trading there. The defendants' conduct was held to constitute injurious falsehood.

Interference with a prospective advantage, even in the social, as distinct from the commercial, sphere, may also be within the ambit of this tort: to deprive a plaintiff of a marriage by falsely informing the intended husband that she was already married has been held to be tortious.[8]

B. DISPARAGEMENT

It is a disparagement if there is some misstatement as to the extent of the plaintiff's interest in his property or as to the quality of his goods. Thus, a false statement by a newspaper owner that the circulation of his newspaper greatly exceeded that of the plaintiff's rival newspaper was held to be capable of being tortious.[9]

A threat of proceedings for infringement of a patent[10] or a trade mark[11] may be enough. Section 70[12] of the Patents Act 1977, and section 26 of the Registered Designs Act 1949, make it a statutory tort for a person by circulars, advertisements or otherwise to threaten proceedings for infringement wherever the defendant is unable to prove that the plaintiff's act constitutes an infringement of the defendant's patent or registered design. On the other hand, an assertion by way of mere 'puffing' that the defendant's goods are better, either generally or in specific respects, than the plaintiff's, is not actionable;[13] the courts will not conduct advertising campaigns for business men by deciding on the relative merits of their competing trade products. The leading case is *White v Mellin*:[14]

---

4 *Shapiro v La Morta* (1923) 130 LT 622, CA. The action failed for other reasons.
5 *Ratcliffe v Evans* [1892] 2 QB 524, CA; *Danish Mercantile Co v Beaumont* (1950) 67 RPC 111 (defendant's bare statement that he is the only authorised importer of certain machines).
6 *Riding v Smith* (1876) 1 ExD 91.
7 [1948] Ch 252.
8 *Sheperd v Wakeman* (1662) 1 Sid 79.
9 *Lyne v Nicholls* (1906) 23 TLR 86; cf *Evans v Harlow* (1844) 5 QB 624.
10 *Mentmore Manufacturing Co Ltd v Fomento (Sterling Area) Ltd* (1955) 72 RPC 157, CA.
11 *Colley v Hart* (1890) 44 ChD 179 at 183 (per NORTH J).
12 See *Johnson Electric Industrial Manufacturing Ltd v Mabuchi-Motor KK* [1986] FSR 280.
13 *Young v Macrae* (1862) 3 B & S 264; *Hubbuck & Sons v Wilkinson, Heywood and Clark* [1899] 1 QB 86, CA.
14 [1895] AC 154, HL.

W bought for sale in his shop bottles of infant food made by M and affixed on them, before selling to customers, a label that Dr V's food for infants and invalids (in fact a product of W) was better in particular respects than any other. An action for injurious falsehood failed, on the ground (*inter alia*) that this mere puff was not a disparagement.[15]

The test is whether a reasonable man would take the claim being made in denigration of the plaintiff's goods as one made seriously.[16]

C. FALSE STATEMENT

The plaintiff has the burden of establishing that the statement was untrue.[17] The statement must be a false one about the plaintiff or his property; it is not enough that a false statement resulted in harm to him.

D. PUBLICATION

Because the essence of the tort is the effect produced by the false statement by persons entering into relations with the plaintiff, the falsehood must be published to persons other than the plaintiff.[18] Whether a negligent or accidental publication is sufficient is undecided. The defendant is liable for a republication which is the natural and probable result of his original publication.[19]

E. MALICE

This is undoubtedly the most difficult and controversial element in this tort. There is weighty authority for the view that, until the late nineteenth century, the plaintiff had only to prove an intention on the part of the defendant to disparage—that only (and here the analogy to defamation is close) if the defendant had set up some *prima facie* privilege, for example, that he was protecting his own interest in the property disparaged, did the plaintiff, in order to succeed, have to rebut this privilege by proving malice.[20] However, the cases decided during the last sixty years[1] have so uniformly insisted on the need for the plaintiff to prove malice, that the former view (however desirable) is no longer tenable.[2]

15 Could M have succeeded on some other tort dealt with in this Chapter?
16 *De Beers Abrasive Products Ltd v International General Electric Co of New York Ltd* [1975] 2 All ER 599.
17 Per LORD DAVEY in *Royal Baking Powder Co v Wright, Crossley & Co* (1900) 18 RPC 95 at 99, HL.
18 Cf *Malachy v Soper* (1836) 3 Bing NC 371.
19 *Cellactite and British Uralite v H H Robertson & Co* (1957) Times, 23 July.
20 See Newark, op cit, and the cases there cited.
 1 See *McDonald's Hamburgers v Burger King UK* [1986] FSR 45 and on malice generally see *Clerk & Lindsell* paras 19–11–19–14.
 2 In *Loudon v Ryder (No 2)* [1953] Ch 423 [1953] 1 All ER 1005, the plaintiff, in her action for slander of title, claimed in the usual way for relief by injunction or otherwise. Although her action failed through want of malice on the part of the defendant, the court nevertheless granted her a declaration that she, and not the defendant, was entitled to the property in issue. Similarly, it was held in *Reuter (R J) Co Ltd v Mulhens* [1954] Ch 50 at 75, CA (per EVERSHED, MR), that such an order might be made 'where the court may think it appropriate to state, in the form of a declaration, its conclusion upon the title of the plaintiff which the defendant has in good faith challenged and continues to challenge'.

Even so, it is difficult to define 'malice' in this context. It has been variously defined as 'improper motive',[3] an intention to injure,[4] or want of honest belief in the truth of the statement.[5] What is significant is that, usually, the courts have not preferred any one of these definitions to the exclusion of the others.[6] Thus, the House of Lords in *White v Mellin* held that either an intention to injure or knowledge of the falsity of the statement would be enough.[7]

It is submitted that LORD COLLERIDGE, LCJ, laid down the correct guiding principle in *Halsey v Brotherhood*:[8]

> although it injures and is untrue ... it is a statement that the defendant has a right to make, unless, besides its untruth and besides its injury, express malice is proved, that is to say, want of *bona fides* or the presence of *mala fides*.

The plaintiff may discharge his burden of proving this element of bad faith in any one of several ways. He does so by proving that the defendant made the statement knowing it to be false, or that he made it recklessly, careless whether it was true or false.[9] A defendant who is shown to have been actuated by ill-will, will be held 'malicious'. He will be liable if his purpose was to damage the plaintiff's business, even, it seems, though he was also acting for the benefit of his own interests.[10] It seems that if the defendant knew his statement to be untrue this is enough—the plaintiff does not also have to prove that the defendant intended (or even knew) that the statement be disparaging.[11]

London Ferro-Concrete Co, Ltd v Justicz affords a typical example of a plaintiff's successful discharge of his burden of proving malice:[12]

> The defendant wrote to a firm of contractors that the plaintiff (who was his competitor for a sub-contract with the firm) used 'inadequate' methods of work. The court held that the defendant knew his statement to be untrue and he was held liable in injurious falsehood.

---

3 Per MAUGHAM J, in *Balden v Shorter* [1933] Ch 427, at 430, [1933] All ER Rep 249 at 250.

4 *Stewart v Young* (1870) LR 5 CP, 122 at 127 (per MONTAGUE SMITH J).

5 Per SCRUTTON LJ in *Greers Ltd v Pearman and Corder, Ltd* (1922) 39 RPC 406 at 417, CA.

6 Indeed, *British Ry Traffic and Electric Co v CRC Co and London County Council* [1922] 2 KB 260, is one of the few cases where the court has held that some particular type of these variants of malice has to be proved; no case where such a holding was essential to the decision is known.

7 The *ratio decidendi* of the judgment of LORD HERSCHELL, LC [1895] AC 154, at 160; cf ATKIN, LJ, in *Shapiro v La Morta* (1923), 130 LT 622 at 628, CA: SCRUTTON, LJ, in *Greers, Ltd v Pearman and Corder Ltd* (1922) 39 RPC 406 at 417-8, CA.

8 (1881) 19 ChD 386 at 388, CA; cf *Wren v Weild* (1869) LR 4 QB 213.

9 Per ATKIN LJ, in *Shapiro v La Morta* (1923) 130 LT 622 at 628, CA.

10 This is the *ratio decidendi* of *Joyce v Motor Surveys Ltd* [1948] Ch 252, and p 127, ante (where the defendant wanted to make his property saleable with vacant possession) and is supported by the judgment of COLLINS MR, in *Alcott v Millar's Karri and Jarrah Forests, Ltd* (1904) 91 LT 722 at 723, CA. Cf *Mentmore Manufacturing Co Ltd v Fomento (Sterling Area) Ltd* (1955) 72 RPC 157.

11 *Wilts United Dairies Ltd v Thomas Robinson, Sons & Co Ltd* [1957] RPC 220; affd (but this point not considered) [1958] RPC 94, CA.

12 (1951) 68 RPC 261, CA.

F. DAMAGE

The plaintiff must prove that the false statement caused him pecuniary loss.[13] A debatable point has been whether the requirement that special damage has to be proved[14] can be discharged by showing general loss of custom without adducing evidence that particular customers have withdrawn their business in consequence of the falsehood. Whether evidence of general loss of business will be sufficient depends on 'the nature and circumstances of the falsehood', for example, the plaintiff cannot be expected to produce individuals who have been affected by a statement in a newspaper, and evidence of general business loss will in such a case be admitted.[15] The same rule has been extended to a circular to customers, where, in the circumstances, the circular was reasonably likely to cause a falling off of business.[16] On the other hand, a plaintiff failed who complained that the defendants had stated in their newspaper that his house was haunted, but who neither produced witnesses giving evidence that the statement had influenced them to the detriment of the plaintiff, nor showed that the house had depreciated in value as a result of it.[17] The expenses of bringing litigation in order to remove a cloud on the title placed by the defendant's statement are special damages.[18]

These common-law rules of damage have been modified by the Defamation Act 1952, section 3 of which enacts:

> In an action for slander of title, slander of goods or other malicious falsehood, it shall not be necessary to allege or prove special damage—(a) if the words upon which the action is founded are calculated to cause pecuniary damage to the plaintiff and are published in writing or other permanent form;[19] or (b) if the said words are calculated to cause pecuniary damage to the plaintiff in respect of any office, profession, calling, trade or business[20] held or carried on by him at the time of the publication.

In the large majority of instances of this tort, it will now no longer be necessary to prove special damage.[1] This is especially important in view of the doubt whether an injunction could be obtained before the Act where damage was merely likely to accrue.[2]

---

13 *Ajello v Worsley* [1898] 1 Ch 274; *Shapiro v La Morta* (1923) 130 LT 622, CA. When the damage complained of is physical injury, this tort is presumably not applicable, but *Wilkinson v Downton* [1897] 2 QB 57, must be relied on; cf *Guay v Sun Publishing Co Ltd* [1952] 2 DLR 479; affd [1953] 3 DLR 577.
14 *Malachy v Soper* (1836) 3 Bing NC 371, decided that the tort is not actionable *per se*.
15 *Ratcliffe v Evans* [1892] 2 QB 524 at 533, CA.
16 *Worsley & Co Ltd v Cooper* [1939] 1 All ER 290; contra, *Lyne v Nicholls* (1906) 23 TLR 86.
17 *Barrett v Associated Newspapers Ltd* (1907) 23 TLR 666, CA
18 *Elborow v Allen* (1622) Cro Jac 642.
19 This includes broadcasting.
20 No doubt these words will have the same meaning here as in defamation, see Ch 23, post.
 1 A plaintiff who relies on s 3 is not allowed also to prove special damage unless he has pleaded it: *Calvet v Tomkies* [1963] 3 All ER 610, CA.
 2 *Dunlop Pneumatic Tyre Co Ltd v Maison Talbot* (1904) 20 TLR 579, CA; cf *White v Mellin* [1895] AC 154 at 163–4, 167, HL. In *Fielding v Variety Incorporated* [1967] 2 QB 841, [1967] 2 All ER 497, CA. LORD DENNING stated that damages for injured feelings were not recoverable for the tort of injurious falsehood.

G. DEFENCES

In those circumstances where a defendant in defamation could plead legislative immunity or absolute privilege, eg statements in judicial proceedings,[3] the same defence would no doubt be available here. Formerly, it might have been apposite to say that the defences of qualified privilege in defamation were similarly applicable, but the present insistence on malice in this tort makes it irrelevant any longer to consider that point.

H. INJURIOUS FALSEHOOD AND DEFAMATION

There are clear similarities between injurious falsehood and the related tort of defamation.[4] But the former is more limited in scope and concerns a person's business interests alone, and the temptation to fall into the trap of regarding the two torts even in relation to business reputation as coterminous must be avoided; the argument might run that in the one the property is defamed, in the other its owner. It is true that some facts might constitute both torts: the statement that a brewer's beer is adulterated is at once an attack upon his business reputation and a disparagement of his product. Yet the torts are substantially different.[5]

1 In defamation, truth is a defence if the defendant proves it; in injurious falsehood, the plaintiff must prove the untruth.
2 In defamation, the plaintiff has to prove malice only if he is rebutting a qualified privilege set up by the defendant; in injurious falsehood, it has been submitted that the plaintiff always has to prove malice.
3 Slander may sometimes be actionable *per se* where an oral falsehood would not be.
4 An action for defamation does not survive the death of either plaintiff or defendant.
5 Above all, defamation fails unless the plaintiff's reputation is besmirched; injurious falsehood will lie even if his reputation is untarnished—the disparagement of the property or other valuable interest is the key interest protected.

---

3 Ch 25, post.
4 See ch 24, post.
5 And see *Hatchard v Mège* (1887) 18 QBD 771.

Chapter 9

Unlawful interference with trade[1]

Allen v Flood[2] established the ground rules for liability in tort for interference with economic interests other than by way of false representations. A person has no right to pursue his trade or livelihood; he merely enjoys a freedom to promote his business and financial interests which the law must reconcile with the equivalent freedoms enjoyed by all his fellows. Where the conduct of one person damages the business interests of another, interferes with his freedom to advance his trade or livelihood, the '... existence of a bad motive, in the case of an act which is not otherwise illegal, will not convert that act into a civil wrong.'[3] For nearly a century subsequent to *Allen v Flood* development of tort liability for interference with trade was sporadic. There appeared to be a haphazard list of torts, inducing breach of contract, interference with contracts, conspiracy, intimidation and random others. LORD DIPLOCK has now enunciated a 'genus' tort, '... interfering with the trade or business of another person by doing unlawful acts.'[4] The other economic torts, he suggests, are merely 'species' of this 'genus' tort.

Two points should be grasped:

1 The underlying principle of English law today is undoubtedly that unlawful acts interfering with economic interests are *prima facie* tortious. This principle links the 'false representation' torts with the 'general' economic torts discussed in this chapter.[5] And in defining unlawful acts the courts over the whole spectrum of the economic torts will take into account that while free competition still underlies our economy, fair competition is seen as equally important.
2 Not all the 'general' economic torts can be said to derive from LORD DIPLOCK's 'genus' tort of unlawful interference. Nor is the scope of the 'genus' tort yet clear. Conspiracy remains an anomalous tort in this field. Direct inducement of breach of contract is probably a separate and independent tort.

SECTION I. CONSPIRACY

The tort of conspiracy takes two forms. It is committed:

1 See generally—Carty 'Intentional Violations of Economic Interests: The Limits of Common Law Liability' (1988) 104 LQR (forthcoming); and P Elias and K Ewing 'Economic Torts and Labour Law: Old Principles and New Feasibilities' [1982] CLJ 321.
2 [1898] AC 1, HL.
3 Per LORD HERSCHELL AT 92.
4 *Merkur Island Shipping Corpn v Laughton* [1983] 2 AC 570 at 608, [1983] 2 All ER 189 at 196.
5 See Heydon 'The Future of the Economic Torts' (1975) 12 UWAL Rev 1 and Carty op cit.

1 when two or more persons combine to do an unlawful act, or to do a lawful act by unlawful means; and

2 when two or more persons combine wilfully to injure another in his trade, and damage to his trade results.[6]

The first form of conspiracy is probably superfluous for if unlawful means[7] are used to interfere in trade the 'genus' tort of unlawful interference in trade will often be committed. The second is anomalous for it contradicts the fundamental assumption in *Allen v Flood* that motive alone cannot make illegal otherwise legal conduct. It can be justified only as 'a crude (and arbitrary) method of attacking an abuse of market power.'[8] In *Lonrho Ltd v Shell Petroleum Co Ltd (No 2)*[9] the House of Lords recognised conspiracy as a 'highly anomalous cause of action' but considered it too well established to be discarded.

A. COMBINATION

The requirement for combination poses little difficulty in the main.[10] The 'antique fiction' that husband and wife were one person in the eyes of the common law no longer prevents spouses being liable together for the tort of conspiracy.[11] Directors and their company may conspire together.[12] Where the combination takes the form of a conspiracy to do an unlawful act it is essential to establish that the act which is the aim of the conspiracy is in fact illegal. In *Marrinan v Vibart*[13] the facts were these: M pleaded that V and X, policemen, conspired to make false defamatory statements about him to the Director of Public Prosecutions, and to give false evidence at the Old Bailey and at a later enquiry by the Masters of his Inn. None of these three statements could ever form the subject of a civil action because of the absolute privilege for judicial proceedings.

It was held that there was no cause of action in conspiracy, because the acts which allegedly caused the damage were not unlawful in any form of civil action.

The judgment illustrates that 'unlawful act' conspiracy is not necessarily limited to interference with economic interests, but has little import. Had the statements not been privileged the defendants would have been liable as joint tortfeasors without the need to add a claim in conspiracy.

Combinations with which the tort of conspiracy is concerned may take various designs: of traders in order to ward off the competition of a rival trader,[14] of trade union officials for the purpose of compelling an employer

6 *Quinn v Leathem* [1901] AC 495, HL.
7 Unless there are acts sufficient to constitute unlawful means for the purposes of conspiracy but insufficient to ground an action in the 'genus' tort of unlawful interference with trade; see post at p 146 et seq.
8 See Carty op cit. And see *Clerk and Lindsell* para 15.21 which pertinently suggests that a combination of two street corner grocers is unlikely to be more oppressive to competitors than the actions of a supermarket chain in single ownership.
9 [1982] AC 173, [1981] 2 All ER 456, HL.
10 See *Clerk and Lindsell* para 15.22 discussing the problems re employer 'conspiring' with employees.
11 *Midland Bank Trust Co Ltd v Green (No 3)* [1982] Ch 529, [1981] 3 All ER 744.
12 *Belmont Finance Corpn Ltd v Williams Furniture Ltd* [1979] Ch 250, [1979] 1 All ER 118.
13 [1963] 1 QB 528, [1962] 3 All ER 380, CA.
14 *Mogul SS Co v McGregor, Gow & Co* [1892] AC 25, HL. Action failed.

to dismiss a non-union man,[15] of wholesalers and distributors against a retailer in order to crush opposition to their policy of supplying newspapers to those setting up new businesses in areas which existing retailers thought to be adequately catered for,[16] of trade union officers and employers against a rival employer to further monopolistic conditions which would lead to better conditions for members of the union,[17] of an employers' federation and a trade union to deprive a worker belonging to another trade union of his job in order to promote collective bargaining in the industry concerned,[18] of employees against their employer threatening a strike unless he dismissed a worker belonging to another union,[19] of members of a theatre audience to hiss an actor off the stage:[20] the courts have had to decide whether these varied combinations have, on the particular facts, constituted actionable conspiracy.

B. THE PURPOSE OF THE DEFENDANTS

Although perhaps no branch of the law of torts contains a higher proportion of House of Lords cases than conspiracy, the principles can be shortly stated. In *Crofter Hand Woven Harris Tweed Co Ltd v Veitch*:[1]

The appellants produced tweed cloth in the Outer Hebrides. Only the weaving of their cloth took place on the island; they imported yarn from the mainland. Other firms had their cloth spun as well as woven on the island. The respondents V and M were trade union officials of the union to which most of the spinners employed in the island mills belonged. Employers of these men informed V and M that the competition of the appellants prevented them from raising wages. The respondents (who were assumed by some of their Lordships to be acting in combination with the millowners) instructed dockers at the island's port to refuse to handle yarn imported from the mainland consigned to the appellants and cloth made by them which they desired to export. Without breaking their contracts of employment the dockers obeyed. The appellants sought to stop this embargo on the ground that it was an actionable conspiracy. They failed, because the House of Lords held that the predominant purpose of the combination was the legimate promotion of the interests of the combiners.

The tort of conspiracy is thus committed only when the predominant purpose of the defendants' combination is deliberately to inflict damage on the plaintiff.[2] Until 1981 the requirement that the defendant's predominant purpose be to injure the plaintiff was thought to apply only to the second form of conspiracy, 'simple' conspiracy where no unlawful means are employed to damage the plaintiff's interests. The House of Lords in *Lonrho Ltd v Shell*

---

15 *Quinn v Leathem* [1901] AC 495, HL. Action succeeded.
16 *Sorrell v Smith* [1925] AC 700, HL. Action failed.
17 *Crofter Hand Woven Harris Tweed Co Ltd v Veitch* [1942] AC 435, [1942] 1 All ER 142, HL. At least one member of the House of Lords (VISCOUNT SIMON, at p 439) thought that the employers were not parties to the combination. Action failed.
18 *Reynolds v Shipping Federation Ltd* [1924] 1 Ch 28. Action failed.
19 *White v Riley* [1921] 1 Ch 1, CA. Action failed.
20 *Gregory v Duke of Brunswick* (1844) 6 Man & G 953. Action succeeded.
 1 [1942] AC 435, [1942] 1 All ER 142, HL.
 2 Ibid at 445, 452, 478, 490, 493.

Petroleum Co Ltd (No 2)[3] held otherwise. The defendants breached sanctions orders against the illegal regime in Rhodesia substantially increasing their profits at the plaintiff's expense. Rejecting the claim in conspiracy the House of Lords found that even if unlawful means were used to further the conspiracy no liability arises in conspiracy unless the defendants acted '... for the purpose not of protecting their own interests but of injuring the interests of the plaintiff.'[4]

Where the defendants' predominant purpose is injury to the plaintiff it will not avail them that they have the subsidiary interest of protecting their own interests. If the predominant purpose is to protect the legitimate trade interests of the defendants, then there is no actionable conspiracy although a subsidiary purpose is to damage the plaintiff. The defendants' legitimate interests extend beyond material ones: if trade union officers further a purpose which is not calculated to improve the financial state of their members but which is honestly believed by them to be desirable and has in fact the support of their members, eg officers of a musicians' union opposing colour discrimination among dance-hall patrons, this is a legitimate interest.[5] Beyond that the meaning of 'legitimate' is not clear: perhaps a combination for the purpose of making the plaintiff pay a debt owed by him to the defendant union, by securing that he should otherwise be deprived of work is an example of an 'illegitimate' interest.[6] Once the *bona fides* of the defendants is established, it is irrelevant that the damage inflicted to secure the purpose is disproportionately severe.[7] The defendants are not liable merely because they were actuated by spite or ill-will.[8] On the other hand, 'it is sufficient if all the various combining parties have their own legitimate trade or business interests to gain, even though these interests may be of differing kinds'.[9]

It is uncertain whether the burden of proving the purpose of damaging the plaintiff is on the plaintiff. Lords Wright[10] and Porter[11] held that the burden is on the plaintiff, Viscount Maugham held that the burden is on the defendant and the other two law lords were silent. It is submitted that the view of the majority is to be preferred[12] and is in accord with earlier House of Lords decisions.[13]

---

3 [1982] AC 173, [1981] 2 All ER 456.

4 At 189, and 464 respectively; on the extent to which *Lonrho* applies to all forms of 'unlawful means' conspiracy, see *Clerk and Lindsell* 15–23.

5 *Scala Ballroom (Wolverhampton) Ltd v Ratcliffe* [1958] 3 All ER 220, CA. After *Rookes v Barnard*, this decision might be different unless no breach of contract was threatened.

6 *Giblan v National Amalgamated Labourers Union of Great Britain and Ireland* [1903] 2 KB 600, CA.

7 Per Viscount Simon, at 447; but see *Trollope v London Building Trades Federation* (1895), 72 LT 342, CA.

8 Per Lord Wright, at 471: I cannot see how the pursuit of a legitimate practical object can be vitiated by glee at the adversary's expected discomfiture; cf. Viscount Simon, at 444–5; Viscount Maugham, at 450. Yet the court must inquire into the state of knowledge of the defendants whenever it is relevant for the ascertainment of their purpose: *Huntley v Thorton*, [1957] 1 All ER 234; *Bird v O'Neill* [AC 907, [1960] 3 All ER 254, PC.

9 Viscount Maugham, *Crofter Hand Woven Harris Tweed Co Ltd v Veitch* [1942] AC 435, at 453 [1942] 1 All ER 142; cf. the judgment of Evatt J, in *McKerman v Fraser* (1931) 46 CLR 343 (High Ct Australia).

10 At 471.

11 At 495.

12 And so applied in *Huntley v Thornton* [1957] 1 All ER 234.

13 Eg *Sorrell v Smith* [1925] AC 700, HL.

C. JUSTIFICATION

Wherever the burden of proof lies, it is clear that the scope of justification in conspiracy is wider than in the other 'general' economic torts. In conspiracy the defendant who proves that his object was to further his legitimate trade interests succeeds; as we shall see, that does not in itself justify procuring a breach of contract. In practice, those combining will almost always be able to satisfy the Court that they were actuated by self-interest. It follows, therefore, that conspiracy is an unimportant tort in this field of economic affairs: the chances of a successful action (where no alternative cause of action would have lain) are remote. This was the inevitable result of the judicial reluctance to look beyond the purposes of the parties to the economic consequences at large of the conduct of the parties. The justification for this has been expressed by LORD WRIGHT as follows:[14]

> '... we live in a competitive or acquisitive society, and the English common law may have felt that it was beyond its power to fix by any but the crudest distinctions the metes and bounds which divide the rightful from the wrongful use of the actor's own freedom, leaving the precise application in any particular case to the jury or judge of fact. If further principles of regulation or control are to be introduced, that is matter for the legislature.'

There are indications that judicial attitudes to competition are changing. Greater emphasis is placed on fairness. Nevertheless the House of Lords in *Lonrho* clearly indicated its distaste for the tort of conspiracy and its role in the sphere of economic relations is now minimal.

SECTION 2. INDUCING BREACH OF CONTRACT

For well over a century a distinct tort of inducing breach of contract has been recognised.[15] The tort is committed when the defendant knowingly induces a third party to break his contract with the plaintiff, and loss to the plaintiff results therefrom. It is not necessary to prove that any unlawful means were employed by the defendant to induce the breach of contract where that breach was the result of *direct* persuasion or intervention by the defendant.[16] Hence inducing breach of contract cannot be regarded as a 'species' of any 'genus' tort of unlawful interference with trade. But the original tort of inducing breach of contract has been extended in various ways:

1 Indirect procurement of a breach of contract may be actionable but only if unlawful means are used.
2 Interference with contract short of procuring an actual breach of contract may be actionable, once again on proof of unlawful means.
3 And LORD DENNING has suggested a broader tort of interfering with contractual relations may exist.[17]

It will be suggested that the first two 'extensions' of inducing breach of

14 *Crofter Hand Woven Harris Tweed Co Ltd v Veitch* (supra) at 472.
15 *Lumley v Gye* (1853) 2 E & B 216.
16 See *D C Thomson & Co Ltd v Deakin* [1952] Ch 646, [1952] 2 All ER 361.
17 *Torquay Hotel Co Ltd v Cousins* [1969] 2 Ch 106 at 137–8.

contract are in fact species of the genus tort of unlawful interference[18] and that the DENNING 'tort' of interference with contractual relations as such without the need to establish unlawful means is non-existent.[19]

An action for enticement of a servant from his master's service was established by the sixteenth century.[20] A separate and generally applicable tort of inducing breach of contract without lawful justification or excuse dates from *Lumley v Gye*.[1]

The court held on plea of demurer that the following facts could constitute a tort.

A singer was under a contract to sing at the plaintiff's theatre but was not the plaintiff's servant. She was induced by the defendant, who knew[2] of this contract, to break it in order to sing at his theatre instead.

This new principle was soon extended from contracts of service to contracts generally; and *dicta* in some cases indeed contemplated its application to advantageous business relations not embodied in contracts[3] but *Allen v Flood*[4] restricted its scope to interferences with actual contracts.

The elements of this tort must now be examined.

A. KINDS OF CONTRACT

Any valid and enforceable contract can found an action upon subsequent interference with it:[5] meagre evidence of its terms is enough.[6] Interference with void contracts is not actionable.[7]

B. BREACH OF CONTRACT

Dicta from earlier this century[8] that the breach must be such as goes to the root of the contract are no longer supportable. Any breach of contract even one that is not actionable in certain respects may now be sufficient. In *Torquay Hotel Co Ltd v Cousins*[9] an injunction was granted against the defendants who, in the course of industrial action, were attempting to stop a supplier

---

18 See Carty op cit.

19 See *Clerk and Lindsell* para 15–05.

20 Separate torts of enticing and harbouring servants were abolished by the Administration of Justice Act 1982.

1 (1853) 2 E & B 216.

2 The plaintiff failed at the subsequent trial because the jury found that the defendant was unaware of the contract.

3 *Temperton v Russell* [1893] 1 QB 715, CA (eg preventing the plaintiff from making a contract); *Bowen v Hall* (1881) 6 QBD 333, CA.

4 [1898] AC 1, HL, *Sorrell v Smith* [1925] AC 700, HL. See ante at pp 103 and 133.

5 Cf *DC Thomson & Co Ltd v Deakin* [1952] Ch 646 at 677 (per EVERSHED MR); [1952] 2 All ER 361, CA, and *Findlay v Blaylock*, 1937 SC 21.

6 *Daily Mirror Newspapers Ltd v Gardner* [1968] 2 QB 762, [1968] 2 All ER 163, CA.

7 *Shears v Mendeloff* (1914) 30 WLR 342 (infant's contract); *Said v Butt* [1920] 3 KB 497 (mistake); *Joe Lee Ltd v Lord Dalmeny* [1927] 1 Ch 300 (gaming); *British Motor Trade Association v Gray*, 1951 SC 586 (contract void in restraint of trade—*obiter* per LORD KEITH).

8 Per PORTER J in *De Jetley Marks v Lord Greenwood* [1936] 1 All ER 863 at 872; doubted by EVERSHED MR in *D C Thomson & Co Ltd v Deakin* [1952] Ch 646 at 689–90.

9 [1969] 2 Ch 106, [1969] 1 All ER 522, CA; and see *Clerk and Lindsell* para 15–04.

fulfilling his contract with the plaintiff. The contract expressly exempted either party from liability for events beyond their control, including labour disputes, which led to a failure to perform. The Court of Appeal interpreted the clause as '... an exception from liability for non-performance rather than an exception from the obligation to perform'.[10] Thus the defendant's conduct still constituted inducing a breach of that latter obligation.

Many actions of this kind are, therefore, concerned largely with interpreting the contract in order to decide whether there has been a breach. Thus, in *Hivac Ltd v Park Royal Scientific Instruments Ltd.:*[11]

> The plaintiffs had been the only English makers of midget valves for hearing aids. Setting up in competition, the defendants employed on this work some of the staff of the plaintiffs in their spare time. It was held that an implied term must be read into the engagement by the plaintiffs of this staff that the latter should not break their fidelity to the plaintiffs by doing an act which would injure the plaintiffs' business, and, in view of the fact that the plaintiffs had a monopoly of this type of work and those members of the staff had a monopoly of the skill, an injunction restraining the inducement of breach of contract should be granted.

On the other hand, if a contract is determinable by either party at pleasure, it is not actionable if the defendant induces a party to determine that contract,[12] for there has been no breach but merely a lawful determination of the contract.

Inducing a strike where there is a no-strike clause in the contract is inducing breach of contract.[13] Giving notice to terminate a contract lawfully cannot give rise to a tort, but most strike notices are not notices to terminate but notice of forthcoming breaches of contract and so union officials inducing strike action are open to liability in the tort.[14] The 'immunities' afforded by statute, albeit now in an attenuated form, are discussed later in this chapter.[15]

Even though the defendant is not responsible for the initial breach of a contract he will be liable if he is responsible for continuing the breach of a still subsisting contract.[16] So, where the defendant had engaged a servant in ignorance of an existing contract of service between the servant and the plaintiff, he was held liable for having continued to employ him after learning the facts.[17]

But is it still necessary to prove a breach of an obligation under the contract? In *Torquay Hotel Co Ltd v Cousins*[18] LORD DENNING contended

---

10 Per RUSSELL LJ at 143
11 [1946] Ch 169, [1946] 1 All ER 350, CA.
12 *McManus v Bowes* [1938] 1 KB 98, [1937] 3 All ER 227, CA.
13 *Rookes v Barnard* [1964] AC 1129, [1964] 1 All ER 367, HL.
14 See *Clerk and Lindsell* para 15.04.
15 At pp149–50.
16 *Smithies v National Association of Operative Plasterers* [1909] 1 KB 310, CA.; cf *Denaby and Cadeby Main Collieries Ltd v Yorkshire Miners Association* [1906] AC 384, HL. There must be a continuing obligation at the time of the breach—in what circumstances then, if any, will the tort be committed if A agrees to sell his house to B and C who knows that A has broken this agreement, buys it from A? For the availability of an injunction see p146, post.
17 *Blake v Lanyon* (1795) 6 Term Rep 221; *Fred Wilkins & Brothers Ltd v Weaver* [1915] 2 Ch 322; cf *Read v Friendly Society of Operative Stonemasons* [1902] 2 KB 88 at 95 (per DARLING J); on appeal, [1902] 2 KB 732, CA. And see *Jones Brothers (Hunstanton) Ltd v Stevens* [1955] 1 QB 275, [1954] 3 All ER 677, CA at p144, post.
18 See supra.

that even if the exemption clause in the contract resulted in there being no breach of contract the defendant remained liable for 'interfering' with the contract. 'Preventing or hindering' performance of a contract was sufficient. There is little support for a tort of such width.[19] Preventing or hindering performance of a contract by unlawful means is actionable as *Dimbleby v NUJ*[20] illustrates. Journalists employed by the plaintiff refused in breach of their contracts of employment to prepare copy. As a result the plaintiff faced severe difficulties in fulfilling his contract with the publishing company. Nevertheless the plaintiff managed to procure alternative copy. SIR JOHN DONALDSON MR held the NUJ liable for unlawful interference with the plaintiff's contractual obligations. Hindrance where unlawful means were employed was sufficient. *Dimbleby & Sons Ltd v NUJ* should be seen as an example of the 'genus' tort of unlawful interference with trade rather than an extension of the distinct tort of inducing breach of contract.[1]

C. KNOWLEDGE OF THE CONTRACT

The defendant must be shown to have had actual or constructive knowledge,[2] at least of the existence[3] of the contract which has been broken.[4] The courts have in recent years been very willing to conclude that the defendant had sufficient knowledge to be aware that he was inducing a breach.[5]

D. 'INDUCEMENT' AND 'INTERFERENCE'

The classic tort of directly inducing a breach of contract established in *Lumley v Gye*[6] has developed apparently in a much broader tort with the emphasis on interference with contractual relations. In *Thomson & Co Ltd v Deakin*[7] JENKINS LJ enumerated the various forms of the tort as he saw it in 1952. These are:

19 See *Clerk and Lindsell* para 15–05; and Carty op cit.
20 [1984] 1 All ER 117, [1984] 1 WLR 67; and see *Shipping Co Uniform Inc v ITWJ* [1985] ICR 245, [1985] IRLR 71.
1 Or as some sort of 'half-way' tort of unlawful interference with contract; see Carty op cit.
2 *British Industrial Plastics Ltd v Ferguson* [1940] 1 All ER 479, HL; in *Lumley v Gye* LORD CAMPBELL directed the jury that 'if the defendant *bona fide* believed that the agreement with the plaintiff had ceased to be binding upon Miss Wagner the *scienter* was not proved and the defendant would be entitled to the verdict', whereupon the jury found for the defendant.
3 He need not know its terms; *J T Stratford Ltd v Lindley* [1965] AC 269, [1964] 3 All ER 102, HL; *Greig v Insole* [1978] 3 All ER 449.
4 *Long v Smithson* (1918) 118 LT 678 Div Ct; *British Homophone Ltd v Kunz and Crystallate Gramophone Record Manufacturing Co Ltd* [1935] All ER Rep 627; in *D C Thomson & Co Ltd v Deakin* [1952] Ch 646 at 687 (per EVERSHED MR); [1952] 2 All ER 361, CA, it is suggested that 'common knowledge about the way business is conducted' would be sufficient constructive knowledge; *Cunard Steamship Co Ltd v Stacey* [1955] 1 Lloyd's Rep 247 (official of seaman's union deemed to know seaman's contract would conform with Merchant Shipping Act 1894). It is enough if the defendant deliberately disregards means of knowledge: *Emerald Construction Co v Lowthian* [1966] 1 All ER 1013.
5 *J T Stratford Ltd v Lindley* [1965] AC 269 at 307, [1964] 3 All ER 102, HL.
6 (1853) 2 E & B 216; see supra at 137.
7 [1952] Ch 646, [1952] 2 All ER 361, CA.

1 direct procurement of a breach of a contract,
2 direct intervention in the contract, for example, disabling a contracting party, and
3 indirect procurement or intervention, for example, secondary industrial action preventing performance of the contract,
4 inconsistent dealings.

Authority establishes that 'interference' in all these four circumstances may be tortious. We shall see that both direct intervention in the contract and indirect procurement or intervention both require proof of unlawful means. Should they better be regarded as 'species' of the embryonic 'genus' tort of unlawful interference with trade?[8]

(1) DIRECT PERSUASION OR PROCUREMENT

Direct persuasion or procurement or inducement applied by the defendant to the contract-breaker is sufficient.[9] If the contract-breaker is a limited company, an approach to some person in the company with actual or ostensible authority to make contracts is required.[10] The issue here seems a straightforward one of causation. There has been much discussion of what has been thought to be a significant distinction between advice and persuasion, but the problem resolves itself into nothing more than whether the breaking of the contract is 'fairly attributable to any such pressure, persuasion or procuration on the part of any of these defendants',[11] and presents just the same difficulties on the facts as other problems of causation in torts:[12] any distinction between advice and persuasion as such is unimportant.[13] For example, a trade union official, who sent to managers of the plaintiffs' public houses a circular questionnaire asking (*inter alia*) for details of the receipts and profits of their houses, was held to have caused the managers to break their contractual obligation not to disclose confidential information; the managers were led to disclose these items because they thought that the defendant's union might ultimately secure them better wages and conditions.[14]

It is important to decide whether the inducement is direct or indirect because if indirect procurement is relied on the breach has to be a necessary consequence and unlawful means have to be used. An inducement may be direct even though a federation transmits it through its members to a contracting party.[15] Where the inducement is direct, it is the other party to the contract, and not the one who is induced, who alone can sue for this tort.[16]

---

8 See Carty op cit; Ellas and Ewing op cit.
9 *Thomson v Deakin* per EVERSHED MR (at 681); JENKINS LJ (at 694).
10 Ibid per EVERSHED MR at 681.
11 Per EVERSHED MR, at 686 (*ratio decidendi*). On the difficulty of deciding whether there is merely a transmission of information, and no inducement, see *Cammellia Tanker Ltd v International Transport Workers Federation* [1976] ICR 274, CA.
12 Eg *Jasperson v Dominion Tobacco Co* [1923] AC 709 PC.
13 *Torquay Hotel Co Ltd v Cousins* [1969] 2 Ch 106 at 147, [1969] 1 All ER 522, CA (per WINN LJ).
14 *Bent's Brewery Co Ltd v Hogan* [1945] 2 All ER 570.
15 *Daily Mirror Newspapers Ltd v Gardner* [1968] 2 QB 762, [1968] 2 All ER 163, CA. In *J T Stratford Ltd v Lindley*, LORD PEARCE alone thought the inducement direct because the employers' association had been notified.
16 *Williams v Hursey* (1959) 103 CLR 30 H Ct Australia. And see *Brekkes v Cattel* [1972] Ch 105, [1971] 1 All ER 1031. The party induced has *locus standi* to obtain a declaration; *Greig v Insole* [1978] 3 All ER 449. If the procurer intentionally damages the party induced he may have a cause of action for unlawful interference; see p 146, post.

(2) DIRECT INTERVENTION

It will be actionable if the defendant intervenes so as to prevent a contracting party from performing his contract, for example, by kidnapping or otherwise restraining him,[17] or by removing from him essential tools.[18] The wrongful act against the one contractor creates a cause of action for interference in the contract of the other. In *GWK Ltd v Dunlop Rubber Co Ltd*:[19]

> A motor car manufacturer had contracted with the plaintiffs that, when he exhibited his car at a motor show, it would have tyres made by the plaintiffs fitted to it. The defendants unlawfully removed the plaintiffs' tyres and substituted their own. That trespass to the car owner's goods created liability to the plaintiffs.

In *D C Thomson & Co Ltd v Deakin* EVERSHED MR[20] limited liability for direct intervention resulting in a breach of contract to tortious acts as in *GWK Co Ltd v Dunlop*. There is some authority that a wrongful act which if effected by the contractor would be a breach of contract is sufficient.[1] Not every breach of a penal statute will be wrongful[2] and some form of unlawful means must always be established thus bringing direct intervention within the 'genus' tort of unlawful interference.

(3) INDIRECT PROCUREMENT

This version of the tort is frequently invoked to stop secondary industrial action. It is committed when the defendant procures a third party to do a wrongful act, normally to breach his contract of employment in order to prevent performance of the main contract. For example, union officials persuade men working for a supplier of parts to a motor car manufacturers to strike, thus preventing their employer from performing his contract with the manufacturers. That conduct involving as it does an unlawful act on the part of the strikers may be actionable at the suit of the manufacturer.

For liability to be established more than 'general exhortations issued in the course of a trade dispute, such as 'stop supplies to A' or 'Treat X as black'[3] must be proved. Such inducements do not necessarily result in a breach of contract. The object might be obtained by lawful means.[4]

But the defendants in *J T Stratford Ltd v Lindley*[5] were found liable.

> S Ltd led out barges on hire to customers. These customers were under a contractual obligation to return the barges to S Ltd's moorings. The defendant union officials instructed their members to break their contracts of employment with S Ltd's customers by not returning the barges. The

---

17 *D C Thomson & Co Ltd v Deakin* [1952] Ch 646 per EVERSHED MR at 678; per JENKIN LJ at 694–5.
18 Ibid per MORRIS LJ at 702.
19 (1926) 42 TLR 376; on appeal 42 TLR 593, CA.
20 Supra at 678.
1   Supra per JENKINS LJ at 694 and *Statnigros v Storhaug & Partners* [1953] CLY 3556 (landlord covenanted with plaintiff tenant to leave open a particular door on Saturday mornings; landlord's agent locked it and held liable in damages on principle of *Lumley v Gye*.)
2   *Lonrho Ltd v Shell Petroleum Co Ltd (No 2)* [1982] AC 173, [1981] 2 All ER 456; see discussion in *Clerk and Lindsell* at para 15–09.
3   *Clerk and Lindsell* para 15–10.
4   *D C Thomson & Co Ltd v Deakin* (supra).
5   [1965] AC 269, [1964] 3 All ER 102.

members obeyed those instructions and did not work the barges back to S Ltd's moorings. The House of Lords held that this amounted to the tort of procuring a breach of the contract between S Ltd and their customers, that the latter should return the barges to S Ltd, for that breach of contract was a necessary consequence of the defendant's conduct.

And in *Falconer v ASLEF*[6] the defendants were held liable to the plaintiff for his hotel expenses incurred when they called railmen out on strike thus preventing the plaintiff from travelling on the ticket he had purchased for a planned journey. The interference with the performance of the contract between British Rail and the plaintiff was found to be a necessary consequence of the defendants' actions. Indirect procurement is actionable only on proof of unlawful means. While this will often consist of breaches of contract by a third party, other unlawful means may suffice.[7] The tort of nuisance committed by demonstrators hindering distribution of the plaintiffs' newspapers constituted the necessary unlawful means in *News Group Newspapers v SOGAT '82.*[8]

(4) INCONSISTENT DEALINGS[9]

In *D C Thomson & Co Ltd v Deakin,* JENKINS LJ further stated that 'there seems to be no doubt that if a third party, with knowledge of a contract between the contract breaker and another, had dealings with the contract breaker which the third party knows to be inconsistent with the contract, he has committed an actionable interference'.[10] This is correct,[11] but it is not always simple to decide whether the defendant, in making the inconsistent dealing, has merely taken advantage of the voluntary decision already made of the third party to discontinue his contract, or whether he has in fact been instrumental in bringing about the breach. *British Motor Trade Association v Salvadori* illustrates the point.[12]

> Third parties had entered into covenants with the plaintiffs not to re-sell motor cars except under certain conditions. The defendants had bought some cars from these third parties with a view to re-sale at a profit in circumstances which amounted to a breach of the covenant with the plaintiffs.

Roxborough J held that the defendants had offered a price for a car high enough to cause a man who would not otherwise have broken his covenant to sell it in breach of covenant and that they were therefore liable.[13] He did add, however, that 'any active step taken by a defendant having knowledge of the covenant by which he facilitates a breach of that covenant is enough',

---

6 [1986] IRLR 331 (County Court).
7 *Merkur Island Shipping Corpn v Laughton* [1983] 2 AC 570, [1983] 1 All ER 334.
8 [1987] ICR 181.
9 For critical analysis of this version of the tort see *Clerk and Lindsell* para 15–05 and Carty op cit.
10 At 694; not considered by the other judges.
11 At least if the word 'dealings' is limited to 'the making of a contract'. JENKINS LJ may have intended to include other dealings eg accepting benefits under a contract already made. In *De Francesco v Barnum* (1890) 63 LT 438, an action succeeded against a theatrical manager, who continued to employ show girls after receiving notice of a prior inconsistent contract which they had with the plaintiff.
12 [1949] Ch 556, [1949] 1 All ER 208.
13 At 565.

and that 'a defendant by agreeing to buy, paying for and taking delivery of a motor-car known by him to be on offer in breach of covenant' commits the tort.[14] With this case can be contrasted *Batts Combe Quarry Ltd v Ford*.[15]

> On selling his quarry to the plaintiffs, a father contracted not to assist in setting up any rival quarry in the neighbourhood. His son, the defendant, decided to set up such a quarry, and the father financed him in this enterprise. It was held that the acceptance of this gift by the son was not an actionable interference with the contract of the plaintiff.

E. STATE OF MIND OF THE DEFENDANT

A defendant is liable if he intends to bring about a breach of the contract; it is irrelevant that he did not act with malice in the sense of spite or ill-will.[16] The decision of the Court of Appeal in *Exchange Telegraph Co v Gregory & Co*[17] illustrates:

> The plaintiffs had a monopoly of information about Stock Exchange prices and circulated this information to subscribers who had contracted not to communicate it to others; they also published it in a newspaper, issued six times daily. The defendant, a stockbroker, induced a subscriber to give him information contained in the plaintiffs' circular, and posted it in his own office for the benefit of his clients. He was held liable for interfering with a contract.

If the defendant does an act the substantially certain consequence of which is to bring about a breach of a contract of which he is aware, then he will be presumed to have intended it, and be held liable unless the presumption is rebutted.[18] A negligent interference with a contract does not constitute this tort.[19]

---

14 *British Industrial Plastics Ltd v Ferguson* [1940] 1 All ER 479, HL.
15 [1943] Ch 51, [1942] 2 All ER 639, CA.
16 There are *dicta* in *Lumley v Gye* and *Bowen v Hall* supra, that malice is essential, but later cases such as *Quinn v Leathem*, [1901] AC 495 at 510, HL (per LORD MACNAUGHTON), *South Wales Miners' Federation v Glamorgan Coal Co* [1905] AC 239, HL, and *D C Thomson & Co Ltd v Deakin* supra per EVERSHED MR at 676, have made it abundantly clear that spite or ill-will is not required. Good faith is no defence; *Greig v Insole* [1978] 3 All ER 449.
17 [1896] 1 QB 147, CA; *British Motor Trade Association v Salvadori*, [1949] Ch 556, [1949] 1 All ER 208; *Emerald Construction Co v Lowthian*, [1966] 1 All ER 1013
18 *White v Riley* [1921] 1 Ch 1. And see *Emerald Construction Co v Lowthian* [1966] 1 All ER 1013 at 1019 (per DIPLOCK LJ). Dealing with a plea that the tort is not committed when the defendant has an honest doubt whether he was interfering with the contract, BROWNE-WILKINSON, J held in *Swiss Bank Corporation v Lloyds Bank Ltd* [1979] Ch 548 at 580, [1977] 2 All ER 853 at 877–9 that if a defendant chooses to adopt a course which to his knowledge will undoubtedly interfere with the plaintiff's contract on one view of the law, he must at least show that he was advised and honestly believed he was legally entitled to take that course.
19 *Cattle v Stockton Waterworks Co* (1875) LR 10 QB 453; *La Société Anonyme de Remorquage à Hélice v Bennetts* [1911] 1 KB 243.

F. DAMAGE

It must be proved that the breach of the contract has caused damage, or at least that damage can be inferred from the circumstances.[20]

An illustration of this need to prove damage is furnished by *Jones Brothers (Hunstanton) Ltd v Stevens*:[1]

> The defendant continued to employ a servant, after learning that the servant, in entering into his employment, was breaking his contract with the plaintiffs. It was shown, however, that in any event, the servant would not have returned to the plaintiffs' employment. It was held, therefore, that the plaintiffs' action based on this tort failed—for they had suffered no damage.

G. JUSTIFICATION

It is established that, exceptionally, circumstances may justify interference with contracts. As yet the courts have not laid down any detailed rules for this defence. The *dictum* of ROMER LJ, is widely cited:[2]

> 'regard might be had to the nature of the contract broken; the position of the parties of the contract; the grounds for the breach; the means employed to procure the breach; the relation of the person procuring the breach to the person who breaks the contract; and ... to the object of the person in procuring the breach.'

In that case it was held that the defendants were not justified in calling the miners out on strike in order to keep up the price of coal by which the miners' pay was regulated.[3] The breach by a plaintiff of his contract with the defendant will not justify the defendant in inducing a third party to break his contract with the plaintiff.[4]

Brimelow v Casson is one of the rare cases where the defence succeeded.[5]

> The defendants were representatives of various theatrical unions, and the plaintiff owned a touring theatrical company. The defendants induced a theatre manager to break his contract with the plaintiff because the plaintiff was paying such low wages to his company that some chorus girls were

---

20 *Exchange Telegraph Co v Gregory & Co*, [1896] 1 QB 147, CA; *Goldsoll v Goldman* [1914] 2 Ch 603; on appeal, [1915] 1 Ch 292, CA; *Bents Brewery Co Ltd v Hogan* [1945] 2 All ER 570.

1 [1955] 1 QB 275, [1954] 3 All ER 677, CA.

2 *Glamorgan Coal Co v South Wales Miners Federation* [1903] 2 KB 545 at 574–5, CA, approved by LORD LINDLEY in HL *sub nom South Wales Miners' Federation v Glamorgan Coal Co* [1905] AC 239 at 252.

3 Cf *Temperton v Russell* [1893] 1 QB 715, CA, trade union officials not justified in interfering in order to enforce certain conditions of labour in a particular trade; *Read v Friendly Society of Operative Stonemasons* [1902] 2 KB 88.

4 *Smithies v National Association of Operative Plasterers* [1909] 1 KB 310, CA. Of course if a contract which X has made with Y is so inconsistent with an earlier contract between X and Z that the later contract interfered with the performance of the earlier one, the very act of X in making the contract with Y constitutes a tort. And see the analysis of this defence by GOFF J in *Pritchard v Briggs* [1980] 1 All ER 294 at 326, et seq.

5 [1924] 1 Ch 302; but SIMONDS J, in *Camden Nominees Ltd v Forcey* [1940] Ch 352 at 366, treated that decision as being based on the separate ground of *ex turpi causa non oritur actio* see p 137, ante.

compelled to resort to prostitution. The interest which the defendants had in keeping up the standards of the theatrical profession was held to justify their procuring the breach.

It may be that, if the means whereby the breach is effected are wrongful in themselves, this defence of justification is not available.[6] In any event, it is obvious that the defence is not very wide, and the facts which would absolve the defendants in the tort of conspiracy on the ground that the acts were done for the purpose of protecting the trade interests of the defendants will not constitute justification for the tort of procuring a breach of contract.[7] The interest in maintaining the security of contracts is greater than the interest in protecting free trade.

H. REMEDIES

(1) DAMAGES

Higher damages will often be recoverable in this tort than could be obtained in an action for breach of contract against the contract-breaker.[8]

a The damages will be assessed in the light of the facts as at the date of breach, not when the contract was made.

b Any damage which the defendant intended to cause is recoverable in tort, eg if the defendant intended to make the plaintiff bankrupt.[9]

c The damages may be more extensive than those awarded in contract under the rule of *Hadley v Baxendale*.[10]

d Damages are at large in this tort; thus in *GWK Co Ltd v Dunlop Rubber Co Ltd*[11] the court included compensation for loss of prestige in its award of general damages. In *British Motor Trade Association v Salvadori*, holding that 'the maintenance of fixed prices and the covenant system as an integral feature of that policy is a trade interest which the plaintiffs are entitled to protect against unlawful interference', ROXBURGH J held that the expenses incurred in unravelling and detecting the devices of the defendants for evading the covenant system were recoverable.[12]

Sometimes the action in tort will succeed where that in contract would fail, eg if physical restraint is used, frustration might be pleaded in contract.

---

6 *Camden Nominees Ltd v Forcey* [1940] Ch 352; cf *Green v Button* (1835) 2 Cr M & R 707.
7 See pp 134–6 et seq, ante.
8 Per ERLE CJ in *Lumley v Gye* at 233–4.
9 Ibid.
10 Cf *Gunter v Astor* (1819) 4 Moore CP 12 (enticement of servants by a rival piano manufacturer; although only in breach for one half day, the court rejected a claim that the damages in tort be so restricted, and awarded two years loss of profits).
11 See pp 141–2 ante and *Times* newspaper, 21 January, 1926 and 10 February, 1926.
12 [1949] Ch 556 at 568–9 [1949] 1 All ER 208. (1) There may be other reasons for preferring the action in tort. Complications which arise from the plaintiff's election whether to sue his contractee in deceit or breach of contract will be avoided in this action: see pp 442–3 post. (2) The duty of the plaintiff to mitigate his damage may be less strict when he is the victim of an intentional tort: so held in *Carmen v Fox Film Corporation* (1923) 204 App Div 776 (NY); cf Williams, *Joint Torts* 285 'a plaintiff is never under a duty to mitigate intended damage'. Interesting problems about the effect of satisfaction of a judgment in contract on the claim in tort remain unsolved; cf *Bird v Randall* (1762) 3 Burr 1345.

(2) INJUNCTION

The remedy often sought is that of injunction: as with other torts, an injunction may be refused, although the tort is established.[13] An injunction may lie, although an action for damages fails.[14] On the other hand, an injunction will be refused against a defendant who persuades an employee of the plaintiff to leave his employment and work for the defendant, where the effect of the injunction would be to tie a reluctant employee to the plaintiff.[15] Thus, Lumley failed to recover damages from Gye because Gye was unaware of the contract, but he obtained an injunction against him.[16] An injunction may also be granted to prevent conduct which will lead to a breach of contract although it is not sufficient 'interference' for the tort action in damages—the basis for such an injunction is that the 'proprietary interest'[17] may be protected.[18]

The common practice has been for plaintiffs initially to apply for an injunction ex parte, pending hearing the defendants the court will often grant an interlocutory injunction on the basis of the plaintiffs affidavit. This happened for example in *J T Stratford & Son Ltd v Lindley*[19] and *Torquay Hotel Co Ltd v Cousins*.[20] The court must be satisfied that the balance of convenience favours granting the injunction.[1]

SECTION 3. UNLAWFUL INTERFERENCE WITH TRADE

The precise extent to which business and trading interests are protected against actions which do not constitute either conspiracy or interference with contractual obligations remain unclear. LORD DIPLOCK's 'genus' tort '... interfering with the trade or business of another person by doing unlawful acts'[2] awaits definition and confirmation. Intimidation, the use of unlawful

---

13 Eg *Rely-a-Bell Burglar and Fire Alarm Co Ltd v Eisler* [1926] Ch 609, where the effect of granting an injunction would have been to prevent the servant from working at all, an injunction against the new employer who enticed him was refused.

14 In *Esso Petroleum Co Ltd v Kingswood Motors (Addlestone) Ltd* [1974] QB 142, [1973] 3 All ER 1057, a mandatory injunction was ordered requiring the reconveyance of a garage sold in breach of a solus tie agreement.

15 *Lotus Cars Ltd v Jaguar Cars Ltd* (1982), *unreported*.

16 *Lumley v Wagner* (1852) 1 De G M & G 604.

17 Cf KITTO J in *A-G for New South Wales v Perpetual Trustee Co Ltd* (1951) 85 CLR 237, at 297: 'a person has a right, a right in *rem* in respect of the contractual rights, the rights in *personam*, which he possesses as against the other party to his contract'.

18 *Manchester Ship Canal Co v Manchester Racecourse Co* [1901] 2 Ch 37, CA, applying *Lumley v Wagner* where A agreed to sell land to B, and then contracted to sell to C, injunction granted to B restraining C from performing his contract; *Earl Sefton v Tophams Ltd and Capital and Counties Property Co Ltd* [1965] Ch 1140, [1965] 3 All ER 1 reversed on other grounds, [1967] 1 AC 50, [1966] 1 All ER 1039, HL. Injunctions are freely given under this head when disclosure of trade secrets is involved: *Printers and Finishers Ltd Holloway* [1964] 3 All ER 731 and 738 n. And see *Swiss Bank Corporation v Lloyds Bank Ltd* [1979] Ch 548, [1977] 2 All ER 853 and *Pritchard v Briggs* [1980] Ch 338, [1980] 1 All ER 294.

19 [1965] AC 269 at 307.

20 [1969] 2 Ch 106, [1969] 1 All ER 522, CA.

 1 *NWL v Woods* [1979] 3 All ER 614, [1979] 1 WLR 1294, ML. On the factors to be considered in deciding whether a court in its discretion grants an interlocutory injunction, see *Hadmor Productions Ltd v Hamilton* [1983] 1 AC 191, [1982] 1 All ER 1042, HL and *American Cyanamid Co v Ethicon Ltd* [1975] AC 396, [1975] 1 All ER 504, HL. *Dimbleby & Sons Ltd v NUJ* [1984] 1 All ER 751, [1984] 1 WLR 427, HL.

 2 *Merkur Island Shipping Corpn v Laughton* [1983] 2 AC 570 at 608.

threats to harm the plaintiffs' business is clearly established a 'species' tort. The scope of the remainder of the 'genus' tort is bedevilled by two problems. Does it embrace any harm to economic interests not adequately protected by conspiracy, interference with contract in all its forms or intimidation? And what constitutes unlawful means?

A. INTIMIDATION: UNLAWFUL THREATS

The tort of intimidation is committed whenever unlawful threats are invoked to prevent another person from doing some act which he is entitled to do and harm results either to the subject of the threats[3] or to a third party.[4] Early authorities on intimidation involved threats of violence. The modern tort of intimidation is defined in *Rookes v Barnard*[5]

> The plaintiff was an employee of BOAC who had resigned from his trade union. The defendants were union officials. They threatened BOAC that all union members employed at BOAC would strike unless the plaintiff was dismissed. BOAC consequently gave the plaintiff notice and (lawfully) dismissed him.

The House of Lords held that the unlawful threat of a breach of contract by union members contributed the unlawful means necessary to create a cause of action in intimidation. The tort requires an intent to injure coupled with threats of unlawful action. If the threat is to do something that the defendant is entitled to do the tort is not committed.[6] As LORD REID put it in *Rookes v Barnard*[7] 'so long as the defendant only threatens to do what he has a legal right to do he is on safe ground.'

The crucial issue then is what for the purposes of the tort of intimidation constitutes unlawful means.[8] The commission of any tort will suffice. A breach of contract will be enough in the case of 'three-party' intimidation,[9] though not in 'two-party' intimidation where the threatened breach is of the defendant's[10] own contract. Breach of equitable obligations may be sufficient.[11] That an act is criminal in breach of a penal statute may not, if that statute was not intended to create private rights.[12]

B. UNLAWFUL ACTS

In *Barrets & Baird (Wholesale) Ltd v IPCS*[13] the plaintiffs were members of the Association of British Abbatoir Owners and companies in the meat trade.

---

3 'Two-party' intimidation.
4 'Three-party' intimidation; as to the extent to which the principles of law differ depending on whether it is a case of 'two-party' or 'three-party' intimidation see *Clerk and Lindsell* para 15–17.
5 [1964] AC 1129, [1964] 1 All ER 367, HL.
6 *Ware and De Freville v Motor Trade Association* [1921] 3 KB 40, CA.
7 At 1168–9.
8 See *Clerk and Lindsell* para 15–15.
9 *Rookes v Barnard* (supra).
10 Ibid at 15–17 and see Carty op cit.
11 *Dixon v Dixon* [1904] 1 Ch 161.
12 *Lonrho Ltd v Shell Petroleum Ltd (No 2)* [1982] AC 173, [1981] 2 All ER 456, HL.
13 [1987] IRLR 3.

The defendant trade union represented fatstock officers employed by the Meat and Livestock Commission in connection with the certification of slaughtered meat among other functions. The union on their behalf was engaged in a dispute with the MLC over pay and conditions. The officers voted to take strike action and a one day strike had already created considerable difficulties for the plaintiffs' business. They alleged that the defendants were liable for interfering in their business by unlawful means either by inducing breach of the officers' contracts of employment or breach of statutory duty by the MLC. HENRY J attempting to define the tort of unlawful interference held that four ingredients to the tort must be established. There must be:

1   interference with the plaintiff's trade or business;
2   unlawful means;
3   intent to injure the plaintiff; and
4   actual injury.

He refused the plaintiffs application for an interlocutory injunction on two grounds. The alleged breach of statutory duty by the MLC was not made out. Statute required them to provide a system of inspection not a strike free system. Even if the breach of their contracts of employment by the fatstock officers constituted unlawful means, no intention to injure the plaintiff was proved.

It is around the two bones of contention in *Barrets & Baird v IPCS*, intent to injure and unlawful means, that the debate on the limits of an unlawful interference tort will rage. Unlawful acts which constitute torts in themselves will suffice. Breaches of contract are sufficient for the tort of intimidation. If a threatened breach of contract can ground an action, it would seem inconsistent if an actual breach cannot. Other civil wrongs may be enough in this context. Restraint of trade alone is insufficient.[14] The central problem again revolves around criminal acts. In certain cases policy considerations may militate against implementation of civil liability as in *Chapman v Honig*[15] where, even though the landlord maliciously evicting a tenant subpoenaed to give evidence against him acted in contempt of court, no action was found to lie in tort. The House of Lords judgment in *Lonrho Ltd v Shell Petroleum Ltd (No 2)*[16] poses difficulties of a far more general nature.

The plaintiffs complied with sanctions orders prohibiting the supply of oil to the illegal regime in Southern Rhodesia. The defendants in breach of the orders continued to supply oil to that regime. The plaintiffs alleged that those unlawful acts resulted in losses to them caused by the prolongation of the illegal regime increasing the defendants' business at the plaintiffs' expense.

14 *Mogul SS Co v McGregor Gow & Co* [1892] AC 25.
15 [1963] 2 QB 502; and see *Hargreaves v Bretherton* [1959] 1 QB 45, [1958] 3 All ER 122 (no cause of action arising in respect of harm resulting from the defendant's perjury); but in *Acrow (Automation) Ltd v Rex Chainbelt Inc* [1971] 3 All ER 1175, [1971] 1 WLR 1676, CA the defendants were held liable for business losses resulting from the defendant's aiding and abetting breach of an injunction not to impede the plaintiffs' manufacture of certain equipment.
16 [1982] AC 173, [1981] 2 All ER 456.

The plaintiffs sought to establish liability for their business losses on three grounds, conspiracy, breach of statutory duty and interference with trade by unlawful means. Conspiracy failed because no intent to injure as opposed to promote the interests of the defendants was proved.[17] Breach of statutory duty failed because the statutory prohibition on supplying oil was not shown to be a duty imposed for the benefit or protection of a class of which the plaintiffs were members.[18] The plaintiffs were thus forced in pursuit of their third claim to rely heavily on the broad principle enunciated by LORD DENNING in *Ex p Island Records*[19] that '... whenever a lawful business carried on by one individual in fact suffers damage as the consequence of a contravention by another individual of any statutory prohibition the former has a civil right of action against the latter for such damage.'[20] LORD DIPLOCK in *Lonrho* expressly rejected such a wide principle of liability for economic loss. The correct approach was one of 'construction' of the statute. Was it intended to create private rights? The judgment in *Lonrho* received further support from the Court of Appeal in *RCA Corpn v Pollard*.[1] The defendants were selling bootlegged Elvis Presley records, a criminal offence in contravention of the Dramatic and Musical Performers' Protection Act. The Court of Appeal refused an injunction to the plaintiffs who enjoyed exclusive recording contracts for Presley records. The loss of commercial benefits resulting to them from the defendants' statutory crime did not give rise of itself to a cause of action in tort or any right to an injunction.

It is difficult then to evaluate whether there remain circumstances in which a statutory crime which is not independently a civil wrong will be sufficient to constitute unlawful means for the purposes of this tort. LORD DIPLOCK's rejection of the 'wide principle' of liability for business losses must however be seen in context. No intent to injure Lonrho was proved. That intent was said in *Barrets & Baird v IPCS* to be an essential ingredient of the tort of unlawful interference. It remains open to a higher court to establish that while liability for business losses resulting from statutory crimes does not follow automatically, where intention to injure the plaintiff is established statutory crime may constitute the necessary unlawful means.[2]

Two further questions await judicial clarification:

1 What precise interests are protected? Trade or livelihood is the common term used, but are economic interests more generally embraced by the tort. *Falconer v ASLEF*,[3] admittedly only a County Court decision, resulted in an award to a disappointed rail traveller where a strike involved him in hotel expenses.
2 To what extent if at all does a defence of justification apply to this emergent tort?

---

17 See ante at pp 134–5.
18 See post at p 364.
19 [1978] Ch 122, [1978] 3 All ER 824.
20 Per LORD DIPLOCK in *Lonrho* at   .
 1 [1983] Ch 135, [1982] 3 All ER 771, CA. The court was careful to state that it was not pronouncing on the soundness of earlier cases such as *Springhead Spinning Co v Riley* (1868) LR 6 Eq 551 where property rights were protected by injunction.
 2 See the discussion in *Clerk and Lindsell* at para 15–15 and Carty op cit.
 3 [1986] IRLR 331.

SECTION 4. ECONOMIC TORTS AND TRADE UNIONS[4]

It is virtually impossible for a trade union to take effective action in the traditional manner (ie by invoking in the last resort industrial action by way of strikes or threats of strikes) without risking liability arising from one of the economic torts discussed earlier. Calling men out on strike may constitute inducing breach of contract. Threatening a strike to preserve a 'Closed Shop' or protect a demarcation agreement risks liability for intimidation. Thus since 1906[5] the common law has to a greater or lesser extent been modified by statutory immunities afforded to unions and their officials for acts done in contemplation or furtherance of a trade dispute. The extent of trade union immunities has depended on the political complexion of the government of the day and the reaction of the judiciary. By restrictive interpretation of the definition of trade disputes and the scope of statutory immunities the judiciary has often narrowed the intended immunities granted by Labour governments to unions. For example, in *Rookes v Barnard*[6] in 1964 the House of Lords held that the Trade Disputes Act 1906 provided no protection against interference with trade, business or employment effected by unlawful threats. So in 1965 Parliament enacted a Trade Disputes Act 1965 (later replaced by section 13 (1) of the Trade Union and Labour Relations Act 1974). This provided that an act done in contemplation or furtherance of a trade dispute should not be actionable in tort on the grounds only

> '... that it consists in his threatening that a contract (whether one to which he is a party or not) will be broken, or its performance interfered with or that he will induce another person to break a contract or interfere with its performance.'

Now the Employment Acts of 1980 and 1982 and the Trade Union Act 1984 have largely eroded the liberal immunities afforded by the Trade Union and Labour Relations Act 1974. Secondary action is excluded from protection. Unions themselves are subjected to liability with complicated rules concerning 'vicarious' liability for actions by members. And immunities under the 1974 Act which remain are lost unless industrial action is supported in a ballot of the membership.

The details of trade union immunities are (thankfully) beyond the scope and space available for a work on torts. What has to be addressed by students of tort is whether the ebb and flow of statutory immunities is a sensible way to deal with conflicts between employers and unions. Would clear definition of trade union rights, rights which enjoyed equal status to the employer's interests in pursuing his trade, be a preferable means of resolving the conflict?[7]

---

4 For full treatment of this topic see Wedderburn *The Worker and the Law* (3rd edn 1986). For an excellent article on economic torts in the context of labour law see P. Elias and K Ewing 'Economic Torts and Labour Law: Old Principles and New Liabilities' [1982] CLJ 321.
5 Trade Disputes Act 1906.
6 [1964] AC 1129, [1964] 1 All ER 367.
7 See Elias and Ewing op cit.

Chapter 10

Intellectual property interests[1]

SECTION 1. COPYRIGHT, PATENTS AND SIMILAR INTERESTS

Intellectual property can be roughly defined as the intangible products of a person's mind and skill. Tangible property, be it land or goods, is protected from intentional interference by trespass and conversion and from negligently inflicted harm by the tort of negligence. Intangible property takes several forms. Contractual rights are, as we have seen, safeguarded to a limited extent by the general economic torts. Goodwill built up in the course of a business is protected in part by the tort of passing off. But what of a person's interest in the results of his intellectual efforts? To what extent are works of literature or art, or scientific inventions afforded protection by the law of torts? Interests in such intellectual property are predominantly defined and protected by statute. The Copyright Act 1956 protects authors, artists and musicians from those who would 'pirate' their efforts.[2] The Patents Act 1977 safeguards new scientific and technological inventions.[3] The Trade Marks Act 1938 supplements the tort of passing off by enabling traders to register their mark, rendering any infringement of that mark actionable.[4] Designs are also protected by statute.[5] But the pace of current technological development, particularly in relation to computer software, has exposed gaps in the statutory protection of intellectual property and new legislation is in the pipeline.[6]

The detailed provisions of the relevant statutes are beyond the scope of this work. Protection of intellectual property must inevitably be, in the main, a matter for legislation. Rules must be made to allow the 'owner' of the 'property' to register his claim. The author of a literary work needs to establish its originality. To do this when the work is just published makes more sense than fighting out that issue several years later when the author alleges that his work has been 'stolen'.

Complex questions bedevil copyright in the different stages of production of a book. Who has rights in the substance, in the typography, in a particular edition? All may be 'owned' by different persons. Should any rights in information be absolute? Provision must be made to override such rights on occasion in the public interest, or copyright could be used to conceal vital information.[7]

---

1 See W R Cornish *Intellectual Property* (1981); J Phillips *An Introduction to Intellectual Property Law* (1986).
2 See further *Clerk and Lindsell* ch 27.
3 See ibid ch 28.
4 See ibid ch 29.
5 See *Cornish* op cit App 3.
6 See the White Paper on *Intellectual Property and Innovation* (Cmnd 9712) and the Copyright, Patents and Design Bill now before Parliament.
7 See *Lion Laboratories v Evans* [1985] QB 526, [1984] 2 All ER 417, CA; *Church of Scientology of California v Miller* (1987) Times, 22 October.

Scientific inventions pose equally difficult problems of principle. Are there products on which the grant of a monopoly, which is the effect of a patent, should be refused?[8] For what period should a patent be allowed? Whether rights in a novel invention accrue to an employee or his employer has to be regulated. Provision must be made to ensure that while the profits of his efforts accrue to the inventor, others can benefit from it.

Thus the groundwork for the grant and regulation of intellectual property rights rests largely in statute. Those rights are on occasion protected by the criminal law. The equitable remedy of account of profits can be particularly useful. But the action for infringement of copyright, patents or trade marks remains essentially an action in tort. The plaintiff may seek an injunction or damages or both. The potential in these torts for profit from tort has resulted in a number of judicial statements, that, in respect of infringement of patents at least, exemplary damages may be awarded.[9]

SECTION 2.   BREACH OF CONFIDENCE

A. THE OBLIGATION OF CONFIDENTIALITY

The grant of a patent protects research processes only once they have concluded in a novel invention. At that stage production of a cheaper 'copycat' version may constitute an infringement of the patent. Where details are leaked to a competitor at an earlier stage how does the law of torts protect trade secrets?[10] And what of other confidential information, lists of clients, special manufacturing processes and so on? The common law and equity now extend a degree of protection to all victims of breach of confidence. Where information of a confidential nature is entrusted to another in circumstances where that other is relied on to keep the confidence, an obligation of confidentiality will arise.[11]

In very many instances the confidential information is valuable as part of the plaintiff's business and economic interests. But this is not always so. Personal information is equally protected by the obligation of confidentiality. In *Argyll v Argyll*[12] the plaintiff was granted an injunction to prohibit her former husband disclosing marital confidences. The relationship between doctors and their patients gives rise to an obligation on the doctor to keep his patient's confidences.[13]

The obligation of confidence often arises in contract. The duty of fidelity owed by an employee not to disclose his employer's trade secrets derives from his contract of employment. But contract is not a pre-requisite of the obligation of confidence. In *Seager v Copydex Ltd*:[14]

8 Should, for example, patents ever be granted on genetic materials?
9 See *Morton–Norwich Products Inc v Intercen Ltd (No 2)* [1981] FSR 337 doubted in *Catnic Components Ltd v Hill & Smith Ltd* [1983] FSR 512 and see post at 467.
10 When a competitor seeks to induce an employee to divulge trade secrets an action for inducing breach of contract may lie; *Hivac Ltd v Park Royal Scientific Instruments Ltd* [1946] Ch 169, [1946] 1 All ER 350; see ante at 138.
11 See *Coco v A N Clark (Engineers) Ltd* [1969] RPC 41 at 47; *Dunford & Elliot v Johnston* [1978] FSR 143 at 148, CA, and see generally *Cornish* op cit at 263 et seq.
12 [1967] Ch 302; *Stephens v Avery* (1988) Times, 1 March.
13 See M Brazier *Medicine, Patients and the Law* (1987) ch 3. *X v Y* (1987) Times, 11 November.
14 [1967] 2 All ER 415, [1967] 1 WLR 923.

The plaintiff had told the defendants about a new type of carpet grip. Without conscious plagiarism the defendants developed this idea which had been given to them in confidence. The plaintiff was awarded damages to compensate him for their having used his idea without paying for it. The information must not be in the public domain; it must not be public knowledge.

An action for damages has been found to lie even in circumstances where neither breach of contract nor harm to tangible or intangible property is established. Nevertheless the precise nature of the action for breach of confidence remains unclear. Criteria used to determine the measure of damages indicate a judicial perception of the action as an emergent tort.[15] The duty of confidentiality is discussed in terms reminiscent of the more familiar duty of care. The development of a public interest defence somewhat akin to qualified privilege in defamation again suggests a tort.[16] The Law Commission[17] has proposed clarification of the issue by creating a statutory tort of breach of confidence. For the present though the better view remains that '... whatever the circumstances are which created the confidential relationship, the obligation to remain silent depends on a duty of good faith enforceable in equity.'

Where breach of confidence protects personal information it protects to a limited extent an interest in privacy. It is not, however, to be equated with a tort of invasion of privacy. Privacy, as such, is not yet an interest protected by tort. Where confidential information is obtained and disclosed without any abuse of a confidential relationship no tort is committed.[19] Once such a relationship is established, though, the obligation binding the recipient of confidential information also binds any third party to whom that information is transmitted.[20] Should a disloyal employee or spouse propose to sell trade secrets or marital confidences to the popular Press, an injunction will be granted against the newspaper as well.[1]

B. PUBLIC INTEREST

Disclosure of confidential information may be justified in the public interest.[2] The competing public interests in maintaining the bond of confidence and

---

15 See *Seager v Copydex Ltd* (supra); and see P M North 'Breach of Confidence: Is there a New Tort' (1972) 12 JSPTL 149.
16 *Initial Services Ltd v Putterill* [1968] 1 QB 396 at 405, CA; *Fraser v Evans* [1969] 1 QB 349 at 362; *Khashoggi v Smith* (1980) 124 Sol Jo 149.
17 Law Comm No 110 Breach of Confidence (Cmnd 8388).
18 *Clerk and Lindsell* para 20–27.
19 See, for example, *Malone v Metropolitan Police Comr (No 2)* [1979] Ch 344; no tort involved in 'telephone tapping'. On the protection of privacy generally see *Privacy and the Law* A Report by *Justice* 1970 and Report of the Younger Committee on Privacy 1972 (Cmnd 5012). Consider how other torts incidentally protect privacy e g trespass to land; see *Baron Bernstein of Leigh v Skyways and General Ltd* [1978] QB 479, [1977] 2 All ER 902.
20 *Printers and Finishers Ltd v Holloway* [1964] 3 All ER 731.
1 See generally *Cornish* op cit at 282–4.
2 *Initial Services Ltd v Putterill* (supra). Decisions on confidentiality and the state which suggest that the public interest in its information is accorded a low priority as against state 'secrets' should be treated with caution and confined to their special facts: See *A-G v Jonathan Cape Ltd* [1976] QB 752, [1975] 3 All ER 484, (Crossman diaries) and *A-G v Guardian Newspapers* [1987] 3 All ER 316, [1987] 1 WLR 1248, HL (Spycatcher affair).

access to particular information must be weighed against each other.[3] A legitimate interest in the subject matter of the information must be proved. Prurient curiosity is insufficient. Disclosure of evidence or 'iniquity' will always be justifiable. In *Lion Laboratories Ltd v Evans*[4] the plaintiffs sought to prevent publication of internal memoranda leaked by employees to the Press. The memoranda cast doubts on the reliability of the Intoximeter manufactured by the plaintiffs and used by the police to test alcohol levels in drivers. The Court of Appeal refused to grant an injunction. The public interest in the reliability of the product which could if unreliable result in unfair prosecutions outweighed any private rights of the plaintiff.

The existence of competing interests, the patient's right to confidentiality and the potential risk to third parties, poses acute problems for physicians. May they, for example, breach confidence to warn a patient's sexual partner that the patient is suffering from AIDS? Risk of physical harm to a third party is almost certainly sufficient to release a person from the bond of confidentiality.[5] Indeed in America doctors who failed to warn a young woman of her ex-boyfriend's, their patient's, homicidal tendencies and threats against her, were held liable in negligence to her family after her ex-boyfriend murdered her.[6] The risk of harm must, however, be proved to be a real risk. In *X v Y*[7] publication of the names of two doctors found to be H.I.V. positive was banned by ROSE J. There was no significant risk to their patients which outweighed the doctors' right to confidentiality. Prurient interest does not equal public interest.[8]

C. REMEDIES[9]

The most common remedy in breach of confidence is the injunction. It is clearly preferable to anticipate and prevent the disclosure to the public at large of the relevant information. Damages may be awarded where loss resulting from an actual breach is suffered. It is unclear whether damages for mental distress may be awarded.[10] Where the confidential information is of commercial value an account of profits is often sought.

---

3 *Church of Scientology of California v Miller* (1987) Times, 22 October.
4 [1985] QB 526, [1984] 2 All ER 417, CA.
5 See *M Brazier* op cit.
6 *Tarasoff v Regents of the University of California* 551 P 2d 334 (1976).
7 (1987) Times, 11 November.
8 *Stephens v Avéry* (1988) Times, 1 March.
9 See A S Burrows *Remedies for Torts and Breaches of Contract* (1987) at pp 157–8, 262–3, and 157–8.
10 *Stevens v Avéry* supra.

Part IV

Negligent invasions of interests in person and property and economic interests

CONTENTS

Chapter 11

Duty of care I—the neighbour principle

SECTION 1. INTRODUCTION

Obviously, more persons suffer damage from careless acts of others than from intentional ones, and the provision made for them is of cardinal importance in the law of torts.

English law has long recognised that, in certain circumstances, persons guilty of careless conduct were liable in damages to their victims.[1] So, the liability of those engaged in certain common callings, such as ferrymen, surgeons, smiths, innkeepers and the like, goes back to the fourteenth century. Further, many actions of nuisance and trespass were based on negligent conduct. Gradually, a large variety of situations in which negligence was the common element was subsumed under the action on the case. But not until from, perhaps, 1825, onwards was there any emergence of negligence as a separate tort; there was merely a list of situations where the victims of careless conduct might recover damages. Thenceforth, actions upon the case for negligence became common, no doubt spurred on at first by the increase in negligently inflicted injuries through the use of the new mechanical inventions such as the railways, and later by the abolition of the forms of action.[2] The existence of negligence as a separate tort with a distinct set of principles is now undeniable, and it is easily the most important tort of all. It must be realised, however, that negligent acts do not come within the scope of the tort of negligence only. Regrettable though it be from the symmetrical standpoint, trespass and nuisance, for example, are often available even though the act complained of is not intentional but merely negligent.

It is essential to grasp at the outset that it is not the law that a person suffering damage as a result of careless conduct can sue in tort; careless acts do not necessarily constitute the tort of negligence. In order to protect the interests of others against the risks of certain harms the law prescribes certain standards of conduct to which persons in particular circumstances ought to conform, and, if, from failure to attain those standards, such harm ensues, this is actionable negligence. A plaintiff can claim to have an interest of his 'protected against an unintentional invasion by conduct involving in the thought of reasonable men an unreasonable hazard that such invasion would ensue'.[3] As LORD WRIGHT has authoritatively put it:[4]

> In strict legal analysis, negligence means more than heedless or careless conduct, whether in omission or commission: it properly connotes the complex concept of

---

1 For the history of the tort of negligence, see Winfield (1926) 42 LQR 184–201; (1934) 34 Columbia LR 41–66, reprinted Winfield *Select Legal Essays* pp 70–97.
2 The main milestones were *Vaughan v Menlove* (1837) 3 Bing NC 468; *Winterbottom v Wright* (1842) 10 M & W 109; *Heaven v Pender* (1883) 11 QBD 503, CA.
3 Per CARDOZO J, in *Palsgraf v Long Island Railroad Co* (1928) 284 NY 339.
4 *Lochgelly Iron & Coal Co v M'Mullan* [1934] AC 1, HL at 25.

duty, breach, and damage thereby suffered by the person to whom the duty was owing.

These three elements of the tort—duty, breach of duty, and ensuing damage, will be considered in turn.

This discussion must be prefaced by the warning that there is no substantial measure of agreement among either judges or writers on the limits of these three categories. In many judgments, indeed, the three elements seem fused into one,[5] and there is some justification for that method.[6] Sometimes, the decision whether to treat a particular matter under the heading of duty or breach seems quite arbitrary. There is much to be said for the view that whether we state any of the conclusions in this tort 'in terms of remoteness, duty or negligence seems immaterial so long as we keep our eye on the fundamental problem of what we are doing and who in a given trial can do it'.[7] What follows is to be regarded as one person's attempt to reconcile the need for logic and orderliness in legal presentation with the paramount obligation of stating the law in the terminology commonly employed by English courts, and at the same time to explain the several techniques applied by the courts to the solution of problems in negligence. In negligence alone of the torts (though perhaps to a much slighter extent in nuisance) do the constituent elements lack reasonably clear definition.

SECTION 2.   PROXIMITY AND POLICY

A. IS THERE ANY PRINCIPLE ON WHICH DUTY IS BASED, OR ARE THERE MERELY CATEGORIES OF DUTY-SITUATIONS?

(1) DUTY-SITUATIONS

The concept of duty in negligence[8] is a comparatively modern one, but is now so firmly rooted that there can be no doubt that actions in negligence must fail where duty is not established.[9] There are many strands in this requirement of duty. In the particular circumstances the defendant must be proved to owe a duty at least to somebody to act or refrain from acting; there must be one of those general situations which the law recognises as being capable of giving rise to a duty—in many situations, as we shall see, it has been held that there can be no such duty.[10] Even if the facts fall outside the 'no duty' category the plaintiff must further show that the defendant, when conducting himself in the manner complained of, owed a duty to him. A

---

5 Thus, in *Roe v Minister of Health* [1954] 2 QB 66, at 85, [1954] 2 All ER 131, CA at 138, DENNING LJ thought that the three questions were in many cases simply three different ways of looking at one and the same question, which is this: 'Is the consequence fairly to be regarded as within the risk created by the negligence?' An admission of negligence does not entitle the plaintiff to a verdict, for he has still to prove that the negligence caused his damage; *Rankine v Garton Sons & Co Ltd* [1979] 2 All ER 1185, CA.

6 But this is not the way in which English judges approach these problems, and for that reason is not followed in this text.

7 Wright (1957) 4 Journal of the Society of Public Teachers of Law (NS) 32.

8 Duties similar to these discussed here under common-law negligence may also arise under statutes or contracts.

9 *Heaven v Pender* (1883) 11 QBD 503 at 507 (per BRETT MR), CA; *Thomas v Quartermaine* (1887) 18 QBD 685 at 694 (per BOWEN LJ) CA; *Le Lievre v Gould* [1893] 1 QB 491 at 497 (per LORD ESHER MR), CA; *Grant v Australian Knitting Mills Ltd* [1936] AC 85, PC at 101; *Hay (or Bourhill) v Young* [1943] AC 92, [1942] 2 All ER 396, HL.

10 See p 160, post.

nurse who carelessly jolts ampoules containing fluid for an injection has broken her duty of care to the hospital but is not liable to a patient who is paralysed because phenol solution in which the ampoules are later placed seeps into the fluid (with which he is subsequently injected) through the cracks, invisible to the naked eye, made in the ampoules by the jolt; she owed no duty to the patient in respect of that act.[11] One may have to particularise further and say that, in order to succeed, A must show not merely that B owes him a duty but a duty in respect of that interest of A which B has violated; for instance, B may be under a duty not to cause A personal injury, yet under no duty in respect of mere economic loss. Again, the risk which materialises may not be of the type envisaged by the law when it imposed on B a duty towards A: B must not lend a schoolboy a loaded rifle, for he may fire it at and injure A; B lends him one and the boy drops the rifle on to A's foot—B has broken the duty of care and there is damage, but he has no liability.[12] Obviously we have indeed a 'complex concept of duty' calling for much closer examination.

The law was developed in an empirical manner by decisions that in some particular circumstances there was a duty and that in others there was none. The not unexpected attempt to rationalise these cases was first made in *Heaven v Pender*, by BRETT MR, who produced this formula:[13]

> ... whenever one person is by circumstances placed in such a position with regard to another that everyone of ordinary sense who did think would at once recognise that if he did not use ordinary care and skill in his own conduct with regard to those circumstances he would cause danger or injury to the person or property of the other, a duty arises to use ordinary care and skill to avoid such danger.

An improved and now much more frequently cited rationalisation is the famous *dictum* of LORD ATKIN in *Donoghue v Stevenson*:[14]

> The rule that you are to love your neighbour becomes in law, you must not injure your neighbour; and the lawyer's question, Who is my neighbour? receives a restricted reply. You must take reasonable care to avoid acts or omissions which you can reasonably foresee would be likely to injure your neighbour. Who, then, in law is my neighbour? The answer seems to be—persons who are so closely and directly affected by my act that I ought reasonably to have them in contemplation as being so affected when I am directing my mind to the acts or omissions which are called in question.

This *dictum* cannot be accepted as the *ratio decidendi* of the case[15] and it is probable that LORD ATKIN never intended it to be an exact comprehensive statement of law.[16] The importance of *Donoghue v Stevenson* is twofold. It firmly established a new category of duties, that of manufacturers of goods to eventual users, a category which, as will be seen later,[17] has since developed far beyond the limits of the facts of that case. It finally set at rest any possible doubts whether the tort of negligence was capable of further expansion or was to be rigidly tied down by existing precedents. It was a clear instance of the courts' taking account of the new conditions of mass production and

11 *Roe v Minister of Health* [1954] 2 QB 66, [1954] 2 All ER 131, CA.
12 See ch 18, post.
13 (1883) 11 QBD 503 at 509.
14 [1932] AC 562, HL at 580.
15 See ch 18, post.
16 Cf *Haseldine v Daw & Son Ltd* [1941] 2 KB 343 at 362 (per SCOTT LJ), [1941] 3 All ER 156, CA.
17 See ch 18 et seq, post.

complex marketing of goods wherein there are many intermediaries between manufacturer and consumer, and, by a conscious work of judicial legislation, imposing on manufacturers certain minimum standards of care in favour of the consumer.[18]

There are numerous and extensive categories of situations which are treated by the courts as imposing a duty of care. By way of illustration merely, makers or repairers of goods owe a duty to those who use those goods, a teacher owes a duty to his child-pupil, an occupier of land to visitors there, those engaged in skilled occupations to their customers, those carrying out activities on a highway to other highway users. The rules of many of these are so specialised that they will be separately examined in later chapters.[19] Besides broad categories such as these, there are many instances of more specific duties—hence, before one falls back on some broad principle, one must ascertain whether on similar facts the courts have already recognised a duty—for, remember, whether a duty exists will be a matter of law not fact.

There are other cases where the law has denied the duty: one may carelessly allow a blind man to walk over a cliff without warning him; a landowner may excavate his land in a careless manner in circumstances where he can foresee that by abstracting percolating water from below he will cause a settlement of plaintiff's adjoining buildings; he is not liable because he owes no duty of care in respect of percolating water.[20]

(2) CREATION OF NEW DUTIES

What happens when the facts fall into neither group? It cannot be seriously maintained that the courts cannot hold a duty to exist unless they have previously expressly held that in such circumstances there is a duty. LORD MACMILLAN stated in *Donoghue v Stevenson* that the 'categories of negligence are never closed'[1] which means at least, as ASQUITH LJ said in *Candler v Crane Christmas & Co*[2] 'that in accordance with changing social needs and standards new classes of persons legally bound or entitled to the exercise of care may from time to time emerge'.[3] New duty-situations are continually being recognised. Thus, it has been held that an education authority owes a duty to the driver of a vehicle to exercise reasonable supervision of children in its nursery adjoining the highway so as to prevent them from endangering his safety on the highway, by, for example, running unattended out of the nursery through an unlocked gate on to the roadway and causing him to

18 The clearest exposition of this function of *Donoghue v Stevenson* is in the judgment of LORD DEVLIN in *Hedley Byrne & Co Ltd v Heller & Partners Ltd* [1964] AC 465, [1963] 2 All ER 575, HL.
19 Eg chs 17 and 18.
20 *Langbrook Properties Ltd v Surrey County Council* [1969] 3 All ER 1424; *Thomas v Gulf Oil Refining Ltd* (1979) 123 Sol Jo 787 (oil company had no duty to avoid fissuring its rock strata and thereby depriving neighbouring plaintiff farmer of water in his ponds).
1 [1932] AC 562 at 619.
2 [1951] 2 KB 164 at 192, [1951] 1 All ER 426, CA.
3 Landon (1941) 57 LQR 179 at 183, still maintains that 'the duty to be careful only exists where the wisdom of our ancestors has decreed that it shall exist', but this is in the teeth of modern authority—for an explicit rejection see *Haseldine v Daw & Son Ltd* [1941] 2 KB 343 at 358–9 (per SCOTT LJ), [1941] 3 All ER 156, CA, and cf *London Graving Dock Co Ltd v Horton* [1951] AC 737 at 757, [1951] 2 All ER 1 (per LORD NORMAND), HL.

swerve to avoid injuring them.[4] An electricity authority which had high-voltage wires near a climbable tree was liable to the personal representatives of a child who trespassed off a nearby footpath, climbed the tree, and was killed.[5] The Ministry of Transport, when siting road signs by the side of a highway, owes a duty to a motorist who may inadvertently leave the road and collide with them.[6]

Since 1970 the House of Lords has given important guidance in a series of cases on how the principle of *Donoghue v Stevenson* should be applied to new situations. First, in *Home Office v Dorset Yacht Co Ltd*, LORD REID said:[7]

> The time has come when we can and should say that it [LORD ATKIN's neighbour rule] ought to apply unless there is some justification or valid explanation for its exclusion.

Then LORD WILBERFORCE said in *Anns v Merton London Borough Council*:[8]

> ... the position has now been reached that in order to establish that a duty of care arises in a particular situation, it is not necessary to bring the facts of that situation within those of previous situations in which a duty of care has been held to exist. Rather the question has to be approached in two stages. First, one has to ask whether, as between the alleged wrongdoer and the person who has suffered damage there is a sufficient relationship of proximity or neighbourhood such that, in the reasonable contemplation of the former, carelessness on his part may be likely to cause damage to the latter, in which case a prima facie duty of care arises. Secondly, if the first question is answered affirmatively, it is necessary to consider whether there are any considerations which ought to negative, or to reduce or limit the scope of the duty or the class of person to whom it is owed or the damages to which a breach of it may give rise.

What now has to be examined is the manner in which, and the circumstances in which, this two-stage test propounded by LORD WILBERFORCE is to be applied. Immediately after the judgment in *Anns* the test tended to be applied in a fairly literal fashion. Judges reasoned thus:

1 Had the plaintiff established proximity, that his injury was a foreseeable result of the defendant's negligence and so that he was within the 'neighbour' principle?
2 Was there any valid policy reason to deny the existence of a duty to the plaintiff?[9]

The 'neighbour' principle was seen as the general rule, and the role of judicial policy in defining exceptions to the general rule was expressly recognised by the majority of judges. LORD WILBERFORCE explicitly acknowledged the decisiveness of policy considerations in *McLoughlin v O'Brian*[10]

---

4 *Carmarthenshire County Council v Lewis* supra (in that case the lorry struck a telegraph pole, and the driver was killed); *Barnes v Hampshire County Council* [1969] 3 All ER 746, HL (local education authority liable for letting children out of a school early before parents or others came to fetch them, when traffic accident ensued).
5 *Buckland v Guildford Gas Light and Coke Co* [1949] 1 KB 410, [1948] 2 All ER 1086.
6 *Levine v Morris* [1970] 1 All ER 144, CA.
7 [1970] AC 1004 at 1027, [1970] 2 All ER 294 at 297.
8 [1978] AC 728 at 751–2, [1977] 2 All ER 492 at 498, HL.
9 So that in *Ashton v Turner* [1981] QB 137, [1980] 3 All ER 870 while injury to a fellow burglar travelling as a passenger with his drunken companion in a getaway car was foreseeable, as a matter of policy it was held no duty of care was recognised as owed by one participant in crime to another. And see *McKay v Essex Area Health Authority* [1982] 2 All ER 771 (no duty to a child born deformed to prevent its birth; no claim for 'wrongful life' in England).
10 [1983] 1 AC 410 at 421, [1982] 2 All ER 298 at 303. See 179, post for details of this case on liability for nervous shock.

... at the margin, the boundaries of a man's responsibilities for acts of negligence have to be fixed as a matter of policy.

However, there were those who contested the broad policy function claimed by LORD WILBERFORCE and in the early eighties proposed proximity, the 'neighbour' principle, as the exclusive test of duty. If the results of so extending the categories of duties were untoward, then that was a matter for Parliament to put right. LORD SCARMAN forcefully expressed this minority view, again in *McLoughlin v O'Brian*:[11]

... if principle inexorably requires a decision which entails a degree of policy risk, the court's function is to adjudicate according to principle, leaving policy curtailment to the judgment of Parliament.

For LORD SCARMAN, and LORD BRIDGE who concurred, the risk was that over-conservatism by the courts would freeze the common law into unjust rigidity.[12] The categories of negligence in 1982 looked infinitely expandable. However, two recent decisions of the House of Lords suggest a fundamental reversal in the trend towards the expansion of the categories of duties and thus the scope of the tort of negligence.

First, in *Governors of the Peabody Donation Fund v Sir Lindsay Parkinson & Co Ltd*[13] LORD KEITH deplored the literal manner in which the two-stage *Anns* test had from time to time been applied. Denying a remedy to a development company who sued a local authority for the financial loss occasioned to them by an inadequate drainage system, which they alleged that the authority had negligently approved, he said of the *Anns* test[14]

There has been a tendency in some recent cases to treat these passages as being themselves of a definitive character. This is a temptation to be resisted. ... in determining whether or not a duty of care of a particular scope was incumbent on the defendant it is material to take into consideration whether it is just and reasonable that it should be so.

So, any analysis of the *Anns* test along the lines that if the plaintiff can prove proximity, the defendant must establish overwhelming policy considerations to negative or limit a duty is clearly now condemned by the House of Lords. But it is the second recent decision of their Lordships which threatens more radically to restrict the scope of negligence and may be seen as partially at least closing the categories of negligence.

In *Leigh and Sillivan Ltd v Aliakmon Shipping Co Ltd*[15] a consignment of steel coils was damaged while being shipped from Korea to England. The buyers under their contract with the sellers had not become the owners of the coils at the time that the damage was suffered but they had accepted the risk. So the sellers owned the coils still, but the buyers stood to lose from the damage. Clear authority before 1980 denied any duty in respect of damage to property to any person without a proprietary interest in the property.[16] In

11 At 430 and 310.
12 Per LORD BRIDGE in *McLoughlin v O'Brian* at 441 and 320 respectively.
13 [1985] AC 210, [1984] 3 All ER 529.
14 At 240 and 534 respectively. And see *Curran v Northern Ireland Housing Co-ownership Association Ltd* [1987] AC 718, [1987] 2 All ER 13; *Yuen Kun-Yeu v A-G of Hong Kong* [1987] 2 All ER 705, [1987] 3 WLR 776; *Jones v Dept. of Employment* (1987) Times, 27 November, CA.
15 [1986] AC 785, [1986] 2 All ER 145, HL.
16 See *Margarine Union v Cambay Prince Steamship Co Ltd* [1969] 1 QB 219, [1967] 3 All ER 775; *The Mineral Transporter* [1986] AC 1, [1985] 2 All ER 935, PC.

1982 at first instance the *Anns* test was applied in relatively similar shipping cases to allow the buyers a remedy.[17] They were foreseeably persons at risk from the carriers' carelessness and no sufficient policy considerations were established to negative the prima facie duty created by that proximity. LORD BRANDON in *Leigh and Sillavan Ltd v Aliakmon Shipping Co Ltd*, while he also advanced policy consideration to deny a duty in such cases, condemned the application of the *Anns* test in such a case altogether. He said:[18]

> ... LORD WILBERFORCE was dealing, as is clear from what he said, with the approach to the questions of the existence and scope of a duty of care in a novel type of factual situation which is not analogous to any factual situation in which the existence of such a duty had already been held to exist. He was not, as I understand the passage, suggesting that the same approach should be adopted to the existence of a duty of care in a factual situation in which the existence of such a duty had been repeatedly[19] held not to exist.

LORD BRANDON's limitations on the scope for further growth of duty-situations must itself be regarded somewhat cautiously. *Leigh & Sillavan Ltd v Aliakmon Shipping Co Ltd* concerns the problematic question of liability for economic loss as did the *Peabody Donation Fund*. Moreover both judgments raise difficult issues of the respective functions of contract and tort. The extent to which the BRANDON restrictions on new duty situations apply to duties to avoid physical damage to people or property remains undecided. What is clear is that even in relation to such harm proximity alone will not conclude the issue of whether a duty arises.[20] As LORD KEITH put it in the Privy Council judgment of *Yuen Kun Yeu v A-G for Hong Kong*[1] the two-stage test in *Anns* can no longer be regarded as in all circumstances[2] a suitable guide to the existence of a duty of care.

(3) THE UNFORESEEABLE PLAINTIFF

'English law does not recognise a duty in the air, so to speak; that is, a duty to undertake that no one shall suffer from one's carelessness.'[3] But suppose that the plaintiff is in breach of his duty of care to Z, but that Y also has suffered damage as the result of the same careless act. In the early days of the development of this tort of negligence, there was much support for the view that Y could also recover. In one leading case the view was canvassed by the Court of Exchequer Chamber that where the defendant railway company could have foreseen that sparks from their engine would set fire to an adjoining field, they were liable to the owner of a cottage 200 yards away across a road when the fire, fanned by a strong wind, destroyed the cottage, although they could not have foreseen harm to the plaintiff's cottage.[4]

This approach was challenged in the leading American case, *Palsgraf v Long Island Railroad Co:*[5]

---

17 *The Irene's Success* [1982] QB 481, [1982] 1 All ER 218; *The Nea Tyhi* [1982] 1 Lloyd's Rep 606.
18 At 815 and 153 respectively.
19 But what will count as 'repeatedly'?
20 *Smith v Littlewoods Organisations Ltd* [1987] 1 All ER 710; *Hill v Chief Constable for West Yorkshire* [1987] 1 All ER 1173.
1 [1987] 2 All ER 705, PC.
2 But for an application of the *Anns* test as modified in *Peabody* see *Banque Keyser Ullmann SA v Skandia (UK) Insurance Co Ltd* [1987] 2 All ER 923, [1987] 2 WLR 1300.
3 *Bottomley v Bannister* [1932] 1 KB 458 at 476 (per GREER LJ).
4 *Smith v London & South Western Rly Co* (1870) LR 6 CP 14.
5 (1928) 284 NY 339.

An employee of the defendant railway company, in helping a passenger on to a train, negligently dislodged a parcel which the passenger was carrying. Unknown to the employee, it contained fireworks. These exploded and the shock upset some scales at the other end of the platform. The scales struck the plaintiff, who was standing on the platform. The majority of the court held that the action failed because, although the conduct was careless, no duty was owed to the plaintiff to protect him against this hazard. The minority dissented on the ground that the plaintiff's injuries were the proximate result of the negligent act of the defendant.

This view of the majority, contained in the judgment of CARDOZO CJ, a judge of international reputation, that there was no liability to a plaintiff towards whom harm could not be anticipated, was to have great influence on English judicial thought. The decisive moment came in 1943, in the House of Lords decision in *Hay (or Bourhill) v Young*:[6]

A motor-cyclist carelessly collided with another vehicle. The plaintiff who was outside the area of foreseeable danger suffered nervous shock as a result of hearing the noise of the collision.

The House of Lords held that the fact that the plaintiff was outside the area of foreseeable danger in itself prevented her from succeeding; the House explicitly rejected the argument that because the defendant violated his duty of care to a third party he was responsible for the damage which he inflicted on the plaintiff. As was to be expected, this principle has been consistently followed in subsequent cases.[7] In the important *Overseas Tankship (UK) Ltd v Morts Dock and Engineering Co Ltd, The Wagon Mound*, which is discussed later, the Privy Council expressly approved the rule.[8]

SECTION 3. OMISSIONS

An omission to act where it is foreseeable that failure to act may harm the plaintiff is not necessarily actionable negligence. For instance if X, a passer-by, sees the victim of a road accident lying on the ground in urgent need of medical attention and does not trouble to walk to the nearby telephone booth to summon medical aid, then, although he foresees that the man may die if he does not receive it, he is not liable for his omission.[9] In such a case, the failure to act is the only conduct causally linked with the plaintiff's harm. Only where there is a pure omission in this sense does the exception apply.

In other circumstances omissions may give rise to liability. If the defendant's earlier act creates a duty to take care the fact that an omission is the immediate cause of harm will not prevent the defendant from being liable. If the plaintiff is a passenger in a car driven by the defendant, and is hurt because the defendant fails to apply the brake, he has a claim in negligence.[10]

6 [1943] AC 92, [1942] 2 All ER 396. And see p 178, post.
7 Eg *King v Phillips* [1953] 1 QB 429, [1953] 1 All ER 617, CA; *Roe v Minister of Health* [1954] 2 QB 66, [1954] 2 All ER 131, CA.
8 [1961] AC 388 at 425, [1961] 1 All ER 404; see p 226 et seq, post.
9 See the comparison made between English law and civil law on this matter by LORD GOFF in *Smith v Littlewoods Organisation Ltd* [1987] 1 All ER 710 at 729.
10 In *Johnson v Rea Ltd* [1962] 1 QB 373, [1961] 3 All ER 816, CA, the defendant stevedores (without lack of due care) dropped soda ash on to a surface over which they subsequently invited the plaintiff to pass. Held they had a duty to take care that the surface was safe, and their failure to remove the ash was actionable—this also may be regarded as an omission in the course of the performance of their operation of unloading the bags of soda ash.

In other cases there may be an existing relationship which imposes a positive duty to act, and so a liability for an omission: for example, the relationship of education authority and pupil.[11] The general practitioner who has accepted a patient onto his NHS list may be liable if he negligently omits to treat the patient, refusing to visit or turning him away from the surgery. Accepting responsibility for the patient's NHS care imposes a positive duty to act.

SECTION 4.   THE EXERCISE OF STATUTORY POWERS

One issue of especial difficulty in defining the limits of duties of care has been whether public authorities exercising statutory powers owe any duty to a private individual suffering loss or injury resulting from an authority's negligence. The difficulties are four fold:

1 Many statutory powers confer on the public authority a measure of discretion as to how, and even if, the relevant power should be exercised.
2 If the alleged negligence is a failure to exercise a statutory power the question of liability for omissions is raised in an acute form.
3 Recent case-law may in some instances require the injured individual to pursue a different and more restrictive procedural remedy from the ordinary tort action instituted by writ.
4 And finally, the Court of Appeal recently held that the statutory framework and statutory remedies for adjudication in claims for social security benefits excluded altogether any common law remedy for negligence.[12]

The first two issues of whether a duty of care will ever be imposed in respect of the negligent exercise of statutory powers and the problem of liability for failure to exercise a power can conveniently be considered together. In *Home Office v Dorset Yacht Co Ltd*[13] the facts assumed were these:

A group of Borstal trainees were working and staying overnight in a training party on Brownsea Island in Poole Harbour, Dorset. They were in the custody of three Borstal officers, servants of the Home Office. One night in breach of their instructions, the officers simply went to bed failing altogether to supervise the boys. Several trainees attempted to escape boarding and damaging the plaintiffs' yacht which was moored offshore.

The likelihood of the damage in these circumstances was readily foreseeable. But the Home Office had a wide statutory discretion as to how Borstals be managed, whether open or closed institutions should be operated, and how much freedom should be given to trainees. If the Home Office were held to owe a duty to private individuals injured by escaping trainees it might be inhibited in exercising that discretion properly for the benefit of the boys and the community generally. LORD DIPLOCK[14] offered a solution to the dilemma. The Home Office could not be liable unless it was established that the escape

---

11 Another illustration is where the conduct of the defendant lulls the plaintiff into a false state of dependence on the defendant. A railway company which omitted to lock a crossing on the approach of a train was held liable to a person injured because of its previous regular practice (on which the plaintiff reasonably relied) of locking the crossing at the train's approach. *Mercer v South Eastern and Chatham Rly Co's Managing Committee* [1922] 2 KB 549.
12 *Jones v Dept of Employment* (1987) Times, 27 November, CA.
13 [1970] AC 1004, [1970] 2 All ER 294, HL.   14 At 1059 and 329 et seq respectively.

resulted from an *ultra vires* act, a misuse of power,[15] by the Home Office or its servants. If, as was assumed for the purposes of establishing the point of law, Borstal officers disregarded instructions then their conduct was *ultra vires*. No action lay unless an *ultra vires* act was proved. Once proved it was open to the court to hold in an appropriate case that a duty of care was owed to individuals whose persons or property were damaged by escapees.

LORD DIPLOCK's reasoning was further developed in *Anns v Merton London Borough Council*.[16]

> The plaintiffs' flats were defective because they were built on foundations which were inadequate and did not conform to byelaws. They sued the local authority for negligence in carrying out its statutory powers under public health legislation of inspecting and approving foundations.

The local authority had exercised the power given to it by the Public Health Act 1936 to make byelaws regarding foundations. They were not under a mandatory duty to inspect all foundations. Therefore, the authority argued:

1 it could not be liable for omitting to inspect, and
2 if it were not liable for not inspecting, it could not be liable for negligent inspection.

LORD WILBERFORCE held that where a public body is discharging functions under statute its powers and duties are *prima facie* definable under public not private law. Public law demands that when a discretionary power is entrusted to a body by statute that power be exercised properly with adequate consideration of relevant matters, and must never be cavalierly disregarded or exercised on caprice alone. Such *ultra vires* conduct may create a duty of care to an individual suffering loss or injury, whether the *ultra vires* conduct is a failure to exercise the relevant power at all, or an improper, *ultra vires*, exercise of that power.

The House of Lords went on to draw a distinction between planning or policy decisions on the one hand, and operational decisions on the other. The court would more readily find a duty of care was imposed where there had been an operational error. Broad policy decisions such as the scale of resources to be made available for the discharge of the authority's public health functions were not immune from suit, but convincing evidence would be called for to establish that the decision was *ultra vires* and unlawful.[17] Once the authority had implemented its policy on the scale of inspections carelessness by the inspector, for example, merely giving the site a cursory glance and going off for a drink in disregard of his instructions, would be operational negligence.[18] In both cases a condition precedent of liability is an

---

15 See De Smith's *Constitutional and Administrative Law* (5th edn) ch 28 for a full explanation of the public law principles of *ultra vires*.

16 [1978] AC 728, [1977] 2 All ER 492, HL.

17 See *Just v R in Right of British Columbia* [1985] 5 WWR 570 (claim by plaintiff injured when a boulder fell from a cliff onto his car dismissed: the rock scaling crew was given discretion as to how to deal with dangerous cliff faces; they had inspected as best they could within limited budget resources).

18 Consider also the useful example given in *Anns* itself from an American case *Indian Tow Co v US* 350 US 61 (1955): the power to decide whether to have a lighthouse on a promontory was a policy-planning decision; it would be an operational failure, once a lighthouse had been installed, to allow it to be unlighted in the hours of darkness. But how would you classify a decision to discontinue maintaining the lighthouse altogether?

ultra vires decision but proving *ultra vires* in the second instance would be much less burdensome.[19]

It must not be forgotten however that establishing an *ultra vires* decision by the authority does not of itself conclude the question of whether a common law duty is owed to the injured plaintiff. To establish liability in negligence the loss or injury to the plaintiff must be of a type which one of the purposes of the statutory powers vested in the authority was to prevent or avoid. In *Anns* the plaintiff became the occupier of one of the damaged flats. His health and safety were at risk unless he expended the necessary money on repairs. In a series of later cases where inadequate buildings had nevertheless been approved by local authorities under building regulations the plaintiffs were the development companies who had lost money because the buildings failed to sell and/or involved them in additional expenditure. In the *Peabody Donation Fund*[20] LORD KEITH held that while such economic loss was readily foreseeable, financial loss to the developers was not the type of loss which local authorities' public health powers were vested in them to prevent, at any rate where the builders or developers acted in reliance on independent professional advice.[21]

The implications of the decision in *Anns* are far-reaching. The result of enshrining in English law a distinction between policy and operational decisions and the condition precedent of an *ultra vires* decision has created to some extent a division between a private law tort of negligence and a public law tort.[1] This division has been further entrenched by a series of House of Lords' judgments on the procedure for challenging public authorities. It has been held that *as a general principle* any attempt to quash a decision of a public authority on the grounds that it contravenes public law principles, for example that it is *ultra vires*, must be pursued under the procedure for application for judicial review alone.[2] Two features of the application for judicial review distinguish it sharply from the normal procedure by which tort actions are normally started. The application must *prima facie* be made within three months of the *ultra vires* decision.[3] Leave must be granted by a judge to make the application. It is not a procedure which the citizen has an

19 Application of the *ultra vires* test since *Anns* has been far from consistent and its applicability to claims other than negligence has been disputed. Judges at first instance, in clear contravention of LORD WILBERFORCE's ruling (at 754 and 501 respectively), have tended to disregard the prior requirement that the act be *ultra vires* in cases of operational error regarding the operational negligence alone sufficient. For two examples of application of the strict *Anns* principle see *Fellowes v Rother DC* [1983] 1 All ER 513; *Rigby v Chief Constable of Northamptonshire* [1985] 2 All ER 985. The basis of the policy/operational division is forcefully attacked by S H Bailey and M J Bowman 'The Policy/Operational Dichotomy. A Cuckoo in the Nest' [1986] CLJ 430.

20 [1984] 3 All ER 529. And see *Yuen Kun of Yeu v A-G Hong Kong* [1987] 2 All ER 705, PC, (no duty owed to depositors by Commissioner for Deposit Taking Companies).

21 *Investors in Industry v South Bedfordshire District Council* [1986] 1 All ER 687. (It remains open whether the council might owe a duty to a building owner, who was himself guiltless of negligence or breach of the regulations, and who lacked access to professional advice. An individual having a house built for his own family, as opposed to development companies would fall more readily within the ambit of the authority's intended powers. Consider the facts in *Cynat Products Ltd v Landbuild* [1984] 3 All ER 513.

1 See M Aronson and H Whitmore *Public Torts and Contracts* (1982).

2 *O'Reilly v Mackman* [1983] 2 AC 237. For the details of the procedure for application for judicial review see Supreme Court Act 1981 s 31 and RSC Ord 53; and see De Smith's *Constitutional and Administrative Law* (5th edn) ch 29.

3 See RSC Ord 53 r 4. In exceptional cases leave may be granted to apply beyond the three month limit.

unfettered right to invoke. Now the vast majority of applications for judicial review are concerned not with alleged negligence but with unfair disciplinary hearings, refusal of state benefits and such like. But the judgment in *Cocks v Thanet District Council*[4] illustrates the problems that this series of cases may pose for the tort lawyer.

Mr Cocks became homeless. He asked the defendant council to house him under the Housing (Homeless Persons) Act 1977. They refused on the grounds they considered that he was intentionally homeless. Mr Cocks issued a writ for breach of statutory duty.

The House of Lords ruled that because in order to have a common law claim for breach of statutory duty he must first prove that the authority's decision that he was intentionally homeless was *ultra vires*, his action started by writ would be struck out. He could only proceed by way of an application for judicial review with his claim for damages, if the court found in his favour, annexed to that application.

Cocks v Thanet District Council does not mean you can never sue a public authority via a normal negligence action. A person run over by a local authority dustcart, or given duff advice by a planning official,[5] is in the same position as a person run over by a private citizen or given careless advice by an architect. What *Cocks* does appear to say is that, if for a duty to the private individual to be imposed, a decision of the authority must first be found to be *ultra vires*, that finding of *ultra vires* must be obtained by way of the specialised public law procedure of application for judicial review. Bearing in mind that the normal time-limit for such an application is three months consider the problems any plaintiff in Mr Anns's position would face, who discovers only several years later the damage that an authority's negligence has occasioned him.

Three comments must be made:

1 The exclusive nature of an application for judicial review is stated as a general principle only allowing of exceptions.
2 Such an exception has been found where the relationship between the authority and the plaintiff was originally founded in contract thus giving him private law rights which preceded any public law decision by issue.[6] Could it be argued that the proximity giving rise to a duty of care in cases like *Anns* creates a private law right of which the public law decision-making element is merely an incident? Alas such an analysis is difficult to reconcile with LORD WILBERFORCE's clear statement on *Anns*.

A plaintiff complaining of negligence must prove, the burden being on him, that action taken was not within the limits of a discretion bona fide exercised *before* (my italics) he can begin to rely on a common law duty of care?[7]

3 Finally the judiciary may just close their eyes to the implication of *Cocks v Thanet DC* in a deserving case as they have tended to ignore on many occasions the technical requirement to establish *ultra vires* in cases of operational negligence. But the procedural obstacle course created by the

---

4 [1983] 2 AC 286.
5 *Davy v Spelthorne DC* [1984] AC 262 (consider LORD WILBERFORCE's forceful criticism of attempts to create via case-law a division between public and private law).
6 *Wandsworth BC v Winder* [1985] AC 461.
7 At 755 and 499 respectively.

marriage of *Anns* and *Cocks v Thanet DC* adds force to the case of those who criticise the whole concept of distinct and separate criteria for public law and private law negligence.[8]

SECTION 5.   DUTY AND THIRD PARTIES

There is in general, apart from circumstances of vicarious liability,[9] no duty imposed on one person in respect of loss or injury occasioned to another by a third party, even if that loss or injury is readily foreseeable and preventable.[10] My omission to warn my next door neighbour that she has left a door open, or my failure to telephone the police when I see a suspicious person in her garden, results in no liability on my part for the burglary committed by that person. For a positive duty to act to be imposed in respect of the consequences of third parties' actions two conditions must be met over and above the foreseeability of those actions:

1 There must exist either between the defendant and the third party, or between the defendant and the plaintiff, some special relationship which properly demands of the defendant that he safeguard the plaintiff from the wrongful conduct of the third party.
2 The damage done by the third party must be closely related to, a very probable result of, some failure in care by the defendant.

Whether both these issues go to the existence of a duty, or the first to duty, and the second to remoteness of damage, is a nice point. We shall so divide them for convenience and deal with the second condition later in the chapter on causation. However, illustrating that, while analysis of the tort of negligence into component parts of duty, breach and remoteness is useful for an understanding of the tort, the three are nevertheless closely inter-related, OLIVER LJ put the question thus:[11]

> ... I think that the question of the existence of duty and that of whether the damage brought about by the act of a third party is too remote are simply two facets of the same problem: for if there be a duty to take reasonable care to prevent damage being caused by a third party then I find it difficult to see how damage caused by that third party consequent on the failure to take such care can be too remote a consequence of the breach of duty. Essentially the answer to both questions is to be found in answering the question: in what circumstances is a defendant to be held responsible at common law for the independent act of a third person whom he knows or ought to know may injure his neighbour?

There is alas, for the student, no one principle applicable to all cases where a duty may arise in respect of the wrongdoing of others. Three categories may be suggested but they are by no means exhaustive.[12]

(1) Where the defendant has the right to control the conduct of the third

---

8 See S H Bailey and M J Bowman 'Negligence in the Realms of Public Law—A Positive Obligation to Rescue' [1984] PL 277.
9 See post ch 27.
10 *Weld-Blundell v Stephens* [1920] AC 956 per LORD SUMNER at 986; *Smith v Leurs* (1945) 70 CLR 256 per LORD DIXON CJ at 261–262.
11 *Perl (P) (Exporters) Ltd v Camden LBC* [1983] 3 All ER 161 at 167.
12 See in particular the judgment of LORD GOFF in *Smith v Littlewoods Organisation Ltd* [1987] 1 All ER 710 at 728 et seq.

party, a failure of control resulting in the very kind of damage likely to result from lack of control may be actionable by the injured plaintiff. So where parents or teachers fail to supervise young children adequately, they may be in breach of duty not only to the child if she injures herself, but also to any other person injured by intentional or negligent wrongdoing by that child.[13] In *Home Office v Dorset Yacht Co Ltd*[14] the Home Office's contention that no duty could arise in the case of a wrong committed by a person of full age and capacity, who was not the servant of or acting on behalf of the defendant, failed. The statutory right to control the trainees conferred on the borstal authorities imported a duty of care to those who were at immediate risk of loss or damage from negligent failure to control the trainees. Their 'special relationship' with the trainees and the existence of an identifiable and determinate class of potential victims (the yacht owners) created the duty owed to the latter.[15] Both these factors were absent in *Hill v Chief Constable of West Yorkshire*[16] where the mother of the Yorkshire Ripper's last victim sought on behalf of her daughter's estate to sue the police for negligence in failing to apprehend Sutcliffe earlier. The general duty owed by the police in public law to prevent crime did not give rise to a common law duty to victims of crime. The class of potential victims was indeterminable. And more crucially there was before his arrest no right vested in the West Yorkshire police to control his conduct; there was no 'special relationship' either between the police and Sutcliffe or the police and his unfortunate final victim. Overall, as Fox LJ put it, applying LORD KEITH's observations in the *Peabody Donation* to a personal injuries claim, Mrs Hill failed to establish that it was 'just and reasonable' to impose a duty on the police in respect of Sutcliffe's deliberate and murderous act.[17]

(2) Where the defendant has created some special source of danger,[18] or presented a third party with the means of committing a tort, he may be under a duty to those placed at risk by his folly. For example, handing a loaded gun to a small boy in the street, who then shoots the next passer by, will result in liability on the part of the foolish adult who created the danger. But this is a category which must be carefully confined. Do I owe a duty of care to road users placed at risk by a student whom I know to be drunk, but to whom I lend my car to drive home? Do I owe a similar duty in respect of the conduct of guests at my dinner party, when I am aware they came by car, but whom I continue to ply with alcohol?[19]

(3) Most hotly disputed recently has been the scope of the duty imposed on owners of adjoining property in respect of the security of their property. For there clearly is a duty to take care that property you occupy is not a source

---

13 For example when lack of supervision leads to a child straying onto the road where a driver is injured swerving to avoid him; see *Carmarthenshire CC v Lewis* [1955] AC 549, [1955] All ER 565.

14 [1970] AC 1004, [1979] 2 All ER 294.

15 Had the trainees made good their escape from the island it is clear that the Home Office would not have been held liable for subsequent crimes committed by them on the mainland even though a presumption of general criminal activity by the boys is more than foreseeable.

16 [1987] 1 All ER 1173, CA.

17 Would the police have been under a duty to a victim attacked after Sutcliffe's arrest had negligence by officers guarding him at the police station allowed him to escape?

18 *Haynes v Harwood* [1935] 1 KB 146 (leaving horses and van unattended in the street acting as an allurement to mischievous boys to untie them and let them loose).

19 See *Paterson Zonchonis & Co Ltd v Merfarken Packaging Ltd* [1980] 3 All ER 522 per ROBERT GOFF LJ at 540–542.

of danger to adjoining premises so that, for example, failure to maintain the property in good repair, allowing fire to spread from one to the other, may all in appropriate circumstances be actionable. In *Perl (P) (Exporters) Ltd v Camden LBC*[20] the facts were these:

> The local authority owned a block of flats the basement flat of which was unoccupied. The plaintiffs were tenants of an adjoining flat. The empty flat was left unsecured and there had been several burglaries in the area. Burglars entered the empty flat, knocked a hole through the 18″ common wall and burgled the plaintiffs' property.

The Court of Appeal found that the authority owed the plaintiffs no duty of care in respect of the loss inflicted by the burglary. The relationship of neighbouring property owners was of itself insufficient to impose on one the duty to guard the other against the foreseeable risk of burglary by way of an unsecured property. And in *Smith v Littlewoods Organisation Ltd*[1] the House of Lords rejected a claim for damage caused by a fire started by vandals in a disused cinema owned by the defendants which spread to the plaintiffs' property. Of crucial importance in both judgments was the issue of, if a duty were imposed how could it be fulfilled? If the only effective precaution was a twenty four hour guard on the premises, was this an obligation which could fairly be laid on the defendant, or did responsibility for securing his own premises, albeit in difficult circumstances, remain with the plaintiff. And the policy implications of extending the duty to neighbouring owners to embrace the conduct of thieves and vandals were clearly of the highest relevance.

> Is every occupier of a terraced house under a duty to his neighbours to shut his windows or lock his door when he goes out, or to keep access to his cellars secure, or even to remove his fire escape, at the risk of being held liable in damages if thieves thereby obtain access to his own house and thence to his neighbour's house? I cannot think that the law imposes any such duty.[2]

Two notes of caution must be mentioned. In relation to the duties of neighbouring property owners consideration must always be given to potential duties created by the torts of nuisance and *Rylands v Fletcher*, as well as negligence alone. None of the series of judgments excludes the possibility of either an exceptional case imposing a duty of care on neighbouring property owners in respect of damage done by third parties, nor of some other new category of special relationship imposing liability for third parties arising in an appropriate case in the future.

SECTION 6.   DUTIES IN TORT AND CONTRACT

There are now many circumstances when liability for negligence arises concurrently in tort and contract. An implied duty of care derives from the contract between the parties.[3] This proximity creates a concurrent duty in tort. Concurrent liability has always been recognised where the defendant

---

20 [1984] QB 342, [1983] 3 All ER 161.
 1 [1987] 1 All ER 710.
 2 *Perl (P) (Exporters) Ltd v Camden LBC* [1984] QB 342, [1983] 3 All ER 161 at 360 and 172 respectively.
 3 For an example of a duty of care implied by statute into a contract for services see the Supply of Goods and Services Act 1982 discussed post at p 293.

exercised a 'common calling', for example, a blacksmith, innkeeper or common carrier. Those 'callings' imposed a duty to show the degree of skill normally expected of a person exercising that particular 'calling', irrespective of contract. But in the case of many professionals, such as solicitors and architects, it was once held that, where there was a contract between the parties, the plaintiff was confined to his remedy in contract alone.[4] A series of Court of Appeal judgments established that such a restrictive rule is no longer applicable. Where the defendant undertakes to provide a service, and the plaintiff relies on the careful performance of that service, a duty of care will normally arise from the parties' relationship concurrent with any duty implied into a contract.[5]

Nevertheless the duties of care owed in contract and tort must not be equated absolutely. Consider the cautionary words of LORD SCARMAN in *Tai Hing Cotton Mill Ltd v Liu Chang Hing Bank Ltd.*[6]

> Though it is possible as a matter of legal semantics to conduct an analysis of the rights and duties inherent in some contractual relationships ... either as a matter of contract law when the question will be what, if any, terms are to be implied or as a matter of tort law when the task will be to identify a duty arising from the proximity and character of the relationship between the parties, their Lordships believe it to be correct on principle and necessary for the avoidance of confusion in the law to adhere to the contractual analysis, on principle because it is a relationship in which the parties have, subject to a few exceptions, the right to determine their obligations to each other, and for avoidance of confusion because different consequences do follow according to whether liability arises from contract or tort, eg in the limitation of action.

A literal application of LORD SCARMAN's words in this Privy Council judgment would necessarily result, in practice, in a return to the restrictive rules of *no* concurrent contractual and tortious liability. It might be accepted in theory that the obligation to take care derives both from contract and tort, but in practice should the courts elect for the contractual analysis alone? The series of appellate judgments rejecting such an approach are not cited or considered in *Tai Hing Cotton Mill Ltd.* Accordingly STEYN J in *Banque Keyser Ullman SA v Skandia (UK) Insurance Co Ltd*[7] felt free to hold that the contractual relationship between insured and insurers did not prevent a concurrent duty in tort owed by the former to the latter. LORD SCARMAN's warning was to be taken as tentative in character. It should be taken note of by those who would too glibly abandon all distinction between contract and tort. It does not mark a return to a contract only rule.

That contract and tort may create concurrent, but by no means coterminous duties, is illustrated further by the consequences of electing to sue in tort or contract where such an election is permissible. The limitation period in contract starts to run from the date of the relevant breach of duty. In tort that start may be delayed until a date when the plaintiff could reasonably have become aware of the damage caused by the breach.[8] Contributory

---

4 *Bagot v Stevens, Scanlan & Co Ltd* [1966] 1 QB 197, [1964] 3 All ER 577.
5 *Esso Petroleum Co Ltd v Mardon* [1975] QB 819, [1975] 1 All ER 203, CA; *Midland Bank Trust Co Ltd v Hett, Stubbs & Kemp* [1979] Ch 384, CA; *Batty v Metropolitan Property Realisations Ltd* [1978] QB 554, [1978] 2 All ER 445.
6 [1986] AC 80 at 107 (vigorously criticised by R Martin 2 Prof Neg 17).
7 [1987] 2 All ER 923, [1987] 2 WLR 1300.
8 See post at p 505.

negligence is a partial defence to the tort of negligence but may not be available in an action for breach of contract.[9]

The limits of a tort action in comparison with contract must be noted in this context. A surgeon treating a NHS patient can owe him no obligation higher or stricter than that of care. He does not contract with his patient to 'guarantee' success. In *Thake v Maurice*[10] the plaintiff paid for a private vasectomy. The operation was carefully and competently performed. Some time later the minute risk of natural reversal of the surgery materialised. The plaintiff's wife conceived again. In his action for breach of contract the plaintiff's counsel argued thus. The surgeon never mentioned the possibility of the vasectomy 'failing'. Therefore he contracted to render Mr Thake sterile. When he failed to do so he was in breach of contract. The Court of Appeal finally dismissed that claim holding that in such a contract a term 'guaranteeing' success could not reasonably be implied.[11] But the argument could never even have been attempted in tort.

Consider also the famous American case of *Hawkins v McGee*.[12] The plaintiff severely burned his hand. The defendant, a plastic surgeon, undertook to treat the hand and restore it to perfect condition. After treatment the hand was in fact much worse than before. The measure of damages awarded in contract was the difference between the hand after treatment and a perfect hand. In tort it would have been the difference between the burned hand and the hand after surgery. In contract the plaintiff is awarded damages for not obtaining the result he contracted for. In tort he is awarded only compensation for the consequences of any lack of care.

The relationship between tort and contract is relevant not only to questions of concurrent liability but also to cases where a third party seeks to establish that A who owes a duty in contract to B also owes a duty in tort to him. *Donoghue v Stevenson*[13] dismisses the fallacy that privity of contract *per se* prevents such a duty to the third party ever arising. If there is the necessary proximity between the parties then a duty in tort may arise independently of any contract between A and B. Nevertheless in relation to claims for economic loss in particular[14] the courts are wary of abandoning distinction between tort and contract altogether. In *Balsamo v Medici*[15] the plaintiff authorised his agent to sell a car and pay the proceeds to a relative. The agent entrusted the task to a sub-agent. He carelessly handed the proceeds of the sale to an imposter. The action in negligence against the sub-agent failed. The plaintiff's remedy lay against his agent alone. Any other result, the judges held, would undermine privity of contract.

---

9 See post at p 246.
10 [1986] QB 644, CA.
11 The plaintiff lost 2–1 in the Court of Appeal. See though the judgment at first instance [1984] 2 All ER 513. Peter Pain J held for the plaintiff in contract and his judgment is instructive on the relationship between tort and contract.
12 84 NH 114, 146 A 641 (1929).
13 [1932] AC 562; see ante at 159.
14 See post at p 190; and see P Cane 'Contract, Tort and Economic Loss' in *The Law of Tort* ed by M Furmston (1986).
15 [1984] 2 All ER 304, [1984] 1 WLR 951.

Chapter 12

Duty of care II: recognised harm

SECTION 1.   INTRODUCTION

'The rule that you are to love your neighbour becomes in law, you must not injure your neighbour . . .'

LORD ATKIN's famous and elegant phrase begs one vital question. What kinds of injury must you take care to avoid inflicting on your neighbour? Failing to return his love may hurt him deeply. No-one would suggest that he can sue you for his distress. The previous chapter examined how subsequent case-law has outlined broad principles within which the ATKIN 'neighbour principle' is used as a starting point when considering whether a duty of care arises. This chapter concentrates on what is perhaps the most crucial issue in the process of defining duty-situations. What kinds of harm give rise to a duty of care in tort?

Restrictive interpretations of the ATKIN principle in the years immediately following *Donoghue v Stevenson* sought to limit its application to personal injuries alone.[1] Over thirty years passed before it was considered applicable to claims for economic loss.[2] Today, in principle, recognition is accorded in an appropriate case to duties to avoid physical damage to persons and property, including emotional harm to persons and damage to real property, and to duties to avoid inflicting economic loss alone. Without doubt it is still much easier to obtain recognition of a duty to avoid physical damage than a duty to avoid 'pure' economic loss. But that does not mean that determining the scope of a duty to avoid personal injuries is in all instances free of controversy. Problems arise in relation to the foreseeability of injury to a particular plaintiff, the limits of liability for emotional harm and whether social policy requires that certain types of harm to persons go uncompensated in the 'public interest'. Nor does the more ready recognition of physical damage as a source of duty mean that the distinction drawn between physical damage and 'pure' economic loss is clear and undisputed. And the case-law illustrates too the artificiality of attempting systematically to define exact and immoveable boundaries between questions of duty, breach and remoteness of damage. The essence of the issue of what kinds of harm are remediable in tort is the determination of the limits of the tort of negligence in 1988. The umbrella of the scope of the duty of care provides a convenient mechanism within which to explore those limits.[3]

The following principles must be borne in mind throughout this chapter.

1 There are kinds of harm which are irremediable in English law even if intentionally and maliciously inflicted. Invasion of privacy and interference

---

1 Eg *Deyong v Shenburn* [1946] KB 227, [1946] 1 All ER 226.
2 *Hedley Byrne & Co v Heller & Partners Ltd* [1964] AC 465, [1963] 2 All ER 575.
3 For powerful criticism of the concept of duty of care in negligence see J C Smith *Liability in Negligence* (1984) Carswell and read in particular ch 1 'The Mystery of Duty'.

with business, without otherwise unlawful means, are just two examples. When the harm of which the plaintiff complains does not give rise to a tort if committed intentionally, the courts will be naturally reluctant to say that such harm gives rise to a cause of action if inflicted carelessly.

2 Liability for careless acts and omissions has to be confined within manageable proportions. The courts will strive to avoid liability 'in an indeterminable amount for an indefinite time to an indeterminate class.'[4]

3 Once again the proper functions of tort and contract and the borderline between them are in issue. Where the substance of the plaintiff's claim is that the defendant failed to provide value for money for services performed, and no contract existed between them, is imposing a duty of care in such circumstances trespassing on the sanctity of privacy of contract? Does it matter?

SECTION 2.   HARM TO PERSONS

A. DUTY TO RESCUERS

Recognition of a duty owed in respect of physical and emotional injury to rescuers raises two important questions about the ambit of the duty to avoid harm to persons. The rescuer is only indirectly at risk from the negligent conduct. Is he then a foreseeable plaintiff? As a rescuer 'elects' to undertake the rescue can he properly claim that the originator of the danger owes him any obligation in respect of his safety which he has 'chosen' to imperil?

In 1935 the Court of Appeal held for the first time that a defendant who owed a duty to another also owed a duty to those who might foreseeably attempt to rescue him from the acute peril in which the defendant's negligence had placed him.[5] Subsequent case-law consistently confirmed a judicial policy to encourage and commend rescue attempts. 'Danger invites rescue. The cry of distress is a summons to relief.'[6] Consequently arguments that no duty is owed to the rescuer electing to imperil his own safety have fallen on deaf ears. Whether the rescuer is a member of the emergency services, whose public duty it is to embark on the rescue mission, or a well-meaning member of the public,[7] the courts will now hold that a duty is owed to him.

The duty owed to rescuers is independent of proof of any breach of duty to another person. In *Videan v British Transport Commission*[8] it was held that a duty was owed to a stationmaster rescuing his small son who had been trespassing on the lines. Albeit that, at that time, no duty was owed to the child trespasser, the stationmaster's presence on the tracks dealing with an emergency was foreseeable thus creating a duty to him directly and personally. The independent duty to a rescuer is now imposed, not only on those who endanger other people or their property so as to invite rescue, but also on anyone endangering himself or his own property so as to create the likelihood of rescue. A householder whose negligent use of a blowlamp resulted in his

---

4 *Ultramares Corpn v Touche* 255 NY 170 (1931) per Cardozo CJ at 444.
5 *Haynes v Harwood* [1935] 1 KB 146, CA.
6 *Wagner v International Rly Co* (1921) 232 NY Rep 176.
7 *Baker v T E Hopkins & Son Ltd* [1958] 3 All ER 147, CA (damages awarded to the widow of a doctor rescuer); *Chadwick v British Transport Commission* [1967] 2 All ER 945, [1967] 1 WLR 912 (nearby resident coming to the aid of victims of a rail disaster and suffering nervous shock).
8 [1963] 2 QB 650, [1963] 2 All ER 860, CA.

setting his roof on fire was held liable to the fireman injured fighting the blaze.[9]

Before the English courts contentions that members of the emergency services should not, as a matter of policy, receive compensation for undertaking the very duty which they are engaged to perform, have received scant consideration. The rescue cases in England are marked by an emphatic desire by the judiciary to 'reward' desirable conduct and encourage in this limited sphere 'Good Samaritanism'. The economic issues behind the imposition of liability to firemen and police officers are ignored. What the courts are in fact doing on one interpretation is transferring the loss from the public purse to the shoulders of the negligent citizen, imposing a tax on carelessness.[10]

B. DUTY TO THE UNBORN

Whether a duty of care was owed to a child damaged by another's negligence before its birth remained unresolved at common law. The potential for and horror of such damage was graphically illustrated by the thalidomide tragedy when children all over the world were born with serious deformities caused by a sedative taken by their mothers in early pregnancy. The Congenital Disabilities (Civil Liability) Act 1976 provides that a child who is born alive but disabled as a result of an occurrence before its birth may in certain circumstances have a cause of action in negligence against the person responsible for that occurrence.[11] The Act supersedes the common law in respect of births after its passing.[12] The duty imposed relates to any occurrence, whether it be one affecting the reproductive capacity of either parent before conception (for example toxic chemicals which damage the father's sperm so as to cause him to beget disabled children), or one affecting the mother during pregnancy (such as a drug causing deformities to the foetus in the womb). The peculiarity of the duty to the child is that it is derivative only. The relevant occurrence must have resulted in liability in tort to the affected parent although it is no answer that the parent suffered no actionable injury '... if there was a breach of legal duty which, accompanied by injury, would have given rise to the liability.'[13] But if there was no injury, wherein lies the breach of duty? It can only be argued that it lies in the breach of duty to the parent to avoid inflicting on her the harm naturally resulting from giving birth to a damaged child. The 1976 Act in general imposes a duty towards parents to avoid inflicting injury to their reproductive functions. The cause of action conferred on the child when born is simply a by-product of the breach of duty to the affected parent.

Not surprisingly then mothers[14] are expressly immune from general liability under the Act. How could a mother damaging her baby by smoking or drinking too much be in breach of duty to herself? Or would she be in breach of duty to the father in damaging *his* child? But section 2 does expressly

---

9 *Ogwo v Taylor* [1987] 3 All ER 961, HL.
10 See the American judgments cited in *Ogwo v Taylor* [1987] 1 All ER 668 at 674–675, CA.
11 Section 1(1).
12 Section 4(5).
13 Section 1(3).
14 See s 1. Fathers are not so immune. But what sorts of circumstance could create parental liability—infecting mother and baby with AIDS?

provide for the only direct duty owed to the unborn. A woman may be liable for damage to her child inflicted by her negligent driving of a motor vehicle when she knows or ought to know herself to be pregnant.

The complexity of the 1976 Act has to be seen to be believed. Its failure to address the issue of causation, the greatest problem in any case of pre-natal injury, has resulted in it being a largely useless and unused piece of legislation. But one crucial question in relation to pre-natal injury and the scope of recognition of harm to persons has been ventilated in the courts. In *McKay v Essex Area Health Authority*[15] the Court of Appeal held that in England the common law recognised no claim for 'wrongful life'. The plaintiff was born, before the passing of the 1976 Act, with terrible disabilities resulting from her mother having contracted rubella (German measles) in pregnancy. The mother had undergone tests when she realised that she had been in contact with the disease and had been negligently told that the tests were negative. She would have opted for an abortion had tests proved positive. The child through its parents sued in respect of the harm caused to her by her birth encumbered by her manifold disability. The Court of Appeal held that it was impossible to measure the harm resulting from entry into a life afflicted by disability where the only alternative was no life at all. Nor were they prepared to impose on doctors a duty of care which was in essence a duty to abort.

In respect of births subsequent to the 1976 Act ACKNER LJ[16] said that the Act gave a cause of action only in respect of occurrences causing disabilities which would otherwise not have afflicted the child. It did not afford a remedy to a child whose birth, afflicted by pre-existing disability, was caused by the defendant's alleged negligence. His Lordship's finding that the Act was inapplicable to a claim for 'wrongful life' was seen by him as preventing such claims arising in future. However, one alternative result of ACKNER LJ's finding that the 1976 Act does not allow 'wrongful life' suits is that that Act is irrelevant to such suits and that the issue of 'wrongful life' with all its ethical and moral implications remains open for review by the House of Lords.[17]

C. NERVOUS SHOCK

Damages cannot be awarded, at common law, for ordinary grief and sorrow experienced when a relative or friend is killed or injured, or when a person is distressed by some dreadful incident or disaster. The courts have in the past been cautious about awarding damages for any non-physical harm to the person, even when that harm goes well beyond normal distress resulting in some cases in obvious physical symptoms. The reasons for caution are easy to catalogue. They are the difficulties of putting a monetary value on such harm, the risk of fictitious claims and excessive litigation ('opening the floodgates'), and the problems of proving the link between the defendant's negligence and the injury to the plaintiff. Gradual, if belated, judicial recognition that psychiatric evidence can establish that link between mind and body led to the abandonment of the nineteenth century attitude that non-

15 [1982] QB 1166, [1982] 2 All ER 771, CA.
16 Ibid at 1187 and 786.
17 See CR Symmons 'Policy Factors in Actions for Wrongful Birth' (1987) 50 MLR 269; J Fortin (1987) JSWL 306.

physical harm was always irrecoverable.[18] 'Nervous shock' 'psychiatric damage'[19] became a recognised kind of harm.[20]

The primary limitation on recovery for nervous shock remains the need to prove harm over and above ordinary grief or distress. Generally, this means that the plaintiff must bring medical evidence to prove that as a result of the shock occasioned to him by the defendant's negligence he has suffered a recognised physical or psychiatric disorder.[21] When then does a duty to avoid such harm arise? The foreseeability of such harm must be established and in laying down criteria for proximity in cases of nervous shock the courts have proceeded on a case by case basis. The option of simply relying on psychiatric evidence to determine where a traumatic event is likely to produce in the average individual a foreseeable psychiatric illness has been expressly rejected.[1]

First, in *Dulieu v White & Sons*[2] damages were awarded to a pregnant woman who suffered a miscarriage resulting from shock and fear for her own safety when she narrowly missed being hit by a vehicle carelessly driven by the defendant. In *Hambrook v Stokes Bros*[3] the trial judge's ruling that recovery for shock was limited to persons in immediate physical danger and fearful for their own safety alone was overturned by the majority of the Court of Appeal. The plaintiff's pregnant wife suffered a miscarriage, and later died, after the shock of seeing a driverless lorry career down a steep road from the direction of the bend round which her children had just passed from her sight. BANKES LJ found that if the shock resulted from fear for herself *or for her children* derived from what she saw or realised by her own unaided senses, and not from what others subsequently told her, she could recover.

What the plaintiff must be able to prove is that harm to him is a foreseeable result of the defendant's conduct. So in *Bourhill v Young*[4]

> The plaintiff, a pregnant Edinburgh fishwife, having alighted from a tram, was removing her basket from the offside of the driver's platform. A motor-cyclist, driving carelessly, but unseen by the plaintiff, passed the tram on the near side and collided with a car 45 to 50 feet from where the plaintiff was standing. Through hearing the noise of the impact and, apparently, later seeing a pool of blood on the roadway, but without herself ever seeing the cyclist or fearing immediate bodily injury to herself, she suffered nervous shock and a consequent miscarriage.

The House of Lords dismissed the action holding that the cyclist owed no duty of care to persons whom he could not reasonably anticipate suffering

---

18 For the C19 view see *Victorian Railways Comrs v Coultas* (1888) 13 App Cas 222, PC.

19 The term preferred by Bingham LJ in *Attia v British Gas plc* [1987] 3 All ER 455 at 462, CA.

20 As to what we now mean by the 'hallowed expression "nervous shock"' see per LORD WILBERFORCE in *McLoughlin v O'Brian* [1982] 2 All ER 298 at 301.

21 Although in *Whitmore v Euroways Express Coaches Ltd* (1984) Times, 4 May COMYN J awarded a wife damages for the 'ordinary' shock at witnessing her husband's injuries without any supporting medical evidence. The principle that the plaintiff must establish '... not merely grief, distress or any other normal emotion, but a positive psychiatric illness' was reiterated by LORD BRIDGE in *McLoughlin v O'Brian* (supra) at 311. *Whitmore* must be explained either as (a) an aberration (b) creating a new class of 'ordinary' shock distinct from true 'nervous' shock (c) or an example of compensation for mental distress consequent on physical injury: see post at ch 29.

1 *McLoughlin v O'Brian* (supra) at 311–313.

2 [1901] 2 KB 669.

3 [1925] 1 KB 141, CA.

4 [1943] AC 92, [1942] 2 All ER 396, HL.

either physical injury or nervous shock as a result of his carelessness. Their Lordships found that no-one would reasonably expect a person of normal susceptibility to shock to suffer any injury as a result of what the plaintiff saw or heard that day. It is suggested in one of the judgments that had the cyclist's negligence been more gross and the whole circumstances of the accident more traumatic recovery might have been allowed.[5] The judgments are not completely in accord, but the majority in *Bourhill v Young* were of the opinion that even though the plaintiff was in no physical danger, beyond the range of foreseeable impact, she would still have recovered should injury by nervous shock reasonably have been contemplated. And that must be the correct test. Nothing in the judgment suggests that simply proving that the plaintiff is within the area of physical impact it follows that there is a duty not to inflict shock on him.[6] Of course, in many cases a plaintiff who narrowly misses physical injury will be able to prove that shock occasioned by his fear for his own safety was foreseeable. But should a speeding car skid to a standstill just short of me on the pelican crossing I must still establish that in those circumstances any psychiatric consequences I suffer as a result of that everyday event should have been anticipated by the careless driver, and I may well have difficulty doing so.[7]

Case-law subsequent to *Bourhill v Young* elaborated the circumstances in which the courts were ready to find shock foreseeable and proximate to the defendant's negligence. In *Boardman v Sanderson*[8] the defendant negligently backed a car over the foot of the plaintiff's young son. The father was within earshot and heard the boy's screams but did not witness the accident itself. He recovered damages for nervous shock and the court rejected the contention that only those actually seeing what happened can recover for shock. The plaintiff in *Chadwick v British Transport Commission*[9] became severely ill after going to help for several hours in the rescue of passengers after a particularly horrific rail accident. The court found that the circumstances of the injuries and the terror caused by the accident made it foreseeable that those witnessing its results would suffer shock. A duty is owed to rescuers and therefore, shock being foreseeable to a rescuer, the defendants were liable to Mr Chadwick.

The limits on liability established by analysis of the case-law up to 1982 appeared to be that the plaintiff should be present at the scene of the accident, or very near to it, so that with his unaided senses he realised what had happened, and that generally he must be very closely related to the person suffering physical injury. Indeed in the vast majority of cases the plaintiff has been the parent of a young child.

In *McLoughlin v O'Brian*[10]

The plaintiff's husband and three children were in a car which was involved in an accident caused by the defendants' negligence. All four of her family

5 Per Lord Porter at 118.
6 Cf Singleton LJ in *King v Phillips* [1953] 1 QB 429 at 437.
7 Where actual physical injury is suffered by the plaintiff consequential damages for shock and distress may now be awarded: see *Kralj v McGrath* [1986] 1 All ER 54 and *Whitmore v Euroways Express Coaches* supra at 178.
8 [1964] 1 WLR 1317, CA.
9 [1967] 2 All ER 945; and see *Dooley v Cammell Laird & Co* [1951] 1 Lloyd's Rep 271 (crane operators recovered for shock occasioned by fear for his workmates when an unsound rope caused his load to crash into the hold where his fellows were working).
10 [1983] 1 AC 410, [1982] 2 All ER 298, HL.

were injured, one so seriously that she died almost immediately. An hour afterwards a friend told her at her home two miles away of the accident. He drove her to the hospital where she was told of the death and saw the three injured. The plaintiff, a woman of reasonable fortitude, suffered in consequence severe shock, organic depression and a change of personality; there were numerous symptoms of a physiological character.

The Court of Appeal rejected her claim limiting the duty to avoid shock to those at or very near the scene of the accident. The House of Lords unanimously overturned their ruling. They held that the plaintiff had to establish proximity to the traumatic events but coming as she did upon the 'immediate aftermath' of the accident in which her family had been so grievously injured she was well within the scope of the duty to avoid nervous shock. Beyond that there are distinct differences of approach among their Lordships as to where to set the limits of the duty to avoid inflicting shock and in particular whether the test should be forseeability alone or whether policy limits should be used to confine the scope of recovery for shock.

LORD BRIDGE and LORD SCARMAN would define liability for shock by reference to foreseeability alone disregarding policy as inappropriate for the court. 'Space, time, distance, the nature of the injuries sustained and the relationship of the plaintiff to the immediate victim of the accident are factors to be weighed, but not legal limitations, when the test of reasonable foreseeability is to be applied'.[11]

LORD EDMUND-DAVIES disagreed in that he found policy factors to be 'justiciable' in such claims, but could discern no valid policy reasons for denying damages to Mrs McLoughlin. LORD RUSSELL declined to speculate in advance on when policy might militate against such a claim. LORD WILBERFORCE saw '... a real need for the law to place some limitation on the extent of admissible claims.'[12] But he too refused to set immovable limits on recovery for nervous shock. He gives indications of the broad criteria within which a duty is owed. The closer the tie between the accident victim and the plaintiff, the closer the proximity between the plaintiff and the scene of the accident, the more likely it is that liability will be found. He offers no firmer rules save to say that shock resulting solely from a communication from a third-party should remain irrecoverable. 'The shock must come through sight or hearing of the event or of its immediate aftermath. Whether some equivalent of sight or hearing, eg through simultaneous television, would suffice may have to be considered.'[13]

The disagreement among their Lordships in *McLoughlin v O'Brian* as to whether proximity alone determined the limits of liability for shock is likely today to be resolved in favour of accepting the justiciability of policy factors. Recent pronouncements by their Lordships have moved well away from the high watermark of simple application of the 'neighbour principle' advocated by LORD SCARMAN in *McLoughlin v O'Brian*.[14] The limitations on liability for shock which may be maintained in the future as a matter of policy are two-fold:

11 Per LORD SCARMAN at 431 and 311 respectively.
12 At 421 and 304.
13 At 423 and 305.
14 See supra at p 162.

1 The requirement that the plaintiff must show that a person of normal disposition and phlegm would have been harmed by the shock will be hard to displace.

It is as WALLER J said in *Chadwick v British Transport Commission*[15] more than foreseeable that within the community some people are more vulnerable to stress than others. Forseeability of the psychiatrically vulnerable plaintiff may be insufficient to create a duty to him. But if some material effect on the normal person is foreseeable the fact that the degree of that effect, the extent of the illness suffered by the vulnerable plaintiff, is much greater than what would be expected of a normal person will not deny him full compensation. The 'eggshell skull' rule applies to psychiatric injury as well as physical harm.[16]

2 The plaintiff will still be required to prove that the harm to him resulted from what he saw or heard himself and not solely from what he was told.

Whether this is always a just and fair rule may be tested on this example. A young child is grievously injured when an explosion wrecks her school. Police go to her home a mile away to tell her elderly parents. Her father collapses and later becomes seriously ill. Her mother rushes to the scene and then seeing her dying child, collapses and later succumbs to symptoms identical to her husband's. Is it right to deny a remedy to the father? What relevant policy factors demand that you do so?

Beyond these two limitations it seems less likely that even in the more cautious climate of 1988 further boundaries will be set on nervous shock.[17] Recovery for example by non-relatives will be rare but not impossible. The scale of the accident and its horror will dictate the scale of potential recovery of shock extending in an extreme case perhaps to mere bystanders. But what of LORD WILBERFORCE's speculations about televised horror? When I see on the television news pictures of the capsized ferry at Zeebrugge and watch the injured and the dead brought ashore, I may be expected to have sufficient fortitude to survive the experience distressed but unscathed. Will the hundreds of relatives who watching that same programme feared for, or actually saw, their own family in the carnage be afforded a remedy if the experience overwhelmed them and they succumbed to illness?

SECTION 3.   POLICY AND PUBLIC INTEREST

The ebb and flow of judicial readiness to limit liability for foreseeable harm by invoking 'public policy' is at the core of the discussion in both this and the previous chapter.

Let us clarify one issue first. The concept of public policy applied by the courts to limit duties of care in tort has in many cases little to do with the public interest in the sense of public morality. We shall look a little later at those situations where it does mean just that, and overlaps with the concept of public policy and public interest invoked in contract and criminal law.

15 [1967] 2 All ER 945; and see *Jaensch v Coffey* (1984) 54 ALR 417.
16 *Brice v Brown* [1984] 1 All ER 997.
17 See, for example, *Attia v British Gas plc* [1987] 3 All ER 455, [1987] 3 WLR 1101, CA where the plaintiff recovered for shock occasioned by seeing her house destroyed by fire.

Policy, as we have seen it in operation so far in tort, is concerned far more with the following factors:

1 Is the imposition of a duty in the relevant circumstances feasible and enforceable? Harm to my neighbour's person or property is easily fore-seeable if I leave my home so insecure that a burglar or a rapist can use my house to gain a concealed exit to hers. But what steps am I required to take to secure her security?
2 Is the imposition of a duty fair? When is the law properly to demand that X safeguards the interests of Y rather than requiring Y to take care of himself?

So both in the judgments relating to liability for vandals and burglars obtaining entry to neighbouring property, and the decisions on the exercise of statutory powers, judicial policy has come down on the side of individual responsibility rather than promoting a broad duty of 'community care' for each other.

3 What are the implications for insurance cover of extending the scope of duty situations?

This factor is rarely voiced publicly but is crucial. Extending duties of care to cover deserving cases is all very well in the abstract, but futile if the defendant lacks funds to pay any damages. Insurance cover requires some certainty in defining the scope of potential liability in order to set realistic premiums and to delineate the conditions of the policy. So in nervous shock claims the range of possible victims suffering grief or distress as a result of a relative or friend's injury or death is more or less unlimited. The law to a greater or lesser extent, dependent on the current judicial trends, imposes arbitrary limits.

Feasibility, fairness and stability are the key policy issues usually invoked by the courts in tort. They are criteria designed to attempt to create a balanced framework defining the relationships between individuals in society. They are concerned with where X stands in relation to his 'neighbour' Y. Of course in utilising concepts of fairness, of what is 'just and reasonable' social judgments are made. For example, the promotion of the virtue of self-reliance is taken for granted. But in general in the majority of cases so far considered no obvious and fundamental moral or ethical issues have been at stake.

How will the courts approach the issue of the imposition of a duty of care where genuinely moral questions are posed? Two examples of denying the existence of a duty in such cases have already been touched on. In *Ashton v Turner*[18] EWBANK J declined to recognise a duty of care owed by one participant in crime to another. And in *McKay v Essex Area Health Authority*[19] the Court of Appeal refused to impose a duty to a child to terminate her existence before her birth.

But in other recent judgments the courts have shown themselves unwilling to mount the unruly horse of public policy in claims where the policy factors raised were essentially matters of public morality and society's values. The applicability of this sort of public interest limitation on the scope of the tort of negligence has been tested in a series of cases concerning whether damages

18 [1981] QB 137 supra at p 161.
19 [1982] QB 1166, [1982] 2 All ER 771, CA supra at p 161.

are recoverable in respect of the birth of an unplanned baby subsequent to a negligently performed sterilization. At first, in *Udale v Bloomsbury Area Health Authority*,[20] JUPP J refused the mother compensation towards the upkeep of the child despite the defendant's admission of negligence. He limited her damages to compensation for the discomfort of her pregnancy. The birth of a child was, he said, a 'blessing'[1] and the financial cost of such a 'blessing' was irrecoverable. It offended society's notions of what is right and the value afforded to human life, and the knowledge that his parents had claimed damages in respect of his birth might distress and damage the child emotionally as he grows to maturity.

A year later the Court of Appeal in *Emeh v Kensington Area Health Authority*[2] overruled JUPP J on the policy issue. They were unconvinced that the policy objections should prevent recovery of damages. There might be an incentive to late abortions. The unity of the family and the welfare of the child might well be strengthened not harmed by financial help with his upkeep. Above all their Lordship's expressed a disinclination to place limits on the scope of the duty owed to the mother by reference to what was 'socially unacceptable'. That exercise, echoing LORD SCARMAN in *McLoughlin v O'Brian*, they preferred to leave to parliament.[3]

The decision in *Emeh* prompts a number of questions. Will the judicial tendency manifested in *Emeh* to avoid questions of social policy as devices to limit duty-situations survive the new activist tendency to invoke policy more readily, recently exhibited by the House of Lords? How should the loss of which Mrs Emeh complained properly be classified? Was it harm to the person, simply another consequence of the bungled sterilization along with the discomfort and danger of her unwanted pregnancy? Or is it more properly to be regarded as economic loss on a par with wasted expenditure and/or loss of profits?

SECTION 4.   PHYSICAL DAMAGE TO PROPERTY

Recognition of a duty to avoid proximate physical damage to another's property, as much as to his person, raises no unique problem of principle. Should a negligent driver manage by the narrowest of margins to prevent his vehicle actually injuring me, but the impact does ruin my new Parisienne dress, I may recover the cost of the dress without problems. Should the careless driver, swerving to avoid me, crash into my neighbour's front wall, the neighbour may recover the cost of repairing the wall. Whether the damaged property comprises chattels or real property, a duty not to inflict that kind of harm arises in appropriate circumstances although quite often where the parties are literally neighbours the source of the duty lies in nuisance rather than negligence *simpliciter*.[4]

The class of persons to whom a duty in respect of damage to property is

---

20 [1983] 2 All ER 522, [1983] 1 WLR 1098.
  1 '... I would have to regard the financial disadvantages as offset by her gratitude for the gift of a boy after four girls'! ibid per JUPP J at 531 and 1109 respectively.
  2 [1985] QB 1012, [1984] 3 All ER 1044.
  3 At 1021 and 1053 respectively and see *Scuriaga v Powell* (1979) 123 Sol Jo 406 (damages in contract for birth of child after failed abortion); and *Thake v Maurice* [1986] QB 644, [1986] 1 All ER 497; *Gold v Haringey Health Authority* [1987] 2 All ER 888.
  4 See ch 19.

owed and the manner in which harm is classified as physical damage to property as opposed to 'pure' economic loss do however call for careful consideration. The House of Lords in *Leigh and Sillivan Ltd v Aliakmon Shipping Co Ltd*[5] confirmed the rule that a duty in respect of loss or damage to property is owed only to a person having '... legal ownership of or a possessory title to the property concerned at the time when the loss or damage occurred ...'[6] Should an old house in the process of conversion to flats be destroyed by a fire caused by negligence, only the owner of the house, or a tenant, will recover compensation. The builders, the plumbers, the decorators all of who lose out on valuable contracts to convert the property are left remediless. Contractual rights in relation to property may well be adversely affected by loss or damage to that property, but they are insufficient to give rise to a duty of care.

Where the plaintiff has the necessary title to the damaged property the further question arises of how harm is classified. All harm, be it personal injuries or physical damage to property, is at the end of the day quantified in economic terms. What loss of earnings did the plaintiff's injuries occasion him? How much is it going to cost to repair or replace a damaged wall? What test then can be applied to determine if harm is primarily physical, or primarily solely economic, so taking it into the problematic field of the limited scope of the duty to avoid 'pure' economic loss?

No one simple test will suffice. Two guidelines may be borne in mind. First, physical damage to, or physical defects in, property which render it less than value for money, but not dangerous, will generally be categorised as economic loss only. Consider the position with a negligently manufactured central heating boiler. Should the relevant defect cause it to explode damaging the fabric of the house in which it is installed, or destroying furniture, or injuring the occupants that damage is physical harm and may be recoverable from the manufacturers. But should the defect simply render the boiler useless, a waste of money, the loss suffered is economic loss alone and its recoverability subject to the restrictive rules governing that kind of harm. More difficult though is the classification of the kind of harm where the defect in the boiler renders it potentially dangerous to persons and other property but is discovered before the danger materialises. The end result is identical to the case of the useless boiler. Money must be expended to replace it. Yet it seems that providing present or imminent danger to health or safety can be established the relevant loss will usually be treated on the same basis as physical harm to persons or property.[7]

The second consideration to be borne in mind when attempting to categorise loss as physical harm or economic loss is this. What is the nature of the enterprise involving the use of the relevant property? Owner occupiers who discover that their homes are at risk of collapse because of failure to comply with building regulations may, as we have seen, be able to recover compensation from the local authority which negligently passed the building work as satisfactory and in compliance with the regulations. Development companies whose property suffers exactly the same fate for the same reason

5 [1986] AC 785, [1986] 2 All ER 145; and see *The Mineral Transporter* [1986] AC1, [1985] 2 All ER 935, PC; *Tate & Lyle Industries Ltd v GLC* [1983] 2 AC 509, [1983] 1 All ER 1159.

6 Ibid at 149; *Simaan General Contracting Co v Pilkington Glass Ltd* (1988) Times, 18 February, CA.

7 *Batty v Metropolitan Property Realisations Ltd* [1978] QB 554 at 00, [1978] 2 All ER 445 at 457; *Anns v Merton London Borough Council* [1978] AC 728, [1977] 2 All ER 492, HL. And see *Rimmer v Liverpool City Council* [1985] QB 1, [1984] 1 All ER 930.

will not. And one reason for the refusal to impose a duty to the developer is the classification of their loss as economic.[8] The rationale for the distinction is two-fold and far from undisputed:

1 The developers own the property to make money. Their ownership is temporary and incidental to their ultimate purpose. The owner occupier's sole interest is in his possession of his home.
2 Much emphasis is placed in *Peabody* on the risk that the imminent danger of damage to the property poses to the health and safety of persons. Perhaps what we must conclude is that harm to persons ranks higher in the list of priorities to damage to property.[9]

SECTION 5. ECONOMIC LOSS

A. STATEMENTS AND 'SPECIAL RELATIONSHIPS'

Two difficulties beset the imposition of a duty to avoid making careless statements. There is, first, the very obvious differences between words and acts. As LORD REID put it in *Hedley Byrne & Co Ltd v Heller & Partners Ltd:*[10]

> Quite careful people often express definite opinions on social or informal occasions, even when they see that others are likely to be influenced by them; and they often do that without taking that care which they would take if asked for their opinion professionally, or in a business connexion.

And moreover, while negligent acts will generally have a limited range of impact negligent words may be widely broadcast without the consent or foresight of the speaker. Second, and more important in relation to liability for careless statements is the fact that in the majority of cases the loss sustained will be pecuniary or economic, and not damage to persons or property.

Where physical damage has resulted from careless statements the courts have shown little reluctance to impose a duty of care.[11] So a doctor whose negligent certification of the plaintiff as a person of unsound mind led to his detention in a mental hospital was held liable in negligence as long ago as 1927.[12] The courts are particularly likely to recognise such a duty where the case is similar to a fact-situation in which a duty of care is well established. In *Dutton v Bognor Regis UDC*[13] the defendants were held liable, after their building inspector had negligently and erroneously certified that a new house

---

8 *Peabody Donation Fund (Governors) v Sir Lindsay Parkinson & Co Ltd* [1985] AC 210, [1984] 3 All ER 529 3, HL; *Investors in Industry Commercial Properties v Norwich City Council* [1986] QB 17, [1985] 3 All ER 257, CA.
9 The artificiality of distinctions drawn between physical and economic damage is expressly recognised by LORD ROSKILL in *Junior Books Ltd v Veitchi Co Ltd* [1982] 3 All ER 201 at 213. But see *Simaan General Contracting Co v Pilkington Glass Ltd* (supra).
10 [1964] AC 465 at 487, [1963] 2 All ER 575 at 580.
11 See *Sharp v Avery and Kerwood* [1938] 4 All ER 85, CA (defendant cyclist negligently performed his undertaking to guide the vehicle in which the plaintiff was a passenger; liable to the plaintiff for his ensuing injuries); and see *Bird v Pearce* (1979) 77 LGR 753, CA; *Clayton v Woodman & Son* [1961] 3 All ER 249 (revd on other grounds [1962] 2 All ER 33, CA) (careless instruction on how to proceed with building work resulting in physical harm to the bricklayer).
12 *De Freville v Dill* (1927) 96 LJKB 1056.
13 [1972] 1 QB 373, [1972] 1 All ER 462, CA.

complied with bye-laws on foundations, to a subsequent buyer for cracked windows and other observable damage caused to the house two years later by subsidence.

Nevertheless, whenever it is contended that a duty lies in respect of careless words, spoken or written, the criteria invoked to limit liability for words inflicting economic loss must sometimes also be borne in mind in relation to physical damage. Should I, late at night at a University party, complain to the Professor of Surgery of giddiness and nausea, I cannot sue if he mistakenly suggests to me that I have had too much to drink rather than diagnosing the heart disease of which I collapse a couple of days later. That said, the problems of liability for careless statements resulting in economic loss are still much more substantial. And the development of the duty to avoid statements causing pecuniary loss is inextricably linked to the troubled history of liability for economic loss in general. The original difficulty resulting to pecuniary loss resulting from careless statements was this. A person suffering economic loss through relying on a fraudulent statement could sue in the tort of deceit. In *Derry v Peek*[14] the House of Lords had held that to establish deceit the plaintiff must prove fraud—that the defendant knew that his statement was untrue. Negligence was insufficient. In *Candler v Crane, Christmas & Co*[15] the Court of Appeal relied on *Derry v Peek* to refuse a remedy to the plaintiff who had invested funds in a company on the basis of accounts negligently prepared by the defendant. Without evidence of fraud they held that economic loss resulting from misstatement was irrecoverable.

The fallacy inherent in *Candler v Crane, Christmas & Co* was exposed by the House of Lords in the landmark judgment in 1963, *Hedley Byrne & Co Ltd v Heller & Partners Ltd.*[16]

> The plaintiffs asked their bankers to inquire into the financial stability of a company with which they were having business dealings. Their bankers made inquiries of the company's bankers, who carelessly gave favourable references about the company. Reliance on these references caused the plaintiffs to lose £17,000. The plaintiffs sued the defendants for their careless statements. The action failed because the defendants had expressly disclaimed any responsibility.

Nevertheless all five law lords proceeded to re-examine the authorities on liability for careless statements. They rightly limited the rule in *Derry v Peek* to its proper function of defining the limits of the tort of deceit and thus irrelevant to the issue of whether a duty of care arose in negligence. Nor did the absence of a contract deny the plaintiff a remedy. As LORD DEVLIN said:[17]

> 'A promise given without consideration to perform a service cannot be enforced as a contract by the promisee, but if the service is in fact performed and done negligently the promisee can recover in an action in tort'.

But their Lordships were not prepared simply to recognise a duty of care in respect of statements on the basis of the *Donoghue v Stevenson* neighbour principle alone. For liability for statements resulting in economic loss to be

14 (1889) 14 App Cas 337, HL and see p 109, ante.
15 [1951] 2 KB 164, [1951] 1 All ER 426, CA (but see the powerful dissenting judgment of DENNING LJ).
16 [1964] AC 465, [1963] 2 All ER 575.
17 Ibid at 526 and 608 respectively.

imposed some narrower test than the foreseeability of the loss must be satisfied.[18] The House of Lords was not prepared to formulate rules which might expose a maker of careless statements to liability to a large indeterminate class of plaintiffs. For instance, newspapers were not to be accountable to everybody who read their advice columns and suffered loss through relying on their negligent advice.[19] The plaintiff to recover for negligent misstatements must establish that the statement was made within a relationship where the plaintiff could reasonably rely on the skill and care of the defendant in making the statement. He must show some 'special relationship' with the defendant which properly resulted in the defendant undertaking responsibility for the accuracy of the statements made.

What sorts of relationships did later case-law find to be sufficiently special? LORD DIPLOCK in the Privy Council case of *Mutual Life and Citizens' Assurance Co Ltd v Evatt*[20] sought to narrow the scope of liability for misstatements.

> The plaintiff was a policy holder in the defendant insurance company and asked them for advice on the financial stability of an associated company of theirs. Knowing that if the advice were favourable he would invest in that company, the defendants carelessly gave him erroneous information, through relying on which he lost money on his investment in it.

The majority of the Judicial Committee held that he was owed no duty by the defendants. A duty in respect of careless statements arose only in respect of advice given in the course of a business where giving advice was its primary purpose or where the defendant had expressly let it be known that he claimed special skill and competence in advising. In a vigorous minority dissent LORD REID and LORD MORRIS found the business context in which the advice was given and relied on sufficient to create the necessary relationship to give rise to a duty.

The limitation on *Hedley Byrne* essayed in *Evatt* has so far been rejected by a stream of English authority since 1971. The Court of Appeal in *Esso Petroleum Co Ltd v Mardon*[1] expressly preferred the minority view in *Evatt*. And the definition of what constituted a sufficient 'special relationship' has been drawn liberally. When advice or information is given in a professional context, the professional will be under a duty, clearly to any client for whom he expressly prepares the advice, but also to others who will be very likely to rely on that advice.[2] It is not a condition precedent of liability for a careless statement that the defendant should *voluntarily* have assumed responsibility for that statement. Circumstances may impose on the defendant the required relationship with the plaintiff.[3] A duty may arise as much in a business context as with a professional relationship. Thus a potato wholesaler who gave a

---

18 See per LORD REID at 483 and 580 and per LORD PEARCE at 537 and 616.
19 Though see *De la Bere v Pearson Ltd* [1908] 1 KB 280.
20 [1971] AC 793, [1975] 1 All ER 150, PC.
 1 [1975] QB 819, [1975] 1 All ER 203, CA.
 2 *J E B Fasteners Ltd v Marks, Bloom & Co (A Firm)* [1983] 1 All ER 583 (accountants); *Arenson v Casson Beckman Rutley & Co* [1977] AC 405, [1975] 3 All ER 901; *Sutcliffe v Thackrah* [1974] AC 727, [1974] 1 All ER 859, HL (auditors and valuers; see also the failure of the contention in both cases that the auditor or valuer shared arbitrators' immunity for negligent performance of their duties); *Cherry Ltd v Allied Insurance Brokers Ltd* [1978] 1 Lloyd's Rep 274 (insurance brokers); *Yianni v Edwin Evans & Sons* [1982] QB 438, [1981] 3 All ER 592 (building society surveyor liable to mortgagor).
 3 *Ministry of Housing and Local Government v Sharp* [1970] 2 QB 223, [1970] 1 All ER 1009, CA. But see *Yuen Kun Yeu v A-G for Hong Kong* [1987] 2 All ER 705, PC.

dealer wrong advice about another dealer's credit worthiness,[4] an inter-
mediary who invited the plaintiff to apply for an overseas post and had
carelessly led him to assume that he was qualified, whereas he was eventually
dismissed for lack of qualifications,[5] and an oil company which misled a
retailer about the site's petrol throughout were all held liable under the *Hedley
Byrne* rule[6] Public bodies, both central[7] and local,[8] have been found to owe
a duty of care both to other public authorities[9] and to members of the public.

It is important of course to remember that proof of a duty to act carefully
in giving advice or information is only the first stage in the claim. Claims will
fail for the same reason as other actions in negligence. Want of care may not
be proved.[10] Or the plaintiff may fail to show that his loss resulted from the
defendant's carelessness. If the plaintiff, albeit he believed the information,
would have acted as he did regardless of the defendant's negligence his loss
is not caused by that negligence.[11] One peculiarity relating to the duty to avoid
careless statements is the immunity afforded to one class of professionals.
Barristers are on policy grounds immune from liability for negligent advice
given in the course of litigation.[12]

B. STATEMENTS AND *DONOGHUE V STEVENSON*

The reasoning of the House of Lords in *Hedley Byrne* presupposed the
inapplicability of the 'neighbour principle' as such to economic loss and
proceeded to create a narrow category of cases within which exceptionally
economic loss might be recoverable. At least that was how *Hedley Byrne* was
interpreted for several years. But, as at any rate LORD DEVLIN's judgment
makes clear, their Lordships did not see liability for misstatement as entirely
confined within the concept of the 'special relationship' developed in that
judgment. LORD DEVLIN expressly accepted that

> Cases may arise in the future in which a new and wider proposition, quite inde-
> pendent of contract, will be needed. There may, for example, be cases in which a
> statement is not supplied for the use of any particular individual.[13]

So could *Hedley Byrne* properly be read not as defining the limits of a duty
to avoid economic loss from misstatement but opening the doors more

---

4 *W B Anderson & Sons Ltd v Rhodes (Liverpool) Ltd* [1967] 2 All ER 850.
5 *McNally v Welltrade International Ltd* [1978] IRLR 497. And in *Lawton v BOC Transhield
   Ltd* [1987] 2 All ER 608 employers were held to owe a duty to former employees when giving
   references.
6 *Esso Petroleum Co Ltd v Mardon* [1975] QB 819, [1975] 1 All ER 203, CA.
7 *Culford Metal Industries Ltd v Export Credit Guarantee Department* [1981] Com LR 127
   (negligent advice by the department to the Secretary of State about the plaintiff's insurance
   export cover could result in liability).
8 *Coats Patons (Retail) Ltd v Birmingham Corpn* (1971) 69 LGR, 356, defendants liable for
   careless answers to 'Enquiries of Local Authority' form.
9 *Ministry of Housing and Local Government v Sharp* (supra).
10 *Stafford v Conti Commodity Services Ltd* [1981] 1 All ER 691; *Argy Trading Developments
   Co Ltd v Lapid Developments Ltd* [1977] 3 All ER 785.
11 *J E B Fasteners Ltd v Marks Bloom & Co* [1983] 1 All ER 583, CA (plaintiff failed to prove
   that he relied on negligently prepared accounts when making his investment).
12 *Rondel v Worsley* [1969] 1 AC 191, [1967] 3 All ER 993; *Saif Ali v Mitchell (Sydney) & Co*
   [1980] AC 198, [1977] 3 All ER 1033 (immunity extends to pre-trial work intimately connected
   with the cause in court and extends to solicitor–advocates too).
13 At 530 and 611 respectively.

generally to recovery of economic loss? This was how MEGARRY VC approached the question in *Ross v Caunters*:[14]

> The defendant solicitor negligently drew up a will so that he failed to carry out his client-testators instruction to benefit the plaintiff. The plaintiff sued the solicitor in negligence.

The plaintiff could in no sense be said to have relied on the solicitor yet his action succeeded. The judge held that the law had by 1979 so developed that he should apply the neighbour principle in *Donoghue v Stevenson* in the absence of any policy factors negativing or limiting the scope of such a duty. There was close proximity between the plaintiff and the defendant. His contemplation of her was 'actual, nominate and direct' and that proximity arose out of the duty he undoubtedly owed to the testator. It was in no way 'casual, accidental or unforeseen.' And finally the liability arising from the duty was to one person alone.[15] The spectre of indeterminate liability was of no assistance to the defendant. Since *Ross v Caunters* several further claims for loss arising from misstatement have succeeded on the basis of the 'neighbour principle' alone rather than within the narrower 'special relationship' rule of *Hedley Byrne*.[16] And *Ross v Caunters* may further be seen as beginning the trend to regard economic loss as generally recoverable where the plaintiff suffering that loss was identifiable and no policy factors militated against the imposition of a duty to avoid economic loss. That trend now seems to have been reversed, as we shall see, and *Ross v Caunters* may have to be regarded as a decision fairly closely confined within its special facts. It has to be asked whether a straight application of the proximity and policy test is in future going to be regarded as correct[17] at all in claims for economic loss even where that loss results from negligent information or advice. In *Yuen Ken Yeu v A-G for Hong Kong*[18] the lack of any 'special relationship' between the Commission for Deposit Taking Companies and the plaintiffs, depositors in a company registered by the Commission which went into liquidation so that they lost all the money which they had deposited, was held to be fatal to their claim that a duty of care was owed to them by the Commissioner. But before rushing to greet the Privy Council judgment as the definitive resurrection of a need for 'special relationship' consider the following matters. Is *Yuen Ken Yeu* a case about liability for negligent statements or conduct? Note that it takes the prize for raising all the difficult questions concerning duty of care. *Inter alia* it raises issues of liability for exercise of statutory powers, control of third parties, and the problems of liability to a large section of the public.

14 [1980] Ch 297, [1979] 3 All ER 580. And see *Al-Kandari v Brown (JR) & Co* [1987] QB 514, [1987] 2 All ER 302; affd by the CA (1988) Times, 27 February.

15 See *Caltex Oil (Australia) Pty Ltd v Dredge Willemstad* (1976) 136 CLR 529 (High Court of Australia) (note the importance in relation to economic loss of there being one identifiable plaintiff and not a diffuse class of potential plaintiffs).

16 *J E B Fasteners Ltd v Marks, Bloom & Co* [1983] 1 All ER 583, CA; *Yianni v Edwin Evans & Sons* [1982] QB 438, [1981] 3 All ER 592; on what basis 'special relationship' or 'neighbour principle' do you think *Ministry of Housing and Local Government v Sharp* [1970] 2 QB 223, [1970] 1 All ER 1009 was decided? Where decisions purport to rest on neighbourhood alone could a 'special relationship' nevertheless be deduced from the facts?

17 It was so regarded in *Al-Kandari v Brown* (1988) Times, 27 February, CA.

18 [1987] 2 All ER 705, PC.

C. ECONOMIC LOSS AND NEGLIGENT CONDUCT

The case by case development of the scope of the duty to avoid inflicting economic loss by careless statements was not matched by similar progress in relation to economic loss resulting from negligent conduct. In 1966 three years after *Hedley Byrne* the difficult but instructive case of *Weller & Co v Foot and Mouth Disease Research Institute*[19] was decided. The defendants had carelessly allowed cattle to become infected by foot and mouth disease. The plaintiffs were auctioneers whose business suffered badly when quarantine restrictions prevented them holding auction sales of cattle. WIDGERY J said no duty of care was owed to the plaintiffs for their loss of profits. The scope of any duty owed was limited to cattle owners who suffered physical damage to their property when cattle had to be destroyed. The loss occasioned to the auctioneer was readily foreseeable but so was economic loss to countless other enterprises: the pubs, the cafes, the carparks, the shops who would benefit from the influx into the town of crowds on marketday. Policy required that a cut-off point be set. WIDGERY J set it at those suffering physical harm and on the facts of *Weller* it is easy to understand why.

A series of judgments on the damages recoverable when services such as water, gas or electricity were negligently interrupted confirmed WIDGERY J's finding that economic loss unrelated to physical damage was irrecoverable. In *British Celanese Ltd v Hunt*[20] and *SCM (UK) Ltd v WJ Whittall & Son Ltd*[21] the cutting off of electricity supplies damaged the plaintiff's machines and materials resulting in a loss of production. The plaintiffs recovered both their additional expenditure in replacing and repairing machinery and their loss of profits on the lost production run. The Court of Appeal in the latter case holding that the economic loss, the loss of profits, was recoverable as it was immediately consequent on physical damage to the plaintiff's property.

Then in 1973 the Court of Appeal again considered economic loss in *Spartan Steel and Alloys Ltd v Martin & Co (Contractors) Ltd.*[1] The defendants' negligence caused the cable carrying electricity to the plaintiff's factory to be cut through interrupting the supply for $14\frac{1}{2}$ hours. To avoid molten metal solidifying in the furnaces the plaintiffs used oxygen to melt it and pour it out of the furnaces. This reduced the value of the metal and lost the plaintiffs the £400 profit they would have expected to make on that melt. The plaintiff also lost a further £1767 on the other four melts which they would normally have completed in the time that the electricity was cut off. The majority of the Court of Appeal held that they could recover only the loss in value of the metal actually in the furnaces and the loss of profit on that melt. The remaining loss was pecuniary loss unrelated to any physical damage and irrecoverable. EDMUND-DAVIES LJ dissenting considered that such foreseeable and direct economic loss should be recoverable. The occurrence or non-occurrence of physical damage was a fortuitous event with no relevance in legal principle. If that very kind of economic loss to that plaintiff was a reasonably foreseeable and direct consequence of want of care, a duty to

---

19 [1966] 1 QB 569, [1965] 3 All ER 560. And see *Cattle v Stockton Waterworks Co* (1875) LR 10 QB 453 (plaintiff could not recover for loss on contract to tunnel on land belonging to another after that land had been flooded by the defendant's negligence).
20 [1969] 2 All ER 1252, [1969] 1 WLR 959.
21 [1971] 1 QB 337, [1970] 3 All ER 245, CA.
1 [1973] QB 27, [1972] 3 All ER 557, CA and see *Electrochrome Ltd v Welsh Plastics Ltd* [1968] 2 All ER 205. *The Kapetan Georgis* (1987) Financial Times, 21 October.

avoid that kind of loss arose. The words used are different but the substance of EDMUND DAVIES LJ's dissent concurs with *Ross v Caunters*. Where an identifiable plaintiff, rather than an indeterminate class, is at risk of economic loss, in the absence of specific policy reasons to the contrary that loss should be actionable.

The judgment of the House of Lords in *Junior Books Ltd v Veitchi Co Ltd* in 1982[2] appeared, at first, to vindicate such a liberalised approach to recovery for economic loss and to confirm the application of the 'neighbour principle' as the prima facie test for economic loss generally and not simply relevant to liability for economic loss resulting from misstatements.

> The plaintiffs contracted with main contractors to have built a new factory in Scotland. The defendants were nominated sub-contractors, specialist flooring experts, who laid the floor in the main production area. Due to the defendants' negligence the floor was so defective that it had to be taken up and relaid. The plaintiffs sought to recover (a) their expenditure in replacing the floor and (b) loss of profits caused by disruption to their business.

No allegation was made in the pleadings that the floor was dangerous. No information was provided as to the terms of either the main or the sub-contract in particular as to whether there was any relevant exemption clause in either contract. The House of Lords nevertheless held by a majority of 4–1[3] that the plaintiffs' losses were recoverable. LORD ROSKILL applying the two-stage test from *Anns* and finding the necessary proximity between the parties looked for any reason why a duty of care should not be owed by the defendants to avoid exposing the plaintiffs to the financial loss which would necessarily result from laying a floor so defective that it had to be replaced before the plaintiffs could proceed with their business. He described the parties' relationship as 'almost as close a commercial relationship as it is possible to envisage short of privity of contract.'[4] He further disapproved the drawing of the boundary of liability in tort on the basis of 'somewhat artificial distinctions between physical and economic or financial loss', and the concomitant contention that liability for financial loss of the type suffered by Junior Books lay in contract alone. He left open the issue of whether in the light of the majority's application of the proximity and policy approach to economic loss *Spartan Steel* could any longer be regarded as correctly decided.

But the narrow nature of the *ratio* in *Junior Books* must be appreciated. LORD ROSKILL found that a duty arose on the basis of the facts agreed, *inter alia*, that the defendants were specialists nominated for the job by the plaintiffs in the clear knowledge that the plaintiffs relied on their skill and would suffer financial loss if the floor was defective.[5] In effect the defendants liability arose from their very 'special relationship' with *Junior Books*. Their Lordships general remarks about the readiness with which the courts will compensate economic loss, 'damage to the pocket', must be treated as just that. The broader principles outlined in *Junior Books* could, as ATKIN's 'neighbour principle' did in *Donoghue v Stevenson*, have signalled a new dawn in the

---

2 [1983] 1 AC 520, [1982] 3 All ER 201, HL; (although this case originated in Scotland (like *Donoghue v Stevenson*) it is fully authoritative on English law).
3 Read carefully LORD BRANDON's instructive dissenting judgment.
4 At 542 and 211 respectively.
5 The ratio of LORD KEITH's judgment is effectively a finding of liability on the special facts alone.

development of the tort of negligence. But in the light of decisions *post Junior Books* it seems they did not[6].

The first case of any importance to test the scope of a duty to avoid economic loss after *Junior Books* was the Court of Appeal judgment in *Muirhead v Industrial Tank Specialities Ltd*:[7]

> The plaintiff was a fish merchant who conceived a plan to buy lobsters in the summer when the price is cheap, store them until December and then sell them for great profit on the Christmas market. The lobsters were to be stored in tanks through which sea-water was constantly pumped, filtered, and re-circulated. The pumps proved to be defective because the electric motors were not suitable for use in the UK. The plaintiffs sued the manufacturers of the electric motors for (1) the loss of several lobsters who died in the tanks, (2) expenditure on attempts to correct the faults, and (3) their loss of profit on the whole enterprise.

It was held that the plaintiff was entitled to damages for the loss of his property, the lobsters, and for any loss of profit on the dead lobsters. But he could not recover from the manufacturers of the motors for either his wasted expenditure or his general loss of profits. The Court of Appeal in effect returned to the earlier approach of *Spartan Steel*, that only financial loss consequent on physical damage was recoverable. The plaintiffs' lack of express reliance on the manufacturers and the absence of the close proximity which existed between the parties in *Junior Books* took them beyond the bounds of any special rules on economic loss created by that judgment. Indeed the formula used by ROBERT GOFF LJ that *Junior Books* was a case which 'on its particular facts' created such close proximity as to give rise to a duty may be seen as the polite judicial way of saying that the House of Lords had got it wrong!

The decisions of the House of Lords in the *Peabody Donation*[8] judgment and *Leigh & Sillivan Ltd v Aliakmon Shipping Co Ltd*[9] further confirmed the prevailing trend to deny a duty to avoid economic loss arising from negligent conduct, and confine *Junior Books* to its special facts. The distinction between physical and economic harm, artificial as it often is, remains at present entrenched in English law. Is this for no better reason perhaps than it is the simplest means of closing the floodgates? Or does a further examination of the fact situations in *Junior Books* and the later judgments, which fail to take up the invitation to fling open the doors to more liberal recovery of economic loss, reveal a more fundamental problem in imposing a duty in tort to avoid economic loss?

No evidence was before the court in *Junior Books* as to whether the main contract expressly limited the main contractors' liability to the plaintiffs, or the sub-contract the sub-contractors' liability to the main contractors. How would such exemption clauses affect the scope of any duty in tort owed by the sub-contractor to the plaintiffs? Speaking of an exemption clause in the *main* contract LORD ROSKILL ventured the view[10] that 'such a clause might ... in some circumstances limit the duty of care'. But it is difficult to see the

---

6 *Simaan General Contracting Co v Pilkington Glass Ltd* (1988) Times, 18 February, CA.
7 [1985] 3 All ER 705, [1985] 3 WLR 993.
8 *Peabody Donation Fund (Governors) v Sir Lindsay Parkinson & Co Ltd* [1985] AC 210, [1984] 3 All ER 529.
9 [1986] AC 785, [1986] 2 All ER 145.
10 At 546 and 214 respectively.

relevance of the main contract in setting the standard by which the duty owed by the sub-contractors should be judged. Perhaps LORD ROSKILL meant the contract under which the services were provided, the sub-contract. If so then his view was in accordance with that of LORD FRASER[11] who opined that a plaintiff suing in tort could be no better off than if the contracting party sued. He was bound by any terms as to the quality of goods set in the contract under which the services were originally agreed. The proposition that where X contracts with Y to provide services or goods which he well realises may cause loss to Z if negligently performed or manufactured, then X's duty to Z is defined by reference to the terms of the contract with Y found favour with ROBERT GOFF LJ in his minority judgment in the Court of Appeal in *Leigh & Sillivan Ltd v Aliakmon Shipping Co Ltd.*[12] The duty owed to the buyers of the steel coils by the shippers could be qualified by any exclusions of liability in the contract of carriage. But it attracted nil support from the House of Lords.[13] The inescapable difficulties confronted once one attempts to define a duty in tort to avoid inflicting economic loss by reference to the terms of a contract to which the plaintiff is not a party can be resolved in a number of ways.

1 The existence of the problem could be regarded as grounds to deny the existence of any duty in tort leaving all the parties involved to their contractual remedies. After all the plaintiffs in *Junior Books*, for example, could had they so wished have contracted directly with the defendants and thus settled all contentious issues concerning terms as to quality by negotiation.

2 The liability of the defendants who negligently provide services or manufacture goods may correctly be seen in lay terms as liability for breach of 'promise'. The plaintiffs in *Junior Books* relied on *Veitchi*. *Veitchi* let them down. Should it be the law of contract not tort to which the plaintiffs look for their remedy? Is it restrictive English rules on privity of contract denying a remedy to persons not party to a contract which are at fault?[14]

3 Can, as ROBERT GOFF LJ suggested, the scope of the duty in tort be defined by the contractual terms undertaken by the defendant? Should those terms be subject to scrutiny by the court as to whether they are 'reasonable' as between the defendant and the plaintiff?[15] Is any exclusion clause in any contract between the plaintiff and any intermediate party relevant on the grounds that the plaintiff electing to sue in tort should not get a better deal than if he had sued in contract?

---

11 Ibid at 534 and 204–5 respectively.
12 [1985] QB 350 at 399, [1985] 2 All ER 350 at 399.
13 [1986] 2 All ER 145 at 157.
14 See *Remedies for Torts and Breaches of Contract* by A S Burrows at 4–7. And see generally on economic loss D Harris and C Veljanowski 'Liability for Economic Loss in Tort' and P Cane 'Contract Tort and Economic Loss' in *The Law of Tort* ed by M Furmston (1986).
15 As is required by the Unfair Contract Terms Act 1977.

Chapter 13

Breach of duty

SECTION 1. THE STANDARD OF CARE

A. LAW, NOT FACT

So far, only the range of persons to whom the defendant owes a duty of care and the types of harm to which the duty of care extends have been considered. Although it is not uncommon for the standard of care to be treated as part of the 'duty', it seems preferable to confine 'duty' to the question of whether the defendant is under an obligation to the plaintiff and to treat separately the question of the extent of the duty owed. The conduct of the defendant, and especially the nature of the duty of care imposed on him, must next be looked at. It certainly is a matter of law and not fact to decide the rules to be applied in deciding whether the defendant has broken a duty of care which he owed to the plaintiff. It will be seen that the standard required of the defendant is that of the reasonable man, which is a legal standard.

Some House of Lords cases will make the point clear. In *Glasgow Corporation v Muir*, LORD THANKERTON explained that, after deciding that the appellants owed a duty to take reasonable care for the safety of children on the premises, the further question had to be settled: 'the test by which ... the standard of care is to be judged'.[1] In *Paris v Stepney BC*,[2] where the House of Lords considered a claim in negligence brought by a one-eyed workman whose good eye was injured in the course of work which involved risk to the eyes while not wearing goggles, LORD OAKSEY first held that 'the duty of an employer towards his servant is to take reasonable care for the servant's safety in all the circumstances of the case' and then defined the standard of care required. Similarly, in *Bolton v Stone*, LORD NORMAND commenced his judgment as follows:[3]

> My Lords, it is not questioned that the occupier of a cricket ground owes a duty of care to persons on an adjacent highway or on neighbouring property who may be in the way of balls driven out of the ground by the batsman. But it is necessary to consider the measure of the duty owed.

It is a matter of law that if A owes B a duty of care he must attain the standard of 'a reasonable man'—a further examination of the legal meaning of this phrase will be made later.[4] There are other principles of law going to the standard of care. The fundamental problem of principle is how to strike a balance between the utility of the activities of the defendant and the threat of harm to the plaintiff which these activities engender. One must take into

---

1 [1943] AC 448 at 454, [1943] 2 All ER 44, HL.
2 [1951] AC 367 at 384, [1951] 1 All ER 42, HL.
3 [1951] AC 850 at 860, [1951] 1 All ER 1078, HL.
4 See p 201 et seq, post.

account these two basic factors in deciding whether one who owes a duty to another has shown reasonable care.[5]

The function of the courts in ascertaining the balance between the individual's right to freedom from harm and the social utility of the defendant's activity can be seen to involve determinations of the general public interest. This can mean that matters extraneous to the specific issues in dispute between the plaintiff and the defendant may be taken into account in assessing the standard of care required of the defendant. A good illustration of such an approach can be found in the caselaw concerning the standard of care demanded of doctors counselling patients on the risks of proposed medical treatment. In *Sidaway v Bethlem Royal Hospital*[6] the House of Lords held by a majority of 4–1 that the test should be whether the doctor conformed to a practice of disclosure sanctioned by responsible medical opinion. In rejecting the contention that the standard of care ought to be what the reasonable patient would want to know,[7] rather than what the reasonable doctor was prepared to tell, their Lordships made several references to what they saw as undesirable social consequences of adopting a patient centred standard. These included that patients might irrationally reject necessary treatment, that, in general,[8] lay people would not understand further information if they were given it, and their Lordships' view that most people were in any case content to leave the decision on the risk versus benefit equation of proposed treatment to their doctors.

In *Budden v BP Oil Ltd*[9] the Court of Appeal struck out the following claim.

> An action was brought on behalf of a child alleging that the child had suffered brain damage caused by excessive lead in his blood. The high level of lead was assumed to result from lead particles emitted from vehicles using petrol supplied by the defendants. The lead had been deliberately added to the petrol. Parliament was progressively phasing down the permitted lead content in petrol. At the time of the damage to the child the level of lead in petrol complied with the permitted limits but would not have done later. The relevant legislation did not provide that it was a defence to any action that the limit was not exceeded—it merely made it a crime to exceed the limit.

The appeal court found that Parliament in setting the limit must be regarded as having conclusively determined in the public interest, taking into account all factors of which health risk was only one, that at the relevant time it was reasonable to add that amount of lead to petrol. Should the courts have felt themselves precluded by Parliament in that instance from making an independent judgment on the standard of care in a negligence action? The legislation was silent on civil liability for lead induced injury. Compare *Budden v BP Oil Ltd* with *Froom v Butcher*.[10] In the latter case the key

5 Eg per PEARSON J in *Donaldson v McNiven* [1952] 1 All ER 1213 at 1216, affd [1952] 2 All ER 691, CA.
6 [1985] 1 All ER 643, [1985] AC 871, HL.
7 The 'prudent patient' is the standard adopted in a number of American states; see *Canterbury v Spence* (1972) 464 F 2d 772 at 780; this was the approach endorsed by LORD SCARMAN in his dissenting judgment in *Sidaway*.
8 But not where the lay person happened to be a highly educated Law Lord see per LORD DIPLOCK at 659.
9 (1980) 124 Sol Jo 376, CA.
10 [1976] QB 286, [1975] 3 All ER 520. See further post at p 244.

issue was whether the plaintiff was contributorily negligent in not wearing a seatbelt. At the time of the accident legislation to make wearing seatbelts compulsory and not wearing them a crime had not yet passed through Parliament. The Court of Appeal felt free to find that failing to wear a seatbelt clearly constituted contributory negligence.

B. THE GUIDING PRINCIPLES OF LAW

(1) THE LIKELIHOOD OF HARM

LORD WRIGHT in *Northwestern Utilities Ltd v London Guarantee and Accident Co Ltd* said[11]

> The degree of care which that duty involves must be proportioned to the degree of risk involved if the duty of care should not be fulfilled.

The amount of caution required tends to increase with the likelihood that the defendant's conduct will cause harm. Of course, in certain instances, the chance of harm may be so small that a man is held to be taking reasonable care although he does not guard against such remote possibilities. The degree of risk of harm is merely one factor to be taken into account, along with the other factors now to be enumerated, in deciding whether in all the circumstances reasonable care has been taken.[12]

(2) THE SERIOUSNESS OF THE RISK AND THE RISK OF SERIOUS INJURY

Not only is it a principle of law that a greater risk of injury is a material factor in framing the standard of care, but it is also a legal rule that the risk of greater injury is material. In *Paris v Stepney BC*[13] the Court of Appeal had held that, where the disability of a workman did not increase the risk of an accident, but only increased the risk of serious injury if such an accident did befall him, the disability was irrelevant in determining the standard of care. The House of Lords reversed this, holding that the gravity of the consequences if an accident did occur had to be taken into account in fixing the measure of care.[14]

(3) THE UTILITY OF THE ACT OF THE DEFENDANT

In *Paris v Stepney BC* the House of Lords was also careful to point out that 'the seriousness of the injury or damage risked and the likelihood of its being in fact caused may not be the only relevant factors'.[15] The reference was

---

11 [1936] AC 108 at 126, PC, approved by LORD NORMAND in *Paris v Stepney Borough Council*, [1951] AC 367 at 381, [1951] 1 All ER 42, HL; cf CARDOZO J, in *Palsgraf v Long Island Railroad Co* (1928) 248 NY 339: 'The risk reasonably to be perceived defines the duty to be obeyed', and LORD MACMILLAN in *Glasgow Corporation v Muir* [1943] AC 448 at 456, [1943] 2 All ER 44, HL: 'the degree of care required varies directly with the risk involved.'
12 *The Wagon Mound (No 2)* [1967] 1 AC 617 at 642–3, [1966] 2 All ER 709, PC (per LORD REID).
13 [1950] 1 KB 320, [1949] 2 All ER 843, CA.
14 [1951] AC 367, [1951] 1 All ER 42; but see *Withers v Perry Chain Co Ltd* [1961] 3 All ER 676, CA (the health risk to the plaintiff had to be balanced against her interest in keeping her job), p 251, post.
15 Per LORD NORMAND at 382.

plainly to that other basic consideration mentioned earlier, the utility of the act of the defendant. *Daborn v Bath Tramways Motor Co Ltd*, illustrates it:[16]

> The relevant issue was whether the driver, in war-time, of a left-hand-drive ambulance had been negligent in turning into a lane on the off-side of the road without giving a signal.

Holding that she had not broken her duty of care, ASQUITH LJ, said:[17]

> In determining whether a party is negligent, the standard of reasonable care is that which is reasonably to be demanded in the circumstances. A relevant circumstance to take into account may be the importance of the end to be served by behaving in this way or that. As has often been pointed out, if all the trains in this country were restricted to a speed of five miles an hour, there would be fewer accidents, but our national life would be intolerably slowed down. The purpose to be served, if sufficiently important, justified the assumption of abnormal risk. The relevance of this applied to the present case is this: during the war which was, at the material time, in progress, it was necessary for many highly important operations to be carried out by means of motor vehicles with left-hand drives, no others being available. So far as this was the case, it was impossible for the drivers of such cars to give the warning signals which could otherwise be properly demanded of them. Meanwhile, it was essential that the ambulance service should be maintained. It seems to me, in those circumstances, it would be demanding too high and an unreasonable standard of care from the drivers of such cars to say to them: 'Either you must give signals which the structure of your vehicle renders impossible or you must not drive at all.'

Similarly, what might be want of care towards an employee in a commercial enterprise will not necessarily be want of care towards a fireman, for 'one must balance the risk against the end to be achieved', and 'the commercial end to make profit is very different from the human end to save life or limb'.[18] And the extent of the duty owed by a police officer to a suspect whom he is pursuing must similarly be judged in the light of the end to be attained ie the lawful arrest of the suspect.[19]

(4) THE COST OF AVOIDING THE HARM

It is relevant to consider how extensive and costly the measures necessary to eliminate the risk would be. In *Latimer v AEC Ltd*[20] DENNING LJ, said:

> In every case of foreseeable risk, it is a matter of balancing the risk against the measures necessary to eliminate it.

In this case an exceptional storm had caused a factory floor to become flooded; when the water receded, the floor was found to be covered with a

---

16 [1946] 2 All ER 333, CA.
17 At 336. Cf *Quinn v Scott* [1965] 2 All ER 588 at 593 (per GLYN-JONES J): 'the safety of the public must take precedence over the preservation of the amenities and [I] cannot hold that the [National] Trust's duty to care for the countryside diminishes to any degree the duty not to subject users of this highway to unnecessary danger'.
18 Per DENNING LJ, in *Watt v Hertfordshire County Council* [1954] 2 All ER 368, CA at 371.
19 *Marshall v Osmond* [1983] QB 1034; and see *Rigby v Chief Constable of Northamptonshire* [1985] 2 All ER 985, [1985] 1 WLR 1242 (police firing CS gas canister into a shop to flush out a dangerous psychopath).
20 [1952] 2 QB 701 at 711, [1952] 1 All ER 1302 at 1305, CA; cf *Watt v Hertfordshire County Council* [1954] 2 All ER 368, CA (duty of fire authority to firemen in respect of equipment) where the *dictum* of ASQUITH LJ, in *Daborn v Bath Tramways Motor Co Ltd* supra, was also approved.

slimy mixture of oil and water so that its surface was slippery. The issue was the liability of the factory owners to a workman who some hours later, was injured through slipping on the floor. The House of Lords affirmed the decision of the Court of Appeal that there was no negligence at common law, LORD TUCKER saying:[1]

> The only question was: Has it been proved the floor was so slippery that, remedial steps not being possible, a reasonably prudent employer would have closed down the factory rather than allow his employees to run the risks involved in continuing work?

In *The Wagon Mound (No 2)* the Judicial Committee stated:[2]

> A reasonable man would only neglect ... a risk [of small magnitude] if he had some valid reason for doing so, eg, that it would involve considerable expense to eliminate the risk.

C. THE RELATION BETWEEN STANDARD OF CARE AND DUTY

Accepting then, that it is a matter of law that the considerations just discussed are to be taken into account in determining whether the defendant has been negligent, one must ask the further question whether the standard of care has to be particularised in detail in terms of 'duty'. A motorist fails to sound his horn at a crossing and is held liable in negligence to another motorist with whom he collides, the court holding that he should have sounded his horn. Would such a decision thenceforth be authority for the proposition that a motorist has a duty at law to sound his horn when approaching an intersection? The case of those who contend that negligence is made up of a series of such detailed rules of law governing conduct in particular circumstances is clearly put in the following passage.[3]

> ... situations tend to repeat themselves, persons find that if they do what was found to be reasonable under similar circumstances they will themselves be free from liability, and accordingly the general rule of reasonable conduct tends to be split up into a number of branches, each of which contains directions as to the way in which a reasonable man would behave under the circumstances in question. This result is both inevitable and beneficial. One of the objects of law is to prescribe rules of conduct so that the individual will know how to act in any given set of circumstances, and to direct him to act as a reasonable man without telling him in more detail how a reasonable man is found by experience to act under those circumstances is to give him very little guidance. When new sets of circumstances arise, it is necessary to fall back on the general test of reasonable conduct viewed in the light of such of the existing rules of conduct as seem most nearly appropriate to the case.

The crucial point of this argument is whether the assumption on which it is based is well founded, viz, that the situations of fact in negligence are usually the same as some case previously decided, and not infinitely various.[4] So, in

---

1 [1953] AC 643 at 659, [1953] 2 All ER 449 at 455, HL.
2 [1967] 1 AC 617 at 642, [1966] 2 All ER 709. For the relevance of the defendant's financial resources, see *Goldman v Hargrave* [1967] 1 AC 645 at 663, PC.
3 *Charlesworth* p 24. See also the similar views of Holmes *The Common Law* pp 110–29.
4 Winfield's case note on *Woods v Duncan* in (1946) 62 LQR 205, indicates that he subscribed to the view that the question whether the defendant's conduct was careless in the particular circumstances is one of duty and not breach of duty.

running down cases, it will usually be relevant to consider the speed of the vehicles, visibility, the state of the road, the distance within which the vehicles pulled up—but how often in any given case will these factors exactly correspond with those of a previously decided case? Are not the special circumstances of each case almost always unique, so different in at least one material point, that a catalogue of duties based on conduct can hardly be compiled?

What, then, is the judicial practice in the matter? It is doubtful whether any consistent attitude can be found. There is no lack of cases where the courts have forcefully rejected attempts to particularise duties. For instance, in *Baker v E Longhurst & Sons Ltd,*[5] SCRUTTON LJ appeared to lay down a principle that a person driving in the dark must be able to pull up within the limits of his vision. Shortly afterwards, in another road traffic case, LORD WRIGHT said of cases such as *Baker v Longhurst*:[6]

> ... that no one case is exactly like another, and no principle of law can in my opinion be extracted from those cases. It is unfortunate that questions which are questions of fact alone should be confused by importing into them as principles of law a course of reasoning which has no doubt properly been applied in deciding other cases on other sets of facts.

When counsel again relied on the *dictum* of SCRUTTON LJ, in *Morris v Luton Corporation*, LORD GREENE adopted the *dictum* of LORD WRIGHT 'in the hope that this suggested principle [of SCRUTTON LJ] may rest peacefully in the grave in future'.[7]

Most important of all is the 1959 decision of the House of Lords in *Qualcast (Wolverhampton) Ltd v Haynes*.[8] The House went out of its way to stress that a judge's reasons for finding want of reasonable care are matters of fact, not law, for otherwise 'the precedent system will die from a surfeit of authorities'.[9] That judges now give reasons for conclusions formerly arrived at by juries without reasons must not be allowed to elevate these decisions of fact into propositions of law.

The contrary view would be that it is a matter of duty and of law as to what detailed rules of conduct in particular circumstances a defendant, owing a duty of care to the plaintiff, must conform. Although no authoritative decision expressly adopting that contrary view has been traced, a difference in approach of judges to cases of negligence, and one which may be important, can be discerned. Some judges regularly preface their judgments by a general statement of the standard of care and then expressly treat the details as matters of fact going to breach, while others (in their language at least) particularise their statement of the duty. In *Caminer v Northern and London Investment Trust Ltd,*[10] a rotten elm tree on the defendant's estate had fallen, causing damage to a user of an adjoining highway; he sued in negligence. For LORDS REID and NORMAND the duty of an estate owner was to take such

5 [1933] 2 KB 461 at 468, CA.
6 *Tidy v Battman* [1934] 1 KB 319 at 322, CA; cf *SS Heranger (Owners) v SS Diamond (Owners)* [1939] AC 94, HL at 101 (per LORD WRIGHT).
7 [1946] KB 114 at 116, [1946] 1 All ER 1 at 3, CA. And see *Easson v LNE Ry Co* [1944] KB 421, [1944] 2 All ER 425, CA. The Court of Appeal in *Foskett v Mistry* [1984] RTR 1, stressed that the test in running down cases was had reasonable care been taken in all the circumstances and said citation of authorities in such cases was rarely justified.
8 [1959] AC 743, [1959] 2 All ER 38.
9 At 43–4 (per LORD SOMERVELL).
10 [1951] AC 88, [1950] 2 All ER 486, HL.

steps as a reasonable and prudent landowner would take, and the question was one of fact whether the conduct of the defendant infringed this requirement; for LORD PORTER, on the other hand, the issue was whether there is a duty to lop middle-aged elm trees. In *Workington Harbour and Dock Board v SS Towerfield (Owners)*[11] the liability of the port authority in respect of a ship which had run aground in the harbour fell to be decided. LORD NORMAND held that the duty was to exercise reasonable care to prevent the peril of damage to ships resorting to the harbour; LORD PORTER expressed it as a duty to warn of the dangerous condition of the port. If those judges who use the term 'duty' as LORD PORTER has done are to be taken to mean a duty in law, then one can only say that there is a sharp and important cleavage in the courts. But an observation of LORD GREENE in *Morris v Luton Corporation* raises doubts whether it can be assumed that such a legal duty is always intended by them:[12]

> There is sometimes a temptation for judges in dealing with these traffic cases to decide questions of fact in language which appears to lay down some rule which users of the road must observe. That is a habit into which one perhaps sometimes slips unconsciously—I may have done it myself for all I know—but it is much to be deprecated, because these are questions of fact dependent on the circumstances of each case.

It is, then, impossible to be dogmatic on this point. In a few instances the courts have regularly framed a duty in more specific terms. It may even be that it is to some extent a matter of convenience to what degree the details of the standard of conduct are to be particularised as legal duties, it may even depend in respect of any specific category of duty on how the courts formulated the rule when the new category of negligence was first developed.[13] It is submitted, however, that because of the tendency of facts to differ in some vital, although perhaps small, detail from case to case, it is undesirable to state conduct in terms of legal duty. *Worsfold v Howe* shows how important the point is:[14]

> The defendant car driver edged blind from a side road across stationary tankers and collided with a motor cyclist approaching on the main road past the tankers. Because the Court of Appeal had held in a previous case that a driver so edging out was not negligent the trial judge felt bound to absolve the defendant from liability.

The Court of Appeal held that the previous decision laid down no legal principle, that such decisions were to be treated as ones of fact, and held the defendant negligent.

Even if the details of conduct (but not the general standard which is, as shown above,[15] in any event undoubtedly a matter of law) are, as is here advocated, to be treated as matters of fact relative to the question whether

---

11 [1951] AC 112, [1950] 2 All ER 414, HL.
12 [1946] KB 114 at 115, [1946] 1 All ER 1 at 3; cf DU PARCQ LJ, in *Easson v LNE Ry Co* [1944] KB 421, [1944] 2 All ER 425, CA.
13 Eg the tripartite division of the duty of an employer to his workman, p 281 et seq, post.
14 [1980] 1 All ER 1028, CA.
15 See p 194, ante.

there has been a breach of duty,[16] it is still a question of law whether the facts constitute sufficient evidence upon which to base a finding of fact that there was in the circumstances a breach of duty to take care: a court empowered merely to reverse on points of law can do so on the ground that there is no evidence of want of reasonable care.[17] At most the relevance of previous decisions on these issues of evaluating facts is to afford a guide to the limits within which there may be said to be reasonable grounds for drawing a particular inference.[18]

SECTION 2.   THE REASONABLE MAN

Here, as in so many aspects of negligence in English law, it is difficult to track down authorities precisely stating the law. The starting point is the *dictum* (of unchallengeable authority) of ALDERSON B, in *Blythe v Birmingham Waterworks Co*:[19]

> Negligence is the omission to do something which a reasonable man, guided upon those considerations which ordinarily regulate the conduct of human affairs, would do, or doing something which a prudent and reasonable man would not do.

The legal standard is not that of the defendant himself but that of 'a man of ordinary prudence',[20] a man using 'ordinary care and skill',[1] a 'hypothetical' man.[2] LORD MACMILLAN has said:[3]

> The standard of foresight of the reasonable man ... eliminates the personal equation and is independent of the idiosyncrasies of the particular person whose conduct is in question.

Yet it is inadequate, not to say question-begging, to say that the standard then is an objective one. The definition of the reasonable man is not complete unless the words 'in the circumstances'[4] are embodied. Plainly, these words may prevent the test from being wholly objective, for the boundary between the external facts and the qualities of the actor is ill-defined. How far, then, is the standard of the 'reasonable man' an objective one?

---

16 Of course, it is not denied that judges, in deciding whether to interfere with the decision of the lower court, may well be influenced by the determination of standards of care in particular and approximately similar cases which they have previously tried—but that is not to say that the issue is thereby transformed into one of duty. And see Holmes *The Common Law* at pp 126–9.
17 And see p 214, post.
18 See *Hazell v British Transport Commission* [1958] 1 All ER 116, and Devlin *Trial by Jury*, *passim*.
19 (1856) 11 Exch 781 at 784.
20 *Vaughan v Menlove* (1837) 3 Bing NC 468 at 475 (per TINDAL CJ).
 1 *Heaven v Pender* (1883) 11 QBD 503 at 507 (per BRETT MR).
 2 *King v Phillips* [1953] 1 QB 429 at 441 (per DENNING LJ), [1953] 1 All ER 617, CA; for A P Herbert's amusing definition, see *Misleading Cases in the Common Law* (1930) p 12 et seq.
 3 *Glasgow Corporation v Muir* [1943] AC 448 at 457, [1942] 2 All ER 44, HL; cf the earlier *dictum* of HOLMES J in *The Germanic* (1904) 196 US 589: 'The standard of conduct ... is an external standard, and takes no account of the personal equation of the man concerned.'
 4 Eg *Glasgow Corporation v Muir* ante at 457 (per LORD MACMILLAN).

A. CHILDREN

Children must, it seems, be treated as a category apart. In many cases infants have been held not guilty of *contributory* negligence where adults would, on similar facts, have been deemed to be contributorily negligent—the test is: what degree of care for his own safety can an infant of the particular age reasonably be expected to take?[5]

In *McHale v Watson*[6] a twelve-year-old boy threw a spike at a post. Unfortunately the spike ricocheted off the post and hit the plaintiff (a girl of nine) in the eye. The High Court of Australia held that the standard of care to be demanded of the boy must be judged by the 'foresight and prudence of an ordinary boy of twelve'. One judgment at first instance has been traced in England holding that it is the standard of a reasonable child of the defendant's age which should be adopted to govern the liability of children. A twelve-year-old boy was found liable for flinging a tennis ball into a classroom at another boy and hitting a dinner lady.[7] An unresolved question, in relation to the standard of care demanded of children, is whether the test is entirely objective or will take into account the child's actual mental ability, maturity and experience.[8]

B. OTHER CATEGORIES OF PERSONS

It is unclear to what extent if at all the standard of the reasonable man will be adjusted to allow for the incapacities and infirmities of individual adults. It may be that the other category of legal incapacity, mentally disordered persons, is so akin to children that the same rule should apply to them. It would be unwise however, to assume, in view of the absence of decided cases, that subjective factors are to be taken into account in the case of classes of persons other than children and mentally disordered persons.[9]

Consider whether the standard of care is (or should be) affected if the defendant is elderly, or deaf, or minus a limb? There is a little authority to the effect that the standard is so affected where *contributory negligence* is being considered. So, in *Daly v Liverpool Corporation*[10] it was held that in deciding whether a sixty-seven-year-old woman was guilty of contributory negligence in crossing a road, one had to consider a woman of her age, not a hypothetical pedestrian. The point will be in issue only rarely in respect of the standard required of defendants for the following reason. A person with such defects will usually be negligent, not because of want of care at the time of the accident, but because, being aware of his defect, he allowed himself to be in the situation; a deaf motorist who collides with another car through not hearing the horn of the other, though not negligent in not hearing it, is

---

5 *Yachuk v Oliver Blais Co Ltd* [1949] AC 386, [1949] 2 All ER 150, PC; cf *Culkin v McFie* [1939] 3 All ER 613; *Gough v Thorne* [1966] 3 All ER 398, CA.
6 (1965) 111 CLR 384.
7 *Staley v Suffolk CC and Dean Mason* (26 November 1985, unreported); see *Clerk and Lindsell* Suppplement 10–64.
8 *Yachuk v Oliver Blais Co Ltd* supra at 396; *McHale v Watson* supra per OWEN J 'child of the same age, intelligence and experience'.
9 Yet, in a case of contributory negligence affecting stevedores, LORD PORTER held that one must consider 'the characteristics of the type of men affected'; *Grant v Sun Shipping Co Ltd* [1948] AC 549 at 555, [1948] 2 All ER 238, HL.
10 [1939] 2 All ER 142.

negligent in driving at all when deaf. Yet when this issue has to be faced squarely, it may be expected that the courts will follow the example of contributory negligence. If, for example, a blind man walked on, and damaged, a valuable package on the pavement in circumstances which would have amounted to lack of care on the part of a normal person, it is thought that he would not be liable in negligence if, judged by the standards of the blind, he were taking reasonable care. It is frequently stated that the defendant's physical characteristics, but not his mental powers, must be considered.[11] This physical/mental division is open to the objection that it does not meet the case of children; the statement of Holmes is therefore preferable:[12]

> When a man has a distinct defect of such a nature that all can recognise it as making certain precautions impossible, he will not be held answerable for not taking them.

This has the further merit of providing a clue to the attitude of the courts. One might expect them to take into account a man's observable physical defects, and yet to be reluctant to embark on an assessment of his mental powers—to consider the latter would be inconsistent with their customary aversion from problems of psychology and the like.

Where the defendant is a vehicle driver the courts are reluctant to take account of any incapacity, so determined are they, with their policy of facilitating speedy and cheap settlement of road accident claims, to apply objective standards of care.[13]

In *Roberts v Ramsbottom*[14] the defendant suffered a slight stroke just before getting into his car. He was completely unaware that he had had a stroke although he admitted that he felt somewhat dizzy. A few minutes after starting his journey he was involved in a collision injuring the plaintiff. It was held that even though his carelessness resulted from impaired consciousness of which the defendant was unaware, he was liable in negligence. His standard of care when driving on a public road was to be assessed objectively disregarding any mental incapacity, just as any physical infirmity or inexperience would be disregarded if the defendant elected to drive. Furthermore the court held that even were he to be exculpated from liability for his actual carelessness when driving, if he were to be regarded as in a state of automatism, he would still be liable because before the accident happened he was aware of his disabling symptoms.

C. INTELLIGENCE

The defendant's actions must conform to certain criteria expected of a person of normal intelligence in a given situation. It is no defence that a man acted 'to the best of his own judgment', if his 'best' is below that of the reasonable man.[15] A man whose reactions are slower than average is not thereby excused. Probably, a man whose intelligence is superior or whose reactions are quicker than average is not liable for failing to use those above-average qualities,[16]

11 Eg Williams *Joint Torts* p 357.
12 *Common Law* p 109.
13 And see *Nettleship v Weston* [1971] 2 QB 691, [1971] 3 All ER 581, CA, p 205, post.
14 [1980] 1 All ER 7, [1980] 1 WLR 823.
15 *Vaughan v Menlove* (1837) 3 Bing NC 468 at 474 (per TINDAL CJ).
16 See *Wooldridge v Sumner* [1962] 2 All ER 978, CA, infra.

unless he has professed to have some special skill or expertise in which case the law demands that he must manifest that skill or expertise. So it is no answer in an action for negligence against a consultant gynaecologist for him to contend that he delivered the baby with the skill to be expected of the average general practitioner.

D. KNOWLEDGE

Two branches of knowledge must be considered separately: the first, that of memory and experience. If X had been on a certain highway several times, and a reasonable man who had been there as often would know that it was busy, then X also is expected to know, even though his memory is so poor that he does not remember it. Similarly, a man is deemed to know those things which adults from their experience are expected to know: that some things easily explode, that others burn, that there is a law of gravity—this minimum amount of knowledge of matters of everyday experience he is deemed to possess.[17] There is one refinement of this rule: where, in the circumstances, the status of the defendant is relevant then the standard is that of a person in that position;[18] so, in *Caminer v Northern and London Investment Trust* the knowledge required of a landowner with regard to elm trees on his estate, their proneness to disease, lack of wind resistance and the like, was of a standard between that of an urban observer and a scientific arboriculturist.[19] In *The Wagon Mound (No 2)* case the Judicial Committee of the Privy Council said that the shipowner was liable for a fire caused by discharging oil in Sydney harbour because the chief engineer should have known that the discharge created a real risk of the oil on the water catching fire.

Secondly, what knowledge of the facts and circumstances surrounding him must the defendant have? He will not be excused for failing to observe what a reasonable man would have observed—a dock authority who did not know, but ought to have known, that the dock was unsafe, was negligent.[20] Further, even if a reasonable man himself could not be expected to know, he may be required to get and follow expert advice: the landlord of flats must therefore consult a specialist engineer about the safety of his lift.[1] It is clear that actual knowledge of the circumstances on the part of the defendant increases the standard of care imposed,[2] but it ought not to be assumed from this that the greater one's memory or experience the greater is the measure of the care imposed, for no cases on this are known.

Knowledge, in particular expert knowledge, does not remain static over the years. Scientific and technological advances lead to constant revision of and improvements in safety standards. In an action in negligence the defend-

---

17 *Caminer v Northern and London Investment Trust* [1951] AC 88, [1950] 2 All ER 486, HL carries the point: cf *Haynes v Harwood* [1935] 1 KB 146, CA at 153 (per GREER LJ).
18 *Clarke v Holmes* (1862) 7 H & N 937 Ex Ch (employer required to know more about the dangers of unfenced machinery than workman).
19 [1951] AC 88 at 100 (per LORD NORMAND), [1950] 2 All ER 486, HL. And see *Quinn v Scott* [1965] 2 All ER 588.
20 *Mersey Docks Trustees v Gibbs* (1866) LR 1 HL 93.
1 *Haseldine v Daw & Son Ltd* [1941] 2 KB 343 at 356, [1941] 3 All ER 156, CA (per SCOTT LJ).
2 *Brooks v LNW Ry Co* (1884) 33 WR 167, Div Ct.

ant must always be judged in the light of the state of scientific, technological or other expert knowledge which should have been available to him at the time of the alleged breach of his duty of care. Concrete evidence that a drug damages the foetus is not conclusive evidence that either the doctor prescribing the drug, or the pharmaceutical company marketing the drug were negligent.[3] The test in negligence[4] must be at the time when the drug was prescribed or marketed should the risk of injury to the foetus have been foreseen. As LORD DENNING put it, when a plaintiff claimed in respect of a medical accident which had never occurred before in *Roe v Minister of Health*[5] 'We must not look at the 1947 accident with 1954 spectacles'.

E. SKILL

It has been seen that a person's conduct must conform to the standard of a person of normal intelligence. When a person has held himself out as being capable of attaining standards of skill either in relation to the public generally, for example, by driving a car,[6] or in relation to some person for whom he is performing a service, he is required to show the skill normally possessed by persons doing that work. A doctor failing to diagnose a disease cannot excuse himself by showing that he acted to the best of his skill if a reasonable doctor would have diagnosed it.[7] Nor can a young hospital doctor plead that he is inexperienced or overworked if he fails to attain the level of competence to be expected from a person holding his 'post' and entrusted with his responsibilities.[8] The same principle presumably applies to newly qualified solicitors.[9] One must, in this class of case, be careful to ascertain exactly what skill the defendant held himself out to have:

> Where the plaintiff had her ears pierced by a jeweller in order to wear earrings and subsequently contracted a disease that might have been avoided had the work been done with normal medical skill, the jeweller was required only to show the skill of a jeweller doing such work, not that of a doctor.[10]

In *Wells v Cooper*:[11]

> A householder fitted a new door handle so insecurely that the plaintiff, when pulling it, lost his balance and was injured.

3 The drug thalidomide undoubtedly caused serious deformities in babies whose mothers took the drug in early pregnancy. One of the major obstacles confronting claims for compensation by the damaged children was doubt whether at the time the drug was first available, as opposed to after the births of several deformed babies, doctors and embryologists appreciated that drugs could cross the placental barrier and injure the foetus.

4 Hence the argument that product liability at least should be strict. See post ch 18, and in particular the effect of incorporating the 'development risks' defence into the new strict liability regime.

5 [1951] 2 QB 66 at 84.

6 *Nettleship v Weston* [1971] 2 QB 691, [1971] 3 All ER 581, CA.

7 In *Bolam v Friern Hospital Management Committee* [1957] 2 All ER 118, it was held that a doctor who conforms to practices accepted as proper by some responsible members of his profession is not liable merely because other members would take a different view.

8 *Wilsher v Essex Area Health Authority* [1986] 3 All ER 801 rvsd on a different point (1988) The Independent, 11 March, HL.

9 *Nettleship v Weston* [1971] 2 QB 691 per MEGAW LJ at 709.

10 *Philips v William Whitely Ltd* [1938] 1 All ER 566.

11 [1958] 2 QB 265, [1958] 2 All ER 527, CA.

The Court of Appeal held that the householder was required to show the standard of care, not of a professional carpenter nor of a person having such skill as the defendant actually possessed, but that of a reasonably competent carpenter doing such a trifling domestic job.[12] Where a man has not held himself out as having special skill, he is not liable when he shows average skill in the circumstances although he has special skill.[13] One of the main reasons why the courts insist on applying a uniform standard of skill is the practical difficulty of assessing a particular persons' actual skill or experience.[14]

Skill, just like every other aspect of the standard of care, has to be assessed in the light of all the circumstances surrounding the alleged breach of duty. No defendant will be expected to attain the same degree of skill under pressure in an emergency, 'in the heat of the moment', as would be demanded in less stressful circumstances.[15] Thus police chasing a suspect must still drive carefully but the hot pursuit of the offender will be taken into account in ascertaining whether the officers concerned fell below the appropriate standard of driving competence.[16] Where negligence is alleged in the course of playing a sport, the fact that the object of competitive sport is to win and that spectators attend sporting occasions to see competitors exhibit their skill at the game will be relevant. So in *Wooldridge v Sumner*[17] DIPLOCK LJ (as he then was) held that where a showjumper was concentrating his attention and exerting his skill to complete his round of the showjumping circuit this must be taken into account in determining whether a momentary misjudgment constituted negligence. By contrast in *Condon v Basi*[18] a footballer sued in negligence when he suffered a broken leg as a result of a tackle by the defendant found by the referee to be serious foul play. The defendant was held liable and upholding, the judgment, at first instance the Court of Appeal held that a clear breach of the rules of the game would be a relevant but not conclusive consideration in deciding whether there had been actionable negligence. The overall test was did the defendant show that degree of reasonable regard for the safety of others to be expected of a competent player of his class?

F. THE CIRCUMSTANCES OF THE PLAINTIFF

The defendant's actual knowledge of the circumstances may increase his measure of care. The measure of care owed to a woman known to be

---

12 If the householder employed a professional carpenter no doubt the latter would be under a contractual duty to him to use the skill of a professional, but what standard would the professional owe to members of the public?

13 *Wooldridge v Sumner* [1962] 2 All ER 978 at 989 (per DIPLOCK J); and see p 250, post, for the facts.

14 That was one reason why the Court of Appeal in *Nettleship v Weston* supra, held that a learner-driver has to reach the standard of any other driver even towards his instructor-passenger.

15 Many of the cases on the standard of care in emergencies deal with contributory negligence, see *Jones v Boyce* (1816) 1 Stark 493 discussed post at 244; on primary liability and emergency see *Parkinson v Liverpool Corpn* [1950] 1 All ER 367.

16 *Marshall v Osmond* [1983] QB 1034, [1983] 2 All ER 225.

17 [1963] 2 QB 43, [1962] 2 All ER 978.

18 [1985] 1 WLR 866.

pregnant,[19] or to a workman with one eye,[20] may, according to particular circumstances, be greater. If the defendant neither knows nor ought to know of these circumstances, they do not affect the measure of his duty. As LORD SUMNER has said:[1]

> ... a measure of care appropriate to the inability or disability of those who are immature or feeble in mind or body is due from others, who know of or ought to anticipate the presence of such persons within the scope and hazard of their own operations.

In *Haley v London Electricity Board*[2] the House of Lords applied LORD SUMNER's dictum when they held that a body conducting operations on a city highway should foresee that blind persons would walk along the pavement, and that it owes a duty to take those precautions reasonably necessary to protect them from harm; on the facts it was held liable although a sighted person would not have been injured in consequence of its operations.

The principles of the preceding paragraph illustrate a general principle relating to standard of care: that the particular circumstances may always be material. For instance, a pedestrian is injured by a motor cycle: if the defendant is a competitor in a race and the plaintiff a spectator the defendant is entitled to take risks which would have amounted to negligence had there been no race, but even then his behaviour may be so foolhardy as to constitute negligence.[3]

G. DEGREES OF CARE

It follows from what has been discussed that English law knows no sharp categories of care—for instance, it has no division corresponding to the two divisions in the civil law of gross carelessness and slight carelessness.[4] No more can be said than that the 'degree of care and diligence which a ... [defendant] must exercise corresponds with the degree of negligence for which he is responsible';[5] the defendant must do what is reasonable in the circumstances.[6]

19 *Hay (or Bourhill) v Young* [1943] AC 92 at 109 (per LORD WRIGHT), [1942] 2 All ER 396; cf LORD WRIGHT (1951) 14 MLR at 400.
20 *Paris v Stepney Borough Council* [1951] AC 367, at 385, 386, HL (per LORD OAKSEY and LORD MORTON, respectively).
1 *Glasgow Corporation v Taylor* [1922] 1 AC 44 at 67; of course, there are numerous cases where defendants have not been held in breach of duty to infants (eg *Donovan v Union Cartage Co Ltd* [1933] 2 KB 71, Div Ct) or to blind persons (eg *Pritchard v Post Office* (1950) 114 JP 370, CA).
2 [1965] AC 778, [1964] 3 All ER 185, HL.
3 *Wilks v Cheltenham Homeguard Motor Cycle and Light Car Club* [1971] 2 All ER 369, CA.
4 Cf LYNSKEY J, in *Pentecost v London District Auditor* [1951] 2 KB 759 at 764, [1951] 2 All ER 330.
5 Per LORD CHELMSFORD in *Giblin v McMullen* (1869) LR 2 PC 317 at 337.
6 Attempts made to introduce categories of ordinary, gross and slight, care, eg in *Coggs v Bernard* (1703) 2 Ld Raym 909, have been successfully resisted; *Wilson v Brett* (1843) 11 M & W 113 at 115 (per ROLFE B); *Grill v General Iron Screw Collier Co* (1866) LR 1 CP 600 at 612 (per WILLES J). In *O'Connor v British Transport Commission* [1958] 1 All ER 558, the Court of Appeal rejected the contention that carriers had to maintain towards passengers a standard of care higher than the ordinary standard of care.

H. REASONABLE ANTICIPATION

In decided cases there is a recurrent emphasis on what could reasonably be anticipated or foreseen as constituting the standard of the reasonable man.[7] This serves to emphasise both that one must not look at the circumstances in the light of what has in fact happened[8] and that it is immaterial that, since the accident, the defendant has taken precautions against a further such accident.[9] 'It is elementary law that a man cannot be expected to take precautions against dangers which he cannot reasonably be expected to anticipate.'[10]

I. FORESEEABLE ACTS OF THIRD PARTIES

Even where the courts are prepared to find a duty in respect of the act of third parties,[11] it will often be difficult to decide,[12] when there has been an intervening act of a third party, whether the defendant's act has caused the damage suffered by the plaintiff. It is important to note that that issue of causation becomes material only after the failure of the defendant to take due care has been proved. Whether the defendant has shown that standard of care will frequently depend on what acts or omissions of another he could reasonably have anticipated. If the plaintiff is injured because a third party has done something which the defendant could not reasonably foresee that he would do, the defendant is not liable.[13] Yet, in *LPTB v Upson*,[14] the House of Lords reversed the ruling of LORD GREENE MR, in the court below that 'drivers are entitled to drive on the assumption that other users of the road, whether drivers or pedestrians, will behave with reasonable care'.[15] LORD UTHWATT added:[16]

> It is common experience that many do not. A driver is not, of course, bound to anticipate folly in all its forms, but he is not, in my opinion, entitled to put out of consideration the teachings of experience as to the form those follies commonly take.

Nor can one excuse one's self by relying on another to do an act unless that reliance were reasonable. *Manchester Corporation v Markland* illustrates this:[17]

---

7 *Glasgow Corporation v Muir* [1943] AC 448, [1943] 2 All ER 44, HL; *Paris v Stepney Borough Council* [1951] AC 367, [1951] 1 All ER 42, HL.
8 'Nothing is so easy as to be wise after the event' per BRAMWELL B, in *Cornman v Eastern Counties Ry Co* (1859) 4 H & N 781 at 786. This principle serves to re-emphasise the point that negligence must be judged on the state of scientific and technological knowledge at the time of the alleged carelessness, discussed ante at p 205.
9 *Hall v Brooklands Auto Racing Club* [1933] 1 KB 205 at 225, CA (per GREER LJ).
10 *Tilley v Stevenson* [1939] 4 All ER 207 at 210 (per SLESSER LJ), CA.
11 See ante at pp 169–171.
12 See post at p 234.
13 *Donaldson v McNiven* [1952] 2 All ER 691, CA.
14 [1949] AC 155, [1949] 1 All ER 60, HL.
15 [1947] KB 930 at 938.
16 At p 173; cf *Grant v Sun Shipping Co Ltd* [1948] AC 549 at 567 (per LORD DU PARCQ), [1948] 2 All ER 238, HL.
17 [1936] AC 360, HL.

The appellants were the statutory authority for the supply of water to the borough of Eccles. One of the appellants' service pipes in a road in Eccles burst; three days later, the resulting pool of water froze, and a motor car skidded on the ice knocking down and killing a man. In an action of negligence by the dependants of the deceased against the appellants, it was held to be no defence that the appellants chose to rely on Eccles Corporation to notify them of bursts—they should themselves have taken proper precautions.

J. GENERAL PRACTICE OF THE COMMUNITY

Commonly, a defendant will support his claim to have shown due care by showing that he conformed to the common practice of those engaged in the activity in question. The evidence is relevant.[18] And, as we shall see in the next section, conforming to the practice of the profession will often be conclusive in claims against professionals. So a specialist who failed to diagnose the complaint of the plaintiff was held not to have been negligent when he used the normal methods of British medical specialists, although the use of an instrument usually employed in the United States might have resulted in a correct diagnosis.[19] Yet evidence of general practice is not always decisive. In *Cavanagh v Ulster Weaving Co Ltd*:[20]

> Plaintiff slipped coming down a roof ladder. Despite unchallenged evidence that the 'set-up' was in perfect accord with established practice, the House of Lords restored the jury's verdict that the defendants were negligent.

In *Brown v Rolls Royce Ltd*:[1]

> The defendants failed to provide the plaintiff with barrier cream commonly supplied by employers to workmen doing work like this. They had relied on proper medical advice in not providing the cream. They further maintained that the plaintiff had not proved that the cream would have prevented him from contracting dermatitis. Held that the plaintiff had not discharged his burden of proving that negligence by the defendants caused his dermatitis.

Commercial enterprises must take steps to keep abreast of scientific developments. Growing understanding of the effects of industrial noise and its role as a causative factor in deafness was not matched by action by employers. In *Thompson v Smiths Shiprepairers (North Shields) Ltd*[2] it was held that once there was general awareness of the dangers of noise and

---

18 Building inspectors, after *Anns v Merton London Borough Council* [1978] AC 728, [1977] 2 All ER 492, HL, instituted more stringent practices on inspection. In subsequent negligence actions against them, these new methods were relevant, but only for inspections made after that case: *Worlock v Saws* (1981) 260 Estates Gazette 920.

19 *Whiteford v Hunter* (1950) 94 Sol Jo 758, HL; cf *Vancouver General Hospital v McDaniel* (1934) 152 LT 56, PC; *Wright v Cheshire County Council* [1952] 2 All ER 789, CA.

20 [1960] AC 145, [1959] 2 All ER 745, HL.

 1 [1960] 1 All ER 577, HL. And see *Stokes v Guest Keen and Nettlefold (Bolts and Nuts) Ltd* [1968] 1 WLR 1776, where the negligence of a works doctor in not instituting medical examinations and in not warning of the risks was held to have caused the scrotal cancer of the plaintiff workman.

 2 [1984] QB 405, [1984] 1 All ER 881.

protective equipment became available from about 1963 onwards that defendants were liable for impairment of hearing caused after that date.

Failure to conform to a standard imposed by a statute, although of course it may constitute a breach of statutory duty, is not in itself conclusive evidence of negligence:[3] it may, however, sometimes be *prima facie* evidence.[4]

SECTION 3.   PROFESSIONAL NEGLIGENCE[5]

A. THE BACKGROUND

There is in terms of fundamental principle no distinction between the guidelines ascertaining the standard of care of professionals from those applicable to any other person. Whether the defendant is a plumber or an architect or a consultant surgeon, the primary question is whether in all the circumstances the defendant acted with the skill and competence to be expected from a person undertaking his particular activity and professing his specific skill. The problems which arise in actions against professionals include these:

1   There may be disputes within the profession as to what constitutes proper practice.
2   The implications of professional negligence are likely to be more far flung. When a carpenter makes an error fixing a new door, damage may be inflicted on the fabric of the house, the householder may suffer personal injury if the door falls off, but the range of potential harm is limited. Should an architect designing blocks of tower flats make an error in design, hundreds of people are at risk, the financial cost of correcting the error in several blocks of flats may be astronomic.
3   The potentially high cost of professional negligence has resulted in massive increases in insurance premiums in particular for architects, solicitors, and accountants. Many professions are now calling for statutory limits on damages awards for professional negligence.[6]
4   Particularly acute difficulties affect doctors. Cutbacks in the NHS mean doctors may often be overworked and hospitals under resourced. Junior doctors may be forced to do tasks beyond their competence in the absence of sufficient consultant cover. And patients may wish to play a greater part in decision-making these days.

3 In *Powell v Phillips* [1972] 3 All ER 864, CA, it was held that breach of the Highway Code, despite s 37(5) of the Road Traffic Act 1972, creates no presumption of negligence calling for an explanation; it is just one relevant circumstance on which the defendant is entitled to rely. In *Trotman v British Railways Board* [1975] ICR 95, it was held that breach of a regulation in British Railways' Rule Book created a rebuttable inference of negligence. A breach of a navigational bye-law is particularly cogent evidence of negligence, eg *Cayzer, Irvine & Co v Carran Co* (1884) 9 App Cas 873 at 880–1 (per LORD BLACKBURN), HL, *sed quaere* whether it is conclusive.
4 *Blamires v Lancs and Yorks Ry* (1873) LR 8 Exch 283; *Phillips v Britannia Hygienic Laundry Co* [1923] 1 KB 539 at 548 (per McCARDIE J), affd [1923] 2 KB 832, CA; *Anglo-Newfoundland Development Co Ltd v Pacific Steam Navigation Co* [1924] AC 406 at 413, HL (per LORD DUNEDIN); see also *Harrison v National Coal Board* [1951] AC 639, [1951] 1 All ER 1102, HL; *National Coal Board v England* [1954] AC 403, [1954] 1 All ER 546, HL. And compliance with a statutory requirement does not exclude liability in negligence. *Bux v Slough Metals Ltd* [1974] 1 All ER 262. And see *Budden v BP Oil Ltd* [1980] 124 Sol Jo 376, CA, p 195, ante.
5 For full treatment of this important topic see Dugdale and Stanton, *Professional Negligence*.
6 And the government has set up an inquiry to examine the issue.

For these and many other reasons in practice actions for professional negligence tend to be fraught with difficulty for the plaintiff and to be fought vigorously by the professional backed by his insurers. Some further guidelines will therefore be given on the current state of the law in England relating to professional negligence.

B. DUTY AND BREACH

Very often the duty of care will arise concurrently in tort and within the contract between the professional and his client. The injured client has the option to elect to sue in either tort or contract.[7] Whether there has been a breach of duty will generally be determined on exactly the same principles regardless of whether the action is brought in tort or contract. However, contract may impose duties higher than those of the duty of care. In *Thake v Maurice*[8] a surgeon failed to warn a private patient of the risk that vasectomy may be reversed by nature restoring the patient's fertility. The patient argued that the surgeon contracted to render him sterile. He was therefore liable for that breach of contract regardless of whether or not he was negligent when the patient's wife conceived again. The Court of Appeal eventually held by 2–1 that no reasonable man would infer from his contract with a doctor that the doctor guaranteed success.[9] But *Thake v Maurice* graphically illustrates the separate roles of tort and contract where the plaintiff seeks to establish a liability independent of classic negligence. The argument pursued by the plaintiff could not even have been attempted had he been a NHS patient with no contract with the defendant.

A number of other problems affect the issue of a professional's duty in tort. In a number of professions the essence of the professional's expertise is advice. Liability in negligence then depends on the principles governing liability for negligent statements.[10] What of liability other than to the client? Authority makes it clear that where a person other than the client may reasonably rely on the professional's expertise a duty may lie to that person.[11]

C. THE REASONABLE 'PROFESSIONAL'

The basic test of whether the defendant conformed to the standard of the reasonable man, the reasonable 'professional' in his case, must be elaborated a little.

The defendant must exhibit the degree of skill which a member of the public would expect from a person in his or her position. Pressures on him, even pressures for which he is in no way responsible will not excuse an error on his part. Negligence is not to be equated with moral culpability or general

7 *Midland Bank Trust Co Ltd v Hett, Stubbs & Kemp* [1979] Ch 384, [1978] 3 All ER 571.
8 [1986] QB 644, [1986] 1 All ER 497. And see *Eyre v Measday* [1986] 1 All ER 488 (female sterilisation).
9 But the appeal court unanimously held the surgeon liable in negligence. The failure to warn was held to be negligent and as a result the wife failed to recognise the symptoms of pregnancy soon enough to be able to opt for an abortion.
10 See ante at p 185 et seq.
11 See *Ross v Caunters* [1980] Ch 297, [1979] 3 All ER 580 discussed ante at p 189.

incompetence. In *Wilsher v Essex Area Health Authority*,[12] a premature baby was admitted to a specialist neo-natal unit. An error was made in that medical staff failed to notice that the baby was receiving too much oxygen and the baby became blind. The Court of Appeal held that the doctors were negligent and by a majority that they must be judged by reference to their 'posts' in the unit. It would be irrelevant that they were inexperienced, or doing a job which should have been done by a consultant, or just grossly overworked. The dissenting judge argued that the doctors should be assessed individually. If a particular doctor was too junior for his 'post' then it should be the health authority who were directly liable to the plaintiff for providing inadequate staffing and resources.[13]

In determining the standard demanded in a particular 'post' be it surgical registrar or partner in a firm of solicitors, expert evidence of proper practice must be called. Where practice is disputed, conformity with a responsible body of opinion within the profession will generally suffice.[14] Particularly in claims for medical negligence, judges have tended to refuse to select between differing bodies of responsible professional opinion.[15] A professional departing from orthodox opinion is not liable in negligence on that evidence alone, but will be required to produce evidence to establish that despite his departure from orthodoxy he still acted with all due care and competence.[16]

Errors of judgment are often the essence of professional negligence. An error of itself is not negligence. The issue in all cases is whether the error in question evidenced a failure of professional competence. The virtual immunity offered to doctors for errors of clinical judgment was firmly condemned by the House of Lords in *Whitehouse v Jordan*.[17] As LORD EDMUND-DAVIES put it:

> The test [of negligence] is the standard of the ordinary skilled man exercising or professing to have that special skill. If a surgeon fails to measure up to that standard in any respect ('clinical judgment') or otherwise he has been negligent.

D. PATIENTS AND DOCTORS

Two factors militate to accentuate the problems of an action against a professional where the professional is a medical practitioner.

First, there is the fear that a flood of successful litigation against doctors will trigger the practice of 'defensive' medicine. Your doctor will opt for the treatment least likely to lead to you suing him rather than the treatment which may be best for you medically. Patients will be subjected to unnecessary tests to protect the doctors and the NHS will thus incur unnecessary expenses. No judge has expressly found against a patient plaintiff on this basis[18] but

---

12 [1987] QB 730, [1986] 3 All ER 801 rvsd on the issue of causation (1988) The Independent, 11 March, HL.
13 On the direct liability of health authorities to patients see post at p 453 et seq.
14 *Bolam v Friern Hospital Management Committee* [1958] 1 WLR 582.
15 *Maynard v West Midlands Regional Health Authority* [1984] 1 WLR 634 at 639 '... a judge's "preference" for one body of distinguished professional opinion over another also professionally distinguished is not sufficient to establish negligence'.
16 *Clark v MacLennan* [1983] 1 All ER 416.
17 [1981] 1 WLR 246 at 258, HL.
18 Do you think that this was a factor in *Whitehouse v Jordan* [1981] 1 All ER 267, [1981] 1 WLR 246? (obstetrician held not liable for failing to proceed more swiftly to Caesarean section: did the judges fear a rise in the rate of Caesarean births to protect obstetricians from liability to damage babies?).

the spectre of defensive medicine haunts the growing avalanche of often unsuccessful medical litigation.[19]

Second, there is the thorny problem of 'informed consent'. We saw earlier that failure by a doctor to advise a patient on the risks of treatment does not invalidate the patient's consent so as to give rise to an action in trespass.[20] But counselling a patient so as to aid him to make a sensible decision on whether or not to agree to proposed treatment is part and parcel of the doctor's duty of care.[1] How should the issue of breach of that duty be determined? The House of Lords in *Sidaway*[2] held that the normal test of professional negligence must apply ie accepted professional practice. In *Gold v Haringey Health Authority* the treatment involved was non-therapeutic sterilisation. The plaintiff chose to be sterilised as a means of permanent contraception. A further pregnancy would not have endangered her health. The judge at first instance[3] said the doctor's duty in counselling her on the risks and disadvantages of sterilisation should be judged by what she, as a reasonable woman, would want to know. She was not receiving therapeutic treatment needed for her health and so *Sidaway* could be distinguished. The Court of Appeal quashed his decision. The test in all cases, they proclaimed, should be accepted professional practice.[4]

The debate on 'informed consent' illustrates that negligence, like trespass, could have a role in defining our individual rights, and promoting individual autonomy. *Who* should decide whether the benefits of proposed treatment outweigh the risks? That is the question of principle. The courts have so far refused to distinguish between negligent treatment as such, and a failure by the doctor in his delicate task of assisting his patient to make his own choices on treatment[5] to exercise his right to self-determination.[6] Judicial fear of a flood of medical litigation, as has happened in the USA, and fraternal regard to the medical profession have induced the English courts so far to decline the opportunity to use the law of torts to uphold patients' rights.

SECTION 4.   PROVING NEGLIGENCE

A. LAW AND FACT

The law of negligence, and—even more so—the reported cases cannot be understood unless the background of procedure is appreciated.[7] Almost all actions of negligence in the High Court are now tried by a judge sitting without a jury; the judge himself tries issues of both law and fact: it will not therefore be surprising if the judgments in such cases do not meticulously mark off matters of law and fact from one another. Formerly, most of these

19 See Jones (1987) 3 Professional Negligence 43.
20 See ante at p 77.
 1 *Chatterton v Gerson* [1981] QB 432, [1981] 1 All ER 257.
 2 *Sidaway v Governors of Bethlem Royal Hospital and the Maudsley Hospital* [1985] AC 871, [1985] 1 All ER 643.
 3 (1986) Times, 17 June.
 4 [1987] 2 All ER 888, [1987] 3 WLR 649, CA.
 5 See in particular the judgment of LORD DIPLOCK in *Sidaway* supra.
 6 See H Teff 'Consent to Medical Procedures: Paternalism, Self Determination, or Therapeutic Alliance, (1985) 101 LQR 432; M Brazier 'Patient Autonomy and Consent to Medical Treatment' (1987) 7 LS 169.
 7 What is discussed in this section is generally applicable to all torts, but is conveniently treated here.

actions were tried by a judge sitting with a jury; it was then sufficiently accurate[8] to say that matters of law were for the judge and matters of fact for the jury.

Appellate cases may be of three types:

1 Most of them are appeals from judges sitting alone.
2 Some are appeals from county court judges often on points of law only.[9]
3 Many old, but a very few recent, cases are appeals from a judge sitting with a jury.

It is useful in view of the distinction between law and fact, which is especially relevant in cases (2) and (3) above, to summarise the respective provinces of law and fact in negligence. The following are matters of law:

1 All questions of duty—was the duty owed to the plaintiff, was it within the hazard, and the like?
2 The Standard of Care—what the standard is, and whether there is any evidence of failure to conform to it.
3 The principles to be applied in determining whether the damage was too remote, and whether there was any evidence of such damage; whether any recognised heads of damage have not been taken into account.

Matters of fact are:

1 Resolving conflicts in the evidence and determining what the circumstances were and what the parties did.
2 Evaluating the conduct of the parties in the light of the facts found and deciding whether it constituted a failure to take care, having regard to the standard of care required of the defendant.
3 Deciding, in the light of the facts found, whether the damage was caused by the defendant and the extent of the damage;[10] assessment of damages.[11]

If, then, an appellate court is concerned with an appeal from either a judge sitting with a jury or from a county court judge,[12] it considers only the several matters defined above as matters of law. If, on the other hand, it is hearing an appeal from a judge sitting without a jury, it is not so restricted. '[It] has ... jurisdiction to review the record of the evidence in order to determine whether the conclusion originally reached upon that evidence should stand; but this jurisdiction has to be exercised with caution.'[13] The court should be 'satisfied that any advantage enjoyed by the trial judge by reason of having seen and heard the witnesses, could not be sufficient to explain or justify the trial judge's conclusion',[14] before it disturbs his findings of fact. On the other hand, where, as often happens, the facts are not in dispute, but the case rests

---

8 But see Pollock in *Pollock-Holmes Letters* vol 92.
9 Many old reported cases were decided at a time when appeals from county courts were on points of law. That general restriction has been revised, and the right of appeal is now in such circumstances as Rules of the Supreme Court and regulations by the Lord Chancellor prescribe; Supreme Court Act 1981, Sch 3, para 14.
10 These and (2) are matters of inference from (1).
11 See ch 29.
12 But see n 18, supra.
13 Per VISCOUNT SIMON in *Watt v Thomas* [1947] AC 484 at 486, [1947] 1 All ER 582, HL.
14 Per LORD THANKERTON, *Watt v Thomas* supra at 488.

on the inference to be drawn from them, an appellate court is in as good a position as the trial judge to decide the case.[15]

B. ONUS OF PROOF

Whether what is in issue is the veracity of primary facts or the validity of the inferences to be drawn from those facts, the burden of establishing:

a that the defendant was negligent, and
b that his negligence resulted in the plaintiff's loss or injury

rests on the plaintiff. Should the evidence be equally balanced so that the accident might have been the result of lack of care or competence, but might just as easily have occurred without carelessness the plaintiff fails. He has not established negligence. Thus in *Ashcroft v Mersey Regional Health Authority*[16] the plaintiff suffered a partial paralysis in her face when in the course of surgery on her left ear the surgeon cut into a facial nerve. Expert evidence showed that this was often an inherent risk of such surgery even when performed with the greatest skill, but all the experts accepted it also sometimes happened because of a failure in skill. The plaintiff's claim failed.

At least Mrs Ashcroft knew what had happened even though her counsel failed to establish that the facts proved constituted negligence. In many cases of alleged negligence the plaintiff knows only that he has been injured. How he came to be hit on the head by a falling object or a collapsing wall, why a swab remained in his abdomen after surgery is a closed book to him. In a number of cases the plaintiff may be able to invoke the principle of *res ipsa loquitur*.

C. *RES IPSA LOQUITUR*

In *Scott v London and St Katherine's Docks Co*[17] the facts were:

The plaintiff, a customs officer, while near the door of the defendants' warehouse, was injured by some sugar bags falling on him. The judge directed the jury to find a verdict for the defendants on the ground of lack of evidence of negligence by the defendants, who called no evidence. On appeal a new trial was directed.

The court justified this direction of a new trial in the following terms, which have since become known as *res ipsa loquitur*:[18]

15 *Powell v Streatham Manor Nursing Home* [1935] AC 243 at 267, [1935] All ER Rep 58 at 67 (per LORD WRIGHT), HL. See also *Benmax v Austin Motor Co Ltd*, [1955] AC 370, [1955] 1 All ER 326, HL. Appellate courts are now exercising this power so freely that many appellate decisions now turn solely on matters of inference from facts. *Morris v West Hartlepool Steam Navigation Co Ltd* [1956] AC 552, [1956] 1 All ER 385, HL is a typical example of the House of Lords substituting its own evaluation of the facts for that of the trial judge: nothing else is in issue, yet the case appears in the Law Reports. And see *Whitehouse v Jordan* [1981] 1 All ER 267, [1981] 1 WLR 246, HL.
16 [1983] 2 All ER 245, affd [1985] 2 All ER 96n.
17 (1865) 3 H & C 596 Ex Ch.
18 Per ERLE CJ at 601. It is not necessary to plead the doctrine; it is enough to prove facts which make it applicable; *Bennett v Chemical Construction (Great Britain) Ltd* [1971] 3 All ER 822, CA.

There must be reasonable evidence of negligence. But where the thing is shown to be under the management of the defendant or his servants, and the accident is such as in the ordinary course of things does not happen if those who have the management use proper care, it affords reasonable evidence, in the absence of explanation by the defendants, that the accident arose from want of care.

In the past there has been a tendency to elevate *res ipsa loquitur* to the status of a principle of substantive law or of at least a doctrine. In the 1970s the Court of Appeal decisively swung away from that approach. In *Lloyde v West Midlands Gas Board*, MEGAW LJ said:[19]

> I doubt whether it is right to describe *res ipsa loquitur* as a 'doctrine'. I think that it is no more than an exotic, although convenient, phrase to describe what is in essence no more than a commonsense approach, not limited by technical rules, to the assessment of the effect of evidence in certain circumstances. It means that a plaintiff *prima facie* establishes negligence where: (i) it is not possible for him to prove precisely what was the relevant act or omission which set in train the events leading to the accident, but (ii) on the evidence as it stands at the relevant time it is more likely than not that the effective cause of the accident was *some* act or omission of the defendant or of someone for whom the defendant is responsible, which act or omission constitutes a failure to take proper care for the plaintiff's safety.

It is still necessary to examine the content of *res ipsa loquitur*, but always with that warning in mind.

Three separate requirements must be satisfied:

(1) 'THE DOCTRINE IS DEPENDENT ON THE ABSENCE OF EXPLANATION'[20]

This merely means that if the court finds on the evidence adduced how and why the occurrence took place then there is no room for inference. So, in *Barkway v South Wales Transport Co Ltd*[1] where the tyre of an omnibus burst and the omnibus mounted the pavement and fell down an embankment, *res ipsa loquitur* did not apply because the court had evidence of the circumstances of the accident and so was satisfied that the system of tyre inspection in the garage of the defendants was a negligent one. Yet the word 'explanation' must be qualified by the adjective 'exact'.[2] This is to make it clear that a plaintiff who is able to present a partial account of how an accident happened is still not precluded from relying on *res ipsa loquitur* for further inferences essential to the winning of his case. The partial explanation

---

19 [1971] 2 All ER 1240 at 1246. The Court of Appeal in *Turner v Mansfield Corporation* (1975) 119 Sol Jo 629 unanimously affirmed that judgment.

20 Per LORD PORTER in *Barkway v South Wales Transport Co Ltd* [1950] 1 All ER 392 at 394, HL.

1 Ibid. And see *Swan v Salisbury Construction Co Ltd* [1966] 2 All ER 138, PC. In *Richley v Faull* [1965] 3 All ER 109 D's car hit P's car when D's car was on the wrong side of the road. D proved that he skidded. Without mentioning *res ipsa loquitur*, the court reached the solution supported by common sense that D was liable unless he showed that the skid occurred through no fault of his. Similarly in *Henderson v Henry E Jenkins & Sons* [1970] AC 282, [1969] 3 All ER 756, HL, the sudden failure of brakes on a lorry owing to a corroded pipe in the hydraulic braking system was held to impute negligence to the owners.

2 Per LORD DUNEDIN in *Ballard v North British Ry Co* 1923 SC 43 at 54, HL.

may make it more obvious that an inference of negligence can be drawn. Of course, as in the *Barkway case*, even if *res ipsa loquitur* is inapplicable because all the material facts are proved, those facts may be found to constitute negligence.[3]

(2) THE HARM MUST BE OF SUCH A KIND THAT IT DOES NOT ORDINARILY HAPPEN IF PROPER CARE IS BEING TAKEN

The courts will apply the doctrine to things falling from buildings,[4] and to accidents resulting from defective machines, apparatus or vehicles.[5] It applies where motor cars mount the pavement,[6] or where aircraft crash on taking off.[7] On the other hand, it was held inapplicable where a fire having been left by a lodger in his grate, neighbouring rooms were damaged by fire spreading from his room.[8]

It will be recalled that the classic definition of ERLE CJ, referred to accidents happening 'in the ordinary course of things'. *Mahon v Osborne*[9] raised the issue whether this means that it must be a matter of common experience, so that the experience of the expert is irrelevant. GODDARD LJ, held that the doctrine applied where swabs had been left in the body of a patient after an abdominal operation[10] but SCOTT LJ, thought that where the judge could not, as with surgical operations, have enough knowledge of the circumstances to draw an inference of negligence, the doctrine did not apply.[11] Since then, the Court of Appeal has held it to be *prima facie* evidence of negligence that a man, on leaving hospital after a course of radiography treatment to his hand and arm, had four stiff fingers and a useless hand;[12] and a court of first instance has been influenced by expert evidence in rejecting the application of *res ipsa loquitur* to a case where a patient sustained a fractured jaw as a result of a dental extraction.[13] Though, on the authorities, the point remains open, it is suggested that where an unexplained accident occurs from a thing under the control of the defendant, and medical or other expert evidence shows that such accidents would not happen if proper care were used, there is at least evidence of negligence for a jury.

3 Conversely, a defendant is not liable for an unexplained accident, to which *res ipsa loquitur* might otherwise apply, if he establishes that he himself was not negligent; *Barkway v South Wales Transport Co Ltd* [1948] 2 All ER 460 at 463 (per BUCKNILL LJ).
4 *Byrne v Boadle* (1863) 2 H & C 722 (flour barrel falling from upper window on to plaintiff, walking on the street below); *Kearney v London and Brighton Ry Co* (1870) LR 5 QB 411.
5 *Ballard v North British Ry Co* 1923 SC 43, HL (defective coupling on train); *Kealey v Heard* [1983] 1 All ER 973, [1983] 1 WLR 573 (collapsing scaffolding).
6 *McGowan v Stott* (1923), in (1930) 99 LJKB 357, CA; *Ellor v Selfridge & Co Ltd* (1930) 46 TLR 236; *Laurie v Raglan Building Co Ltd* [1942] 1 KB 152, [1941] 3 All ER 332.
7 *Fosbroke-Hobbes v Airwork Ltd and British-American Air Services Ltd* [1937] 1 All ER 108.
8 *Sochacki v Sas* [1947] 1 All ER 344.
9 [1939] 2 KB 14, [1939] All ER 535, CA.
10 At 50.
11 At 23. It is impossible to be certain of the view of MACKINNON LJ, in view of the conflicting reports, perhaps the fullest of which is (1939) 108 LJKB 567.
12 *Cassidy v Ministry of Health* [1951] 2 KB 343, [1951] 1 All ER 574, CA. *Saunders v Leeds Western Health Authority* [1985] CLY 2320 (child suffering cardiac stoppage under anaesthetic).
13 *Fish v Kapur* [1948] 2 All ER 176; contra, if the patient swallows a throat pack; *Garner v Morrall* (1935) Times 31 October.

(3) THE INSTRUMENTALITY CAUSING THE ACCIDENT MUST BE WITHIN THE
EXCLUSIVE CONTROL OF THE DEFENDANT

(a) The meaning of 'control'

If the defendant is not in control *res ipsa loquitur* does not apply. In *Turner
v Mansfield Corporation*.[14]

> The plaintiff driver of the defendant's dust cart was injured when its back
> raised itself up as the plaintiff drove it under a bridge. It was held that
> since the plaintiff was in control it was for him to explain the accident and
> since he could furnish no evidence from which negligence could be inferred,
> he failed.

McGowan v Stott[15] is an important case in that it called a halt to previous
attempts to insist on complete control of *all* the circumstances before the rule
could apply. Previously, FLETCHER MOULTON LJ, had indicated[16] that the
scope of *res ipsa loquitur* was severely limited in highway accidents because
all the essential surrounding circumstances were seldom under the defendant's
control, but the court in *McGowan v Stott* refused to follow this, and declared
the doctrine applicable to accidents on the highway where the defendant was
in control of the vehicle causing the damage. Two actions brought against
railway companies by plaintiffs who had fallen out of trains illustrate the
degree of control essential for the doctrine to apply.

In *Gee v Metropolitan Ry Co*,[17] a few minutes after a local train had started
its journey, the plaintiff leaned against the offside door, which flew open.
This was held evidence of negligence on the part of the railway company.

In *Easson v LNE Ry Co*,[18] the plaintiff's claim failed, GODDARD LJ, holding
that 'it is impossible to say that the doors of an express corridor train
travelling from Edinburgh to London are continuously under the sole
control of the railway company'.

(b) Where one of two or more persons is in control

If the instrumentality is in the control of one of several servants of the same
employer, and the plaintiff cannot point to the particular servant who is in
control, the rule may still be invoked so as to make the employer vicariously
liable: thus, a hospital authority has been held answerable for negligent
treatment where the plaintiff could not show which of several members of
the staff was responsible.[19] Further, if a surgeon is shown to be in general

---

14 The case is briefly reported at (1975) 119 Sol Jo 629, CA, but the author based the text on
   a full Court of Appeal transcript.
15 (1923) in (1930) 99 LJKB 357n, CA. Where the apparatus is in the plaintiff's house, eg gas
   apparatus, the onus is on the plaintiff to show that it was improbable that persons other
   than the defendant could have interfered with it—only then can he invoke *res ipsa loquitur*:
   Lloyde v West Midlands Gas Board [1971] 2 All ER 1240, CA. In *Ward v Tesco Stores Ltd*,
   [1976] 1 All ER 219, CA, the plaintiff slipped on yoghurt spilled on the floor of the defendants'
   supermarket. Even though there was no evidence as to how long the yoghurt had been on
   the floor it was held to be a case of *prima facie* negligence.
16 *Wing v London General Omnibus Co* [1909] 2 KB 652 at 663–4, CA.
17 (1873) LR 8 QB 161.
18 [1944] KB 421 at 424, [1944] 2 All ER 425, CA.
19 *Cassidy v Ministry of Health* [1951] 2 KB 343, [1951] 1 All ER 574, CA. For more detailed
   examination of this from the standpoint of vicarious liability, see p 453, post.

command of an operation, and the patient cannot establish whether it was the malpractice of the surgeon or one of the theatre staff which inflicted damage on him in the course of that operation, it seems that *res ipsa loquitur* applies in an action of negligence against the surgeon.[20] If, on the other hand, the surgeon is not in control of all the relevant stages of the treatment, and if the plaintiff cannot prove that the act complained of took place at a time when the defendant surgeon was in control, *res ipsa loquitur* cannot be relied on.[1] *Walsh v Holst & Co Ltd*[2] extends the doctrine further: when the defendant's duty is so extensive that he is answerable for the negligence of his independent contractor, and an accident occurs while the independent contractor is performing the work delegated to him, the plaintiff can invoke *res ipsa loquitur* against both the defendant and his independent contractor.[3]

A related, though distinct, problem is the position of a plaintiff who establishes, without invoking the rule of *res ipsa loquitur*, that the damage to him was caused either by the negligence of A or the negligence of B. If he is merely able to show that only A or B but not both must have been negligent then he is not entitled to a verdict against both unless the defendants have refused to give evidence, in which case adverse inferences against them may be drawn.[4] It is, however, the duty of the trial court to come to a definite conclusion on the evidence—it must not dismiss the action because of uncertainty as to which party was free from blame.[5] If the inference is that one or other or both have been negligent the plaintiff has made out a *prima facie* case against either A or B, or both.[6] These decisions illustrate a trend towards easing the burden on the plaintiff of proving negligence, a trend the more surprising in view of the many 'defendant's decisions' in recent years in other aspects of negligence. Of course, if the circumstances do not warrant the inference that one or other has been negligent, the plaintiff fails.[7]

Beyond setting out the above rules, it is submitted that one cannot define the circumstances where the doctrine applies. As usual in negligence, some

---

20 *Mahon v Osborne* [1939] 2 KB 14, [1939] 1 All ER 535, CA. So held by GODDARD LJ, with whom MACKINNON LJ, appeared to agree, SCOTT LJ, dissenting.

1 *Morris v Winsbury-White* [1937] 4 All ER 494; perhaps SOMERVELL LJ disagreed with this statement of law in *Roe v Minister of Health* [1954] 2 QB 66 at 80, [1954] 2 All ER 131 at 135, CA.

2 [1958] 3 All ER 33, CA. *Kealey v Heard* [1983] 1 All ER 973, [1983] 1 All ER 973, [1983] 1 WLR 573.

3 Apparently, the employer conceded that he is liable even though the plaintiff had not established that the act did not occur within that area of the independent contractor's operations for which the employer is not answerable, viz, acts of collateral negligence—see p 455, post.

4 *Baker v Market Harborough Industrial Co-operative Society Ltd* [1953] 1 WLR 1472, CA; *Cook v Lewis* [1952] 1 DLR 1, decides that where either A or B has committed a tort against P and it is the careless act of both of them which prevents P from knowing which caused the harm, both are liable (A and B were hunters, one or other of whom fired the shot which hit P).

5 *Bray v Palmer* [1953] 2 All ER 1449, CA.

6 *Roe v Minister of Health* per DENNING LJ (ratio), [1954] 2 QB 66, [1954] 2 All ER 131, CA; *France v Parkinson* [1954] 1 All ER 739, CA; where vehicles collide either at cross roads or on the brow of a hill, and both drivers are dead, a passenger has a *prima facie* case, in the absence of other evidence, against both drivers or either of them; *Davison v Leggett* (1969) 133 JP 552, CA, (head on collision centre lane, negligence by both drivers inferred), and more fully reported in *Knight v Fellick* [1977] RTR 316, CA.

7 *Salt v Imperial Chemical Industries Ltd* (1958) Times, 1 February, CA. A consigned caustic soda to carrier B, the container leaked and injured P. The Court of Appeal refused to interfere with the trial judge's finding of no negligence, because this was not a case where either A or B must have been negligent. And see *Knight v Fellick* supra.

writers list all the circumstances where *res ipsa loquitur* has been applied as if they were precedents on points of law. But the Court of Appeal has held[8] that these cases do not lay down any principles of law; they are merely a guide to the kind of circumstance where the doctrine might successfully be invoked.

D. THE EFFECT OF *RES IPSA LOQUITUR*[9]

In some cases the inference to be drawn by resorting to the rule is twofold: that the defendant caused the accident, and that he was negligent. In others, the cause is known, and only the inference of negligence arises.[10]

As has been seen above,[11] on the proved facts it may be just as likely that the event happened without negligence as that it happened in consequence of negligence, in which case there is no evidence of negligence. If, however, in such circumstances, *res ipsa loquitur* applies, its effect is to make it 'relevant to infer negligence'[12] from the fact of the accident—there is in law evidence of negligence on which a jury may properly find for the plaintiff.[13] The distinctive function of the rule is to permit an inference of negligence from proof of the injury and the physical instrumentality causing it, even though there is no proof of the facts identifying the human agency responsible. Looked at this way, its affinity to the ordinary rule of evidence that circumstantial evidence is admissible to prove negligence is clear. As ATKIN LJ, has said:[14]

> ... all that one wants to know is whether the facts of the occurrence do as a matter of fact make it more probable that a jury may reasonably infer that the damage was caused by want of care on the part of the defendants than the contrary.

It is clear then that at least the effect of *res ipsa loquitur* is to afford *prima facie* evidence of negligence. But does it go further and shift the burden of proof in the sense that in the absence of rebutting evidence from the defendant there *must* be a verdict for the plaintiff? In one or two instances some judges in England (but not in other parts of the Commonwealth) have leaned towards the view that it does so shift the burden.[15]

---

8 *Easson v LNER* [1944] KB 421 at 423 (per GODDARD LJ), [1944] 2 All ER 425, CA.
9 For the clearest judicial statement, see the eight rules laid down by EVATT J in *Davis v Bunn* (1936) 56 CLR 246 at 267–8.
10 *Barkway v South Wales Transport* [1950] 1 All ER 392 at 399–400 (per LORD NORMAND), HL.
11 See p 215, ante.
12 *Ballard v North British Ry Co* 1923 SC (HL) 43 at 54.
13 *Cole v De Trafford (No 2)* [1918] 2 KB 523 at 528 (per PICKFORD LJ); of course, when the appellate court hears an appeal from a judge sitting alone, 'the true question is not whether the appellant adduced some evidence of negligence, but whether on all the evidence she proved that the respondents had been guilty of negligence in a relevant particular', per LORD RADCLIFFE in *Barkway v South Wales Transport Co Ltd* [1950] 1 All ER 392 at 403, HL.
14 *McGowan v Stott* (1923), in (1930) 99 LJKB 357 at 360, CA; cf GREER LJ in *Langham v Governors of Wellingborough School and Fryer* (1932) 101 LJKB 513 at 518, CA.
15 Eg LORD EVERSHED MR in *Moore v R Fox & Sons Ltd* [1956] 1 QB 596, [1956] 1 All ER 182, CA. (The Court of Appeal in *Turner v Mansfield Corporation* (1975) 119 Sol Jo 629 held that this case should no longer be regarded as an authority on *res ipsa loquitur*.) *Ludgate v Lovett* [1969] 2 All ER 1275, CA. It is sometimes asserted that the House of Lords decisions in *Woods v Duncan* [1946] AC 401, [1946] 1 All ER 420n, HL, and *Barkway v South Wales Transport Co Ltd* [1950] 1 All ER 392, HL, lend further support, but the High Court of Australia in *Mummery v Irvings Pty Ltd* (1956) 96 CLR 99 at 120, has shown this to be an erroneous interpretation of those cases.

It is submitted, with respect, that *res ipsa loquitur* does not necessarily mean that, without more, the court must find for the plaintiff. Once the rule has been applied the ordinary rules of procedure operate: there is evidence of negligence and therefore the case could be withdrawn from a jury and an appellate court could not set aside a verdict in favour of the plaintiff on the issue of negligence. However, the evidence may be so cogent that a finding by a jury of no negligence could be set aside as a perverse verdict. As DU PARCQ LJ, said:[16]

> The words *res ipsa loquitur* ... are a figure of speech, by which sometimes is meant that certain facts are so inconsistent with any view except that the defendant has been negligent that any jury which, on proof of these facts, found that negligence was not proved would be giving a perverse verdict. Sometimes, the proposition does not go as far as that, but is merely that on proof of certain facts an inference of negligence may be drawn by a reasonable jury ...

To sum up, the effect of *res ipsa loquitur* depends on the cogency of the inference to be drawn, and will vary from case to case: if, for instance, a vehicle mounts the pavement, this is evidence of negligence, but reasonable men may differ about the inference to be drawn from it, so that a verdict of no negligence would not be upset although a withdrawal from the jury would be—yet something may fall from the defendant's window in such circumstances that only an inference of negligence can be drawn, whereupon a verdict of no negligence might be set aside.

The effect of *res ipsa loquitur* where the defendant gives evidence must also be considered. Plainly the effect of the doctrine is to shift the onus to the defendant in the sense that the doctrine continues to operate unless the defendant calls credible evidence which explains how the accident may have occurred without negligence, and it seems that the operation of the rule is not displaced merely by expert evidence showing theoretically possible ways in which the accident might have happened without the defendant's negligence. But beyond this the courts describe the effect in two different ways. Sometimes they state that once the defendant has furnished evidence of the cause of the accident consistent with his having exercised due care it becomes a question whether upon the whole of the evidence the defendant was negligent or not and the defendant will succeed unless the jury is satisfied that he was negligent.[17] On other occasions they state that the defendant loses unless he proves that the accident resulted from a specific cause which does not connote negligence on his part but on the contrary points to its absence as more probable.[18] Probably there is no inconsistency in these judicial

---

16   *Easson v LNE Ry Co* [1944] KB 421 at 425, [1944] 2 All ER 425.

17   Eg *Ballard v North British Ry Co* 1923 SC (HL) 43 at 54 (per LORD DUNEDIN); *The Kite* [1933] P 154, [1933] All ER Rep 234; *Colvilles Ltd v Devine* [1969] 2 All ER 53, HL.

18   Eg *Moore v R Fox & Sons Ltd* [1956] 1 QB 596, [1956] 1 All ER 182, CA. The solution of this problem is not made easier by the uncertain scope and effect of the rule in *The Merchant Prince* [1892] P 179, CA, which held that where the defendant ship under way ran into the plaintiff ship at anchor the defendant had the burden of proving inevitable accident. Does this rule also apply to 'a lorry or a horse and a cart which gets out of control and runs off the road into a house' as DENNING LJ held in *Southport Corporation v Esso Petroelum Co* [1954] 2 QB 182 at 200, [1954] 2 All ER 561, CA at 573 (but see SINGLETON LJ and MORRIS LJ in the same case)? Are there then two separate rules about burden of proof, *res ipsa loquitur*, and the rule in *The Merchant Prince*, as PARKER LJ held in *Newby v General Lighterage Co Ltd* [1955] 1 Lloyds Rep 273, CA at 279: 'At the lowest, it is an ordinary case of *res ipsa loquitur* and in such a case, though the legal burden of proof remains throughout on the plaintiff, he will succeed unless the defendant can point to a possible cause of the

utterances; all may depend on the context of the cases and the cogency of the rebutting evidence in the particular case.

accident which is just as consistent with it having happened without his negligence as with it. At the highest, it is an example of the principle applied in *The Merchant Prince*, in which the legal burden itself is put fairly and squarely on the shoulders of the defendant to disprove negligence.'? Yet in *The Louis Sheid* [1958] 1 Lloyd's Rep 606, KARMINSKI J held that the two rules were identical in effect.

Chapter 14

Causation: remoteness of damage[1]

This topic is relevant in all torts, and because it is dealt with in the Part on Negligence, it must not be thought that its problems concern this tort only. It is convenient to deal with it here for two reasons. First, most of the cases on the topic are on Negligence, and secondly, in Negligence, unlike the torts actionable per se previously considered, the law of causation will have to determine not merely to what extent damages are recoverable but also whether the action succeeds at all, for this tort is actionable only if damage is proved.

SECTION 1.   ANALYSIS OF CAUSAL CONCEPTS

Every occurrence is the result of many conditions which are jointly sufficient to produce it. This complex of conditions includes conditions both antecedent and subsequent to the initiating action or event. When a trespasser drops a match in a field, the oxygen in the air, the combustible material in the field, the lighting and throwing away of the match, the breeze which subsequently fans the flames, are all parts of this complex. Each member of this complex is required to complete the set. For any kind of occurrence there may be more than one complex set of conditions each set of which is jointly sufficient to produce that occurrence. No one complex set is necessary; one can only say that it is sufficient. Within a particular complex, however, each condition is necessary. If only one complex sufficient to produce the occurrence is present, then each member of that complex is causally relevant. In this sense only may one speak of a *causa sine qua non* as a requirement of the plaintiff's case: if the event could not have occurred unless that condition were present, the condition is necessary on that occasion. To that extent the notion of *sine qua non* assists in tracing causation in tort.[2]

The reason why one cannot say that a condition is not a cause if the occurrence could have materialised in the absence of that condition is that more than one complex can produce the same result. Suppose A and B simultaneously shoot P through the heart; both A and B have caused the death although the act of neither is a *sine qua non*—either of the two complexes, A's shooting or B's shooting, is sufficient.

Granted that each member of a set is essential to produce an occurrence, one must next consider, when there is only one set present, whether one

---

1 There is an excellent analysis of the general principles of causation in Hart and Honoré, *Causation in the Law* (2nd edn, 1985).
2 In *Barnett v Chelsea and Kensington Hospital Management Committee* [1969] 1 QB 428, [1968] 1 All ER 1068, the defendants negligently failed to treat a casualty. Held that the hospital was not liable for his death because he would have died had he been admitted. But what if he would have died later if he had been admitted?

condition can be selected from the complex as 'the cause'. There is no precise legal rule, but common sense and law unite in looking for the abnormal or the deliberate human act, and regarding that as 'the cause'. Oxygen in the air is normal: the deliberate throwing down of the lighted match is the cause of the fire, although the oxygen remains a necessary condition of the complex.

SECTION 2. EVIDENCE OF CAUSATION

The preliminary problem of causation, then, for the plaintiff is to adduce sufficient evidence to establish that it is more likely than not that the alleged cause (the 'abnormal' act—be it the throwing down of a lighted match or breach of duty by the defendant) resulted in his loss or injury. Did the conduct of the defendant in fact cause the damage complained of? Where a man was sent home without treatment from a Casualty department after complaining of acute stomach pains and sickness and later died of arsenical poisoning, his widow's claim against the hospital failed even though the hospital admitted negligence.[3] The court found that even had he been given prompt and competent treatment, the man would still have died as a result of the arsenic.

Where there is some evidence that the defendant's conduct may have contributed to the plaintiff's injury the burden remains with the plaintiff to establish on the balance of probabilities that it did so.[4] Particularly when the injury is a disease the plaintiff's task may be formidable. Consider the example of a man claiming that he developed dermatitis because of contact with substances at work and that his employer negligently failed to supply him with protective clothing. The likelihood is that the medical evidence will indicate that contact with the substances at work is one possible cause but that several other hypotheses are also possible. He may have an allergy to some food or the washing powder used to launder his clothes and so on.

The issue of whether the plaintiff has produced sufficient evidence of causation, sufficient evidence that 'but for' the defendant's conduct he would not have suffered injury, is a question of law not fact. And the essence of the exercise on which the courts are engaged is selecting from among the plethora of possible causes the 'responsible cause' for the plaintiff's loss or injury.

Where the plaintiff has proved a breach of duty by the defendant and can further prove that that breach of duty materially increased the risk of the injury to which the plaintiff succumbed the defendant will be held liable. Thus in *McGhee v National Coal Board*[5] it was found that failure to provide adequate washing facilities substantially increased the danger to the plaintiff of him developing dermatitis. He recovered damages from his employers, the National Coal Board, even though he could not via conclusive medical evidence prove that his affliction resulted from the absence of washing facilities alone. Furthermore defendants will also be liable on an extension of the *McGhee* principle if it can be shown that their conduct materially enhanced

---

3 *Barnett v Chelsea and Kensington HMC* (supra).

4 *Hotson v East Berkshire AHA* [1987] 2 All ER 909, [1987] 3 WLR 232, HL. And see *Kay v Ayrshire and Arran Health Board* [1987] 2 All ER 417, HL (plaintiff failed to establish deafness resulted from negligent overdose of penicillin rather than the original attack of pneumoccocal meningitis) [1987] 3 WLR 232, HL.

5 [1972] 3 All ER 1008, [1973] 1 WLR 1, HL. *Clowes v National Coal Board* (1987) Times, 23 April.

an existing risk of injury albeit cannot be conclusively proved that the defendant's negligence was actually the sole cause of that risk materialising. But doctors who failed to notice that a premature baby was receiving too much oxygen were not liable for the baby's blindness because, the House of Lords held, that breach of duty was merely one of six possible causes of that sad injury.[6]

The logic of the principle enunciated by the House of Lords in *McGhee* was accepted by the Lordships themselves as being far from faultless. LORDS REID and WILBERFORCE expressly stated that the decision was essentially a matter of common sense and policy rather than principle.[7] In *Hotson v East Berkshire AHA*[8] the House of Lords refused to extend the *McGhee* 'rule' any further. The plaintiff fell several feet from a tree injuring his hip. He was rushed to hospital but his injury was not diagnosed until five days later. The hospital admitted negligence and responsibility for the pain which the boy suffered during the five days for which treatment was negligently delayed. They denied liability for the condition (avascular necrosis) which the boy developed as a result of a failure in the blood supply to the injured hip. The trial judge found[9] that there was a 75% chance that avascular necrosis would have developed as a result of the injury even if promptly treated, and 25% chance that the delay contributed to the development of the condition. He held that the hospital were liable for loss of that chance and awarded damages assessed at 25% of the compensation which would have been payable had the defendants been 100% liable for the plaintiff's condition. The House of Lords quashing the judgment[10] for the plaintiffs held that the finding that the accident itself was more likely than not to have caused the avascular necrosis concluded the issue in the defendants' favour.[11]

Evidence that the defendants' conduct may have caused or contributed to the plaintiffs' injury will therefore apparently only result in an inference that it did cause that injury, where there is no or inadequate evidence of any other causal factor which on the balance of probabilities resulted in the injury. The House of Lords in *Hotson* held that there was no basis in tort for the judge's decision to award the plaintiff 25% damages to represent the lost 'chance' of complete recovery. If the alleged cause could be proved or be inferred to be more likely than not to be the cause of the damage the plaintiff was entitled to full compensation. Otherwise he gets nothing. It was left open whether when a lost chance of recovery, or avoiding loss, could be proved to result from a breach of duty compensation for that lost chance was recoverable in tort.[12]

SECTION 3.   REMOTENESS OF DAMAGE

Defendants are not liable for all the consequences which 'but for' their conduct would not have occurred. At this point we must turn to the case law

---

6 *Wilsher v Essex Area Health Authority* [1986] 3 All ER 801, CA rvsd (1988) The Independent, 11 March, HL (new trial ordered); cf. *Fitzgerald v Lane* [1987] QB 781, [1987] 2 All ER 455.
7 See the dissenting judgment of SIR NICHOLAS BROWNE-WILKINSON VC in *Wilsher v Essex AHA* (supra).
8 [1987] 2 All ER 909, [1987] 3 WLR 232.
9 [1985] 3 All ER 167, [1985] 1 WLR 1036.
10 The judgment of SIMON BROWN J was upheld by the Court of Appeal [1987] 2 WLR 287.
11 See per LORD MACKAY at 240 and per LORD ACKNER at 248.
12 As it clearly is in contract; *Chaplin v Hicks* [1911] 2 KB 786, CA.

in a search for the legal rules which determine for what consequences of his tort a defendant is answerable, or, as it is often put, the rules determining when damages are not too remote a consequence.

A.   *RE POLEMIS* AND *THE WAGON MOUND*

On this principle of remoteness of damage the two most discussed cases have been *Re Polemis and Furness, Withy & Co*[13] and *The Wagon Mound*.[14] In *Re Polemis*:

> Stevedores employed by the charterers of a ship negligently caused a plank to fall into the hold of the ship, which contained a cargo of petrol in tins. In this hold was petrol vapour from the tins. The ship was destroyed by the fire which at once ensued. Arbitrators found that a spark caused by the plank's coming in contact with something in the hold ignited the petrol vapour and caused the fire, and that the causing of the spark could not reasonably have been anticipated from the falling of the plank, though some damage to the ship might reasonably have been anticipated.

The Court of Appeal unanimously held that the charterers were liable for the loss of the ship because it was a direct, although not a foreseeable, consequence of the negligent act of their employees.

In *The Wagon Mound*:[15]

> The defendants carelessly discharged oil from their ship into Sydney Harbour. About six hours later the ship set sail and left the harbour. The oil was carried by wind and tide beneath the plaintiff's wharf, 200 yards away. After being advised that they could safely do so, the plaintiffs continued welding operations on their wharf. Some 55 to 60 hours after the original discharge of the oil, molten metal from the welding operations on the wharf, when fanned by the wind, set fire to some cotton waste or rag floating in the oil beneath the wharf. The waste set fire to the oil whereupon the flames quickly developed into a conflagration which severely damaged the wharf. The oil also congealed upon the slipways adjoining the wharf and interfered with the plaintiff's use of the slips. The defendants neither knew nor ought to have known that the oil was capable of being set afire when spread on water.

The Judicial Committee held that the defendants were not liable in negligence because they could not reasonably have foreseen that the plaintiff's wharf would be damaged by fire when they carelessly discharged the oil into the harbour.

There is room for argument how far *Polemis* and *Wagon Mound* are in

---

13 [1921] 3 KB 560, CA.

14 *Overseas Tankship (UK) Ltd v Morts Dock & Engineering Co Ltd* [1961] AC 388, [1961] 1 All ER 404, PC. The most influential of the many articles on this topic are by Goodhart: see especially his (1960) 76 LQR 567. Other important articles are: Glanville Williams (1961) 77 LQR 467, and Payne (1962) 25 MLR 1.

15 Some of these facts can only be gleaned from the reports in the courts below, [1958] 1 Lloyd's Rep 575, [1959] 2 Lloyd's Rep 697. In subsequent proceedings arising out of the same discharge of oil the owners of other damaged ships recovered damages in negligence on the ground that the damage was foreseeable; *Overseas Tankship (UK) Ltd v The Miller Steamship Co Pty* [1967] 1 AC 617, [1966] 2 All ER 709, PC.

conflict. The discussion is now a sterile one and will not be entered upon here. Our concern is with the present state of English law; the discharge of that task is not assisted by such a discussion. Developments since *Wagon Mound* make it possible to a considerable extent to expound the law of remoteness with precision.

B. FORESEEABLE TYPE OF HARM

The Wagon Mound held that if the damage which materialises is damage by fire, then for the defendant to be liable he must have been able to anticipate damage by fire; that he could anticipate damage by fouling the wharf's slipways was not enough. An unbroken succession of subsequent cases at all levels, House of Lords,[16] Privy Council,[17] Court of Appeal[18] and first instance,[19] has accepted that the harm suffered must be of a kind, type or class foreseeable as a result of the defendant's negligence. So, the test of liability for shock is foreseeability of injury by shock.[20] If a person suffers personal harm through contact, then it must be shown that harm through contact was foreseeable.

Bradford v Robinson Rentals Ltd is a typical illustration of the working of these principles.[1]

The defendant employers carelessly exposed the plaintiff van driver to extreme cold in the course of his duties. In consequence he suffered frost-bite. The court held that the defendants exposed him to severe cold and fatigue likely to cause a common cold, pneumonia or chilblains, and that frost-bite was of the same type and kind as the harms foreseeable, so that the defendants were held liable.

Where a wife sustained foreseeable psychological damage the fact that some of it resulted from the effect of her husband's changed behaviour (he also was injured in the accident) did not prevent her from claiming—the damage was of a foreseeable type and 'the fact that it arises or is continued by reason of an unusual complex of events does not avail the defendant.'[2]

Suppose that I give a loaded gun to a ten-year-old child, which he drops on his foot. I am careless in handing him the gun, I owe him a duty of care, and an injured foot is the consequence, and yet I am not liable. The risk against which I had to guard was his shooting himself, but the harm which materialised was of a totally different kind: damage by impact of the gun is different from damage by the shooting of a bullet from it.

There are areas of uncertainty in defining 'kind' of damage, as *Tremain v Pike* illustrates:[3]

---

16 *Hughes v Lord Advocate*, [1963] AC 873, [1963] 1 All ER 705; *Donaghey v Boulton & Paul, Ltd* [1968] AC 1 at 26 (per LORD REID).

17 *The Wagon Mound (No 2)* [1967] 1 AC 617 at 636.

18 *Stewart v West African Terminals Ltd* [1964] 2 Lloyd's Rep 371 at 375 (per LORD DENNING MR).

19 *Wieland v Cyril Lord Carpets Ltd* [1969] 3 All ER 1006 at 1009 (per EVELEIGH J); *Tremain v Pike*, [1969] 3 All ER 1303 at 1308 (per PAYNE J).

20 *The Wagon Mound*, at 426.

1 [1967] 1 All ER 267.

2 *Malcolm v Broadhurst* [1970] 3 All ER 508 at 511 (per GEOFFREY LANE J). *Brice v Brown* [1984] 1 All ER 997 (foreseeability of shock therefore liable for plaintiff's acute mental illness—no need to foresee exact mental process leading to the ultimate result).

3 [1969] 3 All ER 1303.

The plaintiff herdsman, while working for the defendant farmers, contracted a rare disease, Weil's disease, through coming in contact with rats' urine. Weil's disease was not foreseeable, though other diseases arising from the presence of rats were foreseeable. The defendants were held not liable.

PAYNE J stated:[4]

> [Weil's disease] ... was entirely different in kind from the effect of a rat bite, or food poisoning by the consumption of food or drink contaminated by rats. I do not accept that all illness or infection arising from an infestation of rats should be regarded as of the same kind.

No doubt further difficulties in the classification of harms will arise in the course of applying this rule, but the principle that the damage sustained must be of the same kind as the foreseeable damage is now firmly established.

C. THE MEANS BY WHICH THE HARM WAS CAUSED

With increasing frequency since *The Wagon Mound* the courts say that the defendant may be liable even though he could not envisage that precise set of circumstances which produced harm of the foreseeable kind. The leading case is the decision of the House of Lords in *Hughes v Lord Advocate*:[5]

> H, aged 8, and another boy aged 10 were playing on an Edinburgh highway. Near the edge of the roadway was a manhole some nine feet deep, over which a shelter tent had been erected. Post Office workmen working on underground cables left the area after dark, placed red paraffin warning lamps there and took the ladder from the manhole and laid it on the ground. The boys came up and started meddling with this equipment and H, while swinging one of the lamps by a rope over the hole, stumbled over the lamp, and knocked it into the hole. An explosion followed. H was thrown into the manhole and severely burned. The explosion occurred because paraffin from the lamp escaped, vaporised and was ignited by the flame. This particular development of events was not foreseeable, but the defendant was held liable for the negligence of the workmen.

The defendant was liable because H was injured as a result of the type or kind of accident or occurrence that could reasonably have been foreseen, even though the workmen could not have foretold the exact way in which H would play with the alluring objects that had been left to attract him or the exact way in which in so doing he might get hurt. The workmen's conduct created a risk of the kind of harm, ie personal injuries by fire, which materialised.

If harm of a foreseeable kind occurs, it will normally be no defence that the precise mechanics of the way in which the negligent act results in the harm could not be foreseen.[6] Since it was foreseeable that a defendant's pack of terrier dogs would bowl over and scratch children he was liable when one of them bit the plaintiff child without bowling him over.[7] The fact that an

---

4 At 1308.
5 [1963] AC 837, [1963] 1 All ER 705.
6 *Wieland v Cyril Lord Carpets Ltd* [1969] 3 All ER 1006 at 1009 (per EVELEIGH J).
7 *Draper v Hodder* [1972] 2 QB 556, [1972] 2 All ER 210, CA.

explosion much greater in magnitude than was foreseeable resulted in damage to the plaintiff will be no defence.[8] The trend of the cases is towards the proposition that it is only when the accident is caused by the intrusion of some new and unforeseen factor that the way in which the damage was caused is relevant. LORD REID in *Hughes v Lord Advocate* discussed *Glasgow Corporation v Muir*.[9]

Two picnickers were allowed to carry a tea urn through a passage of the defendants' tea house. For a reason which was not explained, one of them slipped, and children buying sweets at a counter in the passage were scalded. An action by the children in negligence against the defendants failed.

LORD REID said of this case that a person carelessly carrying a hot tea urn near children would not be liable if it were upset and caused damage because the ceiling collapsed; the fall of the ceiling would be an extraneous cause. One case is difficult to reconcile with the principles set out in this sub-section, *Doughty v Turner Manufacturing Co Ltd*.[10]

The defendants placed an asbestos cement cover over a heat treatment bath containing sodium cyanide as a very hot molten liquid. The defendants' employees carelessly dislodged this cover so that it slid into the bath. The molten liquid exploded, erupted from the bath, and damaged the plaintiff workman nearby. Although it was foreseeable that damage by splashing would result from dislodging the cover it was not foreseeable that an explosion would ensue.

The defendants were held not liable, even though the kind of harm, damage by burning, was foreseeable. They would have been liable for damage by splashing; the risk of damage by explosion was not foreseeable and this risk which materialised differed from the one which was foreseeable so substantially that *Hughes v Lord Advocate* was distinguished. The distinction drawn between a burn caused by a splash and one caused by an explosion is a fine one. But if the trend to restrict the ambit of duty is considered together with the refusal of the House of Lords in *Hotson v East Berkshire Area Health Authority*[11] to take an unmovable approach to general causation, may such fine distinctions become the norm?[12]

D. MEASUREMENT OF DAMAGE

We consider now the circumstances where all that happens is foreseeable: the plaintiff has been as much physically incapacitated as might be expected; the goods have been predictably destroyed. It has always been unchallenged law

---

8 *Vacwell Engineering Co Ltd v BDH Chemicals Ltd* [1971] 1 QB 88, [1969] 3 All ER 1681; on appeal, [1971] 1 QB 111n, [1970] 3 All ER 553n.
9 [1943] AC 448, [1943] 2 All ER 44.
10 [1964] 1 QB 518, [1964] 1 All ER 98, CA.
11 [1987] 2 All ER 909, [1987] 3 WLR 232.
12 And see *Crossley v Rawlinson* [1981] 3 All ER 674. The defendant carelessly started a fire on his lorry on the highway. It was foreseeable that an AA patrol man 100 yards away would run down a path to help put out the fire. He slipped in a concealed hole on the path while running to the fire and was injured. The court held that no injury while running along the path was foreseeable and so no action lay. The case seems wrongly decided.

that the defendant cannot plead that the plaintiff was earning more than the average victim, that the goods were exceptionally valuable: damages are not restricted to the average loss of earnings or average value of goods in the circumstances, even supposing that such a sum was calculable. This rule unquestionably survives *The Wagon Mound*. The extent and limitations of this rule are brought out by *Liesbosch (Dredger) v Edison*.[13]

> The plaintiffs' dredger was sunk owing to the negligence of the defendants. Of course the plaintiffs recovered the market price of a comparable dredger and the cost of providing it at the port where the damage occurred. The plaintiffs further proved that the dredger was employed in connection with a harbour contract, that it was a condition of the contract that they had to find a very large sum of cash by way of guarantee and that 'the fact that the actual pecuniary loss sustained ... was more than double what it should have been was not due to the loss of the *Liesbosch* but to the ... terms of their contract with the Patras Harbour Authority, which compelled them to incur heavy expenses'.

There is no suggestion that these penalty clauses were in the ordinary course of things, still less that they were contemplated by the defendants; yet the House of Lords directed that the plaintiffs recover that very loss which they had sustained on *this* contract. The defendant's liability is not restricted to the foreseeable value of the property damaged; you take the plaintiff's economic facts as you find them. The court's caution about protecting economic loss in the tort of negligence, which we have previously noticed,[14] does not prevent the recovery of pecuniary loss which is entailed by physical harm. Equally clearly, the £10 a week labourer who is knocked down when about to fulfil a once-only lucrative television contract will recover his loss of fees. Since these are matters of binding House of Lords authority, it is pointless to compare them with the views of the Privy Council in *The Wagon Mound*. At the same time, the House ruled that any loss of profit which resulted solely from the plaintiff's lack of means was too remote—hence he could not recover the extra cost of hiring a substitute dredger incurred because he lacked capital to buy one.[15] This is to be regarded as a policy decision; the judges' reluctance to compensate for all economic loss has led them to draw the line at this point.[16]

---

13 (1933) 45 Lloyd's Rep 123; these points are not fully made in the briefer [1933] AC 449, cf *The Daressa* [1971] 1 Lloyd's Rep 60.

14 Ch 12, ante.

15 For development of the argument that this last ruling can only be reconciled with another House of Lords case, *Clippers Oil Co Ltd v Edinburgh and District Water Trustees* [1907] AC 291, by confining it to issues of remoteness and leaving untouched the rule in *Clippens* case that the defendant's plea that the plaintiff should have mitigated his loss will fail if the plaintiff shows that he lacked the financial means to mitigate, see Street *Damages* pp 39–41. The view expressed by the author in *Damages* has been accepted in a series of cases, the latest of which is *Perry v Sidney Phillips & Son* [1982] 3 All ER 705 at 711, CA.

16 For the same reason an injured wife cannot recover further damages because her husband, incapacitated in the same accident, and so not requiring a secretary, is no longer able to employ her as a part-time secretary: *Malcolm v Broadhurst* [1970] 3 All ER 508. Nor can injured children recover more because the hysterical obsession of their mother aggravates their symptoms: *McLaren v Bradstreet* (1969) 113 Sol Jo 471. *See also Schneider v Eisovitch* [1960] 2 QB 430, [1960] 1 All ER 169.

E. EXISTING PHYSICAL STATES

Before *The Wagon Mound*, it was established law that the victim could claim damages for the entire harm to his person, even though, owing to some special bodily sensitivity, it was greater than would have been suffered by the ordinary individual. Thus, the haemophiliac[17] or the extreme neurotic[18] who sustained greater damage than the ordinary person have recovered the full extent of their damage, even though the defendant could not have foreseen this extended harm. The courts have held that *The Wagon Mound* has not affected this principle. In *Smith v Leech Brain & Co Ltd*:[19]

> A negligently inflicted burn on P's lip resulted in his dying of cancer, for the tissues of the lip in which the cancer developed were in a pre-malignant condition at the time when the burn made the cancer develop. The defendants were held liable for the damage resulting from the death.

In *Robinson v Post Office*[20]

> The defendants carelessly lacerated plaintiff's leg; a doctor's subsequent anti-tetanus injection caused encephalitis because the plaintiff was allergic to the injected serum. The defendants were held liable.

No cases before or since *The Wagon Mound* decide whether the same principle applies to property damage. By analogy to the rules about measurement of economic loss laid down in *Liesbosch (Dredger) v Edison*, one would expect that the plaintiff can also recover for additional loss resulting from the unforeseen physical state of the property. The plaintiff's car is hit by the defendant's car: the damage to the bodywork is more extensive because of the existing rusty state. This loss should be recoverable.

Presumably, the defendant takes as he finds them not only the physical state of the damaged person or property, but also the surrounding external physical circumstances. This is the crux of *Great Lakes SS Co v Maple Leaf Milling Co*:[1]

> The defendants negligently failed to lighten the plaintiffs' ship at the time stipulated. When the water level fell the ship grounded and was damaged. This damage was more extensive because the ship settled on a large submerged anchor which the defendants neither knew nor could have expected to be there. The defendants were liable for all the damage to the ship.

The decision is correct: the damage was of a foreseeable type; it was of greater extent than foreseeable, not because of internal characteristics of the property, but because of special external circumstances. No doubt the same rule applies

---

17 *Bidwell v Briant* (1956) Times, 9 May.
18 *Love v Port of London Authority* [1959] 2 Lloyd's Rep 541; or exacerbation of pre-existing nervous disturbance: *Malcolm v Broadhurst* [1970] 3 All ER 508. *Brice v Brown* [1984] 1 All ER 997.
19 [1962] 2 QB 405, [1961] 3 All ER 1159.
20 [1974] 2 All ER 737, CA. In *Wieland v Cyril Lord Carpets Ltd* [1969] 3 All ER 1006, the negligently injured plaintiff later fell downstairs because her neck injuries prevented her from using her bifocal spectacles with her usual skill. Her eye defect was a pre-existing physical state, so that although a normal-sighted person might not have recovered for the damage inflicted by the fall, she was able to claim the additional loss. And see *Warren v Scruttons Ltd* [1962] 1 Lloyd's Rep 497.
 1 (1924) 41 TLR 21—on the generally held view that it matters not that the case was in contract, not tort.

to personal injuries: the defendant who negligently causes the plaintiff to stumble, so that he slides off the edge of a precipice concealed from view, will be liable for those consequences of the risk of stumbling, either before or after *The Wagon Mound*. Once the 'stage is set', the defendant's liability is adjudged accordingly.

F. ULTERIOR HARM

'Ulterior harm' is harm caused by a contingency which occurs after the event which the defendant failed to foresee and guard against, and which is causally independent of that event.[2] The defendant is not liable for all ulterior harm. In marking off the limits of his liability it will not ordinarily matter whether we use the language of risk or cause. The man run down by the defendant's negligence cannot recover for the extra damage sustained when a tile falls off a roof on to his head while he is on his way to hospital. This is because the defendant's conduct did not create a special risk of harm from that kind of contingency, or because the falling tile was a coincidence, ie the original negligent driving and the subsequent fall of the tile were independent acts; the conjunction of the two events was abnormal and not contrived by human agency. *Re Polemis* had no effect on these well-recognised rules, for, as LORD PORTER has pointed out in the House of Lords the case accepted that foreseeable consequences were recoverable, whether direct or otherwise.[3]

A few typical cases will illustrate how the courts handle the problem of intervening acts. In the well-known case of *Scott v Shepherd*[4] it was held to be no defence to the man who first threw the squib that the plaintiff would have suffered no loss had not a third party picked it up and thrown it again after the defendant had thrown it because the third party, in throwing it, was acting for his self-preservation. In short, where the act of the defendant has placed a third party or the plaintiff in a situation of 'alternative danger', if that person acts reasonably in the agony of the moment, his act will not make the ensuing damage too remote a consequence of the act of the defendant. The plaintiff's ship lost her compass and charts when the defendant's ship negligently collided with it; and consequently the plaintiff's ship ran aground while trying to make for port: the defendant was liable for this further harm.[5] Also, damage incurred in rescuing a person imperilled by the act of the defendant or by his own folly[6] is not too remote where the possibility of such rescue could have been anticipated;[7] further, a night watchman, injured while trying, in the course of his duty, to extinguish a fire in the premises of his employer, may recover.[8] Where the injuries negligently inflicted by the defendant on a plaintiff's husband induced a state of acute anxiety neurosis

---

2 The spark which followed the careless dropping of the plank in *Re Polemis* was thus not such a contingency.

3 *Morrison SS Co Ltd v Greystoke Castle (Cargo Owners)* [1947] AC 265 at 295, [1946] 2 All ER 696 at 709, HL.

4 (1773) 2 Wm Bl 892.

5 *The City of Lincoln* (1889) 15 PD 15.

6 *Ogwo v Taylor* [1987] 3 All ER 961, HL.

7 *Haynes v Harwood* [1935] 1 KB 146, [1934] All ER Rep 103, CA. The court did, of course, first decide that the careless defendant owed a duty of care to this would-be rescuer; *Baker v TE Hopkins & Sons Ltd* [1959] 3 All ER 225, CA.

8 *D'Urso v Sanson* [1939] 4 All ER 26.

which persisted for eighteen months and caused him to take his own life, the defendant was held liable to the plaintiff.[9] In each of these cases the ulterior harm was within the foreseeable risk; the subsequent events were not sufficiently abnormal responses to the situation created by the defendant's negligence; the kind of happening 'was on the cards', even though of course one could not say that, looked at when the defendant committed his act, this event was 'probable'. For the same reason, when the defendants negligently inflicted neck injuries on the plaintiff so that her neck had to be put in a collar, and she later fell downstairs because she could not use her bifocal spectacles with her usual skill, she recovered for that further injury.[10]

If, however, the plaintiff's subsequent act is unreasonable, then he cannot recover for his additional injuries.[11] Unreasonable conduct on the part of the plaintiff acts as a *novus actus interveniens* breaking the chain of causation. Even if readily foreseeable the courts as a matter of policy will not impose liability on one man for the calculated imprudence of another. But defining unreasonable conduct will not always be easy. In *Emeh v Kensington, Chelsea & Westminster Area Health Authority*[12] the plaintiff conceived again after an operation to sterilise her carried out by the defendant. The defendant admitted negligence but denied liability for the cost of the upkeep of the child. That loss to the plaintiff he contended resulted from her 'unreasonable' decision not to seek an abortion, and the judge at first instance agreed with him. The Court of Appeal held that as by the time the plaintiff realised she was pregnant she was well into the second trimester of pregnancy, it was not unreasonable for her to refuse the trauma and risk of late abortion. SLADE LJ[13] made it clear that save in exceptional circumstances he would never regard it as unreasonable to refuse abortion even earlier in pregnancy when the procedure in pregnancy is relatively simple and free of risk. WALLER LJ[14] is less clear on this point. Do you think it can be held to be 'unreasonable' to refuse an operation (however simple) which is not necessary for your health and to which many people still have moral objections?[15]

These principles are flexible and their application is sometimes difficult. It is, for instance, uncertain when, if at all, the plaintiff can recover for prolongation of his incapacity resulting from careless medical treatment of his initial injuries. It must be frankly admitted that considerations of policy will affect judicial thinking in such cases. This conclusion is the more acceptable when it is understood that in marginal cases the courts have felt free to hold the defendant liable by the risk approach where the ultimate harm was causally irrelevant. For example, a decorator who carelessly left unlocked the house in which he had been working while he went to fetch more wallpaper was liable to the owner in contract for thefts from the house perpetrated by

---

9 *Pigney v Pointer's Transport Services Ltd* [1957] 2 All ER 807; see also *Cavanagh v London Transport Executive* (1956) Times, 23 October.
10 *Wieland v Cyril Lord Carpets Ltd* [1969] 3 All ER 1006.
11 *McKew v Holland & Hannen & Cubitts (Scotland) Ltd* [1969] 3 All ER 1621, HL; (plaintiff with injured leg subsequently fractured his ankle in trying to descend unassisted a steep staircase without handrail—defendant not liable for plaintiff's broken ankle).
12 [1985] QB 1012, [1984] 3 All ER 1044.
13 1044 at 1053.
14 1044 at 1048.
15 On the related issue of the duty to minimise damages by accepting medical treatment see *Selvanayagam v University of the West Indies* [1983] 1 All ER 824, [1983] 1 WLR 585, PC (discussed post at p 468).

a thief while the defendant had left the house empty and unlocked.[16] The courts can more easily take policy considerations into account when they are free, as in that case, to hold the defendant liable within the doctrine of risk although the defendant could not be said to have caused a loss such as this, which resulted from the deliberate, subsequent and independent conduct of a third party. Take the case of the pedestrian who is knocked down in the dark by the defendant's car—application of either risk or causative principles will result in holding the defendant answerable for the further harm inflicted by another motorist who runs over him while lying in the roadway,[17] but only application of the doctrine of risk could make the defendant answerable for the pickpocket who steals the pedestrian's wallet as he lies unconscious.

The central issue then becomes whether the defendant's negligence was responsible in law for the materialisation of their particular risk. Before addressing the question of remoteness two prior matters must be resolved. Did the defendant owe any duty to the plaintiff to safeguard his person or property?[18] If he did, was he negligent? Were there any practicable measures which he could have taken which would have avoided or minimised the risk of the ulterior harm?[19] Only if duty and breach are proved do problems of remoteness arise.

In *Lamb v Camden Borough Council:*[20]

> In 1973 the defendants carelessly broke a water main outside the plaintiff's Hampstead house. The escaping water undermined the foundations and the house subsided so that until repaired it was uninhabitable. Squatters moved into the unoccupied house, and by the time they were evicted had done damage totalling £30,000. The only issue was whether that damage was too remote.

Lord Denning held that it was a question of policy whether the damage was too remote. Considering that the plaintiff could readily have insured against the risk and could have taken more steps to guard against squatting, and that the defendants had no right to enter the premises, policy dictated that the damage be held too remote even though it was foreseeable.[1] OLIVIER LJ wrestled with the contention that the ratio of Lord Reid's judgment in *Home Office v Dorset Yacht Co Ltd*[2] was that the subsequent act was too remote unless that act was likely to happen. He found Lord Reid's statement to be *obiter* and that the subsequent act was neither likely nor reasonably foreseeable. He added that he did not dissent from the view of Lord Denning that on grounds of policy foreseeable acts could still be too remote.[3] WATKINS LJ held that words such as 'possibility' or 'unlikely' did not assist him. Even though the act was reasonably foreseeable it was too remote. He reached this conclusion by making 'a robust and sensible approach'. His conclusion was:[4]

---

16 *Stansbie v Troman* [1948] 2 KB 48, [1948] 1 All ER 599.
17 But see *Knightley v Johns* [1982] 1 All ER 851, [1982] 1 WLR 349 discussed post at p 235.
18 *Maloco v Littlewoods Organisation Ltd* [1987] AC 241, [1987] 1 All ER 710, HL; *Hill v Chief Constable of West Yorkshire* [1987] 1 All ER 1173 CA discussed ante at pp 171–172.
19 *King v Liverpool City Council* [1986] 3 All ER 544, [1986] 1 WLR 890, CA.
20 [1981] QB 625, [1981] 2 All ER 408, CA.
 1 At 637 and 414 respectively.
 2 [1970] AC 1004 at 1030, [1970] 2 All ER 294 at 300, HL.
 3 At 644 and 419 respectively.
 4 At 647 and 421 respectively.

I have the instinctive feeling that squatters' damage is too remote. I could not possibly come to any other conclusions, although on the primary facts I, too, would regard the damage or something like it as reasonably foreseeable in these times.

These judgments eloquently demonstrate the flexibility and inherent uncertainty surrounding the issue of whether a particular subsequent act is to be adjudged too remote a consequence of the defendant's negligence.[5]

SECTION 4. CONCURRENT CAUSES

Various types of act which may be described as 'concurrent' must be looked at separately. If two tortious acts result in damage, and either one would have produced the same damage, as when merging fires burn out a building, then the perpetrator of each act is responsible for the whole damage, because each act is a substantial factor in producing the result. Similarly, if two independent acts simultaneously bring about the same damage, as where two ships negligently collide, injuring a third party,[6] those responsible for the respective negligent acts are each fully liable.

If the defendant commits a tort (or an act which will become a tort if non-remote damage ensues) and, before his act spends its force, some later tortious act combines with it to produce a particular result which would not have been produced without the operation of the second act, then the defendant will be liable if, and only if, it is found, by applying the rules already stated, that his act caused the damage.[7] In *Hale v Hants & Dorset Motor Services Ltd and another*, the facts were:[8]

P Corporation negligently allowed tree branches to overhang a highway; H was a passenger in an omnibus negligently driven by a servant of the defendant omnibus company in such a way that a branch struck the window of the bus with the result that he was blinded by broken glass.

It was held that the Corporation and the omnibus company were each liable

5 And see *Knightley v Johns* [1982] 1 All ER 851, CA, where the defendant negligently overturned his car in a road tunnel and the plaintiff, a police cyclist, riding the wrong way in the tunnel was then injured in a collision with another car, a police inspector having carelessly failed first to order the closure of the tunnel. The plaintiff's injuries were held to be too remote because they were not reasonably foreseeable.

6 *The Koursk* [1924] P 140. Should the first defendant remain liable if the other 'cause' is the non-tortious act of another person, or a natural cause, or the act of the plaintiff himself? Cf *Cummings (or McWilliams) v Sir William Arrol & Co Ltd* [1962] 1 All ER 623. And see p 374, post.

7 *Rouse v Squires*, [1973] QB 889, [1973] 2 All ER 903, CA, at 898 (per CAIRNS LJ). 'If a driver so negligently manages his vehicle as to cause it to obstruct the highway and constitute a danger to other road users, including those who are driving too fast or not keeping a proper lookout, but not those who deliberately or recklessly drive into the obstruction, then the first driver's negligence may be held to have contributed to the causation of an accident of which the immediate cause was the negligent driving of the vehicle which because of the presence of the obstruction collides with it or with some other vehicle or some other person.'

8 [1947] 2 All ER 628, CA; *Robinson v Post Office*, [1974] 2 All ER 737, p 231, ante.

in full to H:[9] each was negligent in not foreseeing that this harm was likely to result in combination with the negligence of the other.

In *Fitzgerald v Lane*[10] the plaintiff was crossing a pelican crossing when he was hit by a car driven by D.1. The collision threw him up on the bonnet of the car and back onto the road where he was struck by a car driven by D.2. He suffered severe injuries including damage to his neck resulting in partial tetraplegia. Whether it was contact with the car driven by D.1 or D.2 which caused the injury to the neck could not be established. The Court of Appeal held that as the carelessness of D.1 and D.2 materially contributed to the risk of such an injury[11] both were jointly liable. Damages were reduced against each defendant in crossing when the lights were green in the traffic's favour.

SECTION 5.   CONSECUTIVE CAUSES

In *Baker v Willoughby*[12] the defendants admitted negligently injuring the plaintiff in the leg. Before the action came to trial burglars shot the plaintiff in that same leg and it had to be amputated. The House of Lords held that the defendants remained liable for the loss of amenity occasioned by the injury inflicted by them. The fortuitous event of the second tort did not relieve them of liability. But in *Jobling v Associated Dairies Ltd*[13] the plaintiff was partially incapacitated by an accident at work. Later but before the trial he became incapacitated by a supervening illness. The House of Lords distinguishing *Baker v Willoughby*, on flimsy grounds, held that the defendants were only responsible for the plaintiff's loss of earnings up until the time he succumbed to illness. Justification for this distinction between a second tort and supervening illness rests on the flimsy ground that the second tortfeasor would have been liable only for the additional damage inflicted by him and not the whole of the plaintiff's incapacity. It must never be forgotten that the object of damages in tort is to put the plaintiff as far as possible in the position which he would have been 'but for' the tort. Plaintiffs are not supposed to profit. Hence the principle of common law that a widow's damages for loss of her husband would be calculated taking into account her

---

9 In *Robinson v Post Office* [1974] 2 All ER 737, CA, a doctor negligently carried out the test dose procedure when injecting the plaintiff after the defendant had negligently injured him; because the plaintiff would have suffered the same harm had the doctor not been negligent, the defendant was wholly and solely liable for the plaintiff's harm. Cf *Burrows v March Gas and Coke Co* (1872) LR 7 Exch Ch; *Ingram v United Automobile Services Ltd* [1943] KB 612, [1943] 2 All ER 71, CA; *Grant v Sun Shipping Co Ltd* [1948] AC 549, [1948] 2 All ER 238, HL; *Hartley v Mayoh & Co* [1954] 1 QB 383, [1954] 1 All ER 375, CA, is another example; the electricity authority had negligently crossed wires in a factory so that the 'main' switch did not in fact control all the current. The plaintiff fireman was electrocuted while fighting a fire after the 'main' switch had been turned off. *Held* that the factory owners, as well as the electricity authority, were liable because they ought to have known which was the main switch, and, if that had been switched off, the accident would not have happened. See *Carlsholm (Owners) v Calliope (Owners), The Calliope*, [1970] P 172, [1970] 1 All ER 624, on the problem of the consequential damage being caused jointly by the negligence of the plaintiff and the continuing negligence of the defendant.
10 [1987] QB 781, [1987] 2 All ER 455.
11 Applying *Wilsher v Essex Area Heath Authority* [1987] QB 730, [1986] 3 All ER 801, CA discussed ante at p 225.
12 [1970] AC 467, [1969] 3 All ER 1528.
13 [1982] AC 794, [1981] 2 All ER 752.

prospects of re-marriage![14] The plaintiff in *Jobling* would eventually have been unable to work even if the tort had never happened. Disease is a vicissitude of life. The House of Lords on policy grounds refused to make the defendants responsible for that vicissitude.

In conclusion, it must be stressed again that causation and remoteness appertain to all torts. The analysis of the concept of cause is common to all, and so are the rules about measuring items of damage and the 'take the plaintiff as you find him' rule and the principles of multiple causation.[15] We consider in turn the application of risk in the context of particular torts, but we may anticipate the general conclusion—that most torts require that the harm must be of that kind which the judges had in mind when they fashioned the tort. The role played by policy and judicial instincts as to fairness must never be overlooked when considering any problem of causation.

14 No longer, thanks to Parliament. See post at p 495.
15 See eg p 527, post.

Chapter 15

Defences to negligence

SECTION 1. CONTRIBUTORY NEGLIGENCE

At common law it was a complete defence if the defendant proved that the plaintiff was guilty of contributory negligence. The Law Reform (Contributory Negligence) Act 1945 now provides that contributory negligence no longer affords a complete defence, but merely reduces the damages to the extent to which the plaintiff has been contributorily negligent. In the old leading case of *Butterfield v Forrester* the facts were[1]:

The defendant partially obstructed the highway by putting a pole across part of it. The plaintiff, riding violently at dusk, did not observe the pole and ran into it, and suffered injuries, but would have seen it had he been using ordinary care.

Holding that the plaintiff failed despite the wrongful act of obstruction by the defendant, LORD ELLENBOROUGH said:[2]

'One person being in fault will not dispense with another's using ordinary care for himself. Two things must concur to support this action, an obstruction in the road by the fault of the defendant, and no want of ordinary care to avoid it on the part of the plaintiff.'

In order to establish contributory negligence the defendant must plead[3] and prove:

A. That the injury of which the plaintiff complains results from that particular risk to which the negligence of the plaintiff exposed him.
B. That the negligence of the plaintiff contributed to his injury.
C. That there was fault or negligence on the part of the plaintiff.

We then have to consider

D. The scope of the Law Reform (Contributory Negligence) Act 1945.
E. Apportionment of damages between the plaintiff and defendant.

A. RISK

This is a requirement which may be compared with the rule that the plaintiff, in an action based on negligence, must prove that the risk which in fact materialises is the one which the defendant was under a duty to guard against.[4] Here the defendant must show that the harm sustained by the plaintiff belongs

---

1 (1809) 11 East 60.
2 Ibid at 61.
3 *Fookes v Slaytor* [1979] 1 All ER 137, CA.
4 See p 277, post.

to that general class of perils to which the plaintiff was exposed by his own negligent conduct. The important and difficult case of *Jones v Livox Quarries Ltd* illustrates this:[5]

> The plaintiff was riding down a slope leading to the bottom of a quarry on the back of the defendants' vehicle, contrary to their orders, when another vehicle of the defendants was negligently driven into the back of the first vehicle. As a result, the plaintiff was injured. By so riding, the plaintiff exposed himself not only to the risk of falling off the vehicle but also of being injured in the way in which he was injured, and therefore the court found that he was contributorily negligent.

It is plain from the judgments delivered that, if the damage sustained by the plaintiff had been foreign to the risk to which his negligent conduct subjected him, the defence would have failed.[6]

B.   THAT THE NEGLIGENCE WAS CONTRIBUTORY

This is undoubtedly the aspect of the defence of contributory negligence which calls for the most careful examination. The key to the proper understanding of the development of the case law on this subject is the full appreciation of the seriousness of the rule of common law which deprived the plaintiff of a remedy, if he himself were guilty of any fault, however slight, contributing to the damage which he suffered.

The essence of the matter is causation. As LORD ATKIN has said:[7]

> ... if the plaintiff were negligent but his negligence was not a cause operating to produce the damage there would be no defence. I find it impossible to divorce any theory of contributory negligence from the concept of causation.

Not unnaturally, the courts sought to mitigate the harshness of this doctrine of contributory negligence.[8] In doing so they evolved various tests to cover different sets of circumstances. The best-known test was the so-called 'last-opportunity rule'. *Davies v Mann*[9] is the leading case:

> The plaintiff negligently left his ass, fettered by its forefeet, in a highway. The defendant drove his waggon and horses at a smartish pace against it and killed it. Had he used proper care, the defendant could have avoided injuring the ass, but he was driving too fast. It is uncertain when he saw the ass, if he saw it at all.

It was held that, notwithstanding his own negligence, the plaintiff could recover because the defendant could still have avoided the consequences of

---

5 [1952] 2 QB 608, CA.
6 SINGLETON LJ at 612, thought that there would be no defence where a plaintiff negligently sat upon an unsafe wall, and a driver negligently ran into the wall and injured the plaintiff, and DENNING LJ at 616, thought that the plaintiff would succeed, if, while riding on the vehicle as he was in the case, he had been hit in the eye by a shot from a gun fired by a negligent sportsman.
7 *Caswell v Powell Duffryn Associated Collieries Ltd* [1940] AC 152 at 165, [1939] 3 All ER 722 HL.
8 LORD PORTER in *Stapley v Gypsum Mines Ltd* [1953] AC 663 at 677, [1953] 2 All ER 478 HL.
9 (1842) 10 M & W 546.

that negligence.[10] Subsequently, attempts were made to establish as rules of law further classifications of facts based on the time of the several acts and the knowledge of the parties.[11]

The Maritime Conventions Act 1911 authorised the court, in the case of collisions at sea, to apportion the loss according to the degree to which each party was at fault, and this principle was made generally applicable by the Law Reform (Contributory Negligence) Act 1945.[12]

With the passing of these Acts, the practical need for the courts to select some particular cause as the predominant one has disappeared. These Acts do not alter the law of causation upon which contributory negligence depends: since a plaintiff whose acts contributed to his damage is now no longer altogether defeated, but merely has his damages proportionately reduced to the extent to which he was at fault, the courts are free to look for all the causes and apportion accordingly. As LORD PORTER has put it:[13]

> It [the 1945 Act] enables the court (be it judge or jury) to seek less strenuously to find some ground for holding the plaintiff free from blame, or for reaching the conclusion that his negligence played no part in the ensuing accident, inasmuch as, owing to the change in the law, the blame can now be apportioned equitably between the two parties.

Plainly, the courts are no longer concerned with the subtleties and refinements of last opportunity and the like. The purpose here is to state the existing law as the courts apply it. Much of the old learning can therefore now be discarded.

In order to decide whether the plaintiff's negligent conduct, within the risk, is contributory, one applies exactly those rules of causation previously set out.[14] The earliest important case, and, moreover, one on which the courts still rely, was *Admiralty Commissioners v SS Volute*.[15] It was actually decided under the Maritime Conventions Act, and the facts were:

> *The Volute,* a convoy leader, changed her course without signalling. The *Radstock,* on discovering that she was being thereby endangered, negligently put on full steam ahead. Although this negligence was subsequent to that of *The Volute,* both vessels were held to blame for their ensuing collision, and apportionment under the Act was directed.

In a judgment warmly supported by the other law lords, VISCOUNT BIRKENHEAD pointed out that, despite the fact that cases of 'strictly synchronous negligence' were rare, the courts could, nevertheless, still find that the negligence of both parties contributed to the resulting injury even though their acts were not 'synchronous'. He added:[16]

> Upon the whole I think that the question of contributory negligence must be dealt with somewhat broadly and upon common-sense principles as a jury would probably deal with it. And while, no doubt, where a clear line can be drawn, the

---

10 Perhaps the most important of the cases following it is *Radley v London and North Western Ry Co* (1876) 1 App Cas 754 HL.
11 Especially *British Columbia Electric Ry Co Ltd v Loach* [1916] 1 AC 719 PC; *The Eurymedon* [1938] P 41 at 49–50, [1938] 1 All ER 122, CA (per GREER LJ).
12 Section 1 of each Act.
13 *Stapley v Gypsum Mines Ltd* [1953] AC 663 at 677, [1953] 2 All ER 478 HL.
14 See ch 8 ante.
15 [1922] 1 AC 129 HL.
16 [1922] 1 AC 129 at 144.

subsequent negligence is the only one to look at, there are cases in which the two acts come so closely together, and the second act of negligence is so much mixed up with the state of things brought about by the first act, that the party secondly negligent, while not held free from blame under the *Bywell Castle* rule, might, on the other hand, invoke the prior negligence as being part of the cause of the collision so as to make it a case of contribution. And the Maritime Conventions Act with its provisions for nice qualifications as to the quantum of blame and the proportions in which contribution is to be made may be taken as to some extent declaratory of the Admiralty rule in this respect ...

The test, he pointed out, is whether the plaintiff 'in the ordinary plain common sense of this business ... contributed to the accident'. This does not, of course, mean that, whenever the negligence of the defendant is preceded by negligence on the part of the plaintiff, there is always contributory negligence; the acts may be so severable that only that of the defendant can be said to have contributed to the damage, but there is no need to retain a separate rule of law called 'last opportunity' in order to reach this conclusion. EVERSHED LJ explained this clearly in *Davies v Swan Motor Co (Swansea) Ltd*:[17]

> As I understand the *Davies v Mann* principle ... it is this: in that case the plaintiff's negligence or fault consisted in placing the donkey upon the highway; but it having been observed in due time by the defendant ... the negligence of the plaintiff had really ceased to be an operating factor in the collision ... the plaintiff ... as a negligent actor, was at the material time, *functus officio,* one might say *functus culpa.*[18]

The difficulties encountered in determining whether the plaintiff's negligence is contributory are usually not of law but of fact: there is room for difference of opinion on whether, in any particular case, the negligence of the plaintiff has ceased to be an operating factor. But only if this inference is made does the plaintiff's conduct cease to be contributory negligence.

The House of Lords has, since *The Volute,* frequently stressed this test of causation in contributory negligence. Thus, in *Swadling v Cooper*[19] (where the Court of Appeal had attempted to frame elaborate classifications),[20] the House of Lords reversed the decision and upheld the direction of the trial judge to the jury, which in substance was: 'Whose negligence was it that substantially caused the injury?'[1] The Judicial Committee, too, has followed *The Volute* and issued a forceful warning against the dangers of 'attempts to classify acts in relation to one another with reference to time or with regard to the knowledge of one party at a particular moment of the negligence of the other party'.[2]

These principles may be clarified by an examination of some of the more important cases decided since the passing of the Act of 1945. In *Henley v Cameron*:[3]

17 [1949] 2 KB 291 at 317, [1949] 1 All ER 620, CA.
18 Cf VISCOUNT SIMON in *Boy Andrew (Owners) v St Rognvald (Owners)* [1948] AC 140 at 149 HL: 'The negligence of the donkey-owner was therefore a fault not contributing to the collision: it was merely a *causa sine qua non.*'
19 [1931] AC 1, [1930] All ER Rep 257 HL (collision at cross roads between defendant's motor car and the motor cycle of the plaintiff's husband, who was killed).
20 [1930] 1 KB 403.
 1 See all the judgments in *Stapley v Gypsum Mines Ltd* [1953] AC 663, [1953] 2 All ER 478, but especially that of LORD REID.
 2 *Marvin Sigurdson v British Columbia Electric Ry Co Ltd* [1953] AC 291 at 299, PC.
 3 [1949] LJR 989, CA; cf *Harvey v Road Haulage Executive* [1952] 1 KB 120, CA; *Rouse v Squires* [1973] QB 889, [1973] 2 All ER 903, CA.

The defendant chose to leave his car unlighted on the highway at night, and the husband of the plaintiff, riding a motor cycle, carelessly collided with it and was killed. An apportionment under the 1945 Act was made.

Applying the rule laid down in *The Volute,* TUCKER LJ pointed out that 'it must always remain a question of fact whether the negligence of B is "so mixed up" with the state of things brought about by A's negligence as to make the negligence of both contributory causes to the accident',[4] and he pointed out the illogicality of asserting that the rules of contributory negligence differ from those of remoteness, saying:[5]

> I cannot understand how, when considering whether the negligence of A or B or of both has been the effective cause of an accident, the answer can depend on whether A or B happens to be the plaintiff in the action or whether they are both defendants.

In *Boy Andrew (Owners) v St Rognvald (Owners),*[6] as one vessel negligently overtook another, the latter negligently changed course, collided with the first vessel, and sank. The House of Lords followed *The Volute* and found both parties blameworthy. VISCOUNT SIMON said:[7]

> The suggested test of 'last opportunity' seems to me inaptly phrased and likely in some cases to lead to error, as the Law Revision Committee said in their report (Cmd 6032 of 1939, p 16):
> > 'In truth, there is no such rule—the question, as in all questions of liability for a tortious act, is, not who had the last opportunity of avoiding the mischief, but whose act caused the wrong?'

In *Davies v Swan Motor Co (Swansea) Ltd* the facts were:[8]

> Contrary to orders, the plaintiff was standing on steps at the off-side of a dust lorry. The driver of the lorry turned to the right without warning just as a following vehicle was overtaking him, and the plaintiff was injured in the ensuing collision. Both drivers were negligent, but it was also held that the plaintiff was contributorily negligent.

EVERSHED LJ, after considering separately the *Davies v Mann* type of case (where the negligence of the defendant alone, in his opinion, caused the accident), said of the 'last opportunity' rule:[9]

> Now that as a doctrine I venture to think has suffered a demise independently altogether of the Act of 1945 ... No doubt, in practice, such a rule was found useful by judges who were anxious in the interests of justice to avoid coming to a conclusion wholly adverse to a plaintiff merely because, at the material time, the plaintiff was still a negligent actor to some perhaps quite trivial extent. Now the Law Reform (Contributory Negligence) Act 1945, has rendered it no longer necessary to resort to devices of that kind.

DENNING LJ stressed that the matter is purely one of causation. Of the *Davies v Mann* type of case where the plaintiff negligently leaves an obstruction in

---

4 [1949] LJR 989 at 992–3.
5 [1949] LJR 989 at 993.
6 [1948] AC 140 HL.
7 Ibid at 149.
8 [1949] 2 KB 291, [1949] 1 All ER 620, CA.
9 Ibid at 318. In *The Road to Justice* p 111, DENNING LJ said: 'The doctrine of "last opportunity" or "last clear chance" has also gone. No one ever mentions it in the English courts'.

the highway and the defendant negligently runs into it, he said that the fact that the defendant sees the obstruction 'may mean in some cases that the obstruction is not the cause of the accident': in short, one does not apply a mechanical rule of 'last opportunity', but one asks whether 'his conduct would be so powerful a factor in producing the damage that the presence of the parked vehicle would not be itself a cause of the damage'.[10] Similarly, in *Jones v Livox Quarries Ltd*[11] DENNING LJ said:

> There is no clear guidance to be found in the books about causation. All that can be said is that causes are different from the circumstances in which, or on which, they operate. The line between the two depends on the facts of each case. It is a matter of common sense more than anything else ... The man's negligence here was so much mixed up with his injury that it cannot be dismissed as mere history. His dangerous position on the vehicle was one of the causes of his damage ...

C. THE NEGLIGENCE OF THE PLAINTIFF

Here is an important difference between the defence of contributory negligence and the tort of negligence. To set up this defence, the defendant need not prove that the plaintiff owed him a duty of care: for, as was said in *Nance v British Columbia Electric Ry Co Ltd*:[12]

> ... all that is necessary to establish such a defence is to prove to the satisfaction of the jury that the injured party did not in his own interest take reasonable care of himself and contributed, by this want of care, to his own injury.

It may perhaps be assumed that decisions on the standard of reasonable care required of the defendant in negligence apply to determine whether the plaintiff has taken reasonable care for his own safety.[13] Many of the problems relating to the standard of reasonableness discussed with reference to the standard of care in the tort of negligence arise here—especially the standard required of children (where, it will be recalled, the age of the child is considered material)[14] and the rule that 'a prudent man will guard against the possible negligence of others when experience shows such negligence to be common'.[15] The warning given when discussing breach of duty in negligence must be repeated in the present connection—decisions on facts must not lightly be regarded as establishing legal principles.[16] The Court of Appeal is as free to infer contributory negligence and thereby reverse the trial judge as it is to infer negligence.[17] A moped driver who does not wear a crash helmet is

---

10 [1949] 2 KB 291 at 323.
11 [1952] 2 QB 608 at 616, CA; see p 239, ante for the facts.
12 [1951] AC 601 at 611 PC (per VISCOUNT SIMON), [1951] 2 All ER 448; cf *Jones v Livox Quarries Ltd* [1952] 2 QB 608 at 615, CA (per DENNING LJ).
13 Whereas a workman suing for breach of statutory duty is not necessarily 'contributorily negligent' because his conduct would have been sufficiently careless to make his employer vicariously liable the standard of care required of a workman who sues in negligence is apparently the same as that required of him as a defendant in negligence; *Staveley Iron and Chemical Co Ltd v Jones* [1956] AC 627, [1956] 1 All ER 403 HL.
14 See p 202, ante and *Gough v Thorne* [1966] 3 All ER 398, CA. Where a workman's contributory negligence lay in not complying with instructions, the court refused, with respect to this issue of contributory negligence, to take account of his known low intelligence but agreed that it was relevant in measuring the standard of care required of the defendant employer: *Baxter v Woolcombers* (1963) 107 Sol Jo 553.
15 Per LORD DU PARCQ in *Grant v Sun Shipping Co* [1948] AC 549 at 567, [1948] 2 All ER 238 HL.
16 *SS Heranger (Owners) v SS Diamond (Owners)* [1939] AC 94 at 101 HL.
17 *Hicks v British Transport Commission* [1958] 2 All ER 39, CA.

contributorily negligent;[18] and so is a car passenger who does not wear a seat belt,[19] or who knows that the car's footbrake does not work.[20] A passenger injured by negligent drunken driving is contributorily negligent if either he travelled knowing that his driver was so drunk that his capacity to drive carefully was impaired, or, if, knowing that he was later going to be a passenger, he accompanied the driver on a drinking bout, which affected both the driver's capacity to drive safely and his own capacity to appreciate the danger.[1] And a pedestrian who crossed a pelican crossing with the lights at green for the traffic was held contributorily negligent.[2] On the other hand, a house buyer who relies on the valuation of his building society's surveyor is not contributorily negligent in not having his house independently surveyed.[3]

If the negligence of the defendant puts the plaintiff in a position of imminent personal danger, conduct by the plaintiff which in fact operates to produce harm to him, but which is nevertheless reasonable in the agony of the moment, does not amount to contributory negligence. *Jones v Boyce* is the best known case:[4]

> The plaintiff, a passenger in a coach, reasonably believed that the coach was about to overturn through the negligent driving of the defendant, the coach proprietor, and jumped off, breaking his leg. The coach did not overturn, but he was adjudged not contributorily negligent and recovered from the defendant.

The question is merely whether the plaintiff behaved reasonably in the dilemma in which the defendant had placed him, due account being taken of the alarm which such a situation would engender in the plaintiff.[5]

The rule has been extended in *Brandon v Osborne, Garrett & Co*:[6]

> The plaintiff and her husband were in the defendants' shop as customers. Owing to the negligence of the defendants, broken glass falling from the roof imperilled the husband of the plaintiff, who instinctively clutched her husband to try to bring him to a place of safety and was herself injured. Had she remained in her original position she would not have been injured. Her injury was held not to be the result of her own contributory negligence.

These cases mark the limits to which the courts have taken the doctrine; whether it extends to instinctive acts to protect strangers, or to protect interests other than personal safety, is undecided.

Where the plaintiff is exercising some right such as passage along a highway, or obtaining access to it, or some common approach to his premises which the landlord has retained, for him deliberately to encounter a risk of danger created by the defendant is not contributory negligence. It is only contributory

18 *O'Connell v Jackson* [1972] 1 QB 270, [1971] 3 All ER 129, CA.
19 *Froom v Butcher* [1976] QB 286, [1975] 3 All ER 520. Although in *McKay v Borthwick* 1982 SLT 265 (Scotland) it was held that a woman with a hiatus hernia who did not wear a seatbelt on a short journey was not contributorily negligent. Failure to wear a seatbelt is now a criminal offence. Motor Vehicles (Wearing of Seat Belts) Regs 1982 (SI 1982 No 1203).
20 *Gregory v Kelly* [1978] RTR 426.
 1 *Owens v Brimmell* [1977] QB 859, [1976] 3 All ER 765.
 2 *Fitzgerald v Lane* [1987] QB 781, [1987] 2 All ER 455; cf *Tremayne v Hill* [1987] RTR 131, CA.
 3 *Yianni v Edwin Evans & Sons* [1982] QB 438, [1981] 3 All ER 592.
 4 (1816) 1 Stark 493.
 5 For accidents at sea, the rule is known as the rule in *The Bywell Castle* (1879) 4 PD 219.
 6 [1924] 1 KB 548.

negligence if, after making due allowance for his right to be there, the plaintiff is showing an unreasonable neglect of his own safety.[7]

Just as the defendant may be answerable for the negligence of his servant, so also does the contributory negligence of a servant of the plaintiff afford the defendant a good defence where the servant is acting in the course of his employment. On the other hand, the contributory negligence of an independent contractor is not imputed to the principal, and that of a driver is not imputed to a passenger,[8] nor is that of a spouse imputed to the wife or husband.[9] When a child is accompanied by an adult the contributory negligence of the adult is not imputed to the child.[10] Thus, in *Oliver v Birmingham and Midland Motor Omnibus Co Ltd*:[11]

> The plaintiff, an infant in the care of his grandfather, was crossing a road when he was injured in consequence of the negligent driving of the defendant's omnibus by their servant. Although his grandfather was also negligent, the infant was held entitled to recover in full.

D. THE SCOPE OF THE LAW REFORM (CONTRIBUTORY NEGLIGENCE) ACT 1945[12]

The primary object of the 1945 Act is to provide that, where the defence of contributory negligence was previously available, the courts may now, instead of exonerating the defendant from liability, reduce the damages awarded

---

7 *Clayards v Dethick and Davis* (1848) 12 QB 439 (the plaintiff, a cabman, was prevented from taking his horse out of a mews by the only access to the highway because the defendants had dug and negligently fenced a trench at the junction of the mews and highway. In trying to get his horse out, he caused injury to the horse. His action for damages succeeded despite the defendants' plea of contributory negligence); *Behrens v Bertram Mills Circus Ltd* [1957] 2 QB 1, [1957] 1 All ER 583.

8 *Mills v Armstrong, The Bernina* (1888) 13 App Cas 1, HL, where the same principle was held to apply in the case of ships.

9 *Mallett v Dunn* [1949] 2 KB 180, [1949] 1 All ER 973; *Berrill v Road Haulage Executive* [1952] 2 Lloyds Rep 490 (wife driving husband's car not as his servant or agent; her contributory negligence did not prevent husband recovering in full for damage to car). The case last cited, and *France v Parkinson* [1954] 1 All ER 739, CA, also decide that the contributory negligence of a bailee is not to be imputed to a bailor. *Lampert v Eastern National Omnibus Co Ltd* [1954] 2 All ER 719n, decided that where a wife-owner-passenger is injured in a collision between her car driven by her husband and another, in which the two drivers are equally to blame, the wife's damages are to be reduced by one half. Although the wife would be liable to the other driver for her husband's negligence (see p 527 post) why should her liability to third parties be equated with failure to take care for her own safety? Cf *Dawrant v Nutt* [1960] 3 All ER 681.

10 Where a disabled child's cause of action rests on the Congenital Disabilities (Civil Liability) Act 1976 (see p 176 et seq, ante) his damages are reduced if it is shown that the parent affected shared the responsibility for his being born disabled; s 1(7).

11 [1933] 1 KB 35, [1932] All ER Rep 820, Div Ct; cf *Murray v Harringay Arena Ltd* [1951] 2 KB 529, [1951] 2 All ER 320 CA, at p 249, post. *Dicta* in cases where children are suing landowners for personal injuries to the effect that if the child 'is so young as not to appreciate what it is doing, it is for its parents, and not for the landowner on whose land it enters without invitation, to protect it', per SCRUTTON LJ, in *Liddle v North Riding of Yorkshire County Council*, [1934] 2 KB 101 at 110, [1933] All ER Rep 222 at 226, CA, do not conflict with the text; they merely make the separate point that those landowners owe no duty of care to those children, so that contributory negligence never arises on the other hand, a motorist clearly owes a duty to young children on the highway.

12 See (1986) 49 MLR 102; (1981) 55 ALJ 278.

against him to the extent to which the plaintiff was contributorily negligent.
But the detailed provisions of the Act call for further study. Section 1(1)
reads:

> Where any person suffers damage as the result partly of the fault of any other
> person or persons, a claim in respect of that damage shall not be defeated by
> reasons of the fault of the person suffering the damage, but the damages recoverable
> in respect thereof shall be reduced to such extent as the court thinks just
> and equitable having regard to the claimant's share in the responsibility for the
> damage.

Section 4 defines 'damage' as including loss of life and personal injury, and
thus probably embraces any loss for which damages can at common law be
awarded.[13] The use of the word 'result' is a neutral term regarded by the
courts as leaving them free to continue to treat contributory negligence as a
matter of causation.[14] What is clear is that under the Act contributory
negligence which contributes to the extent of the injuries suffered by the
plaintiff is as relevant as contributory negligence contributing to the incident
in which the injuries are suffered. Thus a passenger failing to wear a seat belt
cannot be said to be in any way responsible for the collision in which he is
thrown against the steering wheel. He is responsible for the extent of his
injuries to the degree that those injuries would have been avoided had he
worn a belt.[15] The correct question is not what was the cause of the accident
but rather what was the cause of the damage.[16]

It is the definition of 'fault' in the 1945 Act which has proved most
problematic recently. 'Fault' is defined in section 4 as 'negligence, breach of
statutory duty or other act or omission which gives rise to liability in tort or
would, apart from this Act, give rise to the defence of contributory negligence.' The first limb of the definition of 'fault' thus makes the partial defence
of contributory negligence apparently applicable to all torts. Section 11 of the
Torts (Interferences with Goods) Act 1977 expressly excludes contributory
negligence as a defence to conversion or intentional trespass to goods. As far
as other intentional torts are concerned the balance of authority now favours
the availability of the defence at any rate to trespass to the person.[17]

The key question is whether the defence of contributory negligence can be
invoked in an action for breach of contract.[18] As we have seen, where a duty
of care arises within a contractual relationship the plaintiff may opt to sue in
either contract or tort. So a private patient suing in respect of the negligent
delivery of her baby has a choice of remedies,[19] as does the client of an
allegedly negligent solicitor.[21] A N.H.S. patient, or some third party other

13 In *Drinkwater v Kimber* [1951] 2 All ER 713, the trial judge held that it excluded pecuniary
   loss, but the Court of Appeal [1952] 2 QB 281 at 290 (per SINGLETON LJ), though affirming
   the decision, did so on other grounds and disagreed with this narrow interpretation of
   'damage'.
14 Thus where the plaintiff's own negligence prior to his act of rescue contributed to his injuries,
   his damages were reduced. The plaintiff (a train guard) went to the rescue of the defendant
   who was negligently trying to board a moving train without first applying the emergency
   brake: *Harrison v British Railways Board* [1981] 3 All ER 679.
15 See post at p 248.
16 *Froom v Butcher* [1976] QB 286, [1975] 3 All ER 520; and see *O'Connell v Jackson* [1972] 1
   QB 270, [1971] 3 All ER 129 (injured motor cyclist not wearing helmet).
17 *Murphy v Culhane* [1977] QB 94, [1976] 3 All ER 533; *Barnes v Nayer* (1986) Times, 19
   December. Contributory negligence is expressly included as a defence to product liability
   under the Consumer Protection Act 1987. See post at pp 304–5.
18 *De Meza and Stuart v Apple, Van Straten, Shene and Stone* [1975] 1 Lloyd's Rep 498.
19 See *Kralj v McGrath* [1986] 1 All ER 54.
20 *Midland Bank Trust Co Ltd v Hett, Stubbs and Kemp* [1979] Ch 384, [1978] 3 All ER 571.

than the paying client who has suffered loss from, the solicitor's negligence[21] has no such choice. What basis in common sense is there for saying that X who was provided with services under a contract will not be penalised for her own lack of care, but Y whose only action lies in tort will? And, if the answer is that X by providing consideration acquired a higher obligation than Y whose only remedy lies in tort, how do you justify distinguishing between the case where X elects to sue on one obligation rather than the other? In those many cases where he has the option, the choice of remedy could then dictate the outcome of the case and the level of damages which he receives.

The case-law is unclear. While there is general consensus, and rightly so, that contributory negligence is no defence for breach of strict contractual obligation[1] the authorities diverge on the availability of the defence when the essence of a claim is breach of the contractual duty of care. The purists held that contributory negligence can never be invoked in contract.[2] The second limb of section 4 of the 1945 Act defining 'fault' suggests that apart from tort contributory negligence is only available as a partial defence now where before 1945 it was available as a complete defence. The balance of opinion is that it was not so available in contract. The realists (recently endorsed by the Court of Appeal)[3] argue that distinguishing between tortious and contractual duties of care is pedantry. Contributory negligence should be available where the defendant's liability in contract is the same as his liability in the tort of negligence independently of the existence of any contract.[4] If the substance of your claim whatever you call it, is tort you should not be able to evade tort rules. Where the action concerns breach of a contractual duty of care independent of and distinct from any concurrent duty in tort it seems that the wording of the Act again excludes contributory negligence as a defence. The only sensible resolution of the present conflict on contributory negligence and contract is to seek clarification and statutory amendment of the 1945 Act.[5]

E. APPORTIONMENT OF DAMAGES

The 1945 Act directs courts to reduce the award of damages as they think 'just and equitable having regard to the claimant's share in responsibility for the damage.' If the plaintiff's lack of care is found to have contributed to his damage some reduction must be made. His carelessness cannot be totally disregarded on the ground that that course of action would be 'just and equitable'.[6] Apportionment will generally be on a common sense basis and the Court of Appeal will only interfere with the trial judge's conclusions on apportionment if he can be shown to be plainly wrong.[7] LORD REID summed up the basic guidelines for apportionment in *Stapley v Gypsum Mines Ltd*[8]

---

21 Such as the disappointed legatee in *Ross v Caunters* [1980] Ch 297, [1979] 3 All ER 580.
 1 *Forsikringsaktieselskapet Vesta v Butcher* [1986] 2 All ER 488, 508–510 (1987) Times 27 November, CA.
 2 *AB Marintrans v Comet Shipping Co Ltd* [1985] 3 All ER 442, [1985] 1 WLR 1270.
 3 *Forsikrings Vesta v Butcher* (1987) Times, 27 November, CA.
 4 *Forsikrings Vesta v Butcher* (supra); and see *Sayers v Harlow UDC* [1958] 1 WLR 623 at 625.
 5 For a cogent rehearsal of all the arguments proposing the view that only statutory reform can clarify the present confusion see A S Burrows *Remedies for Torts and Breach of Contract* pp 73–78.
 6 *Bootham v British Northrop Ltd* (1972) 13 KIR 112, CA.
 7 *Hannam v Mann* [1984] RTR 252.
 8 [1953] AC 663 at 682.

A court must deal broadly with the problem of apportionment, and, in considering what is just and equitable, must have regard to the blameworthiness of each party, but the claimant's share in the responsibility for the damage cannot, I think, be assessed without considering the relative importance of the acts in causing the damage apart his blameworthiness.

Two factors therefore have to be considered, the causative potency of the act,[9] and the extent to which the plaintiff deviates from the standard of the reasonable man careful of his own safety.[10] Where there are two or more defendants the fault of each negligent party must be weighed against that of each to the others. Thus where the plaintiff negligently crossed a pelican crossing with the lights at green for the traffic, was struck by a car negligently driven by D.1, ricocheted onto the road and was hit by D.2, his contributory negligence had to be measured separately against each of the defendants.[11]

One common example of contributory negligence, failing to wear a seat belt will suffice to give an example of how apportionment works in practice. LORD DENNING in *Froom v Butcher*[12] suggested norms of 25% reduction if wearing the seat belt would have prevented the injury, and 15% where it would simply have reduced the severity of the injuries. In *Gregory v Kelly*,[13] however, where the plaintiff not wearing his seat belt knew that the car also had a faulty footbrake a reduction of 40% was made. Of course if the plaintiff would still, even had he worn his belt, have suffered injuries of equal severity albeit of a different type no reduction at all may be ordered.[14]

SECTION 2. VOLUNTARY ASSUMPTION OF RISK

A. IS ASSUMPTION OF RISK PROPERLY REGARDED AS A DEFENCE?

It has been explained previously that the consent of the plaintiff may take two forms, consent to the actual invasion of his interest, eg where he invited someone to walk on to his land; or consent to the *risk* of a tort being committed.[15] The latter will be discussed now, for although it is not solely concerned with negligence, the risk assumed by the plaintiff is usually that of the defendant's negligent conduct. The Latin maxim, *volenti non fit injuria*, is commonly used to embrace both these aspects of consent. Assumption of risk has been summarised thus:[16]

---

9 *Davies v Swan Motor Co (Swansea) Ltd* [1949] 2 KB 291 at 326.
10 The expression 'blameworthiness' used by LORD REID suggests a moral term; it is submitted that the High Court of Australia in *Pennington v Norris* (1956) 96 CLR 10, rightly rejected this standard in favour of the stand of the 'reasonable man'. *Quintas v National Smelting Co Ltd* [1961] 1 All ER 630, [1961] 1 WLR 401, CA, could on one reading suggest that if the trial judge finds the defendant liable for breach of statutory duty, and the Court of Appeal reverses that finding, but holds the defendant liable for negligence, this is a ground for reducing the amount deducted from the plaintiff's damages for his contributory negligence.
11 *Fitzgerald v Lane* [1987] QB 781, [1987] 2 All ER 455.
12 [1976] QB 286, [1975] 3 All ER 520. See also *O'Connell v Jackson* (supra) (motor cyclist— 15% reduction for not wearing a crash helmet); consider *Owens v Brimmel* [1977] QB 859, [1976] 3 All ER 765 where passenger accepts a lift knowing the driver is drunk. See Symmons (1977) 40 MLR 350; Gravells (1977) 93 LQR 581.
13 [1978] RTR 426.
14 [1978] RTR 483.
15 See p 75 ante.
16 *Letang v Ottawa Electric Ry Co* [1926] AC 725 at 731 PC, citing *Osborne v London and North Western Ry Co* (1888) 21 QBD 220.

If the defendants desire to succeed on the ground that the maxim *volenti non fit injuria* is applicable, they must obtain a finding of fact that the plaintiff freely and voluntarily, with full knowledge of the nature and extent of the risk he ran, impliedly agreed to incur it.

Assumption of risk is looked at by the courts in two different ways. On one view it imports that the defendant has not in the circumstances broken a duty of care; on the other, there is a breach of duty, but a plea of assumption of risk removes the effect of that negligence. Whichever of these two judicial approaches is made, the consequences are likely to be the same, although understanding of the application of *volenti* may sometimes be readier under the first approach.

Examples will illustrate the two different judicial techniques. Suppose that X is walking along a busy highway when he is hit by a golf ball struck from a tee placed dangerously near to that highway. If X is an ordinary pedestrian he may be able to sue the golf club in negligence, but if, on the other hand, he is a golfer who is crossing the highway in order to reach the next tee he would fail. One could say that the plaintiff fails if the defendant shows that the plaintiff assumed the risk of the defendant's negligence. On the other hand, that the plaintiff is a golfer is merely one of the circumstances going to the question whether the defendant took reasonable care in respect of *this* plaintiff. Sometimes it will not emerge from the plaintiff's evidence that the plaintiff comprehended the risk, and then of course the defendant will himself have to prove that fact if he seeks thereby to rebut the plaintiff's claim. For example, a plaintiff who has been injured while riding in the defendant's car may make out a *prima facie* case without revealing that the defendant was, to the plaintiff's knowledge, drunk; if the defendant wishes to rely on that further factor, he must prove it. On one view he is merely adducing evidence of factors which are material in deciding whether, in all the circumstances of the case, there has been a breach of the duty to take care.[17] Alternatively, one could say that the plaintiff consented to the risk of negligent driving.

A case such as *Murray v Harringay Arena Ltd* is more easily understood by treating it as one where there was no breach of duty:[18]

A six-year-old boy was injured when the puck at an ice-hockey match was hit out of the rink in course of play and landed among the spectators. The Court of Appeal held that his claim in negligence failed.

It would be straining logic to say that this child had in fact assumed the risk. Indeed it may be regarded as a policy decision that organisers of sporting events owe no duty to any spectators to guard against certain dangers incidental to the ordinary conduct of the game.

17 *Insurance Commissioner v Joyce* (1948) 77 CLR 39 (H Ct Australia). *Nettleship v Weston* [1971] 2 QB 691, [1971] 3 All ER 581, CA (and see p 205, ante) shows both techniques in use. SALMON LJ applied this one to the question whether a learner-driver was liable for injuring his car passenger whereas LORD DENNING MR made the standard *volenti* approach. *Watt v Hertfordshire County Council* [1954] 2 All ER 368, CA, is another good example. The plaintiff fireman was injured because a jack on the back of the lorry on which he was travelling in the course of his duties slewed forward when the driver had to apply his brakes suddenly: the court held that *volenti non fit injuria* was irrelevant; the issue was whether, in the circumstances, the employers were negligent in requiring the plaintiff to travel on the back of a lorry together with an unlashed heavy jack and found that there was no failure to take reasonable care.

18 [1951] 2 KB 529, [1951] 2 All ER 320, CA.

Some judges clearly favour the 'no negligence' approach. Thus ASQUITH J has said:[19]

> As a matter of strict pleading it seems that the plea *volenti* is a denial of any duty at all, and, therefore, of any breach of duty, and an admission of negligence cannot strictly be combined with the plea.

The 1962 decision of the Court of Appeal in *Wooldridge v Sumner* is important.[20]

> A non-paying spectator, a photographer, was injured by a horse competing at a jumping show. Held that the rider was not liable in negligence even if he was guilty of an error of judgment.[1]

The court explained that *volenti non fit injuria* did not apply 'to negligence *simpliciter* where the duty of care is based solely upon proximity or "neighbourship" in the Atkinian sense. The maxim in English law presupposes a tortious act by the defendant'.[2]

On the other hand, in *Imperial Chemical Industries Ltd v Shatwell*[3] the House of Lords made no use of this approach. It held that an injured shot-firer could not sue his employer for the conduct of a fellow shot-firer because he had in the special circumstances of the case[4] assumed the risk of his fellow shot-firer's negligence. Perhaps the House of Lords found it more convenient to exempt the employer by finding a defence of consent to negligence than it might have done had it asked whether there was in the circumstances a breach of duty. That is why the survival of both approaches to assumption of risk is to be expected.

B. WHEN THE PLAINTIFF IS DEEMED TO HAVE ASSUMED THE RISK

(1) SUITS BY WORKMEN AGAINST EMPLOYERS

The defendant is not liable whenever the plaintiff is deemed to have absolved him from liability for the consequences. The rule used to be especially important in actions by workmen alleging negligence by their employers. Nineteenth-century cases in which workmen sued employers for injuries sustained at work in effect held that, if the employee knew of the danger, this was enough. The House of Lords (no doubt reflecting the changing social and economic attitudes) changed this by disapproving of the latest of these cases, *Thomas v Quartermaine*,[5] in *Smith v Baker & Sons* where the facts were:[6]

19 *Dann v Hamilton* [1939] 1 KB 509 at 512, [1939] 1 All ER 59.
20 [1962] 2 All ER 978. *Baker v T E Hopkins & Son Ltd* [1959] 3 All ER 225 at 243 (per WILLMER LJ), provides another sound exposition on the principle, when it said of a claim by an injured rescuer 'that, once it is determined that the act of the rescuer was the natural and probable consequence of the defendant's wrongdoing, there is no longer any room for the application of the maxim *volenti non fit injuria*'.
1   He would be liable if he failed to take the care expected of a reasonable competitor in a sporting event: *Wilks v Cheltenham Homeguard Motor Cycle and Light Car Club* [1971] 2 All ER 369 CA.
2   At 990 (per DIPLOCK LJ).
3   [1965] AC 656, [1964] 2 All ER 999.
4   See p 251, post.
5   (1887) 18 QBD 685, CA.
6   [1891] AC 325, HL; cf *Yarmouth v France* (1887) 19 QBD 647, CA.

The plaintiff, a servant of the defendants, railway contractors, was employed in drilling holes in a rock cutting, and was aware of the danger caused by a crane continually swinging crates of stones above his head. A stone fell out of a crate and injured him. He brought an action of negligence against the defendants, who pleaded *volenti non fit injuria*.

The House of Lords held that, notwithstanding the plaintiff's knowledge of the risk, the evidence justified a finding by the jury that he had not voluntarily undertaken it. Although the House of Lords accepted that 'a particular consent may be inferred from a general course of conduct',[7] it was held that knowledge alone is not enough, but that the jury must affirm 'that he consented to the particular thing being done which would involve the risk, and consented to take the risk upon himself'. LORD WATSON said:[8]

> The question which has most frequently to be considered is not whether he voluntarily and rashly exposed himself to injury, but whether he agreed that, if injury should befall him, the risk was to be his and not his master's. [Whether continuing at work knowing of the danger is an assumption of the risk] depends ... upon the nature of the risk, and the workman's connection with it, as well as upon other considerations which must vary according to the circumstances of each case.

Since then, there has been a series of employer–employee cases in which this defence has been negatived on the ground of the employee's want of consent.[9] *Bowater v Rowley Regis Corporation* is typical:[10]

> The plaintiff carter was ordered by the defendants, his employers, despite his protests, to take out a horse known by them to be unsafe. Eventually, he took out the horse, but was thrown off the cart when the horse ran away. He sued in negligence for the injuries which he sustained.

The Court of Appeal rejected the defence of *volenti non fit injuria*, GODDARD LJ saying of the defence:[11]

> ... it can hardly ever be applicable where the act to which the servant is said to be '*volens*' arises out of his ordinary duty, unless the work for which he is engaged is one in which danger is necessarily involved.

Yet where the plaintiff was susceptible, to her and her employer's knowledge, to dermatitis, and her employer found work for her which entailed slight risk of the disease, the employer was not liable for her then contracting it. He was not obliged either to dismiss her or to make the work safe for her with her particular susceptibility; she took the risk and could not then complain.[12] In *Imperial Chemical Industries Ltd v Shatwell*[13] the House of Lords expressly supported the general principle that assumption of risk will not ordinarily defeat a claim by an employee against his employer. At the same time, it recognised that where the claim rested on vicarious liability for joint and

---

7 Per LORD HALSBURY LC, [1891] AC 325 at 338.
8 [1891] AC 325 at 355.
9 See Williams *Joint Torts* ch 12, for a list of them.
10 [1944] KB 476, [1944] 1 All ER 465, CA.
11 Ibid at 480–1.
12 *Withers v Perry Chain Co Ltd* [1961] 3 All ER 676, CA (Is this a decision better explained in terms of no breach of duty in the circumstances? See ante at p 196); cf *Paris v Stepney BC* [1951] AC 367, [1951] 1 All ER 42, p 196 ante.
13 [1965] AC 656, [1964] 2 All ER 999.

flagrant disobedience of a safety rule by the plaintiff and his wrongdoing fellow-servant, and where the latter was not the superior of the plaintiff or one whose orders he was bound to obey, the employer would have the defence available against the plaintiff employee.

(2) OTHER CASES

The effect of the principle must also be examined in actions other than those of workman against employer. *Dann v Hamilton*, though only a decision at first instance, merits attention:[14]

> The plaintiff voluntarily accompanied the defendant as a passenger in a car driven by him, knowing that the defendant was under the influence of drink to such an extent that the chances of a collision from negligent driving were substantially increased. She was injured by his negligent driving and her action was held not to be barred by the defence of *volenti non fit injuria*.

ASQUITH J held that the maxim applied 'where a dangerous physical condition has been brought about by the negligence of the defendant, and, after it has arisen, the plaintiff, fully appreciating its dangerous character, elects to assume the risk thereof'.[15] Although he appeared to doubt whether the defence could lie where the consent of the plaintiff preceded the subsequent act of negligence complained of, the *ratio decidendi* of his judgment probably is no more than a finding of fact that 'the plaintiff, by embarking in the car ... with knowledge that through drink the driver had materially reduced his capacity for driving safely, did not impliedly consent to, or absolve the driver from liability for any subsequent negligence on his part whereby she might suffer harm'.[16] So regarded, the law laid down in the case is unexceptionable, although there is room for disagreement on its application to the facts.[17] The importance of the case is that it demonstrates the freedom of the courts in making the decision of fact whether the inference is to be drawn in a particular case that the plaintiff has consented to relieve the defendant of liability.

Of course, the defendant must show that the plaintiff consented not only to some risk of harm but also to that particular risk which culminated in the injury to him. *Gillmore v London County Council* illustrates this:[18]

> The plaintiff was a member of a physical training class run by the defendants. During an exercise in which the members of the class were lunging at each other, he was injured through losing his balance on a floor which was slippery owing to the negligence of the defendants.

DU PARCQ LJ held[19] that the plaintiff had not consented to the risk incidental to doing physical training on a slippery floor (although, of course, he had

---

14 [1939] 1 KB 509, [1939] 1 All ER 59.
15 Ibid at 517.
16 Ibid at 518, approved in *Slater v Clay Cross Co Ltd* [1956] 1 QB 264, [1956] 2 All ER 625, CA. But note the partial defence of contributory negligence may be available to the drunken driver; *Owens v Brimmell* [1977] QB 859, [1976] 3 All ER 765 ante at p 248).
17 Cf the Australian cases of *The Insurance Commissioner v Joyce* (1948) 77 CLR 39, and *Roggenkamp v Bennett* (1950) 80 CLR 292, in both of which drunken drivers successfully pleaded the defence when sued by passengers, knowing of their condition, who were the victims of their negligent driving.
18 [1938] 4 All ER 331.
19 Ibid at 336.

consented to the physical contacts which might occur in the course of the lunging exercise) and therefore the defence of assumption of risk failed.[20]

The test of acceptance of the risk is objective. In *Bennett v Tugwell*:[1]

> The car in which the plaintiff accepted a lift from the owner's son had a notice stating that passengers travelled at their own risk. The owner's insurance policy covered injuries to passengers while the son was driving. Both the son and the plaintiff passenger thought that the notice did not affect the liability of the insurers. The defence of *volenti* succeeded when the son negligently drove the car and injured the plaintiff.

C. VOLUNTARY ACT

Not only must the plaintiff consent to the risk, but also he must assume the risk freely and voluntarily. The decision on suits by workmen constitute, in effect, judicial recognition that economic pressures negative voluntary conduct in the sense indicated by SCOTT LJ in *Bowater v Rowley Regis Corporation*:[2]

> For the purposes of the rule ... a man cannot be said to be truly 'willing' unless he is in a position to choose freely, and freedom of choice predicates, not only full knowledge of the circumstances on which the exercise of choice is conditioned, so that he may be able to choose wisely, but the absence from his mind of any feeling of constraint so that nothing shall interfere with the freedom of his will.[3]

The courts have, with one early exception,[4] thus consistently refused to allow the defence of *volenti non fit injuria* to lie against rescuers.[5] They are not genuine volunteers. Nor do they in responding to the call for rescue, even if their job requires them to go to a citizen's aid,[6] take upon themselves the risk of injury and impliedly waive any duty owed to them.[7]

It may be said too, that if the defendant places the plaintiff on the horns of a dilemma, this deprives the plaintiff of his freedom of action with the result that his reaction is not voluntary.[8]

Sometimes, mere knowledge of a risk will bar the plaintiff, for example, if

---

20 *Cleghorn v Oldham* (1927) 43 TLR 465 (plaintiff recovered damages against her golf companion who injured her with a golf club on the course) is explicable on this ground too.
1 [1971] 2 QB 267, [1971] 2 All ER 248; *Birch v Thomas* [1972] 1 All ER 905, CA. See now s 148(2) of the Road Traffic Act 1972 and p 259 post.
2 At 479.
3 Cf HODSON LJ in *Christmas v General Cleaning Contractors Ltd* [1952] 1 KB 141 at 151, [1952] 1 All ER 39, CA; affd *sub nom General Cleaning Contractors Ltd v Christmas* [1953] AC 180, [1952] 2 All ER 1110, HL.
4 *Cutler v United Dairies (London) Ltd* [1933] 2 KB 297, [1933] All ER Rep 594.
5 *Haynes v Harwood* [1935] 1 KB 146, [1934] All ER Rep 103, CA.
6 *Ogwo v Taylor* [1987] 3 All ER 961, HL (fireman).
7 *D'Urso v Sanson* [1939] 4 All ER 26 (night watchman extinguishing fire on employers' premises); cf *Merrington v Ironbridge Metal Works Ltd* [1952] 2 All ER 1101; *Baker v T E Hopkins & Son Ltd* [1959] 3 All ER 225, CA (doctor-rescuer); *Sylvester v Chapman Ltd* (1935) 79 Sol Jo 777 (plaintiff mauled by leopard at an animal show of the defendants, when he crossed the barrier to extinguish a cigarette smouldering in the straw between the barrier and the cage, 'was not rescuing anyone from imminent danger of death, nor even preventing damage to property, since there were people who could easily have done with precautions what he did' (per LORD WRIGHT MR); therefore he had no cause of action against the defendants).
8 See the cases on alternative danger discussed, p 244, ante.

he is the gratuitous bailee of a defective chattel—the defendant can say to the plaintiff: 'Take it or leave it'. Conversely, reasons of policy—it will be obvious that one cannot speak of some constant rigid defence of assumption of risk—sometimes dictate that a plaintiff will not fail even though he has freely encountered a known risk: this is where the plaintiff has a right to face the risk, as where he walks along a highway, or exercises his right of access.[9] This last class of case points up the relation of assumption of risk and the defence of contributory negligence. Although the defendant cannot maintain that the plaintiff has assumed the risk, he may show that nonetheless the plaintiff's conduct was so unreasonable in the light of the risk that it constituted contributory negligence. Because the effect of establishing the defence of contributory negligence used to be the same as that of setting up assumption of risk, the courts have sometimes in the past not been careful to heed the distinctions between them.[10] But, since the passing of the Law Reform (Contributory Negligence) Act 1945 the distinction has become important: for now, if the defence of assumption of risk is made out, the plaintiff still recovers nothing, whereas, as has been seen, a plaintiff guilty of contributory negligence alone has his damages reduced to the extent to which he was responsible for the damage.

Section 148(3) of the Road Traffic Act 1972 applies where vehicles are being used in circumstances where third party insurance is compulsory. It provides:

> ... if any other person is carried in or upon the vehicle while the user is so using it, any antecedent agreement or understanding between them (whether intended to be legally binding or not) shall be of no effect so far as it purports or might be held to negative or restrict any such liability of the user ... [to passengers] ... and the fact that a person so carried has willingly accepted as his the risk of negligence on the part of the user shall not be treated as negativing any such liability of the user.

This Act rules out the defence of *volenti non fit injuria* where there is an antecedent agreement, but it is less clear whether a plaintiff is 'so carried' within the section if he has merely impliedly consented to the risk.[11] The section does not prevent the motorist from pleading contributory negligence, where appropriate.[12]

SECTION 3.   EXCLUDING LIABILITY

The already limited application of the defence of *volenti* is further restricted by the operation of the Unfair Contract Terms Act 1977. That Act, which most unfairly for the student misrepresents itself by its title and is in fact as

---

9 *Clayards v Dethick and Davis* (1848) 12 QB 439, p 245 ante. In *Burnett v British Waterways Board* [1973] 2 All ER 631, CA, a lighterman was injured in the defendant's dock, having read a notice that he entered at his own risk. *Held volenti* did not apply because he had not agreed to be bound by its terms and had no choice in the matter.

10 See Williams *Joint Torts* ch 12.

11 *Ashton v Turner* [1981] QB 137, [1980] 3 All ER 870 decides at first instance that s 148(3) does not nullify the defence of *volenti non fit injuria,* but no reasons are given in the judgment.

12 *Nettleship v Weston* [1971] 2 QB 691, [1971] 3 All ER 581, CA, suggests that where a passenger knowingly accepts a lift from a drunken driver, he may be met by the defence of *ex turpi causa.* Section 148 does not prevent the defendant (or his insurers) from raising that defence.

crucial to tort as contract, also affects unilateral exclusion of liability by the defendant.

The Act applies[13] to 'business liability' only, that is to say liability arising from 'things done or to be done by a person in the course of a business' and the occupation of promises used for 'business purposes'.[14] Section 2 prohibits altogether exclusion or limitation of liability for death or personal injury resulting from negligence.[15] Any contract term or notice purporting so to do will be invalid. In the case of loss other than death or personal injury, or death or personal injury resulting from a tort other than negligence, an exclusion or limitation of liability is invalid 'except insofar as the term of notice satisfies the requirement of reasonableness'.[16] Finally section 2(3) provides:

> Where a contract term or notice purports to exclude or restrict liability for negligence a person's agreement to or awareness of it is not of itself to be taken as indicating his voluntary acceptance of any risk.

Several questions must be asked about the operation of the 1977 Act. Business liability is nowhere comprehensively defined. Professions[17] and central and local government are expressly included within the term. But what of the work of a charity? Is the NSPCC a business? Probably yes. The test does not appear to be whether the defendant is a profit making commercial enterprise. The distinction is rather between the domestic and the business, work, sector of life. In view of section 2(3) can *volenti* ever now operate against a business? There is as yet no authority on the point. Clearly knowledge of the unilateral exclusion of liability by notice will be insufficient but so would it at common law. An agreement per se will not be binding. It remains to be seen whether there are residual circumstances, perhaps when the plaintiff took the initiative, where *volenti* might still operate.

The crux of the question in many cases where the operation of the 1977 Act is in issue will often be twofold. Has a breach of duty been proved and purportedly excluded? In the case of loss other than death or personal injury was exclusion of liability reasonable? The first question may be difficult to answer. Consider a lecturer asked by a student to advise him on a lease for a flat saying to the student 'look this is only general advice. I am not a practising solicitor. I cannot accept liability for what I say'. Is the lecturer excluding liability, or limiting the duty[18] owed to the student if any, or simply indicating the standard of care to be expected from him? As to the issue of reasonableness this is essentially a matter for the court subject to the guide-

13 Section 1. On the Act generally see Palmer and Yates 40 CLJ 108.
14 See post at pp 268 et seq.
15 Section 2(1).
16 Section 2(2).
17 See *Stevenson v Nationwide Building Society* (1984) 272 Estates Gazette 663 (surveyors).
18 Section 13 provides: '(1) To the extent that [the] Act prevents the exclusion or restriction of any liability it also prevents—(a) making the liability or its enforcement subject to restrictive or onerous conditions; (b) excluding or restricting any right or remedy in respect of the liability, or subjecting a person to any prejudice in consequence of his pursuing any such remedy. (c) excluding or restricting rules of evidence or procedure and (to that extent) sections 2 and 5–7 also prevent excluding or restricting liability by reference to terms or notices which exclude or restrict the relevant obligation or duty'. Consider again *Hedley Byrne & Co v Heller and Partners* [1964] AC 465, [1963] 2 All ER 575 (ante at p 186) would the disclaimer then survive s 13(1)?

lines further provided in the Act.[19] What the Act undoubtedly means is that a foolproof exclusion notice or agreement is now a thing of the past.

19 See s 11 and Sch 2. And see *Stevenson v Nationwide Building Society* (1984) 272 Estates Gazette 663; *Smith v Bush* (A Firm) [1987] 3 All ER 179, [1987] 3 WLR 889, CA.

Chapter 16

Liability for defective premises

SECTION I. OCCUPIERS' LIABILITY

A. LIABILITY TO VISITORS

(1) WHO IS AN OCCUPIER?

The leading case on the definition of 'occupier' is the House of Lords decision in *Wheat v E Lacon & Co Ltd.*[1]

> The defendants owned a public house of which R was their manager. R and his wife were allowed by agreement to live in the upper floor, access to which was by a door separate from the licensed premises. Mrs R was allowed to take paying guests on the upper floor. An accident was sustained by a paying guest on the staircase leading to the upper floor. It was held that the defendants were occupiers of the upper floor. Mr R was only a licensee of that part, and the defendants had enough residuary control to be treated as occupiers. In fact the defendants, Mr R and Mrs R, were all occupiers.

The case decides that there may be two or more occupiers at one time,[2] that exclusive occupation is not required, and that the test is whether a person has some degree of control associated with and arising from his presence in and use of or activity in the premises. The following earlier decisions remain sound. A concessionaire without a lease in a fairground is an occupier,[3] a contractor converting a ship into a troopship in dry dock occupies the ship,[4] and a local authority which has requisitioned a house[5] is an occupier (even in respect of those parts of the house in which it is allowing homeless persons to live).[6]

---

1 [1966] AC 552, [1966] 1 All ER 582, HL.
2 In *Fisher v CHT Ltd (No 2)* [1966] 2 QB 475, [1966] 1 All ER 88, CA, the owners of a club and the defendants who ran a restaurant in the club under licence from the club were both held to be occupiers. In *AMF International Ltd v Magnet Bowling Ltd* [1968] 2 All ER 789, a contractor (as well as the owner) was an occupier of the whole building although part of the building was separated by a screen beyond which he went only to attend to heating and lighting. It is doubtful whether someone who has granted a right of way occupies that right of way: *Holden v White* [1982] QB 679, [1982] 2 All ER 328, CA. A highway authority which owns the land but has not adopted the highway is not an occupier of the highway; *Holmes v Norfolk County Council* (1981) 131 NLJ 401. A highway authority does not occupy a footpath on land owned by another although it has a statutory obligation to maintain it; *Whiting v Hillingdon London Borough Council* (1970) 68 LGR 437.
3 *Humphreys v Dreamland (Margate) Ltd* [1930] All ER Rep 327, HL.
4 *Hartwell v Grayson Rollo and Clover Docks Ltd* [1947] KB 901, CA. But not a contractor merely painting a house; *Page v Read* (1984) 134 NLJ 723.
5 *Hawkins v Coulsdon and Purley Urban District Council* [1954] 1 QB 319, [1954] 1 All ER 97, CA.
6 *Greene v Chelsea Borough Council* [1954] 2 QB 127, [1954] 2 All ER 318, CA; *Harris v Birkenhead Corporation* [1976] 1 All ER 341, CA (a local authority, having acquired a house by compulsory purchase, occupies it even before its staff enter it).

Wheat v E Lacon & Co Ltd was a decision on the meaning of 'occupier' for the purposes of the Occupiers' Liability Act 1957 but the judgments show that it applies to all cases, whether at common law or under that Act, or the Occupiers' Liability Act 1984 which now regulates occupiers' duties to trespassers, where it is necessary to determine the duty of care owed by occupiers to entrants.

(2) OCCUPIERS' LIABILITY ACT 1957

(a) Scope

The Occupiers' Liability Act 1957 was enacted to give effect to the recommendations of the Law Reform Committee[7] and to eliminate the confusion that had clouded the common law rules on liability to entrants on premises. The rules enacted by sections 2 and 3 of the Act 'have effect, in place of the rules of the common law, to regulate the duty which an occupier of premises owes to his visitors in respect of dangers due to the state of the premises or to things done or omitted to be done on them'.[8]

(i) *Visitors* At common law it was necessary to distinguish between invitees, licensees and other entrants on premises. The approximate distinction was that an invitee was requested to enter the premises in the interest of the occupier, whereas a licensee was merely permitted to enter. This is because 'visitors' for the purposes of the Act are those persons who were invitees *or* licensees at common law: that is, anyone to whom the occupiers give any invitation or permission to enter or use the premises. Where there is more than one occupier, could a person be a visitor in relation to A but a trespasser vis à vis B?[9]

It remains important to distinguish between visitors on the one hand, and other entrants on the other, because the duties of an occupier to those other entrants are governed not by the 1957 Act but by the later 1984 Act.[10] Those other entrants are often called trespassers, but the class is not confined to those persons whose acts constitute trespass to premises. If they are on the premises of the defendant without his permission, even though they have not gone there voluntarily,[11] eg if they have been thrown there or chased there, then they fall within this group, just as much as if they have committed the tort of trespass. Similarly,

... a person entering any premises in exercise of rights conferred by virtue of an access agreement or order under the National Parks and Access to the Countryside Act 1949, is not, for the purposes of this Act, a visitor of the occupier of those premises,[12]

although he is not a trespasser.[13] A person exercising a public right of way

---

7 Cmd 9305.   8 Section 1.

9 *Ferguson v Welsh* [1987] 3 All ER 777 per LORD GOFF at 785, HL.

10 *Stone v Taffe* [1974] 3 All ER 1016, CA is one of the few cases since the Act to turn on this distinction. (Pub manager in breach of contract allowed P and others to have a party after hours. P, who was unaware of that restriction in the contract, held to be a visitor not a trespasser as against the brewery employer.)

11 If the defendant's negligence causes a licensee involuntarily and unpremeditatedly to encroach slightly on land where he has no permission to go, he retains the rights of a licensee: *Braithwaite v Durham Steel Co Ltd* [1958] 3 All ER 161.

12 Section 1(4).

13 Section 60 of the Act of 1949.

has no claim under the 1957 Act because he was not an invitee or licensee at common law.[14]

The pre-Act cases which determined when permission of the occupier might be implied remain in full force. The House of Lords has held that a licence may not be implied merely because the occupier knows of the plaintiff's presence or has failed to take the necessary steps to prevent his entry.[15]

> There must be evidence either of express permission or that the land-owner has so conducted himself that he cannot be heard to say that he did not give it.[16]

The rules are the same for children, but

> ... an open pathway, as in *Cooke v Midland Great Western Ry of Ireland*,[17] or a knowledge that a track is and has long been constantly used, coupled with a failure to take any steps to indicate that ingress is not permitted, as in *Lowery v Walker*,[18] may well amount to a tacit licence.[19]

Although the mere fact that the occupier has on his premises a dangerous object alluring to children does not make him liable to a child trespasser, its presence in a place accessible to children may aid the inference of a licence,[20] so that a child who might otherwise have been treated as a trespasser might because of the allurement be found to be a visitor. In some circumstances occupiers are deemed only to permit young children subject to the condition that they are accompanied by a responsible adult.[21]

Persons entering as of right, such as police with search warrants and the host of officials empowered by statute to enter premises, are visitors.[1]

(ii) *Against what risks the Act affords protection* The Act plainly regulates the duty of the occupier in relation to structural defects or other dangers due

---

14 *Greenhalgh v British Railways Board* [1969] 2 QB 286, [1969] 2 All ER 114, CA; *Holden v White* [1982] QB 679, [1982] 2 All ER 328, CA, but he may still have a remedy in negligence at common law as in *Thomas v British Railways Board* [1976] QB 912, [1976] 3 All ER 15, CA, where a child was run over by a train on a level crossing which he had reached through a gap near a stile which the defendants had failed to repair.

15 *Edwards v Railway Executive* [1952] AC 737, [1952] 2 All ER 430.

16 Per LORD GODDARD at 747.

17 [1909] AC 229, HL; (defendant railway company kept an unlocked turntable close to a public road; children were in the habit of playing with it, having gained access to it through a well-worn gap in a fence of the defendants—held that the defendants were liable to such a child, who was held to be a licensee, for injuries sustained while playing on the turntable).

18 [1911] AC 10, HL.

19 Per LORD PORTER at 744. See also *R Addie & Sons (Collieries) v Dumbreck* [1929] AC 358 at 372–3 (per VISCOUNT DUNEDIN), HL; cf *Gough v National Coal Board* [1954] 1 QB 191, [1953] 2 All ER 1283, CA.

20 *Hardy v Central London Ry Co* [1920] 3 KB 459, CA; *Latham v R Johnson and Nephew Ltd* [1913] 1 KB 398, CA.

21 *Latham v R Johnson and Nephew Ltd* [1913] 1 KB 398, CA; *Bates v Stone Parish Council* [1954] 3 All ER 38, CA (no circumstances to qualify the permissions given by the defendants to infant children to enter their playground; three-year-old child held to be a licensee). In *Phipps v Rochester Corporation* [1955] 1 QB 450, [1955] 1 All ER 129, DEVLIN J criticised this rule on the valid ground that it was lacking in precision, eg what degree of incapacity on the part of the child and what qualifications of his companion are called for? Nevertheless, the rule stands on the authority of the Court of Appeal.

1 Section 2(6). Police officers pursuing inquiries without a warrant may take advantage of the generally implied licence to approach a front door via the garden path; *Robson v Hallett* [1967] 2 QB 939, [1967] 2 All ER 407; but like other visitors they will cease to have visitor status if they fail to leave immediately if that licence is expressly withdrawn; *Snook v Mannion* [1982] RTR 321.

to the state of the premises themselves.[2] That this is not the limit of its scope is made clear by the fact that in addition to dangers due to the state of the premises the Act refers to duties in respect of dangers due to 'things done or omitted to be done on them'. At the very least, then, the Act covers acts or omissions which have created a dangerous condition of a continuing nature which later causes harm.

An outstanding question is whether the Act also affects acts (whether of the occupier or others) which cause harm to the visitor at the time of their commission. Section 1(2) provides that the Act 'shall regulate the nature of the duty imposed by law in consequence of a person's occupation or control of premises'. At common law an occupier had a duty not to permit a use by others of his premises which would foreseeably harm other persons on the premises.[3] Regardless of whether such cases previously fell within that sub-head of the law of negligence creating special duties of occupiers to invitees or licensees, it is submitted that the joint effect of sub-sections (1) and (2) is to bring those situations within the Act—the duty of care arises in consequence of the fact that the defendant is an occupier.[4] On the other hand, the duty of education authorities to protect their pupils against dangerous conditions[5] was imposed on them at common law, not *qua* occupiers but *qua* educational authorities, and it is submitted that the Act would not apply to such cases. At common law activities of an occupier-defendant, which at the time of their commission caused harm to the visitors, were governed by ordinary principles of negligence, and not by the special rules relating to occupiers.[6] It is thought that the Act will not apply to such activities when works are being carried out on land, or for example, arrows are being shot, (it matters not whether the act is that of the occupier or a contractor or a visitor) for the duty of care is imposed on the actor because he is himself performing an act foreseeably likely to cause harm to others present on the premises, and not because the actor occupies the land.[7]

Before the Act some cases had held that a plaintiff might sometimes have the choice of suing either in ordinary negligence or by virtue of the special duty owed by occupiers.[8] The Act only displaces the common-law rules

2 At common law if the danger confronted the visitor while on the premises, although he actually suffered the harm off the premises, eg falling off an unfenced cliff into the sea, the rules regulating the duties of occupiers towards visitors applied: *Perkowski v Wellington Corporation* [1959] AC 53, [1958] 3 All ER 368, PC. The wording of this section of the Act is also wide enough to cover this situation.

3 *Glasgow Corporation v Muir* [1943] AC 448, [1943] 2 All ER 44; see p 194, ante.

4 All three judges in *Videan v British Transport Commission* [1963] 2 QB 650, [1963] 2 All ER 860, CA were of this same opinion (*obiter*).

5 Eg *Rich v London County Council* [1953] 2 All ER 376, CA. On the duty of parents to safeguard their children from dangers in the home: *Jauffir v Akhbar* (1984) Times, 10 February.

6 See p 271, post. And see *Ferguson v Welsh* [1987] 3 All ER 777, HL.

7 The contention is that the restrictive wording of s 1(2) excludes this class of facts. But it may be argued that s 1(1) *displaces* the common-law rules for all matters covered by s 1(1), regardless of whether those matters also fall within s 1(2). This surprising result would only be avoided if it could be contended that s 1(1) in itself, without the aid of s 1(2), limited the Act to duties arising in consequence of occupation—*sed quaere*.

8 Eg *Slade v Battersea and Putney Group Hospital Management Committee* [1955] 1 All ER 429 (relative visiting sick patient in state hospital injured because polish had recently been spread on floor, and she had not been warned of it, held able to sue in ordinary negligence caused by this current operation): *Thompson v Bankstown Municipal Council* (1953) 87 CLR 619 (H Ct Australia), which appears to hold that where, apart from the occupier-invitee/licensee/trespasser rules relating to the condition of land, the facts are such that one

imposed in consequence of occupation: it follows that if some other duty is imposed by common law or statute for some reason independent of occupation of the premises, the plaintiff may rely on either the Act or the other independent common law or statutory cause of action (or both)—for example, a workman injured on his employer's premises may rely either on the common duty of care laid down in the Act or on the duty of the employer as such to provide a safe system of work or on some statutory duty of the employer to provide safe access or the like.[9]

(b) Common duty of care

(i) *General principles*

> The common duty of care is a duty to take such care as in all the circumstances of the case is reasonable to see that the visitor will be reasonably safe in using the premises for the purposes for which he is invited or permitted by the occupier to be there.[10]

If the entrant does not use the premises for that purpose which entitles him to be there no duty is owed to him under the 1957 Act and any remedy which he might have would be regulated by the 1984 Act on the duty owed to trespassers.

Those entering as of right are not 'invited or permitted' by the occupier for any purpose. Section 2(6) of the Act nonetheless makes the common-law duty extend to them by providing that 'persons who enter premises for any purpose in the exercise of a right conferred by law are to be treated as permitted by the occupier to be there for that purpose, whether they in fact have his permission or not'. Section 2(6) does not extend the category of visitors beyond the common-law definition—it merely extends the circumstances when a visitor will be owed the common-law duty of care by providing that visitors who enter for any purpose in the exercise of a right conferred by law are to be treated as permitted by the occupier to be there for that purpose.[11]

Whether the standard required by the common duty of care has been attained is a question of fact; but of course appellate courts will exercise their ordinary unrestricted power of reviewing inferences of fact[12]—and the important issues will be matters of inference rather than the finding of primary facts.

> The circumstances relevant for the present purpose include the degree of care, and of want of care, which would ordinarily be looked for in such a visitor, so that (for example) in proper cases—
>   (a) an occupier must be prepared for children to be less careful than adults; and

---

of the existing duty-situations would apply, then that action in general negligence may be relied on. Thus, in this case, a boy was electrocuted as a result of the negligent maintenance by the defendants of their overhead electric wires: held, although he was a trespasser, he could invoke the separate duty in negligence of a statutory undertaker supplying electric power to take care in the maintenance of that equipment.

9 Eg *Ward v Hertfordshire County Council* [1970] 1 All ER 535, CA: duties of local authority both as education authority and occupier considered when child hurt by playground flint wall, though defendants held not liable under either head because the wall was not dangerous.
10 Section 2(2).
11 *Greenhalgh v British Railways Board* [1969] 2 QB 286, [1969] 2 All ER 114, CA, especially LORD DENNING MR at 292–3.
12 See p 214, ante.

  (b) an occupier may expect that a person, in the exercise of his calling, will appreciate and guard against any special risks ordinarily incident to it, so far as the occupier leaves him free to do so.[13]

These two examples restate existing rules of common law, and therefore support the view that in deciding the countless issues of fact which will arise in applying the 'common duty of care' it will be proper to consider cases decided before the Act as guides (but certainly no more than guides) in interpreting the duty where no unambiguous rule is laid down in the Act itself.

The following common-law principles remain important. In deciding whether there is a danger, regard must be had to the physical and mental powers of a child visitor;[14] in short, what is not a danger to an adult may be a danger to a child. And this may be so because of the allurement or property of temptation, to a child, of some condition on the land.[15] In determining the standard of care owed to a child who is not accompanied by a guardian, it will be material to inquire whether, in the circumstances, the occupier could reasonably have expected the presence of the infant unaccompanied.[16]

The significance of section 2(3)(b) may be illustrated by decisions at common law concerning window cleaners. A window cleaner injured through the insecurity of some part of the exterior of the premises which he uses as a foothold or handhold for the purpose of cleaning the outside of the windows is expected by the occupier to have guarded against this special risk which is ordinarily incident to the calling of a window cleaner;[17] otherwise, if the window cleaner is injured through some defect in the staircase when going upstairs in the ordinary way to reach the windows on an upper floor.[18] Similarly, an occupier is entitled to expect that a chimney sweep will guard against dangers from flues.[19] But a self-employed plasterer injured when scaffolding collapsed beneath him recovered damages from the occupier. The risk was inherent in the defective state of the premises and not an expected risk of his employment as a plasterer.[20]

(ii) *Warning* At common law an occupier discharged his duty to a visitor by a warning sufficient to convey to the visitor full knowledge of the nature and

---

13 Section 2(3).
14 *Cooke v Midland Great Western Ry of Ireland* [1909] AC 229 at 238 (per LORD ATKINSON), HL; cf *Gough v National Coal Board* [1954] 1 QB 191, [1953] 2 All ER 1283, CA. The cases are legion but they all turn on their particular facts *eg Williams v Cardiff Corporation* [1950] 1 KB 514 [1950] 1 All ER 250 CA (a grassy slope with broken glass at the foot is a trap for a four-year-old child). The principle stated in the text also applied at common law in the case of idiots and the blind, and, it is submitted, will continue to apply to them under the Act.
15 Eg *Glasgow Corporation v Taylor* [1922] 1 AC 44, HL (brightly coloured poisoned berries in a park and within easy reach of the child).
16 *Phipps v Rochester Corporation* [1955] 1 QB 450, [1955] 1 All ER 129, containing an excellent review by DEVLIN J of the rights of child visitors. Applied in *Simkiss v Rhondda Borough Council* (1982) 81 LGR 460.
17 *Christmas v General Cleaning Contractors Ltd* [1952] 1 KB 141, [1952] 1 All ER 39, CA, affirmed on other grounds, [1953] AC 180, [1952] 2 All ER 1110, HL.
18 See *Bates v Parker* [1953] 2 QB 231, [1953] 1 All ER 768, CA Report, § 77(iii).
19 *Roles v Nathan* [1963] 2 All ER 908, CA. A factory occupier owes a lesser standard of care to a fireman trying to put out a fire than to his employees and has no duty to provide alternative escape facilities: *Bermingham v Sher Brothers* 1980 SLT 122, HL.
20 *Kealey v Heard* [1983] 1 All ER 973, [1983] 1 WLR 573.

extent of the danger. That rule is changed by section 2(4)(a) of the Act[1] which provides that

> ... where damage is caused to a visitor by a danger[2] of which he had been warned by the occupier, the warning is not to be treated without more[3] as absolving the occupier from liability, unless in all the circumstances it was enough to enable the visitor to be reasonably safe.

For example, the farmer who warns the veterinary surgeon whom he has summoned to the farm at night to attend a sick cow, 'Be careful how you go down the yard or you may fall into a tank', or the railway company which warns of the dangerous roof over what is the sole approach to the ticket office, no longer absolve themselves from liability by that warning alone. On the other hand, where a customer does not heed the warning of a shopkeeper not to go to the far end of the shop because there is a dangerous hole, it might presumably be held in all the circumstances that the common duty of care owed to him under the Act has been discharged. If the defendant does not know of the danger he cannot rely on section 2(4)(a), although he may still have a defence under section 2(1).[4]

(iii) *Assumption of risk*

> The common duty of care does not impose on an occupier any obligation to a visitor in respect of risks willingly accepted as his by the visitor (the question whether a risk is so accepted to be decided on the same principles as in other cases in which one person owes a duty of care to another).[5]

It has been seen earlier that according to the ordinary principles of negligence a defendant has broken no duty of care towards a plaintiff who has voluntarily assumed the risk:[6] This section makes it clear that this principle applies to the duty under the Act.

(iv) *Visitor's knowledge of the danger* At common law no duty of care was owed to a visitor who had full knowledge of the nature and extent of the danger.[7] Knowledge is not specifically mentioned as a relevant circumstance in determining whether the common duty of care has been discharged. But since the Act expressly provides that voluntary assumption of a risk discharges the duty of care, its silence about the effect of mere knowledge of the risk makes it clear that knowledge on the part of the visitor in itself no longer serves to discharge the duty of care. Yet the visitor's knowledge of the danger remains relevant in deciding whether in all the circumstances it was enough to enable him to be reasonably safe.[8]

(v) *Contributory negligence* Section 2(3) states that in deciding whether the occupier has discharged his common duty of care the want of care which would ordinarily be looked for in such a visitor is a relevant circumstance. It is clear therefore that the apportionment provisions of the Law Reform

1 And see *Roles v Nathan* [1963] 2 All ER 908, CA.
2 Does 'danger' mean the peril or the thing which creates the peril?
3 For examples of 'more,' see Newark, op cit, 212.
4 *White v Blackmore* [1972] 2 QB 651, [1972] 3 All ER 158, CA, and see p 269, post.
5 Section 2(5). But where the occupier occupies the premises for business purposes note s 2(3) of the Unfair Contract Terms Act 1977 ante at p 255 and post at p 269.
6 See p 248, ante.
7 *London Graving Dock Co Ltd v Horton* [1951] AC 737, [1951] 2 All ER 1; HL.
8 *Bunker v Charles Brand & Son Ltd* [1969] 2 QB 480, [1969] 2 All ER 59.

(Contributory Negligence) Act 1945 apply to an action for breach of the common-law duty of care exactly as to any other action for negligence or breach of statutory duty. Many cases under the 1957 Act have applied these apportionment provisions.[9]

(vi) *Liability for independent contractors*[10]

Where damage is caused to a visitor by a danger due to the faulty execution of any work of construction, maintenance or repair[11] by an independent contractor employed by the occupier, the occupier is not to be treated without more[12] as answerable for the danger if in all the circumstances he had acted reasonably in entrusting the work to an independent contractor[13] and had taken such steps (if any) as he reasonably ought in order to satisfy himself that the contractor was competent and that the work had been properly done.[14]

No doubt it will be reasonable to employ a contractor where, as in *Haseldine v Daw & Son Ltd*,[15] the work to be done necessitates special skill or equipment not possessed by the occupier; delegation should also be reasonable where it is the normal commercial practice to employ contractors, for example, for office cleaning. It is a question of fact, subject to the other provisions of section 2, whether an occupier who has employed an independent contractor has discharged his common duty of care.

(c) Some special cases within the Act

(i) *Fixed or movable structures*
Section 1(3), enacts that 'the rules so enacted in relation to an occupier of premises and his visitors shall also apply, in like manner and to the like extent as the principles applicable at common law to an occupier of premises and his invitees or licensees would apply, to regulate (a) the obligations of a

---

9 Eg *Bunker v Charles Brand & Son Ltd* [1969] 2 QB 480, [1969] 2 All ER 59.
10 See generally *Ferguson v Welsh* [1987] 3 All ER 777.
11 This expression is not wide enough to cover one circumstance which falls within the common duty of care (see p 261, ante): where an occupier arranges for another to use the premises for a purpose which involves a risk of harm to visitors. It is now uncertain what rules govern the liability of the occupier for acts of independent contractors in such a case. The expression covers work incidental to construction *AMF International Ltd v Magnet Bowling Ltd* [1968] 2 All ER 789, but does it extend to demolition? Yes. See *Ferguson v Welsh* [1987] 3 All ER 777 at 783, HL.
12 In *Coupland v Eagle Bros Ltd* (1969) 210 Estates Gazette 581, the plaintiff was electrocuted by a live wire which the electrical contractor had not switched off while carrying out electrical work. The occupier knew that the wire was dangerous and had not warned anyone; the 'without more' provision did not absolve him from liability, for he was concurrently careless with the contractor. Even though the cause of harm falls outside these words, eg the stowing of cargo by a stevedore, the defendant occupier of the premises may still discharge his common duty of care by relying on the stevedore as his independent contractor: *Mullis v US Lines Co* [1969] 1 Lloyd's Rep 109. This is because s 2(4) states that s 2(4)(b) is only an 'example' of duty of care.
13 In *Cook v Broderip* (1968) 206 Estates Gazette 128, a flat occupier was not liable to his domestic help who was injured because a contractor had negligently put a new switch fuse in the flat; he was entitled to trust the contractor.
14 Section 2(4)(b). The duty to supervise may extend to acts during the period of delegation and before the work is completed. In *AMF International Ltd v Magnet Bowling Ltd* [1968] 2 All ER 789, it was said that if the occupier is going to invite a third party to bring valuable property on to the site during construction, then to escape liability for negligence he may have to employ a supervising architect.
15 [1941] 2 KB 343, [1941] 3 All ER 156, CA.

person occupying or having control[16] over any fixed or movable structure, including any vessel, vehicle or aircraft'.

The expression 'movable structures' will cover such appliances as gangways and ladders, as well as any vessel, vehicle or aircraft: the criterion probably is whether one might go into or upon the 'structure'. It is, however, much more difficult to interpret the expression 'fixed structure', for 'fixed structure' of section 1(3) and 'premises' mentioned in section 1(1) must be mutually exclusive terms for the purpose of the Act. It is unlikely that 'premises' is confined to land only; it probably includes permanent buildings erected on the land. And yet 'fixed structures' must be taken to connote some non-movable chattels constructed on land. Perhaps the draftsmen doubted whether docks or erections on part of the land such as garden sheds or swings in a playground or even scaffolding or lifts were 'premises' and yet thought that movable structures might not cover them. Beyond doubt all these are within the Act, but it is important whether a structure falls within section 1(1) or section 1(3) because different duties of care may be owed under these respective subsections.

If A provides a defective ladder for his independent contractor to repair A's premises, the Act does not apply for the benefit of the injured contractor, for A has ceased to have enough control of the ladder to be an occupier of it.[17] Yet A may still be liable either as the bailor of goods or as an occupier of premises who intends that the plaintiff should use A's appliances on his land.[18]

The subsection clearly makes the common duty of care apply whenever before the Act the special duties to invitees or licensees in respect of the safety of the premises applied. It is doubtful whether the subsection does not also make the common duty of care apply to dangers due (1) to activities on the premises, and (2) to relations between occupiers and persons who are injured while outside the premises.[19]

(ii) *Damage to property*[20] Section 1(3), discussed in the preceding section, also regulates, in the same way as it has been seen to regulate fixed or movable structures,

> (b) the obligations of a person occupying or having control over any premises or structure in respect of damage to property, including the property of persons who are not themselves his visitors.

Of course this subsection will impose a duty on the occupier to prevent damage to goods on the premises arising from the defective physical condition of the premises—the injured man will be able to recover damages for his bloodstained clothes and presumably for damage to his property, even though

16 An engineering firm did not abandon control of a machine roller when they called in a specialist contractor to modify it, and so they retained the obligations of occupiers within section 1(3)(a), *Bunker v Charles Brand & Son Ltd* [1969] 2 QB 480, [1969] 2 All ER 59.
17 *Wheeler v Copas* [1981] 3 All ER 405.
18 *Wheeler v Copas* supra.
19 The subsection does not state to whom the duty is owed. The words 'in like manner' govern 'apply' not 'regulate'. Perhaps the displacement provision of section 1(1) has not been applied to section 1(3) so that the common-law duty may remain as an alternative. The task of giving a meaning to each phrase of this subsection seems almost insuperable.
20 See North, 30 *Conveyancing and Property Lawyer* (1966) 264.

he is uninjured.[21] If the entrant is carrying the goods of a third party, the Act does not appear to give the third party an action: its protection is confined to the entrant.[1] The expression 'damage to property' is not apt to cover loss of property so that the section will not cover the duty of boarding-house keepers to keep safe custody of visitors' goods—still less will it reverse the common-law decision that a publican owes no duty of care to prevent a customer's motor cycle from being stolen from the yard of the public house.[2] On the other hand it seems, consistent with what was said in the preceding section, that whenever the occupier at common law has a duty to prevent damage to goods on his land, whether due to the state of the premises or acts or omissions thereon, the common duty of care will apply.[3]

(iii) *Liability in contract*   At common law contracts for the use of premises were deemed to contain various implied terms relating to the safety of the premises.[4] In lieu[5] of those implied terms, section 5 enacts

(1) Where persons enter or use, or bring or send goods[6] to, any premises in exercise of a right conferred by contract with a person occupying or having control of the premises, the duty he owes them in respect of dangers due to the state of the premises or to things done or omitted to be done on them, in so far as the duty depends on a term to be implied in the contract by reason of its conferring that right, shall be the common duty of care.

(2) The foregoing subsection shall apply to fixed and movable structures as it applied to premises.

The section is not limited to defects in the condition of the premises, and covers damage to goods. Although an employer may be sued in contract by his workmen if he fails to take due care, it is submitted that the duty of the employer to provide safe premises for his workmen is an independent duty arising from tort, and does not depend on a term to be implied in the contract; therefore those duties are untouched by this section. Indeed it appears that all those who enter premises under a contract have the alternative of suing in tort under section 2(1) of the Act.[7]

An action based on this section is in contract, not in tort.[8]

Section 5(3) reads:

21 *AMF International Ltd v Magnet Bowling Ltd* [1968] 2 All ER 789, and including loss consequential on the damage to property, so that a car-hire firm could recover loss of earnings when their car was damaged.
 1 If the visitor's car is damaged he has a remedy, but not then his finance company if he has it on a credit agreement. He may still have a remedy although his finance company has not.
 2 *Tinsley v Dudley* [1951] 2 KB 18, [1951] 1 All ER 252. It would seem that, whatever the common-law position, the combined effect of s 1(3)(b) and s 1(1) is to deny the visitor a remedy for loss of property if she is injured and, say her valuable necklace falls off her person to be carried away in an adjoining stream.
 3 Supported by *AMF International Ltd v Magnet Bowling Ltd* note 21, ante.
 4 See especially *Francis v Cockerill* (1870) LR 5 QB 501; *Gillmore v London County Council* [1938] 4 All ER 331.
 5 The expression 'the duty ... shall be the common duty of care' shows that the duty replaces, and is not merely alternative to, the terms implied at common law.
 6 In contract under this section the owner of goods who does not enter the premises (eg a finance company which has made a car available on a credit agreement) may have a remedy; *cotra* the action in tort under the Act, note 1 above.
 7 *Sole v WJ Hallt Ltd* [1973] QB 574, [1973] 1 All ER 1032. Although P's contributory negligence would have barred his claim in contract, it merely reduced his damages on his tort claim under s 2(1); and see p 246, ante.
 8 For the consequences of this, see p 471, post.

This section does not affect the obligations imposed on a person by or by virtue of any contract for the hire of, or for the carriage for reward of persons or goods in any vehicle, vessel, aircraft or other means of transport, or by or by virtue of any contract of bailment.

Which existing obligations are imposed by or by virtue of a contract? For example a carrier at common law owed his passenger a duty of care in respect of the state of the vehicle, whether or not a contract was made between the two. It is submitted that if at common law the passenger could sue without founding his claim on the contract his rights in tort now rest on section 1(3)(a) of this Act and are not affected by this subsection. At common law there was held to be an implied term in the contract of a railway passenger that reasonable care would be taken to make the railway platform reasonably safe,[9] whereas the duty owed to other users of the platform was that owed in the ordinary way to invitees and licensees. Since fare-paying passengers use the platform by virtue of a contract of carriage the common-law implied term is preserved, whereas gratuitous users are owed the common duty of care.

(d) Exclusion of liability: the 1957 Act

Section 2(1) provides:

An occupier of premises owes the same duty, the 'common duty of care', to all his visitors, except in so far as he is free to and does extend, restrict, modify or exclude his duty to any visitor or visitors by agreement or otherwise.

The occupier thus had two options if he wished to modify the common duty of care owed to his visitors. Where the visitor entered by virtue of a contract, for example, contractors entering to carry out work on premises or tenants granted access to the common parts of a block of flats, an express term of the contract could be drafted to modify the common duty of care. In other cases a clear and unequivocal notice either affixed at the point of entry to the land,[10] or included in a programme or ticket giving access to the land[11] would suffice. The only major restriction in the 1957 Act on the occupier's freedom to modify, and in practice this will generally mean to exclude his duty, is to be found in section 3 of that Act.

At common law an exemption clause in a contract for the use of premises probably operated against persons not being parties to that contract who entered in pursuance of it. Section 3(1) provides that the duty of care owed by the occupier to such visitors as are 'strangers to the contract'[12] cannot be excluded or restricted by such a contract, but

(subject to any provision of the contract to the contrary) shall include the duty to perform his obligations under the contract, whether undertaken for their protection or not, in so far as those obligations go beyond the obligations otherwise involved in that duty.

Section 3(4) provides:

Where by terms or conditions governing any tenancy (including a statutory tenancy which does not in law amount to a tenancy) either the landlord or the tenant is bound, though not by contract, to permit persons to enter or use premises of which

9 *Protheroe v Railway Executive* [1951] 1 KB 376, [1950] 2 All ER 1093.
10 *Ashdown v Samuel Williams & Sons Ltd* [1957] 1 QB 409, [1957] 1 All ER 35.
11 *White v Blackmore* [1972] 2 QB 651, [1972] 3 All ER 158.
12 Defined as 'a person not for the time being entitled to the benefit of the contract as a party

he is the occupier, this section shall apply as if the tenancy were a contract between the landlord and the tenant.

Section 3(5) enacts:

This section, in so far as it prevents the common duty of care from being restricted or excluded, applies to contracts entered into and tenancies created before the commencement of this Act, as well as to those entered into or created after its commencement; but, in so far as it enlarges the duty owed by an occupier beyond the common duty of care, it shall have effect only in relation to obligations which are undertaken after that commencement or which are renewed by agreement (whether express or implied) after that commencement.

The most important effect of this section is that landlords of a block of flats or office, who continue to occupy common stairs, lifts and passages cannot in the leases exclude their liability for harm suffered by visitors of tenants while using that means of access in consequence of the breach by landlords of the common duty of care, even though they have effectively contracted out of liability to the tenants. Any obligation more stringent than the 'common duty of care' owed to the tenant, whether imposed by the lease or by a statute, may be invoked by the tenant's visitors as well as by the tenant unless the lease provides that its benefit shall be restricted to the tenant.

Section 3(2) enacts:

A contract shall not by virtue of this section have the effect, unless it expressly so provides, of making an occupier who has taken all reasonable care answerable to strangers to the contract for dangers due to the faulty execution of any work of construction, maintenance or repair or other like operation by persons other than himself, his servants and persons acting under his direction and control.

But for this subsection the burden of the defendant under section 3 would have greatly exceeded the common duty of care because he would have been unable to delegate to independent contractors any part of his duty to take care.[13]

The relevance of section 3 is much reduced now because, as we shall see, the Unfair Contract Terms Act 1977 drastically reduces the freedom of a person who occupies premises for business purposes to exclude or restrict liability. The occupier in most if not all of the circumstances likely to be covered by section 3 of the 1957 Act will be an occupier for 'business purposes'.

(e) Exclusion of liability: the Unfair Contract Terms Act 1977[14]

The Unfair Contract Terms Act 1977 renders invalid any contract term or notice purporting to exclude or restrict liability for death or personal injury[15]

to it or as the successor by assignment or otherwise of a party to it, and accordingly includes a party to the contract who has ceased to be so entitled' (s 3(3)).

13 The duty in respect of independent contractors now imposed by sections 3(1) and (2) (see p 264, ante) is not exactly the same as the common duty of care imposed by section 2(4)(b). First, section 3(2) limits the liability not only in respect of, as in section 2(4)(b), 'the faulty execution of any work of construction, maintenance or repair' but additionally in respect of any 'other like operation'. Secondly, whereas section 2(4)(b) specifies in detail what would be reasonable care by the occupier in relation to the conduct of the independent contractor, section 3(2) states that he shall take 'all reasonable care' without further particularising this standard—it cannot be assumed that the two standards are identical.

14 See generally ante at p 254.

15 Section 2(1).

resulting from breach of the common duty of care under the 1957 Act where the premises are occupied for the business purposes of the occupier.[16] In the case of other loss or damage any attempted contract term or notice restricting or excluding liability is subject to the requirement of reasonableness.[17] Agreement to or knowledge of the term or notice will not be evidence that the visitor has assumed the risk of injury giving rise to the defence of *volenti non fit injuria.*[18]

The 1977 Act then quite clearly leaves me free via a notice on my front gate to exclude liability to most of my visitors.[19] Its remit is limited to business purposes[20] and it is the purposes of the occupier alone which are relevant. Some cases are clear. Consider *Ashdown v Samuel Williams & Sons Ltd.*[1]

> By licence of the defendants the plaintiff crossed the defendants' land. A notice board purported to curtail the liabilities of the defendants to licensees. The Court of Appeal held that because the defendants had taken reasonable steps to bring the conditions of the notice to the licensee these conditions (which were interpreted by the court to exclude liability for damage sustained in the way in which the plaintiff's injuries were caused) excluded the defendants' liability in the same way as conditions in a contract (eg the 'ticket' cases), which the defendant has taken reasonable steps to bring to the notice of the other party, exclude liability.

If that case arose since 1977 the defendant could not exclude his liability under the Occupiers' Liability Act. But what if the facts of *White v Blackmore*[2] were repeated now? Notices at the entrance to the track and in the programme handed to spectators and competitors excluded liability for injuries occurring in 'jalopy' races. The races were being run to raise money for charity. In 1972 the notices sufficed to exclude the organisers' and occupiers' liability. Was the track occupied for business purposes? Is a Sunday School within the 1977 Act when a bazaar or jumble sale is being held there, but not on Sunday mornings? Are churches and synagogues occupied for business purposes? What of the housewife who does some part-time hairdressing at home and whose customer is hurt coming downstairs from the bathroom?

The only further attempt at clarification of the definition of 'business purposes' is to be found in section 2 of the Occupiers' Liability Act 1984. That particular section amends the Unfair Contract Terms Act to provide:

> but liability of an occupier of premises for breach of an obligation or duty toward a person obtaining access to the premises for recreational or educational purposes, being liability for loss or damage suffered by reason of the dangerous state of premises is not a business liability of the occupier unless granting that person such access for the purposes concerned falls within the business purposes of the occupier.

The purpose of this tortuously worded provision appears to be to allow farmers and owners of countryside areas to exclude liability to daytrippers. The land is occupied for 'business purposes', farming or forestry, but any

---

16 Section 1(1)(c).
17 Section 2(2).
18 Section 2(3).
19 But when I invite students for a tutorial party, or a postgraduate for a supervision at home, do I then occupy my home for 'business purposes'?
20 Section 14 defines business so as to include a profession and the activities of any government department or public or local authority.
1 [1957] 1 QB 409, [1957] 1 All ER 35.
2 [1972] 2 QB 651, [1972] 3 All ER 158.

duty owed to entrants coming to the land to picnic and so on can now once again be excluded by agreement or notice. But the confused wording of the section may result in it having more widespread implications.[3]

B.　LIABILITY TO UNINVITED ENTRANTS

Liability to trespassers and all other uninvited entrants is now regulated by section 1 of the Occupiers' Liability Act 1984.[4] The Act provides that section 1:

> shall have effect in place of the rules of common law[5] to determine—
> (a) whether any duty is owed by a person as occupier of premises to persons other than his visitors in respect of any risk of their suffering injury on the premises by reason of any danger due to the state of the premises or to things done or omitted to be done on them.
> (b) if so, what that duty is

It seems that the intention of the Act was to limit liability towards trespassers to liability for personal injuries only. Section 1(8) expressly provides that a breach of duty under the Act does not result in liability for 'any loss of or damage to property. But as section 1(1)(a) expressly replaces only the rules of common law regarding injury, common law liability for damage to trespassers'[6] and other uninvited entrants' properly survives the 1984 Act.[7]

A duty to uninvited entrants in respect of any danger due to the state of the premises arises only when three conditions are met:[8]

1 The occupier must be aware of the danger or have reasonable grounds to believe it exists.
2 He knew or had reasonable grounds to know that the uninvited entrant either was or might come into the vicinity of the danger.
3 The risk of injury to an uninvited entrant resulting from that danger was one against which in all the circumstances of the case the occupier might reasonably be expected to offer the uninvited entrant some protection.

The circumstances of the case will clearly include the nature of the entrant's presence on the premises and the entrant's age and capabilities. Burglars can reasonably demand little or no protection. Occupiers aware that children often trespass on the land will be expected to offer some protection to those children however mischievous they may be.[9]

Other relevant circumstances may arguably include personal characteristics

---

3　See Bragg and Brazier (1986) 130 Sol Jo 251 and 274.
4　The Act is based on proposals from the Law Commission Report No 75 'Liability for Damage or Injury to Trespassers and Related Questions of Occupiers' Liability', Cmnd 6428.
5　For the common law rules see *British Railways Board v Herrington* [1972] AC 877, [1972] 1 All ER 749.
6　That such common law liability did arise on the principle in *British Railways Board v Herrington* (supra) see *Tutton v A D Walter Ltd* [1986] QB 61, [1985] 3 All ER 757 (liability for negligently spraying crops so as to kill neighbour's bees: the judge held that the bees were probably not trespassers but that liability to their keeper arose even if the bees were trespassing).
7　See *Clerk & Lindsell* para 12–27.
8　Section 1(3).
9　See M Jones (1984) 47 MLB, 713.

of the occupier. What are his financial resources? Could he afford to eliminate the danger? But subjective factors cannot be taken too far. Section 1(4) provides in terms reminiscent of section 2(2) of the 1957 Act:

> Where ... an occupier of premises owes a duty to another in respect of such a risk, the duty is to take such care as is reasonable in all the circumstances of the case to see that he [the uninvited entrant] does not suffer injury on the premises by reason of the danger concerned

One significant difference from the common duty of care is provided for in section 1(5). Any duty arising under the 1984 Act can ...

> ... in an appropriate case, be discharged by taking such steps as are reasonable in all the circumstances of the case to give warning of the danger concerned or to discourage a person from incurring risk.[10]

The warning does not have to be sufficient to enable the uninvited entrant to remain safely on the land. If the occupier of a building site with dangerous concealed trenches puts up notices[11] around the perimeter of the site 'DANGER: KEEP OUT: CONCEALED TRENCHES', that warning would be insufficient to discharge his liability to visitors. In 'an appropriate case' those notices would discharge his responsibility to trespassers. But what if the trespassers were small children from an adjoining primary school?

C. COMMON LAW LIABILITY AND ACTIVITIES ON LAND

Of course an occupier who intentionally harms a person whom he has permitted to be on his premises is answerable. Regardless of whether the plaintiff has an alternative remedy under the Act of 1957, it is probably safe now to generalise that an occupier owes a duty of care not to conduct activities on his land foreseeably likely to harm persons other than trespassers of whose presence he ought to be aware.[12]

Should the words used to cover the 'activity duty' in the 1957 Act be insufficient to embrace all activities on land, then presumably so are the identical words used to define the duty to trespassers in the 1984 Act. In that case then the 'activity duty' to trespassers presumably remains the duty of 'common humanity' enunciated by the House of Lords in *British Railways Board v Herrington*.[13]

The following cases illustrate typical acts within ordinary negligence. In *Gallagher v Humphrey*:[14]

> Through the negligent maintenance of a crane by the defendant occupier, goods carried by it fell on the plaintiff, whom the defendant had permitted to be on the land.

10 And see s 1(5) on applicability of *volenti*.
11 The Unfair Contract Terms Act 1977 probably does not apply to the duty created by the Occupiers' Liability Act 1984.
12 In *Chettle v Denton* (1951) 95 Sol Jo 802, the defendant, while shooting game on private land, hit the plaintiff, a licensee on the land. The defendant was held liable in negligence in that he would have seen the plaintiff if he had taken reasonable care.
13 [1972] AC 877, [1972] 1 All ER 749; and see *Tutton v A D Walter Ltd* [1986] QB 61, [1985] 3 All ER 757 (duty to 'trespassing' bees).
14 (1862) 6 LT 684.

Holding the defendant liable in negligence, COCKBURN CJ said:[15]

> The grantee must use the permission as the thing exists. It is a different question, however, where negligence on the part of the person granting the permission is super-added.

In 1966 the Privy Council held in *Railways Commissioner v McDermott* that a railway body was liable in negligence for not taking reasonable care to make a level crossing safe.[16] Similarly, the plaintiff, who, having seen off friends on a train, was injured by the open door of the guard's van as the train moved away from the platform, was owed a duty of reasonable care by the railway company although he was only a licensee, and was entitled to sue in negligence.[17] Likewise, where hospitals are negligently administered,[18] or schools badly supervised,[19] the liability is in ordinary negligence. It follows from what has been said above that the setting in motion of machinery also may be within the ambit of these acts of misfeasance.[20]

D. COMMON LAW RULES AND MOVABLE STRUCTURES

Common-law rules relating to the duties of occupiers of premises have ordinarily been held to extend to movable structures. Consequently, the question arises whether a trespasser on a vehicle driven by the servant of the owner of the vehicle, and of whose presence the driver is aware, can sue in ordinary negligence or whether he is subject to the special rules about trespassers injured by defective premises. In *Conway v George Wimpey & Co Ltd*[1] the Court of Appeal held (counsel having conceded that, if the plaintiff were a trespasser, he lost the case) that he was a trespasser and therefore failed. It is submitted that this is erroneous—the injury was sustained not by reason of any defect in the lorry but because of the negligent way in which it was driven.[2] In that event, as DENNING LJ rightly held in *Young v Edward Box & Co Ltd*,[3] the liability of the defendant rests on whether the driver drove the vehicle negligently within the scope and in the course of his employment—

---

15 At 685. Perhaps the clearest statement of the rule is *Tolhausen v Davies* (1888) 57 LJQB 392 at 394–5, Div Ct; affd, 58 LJQB 98, CA.

16 [1967] AC 169, [1966] 2 All ER 162, PC; *Thomas v British Railways Board* [1976] QB 912, [1976] 3 All ER 15.

17 *Thatcher v Great Western Ry Co* (1893) 10 TLR 13, CA. In *Dunster v Abbott* [1953] 2 All ER 1572, CA, a canvasser when leaving premises in the dark was injured, allegedly because the defendant occupier turned off a light too soon. This was held to be a problem in general negligence, not of invitees/licensees.

18 Eg *Collins v Hertfordshire County Council* [1947] KB 598, [1947] 1 All ER 633; and *Cassidy v Ministry of Health* [1951] 2 KB 343, [1951] 1 All ER 574, CA.

19 Eg *Rich v London County Council* [1953] 2 All ER 376, CA; *Jauffar v Akhbar* (1984) Times, 10 February (negligent parental supervision); *Slade v Battersea and Putney Group Hospital Management Committee* [1955] 1 All ER 429; and *Slater v Clay Cross Co Ltd* [1956] 2 QB 264, [1956] 2 All ER 625, CA (plaintiff hit by train while walking in a tunnel through which defendants knew persons habitually allowed to pass). Cf *Thompson v Bankstown Municipal Council* (1953) 87 CLR 619 (H Ct Australia).

20 *Excelsior Wire Rope Co Ltd v Callan* [1930] AC 404, [1930] All ER Rep 1, HL; but not the continued running of a moving staircase; *Hardy v Central London Ry Co* [1920] 3 KB 459, CA.

1 [1951] 2 KB 266, [1951] 1 All ER 363, CA; cf *Twine v Bean's Express Ltd* [1946] 1 All ER 202.

2 This vital fact is not stated in the Law Reports—see [1950] 2 All ER 331 at 332.

3 [1951] 1 TLR 789.

the ordinary rules of negligence and no others apply, except where the injury is caused by the defective condition of the vehicle.

It will be recalled that the view has been expressed earlier that it is an open question to what extent these rules remain unaffected by the Occupiers' Liability Act 1957.[4]

E. LIABILITY TO THOSE OUTSIDE THE PREMISES

The risk created by dangers caused by the defective state of premises is not confined to entrants to those premises. Slates falling from roofs, crumbling walls, and dangerous activities carried out on premises are just a few examples of risks as likely to endanger passers by on the highway, or persons on adjoining premises, as to injure persons actually on the occupier's premises. The circumstances in which a duty of care is owed to such persons by the occupier of premises must therefore be briefly considered.

As will be seen,[5] an action in nuisance, derived from public nuisance, often lies at the instance of those injured on a highway as a result of harmful conditions on adjoining land. Because of this historical anomaly, in a large number of situations a plaintiff may now sue either in negligence or in nuisance (or, as often happens, in both) for personal injuries; and yet the law is the same whichever tort is relied on. So, in several House of Lords cases, it has been a matter of indifference whether the case was decided in negligence or in nuisance, both of which were pleaded.[6] Often, it seems quite fortuitous which tort is relied on: if, for instance, some act of negligent omission stands out, the claim will often be negligence. *Holling v Yorkshire Traction Co Ltd* is a typical example.[7]

> The defendants emitted so much steam and smoke on to the highway from their adjoining factory that the view was obscured and two vehicles collided, killing the plaintiff, who was on the highway. It was held to be negligence on the part of the defendant to fail to post a man at each end of the affected area. They were also held liable in nuisance.

There is, then, no doubt that the ordinary principles of negligence can be applied where highway users are injured became of harmful operations being carried out there.[8]

TO THOSE ON ADJOINING PREMISES

Similarly occupiers are under a general duty to take reasonable care to prevent dangers on their premises damaging persons or property on adjoining premises.[9] This is so whether the danger arises from disrepair on the premises,

4 See p 260, ante.
5 See ch 19, post.
6 *Longhurst v Metropolitan Water Board* [1948] 2 All ER 834, HL; *Caminer v Northern and London Investment Trust Ltd* [1951] AC 88, [1950] 2 All ER 486; *Bolton v Stone* [1951] AC 850, [1951] 1 All ER 1078. Sometimes it is not clear on which tort a judgment is based, eg DENNING LJ in *Mint v Good* [1951] 1 KB 517 at 526, [1950] 2 All ER 1159 at 1168, CA.
7 [1948] 2 All ER 662; cf *Wheeler v Morris* (1915) 84 LJKB 1435.
8 Eg *Hilder v Associated Portland Cement Manufacturers Ltd* [1961] 3 All ER 709, [1961] 1 WLR 1434 (defendant occupiers of field allowed children to play football there; liable to motor-cyclist who, when driving along adjoining highway, was knocked off his machine by a ball kicked by the children from the field).
9 *Hughes v Percival* (1883) 8 App Cas 443: the premises for the benefit of which the present rule applies are those in respect of which someone other than the defendant has a vested interest in possession.

or some natural or man made hazard, for example, fire caused by lightning striking a tree.[10] It has recently been held that where adjoining properties have mutual rights of support, negligently allowing a property to fall into dereliction so as to damage the adjoining premises is actionable in negligence as well as in nuisance.[11] There are two issues of particular difficulty affecting the duties of care owed *inter se* by occupiers of adjoining premises.

First, where a plaintiff tenant sues his landlord for damage resulting from the defective state of repair of premises retained by the landlord the case-law is confused. In *Cunard v Antifyre*[12]

> Some defective roofing and guttering, which formed part of the premises retained by the defendant landlord, fell into a part of the premises let by him to do the plaintiff tenant. As a result, his wife was injured and his goods were damaged. Damages in general negligence were awarded to both the tenant and his wife.

Yet, in *Cheater v Cater*,[13] the Court of Appeal had held that a landlord, who had let a field to a tenant at a time when there was a yew tree on the adjoining premises retained by the landlord, was not liable in negligence when the tenant's horse died through eating leaves from that tree which was then in the same state as at the date of the lease. Then, the Court of Appeal in *Shirvell v Hackwood Estates Co Ltd*[14] doubted *Cunard v Antifyre* and held that a workman of a tenant could not recover in negligence from the landlord whose tree on adjoining land fell on him. The facts in *Taylor v Liverpool Corpn* were:[15]

> The plaintiff, the daughter of a tenant of one of the defendant landlords' flats, was injured by the fall of a chimney stack belonging to these flats into the yard adjoining the premises. The landlords had negligently maintained this chimney, which formed part of the building retained by them.

STABLE J found for the plaintiff in negligence, following *Cunard v Antifyre*, and distinguishing *Cheater v Cater* on the ground that the tenant had there impliedly agreed to take the risk in respect of danger existing on the premises at that time, and treating the observations in *Shirvell*'s case as *obiter* on the ground that no negligence had in any event occurred. The principle in *Cunard v Antifyre* would seem to be preferable to one which affords landlords blanket immunity in respect of retained premises in disrepair.[16]

The second area of difficulty in delimiting the duty owed by an occupier to those on adjoining premises relates to damage inflicted on those adjoining

---

10 *Goldman v Hargrave* [1907] 1 AC 645, [1966] 2 All ER 989. Water normally percolates from the defendant's land to the plaintiff's, and the defendant pumps out the water from his land, and by so stopping the subterranean flow causes settlement damage to the plaintiff's land, the plaintiff has no remedy, because the defendant has no duty to adjoining occupiers in respect of percolating water; *Langbrook Properties Ltd v Surrey County Council* [1969] 3 All ER 1424, [1970] 1 WLR 161.

11 *Bradburn v Lindsay* [1983] 2 All ER 408.

12 [1933] 1 KB 551; the principle on which this case was based was approved *obiter* by PARCQ J in *Bishop v Consolidated London Properties Ltd* (1933) 102 LJKB 257 at 262.

13 [1918] 1 KB 247, CA (not cited in *Cunard v Antifyre*).

14 [1938] 2 KB 577 at 594–5 (per GREER LJ), [1938] 2 All ER 1, CA.

15 [1939] 3 All ER 329.

16 It is submitted that the Court of Appeal in *Shirvell*'s case wrongly thought that the decisions where a landlord, having no control of the defective premises, had been held not liable, applied in the case before them: see pp 279–80, post.

premises by third parties. No duty will generally[17] be found to lie where damage is inflicted on a neighbour's property by vandals or burglars even though the wrongdoers' conduct may have been facilitated by disrepair or lax security on the part of the occupier.[18] This is in line with the general reluctance on the part of the courts to impose on a person, who has no special relationship with a third party, liability for the conduct of that party.[19]

SECTION 2.   LIABILITY OF NON-OCCUPIERS

The development of liability for the defective state of premises resulting from the acts or omissions of persons other than the occupier, builder, owners and landlords, for example, has proceeded piecemeal. It has been bedevilled by two problems. First, at common law until very recently there was judicial reluctance to apply the neighbour principle in *Donoghue v Stevenson* to real property as well as chattels. Second, the existence in a number of cases of a potential contractual remedy was taken to exclude tortious liability, even where the individual injured was unable to take advantage of the contractual remedy because he was not a party to the relevant contract, for example, a wife injured by falling masonry in a house leased by her husband when she was not a party to the contract of tenancy with the landlord. An attempt will be made to survey the current state of liability of the non-occupier discussing separately the liability of different classes of defendants.[20]

A. THE DEFECTIVE PREMISES ACT 1972

The Defective Premises Act 1972 section 1 imposes on any 'person taking on work for or in connection with the provision of a dwelling' a strict liability to ensure that the work he takes on is 'done in a workmanlike, or, as the case may be professional manner, with proper materials and so that as regards that work the dwelling will be fit for habitation when completed.' Thus a builder, who reasonably believing that his materials were suitable, for example, used asbestos in roofing materials at a time before the dangers of asbestos were appreciated would still be in breach of his duty under section 1. Section 1 covers all those involved in building new homes, contractors, architects and developers[1] as well as builders. Alas, while splendid in theory, section 1 is in practice more or less a dead letter.[2] First, houses built under the National House-Building Council scheme, and covered by a National House Building Registration Council Certificate are exempted from the regime of strict liability created by section 1. Most new houses built are

---

17 In *Perl (Exporters) Ltd v Camden London Borough Council* [1984] QB 342, [1983] 3 All ER 161 the Court of Appeal did not entirely rule out *special* circumstances which might give rise to such a duty to adjoining occupiers.
18 *Maloco v Littlewoods Organisation Ltd* [1987] AC 241, [1987] 2 WLR 480, HL.
19 See ante at pp 169–171 et seq.
20 For fuller treatment of the matters touched on here see Holyoak and Allen *Civil Liability for Premises*.
1 See s 1(3) (including local authorities).
2 See Spencer 'The Defective Premises Act 1972—Defective Law and Defective Law Reform' [1974] CLJ 307 and [1975] CLJ 48.

erected within the NHBC scheme.[3] Second, the limitation period begins to run as soon as the dwelling is completed.[4] Whereas in an action for negligence now, by virtue of the Latent Damage Act 1986,[5] the limitation period begins to run only when the plaintiff should reasonably have known of the relevant damage subject to a long-stop of fifteen years after which any action in respect of property damage is banned completely. Defects in timbers, foundations and other parts of the fabric of a building rarely become apparent for several years.

Other provisions of the Defective Premises Act, in sections 3 and 4, concerning the survival of a duty of care after disposal of a duty of care after disposal of the premises, and landlords' duties of care where there is an obligation to repair are, as we shall see, rather more useful in practice.

B. BUILDERS AND CONTRACTORS WHO ARE NOT LANDOWNERS

There is no doubt now that a builder or contractor, who is not a landowner, erecting buildings on land, or making installations in buildings, or carrying out work of conversion or repair, or demolishing premises or parts of premises,[6] owes a duty of care to subsequent occupiers of the premises and to their visitors and probably to trespassers as well where the trespasser's presence is reasonably foreseeable.[7] Any general exemption from a duty of care in respect of real property did not survive the judgment of the House of Lords in *A C Billings & Sons Ltd v Riden*:[8]

> B Ltd, building contractors, were employed to make alterations to the front part of a house. In the course of this work B Ltd failed to take reasonable care to make access to the house safe: in consequence R, a visitor, was injured when leaving the house during the hours of darkness. B Ltd were held liable in negligence.[9]

Later judgments confirm that the original builders of a property are liable for negligent construction of that property, to subsequent occupiers and their visitors to that property, just as are contractors later doing work on a completed building.[10] In *Batty v Metropolitan Property Realisations Ltd.*[11]

---

3 See s 2 and SI 1979 No 381.
4 See for an example of the theoretical scope of s 1 made futile by the limitation provisions; *Rimmer v Liverpool City Council* [1984] 1 All ER 930, CA.
5 See post at p 507.
6 *Miller v South Scotland Electricity Board* 1958 SC 20 (HL).
7 Where the builder or contractor is also the occupier at the relevant time his duty to trespassers will be regulated by the Occupiers' Liability Act 1984. In other circumstances ordinary principles of negligence apply; *Railways Comr v Quinlan* [1964] AC 1054, [1964] 1 All ER 897; *Miller v South Scotland Electricity Board* (supra) (defendants liable to child trespasser when they carelessly disconnected electricity in a building about to be demolished so that child suffered a shock from a live cable).
8 [1958] AC 240, [1957] 3 All ER 1.
9 Overruling earlier cases that liability was limited to installations or repairs of things dangerous in themselves eg *Ball v LCC* [1949] 2 KB 159, [1949] 1 All ER 1056.
10 *Gallagher v N McDowell Ltd* [1961] NI 26; *Sharpe v Sweeting & Sons Ltd* [1963] 2 All ER 455, [1963] 1 WLR 665, CA.
11 [1978] QB 554, [1978] 2 All ER 445, CA.

A builder, together with a development company which owned the land, inspected it, and despite its steep slope to a stream decided that it was safe for house building. The builder erected the houses, and the development company sold them. Three years after the plaintiff bought one from the company there was a severe landslip on adjoining land. The court found that the house was doomed because within 10 years its foundations would slip down the hill. The builder conceded that he owed a duty of care to the purchaser from the company. The court rejected his argument that his duty did not extend to land adjoining the plaintiff's or to defects discoverable only by investigating subsoil. The plaintiff had already suffered sufficient damage to found an action because there was imminent danger to health or safety of occupants.

C. LANDOWNERS

It used to be the case that at common law owners of premises were never liable in respect of defects on the premises once they had disposed of the premises. There was no duty not to sell or let a tumbledown house.[12] Any remedy lay in contract. The bulk of that inequitable principle deriving from the old maxim *caveat emptor* has now been eroded by judicial pronouncement on the liability of owner-builders and developers[13] and by the Defective Premises Act 1972, section 3.

First, a '... landowner who designs or builds a house or flat is no more immune from personal responsibility for faults of construction than a building contractor, or from personal responsibility than an architect, simply because he has disposed of his house or flat by selling or letting'.[14] But this principle covers only negligence in the original construction of the building, not inadequate repairs or maintenance by the original owner and vendor.

Section 3 of the Defective Premises Act goes further providing that where 'work of construction, repair, maintenance or demolition or any other work is done on or in relation to premises, any duty of care owed because of the doing of the work to persons who might reasonably be expected to be affected by defects in the state of the premises by the doing of the work shall not be abated by the subsequent disposal of the premises by the person who owed the duty'. Thus a botched up job in repairing floorboards will create liability to visitors while the owner remains the occupier, and that liability will survive for the benefit of subsequent occupiers and their visitors when the owner sells or lets the house.

But section 3 is not comprehensive. It does not cover all possible sources of danger on premises particularly those caused by omissions. Leaving dangerous refuse on premises, failing to remedy or warn the subsequent occupier of a ruinous defect existing before the vendor came into occupation are probably not covered by the words used in section 3, 'work of construction, repair, maintenance[15] or demolition or any other work'. Thus the

---

12 *Otto v Bolton and Norris* [1936] 2 KB 46, [1936] 1 All ER 960 (sale) *Cavalier v Pope* [1906] AC 428 (letting).
13 *Anns v Merton London Borough Council* [1978] AC 728, [1977] 2 All ER 492, HL; *Dutton v Bognor Regis UDC* [1972] 1 QB 373, [1972] 1 All ER 462, CA; *Batty v Metropolitan Realizations Ltd* (supra), CA.
14 *Rimmer v Liverpool City Council* [1984] 1 All ER 930 at 938.
15 Could *omissions* to remove or repair pre-existing defects be caught by this word 'maintenance'?

common law principle that there is no duty as such not to sell or let a ruinous house probably survives albeit much attenuated. Only the House of Lords can finally take up LORD DENNING's invitation in *Dutton v Bognor Regis UDC*[16] that the old cases should be comprehensively overruled.[17]

D. PROFESSIONAL ADVISERS

The strict liability imposed by section 1 of the Defective Premises Act 1972 in respect of the construction of buildings is equally incumbent on architects and other professionals involved in the design of the building as upon the building contractors. Additionally those professionals owe a duty of care to any person who may be injured on the site in the course of the building work,[18] and to subsequent occupiers of the premises in respect of both their personal safety and damage to the property itself.[19] On subsequent disposal of the premises surveyors engaged to inspect the property will be liable for any failure to value the property competently or to discover and report on relevant defects on the property.[20] Where the surveyor has been engaged by the building society contemplating financing the plaintiff's house purchase he will generally be liable, not only to his client, the society, but also to the purchasers where they have relied on his survey, rather than commissioned an independent surveyor.[1] But where a surveyor is expressly commissioned only to value property he is not under any duty to report on defects generally or advise on possible difficulties with re-sale of the property.[2]

E. LOCAL AUTHORITIES

Local authorities owe duties to tenants and subsequent purchasers of local authority dwellings as builders and contractors. So in *Rimmer v Liverpool County Council* the defendants were held liable to a council tenant injuring himself when he fell against a negligently thin glass panel and the glass shattered. But additionally local authorities may also be liable in respect of their function of inspecting and approving building work done by builders and contractors in the private sector. When houses are built defectively, those defects often do not become evident for many years. The typical case is defective foundations which ultimately result in subsidence. By the time the loss is suffered and known, the builder may well be in liquidation, or untraceable. Not surprisingly, victims have turned increasingly for a remedy against the local authority, whose building inspector may have authorised

---

16　[1972] 1 QB 373 at 394.

17　Eg *Otto v Bolton and Norris* (supra).

18　In *Clay v A J Crump & Sons Ltd* [1964] 1 QB 533, [1963] 3 All ER 687, CA, an architect was held liable for directing a wall to be left standing during demolition whereupon it collapsed on the plaintiff who was working on the site; the court rejected the argument that the architect's only duty was his contractual one to his employer; followed in *Driver v William Willett (Contractors) Ltd* [1969] 1 All ER 665 (consulting engineer liable to workman for failing to advise builder about unsafe hoist which caused plaintiff's injuries).

19　See Dugdale and Stanton *Professional Negligence*.

20　M Brazier (1976) 40 Conv (NS) 179; (1981) 45 Conv (NS) 96.

1　*Yianni v Edwin Evans & Sons* [1982] QB 438, [1981] 3 All ER 592.

2　*Sutcliffe v Sayer* [1987] 1 EGLR 155.

the defective construction. In *Dutton v Bognor Regis UDC*[3] a local authority, when its building inspector negligently and erroneously certified that a new house complied with its byelaws on foundations, was held liable to a subsequent buyer of the house for the damage two years later to the house caused by subsidence. In a similar case of an inspector's negligence, the House of Lords in *Anns v Merton London Borough Council* confirmed the decisions in *Dutton*'s case[4] albeit adopting a somewhat different line of reasoning.[5] The duty owed by the local authority is, however, a duty limited to taking care to protect the health and safety of owner occupiers. Thus developers, at any rate commercial organisations with access to independent professional advice[6] will not be able to recover their economic loss[7] if negligence by the local authority facilitates the erection of defective buildings which either do not sell or result in the developers being held liable to purchasers for the relevant defects.

F. LANDLORDS

The liability of landlords for defects arising from disrepair on premises let by them was originally largely limited to contractual liability. A person other than the tenant had no remedy even if the landlord was in breach of a contractual duty to carry out maintenance and repairs. And like vendors he owed no duty in respect of defects arising before the tenancy was granted. As we have seen, landlords are now liable just like anyone else for negligent installations or repairs in premises let by them.[8] That tortious liability covers tenants, their families and others injured on the premises.

Section 4 of the Defective Premises Act creates important new duties in respect of landlords under an obligation[9] to carry out repairs or maintenance on the premises, or who are empowered to carry out repairs.[10] A landlord owes to all persons who might reasonably be expected to be affected by defects in the state of the premises a duty to take such care as is reasonable in all the circumstances to see that they are reasonably safe from personal injury or from damage to their property caused by relevant defects. The landlord is liable although he did not know of the defect, if he ought to have known.[11] A defect is relevant if it is one in the state of the premises arising from, or continuing because of, an act or omission by the landlord which

---

3 [1972] 1 QB 373, [1972] 1 All ER 462.
4 [1978] AC 728, [1977] 2 All ER 492, HL.
5 In order to tackle the difficult question of liability for exercise of statutory powers, see ante at p 165.
6 It remains open whether a builder who lacked independent advice might have a cause of action against the authority: *Cynat Products Ltd v Landbuild Ltd* [1984] 3 All ER 513; *Investors in Industry Commercial Properties Ltd v South Bedfordshire DC* [1986] QB 1034, [1986] 1 All ER 787.
7 *Governors of the Peabody Donation Fund v Sir Lindsay Parkinson & Co Ltd* [1985] AC 210, [1983] 3 All ER 417; see ante at pp 183–5 where the topic is treated more fully.
8 *Rimmer v Liverpool City Council* (supra).
9 This includes statutory obligations.
10 Section 4(4). This extension to the case where the tenant cannot legally insist on a repair but where the landlord has a power to repair is important in view of cases like *Mint v Good* [1951] 1 KB 517, [1950] 2 All ER 1159, CA, which decides that landlords of small houses let on periodic tenancies, have such a power.
11 Section 4(2).

constitutes or would if he had had notice of the defect, have constituted a failure by him to carry out his obligation to the tenant for the maintenance or repair of the premises.[12] The duty is wide; it extends towards trespassers, and towards those outside the premises, and it applies where the landlord merely has a right to enter to carry out maintenance or repairs.

Despite these substantial increases in liability of non-occupiers some gaps remain. If an owner knows of a defect (not created by him) in his premises before he sells or lets them but neither repairs it nor gives warning of the defect the Act imposes no liability on him for harm which results after he has disposed of them by sale or lease as the case may be, and there is no liability at common law.[13] A landlord who fails to repair where he has no obligation or power to do so has no liability either under the Act or at common law.

12 Section 4(3).
13 *Cavalier v Pope* [1906] AC 428, HL; *Bromley v Mercer* [1922] 2 KB 126; *Davis v Foots* [1940] 1 KB 116, [1939] 4 All ER 4, CA (although because of housing legislation this case would now be decided differently the principle is unaffected).

Chapter 17

Employers' liability to their employees

The risk of personal injury either suffered in an accident at work, or by contracting an industrial disease, is particularly acute in certain types of employment. And naturally employees will look to their employers for compensation for injuries inflicted by carelessness of the employer or of fellow employees. As yet the general liability[1] of employers remains liability in negligence alone[2] but it is one of the most highly developed and thoroughly litigated areas of the law of negligence. Compensation for industrial injuries is provided for by way of the state scheme relating to industrial injuries.[3] But the higher level of common law damages ensure that many employees continue to elect for the common law remedy in negligence. In order to ensure that an employee awarded compensation for negligence against his employer receives the money due to him the Employers' Liability (Compulsory Insurance) Act 1969 requires employers to insure against liability for injury sustained by employees in the course of their employment. Despite the increasing volume of material on employers' liability the basic principles can be stated here quite succinctly.[4]

LORD WRIGHT summed up the employer's duty thus in the leading case of *Wilsons and Clyde Coal Co, Ltd v English*:[5]

a duty which rests on the employer and which is personal to the employer, to take reasonable care for the safety of his workmen, whether the employer be an individual, a firm, or a company, and whether or not the employer takes any share in the conduct of the operations.[6]

A. A PERSONAL, NON-DELEGABLE DUTY

This duty, then, is a personal one of a general nature. As will be seen later,[7] there is another form of tortious liability, known as vicarious liability, where

1 Of course in certain cases specific statutory duties in respect of safety are imposed on employers and in such cases an action for breach of statutory duty may lie; see *post* at ch. 22. Breach of the general statutory code on safety provided for by the Health and Safety at Work Act 1974 is not actionable as a breach of statutory duty. Section 17(1) expressly provides that breach of the code of practice under the Act is not of itself tortious. But it may be that in assessing negligence judges may tend to treat conformity with the code as evidence that reasonable care has been taken; and vice versa?
2 See A Ogus and E Barendt *The Law of Social Security* (2nd edn, 1982 and Supp) ch 8.
3 See Social Security Act 1975.
4 Wedderburn *The Worker and the Law* (3rd edn) pp 425–443.
5 [1938] AC 57 at 84, [1937] 3 All ER 628, HL. Where a workman is hired to another employer that employer who would be vicariously liable for his torts according to the principles of *Mersey Docks and Harbour Board v Coggins and Griffith (Liverpool), Ltd*, [1947] AC 1, [1946] 2 All ER 345, HL, p 447, post, is also the 'employer' who owes him this duty of care: *O'Reilly v Imperial Chemical Industries Ltd* [1955] 2 All ER 567.
6 Cf *Bartonshill Coal Co v Reid* (1858) 3 Macq 266, HL; *Paris v Stepney Borough Council* [1951] AC 367 at 384 (per LORD OAKSEY), [1951] 1 All ER 42, HL.
7 Chapter 30, post.

281

a person is liable not for breach of his own personal duty, but for the tort of his servant. Because, until the Law Reform (Personal Injuries) Act 1948, an employer sued by a workman on account of the employer's vicarious liability for the tort of a fellow-workman could successfully raise the defence of common employment, the personal duties of employers have been kept strictly separate from those for which their responsibility is vicarious. It is true that, since that Act abolishes the defence of common employment, this strict marking off of personal duty has become less important in circumstances where the plaintiff can in any event prove fault by a fellow-servant. Yet, it would be misleading to state that the distinction can now be ignored; for there will still be many cases where the employer is in breach of his personal duty and yet no employee is at fault[8]; further, the distinction remains the basis of judicial thinking on the subject, and the development and implications of the cases cannot be understood if this is not grasped.

It is obvious that industrial responsibilities fall naturally into three divisions: (1) personnel, (2) those concerned with place of work, machinery, tools and raw materials, (3) the general management or system of work—how to use machinery, organise the detailed working, and supervision. In view of the need before 1948 to mark off the scope of this duty closely, and of the tendency of some duties in negligence to receive more detailed definition,[9] it will occasion no surprise that the duty has been consistently divided by the courts into those three parts. So, as we have seen, it was stated in the House of Lords that 'the obligation is threefold—the provision of a competent staff of men, adequate material, and a proper system and effective supervision'.[10]

Once breach of the employer's duty is established, liability will follow even in the absence of any primary negligence by the employer or his employees. The duty of care owed to the employee is non-delegable. In *McDermid v Nash Dredging & Reclamation Co Ltd*[11] the plaintiff was employed by the defendants as a deckhand. He was sent to work on a rig owned by a Dutch company under the control of a Dutch captain employed by that Dutch company. The plaintiff of course had no idea he was not continuing to work on one of his employer's boats under one of 'their' captains. The plaintiff suffered serious injuries when as a result of the Dutch captain's carelessness a rope that the plaintiff was untying as the rig moved off snaked round his legs. The employers denied responsibility because quite rightly they contended they were not vicariously liable for the conduct of someone else's employee. The House of Lords held the defendants liable on these very simple grounds. The evidence showed that the plaintiff was injured because no safe system of work was in operation. The duty incumbent on his employers to devise and operate such a system was not performed. The essential characteristic of the employer's non-delegable duty '... is that, if it is not performed, it is no defence for the employer to show that he delegated its performance to a

---

8 It may be that there is an inadequate system for when culpability can be attached to no one person; or it may be that the individual at fault is not an employee of the employer sued as in *McDermid v Nash Dredging & Reclamation Co Ltd* [1987] 2 All ER 878, [1987] 3 WLR 212, HL.

9 See p 198, ante.

10 *Wilsons and Clyde Coal Co Ltd v English* [1938] AC 57 at 78 (per LORD WRIGHT) [1937] 3 All ER 628, HL.

11 [1987] 2 All ER 878, [1987] 3 WLR 212, HL. And see *Kondis v State Transport Authority* [1984] 154 CLR 672.

person, whether his servant or not his servant, who he reasonably believed to be competent to perform it. Despite such delegation the employer is liable for the non-performance of the duty'.[12]

Although the duty is personal, and is not discharged by entrusting it to competent delegates, it is still a liability for negligence, not a liability imposed regardless of fault. 'The obligation is fulfilled by the exercise of due care and skill' and LORD TUCKER has stressed[13] the importance of not enlarging the employer's duty until it is barely distinguishable from his absolute statutory obligations.[14] An employer may be liable for a mere omission;[15] actual knowledge on his part of a danger is not insisted on if he ought to have known of it.[16] It is a question of fact whether there has been a breach of the duty[17]— the rules about 'customary practice' previously discussed are very important in this regard.[18] Nevertheless once a substantial risk of, for example, industrial disease, is well known, failure to protect employees against that disease will be accruable even if it is the 'customary practice' of the trade to go on ignoring the risk.[19]

The same defences are available as in other forms of negligence; contributory negligence is, of course, important in reducing damages. Although it will be recalled that it is very difficult to establish assumption of risk because the courts are reluctant to find that a workman has voluntarily encountered the danger,[20] yet, if the employment necessarily involves particular risks, eg a cinema stunt man, the employer has then no duty to remove these risks, and a workman injured in consequence of undertaking them will not recover in negligence. However, it must be remembered that the three-fold formulation of the employer's duty by LORD WRIGHT[1] is not exclusive. It may be that the employers duty further embraces warning and counselling prospective employees of inherent risks of the work before the employee accepts the job.[2]

In one respect a distinction has to be made between defective equipment and failure to provide competent staff or a proper system of working. The Employers' Liability (Defective Equipment) Act 1969 applies only to defective equipment, including plant and machinery, vehicles, aircraft and clothing provided by the employer for the purpose of his business.[3] Even though the defect is attributable to the negligence of an independent contractor or other

---

12 Ibid at 223 per LORD BRANDON.
13 *Latimer v AEC, Ltd*, [1953] AC 643 at 658, [1953] 2 All ER 449, HL. In *Richardson v Stephenson Clarke Ltd* [1969] 3 All ER 705, the employers left it to the plaintiff employee to choose his equipment. He chose carelessly and was hurt. *Held*, the employers had discharged their duty by providing safe equipment and leaving the selection of the equipment to the plaintiff; the plaintiff's negligence alone caused the accident. On a difficult problem of causation, see *McGhee v National Coal Board* [1972] 3 All ER 1008, HL.
14 See Part V, post.
15 *Williams v Birmingham Battery Co* [1899] 2 QB 338, CA.
16 *Baker v James* [1921] 2 KB 674 at 681 (per MCCARDIE J).
17 *Latimer v AEC Ltd* [1953] AC 643 at 655 (per LORD OAKSEY); further, *res ipsa loquitur* applies—*Ballard v North British Ry Co* 1923 SC (HL) 43 at 53 (per LORD DUNEDIN), HL.
18 See p 209, ante.
19 *Thompson v Smiths Shiprepairers (North Shields) Ltd* [1984] QB 405, [1984] 1 All ER 881.
20 *Smith v Baker & Sons* [1891] AC 325, HL.
1 In *Wilsons and Clyde Coal Co Ltd v English* (supra).
2 See *White v Holbrook Precision Castings* [1985] 1 RLR 215.
3 The Act will not apply, e g where a domestic cleaner is injured because an electrician has carelessly installed a plug in her employer's home; nor is the employer liable at common law if he has carefully chosen the electrician: *Cook v Broderip* (1968) 206 *Estates Gazette* 128.

third party the employer is still liable to his employee for personal injuries suffered in consequence in the course of his employment. It was uncertain when an employer would be liable to his workmen for other types of negligence on the part of his independent contractor.[4] The effect of the decision of the House of Lords in *McDermid v Nash Dredging & Reclamation Co Ltd* would seem to be (although the point is not fully discussed in the judgments) that 'non-delegable' means just what it says and that in respect of any of the components of the duty owed by the employer delegation of the duty to any third party will be no defence if breach of that duty is proved.

Remembering always that the basic question is whether the employer has failed to take reasonable care for the safety of his employee[5] and that the tripartite division is not necessarily exhaustive of the area of liability in negligence of employers to workmen, it is convenient now to examine shortly the three categories.

B. THE PROVISION OF COMPETENT STAFF

Before 1948, an employee injured by the incompetence of his fellow-employee could recover damages in negligence from his employer only by establishing that the employer was himself negligent in employing the fellow-employee in the circumstances. Now that common employment no longer absolves the employer from vicarious liability, clearly this head is of much less importance. This category will now only be relevant where the plaintiff cannot prove any fault on the part of the other employee and yet can show that his injury results from negligent staffing provision—the commonest case will be where the employer appoints an insufficiently qualified or experienced man for a particular task.[6]

C. ADEQUATE PREMISES AND PLANT

The employer must take care to provide safe premises[7] and plant for his workmen. Both failure to provide some necessary equipment and the pro-

---

4 *Davie v New Merton Board Mills Ltd* [1959] AC 604, [1959] 1 All ER 346, HL (an employer who bought a tool from a reliable source was not liable for a latent defect caused by the negligence of the independent contractor). *Sumner v William Henderson & Sons Ltd* [1963] 2 All ER 712n, CA.

5 Emphasised again by the House of Lords in *General Cleaning Contractors Ltd v Christmas* [1953] AC 180, [1952] 2 All ER 1110, HL; cf *Drummond v British Building Cleaners Ltd* [1954] 3 All ER 507, CA.

6 *Black v Fife Coal Co Ltd* [1912] AC 149, HL (employment of a colliery manager without experience of carbon monoxide in a pit where its presence was a possible danger); especially per LORD SHAW OF DUNFERMLINE at 170. In *Hudson v Ridge Manufacturing Co Ltd* [1957] 2 QB 348, [1957] 2 All ER 229, knowingly to employ a workman continually indulging in horseplay was held to violate this duty.

7 'Whether the servant is working on the premises of the master or on those of a stranger, that duty is still the same; but ... its performance and discharge will probably be vastly different in the two cases. The master's own premises are under his control: if they are dangerously in need of repair he can and must rectify the fault at once if he is to escape the censure of negligence. If, however, a master sends his plumber to mend a leak in a respectable private house, no one could hold him negligent for not visiting the house himself to see if the carpet in the hall creates a trap', per PEARCE LJ in *Wilson v Tyneside Cleaning Co* [1958] 2 QB 110 at 121, [1958] 2 All ER 265 at 271, CA.

vision of defective appliances constitute breaches of this duty. So, the failure of ship-owners to provide essential spare ropes for a voyage was actionable negligence.[8] There is probably a duty not merely to provide the material, but also to maintain it.[9]

D. A PROPER SYSTEM OF WORKING

The scope of this requirement has been considerably increased by the decision of the Court of Appeal in *Speed v Thomas Swift & Co Ltd*:[10]

> The plaintiff was engaged in loading a ship from a barge. Normally, the particular part of this loading operation, which required the port and starboard winches to be used together, was carried out while the ship's rails were left in position; only when one winch was being used was it ordinarily necessary to remove a section of the rails in order to prevent their being caught by the hook. The following special circumstances however, made it dangerous on that occasion to load with two winches without removing the section of the rail. Other sections of the rail had been damaged by accident and had had to be removed; timber was lying against the rails so that it was likely easily to be dislodged; the port winch was not in perfect order. A hook caught in the rail, and the rail and timber fell into the barge, and injured the plaintiff. It was held that he could recover in negligence because the defendants had not, in these particular circumstances, laid out a safe system of work.

LORD GREENE MR, approved the following description of 'system of work'.[11]

> What is system and what falls short of system may be difficult to define ... but, broadly stated, the distinction is between the general and the particular, between the practice and method adopted in carrying on the master's business of which the master is presumed to be aware and the insufficiency of which he can guard against, and isolated or day to day acts of the servant of which the master is not presumed to be aware and which he cannot guard against; in short, it is the distinction between what is permanent or continuous on the one hand, and what is merely casual and emerges in the day's work on the other hand.

and added:[12]

> It ... may include ... the physical lay-out of the job—the setting of the stage, so to speak—the sequence in which the work is to be carried out, the provision in proper cases of warnings and notices, and the issue of special instructions. A system may be adequate for the whole course of the job or it may have to be modified or improved to meet circumstances which arise. Such modifications or improvements appear to me equally to fall under the head of system.

---

8 *Vaughan v Roper & Co Ltd* (1947) 80 Ll LR 119, CA.
9 Dicta in *Wilsons and Clyde Coal Co Ltd v English* [1938] AC 57, [1937] 3 All ER 628, HL, and the much-cited judgment of SIR ARTHUR CHANNEL in *Toronto Power Co Ltd v Paskwan* [1915] AC 734 at 738, PC.
10 [1943] KB 557, [1943] 1 All ER 539; approved by the House of Lords in *Colfar v Coggins and Griffith (Liverpool) Ltd* [1945] AC 197, [1945] 1 All ER 326, HL, where, however, VISCOUNT SIMON LC suggested that the principles there laid down marked the limit of the duty (at 202).
11 At 562, citing *Wilsons and Clyde Coal Co Ltd v English* in the Court of Session 1936 SC 883, at 904.
12 At 563.

On the other hand, in *Winter v Cardiff District Council*,[13] the House of Lords held that a workman, who was injured because a rope provided by the employer for that purpose had not in fact been used to lash a regulator being carried on a lorry in which he was travelling, could not complain of the system of work. LORD PORTER said:[14]

> The difference ... is between a case where sufficient and adequate provisions have been made, which will, if carried out, protect the workman unless one of his fellows does not use proper care in carrying out the system, and a case where the system itself makes no such provision.

The judgment perhaps suggests that provided a safe system is devised any failure in operation of the system will not be actionable as a breach of the employer's personal duty. This proposition must be treated with caution after *McDermid v Nash Dredging and Reclamation Co Ltd*. LORD BRANDON asserted unequivocally that the duty extended to the operation of the system.[15] The crucial factor being in that case perhaps that the relevant carelessness in operating the system was that of the man in control of the operation and not just a fellow employee of the plaintiff.

Clifford v Charles H Challen & Son Ltd[16] and *Woods v Durable Suites Ltd*[17] illustrate once again the error of trying to construct propositions of law out of decisions on the facts. In each case, a workman, who had contracted dermatitis through not using protective cream when working with glue, sued the employers under this head. In the former, he had succeeded, although the cream was provided in the factory. Therefore, in the second case, the court was pressed by counsel to hold itself bound by the previous decision. This the Court of Appeal refused to do, holding that the law applied in the first case was merely that there was a duty resting upon the employers to take reasonable care for the safety of their workmen, that the court had there found as a fact that reasonable care had not been taken—in particular, the foreman had made known to the workman his dislike for the cream and had encouraged slackness—whereas in the second case the employers had taken reasonable care by providing the cream, and by posting warning notices about the consequences of not using it.[18]

The House of Lords also laid down that in considering whether the employers are negligent, regard must be had to their knowledge of physical defects of particular workmen, so that it was relevant, in deciding whether the employers had taken reasonable care to protect a workman from flying metal by providing him with goggles, that the employers knew him to be one-eyed.[19]

It may be useful to recapitulate here the rights of workmen on premises. If the workman is merely employed by an independent contractor of the

---

13 [1950] 1 All ER 819, HL.
14 At 822.
15 [1987] 3 WLR 212 at 223.
16 [1951] 1 KB 495, [1951] 1 All ER 72, CA.
17 [1953] 2 All ER 391, CA.
18 And see *Brown v Rolls Royce Ltd* [1960] 1 All ER 577, HL. Sometimes the workman will succeed even though he cannot suggest what steps the employer should have taken to make the system safe: *Dixon v Cementation Co Ltd* [1960] 3 All ER 417, CA.
19 *Paris v Stepney Borough Council* [1951] AC 367, [1951] 1 All ER 42, HL. On the other hand in *Charlton v Forrest Printing Ink Co Ltd* [1980] IRLR 331, CA, it was held that an employee attacked by robbers after collecting wages from the bank could not sue his employers on the ground that they neglected his safety by not employing a security firm instead.

occupier he will, of course, have the rights of a visitor against the occupier. He will only have the greater rights of an employee against an employer in respect of the defect on the premises if he shows that the defect was tantamount to a failure on the employer's part to take reasonable care to protect his safety as, for instance, in *General Cleaning Contractors Ltd v Christmas*,[20] where the employee of a firm of window cleaners was held to be entitled to recover from the firm for failure to lay out a safe system on the premises of a customer whose windows he was cleaning. Subject to that, he will be limited to the rights of a visitor as laid down in the Occupiers' Liability Act 1957 and to any right of action for breach of statutory duty that there may be.[1] If he is the employee of the occupier, he will then not be limited to the rights of a visitor, but will have those further rights considered here. For example, his employer will be liable for defective equipment negligently provided by a third party in circumstances where under the Occupiers' Liability Act an occupier would not be liable for that independent contractor's fault—and moreover his employer must insure against this risk.[2]

20 [1953] AC 180, [1952] 2 All ER 1110, HL; *Drummond v British Building Cleaners* [1954] 3 All ER 507, CA; *Smith v Austin Lifts Ltd* [1959] 1 All ER 81, HL.
1 See p 198, ante and ch 18, post.
2 The Employers' Liability (Compulsory Insurance) Act 1969.

Part V

Invasions of interests in person and property where intentional or negligent conduct need not always be proved

CONTENTS

The common element in the torts discussed in this Part is that a defendant who has not committed the act complained of either intentionally or negligently, and who is not merely being held accountable for the acts of a servant or an independent contractor, may nevertheless sometimes be liable for the tort. These are often styled torts of 'strict liability'. As LORD MAC-MILLAN has observed, 'strict liability' is an ambiguous term.[1] Moreover, it suggests that there is some set of circumstances common to a series of torts where liability arises for acts which are neither intentional nor negligent:[2] it might even imply that, in this particular class of circumstances, the defendant is liable for all his acts. In fact, the rules differ from tort to tort—therefore the nature and extent of the liability in each of them must be separately considered.[3] 'Strict liability' cannot be assigned a constant meaning.

1 *Read v J Lyons & Co Ltd* [1947] AC 156 at 171, [1946] 2 All ER 471, HL.
2 Cf the view of Winfield (1931) 4 Camb LJ 193–4 that it may be taken to mean liability for the torts of independent contractors, or of anyone except a stranger.
3 Cf LORD PORTER in *Read v Lyons*, supra, at 178.

Chapter 18

Product liability

SECTION 1. INTRODUCTION

The complex history of liability for loss or injury caused by defective products illustrates well the gradual development of, and changing perceptions of the role of, the law of torts and its inter-relationship with the law of contract. The classical common law stance towards faulty or useless goods was *caveat emptor* (buyer beware). The individual buying goods was expected either to take steps to ensure that the goods were safe for use and value for money, or to make contractual arrangements which would provide him with a remedy should the goods prove to be defective. If he failed to protect himself any loss would lie, where it fell, with him. In 1893 Parliament intervened to give protection to purchasers of goods via the first Sale of Goods Act. Conditions were implied into contracts of sale that goods should be merchantable and if the purpose for which the goods were bought had been made known to the retailer then the goods must be fit for that purpose. Where goods had been bought by the person to whom they occasioned loss or injury the burden of liability shifted to the retailer.

The Sale of Goods Act 1893 offered comfort only to the purchasers of goods. A person suffering food poisoning from contaminated tinned fish bought for him by someone else was not assisted by that legislation. But in 1932 in *Donoghue v Stevenson*[1] the House of Lords held that the ultimate user of a product might in certain circumstances have an action in negligence against the manufacturers of a product causing injury to his person or his property. The liability of manufacturers in negligence in respect of defective products developed gradually over the next fifty years, as we shall see. Parliament intervened to strengthen the contractual rights of purchasers of goods[2] and services[3] with increasingly interventionist consumer protection laws. And in respect of certain types of goods the criminal law was invoked to protect safety standards, and an action for breach of statutory duty[4] was expressly created to allow individuals injured by goods in the specified categories to recover compensation from the manufacturers without recourse to an action in negligence.

Thus it can be seen that by 1987 little survived of the principle of *caveat emptor*. The social climate which gave birth to that principle had altered. The conditions in which goods are manufactured and marketed had changed so as to make unrealistic the underlying assumption that a prudent individual could if he wished ensure he got a fair bargain. But the plethora of potential

---

1 [1932] AC 562, [1932] All ER Rep 1, HL.
2 See the Sale of Goods Act 1979.
3 See the Supply of Goods and Services Act 1982 and note also the Unfair Contract Terms Act 1977.
4 Consumer Protection Act 1961 s 3, Consumer Safety Act 1978 s 6; both these provisions are now repealed and replaced by the Consumer Protection Act 1987 s 41.

remedies remained confusing and discriminated between purchasers and other users. The difficulty of proving negligence, always a factor in any claim, became especially problematic in relation to products. Throughout the 1970s several official bodies advocated reform.[5] Manufacturers should be made strictly liable for defective products. It was considered that where a product carried some inherent risk of injury that risk should be borne, not by the hapless consumer on whose shoulders the risk materialised, but by the manufacturer who put the product on the market. He benefits by the enterprise. He should bear its burdens. Moreover, while for every individual to insure himself against any form of personal accident would be costly and impracticable for many members of our community, it was said that manufacturers could simply and conveniently insure against liability and where necessary pass the cost on to the consumer.

As we shall see these arguments were far from universally accepted, especially by industry. The final victory for proponents of strict liability was won in Europe. On 25 July 1985 the Council of the European Communities issued a Directive[6] requiring member states to implement a regime of strict liability for defective products. The United Kingdom government responded by enacting the Consumer Protection Act 1987. But both the Directive and the Act leave existing remedies in respect of defective products unaffected. Contractual claims against the retailer, the action in negligence, and where appropriate actions for breach of statutory duty, remain available side by side with new rules on strict liability. The Act is further limited in its effect in that it provides only for claims in relation to personal injury and damage to private property. Damage to business property and economic loss resulting from defective products are outside the new regime of strict liability. And most crucially and tragically for advocates of strict liability the United Kingdom government has exercised its option to provide for a 'development risks' defence to strict liability claims by consumers.[7] Manufacturers who can prove that the state of scientific and technical knowledge at the time that the product was put on the market was not such that they could be expected to have discovered the relevant defect are exempt from liability. We shall have then to see whether the effect of the introduction of strict liability does more in reality than simply reverse the burden of proof demanded by common law negligence.

SECTION 2.   CONSUMER PROTECTION AND THE CHANGING COMMON LAW

A. THE LIMITATIONS OF CONTRACT

The primary means invoked to protect consumers against faulty goods was via the law of contract. The original Sale of Goods Act 1893 has now been replaced by the Sale of Goods Act 1979. It is that 1979 Act which now incorporates into every contract of sale terms of merchantability[8] and fitness

---

5 See Law Commission Report on Liability for Defective Products (1977) Law Com No 82 Cmnd 6381; Strasbourg Convention on Products Liability in regard to Personal Injury and Death 1977 reproduced as Annex A in Law Com No 82; Royal Commission on Civil Liability and Compensation for Personal Injury (Pearson Report) (1978) Cmnd 7054 Vol 1.
6 85/374/EEC.
7 See s 4(1)(e) of the Consumer Protection Act 1987 discussed post at pp 309–310.
8 Section 14(2)(b).

for purpose.[9] Identical terms are implied into any contract for services in the course of which goods are supplied by the Supply of Goods and Services Act 1982.[10] Thus if in the course of private dental treatment my dentist provides me with dentures which crumble within the week it matters not whether any contract or sale for the dentures exist. I clearly had a contract for services with the dentist and he supplied me with unmerchantable dentures. Terms implied into contracts of sale or service by virtue of the 1979 and 1982 Acts cannot be excluded against the consumer.[11]

The protection given by statute to purchasers is thus considerable. The liability is strict liability. It is irrelevant that the retailer is in no way to blame for the defect and may lack any opportunity to discover the defect. Nor is it limited to protection against injury to person or property. Merchantability is defined as '. . . as fit for the purpose or purposes for which the goods are commonly bought as it is reasonable to expect having regard to the description, the price and all other surrounding circumstances . . .' So providing I buy my own electric blanket I can sue the retailer both if it is unmerchantable because it is faultily wired and I suffer an electric shock and also if it is useless and fails to heat my bed at all. The protection offered by contract to purchasers is far from perfect. The definition of merchantability, or rather the lack of precise definition, has recently been criticised by the Law Commission.[12] Nevertheless at any rate until 1987 purchasers of defective goods were still the privileged elite in relation to compensation for loss or injury occasioned by goods.

The limitations on the effectiveness of contract as a means of general consumer protection against defective goods arise from the rules of privity of contract.[13] A person who is not a party to a contract cannot benefit from that contract. So if my mother bought my electric blanket and gave it to me as a present, I cannot sue the retailer in contract if it proves to be faulty even if I suffer serious injuries. Where I purchase the faulty blanket myself, if the retailer has gone out of business, I have no claim in contract against the wholesalers or the manufacturers. Vertical privity denies me the benefit of conditions of merchantability and fitness for purpose in the first example where I have no contract with the retailer. Horizontal privity denies me a remedy in contract where my contract with the retailer is practically valueless. I cannot latch onto the benefit of contracts further up the chain of sale and distribution.

A number of devices have occasionally been used to evade the consequences of rules of privity. In *Lockett v Charles*[14] husband and wife took a meal together in a restaurant. The husband ordered the food and paid the bill. The wife contracted food poisoning from contaminated food. The court held that the husband acted as his wife's agent and contracted on her behalf. Thus she could sue on the contract for the food. The circumstances which allow an inference of agency will be strictly limited. A mother buying goods for her child cannot be said to act as the child's agent. She may be able to recover any loss to *her* caused by injury to the child. So if a small child is scalded by a faulty hot water bottle purchased by his mother, the mother may sue on

9 Section 14(3).
10 Section 4.
11 Unfair Contract Terms Act s 6.
12 Law Commission Working Paper Report: Cmnd 137.
13 See *Cheshire Fifoot and Furmston's Law of Contract* (11th edn) ch 14.
14 *Lockett v A & M Charles Ltd* [1938] 4 All ER 170.

her contract with the retailer.[15] She will recover the cost to her of caring for her injured child. The child will be unable to recover in contract for his pain and suffering. Any action by the child must lie in negligence, breach of statutory duty, or under the Consumer Protection Act 1987 against the manufacturers.

B. THE ACTION FOR NEGLIGENCE

The development of liability in negligence for defective goods enjoyed a chequered history in the nineteenth century. In *Dixon v Bell*[16] a master who entrusted a loaded gun to his young servant was found liable to a third party injured by the servant's firing the gun on the ground that the goods 'were in a state capable of doing mischief'. The court in *Langridge v Levy*[17] declined an invitation to deduce from *Dixon v Bell* a general principle for putting into circulation things 'of a dangerous nature'. In 1842 in *Winterbottom v Wright*[18] the driver of a coach was seriously injured as a result of a defect in the coach. His action against the defendant who supplied his employers with coaches and horses failed. The court held that as the plaintiff had no contract with the defendant, the defendant owed him no duty in respect of the coach's calamitous state of disrepair. It was, and remains, correct that the plaintiff could not take advantage of express terms in the contract as to the repair and maintenance of the coach. What the court in *Winterbottom v Wright* failed to analyse was the possibility of a separate and independent obligation arising within the tort of negligence.

Case-law between 1851 and 1932 continued to deny or ignore any *general* duty to take care in the manufacture and distribution of goods, but to create exceptional cases where a duty did lie. Liability was eventually recognised in respect of goods 'dangerous in themselves',[19] in respect of known defects of which no warning of the defect was given by the supplier,[20] and occupiers were held liable to their invitees in respect of appliances on their premises which proved to be defective.[1] The boundaries of these instances of liability for defects were unclear and the need to prove knowledge of the defect in the second category was often fatal to the success of a claim.

The judgment of the House of Lords in *Donoghue v Stevenson*[2] heralded a new age.

> D drank a bottle of ginger beer, manufactured by S, which a friend bought from a retailer and gave to her. The bottle allegedly contained the decomposed remains of a snail which were not, and could not be, detected (as the bottle was opaque) until the greater parts of the contents of the bottle was consumed. She alleged that she was ill as a result, and sued S. The House of Lords had to decide whether these averments disclosed a cause of action, and they found for the plaintiff by a majority of 3 to 2.

15 See *Priest v Last* [1903] 2 KB 148.
16 (1816) 5 M & S 198.
17 (1837) 2 M & W 519. The court nevertheless found for the plaintiff on the ground of fraud.
18 (1842) 10 M & W 109.
19 See *Longmeid v Holliday* (1851) 6 Exch 761.
20 *Heaven v Pender* (1883) 11 QBD 503 at 517, CA. *Clarke v Army and Navy Co-op Society* [1903] 1 KB 155, CA.
1 *Heaven v Pender* (supra).
2 [1932] AC 562.

LORD ATKIN first discussed the difficulties of finding a general principle of negligence in English law, and then set forth that doctrine of duty to one's neighbour which has already been examined.[3] In a manner which is most instructive for students of the technique of decision-making, he then considered the cases which might seem to stand in the way of the plaintiff's winning, and found that all could be distinguished, either because the relationship of the parties was so much more distant that no duty arose, or because the dicta went further than was necessary for the determination of the particular issues. He then concluded that, by finding for the plaintiff, the following proposition was being enunciated:[4]

> a manufacturer of products, which he sells in such form as to show that he intends them to reach the ultimate consumer in the form in which they left him with no reasonable possibility of intermediate examination, and with the knowledge that the absence of reasonable care in the preparation or putting up of the products will result in an injury to the consumer's life or property, owes a duty to the consumer to take that reasonable care.

LORD THANKERTON found for the plaintiff on the ground that the manufacturer in cases like this brought himself into such a direct relationship with the consumer that a duty of care was imported. LORD MACMILLAN also distinguished earlier cases, stressed that the categories of negligence could be extended, and held that there was a duty of care towards the intended consumer on the part of him who manufactures food and drink intended for consumption by members of the public in the form in which he issued them.

Donoghue v Stevenson has since been extended in its range of application to goods. The principles of negligence derived from that judgment remain of the utmost importance even after the introduction by the Consumer Protection Act of strict liability for products. They must be examined carefully and the following points evaluated:

1 Are there persons who may be liable in negligence in respect of defective goods who would not be classified as 'producers', who are under the Act the categories of persons classified as liable for the purposes of strict liability?
2 Are there kinds of loss remediable in negligence but not under the Act?
3 Consider the impact of the special limitation rules under the Act.
4 On an overview of the operation of common law negligence and the likely effect of the strict liability rules in the Act, how radical has reform proved to be?

To consider these four issues we must first summarise the detailed rules on liability in negligence.

(1) THE NARROW RULE IN *DONOGHUE V STEVENSON*—DEFECTIVE PRODUCTS

It will be recalled that LORD ATKIN stated the 'narrow rule' as follows:

> ... *a manufacturer of products*, which he *sells* in such a form as to show that he intends them to reach the *ultimate consumer* in the form in which they left him with *no reasonable possibility of intermediate examination* and with the knowledge that the absence of reasonable care in the *preparation or putting up* of the products

---

3 See p 157 et seq ante.
4 At 599. This proposition will henceforth be styled the 'narrow rule' in the case and the 'neighbour' dicta the 'broad neighbour principle'.

will result in an injury to the consumer's *life or property*, owes a duty to the consumer to take that reasonable care.

The courts have not been content to keep within this definition: the italicised key words have been extended in later cases; (sometimes the liability in respect of products has been increased, not by a liberal interpretation of these key phrases, but rather by having recourse to the broad 'neighbour principle' in *Donoghue v Stevenson*).

(2) RANGE OF DEFENDANTS

LORD ATKIN imposed liability on manufacturers. Later case-law extended liability to *inter alia* assemblers[5] and repairers[6] and to suppliers of drinking water.[7] Suppliers of goods whether retailers or wholesalers have been held liable where their function went beyond mere distribution. For example, a car dealer selling vehicles reconditioned by him,[8] and a retail chemist[9] failing to observe the manufacturers' instructions to test the product before labelling it were both found liable to injured users. And indeed wherever the circumstances are such that a supplier would normally be expected to check a product then a duty to do so may be imposed. Second hand car dealers will be expected to check the steering on used cars.[10] Wholesalers who failed to test for themselves a hair dye of dubious provenance were held to be negligent.[11]

A number of categories of persons owing a duty of care will also be categorised as 'producers' for the purposes of strict liability but by no means all are. For example, in the case of suppliers failing to carry out tests their strict liability may, as we shall see,[12] be discharged simply by naming the person who supplied the goods to them. Producers of primary agricultural produce are excluded from the strict liability regime altogether. And repairers are beyond the scope of the new rules as well.

(3) PRODUCTS

'Products' includes today not only food and drink[13] but quite clearly any product in normal domestic use. Underwear,[14] hair dye,[15] motor cars,[16] houses[17] and installations in houses[18] have all been treated as proper subjects

---

5 *Malfroot v Noxal Ltd* (1935) 51 TLR 551 (fitting sidecar).
6 *Haseldine v Daw & Son Ltd* [1941] 2 KB 343 (lift repairer).
7 *Read v Croydon Corpn* [1938] 4 All ER 631; *Barnes v Irwell Valley Water Board* [1939] 1 KB 21, [1938] 2 All ER 650.
8 *Herschtal v Steward and Ardern Ltd* [1940] 1 KB 155, [1939] 4 All ER 123.
9 *Kubach v Hollands* [1937] 3 All ER 907.
10 *Andrews v Hopkinson* [1957] 1 QB 229, [1956] 3 All ER 422; and see *Fisher v Harrods Ltd* [1966] 1 Lloyd's Rep 500 (defendant retailer liable to donee of customer for harm to eyes caused by a jewellery cleaning fluid).
11 *Watson v Buckley, Osborne Garrett & Co Ltd* [1940] 1 All ER 174.
12 See post at p 304.
13 *Barnes v Irwell Valley Water Board* (supra) (water).
14 *Grant v Australian Knitting Mills Ltd* [1936] AC 85, PC.
15 *Watson v Buckley, Oxborne, Garret & Co Ltd*, supra.
16 *Herschtal v Steward and Ardern Ltd*, supra.
17 *Anns v Merton London Borough Council* [1978] AC 728, [1977] 2 All ER 492 and 758–9; *Batty v Metropolitan Property Realisations Ltd* [1978] QB 554 (land and fixtures on land ie houses, are not subjected to the new strict liability rules).
18 *Haseldine v Daw & Son Ltd* [1941] 2 KB 343, [1941] 3 All ER 156.

of a duty of care.[19] Pre–*Donoghue v Stevenson* distinctions[20] between products 'dangerous in themselves' and other goods can now be largely disregarded.[1] The distinction remains relevant only in that the greater the potential danger inherent in a product the more stringent the precaution to protect the user against those dangers must be.[2]

(4) ULTIMATE CONSUMER

It follows from what has been said about products that consumer now covers any user of products. The child scalded by the faulty hot water bottle purchased by her mother can sue in negligence. But less obvious persons at risk may also be within the scope of the manufacturers' duty. In *Barnett v H and J Packer & Co*[3] the proprietor of a sweet shop was injured by a piece of metal protruding from a sweet. He recovered damages from the sweet's manufacturers. And in *Stennett v Hancock and Peters*[4] a bystander was held to be within the rule in *Donoghue v Stevenson*.

> The defendant garage owner negligently reassembled the flange on the wheel of X's lorry. When, later, X was driving the lorry on the highway, the flange came off the lorry, mounted the pavement and injured the plaintiff, a pedestrian. The defendant was held liable for his negligent repair.

(5) SALE

There seems no reason why the rule should not apply even where there is no sale to goods distributed in the course of business, for example, free samples provided by manufacturers.[5] The liability for goods supplied in a domestic or social context is more disputable. Would a housewife who baked a fish pie for a charity fair be liable to the family who bought it and ate the pie and succumbed to food poisoning? Would she be liable to her own children who ate the pie's twin for their tea?[6]

---

19 See generally CJ Miller *Product Liability and Safety Encyclopaedia*.
20 See *Dominion Natural Gas Co Ltd v Collins and Perkins* [1909] AC 640, PC.
 1 See *Billings (AC) & Sons Ltd v Riden* [1958] AC 240, [1957] 3 All ER 1 and see the seventh edition of this work at pp 164–5.
 2 But that must not be construed as a rule distinct from negligence that there is a separate class of dangerous things which the defendant must keep safe at his peril. See *Read v J Lyons & Co Ltd* [1947] AC 156, [1946] 2 All ER 471 per LORD MACMILLAN at 172–3 and see post ch 20.
 3 [1940] 3 All ER 575; cf *Mason v Williams and Williams Ltd* [1955] 1 All ER 808 (manufacturers of chisel liable to the plaintiff when a splinter flew off the negligently made chisel supplied to the plaintiff's employers by them and injured his eye).
 4 [1939] 2 All ER 578.
 5 See *Hawkins v Coulsdon and Purley UDC* [1954] 1 QB 319, [1954] 1 All ER 97 per DENNING LJ at 333, CA.
 6 The 'narrow rule' in *Donoghue v Stevenson* is probably inapplicable to gratuitous transfers. There are cases where liability has been established in respect of dangers known to the transferor: see *Hodge & Sons v Anglo-American Oil Co* (1922) 12 LlL Rep 183; and see *Hurley v Dyke* [1979] RTR 265; where the defect is not known to the transferor there seems no reason in principle why the 'broad neighbour principle' should not apply to impose liability on a gratuitous transferor. What would be the standard of care demanded of the housewife in the example in the text?

(6) INTERMEDIATE EXAMINATION

'Which he sells in such a form as to show that he intends them to reach the ultimate consumer in the form in which they left him with no reasonable possibility of intermediate examination.'

If the rule is to apply, 'the customer must use the article exactly as it left the maker, that is in all material features, and use it as it was intended to be used'.[7] The effect of intermediate examination seems to be this: if someone in the place of the manufacturer would reasonably contemplate that the defect in the goods would remain there at the time of their use by the plaintiff despite their passing through the hands of intermediaries, he is still liable[8]—the test is not whether intermediate examination is possible.[9]

This test with respect to goods is stricter than that for the general conception of negligence under the 'neighbour' rule. In *Clay v A J Crump & Sons Ltd*:[10]

Under the supervision of the defendant architect, demolition contractors were demolishing a building, and builders were to construct a new one. On his advice a wall was left standing on the site. It subsequently fell on the plaintiff employee of the builders.

The defendant pleaded that the demolition and building contractors and their employees had the opportunity of intermediate examination. This was held to be a case, not of the narrow products rule, but of the broad principle, so that this rule of intermediate examination did not apply to defeat the plaintiff's claim against the architect.

(7) PREPARATION OR PUTTING UP

The defect may be in the design[11] or in the container and, probably, in the labelling of the package.[12]

(8) CONTINUING DUTY OF CARE

What if the product when first put on the market was not manufactured with any lack of care? At that time on all the reasonably available evidence the manufacturers could have discovered no defect in their product, but later evidence of risks to person or property posed by a latent defect becomes available. Do the manufacturers owe any duty

a to attempt to recall the goods, and
b to warn affected consumers of the danger?

It is clear beyond doubt that even though originally the design of a product may have complied with all due care, once a design defect becomes patent the manufacturer is liable in negligence if he continues to produce and market

---

7 *Grant v Australian Knitting Mills Ltd* [1936] AC 85 at 104, PC.
8 Ibid at 105; *Haseldine v Daw & Co Ltd* [1941] 2 KB 343 at 376.
9 *Dransfield v British Insulated Cables Ltd* [1937] 4 All ER 382, which is to the contrary, is to be regarded as wrongly decided. It would appear from *Vacwell Engineering Co Ltd v BHD Chemicals Ltd* [1971] 1 QB 88, [1969] 3 All ER 1681 that in other respects the rules of remoteness for this tort are the same as in general negligence.
10 [1964] 1 QB 533, [1963] 3 All ER 687, CA.
11 *Hindustan Steam Shipping Co Ltd v Siemens Bros & Co Ltd* [1955] 1 Lloyd's Rep 167.
12 *Kubach v Hollands* [1937] 3 All ER 907.

the unsafe product.[13] In respect of unsafe products already in circulation it is submitted that a continuing duty of care is owed to do whatever is reasonable to recall the defective product and warn users of the risk the defect may pose to their health and/or property.[14]

(9) ECONOMIC LOSS

The duty of care in respect of defective products remains, in general, limited to a duty to avoid inflicting injury to the ultimate consumer's life or property.[15] Economic loss occasioned by defective goods, whether it takes the form of wasted expenditure on the useless product itself, or loss of profits caused by the defective product not doing the job for which it was acquired, is irrecoverable in the tort of negligence save in special circumstances.[16]

In *Junior Books Ltd v Veitchi Co Ltd*,[17] as we have seen, the plaintiffs recovered damages for their wasted expenditure on defective flooring laid by the defendants and additionally recovered for their loss of profits during the time that their business was disrupted while a new floor was being laid. The defendants were sub-contractors expressly nominated for the task by the plaintiffs because of their expertise and reputation as flooring specialists. The House of Lords held:

a that the broad neighbour principle in *Donoghue v Stevenson* was applicable to economic loss as much as to injury to persons or property, and
b that the very close relationship between the parties in *Junior Books* gave rise to a duty of care to avoid defects in the product likely to result in financial loss.

Subsequent case-law has made it clear that for the present at least no general duty to avoid economic loss, to ensure a product is value for money, is imposed on manufacturers.[18] Manufacturers of electric motors for fishtanks were held to owe no duty to the ultimate purchaser of the tanks for loss of profit on his enterprise and wasted expenditure on the tanks themselves. The plaintiff failed, said the Court of Appeal, to prove any reliance on the manufacturer in that respect or to establish a 'special relationship' of the kind present in *Junior Books*.[19]

(10) PROVING NEGLIGENCE

The scope of liability for negligent manufacture, distribution and repair evolved from the rule in *Donoghue v Stevenson* can thus be seen to be considerable. It is in the formidable task of proving negligence that plaintiffs confront outstanding difficulty. In the classic application of the narrow rule

13 *Wright v Dunlop Rubber Co Ltd* (1972) 13 KIR 255.
14 *Walton v British Leyland UK Ltd* 12 July 1978, (unreported) see Miller & Lovell *Product Liability and Safety Encyclopaedia*; and see *Rivtow Marine Ltd v Washington Ironworks* (1974) 40 DLR (3d) 530 (Canada).
15 The property damage must arise from a use to which the defendant might reasonably have expected the property to be put. There was no liability where waterproofing compound was lost when pails manufactured by the defendant melted in the intense heat of Kuwait; *Aswan Engineering Establishment Co v Lupdine Ltd* [1987] 1 All ER 135, CA.
16 *Simaan General Contracting Co v Pilkington Glass Ltd* (1988) Times, 18 February, CA.
17 [1983] 1 AC 520.   18 See generally ante at p 190.
19 *Muirhead v Industrial Tank Specialities Ltd* [1986] QB 507, [1985] 3 All ER 705, CA; *Aswan Engineering Establishment Co v Lupdine Ltd* 1 All ER 135, CA.

in *Donoghue v Stevenson*—where the ultimate consumer is suing the man at the far end of the chain the manufacturer—it is often verging on impossible to prove by direct evidence absence of reasonable care. The consumer's difficulties may be compounded by problems of causation especially, for example, in claims relating to drug induced injury. Yet the burden of proof remains with the plaintiff. LORD MACMILLAN said in *Donoghue v Stevenson:*[20]

> The burden of proof must always be upon the injured party to establish that the defect which caused the injury was present in the article when it left the hands of the party whom he sues, that the defect was occasioned by the carelessness of that party ... There is no presumption of negligence in such a case at present, nor is there any justification for applying the maxim, *res ipsa loquitur.*

The Privy Council modified this unbending approach in *Grant v Australian Knitting Mills Ltd*[21] where the plaintiff was concerned to prove that the dermatitis contracted by him was caused by the presence of invisible excess sulphites in underwear purchased by him and made by the defendants. It was explained that the test was whether, on the balance of probabilities, it was a reasonable inference to be drawn from the evidence that the harm was so caused.[1] On the issue of negligence, it was said:[2]

> if excess sulphites were left in the garment, that could only be because someone was at fault. The appellant is not required to lay his finger on the exact person in all the chain[3] who was responsible, or to specify what he did wrong. Negligence is found as a matter of inference from the existence of the defects taken in connection with all the known circumstances ...

It is submitted that this approach is eminently practical and good law,[4] and is to be preferred to the *obiter dicta* of LORD MACMILLAN, in so far as the two are in conflict.[5] Where the presence of the defect in combination with the known circumstances give rise to an inference of negligence against the manufacturers the burden shifts to the defendant to rebut that inference. That may be done either by pinpointing the exact cause giving rise to the defect and establishing that it does not arise from any want of care, or by the manufacturer producing evidence as to his system and establishing that the system was consistent with all due care. In *Daniels and Daniels v R White & Sons Ltd*[6] the plaintiff was seriously injured when he drank lemonade containing a large quantity of carbolic acid. The acid presumably came from the washing process used by the defendant manufacturer. The judge accepted evidence of the precautions taken by the defendants to avoid such a contingency and found that the plaintiffs had failed to prove negligence.

The problems faced by the plaintiff are compounded where the relevant

20 [1932] AC 562 at 622.
21 [1936] AC 85 PC.
 1 Ibid at 96–7.
 2 Ibid at 101.
 3 What if the plaintiff does not know whether the negligence is that of the manufacturer, the bottler, the wholesaler, the carrier or the retailer?
 4 For a lucid and similar explanation of the burden of proof see *Mason v Williams and Williams* [1955] 1 All ER 808 at 810 per FINNEMORE LJ. See discussion of *res ipsa loquitur* ante at p 215 et seq.
 5 This was exactly the approach of the House of Lords in the Scottish case, *Lockhart v Barr* 1943 SC 1 where the purchaser of aerated water contaminated with phenol recovered from the manufacturer although he could not prove how the phenol came to be in the aerated water.
 6 [1938] 4 All ER 258.

defect is not a construction defect but a design defect. Construction defects occur where the product properly put together and packaged is harmless, but a number of products are wrongly constructed, for example snails get into the ginger beer, or carbolic acid into the lemonade. Design defects occur where the basic design of the product proves to be inherently dangerous. Because it follows that with a construction defect something has gone wrong which normally does not go wrong construction defects allow the possibility of the court inferring negligence. An inference of negligence in respect of a design defect is impossible. The plaintiff has to prove:

a that the manufacturer should have been aware of the risk of the defect, and

b that he could reasonably have avoided the defect.

The issue all too often becomes one of whether at the time that the product was put on the market scientific and technical knowledge available to the manufacturer should have enabled him to have identified the danger.

The classic example of the difficulties posed in proving negligence can be found in the thalidomide case. All over the world children whose mothers had taken the drug thalidomide were born with serious deformities. But at the time the drug was first marketed embryology was an inexact science. Whether or not drugs crossed the placental barrier was not then clear to scientists. Animal tests for risks to the foetus were far from routine and their usefulness was disputed.[7] An action in negligence required parents to prove that in the state of scientific knowledge at the time of marketing the drug, *before* the tragic births of the thalidomide babies taught us all an unforgettable lesson, the manufacturers should have recognised the risk. They had to make their case in the dark. Every attempt to gain discovery of records of tests and expert reports was fought to the last degree. The thalidomide tragedy became the spur for those who advocated reform of the law.[8]

C. ACTION FOR BREACH OF STATUTORY DUTY[9]

Before moving on to examine the outcome of the campaign to reform the general law of product liability by introducing strict liability, brief mention must be made of the possibility of an action for breach of statutory duty in respect of certain limited categories of goods. Since 1961[10] the Secretary of State has had power to make safety regulations prescribing detailed rules as to the design, manufacture and packaging (*inter alia*) of specified classes of goods. The Minister's powers are now provided for by Part II of the Consumer Protection Act 1987. Breach of safety regulations is a criminal offence but section 41 of the 1987 Act expressly provides that an individual injured by a breach of regulations has an action for breach of statutory duty. The

---

7 For an account of the legal issues arising from the thalidomide tragedy see H Teff and C Munro *Thalidomide: The Legal Aftermath* 1976 Saxon House, London.
8 While very difficult to establish negligence in relation to a design defect it is not impossible; see *IBA v EMI and BICC* (1980) 14 BLR 1.
9 See post ch 22.
10 Consumer Protection Act 1961, s 3: Consumer Safety Act 1978, s 6. Both these sections are repealed and replaced by the Consumer Protection Act 1987, s 41. Note that it is only breach of specific safety regulations which give rise to an action for breach of statutory duty and not infringement of the new general safety duty provided for by s 10 of the 1987 Act.

regulations cover only a limited class of goods and the action for damages lies only where the defect in the goods derives from breach of the regulations and is subject to the defence of due diligence to criminal proceedings provided for by section 39. No reported judgment on the action for breach of safety regulations provided for by earlier consumer protection legislation is known of.

SECTION 3.   THE NEW STRICT LIABILITY REGIME

A. THE EUROPEAN DIRECTIVE AND THE CONSUMER PROTECTION ACT 1987

It can be seen then that where no contractual remedy was available to an English plaintiff injured by a defective product he confronted formidable difficulties in establishing negligence, and where no negligence could be proved the loss continued to lie where it fell. The inequity of leaving the person least well equipped to bear, or protect himself against, the loss, and lack of any logical reason for discriminating between purchasers of goods and other users convinced all those august bodies[11] who reviewed liability for products that strict liability should extend to manufacturers as well as retailers and that any user of the product should be able to invoke strict liability against the manufacturer.

Industry was unsurprisingly generally less enthusiastic about calls for reform. It was strenuously argued[12] that while individual consumers who suffered injury from defective products might benefit from the introduction of strict liability, consumers as a whole would be adversely affected by such a change. The cost of products would rise to cover increased insurance premiums required by the need to insure against strict liability. The variety of goods available would decrease, limiting consumer choice of goods. Companies would protect themselves by sticking to well-known and well-tried products and not take risks with minor variations. Finally, and most cogently, it was contended that research and technological innovation in England would be seriously impeded. Risk is an inextricable component of new developments on the frontiers of knowledge. If companies had to bear the risk of some unknown defect themselves, rather than leaving it with the unfortunate victims, they would simply shut down on research and development. British industry would suffer.

Only when the new rules have been in force for some time can we evaluate whether the gloomy forecasts of sections of industry were correct. Two important features of the implementation of strict liability must be borne in mind. First, the regime provided for in the Consumer Protection Act 1987 derives from the European Community Directive of July 12 1985.[13] Although the Directive allows for some variation in the rules throughout member states the basic regime throughout the Community is the same. British industry is subjected to the same rules as the European competitors. Indeed one of the

---

11 Law Commission; see Report No 82 on Liability for Defective Products (1977) Cmnd 6381; Council of Europe, see Strasbourg Convention on Products Liability in regard to Personal Injury and Death (1977); and the Pearson Commission on Civil Liability and Compensation for Personal Injury (1978) Cmnd 7054 Vol 1.
12 See Law Com No 82 Cmnd 6381.
13 85/374/EEC.

aims of the Directive was to harmonise national laws because as it is put in the preamble

> ... the existing divergences may distort competition and affect the free movement of goods within the common market and entail a differing degree of protection of the consumer against damage caused by a defective product to his health or property.

And, second, in the United Kingdom, industry, in particular the pharmaceutical industries, have persuaded the government to adopt the 'development risks' defence albeit that every official report on product liability has advised against such a course of action.

The detailed provision for strict liability made by the 1987 Act must now be examined. It would have been possible, and would certainly have made life easier for students, to give statutory force in the United Kingdom to the Directive. As it is where the interpretation of the Consumer Protection Act is doubtful it should be construed in the light of the Directive. Should the Act be in contravention of the provisions of the Directive any dispute will ultimately have to be decided by the European Court of Justice in Brussels.[14]

B. WHO CAN SUE UNDER THE ACT?

Wherever a defect in a product wholly or partly causes personal injury or death the victim or his dependants may invoke the rules of strict liability to sue under the Act.[15] The injured individual need not be a purchaser or even a direct user of the faulty goods. If defective brakes in a new car bought by A suddenly fail causing a road accident in which A, his passenger B, and C a pedestrian are seriously injured, all three can sue the car's manufacturer. Where a defective product causes damage to a baby before birth, the baby may sue in respect of its disabilities.[16] The prime aim of the Directive and the Act is to provide protection against personal injuries and death but consumers can also sue under the Act where a defect in a product results in damage to private property (including land) providing the amount to be awarded to compensate for that damage exceeds £275.[17] Damage to property used for business purposes[18] is expressly excluded under the Act and the Directive, as is the loss of or any damage to the product itself.[19] Nor is economic loss arising from defective products within the scope of the new strict liability rules.[20]

C. ON WHOM IS STRICT LIABILITY IMPOSED?

Liability is not limited to manufacturers alone. The Directive imposes liability

14 See *De Smith's Constitutional and Administrative Law* (5th edn) pp 116–121.
15 Section 2(1).
16 Section 6(3).
17 See s 5.
18 Section 5(3).
19 Section 5(2).
20 For the limited circumstances in which damages for economic loss are recoverable in negligence see ante at p 299.

on 'producers'[1] and defines producers so as to ensure that plaintiffs should almost always be able to identify easily and swiftly an organisation or individual deemed responsible for putting the product into circulation. The Act adopts a different formula but identifies the same classes of person as responsible for products. Essentially all those involved in the primary production and marketing of goods are made liable. Repairers and distributors who may owe the consumers a duty of care at common law are generally outside the scope of the new strict liability regime.

Section 2 of the Act imposes liability on the following categories of persons.

1 Liability is imposed on 'producers'[2] defined as
a manufacturers[3]
b in the case of products which are not made, but won or abstracted (for example, coal and minerals) the person who won or abstracted the product,[4] and
c in respect of products which are neither made, nor won or abstracted, (for example, crops) but where essential characteristics of the product are attributable to an industrial or other process, the person carrying out that process.[5]
The cumbersome nature of (c) is, as we shall see, explained by the exemption of primary agricultural produce from the regime instituted by the Act.

2 Liability is imposed on any person who brand names a product or by other means holds himself out as a producer.[6] Should I buy a food processor at Marks & Spencer brand named St Michael, if a part flies out of the machine and injures me in the eye, I may sue Marks & Spencer and it is no defence against me that the processor was actually made by a third party.

3 Liability is imposed on any person importing a product into the European Community from outside.[7] Had I bought a Japanese food processor I need not concern myself with the intricacies of suing in Japan, I can proceed against whichever European Community firm brought the product into the community.

4 The problems of the consumer at the end of a long chain of distributors have been discussed earlier. The ultimate consumer may well not know the identity of the manufacturer. Section 2(3) provides that any supplier of a product will be liable to the injured person unless he complies with a request to name, within a reasonable time, the person supplying him with the product. Distributors may thus be deemed to be subject to strict liability unless they can and do name the next organisation up the chain of distribution. A duty of care when imposed on a distributor cannot be thus shifted up the chain.

5 The Directive expressly defines manufacturers of component parts as 'producers' and so subject to strict liability.[8] The Act achieves the same end by more tortuous means defining 'product' so as to embrace component parts.[9]

---

1 Article 3.
2 Section 2(2)(a).
3 Section 1(2)(a).
4 Section 1(2)(b).
5 Section 1(2)(c).
6 Section 2(2)(b).
7 Section 2(2)(c). Note a person importing a product into the UK from another member state is not made strictly liable under the Act. He may be liable in negligence.
8 Article 3(1).
9 See s 1(2).

The effect is simply illustrated. Should defective brakes in a new car fail causing personal injuries the injured person may sue both the 'producer' of the finished product, the car manufacturers, and the 'producer' of the defective component, the manufacturers of the brakes. Section 1(3), however, provides that a supplier of the finished product shall not be deemed to be liable for defects in all component parts because he cannot name the actual manufacturer of each and every component.

D. PRODUCTS

'Products' are defined in the Act as 'any goods or electricity' and include component parts and in certain cases raw materials.[10] Primary agricultural produce is excluded from strict liability unless it has been subject to some industrial process[11] ('initial process' is the term used in the Directive[12]). A consumer injured by contaminated beefburgers can clearly sue the person responsible for processing the beef from beef into burger. If the contamination existed in the cattle before processing, for example, the cattle had been affected by fallout from a nuclear incident such as Chernobyl, he cannot invoke strict liability against the farmer who originally sold the cattle. But what if the beef were contaminated by hormones of steroids fed to the cattle by the farmer to fatten them up? Would that constitute an 'industrial process'.

In earlier drafts of the Directive blood and human tissues were expressly excluded from the Directive. No express mention is now made of these in the Directive or the Act. So it is unclear whether a patient infected with some disease by a contaminated blood transfusion can hold the transfusion service strictly liable. It seems unlikely that human tissues would be classified as 'goods'. Immovable property, that is land and fixtures on land, is beyond the scope of the Act.[13] Goods which become fixtures within immovable property, for example, central heating boilers installed in private houses are probably within the scope of the Act.[14]

E. DEFINING 'DEFECT'

Strict liability must not be confused with 'no-fault' liability. Proof that a product resulted in injury is not sufficient to establish liability. 'Fault' must still be proved by the plaintiff but the relevant fault becomes that a 'defect' in the product resulted in injury, rather than want of care. If 'defect' can be proved then carelessness as such is irrelevant. Thus if a housewife is badly cut about the face, when the blade from her new food processor flies off the machine, she will succeed in her claim for compensation simply on proof of the obvious, that the processor is unsafe and defective. A child drinking lemonade contaminated by carbolic acid recovers damages without problems.

10 Section 1(2).
11 See the Directive Article 2 and s 1 of the Act.
12 Are the terms 'industrial' and 'initial' synonymous? Does combine harvesting count as an industrial (or an initial) process?
13 Liability for defectively constructed buildings remains subject to the general rules of negligence and the Defective Premises Act 1972 see ante ch 16.
14 See Article 2 of the Directive.

Contaminated lemonade is defective. Evidence that this was inexplicable in view of the system designed by the manufacturers to guard against such a catastrophe is irrelevant.[15]

Defect is defined in Article 6 of the Directive and section 3 of the Act. Section 3 provides that there is a defect in a product if the safety of that product is not such as persons generally are entitled to expect. In assessing what persons generally are entitled to expect all the circumstances are to be taken into account including—

(a) the manner in which, and purposes for which, the product has been marketed, its get-up, the use of any mark in relation to the product and any instructions for, or warnings with respect to, doing or refraining from doing anything with or in relation to the product:

(b) what might reasonably be expected to be done with or in relation to the product: and

(c) the time when the product was supplied by its producer to another;

and nothing in this section shall require a defect to be inferred from the fact alone that the safety of a product which is supplied after that time is greater than the safety of the product in question.

It remains for the plaintiff to prove that taking into account the criteria outlined in section 3 the product is defective. No product on earth is entirely safe and free of risk. The test is whether the risk to person and property posed by the product in the context of its common use or uses exceeds what is generally acceptable. Take the example of a sharp knife. Marketed as a kitchen knife for chopping vegetables and packaged so as to be reasonably child proof on display, if the knife cuts off the tip of my finger I cannot claim that my injury resulted from a defect in the product. Its cutting edge was a risk I accepted as the 'price' for a knife which did its job. But if the self-same knife were marketed as 'Marvellous Magic Dagger' and a child cut himself or his playmate then defect would be easily provable. The risk to children would be generally unacceptable.

The test of 'defect' is likely to involve the courts in risk/benefit equations. This can best be illustrated by examples of liability for drugs.[16] A new and effective antibiotic is put on the market. In 99·5% of cases it works well with fewer nasty side-effects than other antibiotics. Alas, 0·5% of consumers develop serious kidney damage caused by the drug. If an identifiable group of persons should or could have been foreseen as susceptible to damage, then the failure to warn doctors of the potential allergic reaction may conclude the issue of defect. Failure to give adequate instructions is a presentational failure and relevant to defining defect. If the allergic reaction is unforeseeable, so that no liability in negligence could arise, then the issue is whether the general benefit conferred by the drug outweighs the risk to the few. A new minor tranquilliser posing a risk of kidney damage to however small a group would probably be found defective. The benefit of yet another mild sedative would not in society's valuation justify any significant risk. A drug to combat AIDS to prolong victim's lives by contrast would be likely to justify a very high degree of risk to life and health. Where the consumer of the drug faces a prospect of almost certain and painful death any product offering realistic hopes of cure or palliation is generally acceptable, albeit the product itself may be inherently dangerous to some of its users.

15 See *Daniels and Daniels v R White & Sons Ltd* [1938] 4 All ER 258 (discussed ante at p 300).
16 See Newdwick 'Liability for Defective Drugs' (1985) 101 LQR 405.

The application of the broad criteria laid down in section 3 to guide the courts in interpreting 'defect' will have to be worked through on a case by case basis. The presentation of the product and the likely use or uses of the product which are specifically designated as relevant guidelines in defining 'defect' by section 3(2)(a) and (b) are inextricably bound up together with the risk/benefit analysis discussed above. Section 3(2)(c) demands further and separate considerations. It has two implications.

First, the time when the product was put into circulation is obviously relevant to determine whether the defect was inherent in the product or the result of 'fair wear and tear'. When a child's seat belt in a car is eight years old and has been used by three rumbustious children can it be expected to be as safe as when new? Will cost be relevant? Should I expect a food processor which I buy dirt cheap to become not just less useful but less safe too?[17]

Second, section 3(2)(c) provides that safety standards must be judged by the generally acceptable standards at the time which the product was put on the market, and not with hindsight by the standards of the time when the relevant claim comes to court. Take the example of lung cancer induced by cigarettes. A claim against the cigarette's manufacturers comes to trial in 1995. In 1994 cigarettes were banned outright save for special provision for addicts to be prescribed nicotine on the NHS. The medical evidence shows the cancer was well established by 1988. The test must be whether the product was below generally acceptable safety standards in 1988. That cigarettes are regarded as absolutely unacceptable in 1994 is irrelevant. Nor would it be conclusive if by 1994 'safer' (non-carcinogenic) cigarettes had been invented.[18]

The likelihood is that in relation to construction and presentation defects strict liability will be easy to prove. Where the manufacturing process breaks down, letting snails get into ginger beer, or an automated process suffers an unnoticed power failure running out ten cars in a batch of a thousand with defective steering the product will be patently defective. Where instructions on use are inadequate, or warnings as to use fail to make the consumer safe, again defect will be easily established. The need to engage in a rigorous examination of risks and benefits of a product will generally be reserved for design defects. And of course the implication for industry of design defects is much more traumatic. Compensating ten unlucky victims of a freak construction defect is a less daunting enterprise than compensating the hundreds or thousands who may have suffered injury before a design defect becomes patent.

F. GENERAL DEFENCES

Section 4 of the Act provides several defences to strict liability. They include the following:

17 Consider the conceptual basis for product liability discussed by Clark (1985) 48 MLR 325.
18 See s 3 '... nothing in this section shall require a defect to be inferred from the fact alone that the safety of a product which is supplied after that time is greater than the product in question.' Where the plaintiff was himself a smoker any damages awarded would in any case be substantially reduced on the ground of his contributory negligence; see s 6(4) discussed post at p 308. On current safety standards what are the chances of success for a plaintiff who did not herself smoke but contracted cancer from passive smoking? Is alcohol a defective product within s 3?

1 The defect is attributable to compliance with any statute or European Community rule prescribing how the product is made. The defence is not available where there are no statutory rules on how the product is made but there are rules requiring licensing of the product by a public body before it can be marketed.[19]

2 The defendant can prove that he never supplied the product to another[20] for example, experimental drugs are stolen from the research laboratory of a drug company and sold by the thieves.

3 The defendant did not supply the goods in the course of business.[1] I am not strictly liable for defects in the food I serve my colleagues at a dinner party.

4 The defect did not exist in the product when the defendant supplied the product to another.[2] Thus a chocolate manufacturer would not be liable for poisoned chocolates injected with acid by some third party on the supermarket shelves.

5 Manufacturers of components will not be liable where the defect arose in the finished product and was caused by faulty design of the finished product or inadequate installation in the finished product by the manufacturers of that product.[3]

In addition to the defences provided for by section 4, section 6(4) provides that the contributory negligence[4] of the consumer shall be available as a defence to strict liability under the Act.[5] Two difficult questions are posed. The Law Reform (Contributory Negligence) Act provides that when a finding of contributory negligence is made apportionment between the plaintiff and defendant of responsibility, and thus damages, is on the basis of relative fault. Where the plaintiff has been careless of his own safety and the defendant is strictly liable will this mean that generally the plaintiff will have to bear the lion's share of responsibility for his injury? Or will the courts at this stage have to revert to considering any evidence of want of care on the part of the defendant?

More tricky still to resolve in practice, though, will be defining the circumstances in which if a product is put to an improper or imprudent use this is simply evidence of contributory negligence or whether it goes to the fundamental issue of whether the plaintiff's injuries were wholly or partly caused by a defect in the product. A stepladder is bought for cleaning windows by a family. The twenty year old son of the household used it to build an assault course. After ten of his sixteen stone, or so, mates have thundered across it, the wood cracks as the young man himself is on the ladder. He falls and breaks a leg. Is he simply guilty of a degree of contributory negligence, or was the ladder put to a use that it would not generally be expected to withstand?

19 Section 4(1)(a).
20 Section 4(1)(b).
 1 Section 4(1)(c).
 2 Section 4(1)(d).
 3 Section 4(1)(f).
 4 Section 6(4).
 5 See ante, ch 15.

G. THE 'DEVELOPMENT RISKS' DEFENCE

The incorporation of the 'development risks' defence (sometimes referred to as 'state of the art') into the Act via section 4(1)(e) is without doubt the most controversial part of the legislation. Permitting member states to incorporate such a defence was a compromise by the European Community in order to end the long drawn out process of agreeing to implement strict liability at all. At present it appears that divergence throughout Europe on the applicability of the defence will be significant. France is excluding the defence entirely. In West Germany the defence will be made generally available but not applicable to pharmaceutical products. The Directive provides that a review of the effect of the 'development risks' defence in member states shall be commissioned in ten years time.

Section 4(1)(e) provides that a defendant shall not be liable where he can show

> that the state of scientific and technical knowledge at the relevant time was not such that a producer of products of the same description as the product in question might be expected to have discovered the defect if it had existed in his products while they were under his control

The effect of the defence is this. Consider the example of drug-induced injury. A plaintiff establishes that the product fails to comply with society's general expectations for the safety of that type of product. That means he proves that the risks created by the drug outweigh the potential benefit of the product. The defendant may still escape liability by virtue of the 'development risks' defence if he can prove that the nature of the defect was such that at the time he marketed the drug[6] available scientific and technical knowledge[7] would not have revealed the defect. Had the Consumer Protection Act been in force at the time of the thalidomide tragedy the crucial question would have been this. Given the embryonic state of embryology then and the lack of knowledge as to whether drugs did cross the placental barrier, could the manufacturers on the basis of then current scientific knowledge have foreseen the risk to the foetus? The answer might well have been no.

The new rules would have conferred one significant advantage on the parents of the damaged babies. In negligence they had to prove that the defendants should have foreseen the risk. Now the defendants must prove that they could not have anticipated the danger. Self-interest will require manufacturers to disclose all reports of tests on the product and expert opinion made available to them.

The regime of strict liability introduced by the Consumer Protection Act will significantly benefit plaintiffs by:

6 It will not be enough to establish that at the time the design was first put on the market the defect was not discoverable. Once the defect becomes apparent any further marketing of batches of the drug will engage liability both under the Act and in negligence. See *Wright v Dunlop Rubber Co Ltd* (1972) 13 KIR 255; see also ante at p 298 on this issue.

7 The 'development risks' defence as defined in the Directive (Article 7(e)) is worded thus: 'the state of scientific and technical knowledge at the time when he put the product into circulation was not such as to enable the existence of the defect to be discovered.' There is no reference to whether a 'producer of products of the same description might have been expected to have discovered the defect' as in section 4(1)(e) of the Act. The test in the Directive refers to knowledge in general and would embrace evidence from research scientists in general. The test in section 4(1)(e) appears to be the traditional negligence test of what could reasonably be expected from companies in that line of business. The Consumer's Association has asked the EC Commission to examine whether s 4(1)(e) is compatible with the Directive.

a ensuring liability for construction defects in all circumstances, and
b requiring the defendant to provide an explanation for a design defect
    consonant with his having designed the product in order to exclude all
    known and knowable defects.

The risk of the unknown defect continues in the UK to be borne by the
injured individual. Both the Law Commission and the Pearson Commission
regarded the incorporation of a 'development risks' defence which results in
this effect as unacceptable. The Pearson Report put it this way:[8]

> ... to exclude development risks from a regime of strict liability would be to leave
> a gap in the compensation cover, through which, for example, the victims of
> another thalidomide disaster might slip through

As case-law fleshes out the barebones of the rules for liability introduced
by the 1987 Act we shall have to see whether in practice the form of 'strict'
liability adopted has done much more than reverse the burden of proof
demanded by the tort of negligence.

H. CAUSATION

The burden of proving:

a that there was a 'defect' in the product, and
b that the relevant injury or damage was wholly or partly caused by that
    defect

lies on the plaintiff.[9] The troublesome issue of when an improper or unexpected use of the product affects the causation of the injury may be expected
to be problematic. Consider the following hypothetical examples.

1 A new antibiotic is marketed. Information to doctors includes a warning
    not to prescribe the drug to pregnant women. The drug is only available
    on prescription. Dr Stone prescribes the drug for Tom. Tom feels better
    the next day. He discontinues the tablets and gives the remainder to his
    colleague Jane who is ten weeks' pregnant. She takes the tablets and her
    baby is born seriously damaged.[10]
2 A punk buys a lurid pink dye in a dressmaking shop. He uses it to dye his
    hair and suffers acute dermatitis as a result.[11]
3 A wealthy businessman buys domestic gas convector heaters and installs
    them in his swimming pool to heat the pool.[12] One heater explodes destroy-
    ing the pool.

One causation issue is, however, somewhat clearer. Intermediate examination of the product will no longer exculpate the manufacturer from liability

---

8 Pearson Report (1978) Cmnd 7054 Vol 1 para 1259.
9 See section 2(1) of the Act and Article 4 of the Directive.
10 Questions of causation can be seen from this example to be inextricably bound up with the
    definition of a 'defect'. The defendants could argue that the manner in which the product
    was marketed as a 'prescription only' drug with appropriate information supplied to GP's
    rendered it acceptably safe.
11 Should dye intended for use on materials be labelled 'Not to be used on the hair'?
12 This has actually happened! Fortunately no damage occurred the heaters simply did not
    work and the purchasers complained to the manufacturers.

for defects in the product existing at the time that he put the product into circulation. That some third party may share liability for the injury to the plaintiff is relevant only to the issue of contribution between the tortfeasors.[13]

Factual difficulties with causation for the consumer seeking to identify and sue the manufacturer will largely be alleviated by the obligation on each supplier to name his supplier or be deemed strictly liable for the defective goods.[14] Only where the last party identified is bankrupt will problems arise.

In the United States claims have been litigated where the actual manufacturer of the product injuring the plaintiff cannot be traced. Injury is proved to be the result of a drug now identified as defective. The drug may have been prescribed several years ago and the identical chemical compound marketed by several companies. There is no way of determining which branch of the drug was prescribed to individual plaintiffs. Courts in the USA have held liability should be apportioned between all companies manufacturing the drug in proportion to their share in the market for that drug.[15]

I. LIMITATION[16]

Actions under Part I of the Consumer Protection Act introducing strict liability for defective products are subject to two periods of limitation:

1 the action must be brought within three years of the date on which injury or damage was suffered by the plaintiff, or, if later, the date on which the plaintiff becomes aware of the injury or damage.[17] In the case of personal injuries only the court has a discretion to override that three year period.
2 No action may be brought in any circumstances more than ten years from the date on which the defendant supplied the relevant product to another.

Claims such as those now before the courts in the USA for cervical cancer which several young women in their late teens developed as a result of a drug (D.E.S.) taken by their mothers in pregnancy could not thus be brought under the 1987 Act. The young women here would be forced to fall back on their remedy (if any) in negligence.

13 See Article 8(1) of the Directive. Contribution is not limited to tortfeasors but is available between all persons liable for the same damage. See the Civil Liability (Contribution) Act 1978 discussed post at pp 530–533. Retailers liable to purchasers for breach of the implied conditions of the contract of sale will now be able to seek contribution from the manufacturers.
14 See s 2(3) discussed ante at p 304.
15 See *Sindell v Abbott Laboratories* 26 Cal 3d 588 (1980); discussed by Newdick 'Liability for Defective Drugs' (1985) 101 LQR 405.
16 See generally post ch 30.
17 Eg a person who took a particular drug in 1988 only becomes aware of the kidney damage caused by that drug in 1998.

Chapter 19

Nuisance

SECTION 1. NUISANCE AS A SEPARATE TORT[1]

A. MEANINGS OF THE WORD 'NUISANCE'

The essence of the tort of nuisance is interference with the enjoyment of land. The earliest remedy, the assize of nuisance, was restricted to freeholders, and its successor (which eventually became the only common-law action), the action upon the case for nuisance, though not confined to freeholders, still required of the plaintiff an interest in land. It is from this action that the present law of private nuisance is derived.

The generic conception of nuisance can readily be illustrated. It covers interferences with use and enjoyment of land by water, fire, smoke, smell, fumes, gas, noise, heat, electricity, disease or any other like thing which may cause such an inconvenience. Nevertheless, the term 'nuisance' is used in different senses by judges, and this has caused confusion both in the development and in the exposition of this branch of the law of torts. First, it is used by way of factual description of conduct or conditions on land that result in annoyance—the burning of bricks by A on his land, or a heap of refuse there, is styled a 'nuisance'. Secondly, 'nuisance' is used to denote the damage resulting from the activity or condition last mentioned; the householder, who cannot sleep because of his neighbour's loud radio, calls this a 'nuisance'. Thirdly, and this, unlike the previous two meanings, connotes legal liability, the courts may declare that the defendant is committing a nuisance: thus, the defendant who has destroyed neighbours' trees by causing poisonous fumes to be emitted from his land may be held liable in nuisance. How important it is to understand these different meanings will be realised when it is noted that the courts will, for example, sometimes consider whether a particular 'nuisance' gives rise to a liability in tort.[2]

To put the matter in another way, in nuisance one is always concerned with invasions of interests in the enjoyment of land, but whether an action of nuisance lies for that invasion depends on further considerations, especially the character of the defendant's conduct. Here is at once the source of confusion of the tort of nuisance with that of negligence and the key to the solution. Whereas in negligence the stress is on the type of conduct, viz, that styled negligent, in nuisance the emphasis is on the invasion of the interest. That interest may be invaded either by intentional or negligent activity, and, in a few instances, even by non-negligent activity.[3]

---

1 See Winfield 'Nuisance as a Tort' (1931) 4 Camb LJ 189; Newark 'The Boundaries of Nuisance' (1949) 65 LQR 480; Prosser *Torts* ch 13; R A Buckley *The Law of Nuisance* (1981).

2 *Pwllbach Colliery Co Ltd v Woodman* [1915] AC 634, HL, affords an interesting example of the care required in using the term.

3 Cf LORD SIMONDS in *Read v Lyons (J) & Co Ltd* (1947) AC 156 at 183, [1946] 2 All ER 471 (*obiter*): '. . . if a man commits a legal nuisance it is no answer to his injured neighbour that he took the utmost care not to commit it. There the liability is strict . . .'

B. NUISANCE AND NEGLIGENCE

It follows, therefore, that the torts of negligence and nuisance overlap. Of course, nuisance does not cover so much ground as negligence because negligence protects interests in persons and goods as well as in land, whereas nuisance is confined to interests in land. It is usually assumed that negligence does not cover all the field covered by nuisance. Theoretically, this assumption seems challengeable. In practice, no doubt, many interferences will never be complained of in an action based on negligence; this is because most actions of nuisance are based on intentional acts, eg continuing to discharge effluent into a river after being notified that this is destroying fish therein, and, as we have seen, negligence is not in practice invoked where conduct is intentional. Yet it is difficult to envisage facts giving rise to an action of nuisance where a duty to take care not to harm the plaintiff in the user of his land could not possibly be established. Take an example sometimes given of a situation said not to be capable of giving rise to an action of negligence—the blocking of rights of light in buildings: if A, a quarry-owner, so blasted his land that a heap of rubble accumulated on land adjoining the building of the plaintiff to such a height that it interfered with the right of light of the plaintiff, why should he not succeed in a negligence action? That is not to say that the law of nuisance and negligence will be identical in all cases: for example, success in negligence always depends on first establishing a legal duty.[4] At the same time, there can be no doubt that in many actions both negligence and nuisance are relied on when it could make no difference to the result if either of them were argued alone.[5]

C. PRIVATE AND PUBLIC NUISANCE

The confusion resulting from the overlapping of nuisance and negligence is aggravated by the existence of another type of nuisance known to the law, namely, public nuisance. Public nuisance is a crime, covering a miscellany of interferences with rights of the public at large, such as brothel-keeping, obstructing public highways, selling impure food—the list is huge. The commission of a public nuisance is not tortious unless an individual proves that he has suffered particular damage beyond that suffered by the rest of the community. This tort is not, however, the same tort as that of private nuisance; one obvious distinction is that in private nuisance the plaintiff must prove interference with his enjoyment of land, whereas claims based on public nuisance are not necessarily linked with user of land. The tendency to mistake them for one and the same is accentuated because the same act can be both a public and a private nuisance (eg a house in a ruinous condition which might fall either on to the highway or on to adjoining land), and because the rules governing who shall be suable are in some respects the same in both

---

4 See p 157 ante.
5 Almost all the substantial difficulties caused by the principle of 'state of affairs' (p 319 post) could be overcome if negligence alone were relied on in those cases, for, with very few exceptions (eg *Wringe v Cohen* [1940] 1 KB 229, [1939] 4 All ER 241, CA, p 332 post), negligence is an alternative tort in those cases.

torts.[6] Yet there is no sound authority for assuming that the rules of the tort of private nuisance and of that arising from public nuisance are in all other respects the same.[7] The facts giving rise to public nuisance will often afford a cause of action in negligence, and it will rarely matter which is relied on.[8] This close similarity of *public* nuisance and negligence will lead the unwary to false conclusions about the relationship of *private* nuisance and negligence—and, in particular, since personal injuries are protected by the tort derived from public nuisance, it may cause them to assume that damages for personal injuries are normally recoverable in private nuisance.[9]

D. NUISANCE DISTINGUISHED FROM OTHER TORTS

Nuisance has to be distinguished from other torts. It overlaps with the rule in *Rylands v Fletcher*[10] which imposes liability for the escape from land of things likely to do mischief if they escape.[11] Yet, as we shall see,[12] there are marked differences: sometimes the courts appear not to have observed these distinctions as sharply as they might, with consequent confusion in the law.[13] Nuisance and trespass do not overlap.[14] The influence of the old forms of action persists here, so that if injury to land is indirectly caused by the defendant, it cannot be trespass. As will have been realised when trespass to land was being considered, this somewhat blurs a classification of torts based on the interest affected. For it means that if A fires at B's wall, this is trespass, whereas if exactly the same damage is caused by something falling from A's land on to B's wall this cannot be trespass, but may be nuisance.

One further warning must be given before the case-law of nuisance is examined. The remedy for nuisance which is normally sought by a plaintiff is an injunction, not damages. The grant of an injunction is discretionary and, although the tort of nuisance is made out, may be refused if, for instance, the harm is not thought to be sufficiently substantial. Cases refusing an injunction must not, therefore, be taken as necessarily deciding that nuisance has not been committed.

A person, then, may be said to have committed the tort of private nuisance

---

6　See p 342 post.

7　See pp 339 et seq post.

8　Although in *Tate and Lyle Industries Ltd v Greater London Council* [1983] 2 AC 509, [1983] 1 All ER 1159, HL the plaintiffs failed in negligence because they failed to establish damage to their property and succeeded in public nuisance; see further post at p 340. *Wing v London General Omnibus Co* [1909] 2 KB 652, CA, is a striking illustration of how far the courts will sometimes go in considering a case under the heading of public nuisance when to do so can add nothing to a consideration of the case in negligence (action against omnibus company by a passenger injured when the omnibus skidded).

9　See p 328 post.

10　(1868) LR 3 HL 330.

11　Chapter 20 post.

12　See pp 357 et seq post.

13　LORD SIMONDS said in *Read v Lyons (J) & Co Ltd* [1947] AC 156 at 183, [1946] 2 All ER 471, HL, that 'the law of nuisance and the rule in *Rylands v Fletcher* might in most cases be invoked indifferently'.

14　It is often essential for the plaintiff to bring his case within the ambit of trespass. Thus, in *Kelsen v Imperial Tobacco Co (of Great Britain and Ireland) Ltd* [1957] 2 QB 334, [1957] 2 All ER 343, see p 68 ante, had the invasion of the airspace by the sign not been a trespass the plaintiff would have failed because the interference would not have been sufficiently unreasonable and substantial to be a nuisance.

*when he is held to be responsible for an act indirectly causing physical injury
to land or substantially interfering with the use or enjoyment of land or of an
interest in land, where, in the light of all the surrounding circumstances, this
injury or interference is held to be unreasonable.*

SECTION 2.   DAMAGE

One point has been deliberately omitted from this definition, and will be dealt
with first: whether damage must be proved in order to succeed in nuisance.
Nuisance is not actionable *per se* and actual damage must be proved, subject
to the following exceptions.

(1) Where, on the facts, damage can be readily presumed, this presumption of damage will suffice. If, then, a house is built so that one of
the cornices projects over the land of the plaintiff, it may be presumed that
damage will be caused to the land of the plaintiff by rain-water dripping
from the cornice on to that land.[15] Yet the following *dictum* shows that the
limits of this exception are narrow:[16]

But to plant a tree on one's own land infringes no rights, and, if the tree grows
over the soil of another, I cannot discover that any action lies for the encroachment
unless damage can be proved.

(2) Where the interference is with an easement, *profit à prendre* or right
of access. This exception may be justified in two ways. First, acquiescence
by the plaintiff in the conduct of the defendant for twenty years may bar
the plaintiff from founding a cause of action upon the act: hence the
difficulty of the plaintiff in proving that any one act caused damage should
not, in effect, prevent him from maintaining a cause of action in respect of
a course of conduct by the defendant which, if continued, will operate in
derogation of the rights of the plaintiff. Thus, the plaintiff can sue for
interference with a right of way without proving actual damage where
otherwise he might in due course lose altogether his right to complain of
the interference.[17] The second justification is illustrated by *Nichols v Ely
Beet Sugar Factory Ltd*:[18]

Effluent was alleged to have been discharged from the factory of the
defendants into a river in which the plaintiff had a right of fishery. The
court held that if the plaintiff had proved that the act of the defendant
caused this effluent to enter the river, he could succeed without proving
damage.

Lord Wright explained that disturbances of such rights were analogous
to trespass, and, although for technical reasons trespass was impossible
under the old forms of pleading in such cases, the fact that these disturbances were in the nature of interferences with rights absolutely pro-

---

15 *Baten's Case* (1610) 9 Co Rep 53b; *Fay v Prentice* (1854) 1 CB 828.
16 *Lemmon v Webb* [1894] 3 Ch 1 at 11 (per Lindley LJ), not discussed in [1895] AC 1, HL.
17 *Harrop v Hirst* (1868) LR 4 Exch 43; cf *McCartney v Londonderry and Lough Swilly Ry Co*
[1904] AC 301, HL.
18 [1936] Ch 343, CA. See also *Marriage v East Norfolk Rivers Catchment Board* [1949] 2 KB
456; affd [1950] 1 KB 284, CA.

tected was recognised to the extent of importing the rule of trespass that no proof of specific damage was required.[19]

(3) An injunction may be granted in a *quia timet* action where, although harm is reasonably feared to be imminent, no actual harm has yet occurred. In *Leeds Industrial Co-operative Society Ltd v Slack*[20] the House of Lords held that the statutory power[1] to give damages in substitution for an injunction applied to *quia timet* actions.

SECTION 3.   THE NATURE OF THE INVASION OF THE INTEREST IN LAND

The act on which a claim in nuisance is based may be one indirectly causing a physical injury to land, or a substantial interference with its enjoyment, or an interference with servitudes (or rights over land).

A. PHYSICAL INJURY

If, for example, the defendant sets up vibrations which cause the building of the plaintiff to collapse, or, if the fumes emitted from his factory destroy vegetation of the plaintiff, he might be committing an actionable private nuisance. There is sufficient invasion of the interest of the plaintiff if he proves his property to have suffered a sensible material injury which is not merely trifling in its nature and which results in a diminution of the value of the property. This is the effect of the decision of the House of Lords in *St Helen's Smelting Co v Tipping*.[2] This case further decides that where such injury is proved, it is not relevant to inquire whether the locality in which the defendant carried on the activity was a suitable one. So, when the plaintiff there established that his shrubs had been sensibly damaged by fumes from the copper-smelting plant of the defendants and that there had been very considerable diminution in the value of his property, the House of Lords held that the requirement of interference with the land of the plaintiff was satisfied, irrespective of whether the defendants carried on their business in a fit industrial locality.[3]

Because, as we shall see,[4] locality is a factor to be taken into account in deciding whether acts which cannot be brought under the present head are sufficient interferences with land, it is important to define 'sensible material injury to property'. This problem resolves itself into two parts, the first of which is the meaning of 'material injury'. A *dictum* of LORD SELBORNE LC suggests that it is enough if science can trace a deleterious physical change in

---

19 At 349; cf (1936) 52 LQR 463 (case note).
20 [1924] AC 851.
 1 Supreme Court Act 1981, s 50 (formerly Lord Cairns' Act 1858, s 2); even though no damages could be awarded at common law because no actual damage had yet occurred, *Hooper v Rogers* [1975] Ch 43, [1974] 3 All ER 417, CA.
 2 (1865) 11 HL Cas 642, approving a direction to the jury by MELLOR J, embodying these principles; (1863) 35 LJQB 66.
 3 The action might still fail for other reasons: eg that the use was not on the whole unreasonable, pp 321 et seq, post.
 4 See p 319, post.

the property;[5] Jessel MR, however, interpreted 'sensible' to mean damage visible by ordinary persons conversant with the subject matter without having recourse to scientific evidence.[6]

The second and more difficult problem is the meaning of 'property'. In *St Helen's Smelting Co v Tipping*[7] Lord Westbury LC distinguished 'material injury to property' on the one hand, and those interferences 'producing sensible personal discomfort' on the other. Depreciation in value of land and buildings is not in itself 'material injury to property'[8] but damage to goods within the premises is sufficient.[9]

Uncertainties remain about the scope of the sub-rule that the fitness of the place where the defendant carries on his activity is immaterial in deciding whether there has been interference amounting to sensible material injury: the impression is that, in practice, the courts often do consider the suitability of the locality, where a strict application of the rule under discussion would seem to preclude it.[10]

B. SUBSTANTIAL INTERFERENCE WITH ENJOYMENT

Where interference with enjoyment of land is relied on, then a substantial interference must be shown. Perhaps the most-cited formulation of the rule is this:[11]

> ought this inconvenience to be considered in fact as more than fanciful, more than one of mere delicacy or fastidiousness, as an inconvenience materially interfering with the ordinary comfort physically of human existence, not merely according to elegant or dainty modes and habits of living, but according to plain and sober and simple notions among the English people?

Although a trivial interference, then, is not a nuisance, Sir Wilfrid Greene MR has held that the loss of even one night's sleep through excessive noise is not trivial in this sense.[12] Nor need injury to health be proved.[13] The defendant's activities need not impinge on the senses as smoke fumes, smells

---

5 *Gaunt v Fynney* (1872) 8 Ch App 8 at 11–12.

6 *Salvin v North Brancepeth Coal Co* (1874) 9 Ch App 706 n affd (1874) 9 Ch App 705, and expressly by James LJ at 709. Scientific evidence is, however, admissible to prove that visible damage was *caused* by the defendant's operations.

7 (1865) 11 HL Cas 642 at 650–1.

8 *Mayo v Seaton Urban District Council* (1903) 68 JP 7 (erection of public lavatories not a private nuisance, although it depreciated value of plaintiff's premises from which persons proceeding to the lavatories could be seen); cf *Thompson-Schwab v Costaki* [1956] 1 All ER 652, CA, infra post, where the depreciation was not made the basis of a finding of nuisance; and *Russell Transport Ltd v Ontario Malleable Iron Co* [1952] 4 DLR 719.

9 A necessary consequence of the decision in *Halsey v Esso Petroleum Co Ltd* [1961] 2 All ER 145.

10 Often, for example, the plaintiff proves that dust has settled on his property, yet in these cases locality is considered, and the appropriateness of the rule under discussion is not adverted to, eg *Andreae v Selfridge & Co Ltd* [1938] Ch 1, [1937] 3 All ER 255, CA. In *Pwllbach Colliery Ltd v Woodman* [1915] AC 634, HL, where the interference was the settling of dust on the plaintiff's slaughter house and other buildings and the meat and sausages therein, Earl Loreburn at 638 appeared to confirm the view of the trial judge that the character of the locality had to be considered.

11 Per Knight-Bruce VC in *Walter v Selfe* (1851) 4 De G & Sm 315 at 322.

12 *Andreae v Selfridge & Co Ltd* [1938] Ch 1, [1937] 3 All ER 255 at 261, CA.

13 *Crump v Lambert* (1867) LR 3 Eq 409 at 412 (per Lord Romilly MR).

and odours do; it is a nuisance to use adjoining premises for prostitution[14] or as a sex shop.[15] On the other hand, it is not necessarily nuisance for an electric power station to operate near a church.[16] If the activity only damages the plaintiff because he is carrying on some extremely delicate trade on his land which demands exceptional freedom from interference, then this will not be an actionable nuisance.[17] In *Bridlington Relay Ltd v Yorkshire Electricity Board*[18] the defendants' power line interfered with the plaintiffs' business of providing a television relay service to subscribers. It was held that because interference with the recreational amenity of television viewing was not a substantial interference, the business interference complained of resulted only from the exceptional degree of immunity which the plaintiffs' business demanded, so that they could not sue in nuisance. It does not follow that, because a landowner has suffered appreciable financial loss in the use of his land as a result of the activities of the defendant, this will be a 'substantial interference', although the infliction of such business loss may be a factor in deciding whether to grant an injunction.[19] In *Victoria Park Racing and Recreation Grounds Co Ltd v Taylor*[20] the plaintiffs showed that they had lost profits in running their racecourse because the defendant, from a building just outside it, broadcast contemporaneous reports of the races. Their action in nuisance failed because the monopoly of view on the part of the plaintiff was not something which, if interfered with, the tort of nuisance protected.

It is important to distinguish this requirement of substantial interference from that harm actually suffered in respect of which damages are recoverable. So, the Privy Council decided that once the nuisance is established, ie once the substantial interference is proved, the remedies for that interference will extend to a sensitive and delicate operation such as the growing of orchids: for the damage to the orchids was a non-remote consequence of what had already been proved to be a nuisance, and *at that stage* the orchids' hyper-sensitiveness became irrelevant.[1]

(1) DURATION OF THE INTERFERENCE

An interference may, however, be substantial, though only temporary in duration—as in *Matania v National Provincial Bank Ltd and Elevenist Syn-*

14 *Thompson-Schwab v Costaki* [1956] 1 All ER 652, CA.
15 *Laws v Florinplace Ltd* [1981] 1 All ER 659.
16 *Heath v Brighton Corporation* (1908) 98 LT 718.
17 *Robinson v Kilvert* (1889) 41 ChD 88, CA.
18 [1965] Ch 436, [1965] 1 All ER 264, disapproved in *Nor-Video Services Ltd v Ontario Hydro* (1978) 84 DLR (3d) 221 (Ont) on the ground that television viewing is now an important incident of the ordinary enjoyment of property since it is a source of information, education and entertainment.
19 *Thompson-Schwab v Costaki* supra. Picketing premises may be a nuisance if accompanied by violence, obstruction, annoyance or molestation, but not if the intention were merely to obtain or communicate information: *J Lyons & Sons v Wilkins (No 2)* [1899] 1 Ch 255, CA; *Ward Lock & Co Ltd v Operative Printers' Assistants' Society* (1906) 22 TLR 327, CA; *Hubbard v Pitt* [1976] QB 142, [1975] 3 All ER 1, CA. Picketing was also a nuisance where the pickets attempted to regulate and control container traffic to and from the plaintiffs' port terminals and prevent the use of drivers not acceptable to the pickets; *The Mersey Dock & Harbour Co v Verrinder* [1982] IRLR 152.
20 (1938) 58 CLR 479 (High Court of Australia); it is thought that English courts would reach the same conclusion.
 1 *McKinnon Industries Ltd v Walker* [1951] 3 DLR 577, PC at 581 (per LORD SIMONDS).

dicate Ltd[2] where, in the circumstances, temporary noise and dust caused by making alterations to a building were held to be a nuisance.

(2) LOCALITY

In this group of nuisances, unlike those where sensible injury to land is complained of, one must consider the locality where the act is performed in order to determine whether the interference is substantial.[3] In *Sturges v Bridgman*[4] it was held that, in deciding whether the noise made by the mortar and pestle of a confectioner was a nuisance actionable by a neighbouring physician, one must take into account that the area consisted largely of consulting rooms of medical specialists.

(3) 'STATE OF AFFAIRS'

At this stage we must consider a problem which is important, not only in an understanding of the tort of nuisance itself, but also because of the implications bearing upon the relation of this tort with the rule in *Rylands v Fletcher*.[5] In *Castle v St Augustine's Links Ltd* the facts were:[6]

> The plaintiff, while using the highway, was blinded by a golf-ball driven from a tee on the adjoining course. He was held able to recover from the owners of the golf club for damages arising from public nuisance.

Suppose that the ball had been hit on to adjoining land and had harmed an interest of the occupier. The issues would have been the same except that the tort of private nuisance would have been committed. Is 'the substantial interference' required in nuisance the actual injury sustained by the plaintiff, ie does he recover if he is knocked unconscious but not if he is merely bruised? Further, we shall see[7] that many maintain that, if any material injury to property is caused, then the defendant is liable regardless of whether his user is reasonable—if, then, the nuisance is the actual injury suffered, it would follow that all householders whose windows were broken by golf balls hit from a golf course could sue the golf club in nuisance: surely there would then be a greater measure of liability in the absence of fault than this tort normally imposes.

An alternative view is that the test of whether there is 'substantial interference' is not whether harm did occur but whether the defendant was responsible for a condition of affairs on his land which threatened damage. Then the golf club would be responsible in nuisance only if they had so constructed the course that it was foreseeably likely that harm would be caused to occupiers of neighbouring land: if damage did in fact ensue, then an action of nuisance would lie, but the amount of damage would affect only the compensation recovered, not the existence of the cause of action.

It is submitted that the trend of recent cases is towards this latter view. *Bolton v Stone*[8] was a case where (*inter alia*) the liability in highway nuisance

---

2 [1936] 2 All ER 633, CA.
3 *Polsue and Alfieri Ltd v Rushmer* [1907] AC 121, HL; *Vanderpant v Mayfair Hotel Co Ltd* [1930] 1 Ch 138 at 166 (per LUXMOORE J).
4 (1879) 11 ChD 852.
5 (1868) LR 3 HL 330; see ch 20, post.
6 (1922) 38 TLR 615.
7 See p 326, post.
8 [1951] AC 850, [1951] 1 All ER 1078, HL.

of the defendant cricket club to a pedestrian hit by a cricket ball struck by a visiting batsman from the club's ground was in issue. So far as nuisance was concerned, the courts regarded as relevant the question whether the pitch and ground were so sited as to endanger those using the highway. JENKINS LJ said:[9]

> The gist of such a nuisance ... is the causing or permitting of a state of affairs from which damage is likely to result.

Similarly, in *Spicer v Smee*:[10]

> Defective electrical wiring was installed in the defendant's premises. This caused a fire resulting in the destruction of the plaintiff's adjoining bungalow.

Finding for the plaintiff in nuisance, ATKINSON J said:[11]

> ... private nuisance arises out of a state of things on one man's property whereby his neighbour's property is exposed to danger.

In short, what mattered was the defective wiring rather than the fire. Further, in *Sedleigh-Denfield v O'Callaghan*,[12] where the defendants allowed a culvert on their land to remain blocked, and the adjoining land of the plaintiff was consequently flooded, LORD ATKIN said that the defendants 'created a state of things ... from which ... flooding ... might reasonably be expected to result': it was therefore a nuisance. Cases like *Midwood & Co Ltd v Manchester Corporation* are readily understood in the light of this concept of 'state of affairs':[13]

> Faulty insulation caused the bitumen in which the defendants' electric mains were laid to volatise in the form of an inflammable gas. After accumulating for three hours, this exploded and set fire to an adjoining house of the plaintiff. The defendants were liable in nuisance.

That is, the defendants were responsible for a state of affairs, namely, the defective condition of the wiring, threatening substantial harm, and from which the resulting damage ensued.

These cases, then, establish that the requirement of 'substantial interference' is complied with if a state of affairs is existing whereby the user of adjoining premises is rendered hazardous by a threat of damage which is foreseeably[14] likely to result from that dangerous state of affairs. Nevertheless, there must be resulting damage in order to satisfy the requirement of the tort that some damage must be caused—not only does the extent of that damage

---

9 [1949] 2 All ER 851 at 855–6, CA. In the House of Lords negligence only was relied on.
10 [1946] 1 All ER 489.
11 Ibid at 493; cf DIXON J in *Torette House Property Ltd v Berkman* (1939) 62 CLR 637, at 659: 'potential source of nuisance or mischief'.
12 [1940] AC 880 at 895–6, [1940] 3 All ER 349, HL. Applied in *Pemberton v Bright and the Devon County Council* [1960] 1 All ER 792, CA.
13 [1905] 2 KB 597, CA; cf *Charing Cross Electricity Supply Co v Hydraulic Power Co* [1914] 3 KB 772, CA; *British Celanese Ltd v A H Hunt (Capacitors) Ltd* [1969] 2 All ER 1252, defendants' storing metal foil in such a way as to cause an escape of it on an isolated occasion resulting in a flash-over at a nearby electricity sub-station, liable in nuisance for foreseeable harm through power loss to plaintiffs' factory in the vicinity, as explained by THESIGER J and distinguished in *SCM (UK) Ltd v W J Whittall & Son Ltd* [1970] 2 All ER 417 at 430; on appeal [1971] 1 QB 337, [1970] 3 All ER 245, CA.
14 Ie foreseeably likely to a defendant who knows or ought to know the 'state of affairs'.

determine the size of the award of damages, but also it may assist in determining whether the state of affairs was a potential nuisance. The damage itself need not be substantial if the court is otherwise satisfied that the state of affairs was such as to expose the premises to risk of substantial harm.

C. INTERFERENCE WITH SERVITUDES

This topic is more fitting for a text book on real property. It will suffice here to mention that the main rights, interference with which may be actionable, are rights to light and air (through a defined channel), rights to support of land and buildings, and rights in respect of water in rivers. The importance of these rights is such that detailed and separate rules relating to them have been formulated by the courts.

SECTION 4.   UNREASONABLENESS

A plaintiff does not win an action based on nuisance by showing merely that another is responsible for substantial interference with his land resulting in damage to him. Nuisance cases often deal with a conflict of interests between neighbouring landowners, and so the law of nuisance has to adjust the respective rights and privileges of these neighbours. The position has been expressed by the House of Lords to be as follows:[15]

> A balance has to be maintained between the right of the occupier to do what he likes with his own, and the right of his neighbour not to be interfered with. It is impossible to give any precise or universal formula, but it may broadly be said that a useful test is perhaps what is reasonable according to the ordinary usages of mankind living in society ...

Thus, considering whether the burning of bricks near a house was actionable, ERLE CJ said:[16]

> It seems to me that the affairs of life in a dense neighbourhood cannot be carried on without mutual sacrifices of comfort; and that, in all actions for discomfort, the law must regard the principle of mutual adjustment ...

It is convenient to subsume this requirement under the word 'unreasonableness', but it must be understood that this is not the same as asking whether, from the defendant's point of view, his conduct was reasonable: he may be operating his chemical factory with proper care, and yet, taking into account not merely his own interests, the activity may be unreasonable. So many cases cited by text-books for the point that reasonableness is not a defence to nuisance are found, on examination, merely to have decided the quite different point that, even though the defendant may have taken

---

15 *Sedleigh-Denfield v O'Callaghan* [1940] AC 880 at 903, [1940] 3 All ER 349 (per LORD WRIGHT). Cf *Trevett v Lee* [1955] 1 All ER 406, CA, especially BIRKETT LJ at 413.
16 *Cavey v Ledbitter* (1863) 13 CBNS 470 at 476, developed and elaborated by ERLE CJ in his undelivered judgment in *Brand v Hammersmith & City Ry Co* (1867) LR 2 QB 223 at 247–8. Or, as the Court of Appeal put it in *Kennaway v Thompson* [1981] QB 88 at 94, [1980] 3 All ER 329 at 333. 'There must be a measure of give and take, live and let live.'

reasonable care in the carrying out of his activity, he may still be liable in nuisance.[17]

In principle, one should consider whether what has been done is reasonable, not merely from the defendant's viewpoint, but from the plaintiff's also. The courts have not been ready to define with precision the principles according to which this rule is to be applied; thus, to some extent, what follows is a rationalisation from the mass of decided cases. The basic issue is always the same: the weighing of the nature and circumstances of the defendant's activity against the nature and extent of the resulting interference with the plaintiff. The test, then, is objective: the view which the disinterested member of the public would take on this conflict.

The relevant factors include the following:

A.   THE CONDUCT OF THE DEFENDANT

(1)   HIS PURPOSE

The law, in judging what constitutes a nuisance, takes into consideration the main object of the defendant's activity.[18] The fact that an incidental consequence of his acts is to harm the business of his neighbour will, in itself, be immaterial here. If, on the other hand, his primary aim is to injure his neighbour, there is clear authority that this is highly relevant. In *Christie v Davey*[19] the court had to decide whether the making of noises by the plaintiffs and the defendant (who were neighbours) were actionable nuisances: in finding that those made by the plaintiffs were not, NORTH J expressly took into account that those of the defendant were 'made deliberately and maliciously for the purpose of annoying the plaintiffs'. Similarly, in *Hollywood Silver Fox Farm Ltd v Emmett*[20] the court held that the firing of guns out of spite against the plaintiff, with the object of interfering with the breeding of silver foxes by him, was actionable. It emphasised that its finding of malice was an important factor in the decision.

These decisions can, in one sense, be regarded as a judicial determination that conduct has no socially valuable purpose when it is motivated by spite. Conversely, then, the more socially worthwhile the activity is, the less likely it is to be held unreasonable. The country must have power stations, factories, and smelting works, but the need for motor cycle speedway tracks[1] or racecourses[2] is less pressing.[3]

This is not to say that, merely because the plaintiff suffers loss as a result of an act done by the defendant with an improper motive, there is a cause of action. In *Bradford Corporation v Pickles*[4] the defendant abstracted water percolating through undefined channels beneath his land, which would otherwise have reached the plaintiffs' adjoining reservoir. To abstract the per-

---

17 Eg *Reinhardt v Mentasti* (1889) 42 ChD 685; *Bamford v Turnley* (1862) 3 B & S 66.
18 Per VAUGHAN WILLIAMS J in *Harrison v Southwark and Vauxhall Water Co* [1891] 2 Ch 409 at 414.
19 [1893] 1 Ch 316 at 326.
20 [1936] 2 KB 468, [1936] 1 All ER 825.
1 *A-G v Hastings Corporation* (1950) 94 Sol Jo 225, CA.
2 *Dewar v City and Suburban Racecourse Co* [1899] 1 IR 345.
3 This element seems to be material in cases such as *Andreae v Selfridge & Co Ltd* [1938] Ch 1, [1937] 3 All ER 255, CA; see p 324, post.
4 [1895] AC 587, HL.

colating water was in itself lawful, and the fact that the defendant might have acted with bad motive towards the plaintiffs (in that he wanted to make the plaintiffs pay an inflated price for the land, which they required in connection with their reservoir) did not, therefore, make his act an actionable nuisance. Or, to put it another way, the plaintiffs' claim came within the rubric of injuries to servitudes, ie here, rights in respect of water; the rule of Section 3 in this Chapter relating to the nature of the invasion of the plaintiffs' interest in land had not been satisfied by the defendant's conduct because the plaintiffs had no rights in respect of percolating water, and the action necessarily failed, regardless of whether it satisfied any requirement of reasonableness within the present Section.[5]

(2) SUITABILITY OF LOCALITY

In deciding whether the interference is unreasonable one has to consider not only the usefulness of the act, but also whether the defendant is carrying it on in a suitable locality. The courts have recognised that there is a national policy of segregating different uses of land, and have furthered this policy by taking into account whether the defendant is putting his land to a use which is compatible with the main use to which land in that district is put. To operate a factory in a residential area may well be unreasonable, while the same activity might be lawful in an industrial area.[6] Where, for instance, Parliament has authorised the construction of an oil refinery on agricultural land, the issue of whether it constitutes a nuisance to neighbouring villagers must now be decided in the light of the new authorised industrial environment.[7]

(3) ORDINARY USE OF THE LAND

It will be seen later[8] that, where the land of the defendant is being put to its natural use, there is no liability in the analogous tort of *Rylands v Fletcher*: there, 'natural user' has received an increasingly wide interpretation. At the same time, the use of the expression in *Rylands v Fletcher* was, it seems, derived from earlier cases concerned with flooding of mines, which could perhaps be regarded as decisions on, and certainly were within the ambit of,

---

5 In *Langbrook Properties Ltd v Surrey County Council* [1969] 3 All ER 1424, the defendants pumped out water from their excavations, thereby extracting percolating water from plaintiffs' nearby land and causing settlement damage to plaintiffs' buildings; held no nuisance. And in *Home Brewery Co Ltd v William Davis & Co (Leicester) Ltd* [1987] QB 339, [1987] 1 All ER 637 the defendants were held not liable in nuisance for blocking water percolating from the plaintiffs' land. No unreasonable use interfering with the plaintiffs' rights was proved. But insofar as flooding of the plaintiffs' land resulted from water 'squeezed out' directly onto the plaintiffs' land, the defendants were held liable in trespass. Similarly, in *Phipps v Pears* [1965] 1 QB 76, [1964] 2 All ER 35, CA, when the defendant by demolishing his house exposed the plaintiffs' neighbouring house to the weather, whereby damage to it resulted, the plaintiff had no remedy because there is no easement to protection against the weather.

6 *Ball v Ray* decided that providing stables in a residential area was unreasonable, whereas interference to a similar extent in another area or in this area by a domestic non-industrial activity, eg the crying of babies in their nursery, would not be a nuisance (1873) 8 Ch App 467. Cf *Moy v Stoop* (1909) 25 LTR 262.

7 *Allen v Gulf Oil Refining Ltd* [1981] AC 1001 at 1014, [1981] 1 All ER 353 at 357–8 (per LORD WILBERFORCE) HL.

8 See p 345, post.

the tort of nuisance. Prominent among these was *Smith v Kenrick*,[9] which decided that a defendant who, in the ordinary course of extracting minerals from his land, caused the property of an adjoining mine owner to be flooded by water, was not liable for damage caused by that flooding. The case has been followed in mining cases since *Rylands v Fletcher*, in some of which it has not been clear whether the decision was based on *Rylands v Fletcher* or on nuisance.[10]

At the same time, it may be (it is impossible to be sure in view of the confusion of *Rylands v Fletcher* and nuisance in the decided case) that the principle of these mining cases survives in nuisance. There may still be a principle of law (a firm sub-rule within the category of reasonable use) that, if water seeps through adjoining land as a result of the non-negligent extraction of mines or minerals, there is no liability in nuisance, ie that the other elements of 'unreasonable use' now being discussed are irrelevant in this one case of mines.

However, it can be said with confidence that there may still be liability in nuisance where the use is 'natural' in the greatly extended sense of that word in modern applications of *Rylands v Fletcher*. In the case of many of those extensions, the so-called 'natural use' would merely be one factor in deciding whether it was unreasonable in nuisance. So, dripping water from the eaves of a building may give rise to a nuisance, although it would be outside *Rylands v Fletcher*.[11]

The nearest approach to the broad rule of 'natural use' in *Rylands v Fletcher* to be found in nuisance is the *dictum* of BRAMWELL B in *Bamford v Turnley*:[12]

> ... those acts necessary for the common and ordinary use and occupation of land and houses may be done, if conveniently[13] done, without subjecting those who do them to an action [in nuisance].

There is, however, no subsequent reliable authority for so broad a statement.[14] On the other hand, it does now seem to be accepted that where building operations of a temporary character, such as demolition, repairs or conversions, are being carried on with reasonable care so as not to cause undue inconvenience to neighbours, no tort is committed.[15] In *Andreae v Selfridge & Co Ltd* the Court of Appeal applied this legal principle to a case where building operations interfered with a neighbouring hotel, holding that, in some circumstances, even interference caused by the use of pneumatic drills would be lawful.[16] In cases other than temporary building operations, it is

---

9 (1849) 7 CB 515.
10 *Whalley v Lancashire and Yorkshire Ry Co* (1884) 13 QBD 131; cf *Hurdman v North Eastern Ry Co* (1878) 3 CPD 168; *Wilson v Waddell* (1876) 2 App Cas 95, HL.
11 *Fay v Prentice* (1845) 1 CB 828.
12 (1862) 3 B & S 66 at 83.
13 Ie with reasonable care and skill.
14 Although the *dictum* of LORD SELBORNE LC in *Ball v Ray* (1873) 8 Ch App 467 at 469, is perhaps the strongest support for it, it was in wider terms than the facts of the case demanded.
15 *Metropolitan Properties Ltd v Jones* [1939] 2 All ER 202 at 205 (per GODDARD LJ); *Newman v Real Estate Debenture Corporation Ltd and Flower Decorations Ltd* [1940] 1 All ER 131; on the other hand 'if he [the occupier] is using it for purposes for which the building was not constructed' it may then be tortious; per BUCKLEY J in *Sanders-Clark v Grosvenor Mansions Co Ltd and D'Allessandri* [1900] 2 Ch 373 at 375–6.
16 [1938] Ch 1, [1937] 3 All ER 255, CA.

probably safest to conclude that it is a material but not a conclusive factor that the land is being put to its ordinary use.[17]

A defendant may be liable in nuisance for the escape of things which are naturally on his land. Where, as a result of the operation of natural agencies, earth slides from the defendant's conical hill so as to threaten the plaintiff's property below, the defendant may be liable in nuisance.[18]

(4) IMPRACTICABILITY OF PREVENTING OR AVOIDING THE INTERFERENCE

It will always be material whether the defendant could still have achieved his purpose without interfering with the use of his land by the plaintiff if he had taken reasonable practicable steps to prevent the interference. If, without excessive expenditure, the factory owner could have installed equipment which would have avoided substantial interference with the plaintiff's use, the courts may well treat this as almost conclusive that the defendant's activity was unreasonable. On the other hand, except in the case of temporary building work referred to on the preceding page, it will not be conclusive of reasonable use that the defendant had used reasonable care in carrying out his work.[19] Thus in *Moy v Stoop*,[20] the court held that no action lay against a householder whose children were often crying in the nursery, but indicated that it was all a matter of degree, and that the decision might well have been different had the children been crying because they were neglected.[1]

B. THE SERIOUSNESS OF THE INTERFERENCE WITH THE PLAINTIFF'S USER OF LAND

(1) THE EXTENT OF THE HARM

The duration of the interference has, as would be expected, often been held to be important in deciding whether there is an actionable nuisance.[2] Indeed, as we have seen in the case of building operations, it is only when they are temporary that the principle of law applies that such works carried out with proper care are not actionable. On the other hand, the Court of Appeal has

---

17 The view of Luxmoore J in *Vanderpant v Mayfair Hotel Co Ltd* [1930] 1 Ch 138 at 166, must now be construed in the light of *Andreae v Selfridge* supra. And the decision in *De Keyser's Royal Hotel Ltd v Spicer Brothers Ltd and Minter* (1914) 30 TLR 257 that pile-driving was actionable nuisance must be read subject to the observations of the Court of Appeal in *Andreae v Selfridge* about judging the reasonableness of the operations with regard to current building techniques.

18 *Leakey v National Trust for Places of Historic Interest or Natural Beauty* [1980] QB 485, [1980] 1 All ER 17, CA, overruling *Giles v Walker* (1890) 24 QBD 656 and disapproving of *Pontardawe Rural Council v Moore-Gwyn* [1929] 1 Ch 656. And see *Russell v Barnet London Borough Council* (1984) 271 Estates Gazette 699 (highway authority liable for subsidence caused by tree roots from trees growing on the highway). For the extent of the responsibility in such a case, see p 322, post.

19 *Rapier v London Tramways Co* [1893] 2 Ch 588, CA, but the court found that in any event the defendants had tried to economise unduly by crowding too many horses in the stable which was the source of the nuisance.

20 (1909) 25 TLR 262.

1 Cf *Harrison v Southwark and Vauxhall Water Co* [1891] 2 Ch 409; *Manchester Corporation v Farnworth* [1930] AC 171, HL (where, however, the issue was complicated by the question of whether there was the defence of statutory authority to the nuisance).

2 *Harrison v Southwark and Vauxhall Water Co* [1891] 2 Ch 409 at 414 (per Vaughan Williams J).

laid down that an interference for a short time is an actionable nuisance if, on the whole, it is unreasonable.[3] Besides the duration of the harm, one must also consider the degree of harm. Thus, in cases like *Midwood & Co Ltd v Manchester Corporation*,[4] where the defendant has been responsible for a state of affairs resulting in an explosion and a setting fire to the plaintiff's premises, there is a cause of action: in short, there may be a major interference although it lasts only for a short period of time.

(2) THE CHARACTER OF THE HARM

The harm may either take the form of physical injury to land or an interference with personal enjoyment of it. A *dictum* of LORD WESTBURY in *St Helen's Smelting Co v Tipping*[5] has indeed been widely taken as creating a sharp legal distinction between the two types of harm, viz, that is sensible physical injury to property is proved then there is an action regardless of whether, on balance, the user of the land by the defendant was objectively reasonable. This is not believed to be the *ratio decidendi* of any of the judgments in that case.[6]

Thus, in *Watt v Jamieson*[7]

Defendant's ventpipe discharged water vapour from a water heater on to plaintiff's neighbouring flat, and caused plaster disintegration and dry rot.

LORD PRESIDENT COOPER held that the plaintiff did not succeed merely by proving this serious damage and added that 'the critical question is whether what he was exposed to was *plus quam tolerabile* when due weight has been given to all the surrounding circumstances of the offensive conduct and its effects'.[8] In *Stearn v Prentice Brothers Ltd*,[9] the plaintiffs' crops were devoured by rats attracted to the premises of the defendants because the defendants collected bone-manure there. Although this was sensible physical injury to land of the plaintiffs, the action of nuisance failed because what the defendants did was held in the circumstances to be neither unusual nor excessive. Yet it is admitted that it will be relevant to consider which of the two types of harm has been incurred. The key to this is to be found in LORD SELBORNE's judgment in *Gaunt v Fynney*:[10] physical damage is a more tangible and readily proved loss than personal annoyance; English courts are always chary of protecting personal discomforts falling short of physical injury,[11] and this attitude is reflected in their attaching greater weight to appreciable physical injury than to personal discomfort.

(3) THE SUITABILITY TO THE LOCALITY OF THE USE INTERFERED WITH

In deciding whether action lies because of industrial interference, the courts have often taken account of the fact that interference took place in a resi-

---

3 *Matania v National Provincial Bank Ltd and Elevenist Syndicate Ltd* [1936] 2 All ER 633, CA.
4 [1905] 2 KB 597.
5 (1865) 11 HL Cas 642 at 650.
6 And see p 316 ante, for the *ratio decidendi* of the case.
7 1954 SC 56.
8 At 58.
9 [1919] 1 KB 394, Div Ct. Cf *Farrer v Nelson* (1885) 15 QBD 258, Div Ct; *Seligman v Docker* [1949] Ch 53, [1948] 2 All ER 887.
10 (1872) 8 Ch App 8 at 11–12.
11 Eg their attitude to nervous shock, pp 177 et seq ante.

dential area. In *Sturges v Bridgman*,[12] it was held material to the success (in nuisance) of a physician, who complained that his professional work was interfered with by a confectioner, that the locality was one where many medical men practised.[13]

(4) SOCIAL VALUE OF THE USE INTERFERED WITH

It may be expected that, just as the usefulness or merit of the defendant's business is taken into account, so also the social value of the plaintiff's use of the land would be material. Interference with a church service might be more readily classed as actionable than interference with the activities of a bookmaker.

(5) COULD THE PLAINTIFF EASILY HAVE AVOIDED THE CONSEQUENCES OF THE HARM?

Usually, when the facts are that the plaintiff could readily have avoided the consequences of the defendant's act, they will be classed under some other head, eg that the cause of the interference was the plaintiff's own default, or, at the other end of the scale, that it is no defence that the plaintiff came to the nuisance.[14] Occasionally, however, the ease with which the plaintiff might have avoided the consequences of the defendant's act might be relevant in deciding whether his action succeeds.

SECTION 5.   WHO CAN SUE?

A plaintiff can only sue in nuisance if he has an interest in the land affected.[15] Thus, a guest whose enjoyment of the land is interfered with cannot base any claim on nuisance.[16] EVERSHED J, in *Newcastle-under-Lyme Corporation v Wolstanton Ltd*,[17] had to decide whether the plaintiffs, who had no legal or equitable interest in the land but who possessed water pipes there, could sue in nuisance for interference with the right of support for these pipes. He held that, in rare cases like this, a person having possession, though no legal or equitable interest, might sue. He was, however, careful to state that he did not intend to lay down any general principle. With this may be compared *Metropolitan Properties Ltd v Jones*:[18]

12 (1879) 11 ChD 852.
13 In *St Helen's Smelting Co v Tipping* (1865) 11 HL Cas 642 at 653, an unreported case was cited with approval where ROLFE B directed the jury that they must look at the problem whether the annoyance from smoke in Shields was actionable, 'not with a view to the question whether, abstractedly, that quantity of smoke was a nuisance, but whether it was a nuisance to a person living in the town of Shields'.
14 See p 335, post.
15 An occupier may recover in respect of damage which occurred before he acquired the property if the nuisance is continuing and he has incurred a loss in respect of it: *Masters v Brent London Borough Council* [1978] QB 841, [1978] 2 All ER 664, and see *GUS Property Management Ltd v Littlewoods Mail Order Stores Ltd* 1982 SLT 533, HL (Scottish).
16 *Malone v Laskey* [1907] 2 KB 141.
17 [1947] Ch 92, [1946] 2 All ER 447; reversed on other grounds, [1947] Ch 427, [1947] 1 All ER 218, CA. A local authority in whom statute has vested the surface of a highway only can sue in nuisance for interference with that surface: *Lodge Holes Colliery Co v Wednesbury Corporation* [1908] AC 323, HL.
18 [1939] 2 All ER 202.

The plaintiff, a lessee of premises from which his assignee had absconded, was called upon by the lessor to pay the rent owing under the lease. The plaintiff thereupon re-entered the premises, and then complained of a nuisance caused by the defendant. He was held not to have sufficient interest in the land to enable him to sue in nuisance.

Similarly the plaintiffs in *Tate & Lyle Industries Ltd v Greater London Council*[19] failed in their action for private nuisance. New ferry terminals erected by the defendants caused excessive siltation of the River Thames disrupting the business operated by the plaintiffs on the bank of the river and supplies from their private jetty. There was no damage to the plaintiffs' property and the House of Lords held no injury to their private rights as riparian owners was proved. It was their public right to navigate the river which had been damaged and their claim lay in public nuisance alone.

A reversioner can sue if he proves that his interest in the land has been interfered with. This usually means that if he proves harm of a permanent character, eg the blocking of lights by a building, he will succeed.[20] Mere temporary interference is not enough, even if the reversioner shows that it is likely that similar future interference will take place.[1]

An allied question of great difficulty is whether the plaintiff with an interest in the land can recover, in addition, damages for injuries to goods and for personal injuries.

Several cases have decided claims for damage to goods in actions based on nuisance, but in none of them was the point argued. In *Midwood & Co Ltd v Manchester Corporation*,[2] damages were awarded by the Court of Appeal for loss of stock in trade, in *Crowhurst v Amersham Burial Board*[3] they were awarded for loss of a horse, in *Halsey v Esso Petroleum Co Ltd* for damage to washing on a clothes line[4] and in *Moss v Christchurch Rural Council*[5] a tenant recovered for damage to his furniture. On the other hand, a claim (in so far as it was based on nuisance[6]) by the occupier for damage to furniture was refused in *Cunard v Antifyre Ltd*.[7]

Damages for personal injuries are recoverable for the tort arising from public nuisance. No English authority on the point in respect of private nuisance has been traced.[8]

LORD SIMONDS has said that 'he alone has a lawful claim who has suffered an invasion of some proprietary or other interest in land'.[9] This may point to a solution of the problem. It may well be that, once the plaintiff has shown

19 [1983] 2 AC 509, [1983] 1 All ER 1159.
20 *Jesser v Gifford* (1767) 4 Burr 2141; cf *Tucker v Newman* (1839) 11 Ad & El 40 (projecting eaves discharging water on land).
1 *Simpson v Savage* (1856) 1 CBNS 347 (smoke discharged from fire); cf *Jones v Llanrwst Urban Council* [1911] 1 Ch 393 at 404 (per PARKER J).
2 [1905] 2 KB 597.
3 (1878) 4 Ex D 5.
4 [1961] 2 All ER 145.
5 [1925] 2 KB 750.
6 The action succeeded in negligence; and see p 273 ante.
7 [1933] 1 KB 551, [1932] All ER Rep 558 Div Ct. SOMERVELL LJ in *Newcastle-under-Lyme Corporation v Wolstanton Ltd* [1947] Ch 427, CA at 446 (and see 463), [1947] 1 All ER 218, seems to have doubted (*obiter*) whether damages to goods were recoverable.
8 In *Bone v Seal* [1975] 1 All ER 787, CA, smells from a pig farm constituted a nuisance but did not diminish the value of the land and caused no ill health; each plaintiff was awarded £1,000 for this two years' loss of amenity in the enjoyment of his property.
9 *Obiter* in *Read v Lyons (J) & Co Ltd* [1947] AC 156 at 183, [1946] 2 All ER 471, HL.

that he has suffered such an invasion, he can recover as consequential damages injuries to his goods and to his person. Thus, it would seem reasonable that a person proving a nuisance caused by the emission of fumes should recover damages for illness caused thereby.[10] More difficult, however, is the type of nuisance dependent on a state of affairs. If, for example, the nuisance consists of a chimney likely to fall on adjoining land, and part of that chimney does fall on to the head of the plaintiff-occupier of that adjoining land, but does no other damage, can he then recover damages for those personal injuries? Perhaps, there, too, the damages would be recoverable—since that interference with enjoyment which the tort demands has been proved, there seems no good reason for distinguishing this case from the previous one.

SECTION 6.   WHO CAN BE SUED?

A person is liable in nuisance if he bears 'some degree of personal responsibility'.[11]

A. CREATOR

If the actual wrongdoer is invested with the management and control of the premises where the nuisance created by him arises, he is liable irrespective of whether he is an occupier in the normal sense of the word.[12] Even though the person who created the interference was neither at the time of the proceedings nor at the time when he created the interference in occupation or control of the premises from which it emanated, but merely created it with the authority of the occupier of the premises, he may still be liable for creating it—he is not excused because he had no right to enter on the premises in order to abate it.[13] In accordance with ordinary principles of tortious liability, he who authorises another to commit a nuisance is himself also liable. A landlord who lets a field for a particular purpose (eg for quarrying lime or go-kart races[14]) where the known necessary consequence of carrying out that purpose was a nuisance has been held liable.[15] Where, on the other hand, the demised premises had a chimney which caused an interference if coal were burnt in

10 But would damages be recoverable in respect of physical illness from nervous shock caused by blasting?
11 Per LORD ATKIN in *Sedleigh-Denfield v O'Callaghan* [1940] AC 880 at 897, [1940] 3 All ER 349, HL.
12 *Hall v Beckenham Corporation* [1949] 1 KB 716, [1949] 1 All ER 423.
13 *Thompson v Gibson* (1841) 7 M & W 456. In *Southport Corporation v Esso Petroleum Co Ltd* [1953] 2 All ER 1204 at 1207; DEVLIN J said (*obiter*): 'I can see no reason why ... if the defendant as a licensee or trespasser misuses someone else's land, he should not be liable for a nuisance in the same way as an adjoining occupier would be.' Certainly, this *dictum* is in accord with the general opinion of text-book writers, eg *Clerk and Lindsell* p 1162, but no case has been traced where liability was imposed upon a person who had never been in occupation or control of the relevant premises in respect of conduct constituting a private nuisance, and not authorised by anyone who was in occupation of those premises. In Australia a trespasser is not liable in nuisance; *Beaudesert Shire Council v Smith* (1966) 40 ALJR 211 H Ct Australia.
14 *Tetley v Chitty* [1986] 1 All ER 663.
15 *Harris v James* (1876) 45 LJ QB 545; *Sampson v Hodson-Pressinger* (1981) 261 Estates Gazette 891, CA; *Smith v Scott* [1973] Ch 314, [1972] 3 All ER 645 (local authority not liable for allowing in house offensive undesirable tenants whom it knew were likely to cause a nuisance.)

it, but which would have been inoffensive had the tenant (as his predecessor had done) burned coke, the landlord was held not liable for a nuisance caused by the tenant's burning coal.[16] Similarly, the occupier is liable for allowing his licensee to carry on activities naturally resulting in a nuisance.[17]

A defendant is vicariously liable for nuisances created by his servant in the course of his employment,[18] SLESSER LJ has held that, 'if the act done is one which in its very nature involves a special danger of nuisance being complained of', then the defendant is liable also for the failure of his independent contractor to take precautions.[19] The nature of this liability for independent contractors in nuisance was more widely stated by COCKBURN CJ in *Bower v Peate*,[20] when holding a principal liable for his independent contractor's withdrawing support from the buildings of the plaintiff:

> a man who orders a work to be executed, from which, in the natural course of things, injurious consequences to his neighbour must be expected to arise, ... is bound to see to the doing of that which is necessary to prevent the mischief, and cannot relieve himself of his responsibility by employing someone else ...

Yet, in view of later doubts cast on this *dictum*,[1] it may not be safe to assume that the liability is any wider than as stated by SLESSER LJ above.

Where the nuisance arises from 'a state of affairs' the nature and extent of responsibility of the creator present considerable difficulties. The cases seem reconcilable by adopting the *dictum* of LORD ATKIN in *Sedleigh-Denfield v O'Callaghan*.[2] He held that the laying of the pipe with an unprotected orifice was, in the circumstances of that case, a nuisance because

> it created a state of things from which when the ditch was flowing in full stream an obstruction might reasonably be expected in the pipe, from which obstruction flooding of the plaintiff's ground might reasonably be expected to result.

Thus, he who plants poplar trees is liable for indirect injury caused by the spreading of their roots under neighbouring land: this harm is foreseeable.[3] Similarly, the creation of a state of danger in maintaining defective electric

---

16 *Rich v Basterfield* (1847) 4 CB 783; cf *Malzy v Eichholz* [1916] 2 KB 308, CA (to authorise the holding of mock auctions is not to be responsible for nuisance caused by the holding of them).

17 *White v Jameson* (1874) LR 18 Eq 303; *A-G v Stone* (1895) 60 JP 168 (liable for allowing gypsy caravanners on land); contra *Hall v Beckenham Corporation* [1949] 1 KB 716, [1949] 1 All ER 423 (defendants were in control, by statute, of a park in which boys created a nuisance by model aircraft; although it was not denied that the defendants could, if they so desired, have submitted to the appropriate Minister for confirmation a bye-law regulating this activity, the fact that no such bye-law was in existence at the material time, was in itself, held to exempt them from liability in nuisance—they could not at that time have interfered with the boys who were flying the model aircraft in the park).

18 *Spicer v Smee* [1946] 1 All ER 489 at 493 (per ATKINSON J).

19 *Matania v National Provincial Bank Ltd and Elevenist Syndicate Ltd* [1936] 2 All ER 633 at 646, CA.

20 (1876) 1 QBD 321 at 326; cf ATKINSON J following *Bower v Peate* in *Spicer v Smee* supra at 495: 'where danger is likely to arise unless work is properly done, there is a duty to see that it is properly done.' See p 450 et seq post, for a fuller treatment of liability for acts of independent contractors.

1 Eg per LORD BLACKBURN in *Hughes v Percival* (1883) 8 App Cas 443, HL at 446–7; cf *Tarry v Ashton* (1876) 1 QBD 314.

2 [1940] AC 880 at 895–6, [1940] 3 All ER 349, HL.

3 *Butler v Standard Telephone and Cables Ltd* [1940] 1 KB 399, [1940] 1 All ER 121; followed in *McCombe v Read* [1955] 2 QB 429, [1955] 2 All ER 758.

mains affords liability for foreseeable damage which in fact ensues.[4] Yet, in *Ilford Urban Council v Beal.*[5]

> The defendant erected a retaining wall along the bank of a river. Because the wall was not constructed in accordance with the best engineering practice it was later completely undermined by the river; this undermining caused it to move forward a foot or two, so that it pressed against and damaged the plaintiffs' sewer. The defendant neither knew nor ought to have known of the existence of that sewer. The defendant was held not liable in nuisance.

The explanation must be that if the non-remote consequence of the defendant's act is an interference with another's interest in land, but that act does not in itself create a state of affairs foreseeably likely to result in that interference, he is not responsible for it in nuisance.[6]

Difficult problems of responsibility for nuisance are raised where local authorities are sued because of pollution from sewage. *Glossop v Heston & Isleworth Local Board*[7] decided that where a local authority has taken over sewers under the Public Health Acts, and those sewers are a nuisance in that they now cease to deal adequately with the sewage of the area, then the local authority is not liable in nuisance merely because it has failed to exercise its statutory power (not duty) to enlarge its sewerage system.[8] On the other hand, the Court of Appeal held in *Pride of Derby and Derbyshire Angling Association Ltd v British Celanese Ltd*[9] that if the sewage reaches the river (the pollution of which is complained of) through the effluent pipe of the local authority from its sewage works then the local authority is responsible.[10]

B. FAILURE TO REMEDY

Responsibility may also arise from failure to take what are reasonable steps

---

4 *Midwood & Co Ltd v Manchester Corporation* [1905] 2 KB 597, CA.

5 [1925] 1 KB 671.

6 *Radstock Co-operative and Industrial Society Ltd v Norton-Radstock Urban District Council* [1968] Ch 605, [1968] 2 All ER 59, CA, shows the difficulty and importance of deciding whether the defendant created the nuisance within this section or merely failed to remedy it within the next section B. A properly laid sewer in a stream, sixty years later, because of stream scouring over the years, caused eddies which undermined the piles of B's bridge. If the defendant only 'continued' the nuisance within section B, P had the burden of proving D's negligence; if D were deemed to have created it, D had the burden of exculpating himself.

7 (1879) 12 ChD 102, CA.

8 Cf *Smeaton v Ilford Corporation* [1954] Ch 450, [1954] 1 All ER 923 (defendants' sewers overloaded through, as to 98% discharge into their sewers of sewage which they were required to receive, and, as to 2% discharge from a new municipal housing estate; defendants held not liable in nuisance for flooding which ensued).

9 [1953] Ch 149, [1953] 1 All ER 179, CA.

10 DENNING LJ (*obiter*) at 190–1, stated that they would also be liable if the existing system had become inadequate because of new houses built by the local authority or even because of new houses, the erection of which by private persons the local authority had sanctioned by virtue of its powers of control under the Town and Country Planning Acts, since they would then be 'responsible' for the nuisance. In *Page Motors Ltd v Epsom and Ewell District Council* (1981) 80 LGR 337, CA, a local authority which failed for 5 years to find another site for gypsies was held liable to a car dealer who lost business through the gypsy site being nearby.

in the light of the defendant's own financial and other circumstances[11] to remedy a dangerous state of affairs on land.

1 If it is created by a trespasser and the occupier knows or ought to know of it, he is responsible.[12]

2 If it occurs as a result of an act of nature of which the occupier knows or ought to know, he commits the tort.[13]

3 It was held in *Bradburn v Lindsay*,[14] contrary to earlier authorities, that where neighbouring owners have mutual rights of support, failure to repair the defendant's house resulting in damage to the plaintiff's adjacent property constituted an actionable nuisance.

4 If the predecessor of the defendant created it and the defendant knows or ought to know of it, the defendant is liable.[15]

5 In one case, there is responsibility even though due care is shown (an instance where there may be liability in nuisance for an act which is neither intentional nor negligent). In *Wringe v Cohen* the Court of Appeal held:[16]

> ... if, owing to want of repair, premises on a highway become dangerous and, therefore, a nuisance, and a passer-by or an adjoining owner suffers damage by

---

11 *Goldman v Hargrave* [1967] 1 AC 645, [1966] 2 All ER 989, PC; *Leakey v National Trust for Places of Historic Interest or National Beauty* [1980] QB 485, [1980] 1 All ER 17, CA. It is because the defendant has had this state of affairs thrust on him that his financial and physical resources are taken into account in deciding what is reasonable. Presumably, failure by a local authority to exercise a statutory power to remedy a nuisance is actionable only if the omission is *ultra vires* within the rule in *Anns v Merton London Borough Council* [1978] AC 728, [1977] 2 All ER 492, HL, p 166 ante; and see *Potter v Mole Valley District Council* (1982) Times, 22 October.

12 *Sedleigh-Denfield v O'Callaghan* [1940] AC 880, [1940] 3 All ER 349, HL. Note that this principle is concerned with acts of trespassers on the defendant's land not responsibility for the acts of trespassers who gain access to the plaintiff's property via the defendant's premises. On which see *Perl (P) (Exporters) Ltd v Camden London Borough Council* [1984] QB 342, [1983] 3 All ER 161 and *Maloco v Littlewoods Organisation Ltd* [1987] 1 All ER 710, HL, ante at p 171.

13 *Davey v Harrow Corporation* [1958] 1 QB 60, [1957] 2 All ER 305, CA (landowner who allows trees, whether planted or self-sown, to encroach on, whether by branches or roots, and cause damage to his neighbour's land, liable in nuisance); followed in *Morgan v Khyatt* [1964] 1 WLR 475 PC. In *Leakey v National Trust for Places of Historic Interest or Natural Beauty* [1980] QB 485, [1980] 1 All ER 17, CA, the defendant, knowing that its sloping bank of earth threatened the plaintiff's property, was held liable even though the damage arose from natural causes. In *Page Motors Ltd v Epsom and Ewell District Council* supra, it was held that in the case of a local authority in deciding what steps it should reasonably take, account should be taken of the need for it to go through the democratic process of a dialogue with interested parties, and of its political responsibilities. It is not enough that the defendant knows or ought to know that the 'nuisance' exists, eg a tree overhanging a road—in a case like that there must be actual or constructive knowledge that it is also a hazard to traffic, so that the defendant was not liable if it were first realised that such a tree was a hazard when two lorries tried to pass each other while opposite to it; *British Road Services Ltd v Slater* [1964] 1 All ER 816. It is, however, doubtful whether one is liable for the presence of animals *ferae naturae* or failure to remove them: *Farrer v Nelson* (1885) 15 QBD 258; *Seligman v Docker* [1949] Ch 53, [1948] 2 All ER 887. There is a wealth of case law to illustrate (1) and (2) above, but they all turn on the question of whether the defendant knew or ought to have known, and therefore do not merit detailed consideration, eg *Slater v Worthington's Cash Stores (1930) Ltd* [1941] 1 KB 488, [1941] 3 All ER 28; *Leanse v Lord Egerton* [1943] KB 323, [1943] 1 All ER 489.

14 [1983] 2 All ER 408.

15 *St Anne's Well Brewery Co v Roberts* (1928) 140 LT 1, CA *obiter; Wilkins v Leighton* [1932] 2 Ch 106; *Sedleigh-Denfield v O'Callaghan* [1940] AC 880 at 904–5 (per LORD WRIGHT).

16 [1940] 1 KB 229 at 233, [1939] 4 All ER 241, CA. The imposition by the Housing Act 1961 s 32, (see now Landlord and Tenant Act 1985) of heavy statutory obligations to repair houses has greatly increased the importance of *Wringe v Cohen*.

their collapse, the occupier, or the owner if he has undertaken the duty of repair, is answerable whether he knew or ought to have known of the danger or not.

Although the case has been doubted by some writers,[17] it will be seen later that its authority is now firm.[18] The case itself was one where the landlord failed to repair but presumably that which is strictly an *obiter dictum* about occupiers as such, eg tenants, will be applied in the future. It is important to note the limitations of the case: in particular, that there is no authority for applying the rule there enunciated to premises not on the highway,[19] and 'if the nuisance is created, not by want of repair, but, for example, by the act of a trespasser, or by a secret and unobservable operation of nature, such as subsidence under or near the foundations of the premises, neither an occupier nor an owner responsible for repair is answerable, unless with knowledge or means of knowledge he allows the danger to continue',[20] or as the court expressed itself later in the judgment,[1] 'if premises become dangerous, not by the occupier's act or neglect of duty, but as the result of the act of a third party, or of a latent defect, the occupier is not liable'.[2]

6 Where the defendant's failure to repair his property or maintain adequate security arrangements results in damage being inflicted on neighbouring owners by burglars or vandals, no duty of care has yet been held to impose liability in negligence on the lax property owner.[3] There would appear to be no circumstances in which liability in nuisance could be established on these facts where there would not concurrently be liability in negligence.

C. LANDLORD AND TENANT

The respective liabilities of landlord and tenant for conditions on premises the subject of the demise call for separate treatment.[4]

If, at the date of letting, the landlord knows or ought to know of the condition giving rise to the actionable nuisance, then he is liable during the tenancy where he does not take from the tenant a covenant to repair.[5] Even if the tenant lawfully[6] covenants to repair, the landlord is still liable.[7] Even

17 Eg *Salmond* 74.
18 See p 334 post.
19 For the view that *Wringe v Cohen* merely illustrates the rule that in public nuisance the burden of proving inevitable accident is on the defendant, see DENNING LJ in *Southport Corporation v Esso Petroleum Co Ltd* [1954] 2 QB 182 at 198, [1954] 2 All ER 561 at 572; and see p 339 et seq.
20 *Wringe v Cohen* supra at 233.
 1 At 248–9.
 2 What if the plaintiff does not have time to repair an observable defect, eg lightning damage, or he does the repair inadequately but with care, eg unknown to him his materials are faulty?
 3 *Smith v Littlewoods Organisation Ltd* [1987] 1 All ER 710, HL; *Perl (P) (Exporters) Ltd v Camden London Borough Council* [1984] QB 342, [1983] 3 All ER 161, CA; see ante at p 171.
 4 As we have seen p 329 ante, a landlord who authorises his tenant to commit a nuisance is himself liable. In *Hilton v James Smith & Sons (Norwood) Ltd* (1979) 251 Estates Gazette 1063, CA a landlord was held liable in nuisance for his failure to enforce his covenants against lessees whose vehicles constituted a nuisance to the plaintiff by obstructing access.
 5 *Todd v Flight* (1860) 9 CB NS 377; *Gandy v Jubber* (1865) 5 B & S 485; 9 B & S 15 (undelivered judgment); *Bowen v Anderson* [1894] 1 QB 164; *St Anne's Well Brewery Co v Roberts* (1928) 140 LT 1. For the purpose of this rule, the continuation of weekly and other periodic tenancies is not treated as a new tenancy at the recommencement of each period.
 6 Landlord and Tenant Act 1985 imposes certain liabilities on landlords with regard to structural repairs and some installations within houses, and renders ineffective any attempt by landlords to impose these liabilities on tenants.
 7 *Brew Brow Ltd v Snax (Ross) Ltd* [1970] 1 QB 612, [1970] 1 All ER 587, CA.

though the tenant has not covenanted to repair, the landlord will not be liable for such a condition of which he neither knows nor ought to know.[8]

The landlord will be liable for dangerous conditions arising from want of repair during the tenancy if he covenants to repair,[9] if he reserves the right to enter and repair,[10] or even if he has an implied right to enter and repair such as is possessed by landlords of small houses let on periodic tenancies.[11] But the tenant is not exempt because the landlord is liable.[12] It will be recalled that this responsibility for want of repair may in one case be incurred even though due care has been taken.[13]

Doubts have been cast on the principle of *Wringe v Cohen* that there may be liability for want of repair even though there is no want of care, because it is said to be contrary to *Sedleigh-Denfield v O'Callaghan*. The cases are not in conflict, as has been amply demonstrated in *Cushing v Peter Walker & Son*[14] and *Mint v Good*.[15] Thus in *Cushing v Walker:*

> Unknown to the defendants, a slate on the roof of their premises was dislodged by enemy action. A month later, it fell off the roof, and injured the plaintiff.

The court held that *Wringe v Cohen* did not impose liability because the condition did not arise from want of repair and that, in any event, that case expressly excepted from the principle of 'liability without knowledge' cases where the defect arose from an act of a trespasser or a secret unobservable process of nature. Enemy action was equivalent to the act of a trespasser, and the case fell within the principle of *Sedleigh-Denfield v O'Callaghan*. In short, there is liability in nuisance for conduct which is neither intentional nor negligent where a nuisance arises from a failure to repair premises (at least, if they adjoin a highway) provided that the defect is not caused by a trespasser or a secret natural process.

SECTION 7.   MUST THE INTERFERENCE COMPLAINED OF EMANATE FROM LAND?

The land from which the interference has its source need not belong to the defendant.[16] It is sufficient if the interference is from the highway.[17]

---

8 *St Anne's Well Brewery Co v Roberts* (1928) 140 LT 1, CA.
9 *Payne v Rogers* (1794) 2 Hy Bl 350.
10 *Wilchick v Marks and Silverstone* [1934] 2 KB 56; *Heap v Ind Coope and Allsopp Ltd* [1940] 2 KB 476, [1940] 3 All ER 634, CA; *Spicer v Smee* [1946] 1 All ER 489.
11 *Mint v Good* [1951] 1 KB 517, [1950] 2 All ER 1159, CA.
12 *Wilchick v Marks and Silverstone* supra. This was part of the *ratio decidendi* of GODDARD J and is therefore to be preferred to the *obiter dictum* to the contrary of one of the judges (HEATH J) in *Payne v Rogers* supra, which was there justified on the dubious ground that to hold the tenant liable would encourage circuity of action.
13 See p 333 ante.
14 [1941] 2 All ER 693.
15 See note 11 supra.
16 See p 329 ante. *Hooper v Rogers* [1975] Ch 43, [1974] 3 All ER 417, CA, nuisance can emanate from land of P if he is co-occupier with D.
17 *Hubbard v Pitt* [1976] QB 142, [1975] 1 All ER 1056, CA, reviewing earlier authorities, especially *J Lyons & Sons v Wilkins (No 2)* [1899] 1 Ch 255, CA, and *Ward Lock & Co Ltd v Operative Printers' Assistants' Society* (1906) 22 TLR 327, CA, and holding that picketing on a highway is capable of being a nuisance actionable by an adjoining landowner, and followed in *The Mersey Dock & Harbour Co v Verrinder* [1982] IRLR 152. In *A-G v Gastonia Coaches Ltd* [1977] RTR 219 motor coaches parked on the highway in front of the plaintiff's house were held to be a nuisance.

SECTION 8.   DEFENCES

A. PRESCRIPTION

A right to commit a private nuisance may be acquired as an easement by prescription. In order to decide whether this defence avails, then, one must look to the law of real property to discover whether the defendant has complied with the rules relating to the acquisition of an easement. The most common method of creating such an easement is by twenty years' continual user which is neither *vi, clam,* nor *precario*:[18] one may, for example, thus acquire the right to pour effluent in a stream, but not if it is done secretly.[19] Where there is a perpetual change in the amount of inconvenience caused, as in the case of fumes and noise, it is doubtful whether a prescriptive right can be acquired. Of course, if the particular use is prohibited by statute, no prescriptive right can be acquired.[20]

Further, 'acts which are neither preventable nor actionable cannot be relied upon to found an easement'.[1] Thus, where a defendant confectioner had for more than twenty years made certain noises on his land, which then for the first time interfered with the enjoyment of the plaintiff's user of his land when the plaintiff built a medical consulting room at the end of his garden near to the source of the noise, the defendant could not plead a prescriptive right: there had been no invasion of legal right before, nothing which the plaintiff could take steps to prevent.[2]

B. THE RELEVANCE OF THE CONDUCT OF THE PLAINTIFF

Authorities on the several matters under this head are surprisingly scanty. It is no defence that the plaintiff came to the nuisance by occupying land adjoining it.[3] Nor is it a defence that the nuisance has only arisen because the plaintiff has chosen to use a particular part of his land: the law protects a man in the reasonable use[4] of his land against those nuisances which the defendant has not acquired a prescriptive right to commit.[5] Yet, it may be assumed that the plaintiff has the normal duty in tort to take reasonable steps to mitigate his loss: he should, for instance, take reasonable steps to minimise the damage when his land is flooded in consequence of his neighbour's tortious conduct.[6]

The ordinary law of causation applies also in nuisance, and, if the interference is caused not by the defendant but by the plaintiff's own acts, he will

18 No doubt, an easement lawfully acquired by any other method of prescription, eg lost modern grant, will also be a defence.
19 *Liverpool Corporation v H Coghill & Son* [1918] 1 Ch 307.
20 *Liverpool Corporation v H Coghill & Son* supra at 314 (per EVE J).
 1 *Sturges v Bridgman* (1879) 11 ChD 852, CA.
 2 *Sturges v Bridgman* supra.
 3 *Bliss v Hall* (1838) 4 Bing NC 183; *Miller v Jackson* [1977] QB 966, [1977] 3 All ER 338, CA (no defence to cricket club that the ground first became a nuisance only when the plaintiff built close to it).
 4 As we have seen, p 326 ante, the suitability of the use made of the land by the plaintiff is one factor determining whether the act of the defendant was, in all the circumstances, unreasonable.
 5 *Sturges v Bridgman* supra; *Elliotson v Feetham* (1835) 2 Bing NC 134.
 6 'Can a person who sees encroaching roots on his land build a house and wait for it to fall down?' asked JENKINS LJ (*arguendo*), in *Davey v Harrow Corporation* [1958] 1 QB 60 at 63; [1957] 2 All ER 305 at 309, CA; but he did not answer his own question.

not recover.[7] The defences of consent and assumption of risk are also available. *Pwllback Colliery Co Ltd v Woodman*[8] illustrates the working of consent. The issue was whether a lessor who allowed his lessee to carry on the business of coal mining could complain when the latter's non-negligent operations caused coal dust to be deposited on other land of the lessor. The House of Lords held that only if the terms of the lease could be construed as authorising a nuisance was there any defence, and that, since the nuisance was not a necessary result of the carrying on of the trade, in the absence of an express authorisation of the nuisance in the lease, this defence of consent failed. In *Kiddle v City Business Properties Ltd*[9] the plaintiff complained of the damage caused to his shop when flooding from the gutter carrying off the water from a part of the premises retained by the defendant landlord occurred without negligence on the part of the defendant. It was held that the tenant took the premises as he found them and must be deemed to have run this risk: here his action in nuisance failed.

In the absence of clear authority on this point,[10] it would be reasonable to expect that the rules of contributory negligence[11] apply to nuisances based on negligent conduct, but perhaps not where the interference is the intended result of the intentional act of the defendant.[12]

C. STATUTORY AUTHORITY

This is the most important defence. Many activities which interfere with the enjoyment of land are carried out by public or private enterprise in pursuance of an Act of Parliament. If the statute merely confers a permissive power then that power must be exercised so as not to interfere with private rights.[13] If the activity complained of is authorised by the statute it is a matter of statutory interpretation whether an action lies in nuisance for damage resulting from that activity.

In *Allen v Gulf Oil Refining Ltd*:[14]

A statute was interpreted by the House of Lords as authorising the defendant company to acquire compulsorily land near Milford Haven for the purpose of constructing and operating an oil refinery. The company built the refinery and the plaintiffs complained that its smell, noise and vibration constituted a nuisance. The company pleaded the defence of statutory authority.

The House of Lords held that the plaintiffs would first have to establish a nuisance, and that the change in environment authorised by establishing the

---

7 Cf the case in public nuisance, *Almeroth v Chivers & Sons Ltd* [1948] 1 All ER 53, CA.
8 [1915] AC 634, HL.
9 [1942] 1 KB 269, [1942] 2 All ER 216. In *Leakey v National Trust for Places of Historic Interest or Natural Beauty* [1980] QB 485 at 515, [1980] 1 All ER 17 at 26, CA.
10 In *Trevett v Lee* [1955] 1 All ER 406, CA at 412 (case on public nuisance), EVERSHED MR *(obiter)* had no doubt that the Act of 1945 applied, but left open the question whether the standard of fault would be the same as in negligence.
11 Including of course, the apportionment provisions of the Law Reform (Contributory Negligence) Act 1945.
12 *Butterfield v Forrester* (1809) 11 East 60, was itself an action derived from public nuisance.
13 *Metropolitan Asylum District v Hill* (1881) 6 App Cas 193.
14 [1981] AC 1001, [1981] 1 All ER 353, HL.

refinery was relevant on that issue. If a nuisance were proved the company then had the onus of proving that the nuisance was an inevitable result of carrying on a refinery there.[15]

The defendants must thus prove that they used all reasonable care in establishing the operation authorised by statute, and that the nuisance was not to any extent a result of their negligence in doing what Parliament had authorised them to do. In *Tate & Lyle Industries Ltd v Greater London Council*[16] the defendants were held liable in public nuisance where reasonable care in the design and erection of new ferry terminals, which they had been authorised to build by statute, would have at least partially avoided the siltation of the Thames which damaged the plaintiffs' business. As some degree of siltation would have been inevitable even with properly designed terminals the plaintiffs recovered only 75% of their total loss.

One further matter bedevils the defence of statutory authority to nuisance where the defendant is a public authority. In considering alleged negligence by the authority should the distinction in *Anns v Merton London Borough Council*[17] between policy and operational errors be addressed?[18] The case law is hopelessly confused.[19]

D. OTHER DEFENCES

Defences discussed earlier[20] may also be available in nuisance, such as necessity or defence of property or consent.[1] It is no defence that the act of the defendant would not have been a nuisance but for the act of others, too, provided that the defendant knew what the others were doing.[2]

E. FIRE

The Fires Prevention (Metropolis) Act 1774[3] provides that, in an action brought in respect of a fire, it is a defence to prove that the fire began accidentally. But, as ATKINSON J decided in *Spicer v Smee*,[4] the defence has no application where the fire was caused by the negligence of the defendant or intentionally created by him or those for whom he was responsible. Even when a fire started accidentally, if the defendant negligently allowed it to change from a small one to a raging fire, the Act would not afford him a defence for the damage caused by that raging fire.[5] Except perhaps, where a

---

15 Following *Manchester Corporation v Farnworth* [1930] AC 171, HL.
16 [1983] 2 AC 509, [1983] 1 All ER 1159. And see *Department of Transport v North West Water Authority* [1984] AC 336, [1983] 1 All ER 892.
17 [1978] AC 728, [1977] 2 All ER 492.
18 See ante p 165.
19 See S H Bailey and M J Bowman 'The Policy/Operational Dichotomy' [1986] CLJ 430.
20 See Ch 6 ante.
 1 *Leakey v National Trust for Places of Historic Interest or Natural Beauty* [1980] QB 485 at 515, [1980] 1 All ER 17 at 26, CA (per MEGAW LJ) held that it was a defence 'that the plaintiffs, knowing of the danger to their property, by word or deed, had shown their willingness to accept that danger.'
 2 *Thorpe v Brumfitt* (1873) 8 Ch App 650.
 3 The Act applies generally, not merely to London: *Filliter v Phippard* (1847) 11 QB 347.
 4 [1946] 1 All ER 489.
 5 *Goldman v Hargrave* [1967] 1 AC 645, [1966] 2 All ER 989, PC.

person may be liable in nuisance though his conduct was neither intentional nor negligent,[6] the defence has no application to nuisance by fire.

SECTION 9.   REMEDIES

A. DAMAGES

The measure of damages is similar to that in that other tort which protects interests in land, trespass.[7] The plaintiff is entitled to full restitution for his loss. Where, for instance, a house (or crops or the like[8]) is destroyed or damaged then the plaintiff will recover the difference between the monetary value to him of his interest (whether he be landlord, tenant or otherwise) before and after the event.[9] Where business loss is suffered in consequence of the interference, whether by loss of custom[10] or the cost of moving elsewhere,[11] this is compensated for in nuisance.[12] Where, however, an hotel owner complained of loss of custom through building operations, the Court of Appeal reversed an award of damages to the full extent of loss of custom, holding that a certain amount of the interference was in the circumstances reasonable, and yet might have led to loss of custom; the court therefore assessed what proportion of the business loss was attributable to that excess of noise and dust which alone was actionable.[13] In 1966, in *Overseas Tankship (UK) Ltd v Miller Steamship Co Pty Ltd*[14] the Privy Council held that in the tort derived from public nuisance[15] it is not enough that the damage complained of is a direct consequence of the wrongful act—it must be a foreseeable consequence. Dicta in the case treated this rule as applicable also to private nuisance.

To continue a nuisance may amount to a commission of a further tort of nuisance.[16] For example, if a defendant against whom damages for obstructing the plaintiff's right to light had been awarded, continued subsequently to obstruct that right to light, another action would lie. Similarly, where a defendant, who imposed a strain on the plaintiff's wall by piling earth against it, was sued in nuisance it was stated that 'a fresh cause of action arises as each brick topples down, and that there is a continuing cause of action until the root of the trouble is eradicated'.[17] Where, however, in pursuance of its statutory discretionary power,[18] the court refuses an injunction, the award of

---

6 Eg p 334 ante.

7 See ch 5 ante.

8 See *Marquis of Granby v Bakewell Urban District Council* (1923) 87 JP 105, for a detailed calculation on this basis of the value of fish destroyed by pollution of a stream.

9 *Moss v Christchurch Rural District Council* [1925] 2 KB 750 Div Ct. And not the cost of restoring it to its original state: *Lodge Holes Colliery Co v Wednesbury Corporation* [1908] AC 323, HL; *C R Taylor (Wholesale) Ltd v Hepworths Ltd* [1977] 2 All ER 784 (plaintiff not entitled to recover the cost of reinstating his destroyed billiard hall which he did not intend to use for that purpose again—the basis of assessment was the reduced value of the premises).

10 *Fritz v Hobson* (1880) 14 ChD 542.

11 *Grosvenor Hotel Co v Hamilton* [1894] 2 QB 836 at 840 (per LINDLEY LJ), CA.

12 See ch 29 post, for the recovery of damages on account of personal injuries and other consequential loss.

13 *Andreae v Selfridge & Co Ltd* [1938] Ch 1, [1937] 3 All ER 255, CA.

14 [1967] 1 AC 617, [1966] 2 All ER 709, PC.

15 Page 339 post.

16 Cf trespass to land; see ch 5 ante.

17 Per STABLE J, in *Maberley v Peabody & Co of London Ltd* [1946] 2 All ER 192 at 194.

18 Lord Cairns Act 1858 s 2; Supreme Court Act 1981 s 50.

damages which it may make in lieu may take account of future as well as past damages.[19]

B. INJUNCTION

The law of nuisance is complicated by the fact that plaintiffs usually want to prevent the continuance of the nuisance by obtaining an injunction. Thus, a plaintiff may seek both damages and an injunction: a Canadian case has held, in an action seeking both remedies, that damages for permanent depreciation of the land by the interference cannot be awarded, because it is to be presumed that the injunction will be obeyed, so that the land will not so depreciate.[20] It is because the usual relief sought by plaintiffs in an action of nuisance is an injunction that negligent conduct is so rarely relied on: for, if the defendant persists after the plaintiff has complained, so that the plaintiff has to ask for an injunction, obviously his conduct is intentional. What is more important, the injunction is a discretionary remedy, and one may therefore make out an actionable claim for damages and yet be refused an injunction: *Cooke v Forbes*, for example:[1]

> The plaintiff used a certain bleaching chemical in making cocoa-nut matting. Occasionally, emission of sulphuretted hydrogen from the defendant's plant damaged the plaintiff's manufactures. Without prejudice to a claim in damages, the court refused an injunction because the interference was only occasional.

It is sometimes suggested that the power of the courts to decide whether to grant an injunction or to award damages only enables them to regulate the use of the land in the public interest, either by forbidding an activity or by allowing it while requiring the law breaker to pay the social costs resulting from the activity.[2] Yet the courts will not refuse an injunction because the activity benefits a section of the public, if all the requirements of the tort are established.[3] The courts frequently grant an injunction but suspend its operation till the defendants have had time to end the nuisance.[4]

SECTION 10.   PUBLIC NUISANCE

A. ELEMENTS

A miscellany of facts, indeed any omission 'which obstructs or causes incon-

---

19 *Leeds Industrial Co-operative Society v Slack* [1924] AC 851, HL.
20 *Macievich v Anderson* [1952] 4 DLR 507 (Manitoba Ct of Appeal).
 1 (1867) LR 5 Eq 166. *Bracewell v Appleby* [1975] 1 All ER 993 is a recent example of an injunction being refused and an award of damages being made in lieu. Once the plaintiff has proved that substantial interference has already occurred, and is likely to recur in the future, the burden is on the defendant to adduce special circumstances why an injunction should not be granted: per LORD SIMONDS in *McKinnon Industries Ltd v Walker* [1951] 3 DLR 577, PC at 581.
 2 See Ogus and Richardson (1977) CLJ 284.
 3 *Kennaway v Thompson* [1981] QB 88, [1980] 3 All ER 329, CA, refusing to follow LORD DENNING in *Miller v Jackson* [1977] QB 966, [1977] 3 All ER 338, CA.
 4 *Stollmeyer v Petroleum Development Co Ltd* [1918] AC 498n, PC, but it is doubtful whether suspension is appropriate for trespass: *John Trenberth Ltd v National Westminster Bank Ltd* (1979) 253 Estates Gazette 151.

venience or damage to the public in the exercise of rights common to all Her Majesty's subjects'[5] may constitute the crime of public nuisance.

> A public nuisance is a nuisance which is so widespread in its range or so indiscriminate in its effects that it would not be reasonable to expect one person to take proceedings on his own responsibility to put a stop to it, but that it should be taken on the responsibility of the community at large.[6]

Paradoxically, once the plaintiff has proved the crime of public nuisance as so defined, he can maintain an action in tort by showing also that he has suffered particular damage.[7] This particular damage is not limited to special damage in the sense of actual pecuniary loss;[8] it may consist, for example, of inconvenience or delay provided that it is substantial and appreciably greater in degree than any suffered by the general public.[9] Thus a plaintiff could recover in public nuisance for both damage to his vehicle on the highway and for interference with his peaceful sleep in his adjoining house.[10]

The most important area of this tortious liability is that of nuisance on the highway, either by obstructing it[11] or rendering passage along it unsafe.[12] Causing crowds or vehicles to block the highway,[13] leaving dangerous articles such as defective cellar flaps or unlighted scaffolding there,[14] or having ruinous premises adjoining the highway,[15] or conducting operations off the highway which menace the safety of those upon it;[16] these are characteristic illustrations of nuisances on the highway. Similarly, to discharge oil from a ship in the estuary of a public navigable river and thereby damage the plaintiff's foreshore is a public nuisance.[17] And to prevent free navigation of a river by creating excessive siltation will constitute public nuisance.[18]

The recent use of the action for public nuisance to prohibit demonstrations and picketing may be a source of some concern.[19] There can be no doubt

---

5 Stephen, *Digest of Criminal Law* art 235.
6 Per DENNING LJ in *A-G v PYA Quarries Ltd* [1957] 2 QB 169 at 191, [1957] 1 All ER 894, CA.
7 There is a very lucid review of the authorities in the judgment of SCHOLL J in *Walsh v Ervin* [1952] VLR 361; see also *Harper v Haden & Sons* [1933] Ch 298, [1932] All ER Rep 59, CA; *Benjamin v Storr* (1874) LR 9 CP 400; *Wilkes v Hungerford Market Co* (1835) 2 Bing NC 281; *Ricket v Metropolitan Ry Co* (1867) LR 2 HL 175.
8 Eg loss of custom (*J Lyons Sons & Co v Gulliver* [1914] 1 Ch 631; *Blundy Clark & Co Ltd v London and North Eastern Ry Co* [1931] 2 KB 334, [1931] All ER Rep 160) or land depreciation (*Caledonian Ry Co v Walkers Trustees* (1882) 7 App Cas 259, HL). Expenses incurred in dredging river so that plaintiffs could continue to use their ferry at their sugar refinery; *Tate and Lyle Industries Ltd v Greater London Council* [1983] 2 AC 509, [1983] 1 All ER 1159.
9 *Boyd v Great Northern Ry Co* [1895] 2 IR 555; *Walsh v Ervin* supra.
10 *Halsey v Esso Petroleum Co Ltd* [1961] 2 All ER 145. But was VEALE J correct in holding that the plaintiff recovered even though he was unlawfully using the road as a garage for his car when it was damaged?
11 'An obstruction is something which permanently or temporarily removes the whole or part of the highway from public use'; per LORD EVERSHED MR in *Trevett v Lee* [1955] 1 All ER 406 at p 409, CA.
12 For the liability of highway authorities for failure to repair, see p 514 post.
13 Eg *Lyons Sons & Co v Gulliver* [1914] 1 Ch 631.
14 Eg *Penny v Wimbledon Urban District Council* [1899] 2 QB 72.
15 *Harrold v Watney* [1898] 2 QB 320.
16 *Castle v St Augustine's Links* (1922) 38 TLR 615.
17 *Southport Corporation v Esso Petroleum Co Ltd* [1953] 2 All ER 1204, [1954] QB 182, [1954] 2 All ER 561, CA, [1956] AC 218, [1955] 3 All ER 864, HL.
18 *Tate & Lyle Industries Ltd v Greater London Council* (supra).
19 See for a recent example the interlocutory injunction issued against unions demonstrating in Wapping; *News Group Newspapers v SOGAT 82* [1987] ICR 181, [1986] IRLR 337.

that collecting hordes of men to picket employers' premises or to protest against nuclear power can amount to nuisance, just as causing any other type of crowd to obstruct the highway can. But could a demonstration or picket ever be justified by its purpose? Could it constitute reasonable use of the highway?[20]

The rigid categorisation of the law of torts is illustrated here. If someone falls over a projection on the forecourt (not forming part of the public footpath) leading to a shop, then his rights are merely those owed in negligence to visitors to premises—he has no action in nuisance, public or private.[1] Should this happen on the footpath, however, it becomes a case derived from public nuisance. And, if one deviates only slightly from the footpath in order to pass an obstruction, and, while thus off the highway, is injured, this might be within the area of torts originating in public nuisance.[2]

Most commonly, a claim in public nuisance is for personal injuries sustained by a person while passing along the highway. In addition occupiers of premises adjoining the highway may recover in an action based on public nuisance when they suffer special damage as a result of a nuisance on a highway, although the damage complained of is not suffered by them *qua* users of the highway: for example, shopkeepers, access to whose premises has been interfered with,[3] or whose customers have been subjected to noxious smells and darkened rooms as a result of the parking of horses and carts outside their premises, have succeeded in this tort.[4] So also has a householder who was prevented by the erection on a highway of a stand which blocked the view from his house, from letting for hire window seats from which to view a procession.[5] In view of the decision of the Privy Council in *Overseas Tankship (UK) Ltd v The Miller Steamship Co Pty Ltd*[6] the last-cited decision can be supported only if the defendant ought to have foreseen that the view would not be blocked; it would not be enough that the damage was a direct consequence. In that case the plaintiffs' ship was damaged in a fire caused by the defendants' carelessly allowing oil to overflow from their ship into the waters of Sydney Harbour. The defendants were held liable for the tort derived from public nuisance, but only because the fire on the plaintiffs' ship was held to be a foreseeable consequence of the defendants' wrongful act.

B. THE RELATION BETWEEN PUBLIC NUISANCE AND PRIVATE NUISANCE

Is there any authority for the assumption underlying much of what is written about this topic: that the law of public and private nuisance is one and the

20 See H Carty, 'The Legality of Peaceful Picketing on the Highway' [1984] PL 600.
1 *Jacobs v London County Council* [1950] AC 361, [1950] 1 All ER 737, HL; in *Bromley v Mercer* [1922] 2 KB 126, CA, an unsafe wall adjoining a highway which amounted to a public nuisance, collapsed, not on to the highway, but on to private land, and it fell on a child who was playing on that private land, and was not using the highway—the child was held to have no cause of action derived from public nuisance; *Creed v John McGeoch & Sons Ltd* [1955] 3 All ER 123 (road merely under construction, neither dedicated nor taken over by local authority; therefore not highway nuisance).
2 *Barnes v Ward* (1850) 9 CB 392; *Barker v Herbert* [1911] 2 KB 633, CA.
3 *Fritz v Hobson* (1880) 14 ChD 542.
4 *Benjamin v Storr* (1874) LR 9 CP 400.
5 *Campbell v Paddington Corporation* [1911] 1 KB 869.
6 [1967] 1 AC 617, [1966] 2 All ER 709, PC.

same? If that invasion of the interest of the plaintiff which the particular tort demands takes place, then the rules on who is deemed to be responsible for continuing that invasion are the same.[7] Also the courts expressly consider the reasonableness of the conduct in determining whether an action derived from public nuisance may lie. Thus, whether one who has collided with a vehicle left standing without lights at night and obstructing a highway can sue, will depend in part on whether the vehicle has been there for a long time, and whether there was good excuse for its being there.[8] *Trevett v Lee*[9] is an illustration:

> The defendants' house fronted on a quiet country road. In time of drought they laid a hosepipe across the highway to enable water to be brought by gravity from a supply on the other side of the road. The plaintiff fell over this hosepipe on the highway and was injured.

The Court of Appeal held that this did not afford the plaintiff a cause of action derived from public nuisance because the defendants' user of the highway, 'judged both from their own point of view and from the point of view of the other members of the public',[10] was reasonable.

Yet, no case has decided that in other respects the rules of the two torts are identical. Of course, if one could examine the law of torts regardless of the history of the subject, one might say that, whether the inconvenience was to the public or to a landowner, the rules should be the same. But, in the present state of knowledge of the legal development of public and private nuisance, there is no proof that the rules are identical.[11] On the contrary, prescription is no defence to suits derived from public nuisance;[12] victims of private nuisance who show substantial interference need not prove more loss than their fellows. The courts are likely to equate as far as possible the rules of the two torts.[13]

One particular form of private nuisance is interference with access to a highway. Because very often the same facts may also constitute the tort derived from public nuisance and claims based on both torts are joined, it is

---

7 *Sedleigh-Denfield v O'Callaghan* [1940] AC 880 at 893, 899 (per LORD ATKIN) and 907 (per LORD WRIGHT), [1940] 3 All ER 349, HL. Hence public nuisance cases have sometimes been relied on without express mention of that in section 6 of this chapter ante. But DENNING LJ in *Southport Corporation v Esso Petroleum Co* [1954] 2 QB 182 at 198–9, [1954] 2 All ER 561 at 572, appears to have thought that *Wringe v Cohen* [1940] 1 KB 229, [1939] 4 All ER 241, CA (p 332 ante) depended on the fact that it was a public nuisance (a tenable position), and he further stated that the ratio of the obscure decision in *Sadler v South Staffs etc Tramways Co* (1889) 23 QBD 17, was that, in this tort derived from public nuisance, the burden of proving inevitable accident was on the defendant.

8 *Ware v Garston Haulage Co Ltd* [1944] 1 KB 30, [1943] 2 All ER 558, CA; *Maitland v Raisbeck and Hewitt Ltd* [1944] KB 689, [1944] 2 All ER 272, CA. If a motor cyclist collides with a lighted lorry parked on a straight wide section of a highway he may fail in any event because the obstruction did not cause his injuries; he was the sole cause of his harm: *Dymond v Pearce* [1972] 1 QB 496, [1972] 1 All ER 1142, CA.

9 [1955] 1 All ER 406.

10 Per EVERSHED MR at 412.

11 Contra Winfield (1940–1) 18 NYULQR 75: 'Current English Law would not take the distinction,' though he mentions *Fuller* and *Saunders Case*, referred to in *Cranbank's Case* (1618) 2 Roll Rep 49 (defendant laid logs in adjoining highway whereby plaintiff's cart upset—held not private nuisance, but none the less actionable in case).

12 *Mott v Shoolbred* (1875) LR 20 Eq 22.

13 The Privy Council drew no distinction between the two in their judgment in *Overseas Tankship (UK) Ltd v The Miller Steamship Co Pty Ltd* [1967] 1 AC 617, [1966] 2 All ER 709, PC.

necessary to distinguish the two. These rights of access, like other property rights such as easements, now receive, under the influence of the law of real property, an emphasis quite different from that of the remainder of the tort of private nuisance. The issue is: has the plaintiff a right whereupon the defendant violates it at his peril,[14] not whether the defendant's conduct is so unreasonable an interference that it should be deemed tortious?[15] Consequently, interference with access whether to roads or navigable waters,[16] is actionable *per se*.[17]

---

14 Cf *Bradford Corporation v Pickles* [1895] AC 587, HL p 322 ante.
15 Cf *Wright's Cases* 699.
16 *Lyon v Fishmongers Co* (1876) 1 App Cas 662, HL.
17 *Nicholls v Ely Beet Sugar Factory Ltd* [1936] Ch 343, CA; *Walsh v Ervin* p 340 ante.

Chapter 20

Rylands v Fletcher

SECTION 1. INTRODUCTION

A person who, in the course of non-natural user of land, is held to be responsible for the accumulation on it of anything likely to do harm if it escapes is liable for the interference with the use of the land of another which results from the escape of the thing from his land

This is known as the rule in *Rylands v Fletcher*:[1]

> The defendants employed independent contractors to build a reservoir on their land. Through the negligence of the independent contractors, disused shafts upon the site, which communicated with the mine of the plaintiffs beneath the reservoir, were not blocked up. On the filling of the reservoir, the water escaped down the shafts and flooded the mine of the plaintiffs.

Although the defendants were neither themselves negligent nor vicariously liable in the tort of negligence for the negligence of their independent contractors,[2] they were held liable both by the Court of Exchequer Chamber and the House of Lords. BLACKBURN, J, delivering the judgment of the Court of Exchequer Chamber, said:[3]

> We think that the true rule of law is, that the person who for his own purposes brings on his lands and collects and keeps there anything likely to do mischief if it escapes, must keep it in at his peril, and, if he does not do so, is *prima facie* answerable for all the damage which is the natural consequence of its escape.

LORD CAIRNS in the House of Lords concurred in this judgment except that he restricted the scope of the rule to where the defendant made 'a non-natural use' of the land.[4] This liability was something more than negligence; the defendant would be answerable in many circumstances where his acts were neither intentional nor negligent interferences with the interests of the plaintiff.

In its form, at least, the judgment of BLACKBURN, J, does not purport to be making new law, as the following quotation shows:[5]

> The general rule, as above stated, seems on general principle just. The person whose grass or corn is eaten down by the escaping cattle of his neighbour, or whose mine is flooded by the water from his neighbour's reservoir, or whose cellar is invaded by the filth of his neighbour's privy, or whose habitation is made unhealthy by the fumes and noisome vapours of his neighbour's alkali works, is damnified

---

1 (1866) LR 1 Ex 265; affd (1868) LR 3 HL 330.
2 For discussion of vicarious liability and independent contractors, see ch 27 post.
3 At 279–80.
4 At 338–40.
5 At 280.

344

without any fault of his own; and it seems but reasonable and just that the neighbour, who has brought something on his own property which was not naturally there, harmless to others so long as it is confined to his own property, but which he knows to be mischievous if it gets on his neighbour's, should be obliged to make good the damage which ensues if he does not succeed in confining it to his own property.'

Yet, close though the analogy may be to nuisance and other existing torts, the fact remains that *Rylands v Fletcher* was the starting point of a liability which, as developed by the courts in subsequent decisions, was wider than any which preceded it.

This extension of liability gave rise to speculation whether or not some comprehensive theory of strict liability for harm caused to persons by dangerous things was being formulated. Such a theory would tend to associate *Rylands v Fletcher* with negligence—protecting interests in the person, chattels, and land indiscriminately, but, because the foreseeable risk is so much greater in the case of dangerous things, differing from the ordinary forms of negligence in imposing liability for conduct not even careless.

Such a theory, whatever attraction it may have, is no longer tenable after the interpretation put upon *Rylands v Fletcher* by the House of Lords in *Read v J Lyons & Co Ltd*.[6] The facts were:

The appellant, while working in the respondent's factory, was injured by an explosion there. No allegation of negligence was made by her against the respondents, whom she sued in respect of her injuries. The basis of her claim was that the defendants carried on the manufacture of high-explosive shells, knowing that they were dangerous things.

The ground for the decision of the House of Lords in favour of the respondents was that *Rylands v Fletcher* does not apply unless there has been an escape from a place where the defendant has occupation or control[7] over land to a place outside his control. But the importance of the case does not end there. The decision in *Read v Lyons* constitutes a denial of a general theory of strict liability for ultra-hazardous activities: there is liability for non-negligent conduct in a series of defined situations only. If a plaintiff's case falls outside those limits, he must establish intentional or negligent conduct on the part of the defendant. Further, the *dictum* of LORD SIMONDS that 'the law of nuisance and the rule in *Rylands v Fletcher* might in most cases be invoked indifferently'' illustrates how far the House of Lords recognised the affinity of the two torts.[8] The differences remaining between the two will be discussed at the end of this chapter.

Perhaps the most remarkable characteristic of this rule has been its fluidity. Stated in very broad terms by BLACKBURN J, it was at once modified in the case itself by the House of Lords, who confined it to 'non-natural' user. There followed a widespread application of the rule: often cases properly sounding in nuisance only were brought within the fold of *Rylands v Fletcher*. The rule was given a greater measure of elasticity by the interpretation of 'non-natural' user by the Privy Council in 1913, who defined it as 'some special use bringing

6 [1945] KB 216, CA; affd, [1947] AC 156, [1946] 2 All ER 471, HL. All the judgments in both Court of Appeal and House of Lords are important.
7 An escape from property controlled by the defendant on the highway may be sufficient; *Rigby v Chief Constable of Northamptonshire* [1985] 2 All ER 985 at 996.
8 [1947] AC 156 at 183.

with it increased danger to others, and [which] must not merely be the ordinary use of the land or such a use as is proper for the general benefit of the community'.[9] Although this concept may not be quite so wide as that of the 'unreasonableness' of nuisance, it was fluid enough to enable the House of Lords in *Read v Lyons* to doubt whether the operating of a munition works in war-time was a non-natural user, and this, despite the fact that the House of Lords had held, twenty-six years earlier, that *Rylands v Fletcher* did apply to an explosion from a munitions factory in war-time.[10] After 1913, even, *Rylands v Fletcher* continued to be invoked freely, and often it was not sufficiently sharply distinguished from nuisance. And then in 1947 came the reaction in *Read v Lyons*. Before the elements of this tort are considered, the emphatic warning must be given that those pre-1948 decisions of lower courts which appear to have extended the original rule must, in future, be closely scrutinised before they are accepted as good authorities.

SECTION 2.   'THINGS' WITHIN THE RULE[11]

BLACKBURN J spoke of 'anything likely to do mischief if it escapes'. These things must not be summarily described as 'dangerous' and then be equated, and, in turn, confused with those things which have been styled 'dangerous' in the context of negligence. It would be wise to eschew this word 'dangerous', for it means so many different things in different contexts. Thus, water is not 'dangerous' per se, yet it was the 'thing' in *Rylands v Fletcher* itself. As DU PARCQ L J said in *Read v Lyons*,[12] what matters here is whether the thing is likely to do damage on escaping to other land.[13] Whether or not this involves personal danger is quite irrelevant. Thus, filth and water are things within the rule. Nor is the extra-hazardous quality of the thing (in the sense that it might be likely to harm persons who are on the premises where it is kept) of any moment.

It is submitted that the category of things coming under *Rylands v Fletcher* is narrower than that in nuisance in at least one respect. In *Rylands v Fletcher* a tangible thing must be accumulated which, in its nature, is likely to cause mischief, either upon its own escape or upon its giving off fumes, gas, electricity, or, possibly, odours, which themselves escape. In nuisance on the other hand, no physical object having that quality need be on the defendant's land.[14] For example, in *Christie v Davey*[15] a defendant who beat a tray against the wall of his house was held liable in nuisance to his neighbour for the

---

9   *Rickards v Lothian* [1913] AC 263 at 280, PC.
10   *Rainham Chemical Works Ltd v Belvedere Fish Guano Co* [1921] 2 AC 465, HL.
11   There is a detailed study of the cases decided up to that date in Stallybrass, 'Dangerous Things and the Non-natural User of Land' in (1929) 3 Camb LJ 376.
12   [1945] KB 216 at 247, CA.
13   Cf LORD PORTER in *Read v J Lyons & Co* [1947] AC 156 at 176, [1946] 2 All ER 471, HL.
14   The only case apparently inconsistent with this is *Hoare & Co v McAlpine* [1923] 1 Ch 167, a decision at first instance, treating vibrations caused by a pile driver as being within the rule (see Pollock's criticism, (1923) 39 LQR 145); moreover, the case could, perhaps, have been decided in nuisance. The case was disapproved of in *Barrette v Franki Compressed Pile Co of Canada Ltd* [1955] 2 DLR 665 (pile driving vibrations not within *Rylands v Fletcher*, but held to be nuisance). It must, however, be admitted that here, as elsewhere, the law of torts has not attuned itself to scientific discoveries about the nature of matter. Accumulation of something leading to a discharge of electricity is within the rule—see note 20, infra.
15   [1893] 1 Ch 316.

interference caused by the noise; because a tray is likely neither itself to escape not to give off fumes, smells, or even noise, the defendant in that case could not have been liable in *Rylands v Fletcher*. More doubtfully, this category of mischief-making things may be narrower than that for which liability in nuisance is imposed—whereas trees likely to fall may give rise to actions in nuisance, it was held in *Noble v Harrison*[16] that beech trees, at any rate were not sufficiently likely to cause danger so as to be within *Rylands v Fletcher*. The justification for such a distinction may very well be that since the scope of liability in *Rylands v Fletcher* is wider, the propensity of the thing to cause harm on escaping must be the more obvious. Likewise (although it is not in itself a defence to this tort that the defendant was unaware that the thing was likely to do harm), proof that it was not, according to the common experience of mankind, likely to cause harm on escaping will absolve the defendant.[17]

Counsel argued in *Read v Lyons*[18] that the thing must have 'capacity for independent movement' as well as being a potential cause of harm—so that glass, for example, would be outside the rule. Provided that an extension is made to include a thing likely to give off something such as a gas, which itself has capacity for independent movement, this contention has much to commend it, and there is some, though hardly adequate, support for it in the cases.[19]

Things which have been held to be within the rule include electricity,[20] gas likely to pollute water supplies,[1] explosives,[2] fire and things likely to cause, and which in fact cause, fires (including a motor vehicle whether the tank contain,[3] or be emptied of,[4] petrol),[5] things likely to give off noxious gases or fumes,[6] water,[7] sewage,[8] and slag heaps.[9] Cases holding planted yew-trees[10] and chair-o-planes[11] to be within the rule are probably sound: whether a decayed rusty wire-fence[12] and a flag-pole,[13] have been rightly regarded as being within the rule is doubtful. In *Attorney-General v Corke*[14] it was held that the owner of land who allowed caravan-dwellers to live on it was answerable on this principle for the interferences which they perpetrated on adjoining land.

16 [1926] 2 KB 332 at 342 (per WRIGHT J); there were other reasons why an action based on *Rylands v Fletcher* failed.
17 *West v Bristol Tramways Co* [1908] 2 KB 14, CA at 20–1 (per LORD ALVERSTONE).
18 [1947] AC 156 at 158, [1946] 2 All ER 471, HL.
19 Eg *Wilson v Newberry* (1871) LR 7 QB 31 at 33 (per MELLOR J): 'things which have a tendency to escape and to do mischief.'
20 *National Telephone Co v Baker* [1893] 2 Ch 186.
 1 *Batcheller v Tunbridge Wells Gas Co* (1901) 84 LT 765.
 2 *Rainham Chemical Works Ltd v Belvedere Fish Guano Co* [1921] 2 AC 465, HL and CS gas canisters; *Rigby v Chief Constable of Northamptonshire* (supra)
 3 *Musgrove v Pandelis* [1919] 2 KB 43, CA.
 4 *Perry v Kendricks Transport Ltd* [1956] 1 All ER 154, CA.
 5 *Jones v Ffestiniog Ry Co* (1868) LR 3 QB 733 (sparks from railway engine); *Balfour v Barty-King* [1956] 2 All ER 555 (blowlamp), affirmed on other grounds [1957] 1 QB 496, [1957] 1 All ER 156, CA.
 6 *West v Bristol Tramways Co* [1908] 2 KB 14, CA; *Halsey v Esso Petroleum Co Ltd* [1961] 2 All ER 145 (acid smuts).
 7 *Rylands v Fletcher*; *Western Engraving Co v Film Laboratories Ltd* [1936] 1 All ER 106, CA.
 8 *Humphries v Cousins* (1877) 2 CPD 239.
 9 *A-G v Cory Brothers & Co* [1921] AC 521, HL.
10 *Crowhurst v Amersham Burial Board* (1878) 4 Ex D 5.
11 *Hale v Jennings Brothers* [1938] 1 All ER 579, CA.
12 *Firth v Bowling Iron Co* (1878) 3 CPD 254.
13 *Shiffman v The Venerable Order of the Hospital of St John of Jerusalem* [1936] 1 All ER 557.
14 [1933] Ch 89. In *Smith v Scott* [1973] Ch 314, [1972] 3 All ER 645 undesirable tenants were held to be outside the rule, because a landlord has no 'control' over tenants.

SECTION 3.   BRINGING ON THE LAND

BLACKBURN J said that the rule applies to a 'person who for his own
purposes brings on his lands and collects and keeps there' the thing in
question. The thing may or may not be something which in its nature is
capable of being naturally there: what matters is whether the particular thing
has in fact been accumulated there. If, therefore, water flows from A's
underground tunnels into B's mines, whether by force of gravitation or by
percolation, A is not liable in *Rylands v Fletcher* for that escape if the water
was naturally on A's land and he did nothing to accumulate it there:[15]
Rylands v Fletcher applies only to 'things artificially brought or kept upon the
defendant's land'.[16] On the other hand, there was liability in *Rylands v Fletcher*
itself because steps had been taken by the defendant to accumulate the water
on his land by constructing the reservoir.[17] The cases where flooding of
neighbouring land results from pumping or diverting water from the land of
the defendant to that of the plaintiff may be nuisance, but cannot be within
Rylands v Fletcher because the defendant has not accumulated the water.[18]
Similarly, the escape of rocks is outside the rule: there has been no accumulation;[19] if, however, rocks are blasted in quarrying there may then be liability
for accumulating the explosives.[20]

In the case of vegetation, should the facts otherwise be within the rule, it
will be important to consider whether it was planted there, for the planting
of it will constitute an accumulation.[1] *Giles v Walker* (assuming that the case
was decided on *Rylands v Fletcher*) is also relevant here:[2]

> The defendant, in order to redeem some of his forest land, ploughed it up.
> Thistles grew up all over it. Thistle-down escaped from the defendant's
> land to that of the plaintiff, where it seeded itself.

Finding that the thistles were 'the natural growth of the soil', the court held
that this was no tort.[3] Yet it seems, from an interjection of LORD ESHER MR
during the argument, that the result would have been different had the court
found that the defendant was responsible for the thing having come on to
his land: presumably, had there been a finding of fact that the ploughing up
of the land had caused the thistles to come on to the defendant's land and
accumulate there, this requirement of the tort would have been satisfied.[4]

Problems of responsibility for accumulation were considered by the House
of Lords in *Rainham Chemical Works Ltd v Belvedere Fish Guano Co*:[5]

---

15 *Wilson v Waddell* (1876) 2 App Cas 95, HL.
16 *Bartlett v Tottenham* [1932] 1 Ch 114 at 131 (per LAWRENCE LJ). It is probable that, by
     analogy with nuisance, a defendant who has not himself brought the thing on to the premises,
     but is responsible for its accumulation there (eg his predecessor in title brought it on to the
     premises) is himself within the rule.
17 And in *Broder v Saillard* (1876) 2 Ch D 692, where the water was brought onto the land in
     connection with the stabling of the horses of the defendant.
18 Eg *Baird v Williamson* (1863) 15 CB (NS) 376; *Whalley v Lancashire and Yorkshire Ry Co*
     (1884) 13 QBD 131, CA; cf *Hurdman v North Eastern Ry Co* (1878) 3 CPD 168, CA.
19 *Pontardawe Rural Council v Moore-Gwyn* [1929] 1 Ch 656.
20 Cf *Miles v Forest Rock Granite Co (Leicestershire) Ltd* (1918) 34 TLR 500 CA.
 1 *Crowhurst v Amersham Burial Board* (1878) 4 Ex D 5.
 2 (1890) 24 QBD 656 Div Ct, and see 62 LT 933. Cf *Seligman v Docker* [1949] Ch 53.
 3 See also Goodhart *Essays in Jurisprudence* ch 8.
 4 62 LT at p 934. Observations by the Court of Appeal in *Davey v Harrow Corporation* [1958]
     1 QB 60, [1957] 2 All ER 305, CA, support the view taken in the text.
 5 [1921] 2 AC 465, HL.

A and B contracted with the Ministry of Munitions to manufacture explosives on their land. They formed a limited company, C Ltd, and arranged for C Ltd. to perform this contract for them on the land of A and B. Thus C Ltd were, *quoad* A and B, licensees. Neighbouring landowners suffered damage to their land caused by an explosion on the land of A and B while C Ltd were using it, and they sued A and B and C Ltd.

It was decided that a licensee who himself accumulates on land of another is liable for the consequences of that accumulation.[6] Further, the House of Lords held that those who remain in occupation of land are also liable to landowners injured by the escape of that which their licensee accumulates in discharge of a contractual duty owed by the occupiers to a third party.

LORD SUMNER further stated (*obiter*) that if 'they (A and B) ... simply suffered others to manufacture upon the site which they nevertheless continued to occupy' they would be liable for the consequences of an escape.[7] On the other hand, EVE J in *Whitmores (Edenbridge) Ltd v Stanford*[8] held that a landowner, upon whose land some other person had a prescriptive right to accumulate water for his own purposes, was outside the rule. The extent to which an occupier is liable for the accumulation by his licensees cannot be regarded as settled, but it is relevant to observe that in *Rylands v Fletcher* BLACKBURN J spoke only of a person who '*for his own purposes*' brings things on his land.[9] A local authority which is required by statute to permit the discharge of sewage into its sewers is 'responsible', for the present purpose, for the accumulation of that sewage in its sewers.[10]

He who authorises another to commit a tort is normally himself also liable for that tort. Thus, a lessor, who lets land for a particular purpose in such circumstances that he is necessarily taken to have authorised the interference which the lessee in consequence causes, is liable in nuisance.[11] There were *obiter dicta* in *Rainham Chemical Works Ltd v Belvedere Fish Guano Co* to the effect that the same rule applies in *Rylands v Fletcher*—in short, that a defendant may be liable although he does not occupy the land when the thing escapes from it if he has authorised another to accumulate it on the land.[12]

---

6 Where, however, over twenty years had elapsed since the licensee had the right to enter and accumulate water there, he was held not to be accountable for the escape of water, if he no longer had control of the land; *Westhoughton Coal and Cannel Co Ltd v Wigan Coal Corporation Ltd* [1939] Ch 800, [1939] 3 All ER 579, CA. Similarly, a person who brings a dangerous thing onto the highway may be liable if it escapes; *Rigby v Chief Constable of Northamptonshire* [1985] 2 All ER 985, [1985] 1 WLR 1242.

7 At 480.

8 [1909] 1 Ch 427.

9 At p 279. See also *Humphries v Cousins* (1877) 2 CPD 239 (occupier bound to receive sewage in drains on his land, in circumstances where it was presumably not collected for his own purposes, held liable for escape). In *Read v Lyons* at p 170, VISCOUNT SIMON doubted whether a defendant making munitions in his factory at the Government's request in wartime brought things on to his land 'for his own purposes' within the rule. Gas, water and electricity boards, and inland waterways authorities carrying out statutory duties do not accumulate for their own purposes, so that *Rylands v Fletcher* does not apply: *Dunne v North Western Gas Board*, [1964] 2 QB 806, [1963] 3 All ER 916, CA; *Boxes Ltd v British Waterways Board* [1971] 2 Lloyd's Rep 183, CA.

10 *Smeaton v Ilford Corporation* [1954] Ch 450, [1954] 1 All ER 923.

11 See p 329, ante.

12 At 476 (per LORD BUCKMASTER); at 489 (per LORD PARMOOR); cf *A-G v Cory Brothers* (1918) 34 TLR 621, but not considered at [1921] 1 AC 521, HL. Contra, Charlesworth, *Negligence* 241–2 and *obiter dicta* of SCRUTTON LJ and GREER LJ in *St Anne's Well Brewery Co v Roberts* (1928) 140 LT 1 at 5 and 9, respectively, CA.

SECTION 4.   NON-NATURAL USER

BLACKBURN J merely said that the rule applied only to a thing 'which was not naturally there'.[13] In the House of Lords LORD CAIRNS used ambiguous words which have since been construed as meaning[14] that the defendant is only answerable if, in bringing the thing there,[15] he is making 'a non-natural use' of the land. This expression is highly flexible and enables the courts to take account of their own interpretation of contemporaneous needs. The form in which the Privy Council expressed this rule in *Rickards v Lothian* emphasised this flexibility:[16]

> It must be some *special* use bringing with it *increased danger* to others, and must not merely be the ordinary use of the land or such a use as is proper for the general benefit of the community.

VISCOUNT SIMON in *Read v Lyons* thought this statement to be 'of the first importance'[17] and LORD PORTER said:[18]

> ... each seems to be a question of fact subject to a ruling of the judge as to whether ... the particular use can be non-natural, and in deciding this question I think that all the circumstances of the time and place and practice of mankind must be taken into consideration so that what might be regarded as ... non-natural may vary according to those circumstances.

The current tendency is to interpret 'non-natural use' narrowly, and many earlier cases may, therefore, be no longer followed. For instance, in *Read v Lyons*, despite the previous decision of the House of Lords in *Rainham Chemical Works Ltd v Belvedere Fish Guano Co*,[19] it was doubted whether building and running a munitions factory on land in war-time was a non-natural use.[20]

The following instances can confidently be regarded as outside *Rylands v Fletcher* because the land is being 'naturally used': water-pipe installations in buildings[1], trees, even though planted by the defendant (at least if they are not poisonous),[2] the working of mines and minerals on land,[3] building or pulling down walls,[4] the lighting of a fire in a fire-place of a house,[5] necessary

---

13 VISCOUNT SIMON in *Read v Lyons* [1947] AC 156 at 166, [1946] 2 All ER 471, described this as 'a parenthetic reference to' the test of LORD CAIRNS.
14 (1868) LR 3 HL 330 at 337–40. See Newark (1961) 24 MLR 557
15 What matters is whether the accumulation (as distinct from the escape or discharge) is a non-natural use: *Read v Lyons*, at 186 (per LORD UTHWATT).
16 [1913] AC 263 at 280, PC.
17 [1947] AC 156 at 169.
18 Ibid at 176.
19 [1921] 2 AC 465.
20 At 169–70 (per VISCOUNT SIMON); at 173–4 (per LORD MACMILLAN).
1 *Rickards v Lothian* [1913] AC 263; *Tilley v Stevenson* [1939] 4 All ER 207, CA.
2 *Noble v Harrison* [1926] 2 KB 332 Div Ct.
3 *Rouse v Gravelworks Ltd* [1940] 1 KB 489, [1940] 1 All ER 26, CA.
4 *Thomas and Evans Ltd v Mid-Rhondda Co-operative Society Ltd* [1941] 1 KB 381, [1940] 4 All ER 357, CA; *St Anne's Well Brewery Co v Roberts* (1928) 140 LT 1.
5 *Sochacki v Sas* [1947] 1 All ER 344; and also holding a torch at the top of the opening of a grate in order to test chimney draught; *J Doltis Ltd v Isaac Braithwaite & Sons (Engineers) Ltd* [1957] 1 Lloyd's Rep 522.

wiring for supplying electric light,[6] and storing metal foil in a factory.[7] Probably, the provision for sewage disposal by a local authority,[8] and the escape from a ship of generated steam are also outside the rule.[9] On the other hand, it has been held that the storing of water, gas and electricity in bulk in mains, and the like,[10] the operation of a chair-o-plane[11] and the use of a blowlamp to thaw pipes in a loft[12] constitute non-natural user of the land. It is difficult to resist the conclusion that the category of 'non-natural user' is presently a narrow one, and that the current interpretation of the term is likely to restrict the scope of application of the rule in *Rylands v Fletcher*.

SECTION 5. ESCAPE

There must be an 'escape from a place where the defendant has occupation of or control over land to a place which is outside his occupation or control'.[13] Therefore, an explosion which injures the plaintiff within the factory where the explosion occurred,[14] and a yew tree which poisons a horse which ate its leaves by reaching over to the land of the defendant, the tree never having extended beyond the defendant's boundary,[15] are both outside the rule. On the other hand, where something escapes from one place of entertainment in a fairground to a stall tenanted by another but still within the fairground, there is, apparently, sufficient escape.[16]

In *Midwood & Co v Manchester Corporation*[17] one of the two grounds of liability was *Rylands v Fletcher*—on the following facts:

After an explosion in a cable belonging to and laid by the defendants in the highway, inflammable gas escaped into the plaintiff's nearby house and set fire to its contents.

In *Charing Cross Electricity Supply Co v Hydraulic Power Co*,[18] the Court of Appeal, relying on this case, held that there was a sufficient escape when water from a main, laid by the defendants under the highway, escaped and

6 *Collingwood v Home and Colonial Stores Ltd* [1936] 3 All ER 200.
7 *British Celanese Ltd v A H Hunt (Capacitors) Ltd* [1969] 2 All ER 1252; *Mason v Levy Auto Parts of England Ltd* [1967] 2 QB 530, [1967] 2 All ER 62 (storage of spare motor parts and engines having regard to quantities of combustible material, manner of storage and character of neighbourhood).
8 *Pride of Derby and Derbyshire Angling Association v British Celanese Ltd*, [1953] Ch 149 at 189, [1953] 1 All ER 179 at 203 (per DENNING LJ), CA; contra, *Smeaton v Ilford Corporation*, [1954] Ch 450 at 470, [1954] 1 All ER 923 at 932 (per UPJOHN J).
9 *Howard v Furness Houlder Argentine Lines Ltd and Brown Ltd* [1936] 2 All ER 781.
10 *Northwestern Utilities v London Guarantee and Accident Co Ltd* [1936] AC 108. *Western Engraving Co v Film Laboratories Ltd* [1936] 1 All ER 106, CA; water in unusual quantities brought on to land for manufacturing purposes of defendant occupier.
11 *Hale v Jennings Brothers* [1938] 1 All ER 579, CA.
12 *Balfour v Barty-King* [1956] 2 All ER 555, affd on other grounds [1957] 1 QB 496, [1957] 1 All ER 156, CA.
13 *Read v J Lyons & Co* [1947] AC 156 at 168 (per VISCOUNT SIMON), [1946] 2 All ER 471, HL.
14 *Read v Lyons*, supra.
15 *Ponting v Noakes* [1894] 2 QB 281.
16 This point was essential to the decision in *Hale v Jennings Brothers*, [1938] 1 All ER 579, CA, although it may not have been argued. An escape to the lower part of the same building, but in different occupation is sufficient: *J Doltis Ltd v Isaac Braithwaite & Sons (Engineers) Ltd* [1957] 1 Lloyd's Rep 522.
17 [1905] 2 KB 597, CA.
18 [1914] 3 KB 772, CA.

damaged the plaintiff's electric cable which was near to it and under the same highway. The House of Lords in *Read v Lyons* did not overrule these cases, and pointed out that there was in each of them an escape into property, over which the defendant had no control, from a container which the defendant had a licence to put in the highway.[19] And where police fired CS canisters into the plaintiff's shop to flush out an armed man, while it was doubted whether an intentional act could found liability in *Rylands v Fletcher*, the judge confirmed that escape from the highway onto the plaintiff's land constituted a sufficient 'escape' within the rule.[20]

It appears that the actual harm wrought by the escape need not be immediately caused by the thing accumulated. It is submitted, for example, that when explosives are accumulated for quarrying purposes, and rocks are hurled on to adjoining land by the blast resulting from a consequent explosion, the damage actually caused by the rocks (though they are not the thing the accumulation of which makes the tort possible) is recoverable under the rule.[1]

SECTION 6.   INTERFERENCE WITH USE OF LAND BY THE PLAINTIFF

Two questions are raised: first, can a plaintiff, whose interest in land has been interfered with, recover consequential damages for injury to chattels or to the person? BLACKBURN J allowed a claim where sparks from a railway engine set fire to a haystack,[2] and in several other cases the principle of liability for harm to chattels has been approved.[3] The rights of an occupier who sustains personal injuries are more doubtful. It is thought that the *dicta* in *Read v Lyons* doubting whether the plaintiff could recover damages for personal injuries even if escape had been proved must be read in the light of the facts, ie the plaintiff suffered personal injuries but had no interest in land, and that there is no reason to differentiate between damage to the person and damage to chattels in the present context. Further, *Hale v Jennings Brothers* is binding Court of Appeal authority for the proposition that an occupier can recover in respect of personal injuries:[4]

A tenant of a stall at a fair suffered personal injuries as the result of an escape of the defendant's chair-o-plane. She was held to have a good cause of action based on *Rylands v Fletcher*.

19 [1947] AC 156 per LORD PORTER at 177; cf VISCOUNT SIMON at 168 and LORD SIMONDS at 183. *Hillier v Air Ministry* (1962) Times 8 December (cows electrocuted by underground electric cable; liable within rule).

20 *Rigby v Chief Constable of Northamptonshire* [1985] 2 All ER 985, [1985] 1 WLR 1242.

1 It was held in *A-G v Cory Brothers & Co* [1921] AC 521 at 538 (per VISCOUNT FINLAY), HL, that where parts of a coal slag heap escaped and their pressure on a third party's quarry spoil caused that spoil to damage the plaintiff's land, the requirement of *Rylands v Fletcher* was satisfied.

2 *Jones v Festiniog Ry Co* (1868) LR 3 QB 733; cf *Cattle v Stockton Waterworks Co* (1875) LR 10 QB 453 at 457 (per BLACKBURN J).

3 Eg *Midwood & Co Ltd v Manchester Corporation* [1905] 2 KB 597, CA; *Musgrove v Pandelis*, [1919] 2 KB 43, CA; *Collingwood v Home and Colonial Stores Ltd* [1936] 3 All ER 200; cf *Read v J Lyons & Co* [1947] AC 156 at 169 (per VISCOUNT SIMON).

4 [1938] 1 All ER 579, CA. The point is not reported to have been argued but is essential to the decision.

Secondly, can a plaintiff ever recover for personal injuries or damage to his chattels when he has no interest in the land? The point was never discussed before *Read v Lyons*, but decisions of the Court of Appeal in *Miles v Forest Rock Granite Co (Leicestershire) Ltd,*[5] and *Perry v Kendricks Transport Ltd*[6] lend support to the view that an action would lie. But in *Read v Lyons* some law lords doubted whether this was so;[7] indeed, it is probably one of the two *rationes decidendi* of LORD MACMILLAN that such an action does not lie.[8] He added:

> The doctrine of *Rylands v Fletcher* ... derives from a conception of mutual duties of adjoining or neighbouring landowners and its congeners are trespass and nuisance.

This issue can only be settled by the House of Lords, which would have to decide whether to follow the analogy of nuisance so as to keep *Rylands v Fletcher* within as narrow a compass as possible, or whether to move towards a more general recognition of strict liability for ultra-hazardous activities. A plaintiff who has no interest in any land which is menaced by the escape and whose only damage is financial loss cannot sue;[9] there is no decision whether an occupier can recover for merely financial loss.

SECTION 7.   DAMAGE

It is assumed that this is not a tort actionable per se: damage must be proved.

SECTION 8.   DEFENCES

A. STATUTORY AUTHORITY[10]

Sometimes, public bodies storing water, gas, electricity and the like, are by statute exempted from liability so long as they have taken reasonable care. It is a question of statutory interpretation whether, and, if so, to what extent, liability under *Rylands v Fletcher* has been excluded.[11]

Smeaton v Ilford Corporation is a case where this defence alone prevented the plaintiff from recovering in this tort:[12]

> Sewage accumulated by the defendants in their sewers overflowed on to the land of the plaintiff in circumstances which were held to constitute neither nuisance nor negligence. Section 31 of the Public Health Act 1936,

---

5 (1918) 34 TLR 500.
6 [1956] 1 All ER 154; and at first instance in *Shiffman v Venerable Order of the Hospital of St John of Jerusalem* [1936] 1 All ER 557; *Halsey v Esso Petroleum Co* [1961] 2 All ER 145 and *British Celanese Ltd v A H Hunt (Capacitors) Ltd* [1969] 2 All ER 1252.
7 Eg VISCOUNT SIMON at 169 and LORD PORTER at 178.
8 At 173.
9 *Cattle v Stockton Waterworks Co* (1875) LR 10 QB 453 (escape of water made it more expensive for plaintiff to carry out his contract to construct a tunnel); *Weller & Co v Foot and Mouth Disease Research Institute* [1966] 1 QB 569, [1965] 3 All ER 560 (escape of virus which damaged third party's cattle damaged business of plaintiff cattle auctioneer).
10 See p 94, ante. And on public utilities, generally see *Clerk and Lindsell* ch 24.
11 Eg *Green v Chelsea Waterworks Co* (1894) 70 LT 547.
12 [1954] Ch 450, [1954] 1 All ER 923. It was reported in the *Law Journal* (1954), p 619, that the defendants subsequently made a substantial payment to the plaintiff in return for his not proceeding with his appeal to the Court of Appeal.

under which the defendants had acted in receiving the sewage, reads: 'A local authority shall so discharge their functions ... as not to create a nuisance.' Interpreting this to mean that the defendants were absolved from liability provided that they did not create a nuisance, the court held that the defendants had a defence under the statute to an action based on *Rylands v Fletcher*.

B. CONSENT OF PLAINTIFF

If the plaintiff has permitted the defendant to accumulate the thing the escape of which is complained of, then he cannot sue if it escapes.[13] Implied consent will also be a defence. Thus, a person becoming the tenant of business or domestic premises at a time when the condition or construction of adjoining premises occupied by the landlord is such that a happening of the *Rylands v Fletcher* type is likely to ensue, is deemed to have consented to take the risk of such an event actually happening. This afforded a good defence in *Kiddle v City Business Properties Ltd,*[14] when an overflow of rainwater from a blocked gutter at the bottom of a sloping roof in the possession of the landlord, and above the tenant's premises, damaged the stock in the tenant's premises.[15]

If the accumulation benefits both plaintiff and defendant this is an important element in deciding whether the plaintiff is deemed to have consented.[16] Where, therefore, for the benefit of the several occupants of a building, rainwater is collected on the roof,[17] or a water-closet is installed,[18] or water pipes are fitted,[19] the several occupants are deemed to have consented. On the other hand, the defence does not seem to be available as between a commercial supplier of gas (in respect of gas mains under the highway) and a consumer in premises adjoining the highway.[20] In any event an occupier will not be presumed to have consented to installations being left in a dangerously unsafe state.[1]

C. CONTRIBUTORY NEGLIGENCE

Where the plaintiffs worked a mine under the canal of the defendant and had

---

13 *A-G v Cory Brothers & Co* [1921] AC 521, HL (the *ratio decidendi* of the judgments of LORDS FINLAY and ATKINSON).
14 [1942] 1 KB 269, [1942] 2 All ER 216.
15 This principle of implied consent does not apply where the plaintiff and the defendant are not in a tenant-landlord relationship to each other; *Humphries v Cousins* (1877) 2 CPD 239.
16 *Peters v Prince of Wales Theatre (Birmingham) Ltd* [1943] KB 73, [1942] 2 All ER 533, CA. Where the plaintiff by inference has consented to having the benefit of the defendant's watercourse, but contends that he has not consented to a negligent accumulation of water, the onus is on the plaintiff to allege and prove that negligence: *Gilson v Kerrier Rural District Council*, [1976] 3 All ER 343, CA.
17 *Carstairs v Taylor* (1871) LR 6 Exch 217 (*ratio decidendi* of BRAMWELL P's judgment PIGOTT B concurring).
18 *Ross v Fedden* (1872) LR 7 QB 661.
19 *Anderson v Oppenheimer* (1880) 5 QBD 602, CA (the reasoning is muddled, but this is the basis of the decision).
20 *Northwestern Utilities Ltd v London Guarantee and Accident Co Ltd* [1936] AC 108 at 120, PC.
1 *A Prosser & Sons Ltd v Levy* [1955] 3 All ER 577, CA.

good reason to know that they would thereby cause the water from the canal to escape into this mine, it was held that they could not sue in *Rylands v Fletcher* when the water actually escaped and damaged their mine: for, said COCKBURN CJ:[2] 'the plaintiffs saw the danger and may be said to have courted it'. Where the plaintiff is contributorily negligent, the apportionment provisions of the Law Reform (Contributory Negligence) Act 1945 will now apply. Further, 'a man cannot increase the liabilities of his neighbour by applying his own property to special uses, whether for business or pleasure', as was said in *Eastern and Southern African Telegraph Co v Cape Town Tramways Cos.*[3] There the plaintiffs, who complained that the tramways of the defendant caused electrical interference with the receipt of messages through their submarine cable, failed because no damage to the cable itself was caused; the plaintiff suffered loss only because he relied on these cables for the transmission of messages.

D. ACT OF THIRD PARTIES

The liability of the occupier where others accumulate things on his land has already been examined.[4] What must next be considered is when is it a defence that, although the defendant brought the thing on to his land, it has only escaped through the act of a third party.

It is evident from *Rylands v Fletcher* itself that the defendant is liable for an escape attributable to his independent contractors.[5] There is weighty support for the proposition that the defendant is liable for escapes caused by other third parties where the defendant ought reasonably to have foreseen the act of that third party and had enough control of the premises to be able to prevent it. The proprietor of a chair-o-plane was accordingly held liable for the escape of a chair caused by a passenger's tampering with it;[6] the owner of a flag-pole was liable for not anticipating the interference with it of small children (when as a result of that interference, the pole fell on and injured the plaintiff);[7] a gas company laying a main in a highway, when they ought to have foreseen that subsidence might occur owing to the presence of mines underneath, were liable for damage caused by an explosion of gas on the fracture of the main when the surrounding earth subsided.[8] B was not, however, liable where flooding of A's premises was caused by an unknown third party's maliciously turning on a water tap in B's premises and blocking the waste pipe of the lavatory basin,[9] or where the defendant's reservoir overflowed when a third party, conducting operations higher up the stream

---

2 *Dunn v Birmingham Canal Co* (1872) LR 7 QB 244 at 260, affd (1872) LR 8 QB 42.
3 [1902] AC 381, PC, at 393; cf *Hoare & Co v McAlpine* [1923] 1 Ch 167, which left open the question whether a plaintiff who complained that his buildings had been damaged could be met by the plea that they were damaged only because they were dilapidated buildings having insecure foundations.
4 See p 349, ante.
5 See ch 27, post for separate treatment of independent contractors.
6 *Hale v Jennings Brothers* [1938] 1 All ER 579, CA.
7 *Shiffman v The Venerable Order of the Hospital of St John of Jerusalem* [1936] 1 All ER 557 at 561 (per ATKINSON J *obiter* on *Rylands v Fletcher*).
8 *Hanson v Wearmouth Coal Co Ltd and Sunderland Gas Co* [1939] 3 All ER 47, CA.
9 *Rickards v Lothian* [1913] AC 263, PC.

supplying it, discharged downstream an unusually large volume of water into it without any warning.[10] There is now a tendency to restrict the situations where *Rylands v Fletcher* will apply in the absence of negligence. A particular illustration in the present context is the Court of Appeal decision that, once the defendants have proved that the escape was the act of a stranger 'they avoid liability, unless the plaintiff can go on to show that the act which caused the escape was an act of the kind which the owner could reasonably have contemplated and guarded against'.[11]

E. ACT OF GOD

The defence has received in connection with this tort a prominence out of all proportion to its practical importance. If an escape is caused, through natural causes and without human intervention, in 'circumstances which no human foresight can provide against, and of which human prudence is not bound to recognise the possibility',[12] there is then said to exist the defence of Act of God.

In *Nichols v Marsland*[13] the defence succeeded where a most violent thunderstorm caused flooding. The case was put in its proper perspective by the House of Lords in *Greenock Corporation v Caledonian Ry Co*[14] where an extraordinary and unprecedented rainfall was held in similar circumstances not to be an Act of God: the explanation of *Nichols v Marsland* was that there the jury found that no reasonable person could have anticipated the storm and the court would not disturb this finding of fact.

Earthquakes and tornadoes may sometimes be Acts of God, but few other natural phenomena seem likely to be within its scope so as to constitute a defence to *Rylands v Fletcher*.

---

10 *Box v Jubb* (1879) 4 Ex D 76; cf *Black v Christchurch Finance Co* [1894] AC 48 PC. Analogous cases to those last cited are those suggesting that there is no liability where an unobservable defect of nature causes the escape, or where there is flooding because a rat gnaws through a water cistern; *Carstairs v Taylor* (1871) LR 6 Exch 217 (*ratio decidendi* of KELLY CB).

11 Per PARKER LJ (*ratio*) in *Perry v Kendricks Transport Ltd* [1956] 1 All ER 154 at 161; likewise JENKINS LJ, at 160 that once the act of stranger is made out 'one reaches the point where the claim based on *Rylands v Fletcher* merges into the claim in negligence'. Contra, *Salmond* 370 and *Fleming* 332, but it is submitted that the obscure *dicta* of SINGLETON LJ (on which they rely) in *A Prosser & Sons Ltd v Levy* [1955] 3 All ER 577 at 587, CA, cannot stand against the clear-cut decision in *Perry v Kendricks Transport Ltd Northwestern Utilities Ltd v London Guarantee and Accident Co Ltd* [1936] AC 108, on which Salmond also relies, is an isolated case where the Judicial Committee held that there was liability in negligence, but not in *Rylands v Fletcher* for an escape resulting from the foreseeable conduct of a third party and is therefore irrelevant on this point. In support of this interpretation of the last cited case, see Wright, *Legal Essays and Address*, 134 and *Shell Mex and BP Ltd v Belfast Corporation* [1952] NI 72 CA (NI).

12 A definition of LORD WESTBURY in *Tennent v Earl of Glasgow* (1864) 2 Macph (HL) 22 at 26–7, approved and followed by the House of Lords in *Greenock Corporation v Caledonian Ry Co* [1917] AC 556, HL.

13 (1876) 2 Ex D 1.

14 [1917] AC 556, HL.

F. NECESSITY

It has been held[15] that if an intentional release of a substance, in this instance the firing of CS gas canisters by police officers intent on flushing out a psychopath from the defendant's shop, can ground liability in *Rylands v Fletcher*, then the defence of necessity must be available in this tort. Such an intentional invasion of the plaintiff's property seems, however, more properly accountable in trespass.

SECTION 9.   NUISANCE AND *RYLANDS V FLETCHER*

Although the trend is towards bringing *Rylands v Fletcher* closer to nuisance, the rule in *Rylands v Fletcher* must still be examined separately because it will afford a remedy where nuisance will not in the following circumstances.

1 If the defendant has accumulated 'a thing' which escapes, then, regardless of whether he was negligent in allowing it to escape or of whether it was foreseeable that it would in the particular circumstances escape, he is liable (except for the defences of Act of God and Act of a Third Party). In nuisance, the defendant is liable for damage resulting from a state of affairs on his land where that state of affairs was foreseeably likely to result in substantial interference with the plaintiff's use of his land:[16] nuisance then has a much closer affinity than *Rylands v Fletcher* with negligence. Thus, if the ball is hit from a baseball park through a neighbour's window (assuming that this is not a natural use of a park in England) the club will be liable in *Rylands v Fletcher*: they will be liable in nuisance only if it was reasonably likely that this would happen in view of the siting of the pitch in the park. Similarly, a local authority bound by statute to permit the discharge of sewage into its sewers is not thereby, without more, responsible in nuisance for flooding caused by the sewer's being overcharged, but is liable in *Rylands v Fletcher*, unless it can set up the defence of statutory authority.[17]

2 The occupier is liable in *Rylands v Fletcher* for the accumulation of, and the escape caused by, independent contractors. In nuisance the liability for independent contractors is less extensive.[18]

3 Damage by fire may sometimes be the subject of a claim in trespass or negligence, or the separate action on the case for fire.[19] It may also give rise to a claim in nuisance or in *Rylands v Fletcher*. It will be recalled that the Fires Prevention (Metropolis) Act 1774 provides that the person on whose land a fire 'shall accidentally begin' has a defence.[20] This defence is

---

15 *Rigby v Chief Constable of Northamptonshire* [1985] 2 All ER 985 at 996.

16 This explains why *quia timet* injunctions lie for a 'state of affairs' in nuisance but not necessarily for an 'accumulation' in *Rylands v Fletcher*.

17 *Smeaton v Ilford Corporation* [1954] Ch 450, [1954] 1 All ER 923.

18 See ch 19, ante.

19 *Balfour v Barty-King* [1957] 1 QB 496, [1957] 1 All ER 156, CA; *Mason v Levy Auto Parts of England Ltd* [1967] 2 QB 530, [1967] 2 All ER 62. In *H & N Emanuel Ltd v Greater London Council* [1971] 2 All ER 835 CA, it was held than an occupier is liable for an escape of fire caused by the negligence of anyone other than a stranger.

20 P 337, ante.

not available to suits based on *Rylands v Fletcher*[1] although it is sometimes a defence in nuisance.[2]

Beyond these three heads it is difficult to state with confidence further circumstances where the distinction between nuisance and *Rylands v Fletcher* is clear. Possibly, the scope of 'reasonable use' in nuisance is wider than that of 'natural use' in *Rylands v Fletcher* in that the number of relevant factors, e g locality, is greater in nuisance. Further, it is the 'accumulation' which in *Rylands v Fletcher* must be non-natural, whereas it is the use which in nuisance must be unreasonable. It is conceivable that a farmer may accumulate water in an ordinary way and yet irrigate unreasonably so that his flooded neighbour may recover in nuisance but not in *Rylands v Fletcher*. Sometimes it is said that in *Rylands v Fletcher* there may be liability for an isolated escape, whereas the interference required in nuisance must have a certain degree of permanence.[3] This cannot be accepted as an accurate mark of distinction— it does not take account of the rule of 'state of affairs' in nuisance.[4] Provided that there is on the defendant's land a state of affairs likely to cause damage to the plaintiff's land, an action of nuisance may still lie although there is an isolated escape of a thing from the land of the defendant to that of the plaintiff—there is no doubt that if the defendant maintains his chimney stack in a dangerous state, with the result that it falls on to the plaintiff's adjoining premises, the plaintiff will not be prevented from succeeding in nuisance because there is an 'isolated escape'.

Of course, there are many facts within nuisance which are outside *Rylands v Fletcher*, for example:

a *Rylands v Fletcher* is confined to the accumulation of physical objects: nuisance covers damage done by intangibles such as noise even though nothing likely of itself to cause such noise was kept on the defendant's land.
b No accumulation or escape is required in nuisance.
c A use may be natural and yet give rise to liability in nuisance.[5]

---

1 *Musgrove v Pandelis* [1919] 2 KB 43, CA; *Mulholland and Tedd Ltd v Baker* [1939] 3 All ER 253; *Perry v Kendricks Transport Ltd* [1956] 1 All ER 154, CA: *Balfour v Barty-King* supra, at first instance.
2 P 337, ante.
3 Cf Newark (1949) 65 LQR 480 at 488.
4 See p 319, ante.
5 Eg *Sedleigh-Denfield v O'Callaghan* [1940] AC 880 at 888, [1940] 3 All ER 349 at 354 (per VISCOUNT MAUGHAM), HL; *British Celanese Ltd v A H Hunt (Capacitors) Ltd* [1969] 2 All ER 1252.

Chapter 21

Animals

SECTION 1. NEGLIGENCE AND STRICT LIABILITY

Persons who own or control animals are subject to the same duty of care in respect of the care and control of the animal as those responsible for any other chattel.[1] Thus in *Aldham v United Dairies (London) Ltd*[2] the defendant was held liable when his unattended pony became restive and jabbed at a passing pedestrian dragging her down. And in *Draper v Hodder*[3] the owner of a pack of terriers was found liable when the dogs bit a neighbour's child. He was negligent in failing to control and/or train the pack adequately. But liability for damage inflicted by animals extends beyond failure to control the animal properly. The Animals Act 1971[4] provides in certain circumstances for liability without fault.

SECTION 2. DAMAGE DONE BY DANGEROUS ANIMALS

A. DANGEROUS SPECIES

Section 2(1) imposes liability where any damage is caused by an animal which belongs to a dangerous species. A dangerous species is a species which is not commonly domesticated in the British Isles, and whose fully grown animals have such characteristics that they are likely, unless restrained, to cause severe damage or that any damage they may cause is likely to be severe.[5] A species is dangerous if it is likely to cause damage either to persons or to property; the list will not be confined to animals likely to attack man, such as bears, tigers, lions and zebras. An action lies even though the damage caused is not of the kind which made the species dangerous. Liability arises even though the animal has not escaped from control; for example, the keeper will be liable if his elephant slips or stumbles and causes damage, even though there was no failure of control. Damage includes the impairment of any mental condition.[6] Presumably, if someone suffered nervous shock (with resulting physical illness) at the sudden appearance of a monkey there is liability.

---

1 *Fardon v Harcourt–Rivington* [1932] All ER Rep 81 at 83.
2 [1940] 1 KB 507, [1939] 4 All ER 522; And see *Brock v Richards* [1951] 1 KB 529, CA.
3 [1972] 2 QB 556, [1972] 2 All ER 210 (the defendant's contention that while bowling over or scratching by the excited dogs was foreseeable, biting was harm of a distinct and unforseeable type was rejected).
4 Section 8(1) further amends the common law relating to negligence to impose a duty of care in respect of cattle straying on the highway.
5 Section 6(2).
6 Section 11.

B. OTHER DANGEROUS ANIMALS

Section 2(2) imposes liability in certain circumstances for an animal which does not belong to a dangerous species. Three requirements must be met. First, the damage must be of a kind which the animal, unless restrained, was likely to cause or which, if caused by the animal, was likely to be severe. This formulation covers not only say, a dog which attacks a man, but also where an animal with a dangerous disease spreads the infection to other animals. Secondly, the likelihood of the damage or of its being severe must be due to characteristics of the animal which are not normally found in animals of the same species[7] or are not normally so found except at particular times or in particular circumstances.[8] That could cover the bitch with a litter which was prone at such a time only to bite strangers. Thirdly, those characteristics must be known to the keeper or to his servant or member of his household under the age of sixteen.

C. LIABILITY FOR EITHER KIND OF DANGEROUS ANIMAL

Liability is imposed on the keeper, ie the person who owns the animal or has it in his possession, or who is head of the household of which a member under the age of sixteen owns the animal or has it in his possession. The last provision prevents evasion of liability by making a child in the family the nominal owner. If a person ceases to keep, own or possess it, he continues to be liable until another person owns or possesses it.[9]

Liability is imposed regardless of fault. The defendant is not liable for any damage which is due wholly to the fault of the person suffering it.[10] Damages will be reduced under the Law Reform (Contributory Negligence) Act 1945 where the plaintiff's fault contributes to his damage.[11] It is a defence that the damage was suffered by a person who has voluntarily accepted the risk.[12] A person employed as a servant who accepts a risk incidental to his employment shall not be treated as accepting it voluntarily.[13] It is also a defence that the

---

7 The keeper was liable where a horse of unpredictable and unreliable behaviour crushed its groom against the bar of its trailer even though it had no previous tendency to injure people, for that was a characteristic unusual in a horse. *Wallace v Newton* [1982] 2 All ER 106.

8 In *Cummings v Granger* [1977] QB 397, CA, the plaintiff was bitten by the defendant's Alsatian dog which was used as a guard dog in his scrapyard. The dog used to bark and run around when coloured people like the plaintiff approached. This characteristic is not normally found in Alsatian dogs except when used as guard dogs. This was held to be a particular circumstance within s 2(2)(b).

9 Section 6(3). A person who takes possession for the purpose of preventing damage or restoring it to its owner is not thereby made liable; s 6(4).

10 Section 5(1). In *Cummings v Grainger* [1977] QB 397, CA at 404, LORD DENNING appeared to hold that even though the plaintiff trespassed in the defendant's yard, the fact that the dog bit the plaintiff showed that the damage was not wholly due to the plaintiff's fault, but only partly so, with the result that this defence was not available. Yet since the question of a defence could not arise unless the dog had bitten the plaintiff it is difficult to see how, if LORD DENNING is right, that defence could ever succeed.

11 Section 10.

12 Section 5(2). In *Cummings v Grainger* supra the court found that when the plaintiff knew of the dog she must be taken to have voluntarily accepted the risk. The court, especially ORMROD LJ at 408 treated this defence as being wider than the common law defence of *volenti*.

13 Section 6(5).

damage occurred on property where the plaintiff was a trespasser if it is proved either that the animal was not kept there for the protection of persons or property or (if the animal was kept there for the protection of persons or property) that keeping it there for that purpose was not unreasonable.[14] Presumably it would be difficult to maintain this defence in respect of a dangerous species being kept for protection only, because that might well be unreasonable; trespassers will never have a remedy when attacked by an animal of dangerous species not kept for protection.

SECTION 3.   LIABILITY FOR STRAYING LIVESTOCK

Section 4 imposes liability on a person in possession of livestock which stray on to another's land. 'Livestock' means cattle, horses, asses, mules, hinnies, sheep, pigs, goats and poultry[15] and also deer not in the wild state.[16] The liability is for damage done by the livestock to the land or to any property on it.[17] Presumably 'property' includes other animals as well as goods, but the plaintiff cannot recover under section 4 for his personal injuries. Either the person in possession or the owner even though not in possession can recover for damage to his land or property. A plaintiff may incur expense in keeping livestock while it cannot be restored to its owner or while it is detained in pursuance of the power conferred by the Act to detain it.[18] He can recover any such expenses reasonably incurred.[19]

Liability is strict under this section; no fault has to be proved. The defendant is not liable for any damage due wholly to the fault of the plaintiff.[20] This defence applies where the plaintiff could have prevented the damage by fencing[1] only if the plaintiff is in breach of a duty which he owed to a person having an interest in the land from which the livestock strayed and the straying would not have occurred but for that breach.[2] The Law Reform (Contributory Negligence) Act 1945 applies to this tort. It is also a defence that the livestock strayed from a highway and its presence there was a lawful use of the highway.[3]

---

14 Section 5(3). *Cummings v Grainger* supra (reasonable to keep an Alsatian dog, known to be ferocious, to protect old cars in a locked yard). Had the Guard Dogs Act 1975 been in force, LORD DENNING would have held that failure to comply with the requirement of that Act that the dog had to be in the control of a handler would have made the keeping of the dog unreasonable.

15 See s 11.

16 Section 11.

17 This would not cover the case when there is no damage, only loss, eg Ministry of Agriculture, Food and Fisheries makes foot and mouth order restricting movement of cattle, but none of P's cattle is destroyed.

18 Section 7. See *Matthews v Wilks* (1987) Times, 25 May; *Morris v Blaenau Gwent District Council* (1982) 80 LGR 793.

19 Section 4(1)(b).

20 Section 5(1).

1 Fencing includes the construction of any obstacle designed to prevent animals from straying.

2 Section 5(6).

3 Section 5(4).

SECTION 4.   LIABILITY FOR INJURY DONE BY DOGS TO LIVESTOCK

Section 3 provides that where a dog causes damage by killing or injuring livestock[4] its keeper is not liable for the damage, even though he was not negligent. A person is not liable if the livestock was killed or injured on land on to which it had strayed and either the dog belonged to the occupier or its presence on the land was authorised by the occupier.[5] It is a defence that the damage was due wholly to the fault of the person suffering it.[6]

---

4 Livestock for this purpose is slightly wider than under s 4 in that it includes pheasant, partridges and grouse while in captivity; s 11.
5 Section 5(4).
6 Section 5(1). If the plaintiff by his fault has contributed to the damage, the Law Reform (Contributory Negligence) Act 1945 applies to permit a reduction of the damages awarded.

Chapter 22

Violation of interests protected by statute, or the action for breach of statutory duty

SECTION 1. INTRODUCTION[1]

A person suffering damage as a result of a violation of a statute may have an action in tort in respect of that damage, commonly styled an action for breach of statutory duty. The early cases on the tort rested on a broad principle that whenever a violation of a statute caused damage to an individual's interests a right of action in tort arose.[2] Leading nineteenth-century judgments[3] markedly restricted the scope of the tort, requiring that any person claiming for breach of a statutory duty must first establish that the legislature intended that violation of his right or interest be tortious.

LORD DENNING MR attempted to resurrect the broader principle in *Ex p Island Records Ltd*.[4] He contended that if '... a private right which is being interfered with by a criminal act, thus causing or threatening to cause him special damage over and above the generality of the public, then he can come to the court as a private individual and ask that his private right be protected.'[5] Thus, he held that whenever a lawful business carried on by a private person suffered damage as a result of contravention of a statutory prohibition an action for breach of statutory duty would lie.

This 'broad Denning principle', had it taken root, would have transformed the action for breach of statutory duties and opened up the way for greater protection by the law of torts in respect of damage to economic and business interests. Plaintiffs could have taken advantage of the extensive provision made by statute to regulate the economy to obtain compensation for losses which the classic economic torts left irremediable.[6] Relying on *Ex p Island Records* the plaintiffs in *Lonrho Ltd v Shell Petroleum Co Ltd (No 2)*,[7] an oil company who had suffered heavy losses because they complied with government sanctions orders prohibiting trade with the illegal regime in Rhodesia while competitors flagrantly violated those orders, sought to sue their competitors for breach of the orders.

The House of Lords firmly rejected and condemned the 'broad Denning principle', re-asserting that the general rule in a claim for breach of statutory duty is that 'where an Act creates an obligation and enforces performance in a specified manner ... that performance cannot be enforced in any other

---

1 See generally K M Stanton, *Breach of Statutory Duty in Tort* (1986), R A Buckley 'Liability in Tort for Breach of Statutory Duty' (1984) 100 LQR 204.
2 *Couch v Steel* (1854) 3 E & B 402 was the last important case resting on the old broad principle.
3 See *Atkinson v Newcastle and Gateshead Waterworks Co* (1877) 2 Ex D 441, CA; *Groves v Lord Wimborne* [1898] 2 QB 402, CA.
4 [1978] Ch 122, [1978] 3 All ER 824.
5 At 139.
6 See ante ch 9.
7 [1982] AC 173, [1981] 2 All ER 456; and see *RCA Corpn v Pollard* [1983] Ch 135, [1982] 3 All ER 771.

manner'.[8] Where the only manner of enforcing performance for which the Act provides is the criminal process, there are only two classes of exception to this general rule. The first is '... where on the true construction of the Act it is apparent that the obligation or prohibition was imposed for the benefit of a particular class of individuals'.[9] And the second arises where statute creates a public right and an individual member of the public suffers 'particular, direct and substantial damage other and different from that which is common to the rest of the public.'[10] Lonrho's claim fell outside either exception. Sanctions orders prohibiting trade with Rhodesia were intended to end all trade and bring down the illegal regime. They were not imposed for the benefit or protection of any class of business, but to create public rights enjoyable by all citizens wishing to avail themselves of such rights.[11]

The existence of a cause of action for violations of a statute thus becomes primarily a matter of construction of the relevant statute. But in the vast majority of statutes to which the tort has been held to extend Parliament has imposed a duty on the defendant, expressly made breach of that duty a crime, and given no indication of whether a cause of action in tort is intended.[12] Yet the judges readily imply such an intention. Many of the decided cases can for the most part be regarded as decisions of policy whether breach of particular statutory provisions should be compensated for by way of damages awarded to the victim.

The priority afforded to interests in bodily security by the law of torts is reflected in the willingness of the courts to interpret industrial safety legislation so as to confer a right of action on injured workmen. Breaches of statutory rules to fence machinery in the Factories Act[13] and regulations made for miners' safety by the Mines and Quarries Acts[14] represent classic examples of the statutory provisions traditionally held enforceable in tort. Now, the Health and Safety at Work Act 1974 is intended to replace earlier piecemeal legislation on industrial safety. Sections 2–9 impose general safety duties on employers and employees. Breach of these general duties are expressly stated not to be actionable in tort, whereas breach of specific health and safety regulations, made by the Secretary of State under section 15 of the Act, will be actionable unless the regulation in issue provides otherwise.[15]

Interests in land and goods have also been protected against violation of a statute. A mineowner recovered damages from a neighbouring mineowner in breach of his statutory duty to pump water out of the mine.[16] Economic losses may be recoverable where protection of that kind of loss is within the ambit of the statute. In *Monk v Warbey*[17] the plaintiff suffered bodily injuries

8 *Doe d Bishop of Rochester v Bridges* (1831) 1 B & Ad 847 at 859.
9 Per Lord Diplock at 186 and 461 respectively.
10 *Benjamin v Storr* (1874) LR 9 CP 400 at 407.
11 As to this second exception to the general rule see post at p 371 and see Stanton op cit at pp 50–51. Is Lord Diplock himself creating a new category of action for breach of statutory duty?
12 But see the Consumer Protection Act 1987 s 41 which makes breaches of consumer safety regulations made under Part II of that Act expressly actionable in tort; and see Health and Safety at Work Act 1974 s 47(2).
13 *Groves v Lord Wimborne* (supra).
14 *Black v Fife Coal Co Ltd* [1912] AC 149; *National Coal Board v England* [1954] AC 403, [1954] 1 All ER 546.
15 Section 47. Existing actions for breach of statutory duty under earlier legislation remain unaffected.
16 *Ross v Rugge-Price* (1876) 1 Ex D 269.
17 [1935] 1 KB 75.

in a road accident. Alas, the driver of the car was uninsured and impecunious. The plaintiff recovered his consequent financial loss by successfully suing the owner of the car who, in breach of his statutory duty, had allowed his friend to drive the vehicle uninsured against third party risks. In *Rickless v United Artists Corpn*[18] the plaintiffs won a massive award of damages for the defendants' unauthorised use of clips from old Peter Sellers films. The Court of Appeal found that violation of section 2 of the Dramatic and Musical Performers' Protection Act 1958, prohibiting use of such material without the performer's consent, did create a civil right of action. The purpose of the Act was protection of performers' rights and correlative financial interests.[19]

Interference with the statutory right to vote was held actionable in *Ashby v White*.[20] Failure by an employer to comply with statutory rules regarding statements detailing how wages are made up was found to give an aggrieved employee a right of action.[1] What is crucial is not the classification of the plaintiff's interest, as in his bodily security or his goods or his financial prosperity, but whether protection of that interest, whatever its type, is within the ambit of the relevant statute.

In determining whether the interest violated is one protected by the statute, whether the statute was passed for the benefit of a class of which the plaintiff is a member or to provide public rights of which the plaintiff may avail himself, three further general factors should be borne in mind.

First, the courts have not been generally ready to allow an action in tort against public authorities violating general statutory duties to provide public services. So it has been held that no action lies against the Minister of Education for failing to carry out his duty to 'promote the education of the people of England and Wales.'[2] A claim against the Minister of Health for breach of his statutory duty to provide an efficient and comprehensive health service also failed.[3] But an action for breach of the more defined and specific duty cast on local authorities to house homeless persons succeeded.[4] The absence of any prescribed remedy in the Act much influenced the court. Establishing a right of action against the public authority is, however, only the first of the plaintiff's problems. Where performance of the relevant statutory duty requires the exercise of the authority's discretion, then any challenge to the authority will have to be brought not by way of an action started by writ but by means of an application for judicial review.[5]

In determining whether an action lies for breach of statutory duty the courts will, secondly, take account of the existing law of torts. Do other torts, significantly negligence, adequately protect the plaintiff's rights? So several

---

18 [1987] 1 All ER 679, [1987] 2 WLR 945.
19 Leave to appeal to the House of Lords granted.
20 (1703–4) 1 Bro Parl Cas 62; but see now the Representation of the People Act.
 1 *Simmonds v Newport Abercarn Black Vein Steam Coal Co* [1921] 1 KB 616, CA.
 2 *Watt v Kesteven County Council* [1955] 1 QB 408, [1955] 1 All ER 473; but see *Meade v London Borough of Haringey* [1979] 2 All ER 1016, [1979] 1 WLR 637 discussed by Stanton op cit at pp 81–83.
 3 *R v Secretary of State for Social Services ex p Hincks* (1979) as did an action against a local authority for failing to clear snow off the streets; *Saunders v Holborn District Board of Works* [1895] 1 QB 64.
 4 *Thornton v Kirklees Metropolitan Borough Council* [1979] QB 626, [1979] 2 All ER 349; and see *Booth & Co (International) Ltd v National Enterprise Board* [1978] 3 All ER 624.
 5 *Cocks v Thanet District Council* [1983] 2 AC 286, [1982] 3 All ER 1135; on the implications of this procedural division between public and private law see ante at p 167.

claims relating to breach of regulations relating to road safety have failed.[6] And an action by a plaintiff made ill by infected milk bottled for sale by the defendants failed.[7] Existing remedies in tort and contract were thought to be sufficiently comprehensive. Finally, the statutory duty itself must be precise in its terms so as to make enforcing it by way of action fair to the defendant.[8]

SECTION 2.   THE NATURE OF THE ACTION

This action in tort is generally styled an action 'for breach of statutory duty'. This description (in conformity though it may be with the traditional stress on wrongs in the English law of torts) is misleading. From the examples set out above, it is abundantly clear that a plaintiff who merely proves that the defendant broke a statutory duty is far from having established the tort. The emphasis must be on whether in the light of the nature of the plaintiff's interest, that interest was intended to be protected by the statute.[9]

One of the most harmful consequences of this mistaken emphasis on breach of duty has been a serious confusion between this tort and negligence. Proof by the plaintiff that the defendant owes him a duty is the essence of the tort of negligence; what could be more natural than to say that just as in negligence a breach of duty amounting to carelessness must be proved, so also in this tort there must be a negligent breach of statutory duty (and especially when the subject matter of so many of the actions, especially those by workmen against employers, is common both to the present tort and to actions in negligence and when failure to comply with a statute is sometimes treated as evidence of negligence in claims for that tort). The House of Lords has now exposed that error—one which would never have been made but for the false stress on breach of duty. The judgment of LORD WRIGHT in *LPTB v Upson* clarifies the point:[10]

> ... a claim for damages for breach of a statutory duty intended to protect a person in the position of the particular plaintiff is a specific common law right which is not to be confused in essence with a claim for negligence. The statutory right has its origin in the statute, but the particular remedy of an action for damages is given by the common law in order to make effective, for the benefit of the injured plaintiff, his right to the performance by the defendant of the defendant's statutory duty. It is an effective sanction. It is not a claim in negligence in the strict or ordinary sense ... whatever the resemblances, it is essential to keep in mind the fundamental differences of the two classes of claim.

6 *Phillips v Britannia Hygiene Laundry Co* [1923] 2 KB 832; *Clarke and Wife v Brims* [1947] KB 497, [1947] 1 All ER 242.
7 *Square v Model Farm Dairies (Bournemouth) Ltd* [1939] 2 KB 365, [1939] 1 All ER 259, CA; but an action against a local authority for violating its duty to supply pure drinking water succeeded in *Read v Croydon Corpn* [1938] 4 All ER 631.
8 *Cutler v Wandsworth Stadium Ltd* [1949] AC 398, [1949] 1 All ER 544.
9 *Ashby v White* (1703) 2 Ld Raym 938 at 954; *Atkinson v Newcastle and Gateshead Waterworks Co* (1871) LR 6 Exch 404 at 409, (1877) 2 Ex D 441, CA; *Simmonds v Newport Abercarn Black Vein Steam Coal Co* [1921] 1 KB 616 at 631, CA; *Ross v Rugge-Price* (1876) 1 Ex D 269 at 272-3.
10 [1949] AC 155 at 168, [1949] 1 All ER 60, HL; cf *Caswell v Powell Duffryn Associated Collieries Ltd* [1940] AC 152 at 178, [1939] 3 All ER 722, HL (per LORD WRIGHT) and *Chipchase v British Titan Products Co Ltd* [1956] 1 QB 545, [1956] 1 All ER 613, CA (compliance with exhaustively defined statutory regulations did not prevent liability in negligence). And see Stanton op cit at pp 28–30 on the dangers of confusing negligence in a statutory context with breach of statutory duty.

The reason why this tort is classed herein along with the other torts of 'strict' liability will now be clear: it is another tort which lies in some circumstances even though the conduct of the defendant is neither intentional nor negligent; one has to look to the statute to see against what types of conduct, whether intentional, negligent or accidental, the interest of the plaintiff under the statute is to be protected.

The rules (some of them imprecise because of the ever-present problem of statutory interpretation) governing this tort will now be examined.

SECTION 3.   WHAT THE PLAINTIFF MUST PROVE

A. AN OBLIGATION ON THE DEFENDANT

A mandatory duty must be imposed on the defendant if the action is to lie. The imposition of a criminal offence prohibiting members of the public from engaging in certain conduct is insufficient.[11] The conferral of a power to act is not enough. The statute must create a positive obligation incumbent on the defendant. Such an obligation will normally be found in a statute, or in regulations made under a statute. Recent judgments have considered whether an action lies for breach of provisions of the European Community Treaties. In *Garden Cottage Foods Ltd v Milk Marketing Board*[12] it was held that an action lay for breach of the duty imposed by Article 86 not to abuse a dominant position in the common market. Construing Article 30, on the legality of the imposition of import restrictions by the UK government, the majority of the Court of Appeal in *Bourgoin SA v Ministry of Agriculture*[13] refused to award damages in breach of statutory duty. The judgments establish the availability in principle of the action for breach of community legislation. The distinction between them lies in that Article 86 imposes a directly applicable duty on individuals, whereas Article 30 concerns the discretionary powers of public authorities. The implications for the protection of economic interests, which are heavily regulated by community rules to eliminate unfair competition, of the availability of claims in tort for breach of those rules will be far-reaching.[14]

B. THE STATUTE MUST IMPOSE THE BURDEN ON THE DEFENDANT HIMSELF

This issue has been raised most frequently in actions by workmen (who have been injured by some act or omission of fellow workmen) against their employers. It is not always easy to decide whether the duty is imposed on the employer or on the workman. Thus, it was held by the House of Lords in *Harrison v National Coal Board* that duties relating to mines, when expressed impersonally, are imposed on the mineowner, but that the duties relating to shot-firing, since they are expressly imposed on the shot-firer, are not duties

---

11 *Lonrho Ltd v Shell Petroleum Co Ltd (No 2)* [1982] AC 173, [1981] 2 All ER 456 at 462.
12 [1984] AC 130, [1983] 2 All ER 770.
13 [1985] 3 WLR 1027, CA. See post on the tort of misuse of power at p 440.
14 But is an action based on a right directly conferred by E.C. Law properly styled an action for breach of *statutory* duty?

of the mineowner.[15] Obviously, the present tort does not lie against the employer unless the duty imposed on him has been broken.[16]

Once the statute has been interpreted to impose a duty on the employer, the general principle is clear. The House of Lords has held:[17]

> ... the owner cannot relieve himself of his obligation by saying that he has appointed reasonably competent persons and that the breach is due to negligence on their part ...

It would therefore be no defence to an employer of a workman injured by an unfenced machine that the foreman has failed to carry out the instructions to fence which the employer issued to him. The rule is the same where the duty of the employer has been neglected by the independent contractor[18] of the employer.[19] Other problems, however (which will be discussed later),[20] are raised when the defendant has delegated the duty to the plaintiff himself, and the plaintiff is injured as a result of his own failure to perform the delegated duty.

C. THE STATUTE PROTECTS HIS INTEREST BY WAY OF A CAUSE OF ACTION IN TORT

The fundamental issue, as the courts time and time again insist, is simply whether the Act intended to give a right of action in tort.[1] Everything else is subordinate to that. The following considerations are no more than guides, deducible from decided cases, to the principles which the courts utilise in seeking that (usually unexpressed) legislative intention: they must not be elevated to the status of inflexible rules of law overriding the paramount question of the purpose of the statute. As LORD SIMONDS has said:[2]

> The only rule which in all circumstances is valid is that the answer must depend on a consideration of the whole Act and the circumstances, including the pre-existing law, in which it was enacted.

(1) THE STATE OF THE PRE-EXISTING COMMON LAW

Sometimes, the law of torts in force before the passing of the Act is considered to afford adequate compensation to victims in circumstances also covered by the statute, the object of the statute being to regulate certain activities in order to prevent the occurrence of that loss which the existing law of tort

---

15 [1951] AC 639, [1951] 1 All ER 1102, HL. This case was decided on the Coal Mines Act 1911, now repealed by the Mines and Quarries Act 1954, s 150 of which appears to impose a liability on the owner in respect of breaches of duty by a shot-firer.

16 See p 463, post, for a discussion whether the employer is vicariously liable for breach by the employee of a statutory duty imposed on the employee.

17 *Lochgelly Iron and Coal Co Ltd v M'Mullan* [1934] AC 1 at 13 (per LORD WARRINGTON).

18 See p 450, post.

19 *Hosking v De Havilland Aircraft Co Ltd* [1949] 1 All ER 540; *Braham v J Lyons & Co Ltd* [1962] 3 All ER 281, CA; cf *Hole v Sittingbourne and Sheerness Ry Co* (1861) 6 H & N 488.

20 See p 375, post.

1 Eg *Atkinson v Newcastle and Gateshead Waterworks Co* (1877) 2 Ex D 441 at 448 (per LORD CAIRNS LC), CA; *Pasmore v Oswaldtwistle Urban District Council* [1898] AC 387 at 397 (per LORD HALESBURY LC), HL.

2 *Cutler v Wandsworth Stadium Ltd* [1949] AC 398 at 407, [1949] 1 All ER 544, HL.

would redress:[3] then the statute will not usually confer an additional cause of action for damages. For instance, the ordinary law of negligence affords adequate protection for the victims of road accidents: yet, the need to reduce these accidents is so urgent that there is much legislation regulating road traffic—the construction and use of vehicles and the carrying of lights during hours of darkness are random illustrations. But the courts do not generally allow persons injured by motorists in breach of such statutory duties to sue in reliance on the relevant statute: they leave them to pursue their remedy in negligence, and regard the sanctions of the statute as limited to the imposition of the penalty there prescribed.[4]

If, however, the statute merely affirms an interest of the plaintiff which the common law already recognises, and does not purport to be giving that interest statutory protection for some quite different purpose, then the plaintiff may be free to sue for breach of the statute.[5] Thus, in *Ashby v White*, where the right to vote, a common-law right, had been confirmed by statute, HOLT CJ said:[6]

> And this statute . . . is only an inforcement of the common law; and if the parliament thought the freedom of elections to be a matter of that consequence, as to give their sanction to it, and to enact that they should be free; it is a violation of that statute, to disturb the plaintiff in this case in giving his vote at an election, and consequently actionable.

(2) ALTERNATIVE REMEDIES PROVIDED BY STATUTE

Where a statute fails to provide any alternative means of enforcement in the event of breach of the relevant duty, the plaintiff's task to establish that an action in tort was intended by the statute is much eased.[7] The availability of an alternative remedy is not fatal to this case. Administrative remedies and criminal penalties must be considered separately.

Provision is made in many cases where public authorities fail to carry out their duties for administrative machinery to secure compliance with those duties. Representations may be made to the Secretary of State who can order a recalcitrant local authority to fulfil its responsibilities for public health or education. An aggrieved citizen may find that the provision of such an

---

3   Sometimes, as in *Square v Model Farm Dairies (Bournemouth) Ltd* [1939] 2 KB 365, [1939] 1 All ER 259, CA (sale of infected milk), the court might decide that no tort was intended to be created because existing contractual remedies were adequate.

4   *Phillips v Britannia Hygiene Laundry Co* [1923] 2 KB 832, CA (defective axle on lorry, in breach of Motor Cars (Use and Construction) Order, 1904; no action available to owner of another vehicle damaged in consequence of breach); *Clarke v Brims* [1947] KB 497, [1947] 1 All ER 242 (failure to carry a red rear light on a car gave no right of action under this head to plaintiff who collided with the car); *Balmer v Hayes* 1950 SC 477 (failure of driver to disclose, in an application for a driving licence, that he was epileptic, gave no cause of action to a passenger injured when an attack of epilepsy caused the driver to collide with another vehicle). *Verney v Wilkins* (1962) 106 Sol Jo 879 (learner-driver not liable for passenger's injuries merely because in breach of Act he was unaccompanied by qualified driver); *Coote v Stone* [1971] 1 All ER 657, CA (parking on clearway not actionable in itself).

5   *Wolverhampton New Waterworks Co v Hawkesford* (1859) 6 CBNS 336 at 356 (per WILLES J). He may then have the choice of the action for breach of statutory duty or the existing common-law remedy, eg *Simon v Islington Borough Council* [1943] 1 KB 188 at 193, [1943] 1 All ER 41, CA (neglect of abandoned tramway).

6   (1703) 2 Ld Raym 938 at 954.

7   *Thornton v Kirklees Metropolitan Borough Council* [1979] QB 626, [1979] 2 All ER 349; *Booth & Co (International) Ltd v National Enterprise Board* [1978] 3 All ER 624.

administrative remedy is found to prevent any action in tort arising.[8] But this will not be so in all cases. Pupils injured as a result of dangerous school premises have been allowed to sue in tort for breach of statutory regulations[9] despite the provision in the Education Act empowering the Secretary of State to compel local authorities to carry out their statutory duties, including their safety obligations.

Where the 'alternative remedy' is the imposition of a criminal penalty, the onus will be on the plaintiff to establish that his claim falls within one of the two exceptions to the general rule of non-actionability on such a case re-asserted by LORD DIPLOCK in *Lonrho*.[10] He must show that the interest of the statute was not just to regulate a particular activity in the general public interest but to benefit a class of persons to which he belongs.[11] The existence of criminal penalties in the Factories Acts did not bar concurrent remedies in tort. The duties imposed by those Acts were specifically designed to protect workmen.[12] But breach of statutory rules regulating the operation of greyhound tracks and betting thereon did not enable an aggrieved bookmaker to sue.[13] The statute was not passed to safeguard or enhance the business of bookmakers.

(3) PUBLIC AND PRIVATE RIGHTS

The plaintiff seeking to sue in this tort must establish that a right or interest of his has been violated by the breach of duty. It will be easier for him to do this where the duty is imposed for the benefit of a defined and ascertainable group of persons to whom he belongs. Nevertheless he is not precluded merely because the statute is shown by the defence to be designed for the protection of the public. In a *dictum* consistently followed since,[14] ATKIN LJ stated the law as follows:[15]

> ... the question is not to be solved by considering whether or not the person aggrieved can bring himself within some special class of the community or whether he is some designated individual. The duty may be of such paramount importance that it is owed to all the public. It would be strange if a less important duty, which is owed to a section of the public may be enforced by an action, while a more important duty owed to the public at large cannot. The right of action does not depend on whether a statutory commandment or prohibition is pronounced for the benefit of the public, or for the benefit of a class. It may be conferred on anyone who can bring himself within the benefit of the Act, including one who cannot be otherwise specified than as a person using the highway.

---

8 *Wyatt v Hillingdon London Borough Council* (1978) 76 LGR 727 (no action lay by disabled person alleging breach of the duty under s 2 of the Chronically Sick and Disabled Persons Act 1970 in failing to meet her need for home help; she had a statutory remedy of making representations to the Secretary of State).

9 *Reffell v Surrey County Council* [1964] 1 All ER 743, [1964] 1 WLR 358 (was this because representations after the event would be futile?).

10 See ante at p 364.

11 See *Atkinson v Newcastle and Gateshead Waterworks Co* (1877) 2 Ex D 441, CA.

12 *Groves v Lord Wimborne* [1898] 2 QB 402; breach of the duty to stop at a pedestrian crossing is a rare example of road safety regulations being interpreted so as to create a right of action in tort; *London Passenger Transport Board v Upson* [1949] AC 155, [1949] 1 All ER 60; is this perhaps because pedestrians at (zebra) crossings constitute a defined class of person intended to be protected by the statutory rules?

13 *Cutler v Wandsworth Stadium Ltd* [1949] AC 398, [1949] 1 All ER 544.

14 See *Monk v Warbey* [1935] 1 KB 75.

15 *Phillips v Britannia Hygienic Laundry Co* [1923] 2 KB 832 at 841, CA.

And, it will be remembered, that LORD DIPLOCK's second exception[16] to the general rule of non-actionability where alternative criminal remedies were provided by the statute related to special damage resulting to the plaintiff in his enjoyment of a public right (a right available to all Her Majesty's subjects). It is somewhat difficult to discern whether LORD DIPLOCK was simply endorsing the approach of ATKIN LJ (quoted earlier) that certain duties might be designed to benefit each and every member of the public individually, or initiating a new category of breach of statutory duty. Such a new category might on its face enable a person suffering special damage to sue without establishing a specific intention to protect his individual interest. The wording used by his Lordship is obscure and one of the authorities relied on is a leading judgment on public nuisance.[17] Thus any extension of the tort seems unlikely.[18]

D. THE HARM SUFFERED BY HIM IS WITHIN THE SCOPE OF THE GENERAL CLASS OF RISKS AT WHICH THE STATUTE IS DIRECTED

The leading case is *Gorris v Scott*:[19]

A statutory order required that those parts of a ship which were occupied by animals were to be divided into pens of a specified size by substantial divisions. The defendant violated this order in respect of a ship on which he was transporting sheep belonging to the plaintiff. This violation caused the plaintiff's sheep to be washed overboard. The statute was designed to prevent the spread of disease, not to prevent animals from being drowned: an action for breach of statutory duty therefore failed.

The House of Lords has held that the statutory duty on an employer to fence every dangerous part of a machine was confined to the prevention of a workman coming into contact with moving parts of the machine and did not comprehend protecting him from injury caused by ejected or flying pieces of the machine itself, or of the material on which the machine was working.[20] On the other hand, when a bogie was derailed by a stone that had been allowed to fall from the roof of a mine in breach of the defendants' statutory duty, and the plaintiff was injured thereby, the House of Lords held that 'where the object of the enactment is to promote safety there can be no implication that liability for a breach is limited to one which causes injury in a particular way'.[1] This problem of risk is the same as in negligence: in both torts the risk or hazard must be foreseeable or within the Act, but the exact way in which the accident occurs need not be—and the courts, as these cases

---

16 *Lonrho Ltd v Shell Petroleum Co Ltd (No 2)* [1982] AC 173, [1981] 2 All ER 456; see ante at p 364.
17 *Benjamin v Storr* (1874) LR 9 CP 400.
18 See Stanton op cit at pp 49–51.
19 (1874) LR 9 Exch 125.
20 *Close v Steel Company of Wales* [1962] AC 367, [1961] 2 All ER 953; cf *Wearing v Pirelli Ltd* [1977] 1 All ER 339, HL (the defendant employer was liable when the unfenced dangerous part threw his employee's hand against the materials being worked upon).
1 *Grant v National Coal Board* [1956] AC 649 at 664, [1956] 1 All ER 682 at 689, HL (per LORD TUCKER); *Donaghey v Boulton and Paul Ltd* [1968] AC 1, [1967] 2 All ER 1014, HL; *Millard v Serck Tubes Ltd* [1969] 1 All ER 598, CA.

show, inevitably have a wide discretion in deciding where to draw what cannot be a hard and fast line between the two.

E. HE WAS ONE OF THE PERSONS PROTECTED BY THE STATUTE

Breach of a statute may give rise to an action in tort, but not necessarily at the instance of the particular plaintiff, as *Knapp v Railway Executive* shows:[2]

> The Brighton & Chichester Railway Act 1844 provided for the erection of gates at level crossings, and the general supervision and maintenance thereof. K had stopped his car slightly short of a level crossing governed by this Act because it was closed against road traffic. Somehow, the brake of the car was released; the car moved forward and struck the gate. The gate had not been maintained in accordance with the Act, so that it swung back and injured the driver of an oncoming train. It was held that the purpose of these provisions was to protect road users against danger from the railway only, and that an engine driver on the railway was thus not within the scope of the Act.

F. WHEN HE MUST PROVE DAMAGE

Whether the plaintiff has to prove damage depends on the particular statute. The question is: what is the nature of the right or interest protected by the statute? If, for example, it is an interest in personal safety, then the courts will grant a remedy in tort only if the plaintiff shows that he has sustained personal injury in consequence of a breach of the statutory duty.[3]

Where, from its context, it is clear that the statute created a right in the plaintiff so absolute in its content that the plaintiff was to be protected against a violation, even though it caused no damage, then the tort is actionable *per se*. The courts are most likely to interpret in this manner a statute which protects an interest of the plaintiff other than an interest in his person or in his goods. Thus, in *Ashby v White*[4] interference with the statutory right to vote was held actionable per se, and in *Ferguson v Earl Kinnoull*[5] the refusal on the part of the defendant, in the face of a statute, to determine the suitability of the plaintiff, a minister of religion, for a living to which he had been presented, was held actionable per se.

The general unawareness that certain claims are, or can be, based on this present cause of action has been mentioned already.[6] It has for instance, given rise to a strange line of decisions concerning injuries caused by failure to repair highways. It has already been seen[7] that the plaintiff in actions derived from public nuisance on the highways must prove special and par-

2 [1949] 2 All ER 508, CA; cf *Lavender v Diamints Ltd* [1949] 1 KB 585, [1949] 1 All ER 532, CA.
3 Eg *Watts v Enfield Rolling Mills (Aluminium) Ltd* [1952] 1 All ER 1013, CA.
4 (1703) 2 Ld Raym 938; cf *Simmonds v Newport Abercarn Black Vein Steam Coal Co* [1921] 1 KB 616, CA.
5 (1842) 9 Cl & Fin 251, HL.
6 See p 366, ante.
7 See p 339, ante.

ticular damage to himself beyond that suffered by the public at large. Most duties of public bodies with regard to the maintenance of highways and structures thereon are now statutory, and, in some cases, breaches of these duties have been held to give rise to an action for breach of statutory duty,[8] so that the same facts will often give rise to an action for breach of statutory duty and for nuisance. Yet the separate nature of these two actions seems to have become blurred in some cases, with the result that the courts appear to have thought that the rule in nuisance about particular damage also applied to the action for breach of statutory duty. *Blundy Clark & Co Ltd v London North Eastern Ry Co* illustrates the point:[9]

> The plaintiff claimed damages on the ground that his business had been interrupted by failure on the part of the defendant to maintain a canal lock in working order. Having found that the statutory duty in question was one which, if broken, gave rise to an action in tort, the court proceeded on the assumption that the plaintiff could nevertheless only succeed if he proved a particular loss.

It is submitted that ordinarily a plaintiff has to prove no more than that the damage which he has sustained (whether exceptional, particular or otherwise) was caused by breach of the statute. The one possible exception to this principle would be if a statute were interpreted to require that a plaintiff could succeed only by proving a particular loss.

G. THE CONDUCT OF THE DEFENDANT WAS OF SUCH A CHARACTER AS TO VIOLATE THE STATUTE

Whether a defendant is liable for a breach, even though his act is neither intentional nor negligent, depends on the statute. Certainly, the liability is strict in many cases, especially under the Factories Act 1961. For instance, non-negligent failure properly to maintain a lift in efficient working order has been held by the House of Lords to be an actionable breach of the Factories Act 1937 repealed and replaced by the Factories Act 1961.[10] On the other hand, many statutes require the defendant only to do what is 'reasonably practicable'; for example, no mineowner is liable to an action for breach of the duties imposed by the Mines and Quarries Act 1954, 'if it was impracticable to avoid or prevent the contravention'.[11] There is a mass of case-law on the interpretation of statutory provisions laying down standards of conduct: the point to note here is that one must always turn to the statute imposing the duty to discover against what types of conduct on the part of the defendant the plaintiff will be protected by an action in tort. One case may be cited by way of illustration:[12]

> The defendants had a statutory duty to maintain a fence along their railway line. Some cows of the plaintiff were separated from their calves by the line. The cows broke the fence in an attempt to reach their calves and were killed by the defendants' train. Although it would have been no defence to

8 See pp 514 et seq, post.
9 [1931] 2 KB 334, [1931] All ER Rep 160, CA.
10 *Galashiels Gas Co Ltd v Millar* [1949] AC 275; [1949] 1 All ER 319, HL.
11 Section 157.
12 *Cooper v Railway Executive (Southern Region)* [1953] 1 All ER 477.

the defendants that gaps in the fence were caused by trespassers or by accident, the defendants were not liable here because they had provided a fence strong enough to prevent cattle from straying: the Act did not require them to build a fence which would prevent cattle from forcing a way through.

H. A BREACH OF THE DUTY

This presents no further problem: the burden of proof is on the plaintiff.

I. CAUSATION

As with other torts, heads of damage are recoverable only when the breach of the defendant 'caused' them: moreover, as we have seen,[13] in many actions, especially those by workmen for breach of safety requirements, success depends on proof that injury to the plaintiff has been so 'caused'. In this tort 'the employee must in all cases prove his case by the ordinary standard of proof in civil actions: he must make it appear at least that on a balance of probabilities the breach of duty caused or materially contributed to his injury'.[14] Where the plaintiff steel erector would not have worn a safety belt had it been provided the House of Lords held that his employers were not liable to him for breach of their statutory duty to provide one.[15]

SECTION 4.   DEFENCES

A. THE RELATION BETWEEN CRIMINAL AND TORTIOUS LIABILITY

Breaches of particular statutory duties may give rise both to criminal and tortious proceedings. It must not, however, be assumed that the defences in each case are identical. For example, the defences open to mineowners under the Coal Mines Act 1911[16] were held to be wider in criminal proceedings than in actions for breach of statutory duty.[17]

B. ASSUMPTION OF RISK

Wheeler v New Merton Board Mills Ltd,[18] decided that *volenti non fit injuria*

---

13 Chapter 14, ante.
14 *Bonnington Castings Ltd v Wardlaw* [1965] AC 613 at 620, [1956] 1 All ER 615 at 618, HL (per LORD REID); cf *McGhee v National Coal Board* [1972] 3 All ER 1008, HL (an action in common-law negligence). Even though the plaintiff has proved the employer's breach of statutory duty with regard to a machine and that he has sustained injury from the machine, the onus of proving causation remains with the plaintiff; *Lineker v Raleigh Industries Ltd* [1980] ICR 83, CA.
15 *Cummings (or McWilliams) v Sir William Arrol & Co Ltd* [1962] 1 All ER 623, HL.
16 See now the Mines and Quarries Act 1954.
17 *Yelland v Powell Duffryn Associated Collieries Ltd* [1941] 1 KB 154, [1941] 1 All ER 278, CA; cf *Harrison v National Coal Board* [1951] AC 639, [1951] 1 All ER 1102, HL.
18 [1933] 2 KB 669, CA.

is not a defence to an action brought by a workman for breach by an employer of his statutory duty—at least where the statute makes the employer liable whether or not his conduct was intentional or negligent. In *Imperial Chemical Industries Ltd v Shatwell*,[19] the House of Lords approved the *Wheeler* case so far as employer's statutory duties are concerned, but it added that the defence of *volenti* 'should be available where the employer was not himself in breach of statutory duty and was not vicariously in breach of any statutory duty through the neglect of some person who was of superior rank to the plaintiff and whose commands the plaintiff was bound to obey'.[20] The grounds for the *Wheeler* decision are not discoverable: this makes it all the harder, in the absence of any decision outside the sphere of such duties of employers to workmen, to know whether the defence is generally inapplicable to actions for breach of statutory duty.[1] It may well be contrary to public policy for anybody, and not merely employers, to contract out of a duty imposed by Act of Parliament: if this is so, assumption of risk may never be a defence to this action.

C. CONTRIBUTORY NEGLIGENCE

At common law, contributory negligence on the part of the plaintiff was a defence.[2] Apportionment of damages is now possible under the Law Reform (Contributory Negligence) Act 1945.[3] The principles of the defence are the same as those already discussed, subject to this exception.[4] Statutes such as the Factories Act aim to protect workmen against acts of inattention; accordingly a 'risky act due to familiarity with the work or some inattention resulting from noise or strain' will not be contributory negligence, although it might be sufficient negligence to make the employer vicariously liable to a third party negligently injured thereby.[5]

Frequently the employer has delegated to his employee responsibility for the performance of the statutory duty and that employee is negligent. The House of Lords held in *Boyle v Kodak Ltd*[6] that 'once the plaintiff has

19 [1965] AC 656, [1964] 2 All ER 999, HL.
20 At 687.
1 See an *obiter dictum* of Lord Normand in *Alford v National Coal Board* [1952] 1 All ER 754 at 757.
2 *Caswell v Powell Duffryn Associated Collieries Ltd* [1940] AC 152, [1939] 3 All ER 722, HL (unanimous but *obiter*).
3 *Cakebread v Hopping Brothers (Whetstone) Ltd* [1947] KB 641, [1947] 1 All ER 389, CA.
4 It is difficult to accept the view of Denning J, in *Lavender v Diamints Ltd* [1948] 2 All ER 249 (not considered on appeal, [1949] 1 KB 585, [1949] 1 All ER 532) that a contributorily negligent plaintiff in an action for non-negligent violation of statutory duty must be awarded no damages.
5 *Staveley Iron and Chemical Co Ltd v Jones* [1956] AC 627 at 648, [1956] 1 All ER 403 at 410, HL (per Lord Tucker), explaining the similar decision of the House of Lords in *Caswell v Powell Duffryn Associated Collieries Ltd* [1940] AC 152, [1939] 3 All ER 722, HL. In *Mullard v Ben Line Steamers Ltd* [1971] 2 All ER 424, CA, the deduction for contributory negligence was reduced from $\frac{1}{2}$ to $\frac{1}{3}$ because the plaintiff's conduct 'was a momentary error, not to be judged too harshly when balanced against the defendants' flagrant and continuous breach of statutory duty' (per Sachs LJ at 428). On the difficulty of proving contributory negligence in this tort as distinct from that of negligence, see *Westwood v Post Office* [1974] AC 1, [1973] 3 All ER 184, HL, and especially the statements by Lord Kilbrandon at 17, that a workman's disobedience is not the same as contributory negligence.
6 [1969] 2 All ER 439. This decision applied *Ross v Associated Portland Cement Manufacturers Ltd* [1964] 2 All ER 452, HL, and *Ginty v Belmont Building Supplies Ltd* [1959] 1 All ER 414.

established that there was a breach of enactment which made the employer absolutely liable, and that that breach caused the accident, he need do no more.'[7] 'But if the employer can prove that the only act or default of anyone which caused or contributed to the non-compliance was the act or default of the plaintiff himself, he establishes a good defence.'[8]

In *Boyle v Kodak Ltd* the statutory duty to fix a ladder securely while a storage tank was painted was imposed on both the employers and the employee who was injured through its breach. The Court of Appeal dismissed the action on the ground that the plaintiff was the sole cause of the accident, but the House of Lords allowed his appeal. The employers had not proved that they had instructed the plaintiff on how to comply with the regulations; therefore their breach of statutory duty was a cause of the damage. The significance of the plaintiff's also being in breach of his statutory duty was that it constituted a ground for apportionment of the damages: he was awarded one half. Had the statute imposed the duty on the employers alone, the plaintiff's damages would not have been reduced, although performance of the duty was delegated to him by his employers, unless the employers proved that the plaintiff failed to take care for his own safety and so was contributorily negligent.

D. ACT OF THIRD PARTY

This is not a defence where the statute is deemed to impose a liability so strict that the defendant is responsible for such acts: as usual, all depends on the interpretation of the Act.[9]

SECTION 5.   PROPOSALS FOR REFORM

The case law determining when an action in tort will lie for violations of a statute cannot be represented as consistent or in the main well-reasoned. Hence the difficulty in ascertaining a body of principles governing the tort. In 1969 the Law Commission recommended a single reform.[10] The following provision should be enacted.

> Where any Act passed after this Act imposes or authorises the imposition of a duty, whether positive or negative and whether with or without a special remedy for its enforcement, it shall be presumed, unless express provision to the contrary is made, that a breach of the duty is intended to be actionable (subject to the defences and other incidents applying to actions for breach of statutory duty) at the suit of any person who sustains damage in consequence of the breach.

---

7 At 441 (per LORD REID).
8 At 446 (per LORD DIPLOCK).
9 *Cooper v Railway Executive (Southern Region)* [1953] 1 All ER 477 at 478.
10 Law Com Report No 21. *The Interpretation of Statutes* para 38, App A(4).

Part VI

Interests in reputation—defamation[1]

---

1 *Gatley* enjoys a high reputation among judges and practitioners, and has the merit of annotating decisions in the Commonwealth and United States. The Report of the Committee on Defamation Cmnd 5909 (1975), hereinafter called the Faulks Report, is another important source.

CONTENTS

Chapter 23

The tort of defamation

SECTION 1. INTRODUCTION

There are two types of defamation—libel, which, in general, is written, and slander, which, in general, is oral. In some respects, different rules are applicable to each. Both, however, protect the interest in his reputation which everybody enjoys: there is, therefore, no tort unless there has been a communication of the defamatory matter to a third party, for it is the opinion held of the person defamed by others that matters. Insults directed to the plaintiff himself do not in themselves constitute defamation; the tort is not primarily concerned with the plaintiff's wounded feelings.

In many ways defamation is unique among torts. It is less untrue of it than of most torts to say that one cannot comprehend the present law without a knowledge of its historical development, and certainly, the anomalies, not to say absurdities, with which it is beset can be explained only in the light of its history.[1] The tort is of great interest to those law students, who are especially concerned to see how various political and economic forces have shaped the law. Procedural points are of exceptional importance, too.[2]

Until the sixteenth century, general jurisdiction over defamation was exercised by ecclesiastical courts. Then the common-law courts developed an action on the case for words which gained ground in actions for slander where 'temporal', as distinct from 'spiritual' damage, could be established. This progress became too rapid for the judges, who proceeded to hedge the action around with tight restrictions. In the Stuart period, the Court of Star Chamber assumed criminal jurisdiction over all types of libels. The common-law courts succeeded to this jurisdiction on the abolition of that court in 1641. The upshot of this confused story was that the common-law courts then established a distinction between libel and slander on the basis that damage would be presumed in libel, but that the plaintiff would have to prove special damage before slander would lie. In the late nineteenth and early twentieth centuries, liability in defamation was extended because of the menace to reputations occasioned by the new popular Press with its mass circulations. Latterly, the political pressures exercised by the Press under the banner of Free Speech have resulted in a narrowing of the scope of liability.

Many of these changes have been effected by legislation, much of it ill-considered and badly drafted. The tort is also notable for the highly detailed and complex rules which the courts have had ample opportunity to work out, for litigants have shown a great liking for pursuing their private squabbles

1 See Veeder *Select Essays in Anglo-American History* (1909) vol 446–73; *HEL* vol v 205–12, vol vii 333–78.
2 The best introductions to these procedural matters are the Report of the Committee on Defamation Cmnd 5909 (1975) and Duncan & Hoolahan, *Guide to Defamation Practice* (2nd edn, 1958). The Report of the Australian Law Reform Commission 'Unfair Publications' ALRC Nov (1979) has many constructive proposals for change.

under the official umbrella of the law courts. Not surprisingly perhaps, the tort is treated by some judges with that suspicion which they normally reserve for actions by 'gold-digging' plaintiffs who cannot prove physical injury to the body, land or goods. And it must not be forgotten that to sue in defamation, the plaintiff must generally be fairly rich to begin with. Legal aid is available neither to pursue nor to defend an action for defamation.[3] Recently, a number of libel actions have been supported by private funds set up by wealthy individuals such as Sir James Goldsmith who have themselves suffered at the hands of the popular and satirical Press, in particular *Private Eye*. The level of damages has soared with a hefty component of most of those awards being exemplary (punitive) damages. The amount of damages, almost uniquely in this country, is set by a jury. Nor can the Court of Appeal itself reduce the award. It can only order a new trial, at further expense, where it finds the award excessive, or upholds complaints that the judge misdirected the jury.

The proper function of the tort of defamation must be considered in its context today. It exists to protect a person's reputation. Yet only a wealthy person, or one whose cause appeals to wealthy persons, can take advantage of the tort. It is not primarily concerned with invasion of privacy, or breach of confidence, or the terrible hurt occasioned to the plaintiff and his family if stories about his private life and alleged loves are blazoned all over the Sunday newspapers. Yet all these factors obviously operate on the jury's mind particularly in assessing damages. No cause of action survives the defamed person's death.[4] Reputation is thus a transitory interest. It is an interest which by way of the defences available has to be balanced against the public interest. So should I inform the police of my suspicion that a neighbour is abusing his child, providing my suspicion is honestly held, I have a defence of qualified privilege even if my allegations prove to be unfounded. Fair comment protects the Press expressing their views on the actions of politicians, public servants and others in the public eye. But there is no general public interest in information as such to protect the Press if their basic facts are untrue. An article correctly reporting the conduct of a Minister may criticise that conduct with vigour. No defence will avail the newspaper if they get their basic facts wrong. In the USA, broadly speaking, criticism of a public figure can only constitute an actionable defamation if activated by malice, even if parts of the allegations are untrue.

The debate on how to achieve the correct balance between the individual's interest in his good name and freedom of speech is a vital attribute of a democratic society. In attempting to resolve that debate via the development of the tort of defamation the courts are hindered by the elaborate procedural 'game' which characterises most libel actions, the unpredictable role of the jury, and the absence of developed torts of invasion of privacy and breach of confidence. All too often the latter are the heart of libel actions. Were you on a jury hearing evidence that a newspaper tapped a person's telephone, 'set him up' with a meeting with a prostitute, and hounded his young family, could you discount that behaviour when assessing the truth or falsity of the allegations made? Defamation has constitutional significance, certainly, but

---

3 Legal Aid Act 1974, s 7, Sch I, Pt II, para 1. The Faulks Report recommended that legal aid be made available with safeguards. On this and other considerations see *Gatley* ch 20.

4 See Law Reform (Miscellaneous Provisions) Act 1934, s 1(1). Defaming a dead person may still constitute a criminal libel see *Gatley*.

its role as a protection against abuse of freedom of speech is apt to be overestimated.

SECTION 2.   THE CRITERIA FOR DISTINGUISHING LIBEL AND SLANDER

Any medium whereby thought and ideas can be expressed or conveyed may constitute the publication of a defamation—words, pictures, gestures,[5] music or statues are all examples.[6] It is, however, the choice of medium which determines whether there is libel or slander. It is because the rules of the two torts differ in some matters that it is important to distinguish between them.

There can be no doubt but that anything communicated in a form of a permanent character *and* visible to the eye is libel, and that anything temporary *and* merely audible is slander. Thus, books, newspapers, letters and even effigies[7] are libels, and spoken words are slander. What is uncertain is whether matters permanent and only audible, or visible but not permanent, constitute libel. In *Youssoupoff v Metro-Goldwyn-Mayer Pictures, Ltd:*[8]

> In a talkie film the scenes depicted on the screen itself were defamatory, and held to constitute libel.

If the text-books were right in saying that this case decided that talking films are always libel, it would support the view that 'permanency' is the sole test. But the case did not decide this: the defamatory matter was contained not in the 'talkie' but in the pictorial part: SLESSER LJ stated the *ratio decidendi* of the case as follows:[9]

> There can be no doubt that, so far as the photographic part of the exhibition is concerned, that is a permanent matter to be seen by the eye, and is the proper subject of an action for libel, if defamatory. I regard the speech which is synchronised with the photographic reproduction and forms part of one complex, common exhibition as an ancillary circumstance, part of the surroundings explaining that which is to be seen.

Clearly, therefore, the case does not settle, for instance, whether a defamatory anecdote in a film is libel. Although there are *obiter dicta* in other cases suggesting that permanency is enough,[10] and however sensible such a test might be, the point remains undecided. It is not possible, then, to say into which category the following fall: tape recordings, talking parrots, deaf and dumb language, sky-writing, police shadowing.

The dictation of a letter to a typist is, it is submitted, only a slander.[11] The

---

5 See *Cook v Cox* (1814) 3 M & S 110 at 114 (per LORD ELLENBOROUGH).

6 Even the lighting of a lamp in the day-time in the plaintiff's garden, thereby inferring that he keeps a brothel; *Jefferies v Duncombe* (1809) 2 Camp 3; and perhaps even the police shadowing the plaintiff's house.

7 *Monson v Tussauds Ltd* [1894] 1 QB 671, CA (placing of effigy of plaintiff near effigies of convicted murderers in waxworks exhibition).

8 (1934) 50 TLR 581, CA.

9 At 587.

10 Eg LOPES LJ, in *Monson v Tussauds Ltd* [1894] 1 QB 671 at 692 'Libels are generally in writing or printing, but this is not necessary; the defamatory matter may be conveyed in some other permanent form. For instance, a statue, a caricature, an effigy, chalk marks on a wall, signs, or pictures may constitute a libel.'

11 In *Osborn v Thomas Boulter & Son* [1930] 2 KB 226, [1930] All ER Rep 154, CA, this appeared to SCRUTTON LJ and SLESSER LJ to be a slander only, but GREER LJ was inclined to think it libel. When the typist listens to the audio-tape a libel is probably being published.

forwarding of the typed letter itself is undoubtedly libel, and, it is thought, a libel for which the dictator is accountable because he authorised it. The reading aloud of a letter written by another, where those to whom it was read were aware that the speaker was reading from the document, was held to be libel[12] in *Forrester v Tyrrell*, the short report of which, however, does not mention that the point was argued. In *Osborn v Boulter*[13] SCRUTTON and SLESSER LJJ thought that the reading aloud of a document was slander.

The Defamation Act 1952 has, however, modified the common law by enacting that 'for the purposes of the law of libel and slander, the broadcasting of words by means of wireless telegraphy shall be treated as publication in permanent form'.[14] 'Words' embraces television for it includes 'pictures, visual images, gestures and[15] other methods of signifying meaning'.[16] 'Wireless telegraphy' means 'publication for general reception by means of wireless telegraphy within the meaning of the Wireless Telegraphy Act 1949'.[17] 'General reception' is not defined, but presumably excludes, for example, the use by police cars of radio to direct traffic or to report back to headquarters, but would it include the broadcast by an aircraft of a distress message? The Act of 1949 covers broadcasts on all frequencies ordinarily used, and also the rediffusion or relay of such broadcasts by wire.[18] Whether it covers broadcasts from foreign stations is not clear.[19] To the extent that broadcasting is outside the definition of the Act, the common-law uncertainty whether it is libel or slander, of course, remains. The Theatres Act 1968 has provided that the publication of words in the course of performance of a play shall also be treated as publication in a permanent form.[20]

SECTION 3.   THE DIFFERENCES IN THE LAW OF LIBEL AND OF SLANDER

There are two major differences between libel and slander.

A.   SLANDER AS SUCH IS NOT A CRIME

A libel of sufficient seriousness may be punished as a crime; slander is a tort only.[1]

---

12 (1893) 57 JP 532, CA. MACDERMOTT J followed this decision with obvious reluctance in another case where the audience was aware that the defendant was reading out a letter; *Robinson v Chambers (No 2)* [1946] NI 148.

13 Supra. SLESSER LJ left open whether (236) 'the circumstance of dictation, and the dictated matter being brought back and considered by the dictator, may constitute in certain cases a libel'. What of the office cleaner who unintentionally sets off the dictaphone?

14 Section 1. And see, to similar effect, Cable and Broadcasting Act 1984, s 28.

15 The surprising omission of 'all or any' here presumably indicates that the *eiusdem generis* rule must be strictly applied. What, then, of a 'raspberry' or the whistling of 'Colonel Bogey'?

16 Section 16(1).

17 Section 16(3). Comments in morse code will be within the Act.

18 Section 19.

19 The operative part of the Wireless Telegraphy Act, Part I, has territorial application merely (s 6), but the Act is silent about the extent of application of the remainder of its provisions.

20 Section 4, other than certain performances excepted by section 7.

1 Of course, spoken words may constitute a crime where the other elements of that crime are present: eg blasphemy, sedition. On criminal libel generally, see *Gatley* ch 36 and Law Commission Report No 149. Earlier views that to constitute a crime a libel must be calculated to provoke a breach of the peace were disregarded by the House of Lords in *Gleaves v Deakin* [1980] AC 477, [1979] 2 All ER 497.

B. LIBEL ALWAYS ACTIONABLE PER SE

Libel is actionable per se whereas slander, subject to the exceptions next discussed, is actionable only on proof of actual damage.

SECTION 4.   EXCEPTIONAL CASES WHERE SLANDER IS ACTIONABLE PER SE

A. IMPUTATION OF CRIME

The limits of this exception cannot be precisely defined, because it is not settled whether the reason for it is the social ostracism resulting from such a slander, or the putting of the plaintiff in jeopardy, or some other matter.

At least, the following points are incontrovertible. The crime need not be an indictable one, but it must be one for which the plaintiff could be made to suffer corporally, ie by punishment with at least imprisonment in the first instance: 'I know enough to put you in gaol' is therefore actionable per se.[2] A crime is outside these limits if the perpetrator, having been arrested for it, can only be punished by a fine and not by imprisonment;[3] this is still so even though there is a power to commit for non-payment of the fine.[4] Words casting *suspicion* of murder are not within the exception.[5]

The words complained of must be looked at in their context in order to discover what was imputed, as *Thompson v Bernard* shows:[6]

> The words 'T is a damned thief, and so was his father before him; and I can prove it' seem clear enough, but because they were followed by: 'T received the earnings of the ship, and ought to pay the wages', the court directed a non-suit, because only breach of contract was in fact imputed.

This case also illustrates the obvious point that difficult problems of criminal law may have to be solved in order to determine whether the facts imputed constituted a crime punishable by imprisonment or otherwise corporally. If the plaintiff has to rely on some secondary meaning of the words spoken, he must prove that they were reasonably capable of being so interpreted.[7]

Gray v Jones[8] lends support to the view that social ostracism is at least one of the reasons for this exception:

> Having found that the words 'You are a convicted person' might reasonably mean that a crime punishable corporally was imputed, ATKINSON J, in a closely reasoned judgment, held them to be within the exception because, although they would not place the plaintiff in jeopardy, they would tend to make him ostracised socially.

On the other hand, there have been several cases where something criminal in character, but for technical reasons not punishable, has been held to be

---

2 *Webb v Beavan* (1883) 11 QBD 609; this illustration also shows that a general imputation of criminality without reference to a specific offence is enough.
3 *Hellwig v Mitchell* [1910] 1 KB 609; *Ormiston v GW Ry Co* [1917] 1 KB 598.
4 *Michael v Spiers and Pond Ltd* (1909) 101 LT 352.
5 *Simmons v Mitchell* (1880) 6 App Cas 156, PC.
6 (1807) 1 Camp 48.
7 *Gray v Jones* [1939] 1 All ER 798.
8 Supra.

outside the rule, presumably because the plaintiff was not in jeopardy.[9] In *Lemon v Simmons*, for instance:[10]

> To say that a husband stole from his wife while they were living together was held not to impute a crime, because husbands were not at that time punishable for such thefts.

B. CERTAIN TYPES OF DISEASE

To impute that a person has a contagious venereal disease is to commit a slander actionable per se.[11] Whether the exception has any greater scope is doubtful. There is weak authority that leprosy is within the exception[12] and it has sometimes been asserted rather unconvincingly that scarlet fever and the plague are also within it.[13] Even if it is defamatory to impute a communicable disease such as scarlet fever or tuberculosis, it is submitted that, where suffering from the particular disease induces neither moral condemnation nor loathing, it is probably not now actionable per se. Even in the case of venereal disease, it is not actionable per se now to say that the plaintiff has suffered from it in the past.[14]

C. OFFICE, PROFESSION, CALLING, TRADE OR BUSINESS

At common law a slander in respect of an office, profession, trade or business was actionable per se if:

1 it was calculated to disparage him in his office, and
2 it was spoken in relation to his office.

Section 2 of the Defamation Act provides:

> In an action for slander in respect of words calculated to disparage the plaintiff in any office, profession, calling, trade or business held or carried on by him at the time of the publication, it shall not be necessary to allege or prove special damage, whether or not the words are spoken of the plaintiff in the way of his office, profession, calling, trade or business.

and thereby makes the second requirement no longer necessary. It nullifies decisions such as *Jones v Jones*,[15] where the House of Lords held that an allegation that a headmaster had committed adultery with a school-cleaner did not relate to his conduct in his profession, and, regardless of its prejudicial effects on his employment, was not therefore within the exception at common law. Words are actionable per se if they impute some want of integrity or

---

9 E g *Jackson v Adams* (1835) 2 Bing NC 402.
10 (1888) 57 LJ QB 260; *D & L Caterers Ltd and Jackson v D'Ajou* [1945] KB 210; on appeal, [1945] KB 364, [1945] 1 All ER 563, CA, raised, but did not decide, the point whether trading, as well as social, ostracism will be deemed sufficient, for there a crime punishable by imprisonment was imputed to a limited company engaged in trade.
11 *Bloodworth v Gray* (1844) 7 Man & G 334. Even if AIDS is not strictly speaking a venereal disease an imputation that a person has that disease would probably be actionable.
12 *Taylor v Perkins* (1607) Cro Jac 144: 'Thou art a leprous knave,' held actionable per se.
13 See *Gatley*, § 166.
14 *Taylor v Hall* (1742) 2 Stra 1189.
15 [1916] 2 AC 481.

some corrupt or dishonest conduct in the office, whether of profit or of honour.[16] At common law, if they merely imputed imcompetence, a distinction was drawn between offices of profit and offices of honour. An imputation of incompetence in the discharge of an office of profit was actionable per se, and continues to be actionable per se under the Act. In respect of an office of honour, a mere imputation of incompetence was not actionable per se unless the charge, if true, would have been a ground for removing the plaintiff from his office.[17] After the Act, a slander relating to an office of honour is still actionable per se only if it imputes either dishonesty or want of integrity, or such incompetence as would be a ground for removal from office.[18]

D. UNCHASTITY OF A WOMAN

The loosely-worded and short Slander of Women Act 1891 provides that 'words spoken and published ... which impute unchastity or adultery to any woman or girl, shall not require special damage to render them actionable'. 'Unchastity' includes lesbianism,[19] and it is assumed, though the Act does not say so expressly, that it applies only to suits brought by the woman, not her alleged male partner in the act of unchastity. Slang expressions of unchastity are enough, but presumably gestures and other media of communication, not being 'words', are outside the Act.

SECTION 5.   SPECIAL DAMAGE, AND REMOTENESS OF DAMAGE IN DEFAMATION GENERALLY

The question of what special damage must be proved in respect of those forms of slander which are not actionable per se seems so intertwined with the problem of remoteness of damage in defamation that both these topics will be considered under the one heading.

Some material loss is required: for instance, loss of employment,[20] the refusal of persons to enter into contracts with the plaintiff,[1] the loss of hospitality from friends proved to have provided food or drink on former occasions.[2] A threat of material loss is insufficient.[3]

It is uncertain whether loss of consortium, either by husband or wife, is special damage. In *Lynch v Knight*:[4]

> The defendant told the plaintiff's husband that the plaintiff had almost been seduced before their marriage, whereupon the husband made her leave their home. Her action in slander claiming loss of consortium as special damage failed.

16 *Booth v Arnold* [1895] 1 QB 571, CA.
17 *Alexander v Jenkins* [1892] 1 QB 797, CA.
18 *Robinson v Ward* (1958) 108 L Jo 491.
19 *Kerr v Kennedy* [1942] 1 KB 409, [1942] 1 All ER 412.
20 *Coward v Wellington* (1836) 7 C & P 531.
 1 *Storey v Challands* (1837) 8 C & P 234.
 2 *Davies v Solomon* (1871) LR 7 QB 112.
 3 *Michael v Spiers and Pond Ltd* (1909) 101 LT 352.
 4 (1861) 9 HL Cas 577.

The ground of the decision was, not that loss of consortium is not special damage, but that the damage was too remote. It is thought that the opinion of LORD CAMPBELL in that case, that loss of consortium may be special damage, will be followed.[5]

In *Allsop v Allsop*,[6] a plaintiff suffered physical illness as a result of her mental suffering following upon the slander: this was held not to be special damage. Noting that mental distress and bodily harm may be taken account of by way of aggravation in assessing damages in defamation,[7] this case must be taken as deciding that special damages in slander must be damages in respect of a primary interest, ie loss of esteem or association (and not merely a parasitic one), and that the primary purpose of the law of defamation is not to protect against nervous shock, or nervous shock resulting from the apprehension of the effects of defamatory matter being published to third persons.

The extent to which, if at all, the law of causation in defamation differs from that in the remainder of the law of torts remains a difficult problem. In the first half of the nineteenth century, any damage caused by the wrongful act of a third party was too remote a consequence of the defamation of the defendant. Thus, a person dismissed by his employer in consequence of the defendant's slander failed in *Vicars v Wilcocks*.[8] In *Ward v Weeks* it was held that defamers are liable only for the *necessary* consequences of their acts (and this test was plainly thought to be applicable to all torts) and therefore the defendant was held not to be answerable for the repetition of his defamation by another.[9] We have seen that the ordinary law of causation in torts is quite different from this:[10] has the law of causation in defamation changed too? *Vicars v Wilcocks* is now discredited, and will not be followed.[11] Nor can the proposition in *Ward v Weeks* that only damage occurring as a necessary consequence of a defamation is recoverable now be supported. The general test of remoteness is now the same for defamation as it is for other torts.[12] Nor can the narrower rule in *Ward v Weeks* to the effect that there is never liability on repetition of a slander be validly maintained. In *Derry v Handley*[13] the plaintiff was able to recover when a slander communicated to X by the defendant was repeated by X to his wife, the employer of the plaintiff, who in consequence dismissed her: the basis of the direction was that there was a moral duty to repeat the slander. Nor is an intended or authorised repetition too remote. It remains doubtful whether there is liability for the repetition of slander, which, though happening in the ordinary course of things or foreseeable, was neither authorised nor intended, nor made under a moral

---

5 At pp 589–91; it was apparently approved by LORD GODDARD CJ, in *Best v Samuel Fox & Co Ltd* [1952] AC 716 at 732, [1952] 2 All ER 394, HL; and see *Wright v Cedzich* (1930) 43 CLR 493 (H Ct Australia), at 530 (per RICH J), and *Lampert v Eastern National Omnibus Co* [1954] 2 All ER 719n.
6 (1860) 5 H & N 534.
7 Per BRAMWELL B, at 539; and see p 427, post.
8 (1806) 8 East 1.
9 (1830) 7 Bing 211.
10 Chapter 14, ante.
11 *Lynch v Knight* (1861) 9 HL Cas 577 at 590 and 600–1 respectively (per LORD CAMPBELL LC and LORD WENSLEYDALE); *Bowen v Hall* (1881) 6 QBD 333 at 338 (per BRETT LJ and LORD SELBORNE).
12 See *Lynch v Knight*, supra, at 600 (per LORD WENSLEYDALE); *Chamberlain v Boyd* (1883) 11 QBD 407; *Speight v Gosnay* (1891) 60 LJ QB 231 at 232 (per LOPES LJ).
13 (1867) 16 LT 263.

duty;[14] there is nothing to prevent the courts from pursuing what, it is suggested, is the desirable course, namely, of assimilating defamation to the rest of the law of torts, and making publishers liable for repetitions of their defamatory statements in the ordinary course of things.[15]

14 In *Weld-Blundell v Stephens* [1920] AC 956, HL, a case in contract, some members of the House of Lords treated *Ward v Weeks* as good law, but there is no suggestion in their judgments that the rules of remoteness in defamation differ from those in other torts. On the other hand, in *Ratcliffe v Evans* [1892] 2 QB 524 at 530, CA, BOWEN LJ, said that 'verbal defamatory statements ... may be uttered under such circumstances that their repetition follows in the ordinary course of things from their original utterance' and that in such a case the damage is not too remote.

15 This view is supported by dicta in *Ward v Lewis* [1955] 1 All ER 55 at 56 (per DENNING LJ), and at 57 (per MORRIS LJ), CA, where it was stated that a slanderer is liable for a republication, when he knows or ought to know that the slander is likely to be republished. Is a speaker liable for the report of his speech in the media when he knew reporters were present? See *McWhirter v Manning* (1954) Times, 30 October.

Chapter 24

Elements of libel and slander

SECTION 1. DEFAMATORY

A. DEFINITION

The classic definition of a defamatory statement is one 'which is calculated to injure the reputation of another, by exposing him to hatred, contempt or ridicule'.[1] The inadequacy of this definition is now generally recognised, especially in that it does not embrace injury to trading reputation.[2]

LORD ATKIN proposed the following test (though not as a formal definition): 'Would the words tend to lower the plaintiff in the estimation of right-thinking members of society generally?'[3] This test certainly cures some of the defects of the earlier cited definition. Yet the expression 'right-thinking members of society' is ambiguous. It is defamatory to say that a person is insane,[4] and, it seems, that she has been raped,[5] but do right-thinking persons think less well of those unfortunates? On the other hand, that one's associates (being themselves an ordinary cross-section of a respectable part of the community) think less well of one in consequence of a statement does not necessarily make that statement defamatory. Thus in *Byrne v Deane* it was held that to impute that a member of a golf club has sneaked to the police about an illegal fruit-machine kept in the club for the purposes of gambling is not defamatory, although it lowers him in the esteem of his fellow members.[6] A certain class of society may think badly of persons who borrow from

1 *Parmiter v Coupland* (1840) 6 M & W 105 at 108 (per PARKE B).
2 Eg *Capital & Counties Bank v Henty* (1882) 7 App Cas 741, HL, at 771 (per LORD BLACKBURN); *Tournier v National Provincial and Union Bank of England* [1924] 1 KB 461, CA, at 477 (per SCRUTTON LJ) and 486–7 (per ATKIN LJ). Also a plaintiff may be made a laughing stock by, say, a cartoon and be annoyed thereby, and yet not have his character or reputation impaired. This definition is inexact in that the ridicule must be substantial enough to reflect on reputation: see *Emerson v Grimsby Times and Telegraph Co Ltd* (1926) 42 TLR 238, CA, and *Blennerhasset v Novelty Sales Services Ltd* (1933) 175 LT Jo 393 (a full-page advertisement in newspaper was headed 'Beware of Yo Yo' and went on to imply that a Mr Blennerhassett who ate lobster at Pim's, and a worthy man, had now been placed, under supervision, in a quiet place in the country by reason of the fascination of the defendant's toy, the Yo Yo. Although the plaintiff, a Mr Blennerhassett, a stockbroker who lunched at Pim's, showed that his arrival at the Stock Exchange on the day after the publication was greeted with 'jeers, ribaldry and laughter', the statement was held not to be capable of a defamatory meaning). Yet a caricature has been held to be defamatory; *Dunlop Rubber Co v Dunlop* [1921] 1 AC 367, HL; cf *Dolby v Newnes* (1887) 3 TLR 393.
3 *Sim v Stretch* [1936] 2 All ER 1237 at 1240, HL; in *Rubber Improvement Ltd v Daily Telegraph Ltd* [1964] AC 234 at 285, [1963] 2 All ER 151 at 174, HL, LORD DEVLIN said that the test was the effect on the 'ordinary' man, not the 'logical' man.
4 *Morgan v Lingen* (1863) 8 LT 800.
5 *Youssoupoff v Metro-Goldwyn-Mayer Pictures Ltd* (1934) 50 TLR 581, CA.
6 [1937] 1 KB 818, [1937] 2 All ER 204, CA.

their servants, but to impute this practice to anyone is none the less not defamatory.[7]

Certain sections of society would be scandalised by an imputation that a man is a Communist, others would shun any supposed member of the National Front, but can right-thinking members be so affected when a man belongs to a party which the law in no way prohibits? Would it be defamatory to say that someone is illegitimate, impotent, poverty-stricken, the daughter of a murderer, or pictured in an advertisement for whisky? Is it defamatory to say that a worker stayed at work during a strike, or that he is not a member of a union?[8] No confident answers to these questions can be given because English law has not defined 'defamatory' precisely. With diffidence it is suggested that the 'right-thinking' test (which has yet to be subject to an appelate court's close scrutiny in a pertinent case) must be qualified as follows:

1 If most citizens would shun or avoid a man in consequence of the statement, this is defamatory, eg insanity.
2 If a substantial and respectable proportion of society would think less well of a person, provided that this reaction is not plainly anti-social or irrational, then a statement is defamatory.[9]

This accords with *Byrne v Deane* and yet supports the view that to say that a man is a non-unionist or works during strikes, that a bank manager is a Communist, or that a member of White's Club pleads the Gaming Act, is defamatory even though such persons do not go down in the esteem of 'right-thinking' men.

To say that abuse is not defamatory is misleading. The cases relied on for this erroneous statement are cases of slander deciding that special damage must ordinarily be proved.[10] The test to be applied to words of abuse is exactly the same as for other allegedly defamatory statements. Thus it has been held that it may be defamatory to call a man a hypocrite,[11] a villain,[12] a black-sheep,[13] an habitual drunkard,[14] a pansy.[15]

---

7 *Sim v Stretch* [1936] 2 All ER 1237, HL. On the other hand, not merely the golfing fraternity, but right-thinking persons will (it has been held) think worse of an amateur golfer who allows his name to be used in the advertising of chocolates. *Tolley v JS Fry & Sons* [1931] AC 333, HL. Yet, in *Gibbings v O'Dea & Co Ltd* (1948–9), Macgillivray & Le Quesne Copyright Cases 31 it was held not to be libel for defendants to use plaintiff author's name on an advertisement for mattresses in the *Irish Times*.
8 No, thought McCARDIE J, in *Myroft v Sleight* (1921) 90 LJ KB 883.
9 If the words would not in themselves convey to the ordinary person the meaning which a special group of experts would give to them, then this suggested rule would not apply (unless an innuendo, p 391, post were pleaded) because the basic rule that words must be defamatory in their ordinary meaning would not be satisfied: *Mollo v British Broadcasting Corporation* (1963) Times, 2 February: (a book review in *The Listener* of the plaintiff's book on bridge attributed to him a response of two clubs to an opening bid of one spade on a hand set out; the ordinary citizen would see nothing wrong in such a conventional response, and so there was no libel unless innuendo pleaded and proved). Nor is it defamatory for D to say that the plaintiff is Mr X without more, although others have published defamatory articles about Mr X, for the libel complained of must be in the statement published by the defendant: *Astaire v Campling* [1965] 3 All ER 666.
10 Eg *Thorley v Lord Kerry* (1812) 4 Taunt 355.
11 Eg, the widely quoted *dictum* in *Thorley v Lord Kerry*, supra: 'But for mere general abuse spoken, no action lies'.
12 *Bell v Stone* (1798) 1 Bos & P 331.
13 *M'Gregor v Gregory* (1843) 11 M & W 287.
14 *Alexander v Jenkins* [1892] 1 QB 797 at 804 (per KAY LJ).
15 *Thaarup v Hulton Press Ltd* (1943) 169 LT 309, CA. For a recent example of a particularly abusive alleged libel see *Cornwell v Myskow* [1987] 2 All ER 504, [1987] 1 WLR 630, CA.

A statement may nevertheless be defamatory, although the maker states it, not as a fact, but as a mere opinion.[16] One must take into account circumstances of time and place.[17] Thus, in *Slazengers Ltd v Gibbs & Co*,[18] to state, during the war with Germany, that the plaintiffs were a German firm and likely to be closed down, was defamatory. For this reason then earlier authorities on what is defamatory must be treated with caution. Consider *Youssoupoff v Metro-Goldwyn-Mayer Pictures Ltd*[19] where it was held defamatory in 1934 to say of the plaintiff that she had been raped. Would that still be defamatory today?

A few examples at random may further illustrate what is and is not defamatory. To say that a motorist drove negligently is defamatory,[20] but not (in itself) that a trader has been put on a stop-list[1] nor to announce in a newspaper that the plaintiff was married on the day before the date fixed for the wedding.[2]

It is defamatory to impute to a trader or businessman or professional man lack of qualification, knowledge, skill, capacity, judgment or efficiency in the conduct of his trade or business or professional activity, for example, a severe attack on the special anaesthetising technique of a practising dental surgeon.[3]

It is not defamatory merely to criticise the goods; the trader himself must be attacked. If,[4] however, one can read into a criticism of the product a criticism of its maker, that criticism may be defamatory. To say that a baker's bread is always unwholesome is defamatory,[5] but to say that a product does not answer its purpose is not.[6] To say that a trader is bankrupt or insolvent is defamatory,[7] but to say that he has ceased to be in business is not, for it does not reflect on his reputation.[8]

B. WHO MAY BE DEFAMED

Any living person may be defamed.[9] The law of defamation in respect of

---

16 *Braddock v Bevins* [1948] 1 KB 580 at 598, [1948] 1 All ER 450, CA.
17 *Dolby v Newnes* (1887) 3 TLR 393 (a statement, although not defamatory at a private dinner party, may become so if repeated in the magazine *Titbits*).
18 (1916) 33 TLR 35.
19 (1934) 50 TLR 581, CA. (Could the risk of her having contracted AIDS or disease from her attacker be relevant cancelling our changed social attitudes to rape victims?)
20 *Groom v Crocker* [1939] 1 KB 194, [1938] 2 All ER 394, CA.
1 *Ware and De Freville Ltd v Motor Trade Association* [1921] 3 KB 40, CA.
2 *Emerson v Grimsby Times and Telegraph Co Ltd* (1926), 42 TLR 238, CA.
3 *Drummond-Jackson v British Medical Association* [1970] 1 All ER 1094, CA.
4 *Evans v Harlow* (1844) 5 QB 624.
5 Per LORD HALSBURY LC, in *Linotype Co Ltd v British Empire Type-Setting Machine Co Ltd* (1899) 81 LT 331 at 333, HL.
6 *Evans v Harlow*, supra.
7 *Shepheard v Whitaker* (1875) LR 10 CP 502.
8 *Ratcliffe v Evans* [1892] 2 QB 524, CA. Nor is it defamatory to say that his business is suffering as a result of competition; *Stephenson v Donaldson & Sons* (1981) 262 Estates Gazette 148. In some circumstances it may be the separate tort of injurious falsehood, p 126, ante.
9 In the absence of any decision by English courts on the point, it may be presumed that they will follow decisions in other common-law jurisdictions to the effect that words defamatory of dead persons will not sustain an action by relatives who cannot prove that *their* reputation is besmirched; cf Porter Report, § 27. A trade union cannot be defamed: *Electrical, Electronic, Telecommunication and Plumbing Union v Times Newspapers Ltd* [1980] QB 585, [1980] 1 All ER 1097, CA, because the Trade Union and Labour Relations Act 1974, s 2(1) deprives trade unions of legal personality.

trading corporations is the same as for private individuals, except that, in the nature of things, they have no social reputation, but only a commercial one. In their case, therefore, a statement 'must attack the corporation or company in the method of conducting its affairs, must accuse it of fraud or mismanagement, or must attack its financial position'.[10] So, it is defamatory of a trading company to assert that it provides insanitary houses for its employees,[11] or indulges in black-market activities.[12] A local authority can sue for defamation which reflects upon it as a corporate body.[13]

C. THE INTERPRETATION OF DEFAMATORY STATEMENTS; THE INNUENDO

It has so far been assumed that the meaning of the statements complained of is readily ascertainable. Obviously, this is not always so: there are, therefore, certain rules of interpretation which must now be considered.

Where nothing is alleged to give them an extended meaning, words must be construed by the judge[14] in their ordinary and natural meaning.[15] The whole of the statement must be looked at, not merely that part on which the plaintiff relies as being defamatory, although, of course, it may be relevant to take account of the greater importance of some part of a statement, eg the headlines of an article in a newspaper.[16] There may be circumstances where the plaintiff alleges that the statement is defamatory because specific facts known to the reader give to the statement a meaning other than or additional to its ordinary meaning; this is known as a 'true' or 'legal' innuendo. In that case the plaintiff must plead and prove such facts,[17] for the defendant is entitled to know that meaning of the statement on which the plaintiff relies so that he is able to argue either that the statement in that meaning is not defamatory or that it is then true of the plaintiff. There is a third possibility. The words may have a meaning beyond their literal meaning which is inherent in them and arises by inference or implication: this is sometimes known as the 'false' innuendo. The plaintiff has to plead separately any such 'false' innuendo. A 'false' innuendo differs from a 'true' innuendo in that the pleader of a 'false' innuendo does not set out any extrinsic facts in support of his plea.

The judge decides whether a statement is capable of bearing a defamatory

10 *South Hetton Coal Co v North-Eastern News Association Ltd* [1894] 1 QB 133, CA, at 141 (per LOPES LJ).
11 Ibid.
12 *D & L Caterers Ltd v D'Ajou* [1945] KB 364, [1945] 1 All ER 563, CA; cf *Holdsworth Ltd v Associated Newspapers Ltd*, [1937] 3 All ER 872, CA (actionable to say that limited company refused to accept interim wages award of joint conciliation board for the industry). A company may recover substantial damages even though it suffers no financial loss: *Selby Bridge (Co of Proprietors) v Sunday Telegraph Ltd* (1966) 197 *Estates Gazette* 1077.
13 *Bognor Regis Urban District Council v Campion* [1972] 2 QB 169, [1972] 2 All ER 61 (refusing to follow a decision to the contrary in *Manchester Corporation v Williams* [1891] 1 QB 94).
14 Per LORD GREENE in *Turner v Metro-Goldwyn-Mayer Pictures Ltd* [1950] 1 All ER 449 at 465, HL.
15 *Capital & Counties Bank v Henty* (1882) 7 App Cas 741 at 772 (per LORD BLACKBURN), HL.
16 *Shipley v Todhunter* (1836) 7 C & P 680.
17 O 82 r 3(1) provides that 'where the plaintiff alleges that the words or matter complained of were used in a defamatory sense other than their ordinary meaning, he shall give particulars of the facts and matters on which he relies in support of such sense'.

meaning, whether in its normal meaning or by innuendo,[18] and, that being resolved in the affirmative, the jury decides whether it did have that meaning on the occasion complained of.[19] The judge has to construe the words used, to decide whether they are capable of a defamatory meaning; once he decides that they are so capable, the jury decide the meaning of the words in finding whether they are defamatory.[20] The plaintiff may contend that the statement has different defamatory meanings. The judge decides which of those the statement is capable of conveying, and the jury decides which particular meaning within that category the words do bear.[1] If, therefore, an appellate court holds that the words are incapable of a defamatory meaning where a jury, having been entrusted with the decision by the trial judge, has found for the plaintiff, the court will set aside the verdict and enter judgment for the defendant. Conversely, on the very rare occasions when an appellate court holds that a jury could not reasonably have found that the words were not defamatory, it will set aside the verdict and order a new trial.[2] Where the judge has misdirected the jury on the law, its verdict will also be set aside.[3]

Here are typical examples of 'true' or 'legal' innuendoes. The defendant, having engaged the plaintiff, a well-known singer, to perform at a concert, printed her name third in the order on the programme. The court accepted evidence that in the musical world the best singer was placed at the head of the programme and those of lesser reputation in the middle, so that the programme constituted a defamatory innuendo of the plaintiff.[4] A caption under a newspaper photograph of a man and a woman to the effect that it was Mr C and his fiancée conveyed to those who knew that the plaintiff lived with Mr C as his wife the defamatory meaning that she had done so without being married to him.[5] To include a cartoon of a well-known amateur golfer in an advertisement for chocolate implied that he was being paid for the advertisement and so prostituting his amateur status.[6]

In *Hough v London Express Newspaper Ltd*[7] the issue was raised whether a plaintiff relying on an innuendo has to prove that it was published to somebody who interpreted the matter in the defamatory sense alleged:

> The defendants published an account and photograph of the 'curly-headed wife' of a named boxer. The plaintiff, another woman—in fact the boxer's wife—produced witnesses who gave evidence that they had read the statement to mean that the plaintiff was not the wife of the boxer; but they were not misled into thinking that she was not the wife, nor was any person so misled produced as witness.

---

18 *Adam v Ward* [1917] AC 309 at 329 (per Lord Dunedin), HL. *Lloyd v David Syme & Co* [1986] AC 350, [1986] 2 WLR 69, PC.
19 Per Scrutton LJ, in *Cassidy v Daily Mirror Newspapers Ltd* [1929] 2 KB 331 at 340, CA.
20 *Jones v Skelton* [1963] 3 All ER 952, PC.
 1 *Slim v Daily Telegraph* [1968] 2 QB 157, [1968] 1 All ER 497, CA.
 2 *Lockhart v Harrison* (1928) 139 LT 521 at 523 (per Lord Buckmaster), HL; *Australian Newspaper Co v Bennett* [1894] AC 284, PC, is a good example of judicial reluctance to do this. Cf *Broome v Agar* (1928) 138 LT 698, CA (CA refused to direct new trial because jury had decided that it was not defamatory for mistress to say that her chauffeur was a rotter who went out joy-riding in her car.)
 3 *Tournier v National Provincial and Union Bank of England* [1924] 1 KB 461, CA; cf *Dakhyl v Labouchere* [1908] 2 KB 325n, HL.
 4 *Russell v Notcutt* (1896) 12 TLR 195, CA.
 5 *Cassidy v Daily Mirror Newspapers Ltd* [1929] 2 KB 331, CA.
 6 *Tolley v JS Fry & Sons* [1931] AC 333, [1931] All ER Rep 131, HL.
 7 [1940] 2 KB 507, [1940] 3 All ER 31, CA.

It was held that it was unnecessary to 'prove more than that there are people who know the special facts and so might understand the words in a defamatory sense' and that there was no need for 'evidence that some person did so understand them'.[8] The plaintiff therefore succeeded. The plaintiff must plead and prove that some people actually knew the facts,[9] and those facts must exist at the time of publication of the alleged defamatory matter.[10]

Problems also arise with regard to false innuendoes. In the House of Lords case of *Rubber Improvement Ltd v Daily Telegraph Ltd*:[11]

> The defendants published an article which stated that the Fraud Squad of the City of London Police were investigating the affairs of the plaintiff's company.

The article was found defamatory in its primary meaning because the simple statement that the Fraud Squad are inquiring into his affairs may damage his reputation even though it is consistent with his innocence. It would be open for the plaintiff to plead secondly, and for the court to find, as the House did here, that the words were capable of meaning that there was ground for suspicion. This second plea would be merely a false innuendo because no further facts would need to be particularised in the pleading. Thirdly, the statement did not in itself impute guilt of fraud; the plaintiff would have to plead an innuendo that by reason of the further facts he then set out the words were understood to mean that he was guilty of fraud. The courts would hold that if D said that there is a rumour that P is guilty it imputes guilt, but a statement that he is suspected does not necessarily do so. They distinguish between an allegation that the plaintiff is suspected and an allegation of guilt.

When the defendant newspaper described a well-known broadcaster as 'bent' the plaintiff had to set out the meaning of the word on which he relied.[12] If a statement is capable of many different meanings and the plaintiff does not specify those on which he relies the defendant is entitled to justify the statement on any meaning which it reasonably bears.[13] If the plaintiff fails to plead the meanings on which he relies in a long article which contains many different meanings in relation to him the defendant is entitled to have the plaintiff's statement of claim struck out on the ground that it discloses no reasonable cause of action.[14]

The courts seek to ensure that the issues which come to trial are clean cut and to erode the advantage one party can obtain by clever tactics. It is a fundamental principle in an action for defamation that:[15]

---

8 Per GODDARD LJ, at 515. *Theaker v Richardson* [1962] 1 All ER 229, CA (defendant liable for publishing libel to plaintiff's husband although no evidence that husband believed the accusation made against his wife).

9 *Fullam v Newcastle Chronicle and Journal Ltd* [1977] 1 WLR 651, CA.

10 *Grappelli v Derek Block Holdings Ltd* [1981] 2 All ER 272, CA; cf *Hayward v Thompson* [1982] QB 47, [1981] 3 All ER 450, CA, and p 399, post.

11 [1964] AC 234; sub nom *Lewis v Daily Telegraph* [1963] 2 All ER 151, HL.

12 *Allsop v Church of England Newspaper Ltd* [1972] 2 QB 161, [1972] 2 All ER 26, CA.

13 *London Computer Operators Training Ltd v British Broadcasting Corporation* [1973] 2 All ER 170.

14 *DDSA Pharmaceuticals Ltd v Times Newspapers Ltd* [1973] QB 21; [1972] 3 All ER 417, CA.

15 *Polly Peck (Holdings) plc v Trelford* [1986] 2 All ER 84 at 94, [1986] 2 WLR 845 at 945, per O'CONNOR LJ.

... the trial of the action should concern itself with the essential issues and the evidence relevant thereto and that public policy and the interests of the parties require that the trial should be kept strictly to the issues necessary for a fair determination of the dispute between the parties.

D. EFFECT OF THE DEFENDANT'S BEING UNAWARE THAT HIS STATEMENT WAS DEFAMATORY

(1) MECHANICAL DISTRIBUTORS

As we shall see,[16] a person is deemed to publish defamatory matter even though he did not play a primary part in its publication: eg a newsvendor, bookseller and the like. Such persons, however, are not liable for their acts of publication if they are 'innocent' in the sense now to be described.

The leading case is *Vizetelly v Mudie's Select Library Ltd* where the proprietors of a circulating library were held to be mechanical distributors to whom this special rule would apply if they were proved to be 'innocent'. The rule is clearly set out by ROMER LJ in that case:[17]

> [It is a defence to] 'a person who is not the printer or the first or main publisher of a work which contains a libel, but has only taken, what I may call, a subordinate part in disseminating it, ... if he succeeds in showing (1) that he was innocent of any knowledge of the libel contained in the work disseminated by him, (2) that there was nothing in the work or the circumstances under which it came to him or was disseminated by him which ought to have led him to suppose that it contained a libel[18] and (3) that, when the work was disseminated by him, it was not by any negligence on his part that he did not know that it contained the libel ...'

Whether he does so succeed is a question of fact for the jury.[19] In this case the jury found that the proprietors had not established their 'innocence': in a publication taken by the defendants the publishers had circulated a notice asking for the return of copies of a certain book in order to withdraw a particular page containing defamatory matter; the defendants ignored the circular, and, moreover, they did not employ a reader to peruse the novels in their library. Yet libraries need not have *scholarly* works read before circulating them,[20] nor, it seems (and more surprisingly), need the importers of publisher's remainders of American detective stories read them.[1]

Besides newsvendors, booksellers and circulating libraries, a porter delivering parcels has been held to be within the rule.[2] No doubt persons lending books gratuitously or making gifts of them, and gramophone record dealers are also protected. It is irrelevant to determine whether the Post Office, when delivering mail, or British Telecommunications operating its telephone services, are within it, because legislation exempts both of them and their

---

16 See p 400, post.
17 [1900] 2 QB 170 at 180, CA. See also *Emmens v Pottle* (1885) 16 QBD 354, CA. *Goldsmith v Sperrings Ltd* [1977] 2 All ER 566, [1977] 1 WLR 478 (newsvendor).
18 In *Goldsmith v Sperrings* (supra) attempts to strike out actions against several vendors of *Private Eye* as an attempt to suppress that journal altogether failed. There was evidence the vendors ought to have been aware of alleged libels.
19 Cf *Sun Life Assurance Co of Canada v W H Smith & Sons Ltd* [1932] All ER Rep 432, CA.
20 *Weldon v Times Book Co Ltd* (1911) 28 TLR 143, CA.
1 *Bottomley v F W Woolworth & Co Ltd* (1932) 48 TLR 521, CA.
2 *Day v Bream* (1837) 2 Mood & R 54.

servants from any liability in tort in respect of postal packets or the telephone service.[3]

(2) OTHER PUBLISHERS

(a) At common law

'A person charged with libel cannot defend himself by showing that he intended in his breast not to defame'.[4] There can also be no doubt that a person who has no actual knowledge that his statement is defamatory may still be liable. It is usually stated that the liability at common law is absolute, that if the statement is in fact defamatory, it matters not whether the defendant could have taken steps to discover that the statement was defamatory.[5] The leading case is *Cassidy v Daily Mirror Newspapers Ltd*:[6]

> With the authority of Mr C, the defendants published a photograph, taken at a race-meeting, with the following words underneath: 'Mr C, the racehorse owner, and Miss X, whose engagement has been announced'. The defendants published the photograph, not knowing that the plaintiff was married to Mr C, and having taken no steps whatever to find out whether Mr C was already married. The defendants were held liable to the plaintiff.

The case is certainly authority for the proposition that one may be liable for a statement which one does not actually know to be defamatory: neither this, nor any other relevant case has decided that a defendant who has taken all possible steps to ensure the accuracy of his statement, and who could not by any reasonable inquiries have conceivably found that his statement was defamatory, is liable in defamation.[7]

(b) The Defamation Act 1952

The Defamation Act 1952 now provides that the publisher of an 'innocent defamation' in certain circumstances may make an offer of amends as defined in the Act.

Section 4(5) provides that words shall be treated as published innocently:

> if and only if the following conditions are satisfied, that is to say—...
>
> (b) that the words were not defamatory on the face of them, and the publisher did not know of circumstances by virtue of which they might be understood to be defamatory of that other person,
>
> and ... that the publisher exercised all reasonable care in relation to the publication; and any reference in this sub-section to the publisher shall be construed as including

---

3 Post Office Act 1969 and British Telecommunications Act 1981. And see p 513, post. It remains pertinent to ask whether the rediffusion of radio programmes is within the rule in *Vizetelly v Mudie's Select Library Ltd* [1900] 2 QB 170; it is thought that it is. But is it negligence on the part of the promoters of rediffusion not to delay re-transmission until they have checked the contents of broadcasts? BBC relaying a Eurovision programme? a party political broadcast? a newspaper publishing a syndicated article? an advertisement in a newspaper prepared by an advertisement agency?
4 Per LORD LOREBURN LC, in *E Hulton & Co v Jones* [1910] AC 20 at 23, HL.
5 Eg *Winfield*, p 293.
6 [1929] 2 KB 331, CA.
7 So RUSSELL LJ said in the case (at 354): 'They are paying a price *for their methods of business*.'

a reference to any servant or agent of his who was concerned with the contents of the publication'.

The interpretation of these words is difficult.

1 It seems, from the expression 'defamatory on the face', that, if the plaintiff is able, without setting up an innuendo, to establish that the words are defamatory, the defendant cannot plead the section.[8] The rule that, without invoking an innuendo, one can consider the circumstances of time and place, becomes, therefore, increasingly important.[9]

2 Although, in the first place, section 4(5)(b) states only 'did not know' and omits 'ought not to have known', it seems that the later requirement of reasonable care 'in relation to the publication' extends to 'the contents' of the publication. If the defendant knows or ought to know that the statement is defamatory, then he cannot plead the section.[10]

3 If the 'servant or agent' is not innocent then the section does not apply. Many items are contributed by free-lance writers who are independent contractors, but who are certainly not servants, and who, it is submitted, are not necessarily agents in the usual legal meaning of the word. It is not clear whether 'servants or agents' will always include them, and surely it does not include readers whose letters are published.

4 It seems that the defendant has to prove the innocence of himself and all his servants or agents concerned with the contents of the publication.[11]

5 Pertinent to the last point, which servants or agents are 'concerned with the contents of the publication'? Editorial staff certainly but what of the typists, the telephonists, or the typesetters?

6 At common law, where there comes to the knowledge of a servant acting in the course of his employment a fact which he has a duty to communicate to his employer, notice of it is, for the purposes of defamation, imputed to the employer, whether he knows that fact or not.[12] It is thought that this doctrine of imputed notice applies to the section. In that event, even if telephonists are held not to be concerned with the contents in the sense of the Act, knowledge acquired by one in the course of her employment will prevent her employer from pleading the section, although she has not passed on her knowledge to him.

7 We shall see[13] that defamers are, at common law, infected with the malice of certain others. Section 4(6) extends this for the purposes of subsection (1)(b) by providing that the subsection shall not apply unless the defendant proves that the author (whether he be servant, agent, independent contractor, writer of a letter under an assumed name, or from a wrong address) wrote without malice: newspapers, then, can hardly use this statutory defence if they cannot trace the author of a letter.

The application of the Act, once these conditions are satisfied, is also

---

8 If the report read: 'After a few preliminary remarks Miss Jones was *seduced* by the chairman' this would be 'on the face' and not privileged by the section.

9 See p 390, ante, especially *Slazengers Ltd v Gibbs & Co* (1916) 33 TLR 35.

10 Would the defendant be able to invoke the Act if, by mistake, he inserted the photograph of the plaintiff, whom he did not know to be a teetotaller, in a whisky advertisement?

11 Section 4(1)(b).

12 *Sun Life Assurance Co of Canada v W H Smith & Son Ltd* [1933] All ER Rep 432 at 436 (per SCRUTTON LJ), CA; cf *Apthorp v Neville* (1907) 23 TLR 575.

13 See p 415, post.

difficult to unravel. The defendant can then make an offer of amends, supported by an affidavit setting out the facts relied on to show that his publication was 'innocent'. An offer of amends, as defined by section 4(3), means:

(a) in any case, to publish ... a suitable correction ... and a suitable apology to the party aggrieved ...
(b) where copies of a document or record containing the said words have been distributed by or with the knowledge of the person making the offer, to take such steps as are reasonably practicable on his part for notifying persons to whom copies have been so distributed that the words are alleged to be defamatory of the party aggrieved.[14]

Whether any publication of the apology, beyond sending it to the party aggrieved, is required, is not stated. It will be noted that section 4(3)(b) does not require a correction, nor does it apply at all to originals, only to copies. Normally, these difficulties will be avoided if the defendant's offer reproduces the words of the subsection, whatever they may mean.

If the plaintiff accepts the offer, the High Court finally decides, in default of agreement between the parties, how the offer shall be fulfilled: the court would, at this stage, have to interpret section 4(3).

The Act provides that it is a defence, in any proceedings for innocent libel or slander by the plaintiff against the offerer of amends, either that an offer has been made, accepted and performed, or that it has been refused, after having been made as soon as practicable[15] after the defendant received notice that the words were or might be defamatory of the plaintiff, and that the offer had not been withdrawn. This provision might be very unfair to the plaintiff. If he rejects the offer of amends because he thinks that the publication was not 'innocent' or because section 4(3) was not complied with, it seems that he has no means under the Act of securing the performance of the offer of amends should the defendant prove his innocence at the trial.[16] Surely the plaintiff ought to be able to postpone his decision whether to accept the offer pending a judicial ruling whether the section applies at all.

SECTION 2. REFERENCE TO THE PLAINTIFF

'In order to be actionable the defamatory words must be understood to be published of and concerning the plaintiff.'[17] The plaintiff need not be mentioned in the statement, nor need everyone reading it know that he was referred to; it is sufficient if ordinary sensible people, proved to have special knowledge of the facts, might reasonably believe that the statement referred

---

14 No money payment to the plaintiff is required, even if he has suffered special damage.
15 Not after seven weeks' delay: *Ross v Hopkinson* (1956) Times, 16 October. This is the only known decision on s 4. As this case shows, the plea must be made promptly, yet the defendant has to make sure that his affidavit includes all the relevant material: an expensive process which may be difficult to perform in a short time.
16 The defendant can offer no evidence other than of facts specified in the affidavit.
17 Per LORD ATKIN in *Knupffer v London Express Newspaper Ltd* [1944] AC 116 at 121, [1944] 1 All ER 495, HL. Cf *Farrington v Leigh* (1987) Times, 10 December, CA.

to the plaintiff.[18] The damages will be less when only a small proportion of those who read the article would know that it was defamatory of the plaintiff.

A. CLASS LIBELS

Where a statement defamatory of a class of persons is made, the same test is applied to determine whether individuals within the class may sue. If the class is so small that persons would reasonably believe that each member of it is pointed at, then each individual member may sue.[19] Thus, where proceedings were pending against seventeen persons, it was held that one of them could sue a third party who said of them all that 'these defendants helped to murder HF.'[20] No doubt, a similar rule would apply to directors of a company or trustees of an institution. But a statement that 'all estate agents are rogues' would not ordinarily enable any one member of such a large class to sue.

Even where the class is too large to permit every member to sue, an individual within the class may still be able to sue if he can show that the statement was nevertheless particularly referable to him. Often this will rest on an innuendo, which must then be specifically pleaded, and the court will order the plaintiff to give full particulars of the facts on which the claim rests.[1]

Two cases will illustrate the position. First, *Le Fanu v Malcolmson*:[2]

The defendants published an article importing that in some of the Irish factories cruelties were practised upon employees. There were circumstances in the article as a whole, including a reference to Waterford itself, which enabled the jury to identify the plaintiffs' Waterford factory as the one aimed at. The plaintiffs' action succeeded.

Secondly, *Knupffer v London Express Newspaper Ltd*:[3]

The defendants' newspaper, during the war, referred to the quisling activities of the Young Russian party. Although the party was international, and had a British branch of 24 members headed by the plaintiff, the article referred only to the party's activities in France and U.S.A. Since the total membership was several thousands, each member could not be said to be pointed at. No facts were proved in evidence that could identify the plaintiff as being singled out in the article, and therefore his action failed.

---

18 *Morgan v Odhams Press Ltd* [1971] 2 All ER 1156, HL. *Cassidy v Daily Mirror Newspapers Ltd* [1929] 2 KB 331, CA. If the defendant publishes a statement defamatory on its face about someone described but not named, and a later publication by the defendant names the plaintiff so as to identify to readers of the first newspaper article for the first time the person written about, the second publication may be relied on to support the allegation that the first one referred to the plaintiff: *Hayward v Thompson* [1982] QB 47, [1981] 3 All ER 450, CA.

19 Is the true statement 'Either you or Jones stole the money' actionable by Jones? No, held MADDEN CJ in *Chomley v Watson* [1907] VLR 502.

20 *Foxcroft v Lacy* (1613) Hob 89; cf *Browne v D C Thomson & Co Ltd* 1912 SC 359, defendants' newspaper published article stating that in Queenstown the Roman Catholic religious authorities had instructed that all Protestant shop assistants were to be dismissed. The seven persons who alone exercised religious authority on behalf of the Roman Catholic Church in Queenstown were able to sue in libel.

1 *Bruce v Odhams Press Ltd* [1936] 1 KB 697, [1936] 1 All ER 287, CA.

2 (1848) 1 HL Cas 637, HL.

3 [1944] AC 116, [1944] 1 All ER 495, HL.

B. UNINTENTIONAL REFERENCES TO THE PLAINTIFF

The plaintiff may be referred to although the defendant did not intend it—but where the defamation is intentional higher damages may be awarded.[4] In several cases, newspaper proprietors who did not intend to defame the plaintiff have been held liable. In *Hulton v Jones*,[5] the defendants published a fictional article about 'Artemus Jones'; the writer of the article did not know of the plaintiff, of that name, who was a former contributor to the newspaper, but the managing editor, on reading the article in proof, had thought at first that the plaintiff was intended. The defendants were held liable. In *Newstead v London Express Newspaper Ltd*[6] the defendants published an account of the trial for bigamy of 'Harold Newstead, thirty-year-old Camberwell man': the reporter had included the address and occupation of the Harold Newstead of whom this was a correct report, but the sub-editor deleted it; this want of particularity caused readers to think that the plaintiff, another Harold Newstead of Camberwell, of about the same age, was meant; it was held to be no defence that the words were true of, and intended to refer to, another, and the jury was held to be justified in finding that the words referred to the plaintiff. No English appellate decision has been traced, where a defendant who could not possibly have known that the words were referable to the plaintiff, has been held liable.

Suppose that the defendant elects to rely on section 4 of the Defamation Act 1952. That section certainly covers instances where the statements were not known to be defamatory, or where 'the publisher did not intend to publish them of and concerning that other person, and did not know of circumstances by virtue of which they might be understood to refer to him'. It will be recalled, however, that the section applies only where the defendant proves that neither he nor his servants or agents have failed to take all reasonable care. Thus, failure by novelist Antonia White to consult 'Spotlight' deprived her of the defence when she included an actress named June Sylvaine (the plaintiff's stage name) in her book.[7] On facts like those of *Hulton v Jones* and *Newstead v London Express Newspaper Ltd*, the section could not apply because all reasonable care had not been taken. The position, therefore, is that there is no binding authority at common law for the proposition that a publisher, who could not have known that the statement referred to the plaintiff, is answerable—in any event, in such circumstances the Act affords a defence of offer of amends. Moreover, if the defendant knew that the statement referred to the plaintiff, or by the exercise of all reasonable care could have prevented the publication of a statement referring to the plaintiff, the Act would afford him no defence so that his common-law liability would be left untouched.

---

4 *Bridgmont v Associated Newspapers Ltd* [1951] 2 All ER 285, CA.
5 [1910] AC 20, HL.
6 [1940] 1 KB 377, [1939] 4 All ER 319, CA. And see *Grappelli v Derek Block (Holdings) Ltd* [1981] 2 All ER 272, [1981] 1 WLR 822 and *Hayward v Thompson* [1982] QB 47, [1981] 3 All ER 450 (effect of later publications identifying the person defamed).
7 *Ross v Hopkinson* (1956) Times, 16 October.

SECTION 3. PUBLICATION

Publication is 'the making known the defamatory matter after it has been written to some person other than the person of whom it is written'.[8] This requirement of publication to a third party merely underlines that the tort protects not a man's opinion of himself but the estimation in which others hold him.

Because of this rule, it is often important to know when the defendant, who perhaps addressed his remarks to the plaintiff alone, can be held responsible for the fact that third parties have learnt of the defamation. The rule is that if he intended that it should be published to them, or ought to have foreseen such publication, he is liable, but not otherwise.[9] A defendant is not liable for an 'unsuspected overhearing of the words' spoken by him to the plaintiff.[10] He is not liable where a father opens his son's letter,[11] or the butler opens even the unsealed letter of his employer.[12] A correspondent should expect that clerks of the plaintiff, a businessman, might in the ordinary course of business open letters addressed to him at his place of business (and not marked 'personal', 'private', etc), and is therefore responsible for the publication to them.[13] It is also to be expected that a husband will open an unstamped manila envelope lying on the door-mat looking like a circular, even though it is sealed and addressed to his wife.[14]

In general, the original maker of a statement is not liable for its republication by another, but that other will be responsible even though he expressly states that he is merely reproducing what he has been told from a specified source.[15] So, the writer, newspaper proprietor and printer of a defamatory article in a newspaper are each liable for its publication.[16] In accordance with ordinary principles, however, 'where a man who makes a request to another to publish defamatory matter, of which, for the purpose, he gives him a statement, whether in full or in outline, and the agent publishes the matter, adhering to the sense and substance of it, although the language be to some extent his own, the man making the request is liable to an action as the publisher'.[17] A man who knows that reporters are present when he is making a speech is not thereby responsible for its publication in the Press, but he is answerable if he gives the information to them with a view to publication.[18]

---

8 Per LORD ESHER MR, in *Pullman v Hill & Co* [1891] 1 QB 524 at 527, CA.
9 *Huth v Huth* [1915] 3 KB 32 at 38, CA (per LORD READING CJ); *McNichol v Grandy* [1932] 1 DLR 225 (S Ct Canada) held that the burden of proving that it would not be expected that a statement would be overheard is on the defendant.
10 *White v Stone Lighting and Radio Ltd* [1939] 2 KB 827; [1939] 3 All ER 507, CA.
11 *Powell v Gelston* [1916] 2 KB 615.
12 *Huth v Huth*, supra; contra, if the sender knew that the plaintiff was blind, and that the butler often opened letters for her.
13 *Pullman v Hill* [1891] 1 QB 524, CA. But what if one sent a letter marked 'private' to, say, the Prime Minister or even to any other busy public figure, might there not be publication to the secretary who opened it?
14 *Theaker v Richardson* [1962] 1 All ER 229, CA.
15 *M'Pherson v Daniels* (1829) 10 B & C 263.
16 And distributors. In *Goldsmith v Sperrings Ltd* [1977] 2 All ER 566, CA, it was held not to be an abuse of process for Sir James Goldsmith to pursue a claim arising from an article in *Private Eye* against 37 different distributors with a view to making them settle his claim on the basis of their undertaking to cease distributing the magazine.
17 Per MONTAGUE SMITH J, in *Parkes v Prescott* (1869) LR 4 Exch 169 at 179.
18 *Adams v Kelly* (1824) Ry & M 157; *McWhirter v Manning* (1954) Times, 30 October.

The requirement of publication to a third party is satisfied by dictating a letter to one's typist,[19] and probably also when the office-boy press-copies it.[20] A judge at first instance in Northern Ireland has held that a printer does not, by the very act of handing back in a parcel the printed handbills to the customer-author, publish the handbills.[1] The defendant's publication to his own wife is not enough[2] but publication to the wife of the plaintiff is.[3]

Difficulties of proving publication are eased by certain rebuttable presumptions. Proof of proper addressing and posting of a letter gives rise to a presumption of publication to the addressee,[4] and a post card and a telegram[5] (but not an unsealed letter)[6] are presumed to have been published to Post Office officials. On the other hand, where the defendant handed to X a folded unsealed letter which he, without reading or showing to others, handed to the plaintiff, there was held to be no publication.[7]

There is no publication to a person unless the defamatory meaning of the communication would be understood by that third person—a postcard defamatory of, but (to persons unaware of the special facts) not known to be referable to the plaintiff, has been held not to be published to Post Office staff.[8]

There may be publication by omission. Failure by a defendant authorised and able to remove or amend defamatory matter which is the work of another is publication by him—those in charge of a club will therefore be accountable for defamatory matter placed by another on the notice-board of the club if they do not remove it within a reasonable time.[9]

---

19 *Pullman v Hill* [1891] 1 QB 524, CA. The circulation of inter-departmental memoranda within a company is sufficient publication: *Riddick v Thames Board Mills Ltd* [1977] QB 881, [1977] 3 All ER 677, CA.

20 The reports of *Pullman v Hill* do not expressly state that the press-copying in that case was held to be a publication, but Lord Esher, a judge in that case, said in *Boxsius v Goblet Frères* [1894] 1 QB 842 at 849, CA that the case had so decided.

1 *Eglantine Inn Ltd v Smith* [1948] NI 29 (the printer was nevertheless held jointly liable for the subsequent distribution of the handbills by the author's agents).

2 *Wennhak v Morgan* (1888) 20 QBD 635, Div Ct.

3 *Wenman v Ash* (1853) 13 CB 836.

4 *Warren v Warren* (1834) 1 Cr M & R 250.

5 *Sadgrove v Hole* [1901] 2 KB 1, CA.

6 *Huth v Huth* [1915] 3 KB 32, CA (it was stated *obiter* that had post office officials in fact read the letter to check whether it was properly stamped, that would have been publication—does this mean that it is foreseeable that any mail will be thus opened, eg to see whether prohibited articles are sent, or is it limited to unsealed mail?).

7 *Clutterbuck v Chaffers* (1816) 1 Stark 471.

8 *Sadgrove v Hole* [1901] 2 KB 1, CA; so also cipher messages, and sometimes messages in a foreign language.

9 *Byrne v Deane* [1937] 1 KB 818, [1937] 2 All ER 204, CA; contra if the matter is carved in stone, or the defendant is not in control of the place where the libel is exhibited. Is an executor liable for the publication of defamatory matter in probate of a will because he has not exercised his power to apply to the court for its deletion from the probate?

Chapter 25

Defences

Some of the defences already discussed may be available in defamation. In that event, the same rules will apply, and they will not, except for consent and assumption of risk, be dealt with here. In addition, many defences peculiar to defamation have to be described.

SECTION 1. CONSENT AND ASSUMPTION OF RISK

The better opinion is that consent is an independent defence in defamation.[1] A man who telephones to a newspaper false news about himself will not be able to sue in defamation when the newspaper publishes it, but a plaintiff has been deemed not to have consented to the publication in a newspaper of a story which he told about himself at a parish vestry meeting.[2]

Earlier decisions that no consent could be implied to the Jockey Club's publishing in the *Racing Calendar* reports of investigations made by its stewards into alleged breaches of their rules have been circumvented by the club's granting licences to train racehorses under their auspices subject to the express condition that suspensions or withdrawals of licences may be published in the *Calendar*.[3] The extent of the consent is a question of fact: so, although a licence-holder had consented to publication of such matters in the *Racing Calendar*, he was held not to have consented to its further publication in *The Times*.

It is sometimes a difficult question of fact to decide whether a plaintiff has consented to the repetition of a defamatory statement. If, for instance, the plaintiff asked the defendant to repeat it so as to abandon the privilege attaching to the occasion of the original publication, or because he did not properly understand on the first occasion, he would not be consenting.

The defence of assumption of risk was upheld in *Chapman v Ellesmere*.[4] The plaintiff maintained that even if he had consented to the publication of a report of an inquiry by the Jockey Club, he had not consented to its publication in such a form as to contain an innuendo against him. The Court of Appeal rejected this plea on the ground, in effect, that the plaintiff had agreed to run the risk of the particular form that the statement might take.[5]

---

1 But see DENNING LJ, in *Russell v Duke of Norfolk* [1949] 1 All ER 109 at 120, CA. This issue may be crucial if, for example, A asks B for a reference and B is actuated by malice in providing one, unless the consent is deemed to be to a non-malicious reference only.
2 *Cook v Ward* (1830) 6 Bing 409.
3 *Cookson v Harewood* [1932] 2 KB 478 n; [1931] All ER Rep 533, CA; cf *Chapman v Ellesmere* [1932] 2 KB 431; [1932] All ER Rep 221, CA. On the limited extent to which the courts will be prepared now to imply assent to publication see *Tadd v Eastwood* [1985] ICR 132, [1985] IRLR 119, CA.
4 [1932] 2 KB 431; [1932] All ER Rep 221, CA.
5 Per SLESSER LJ at 464.

SECTION 2.   JUSTIFICATION

It is no part of the plaintiff's case to establish that the defendant's statement was untrue: the plaintiff has merely to prove the publication of a statement defamatory of him. If, however, the defendant can prove that his statement is true he has a complete defence, even if he made the statement maliciously. 'For the law will not permit a man to recover damages in respect of an injury to a character which he does not ... possess.'[6] The defendant does not discharge this burden by proving that he honestly believed it to be true—he must prove that it was true in fact.[7] Nor will it avail him to show that he repeated accurately to a third party what he heard from another even though he told that third party that it was a mere repetition.[8] If the words impute the commission of a specific offence, it is not enough to prove that the plaintiff was suspected of the alleged offence.[9] These restrictions on the defence are clearly necessary to prevent it from being abused.

Before deciding whether the defendant can successfully plead justification, one must first discover, in accordance with the rules discussed above, what the statement complained of has been interpreted to mean.[10] If the statement contains an innuendo, that too must be justified.[11] And even if the defendant justifies the innuendo, he will still fail unless he also justifies the primary meaning of the words used; for they form a separate head of claim.[12] If the defendant enters a plea of justification and a traverse of the innuendo, success on the first plea and failure on the traverse means that his defence fails. And just as the plaintiff must specifically plead the meanings he relies on as defamatory, so must the defendant pleading justification '... make it clear to the plaintiff what is the case he is seeking to set up'.[13]

Obviously, then, many problems on justification are merely points of interpretation, where the material question is: 'Does that which is proved to be true tally with that which the defendant's statement is interpreted to mean?' *Wakley v Cooke* is a typical case:[14]

> The defendant called the plaintiff a 'libellous journalist'. He proved that a judgment against the plaintiff for libel had once been obtained. Because the defamatory statement complained of meant that the journalist habitually libelled people, the defendant had not justified it.

The defence will fail if the statement is not substantially true. Thus, if it is

---

6 *M'Pherson v Daniels* (1829) 10 B & C 263.
7 *Peters v Bradlaugh* (1888) 4 TLR 414, Div Ct. Has the defendant merely to adduce a preponderance of evidence that the crime has been committed, or to prove it beyond reasonable doubt? The former, it is suggested, would be sufficient; *Laurence v Chester Chronicle* (1986) Times, 8 February; cf *Hornal v Neuberger Products Ltd* [1957] 1 QB 247, [1956] 3 All ER 970, CA.
8 *M'Pherson v Daniels* (1829) 10 B & C 263.
9 *Rubber Improvement Ltd v Daily Telegraph Ltd* [1964] AC 234 at pp 274–5 (per Lord Hodson).
10 See p 391, ante.
11 *Prior v Wilson* (1856) 1 CB (NS) 95.
12 *Watkin v Hall* (1868) LR 3 QB 396 at 402 (per Blackburn J).
13 *Lucas-Box v Associated Newspaper Group* [1986] 1 All ER 177, [1986] 1 WLR 147, CA.
14 (1849) 4 Exch 511; Is it more defamatory of a woman to allege she has had an extra-marital affair with one man rather than another? See *Khashoggi v IPC Magazines Ltd* [1986] 3 All ER 577, [1986] 1 WLR 1412, CA.

inaccurate only in minor points of detail, the defendant succeeds.[15]. Similarly, 'it is unnecessary to repeat every word which might have been the subject of the original comment. As much must be justified as meets the sting of the charge, and if anything be contained in a charge which does not add to the sting of it, that need not be justified'.[16] In *Clarke v Taylor* the facts were:[17]

> The defendant accused the plaintiff, C, of taking part in a 'grand swindling concern' at Manchester, and added that 'C had been at Leeds for one or two days before his arrival in [Manchester] ... and is supposed to have made considerable purchases there. It is hoped, however, that the detection of his plans in Manchester will be learnt in time to prevent any serious losses from taking place'. The defendant justified the statement that the plaintiff had swindled at Manchester, but not the remainder of the statement. Held, that this was a sufficient plea of justification because the remaining words did not add any further alleged act of criminality.

Many statements contain both statements of fact and opinion: for example, 'X was drunk again last night; his behaviour is disgusting'. If the defendant relies on a plea of justification in respect of this, he must prove not only that X was drunk but also that the statement that his behaviour was disgusting (in so far as that comment adds to the sting of the libel) was accurate, ie implied in the fact that he was drunk; in so far as the further statement introduces new matter or implies the existence of further facts he must prove those further facts which justify the terms in which he has described the plaintiff.[18]

At common law, every material statement had to be justified. If, therefore, the defendant could prove the truth of three charges but not that of a distinct fourth charge, the defence failed, although these circumstances would be relevant in assessing damages. This rule is modified by section 5 of the Defamation Act 1952:

> In an action for libel or slander in respect of words containing two or more distinct charges against the plaintiff, a defence of justification shall not fail by reason only that the truth of every charge is not proved if the words not proved to be true do not materially injure the plaintiff's reputation having regard to the truth of the remaining charges.[19]

It is now therefore important to know when there are several charges, for the section can only apply when the defendant has proved that at least one charge which, having been separated from the remaining charges, is itself incapable of further severance is, in the common-law meaning, substantially true. At common law the courts had also to consider when charges were severable, because any severable charge could be separately justified with a view to reducing damages or, perhaps, establishing some other defence in respect of

---

15 *Alexander v North Eastern Rly Co* (1865) 6 B & S 340 (defendants published notice that plaintiffs had been sentenced to a fine of £1 with alternative of 3 weeks imprisonment: in fact alternative was only 2 weeks imprisonment).
16 *Edwards v Bell* (1824) 1 Bing 403 at 409 (per BURROUGH J).
17 (1836) 2 Bing NC 654.
18 *Cooper v Lawson* (1838) 8 Ad & El 746. There is sometimes another possible defence, viz, fair comment, pp. 422 et seq, post; but this defence is subject to certain requirements, the absence of any of which makes it necessary to rely on justification, eg fair comment may only be pleaded if the matter is one of public interest.
19 A defendant who relies on s 5 must plead it as a defence. *Moore v News of the World* [1972] 1 QB 441, [1972] 1 All ER 915, CA.

other charges. Presumably, the common-law rules on what is a severable charge apply under the Act.[20]

The effect of the Act is illustrated by considering its application to the facts of the pre-Act decision in *Goodburne v Bowman:*[1]

> The plaintiff was alleged by the defendant to have made, in each of his two periods of office as mayor, 2d. a bushel secret profit from the corporation on selling coals to the poor. The defendant justified the statement by pleading that the plaintiff did this in one of these terms of office only. This plea failed because it did not establish the truth of all the material statements in the libel.

Under the Act, it would be open to the jury on similar facts to find that, in view of the truth of one of the two charges, the other did not materially injure his reputation. The plaintiff cannot evade the section by basing his cause of action, in the first place, solely on those residuary parts of the defendant's statement which are not true; if the different parts of an article are not plainly severable the defendant can base a defence of justification (and fair comment) on the whole of the article.[2] Where several defamatory allegations have a common 'sting' they are not to be regarded as separate and distinct. The defendant must justify the 'sting' and '. . . it is fortuitous that what is in fact similar fact evidence is found in the publication.'[3]

If a plaintiff persists in a plea of justification and thereby prolongs the period in which the damage from the publication continues to spread, a greater sum by way of aggravated damages may be awarded against him.[4]

The completeness of the defence of justification must be emphasised. Even if the defendant be inspired by malice, or even if, when he made the statements, he did not believe them to be true, if in fact they are true, his defence is good. This makes the consequences of the failure of the English law of torts to protect privacy so serious.[5] Newspapers are free in this country to rake up a man's forgotten past, and ruin him deliberately in the process, without risk of incurring tortious liability.[6]

---

20 See *Clarkson v Lawson* (1830) 6 Bing 587; *Davis v Billing* (1891) 8 TLR 58, CA; *Fleming v Dollar* (1889) 23 QBD 388, CA.

1 (1833) 9 Bing 667.

2 *S and K Holdings v Throgmorton Publications Ltd* [1972] 3 All ER 497, CA, distinguishing *Plato Films Ltd v Speidel* [1961] AC 1090.

3 *Polly Peck (Holdings) plc v Trelford* [1986] 2 All ER 84 at 102; *Khashoggi v IPC Magazines* [1986] 3 All ER 577, [1986] 1 WLR 1412.

4 *Cassell & Co Ltd v Broome* [1972] AC 1027 at 1125 (per LORD DIPLOCK), HL. As to late entry of a plea of justification see *Atkinson v Fitzworth* [1987] 1 All ER 483, [1987] 1 WLR 201, CA.

5 The Porter Committee justified their refusal to recommend an alteration of the law relating to privacy as follows: (§ 26) 'We think that there are great difficulties in formulating an extended definition of criminal or civil libel which, while effective to restrain improper invasion of privacy, would not interfere with the due reporting of matters which are of public interest. It appears to us, however, that the difficulties which confront this Committee should not form an obstacle to action by the press itself or prevent it from dealing with the problem as one of internal discipline to be regulated by an understanding between the proprietorial and journalistic organisations. The offence is primarily one against good taste, and if a legal remedy has to be created, it must, we think, lie in a sphere which is outside our terms of reference.' The last sentence is the crucial one: privacy cannot be protected within the law of defamation because the protection sought is not for reputation as such, but for the interest which a person has in his private life not being unduly interfered with.

6 This is the more serious now that the Civil Evidence Act 1968, s 13 provides that, if it is relevant in defamation proceedings whether a person committed a criminal offence, proof

The Rehabilitation of Offenders Act 1974 does impose one curb on that freedom in relation to what it terms 'spent' convictions of 'rehabilitated persons'. After the expiry of certain defined periods, the duration of which differs according to the length of sentence, convictions (other than a sentence of life imprisonment or one of more than two-and-a-half years or one of preventive detention) become spent and the person convicted rehabilitated. Section 8 provides that where a plaintiff sues for defamation because a spent conviction has been dug up against him, proof that the matter complained of was true will not avail the publisher as a defence if the publication is proved to have been made with malice. The onus of proving malice, defined as 'some spiteful, irrelevant or unproper motive', lies on the plaintiff.[7]

SECTION 3.　IMMUNITY OF PROCEEDINGS IN PARLIAMENT

By the law of Parliament courts have no jurisdiction over proceedings in Parliament:[8] this is a matter of 'no jurisdiction' or immunity.[9] This immunity extends not only to statements made in the course of parliamentary proceedings but also to all reports, papers, votes, and proceedings published by, or under the authority of, either House.[10]

SECTION 4.　ABSOLUTE PRIVILEGE

Certain occasions are deemed to be so important that those making statements upon them are not liable in defamation even though their statements are untrue and even malicious. These occasions, where the public interest in freedom of communication is paramount, are styled cases of absolute privilege.

of conviction is conclusive evidence that he committed the offence. But see ante at p 152 development of a tort of breach of confidence.

7 *Herbage v Pressdram* [1984] 2 All ER 769, [1984] 1 WLR 1160, CA.

8 Bill of Rights, 1688; *Ex parte Wason* (1869) LR 4 QB 573 at 576 (per COCKBURN CJ). Hence, the frequent challenge by the victim to the MP to repeat outside the House his attacks on the victim's reputation. Petitions addressed to Parliament are within the immunity: *Lake v King* (1670) 1 Saund 131, but there is no general immunity for letters written to MPs: *Rivlin v Bilainkin* [1953] 1 QB 485, [1953] 1 All ER 534.

9 *Rivlin v Bilainkin* supra; 5th Report from the Committee of Privileges, 1956–7, draft report proposed by the Attorney-General, p xxix, and evidence of the Clerk of the House of Commons at paras 397, 431–3. The 2nd Report of the Joint Committee on the Publication of Proceedings in Parliament (1969–70) HL 109, HC 261, paras 26 and 27, recommended a statutory definition which would make it clear that all things said, done or written between MPs, or between MPs and officers of Parliament, or between MPs and Ministers of the Crown for the purpose of enabling any MP or any such officer to carry out his functions should be within the privilege. The Faulks Report, para 203, agreed; and see 3rd Report from the Committee of Privileges, 1976–7 HC 417 para 7.

10 Parliamentary Papers Act 1840, s 1, offsetting *Stockdale v Hansard* (1839) 9 Ad & El 1. Significantly, the section does not confer absolute privilege; it orders the judge to 'stay', whereby the suit 'shall be deemed and taken to be finally put an end to.' Since Command Papers are outside this immunity, the method of bringing them within it is to use an unopposed return under the Parliamentary Papers Act 1840, to make the Command Paper a Parliamentary Paper, but that cannot be done if Parliament is not sitting.

A. EXECUTIVE MATTERS

In the leading case of *Chatterton v Secretary of State for India*[11] it was held that a letter from the Secretary of State for India to his Parliamentary Under-Secretary providing the material for the answer to a parliamentary question was absolutely privileged. It is impossible to say how high in the hierarchy of civil servants a defendant must be before he enjoys this privilege. A message from the High Commissioner for Australia to his Prime Minister about a matter of commerce which concerned the Government of Australia has been held to be privileged.[12] On the other hand, it has been doubted whether those below the status of Minister may claim the privilege.[13] If it were not for the cases relating to military communications now to be considered, one might confidently submit that routine communications between persons not in charge of government departments are outside the privilege, and one might doubt whether the courts would willingly extend it at all beyond the limits reached in the decisions above.

In *Dawkins v Lord Paulet*[14] it was held that a report on the plaintiff from his superior officer to his commander-in-chief could not be the basis of an action for libel. COCKBURN CJ dissented; LUSH J based his judgment on the principle that the army was outside the jurisdiction of the courts,[15] and one of the three grounds of MELLOR J's judgment was that such letters were absolutely privileged.[16] It is submitted that this is not strong enough authority for the proposition that communications within the civil service relating to the character and ability of personnel are absolutely privileged, and does not decide that civil servants below ministerial rank have this absolute privilege. Such communications would be adequately protected by that qualified privilege which doubtless attaches to them.[17]

This privilege must not be confused with the procedural rule that the Crown, whether or not it is a party, cannot be compelled in any litigation to produce, or disclose the existence of, any documents the production or disclosure of which would be contrary to the public interest.[18] In practice, because the Crown could decide at its discretion whether to produce the document, this rule has effectively prevented plaintiffs from maintaining

---

11 [1895] 2 QB 189, CA. The Parliamentary Commissioner Act 1967, s 10(5) also gives an absolute privilege to the Parliamentary Commissioner for his reports to Parliament and for certain of his communications to MPs; the Local Commissioners have a similar absolute privilege under the Local Government Act 1974, s 32.

12 *M Isaacs & Sons Ltd v Cook* [1925] 2 KB 391.

13 *Szalatnay-Stacho v Fink* [1946] 1 All ER 303 at 305 (per HENN COLLINS J); not considered, [1947] KB 1, CA, *Richards v Naum* [1967] 1 QB 620, [1966] 3 All ER 812, CA. On grounds of public policy, arising out of international comity, English courts will concede to foreign governments immunities similar to those accorded by way of privilege to the United Kingdom government. Thus no action for libel lay in respect of an internal memorandum from a foreign embassy; *Fayed v Al-Tajir* [1987] 2 All ER 396, [1987] 3 WLR 102, CA.

14 (1869) LR 5 QB 94.

15 But see *Dawkins v Lord Rokeby* (1873) LR 8 QB 255, Ex Ch, affirmed (1875) LR 7 HL 744.

16 In *Gibbons v Duffell* (1932) 47 CLR 520, the High Court of Australia was confronted with the argument that the police were to be equated with the army, so that communications within the force were absolutely privileged: the court held that they were only the subject of qualified privilege. In *Merricks v Nott-Bower* [1965] 1 QB 57, [1964] 1 All ER 717, CA, the report by one high police officer to another about another police officer was held to be not so clearly the subject of absolute privilege that a claim in libel should be struck out.

17 See p 410 et seq, post.

18 Crown Proceedings Act 1947, s 28. And see *Schneider v Leigh* [1955] 2 All ER 173, CA.

libel suits even for communications within the civil service which were not absolutely privileged.[19]

B. JUDICIAL PROCEEDINGS

Statements made in proceedings before superior and inferior courts of record, and magistrates' courts are privileged. The privilege extends to other tribunals recognised by law,[20] provided that they are 'exercising functions equivalent to those of an established court of justice'.[1] 'In any case of doubt the overriding factor is whether there will emerge from the proceedings a determination the truth and justice of which is a matter of public concern';[2] thus an enquiry before an Inn of Court into the conduct of a barrister was absolutely privileged,[3] even though the body had no power to issue a subpoena, or to take evidence on oath, and sat in private. The disciplinary committee of the Law Society,[4] courts-martial[5] and select committees of the House of Commons[6] are also within the privilege. If the functions are merely administrative, or determine no rights nor the guilt or innocence of anyone, there is no absolute privilege, even though judicial procedures such as hearing evidence or summoning witnesses are used.[7] Justices dealing with applications for liquor licensing,[8] and a meeting of the London County Council for the grant of music and dancing licences,[9] official industrial conciliation processes[10] have been held to be outside the scope of the privilege. Competition proceedings before the European Commission, by contrast, were held to attract absolute privilege despite the administrative nature of their procedures. The public interest in the Commission's duty to enforce European competition law outweighed the private interests of litigants seeking to vindicate their reputations.[11]

The privilege is enjoyed by judges, parties, witnesses,[12] counsel[13] and sol-

---

19 *Home v Bentinck* (1820) 2 Brod & Bing 130; *Beatson v Skene* (1860) 5 H & N 838; and *West v West* (1911) 27 TLR 476, CA, are examples of cases where the rule was successfully used for that purpose. The House of Lords in *Conway v Rimmer* [1968] AC 910, [1968] 1 All ER 874, invested the courts with a residual power to demand production when the public interest does not demand non-disclosure; to this extent the Crown's discretion to withhold documents is curtailed. The House of Lords in recent years has suggested that only in very clear cases will that residual power be invoked, *Air Canada v Secretary of State for Trade (No 2)* [1983] 2 AC 394, [1983] 1 All ER 161.

20 Either under statute or royal prerogative of justice: *Lincoln v Daniels* [1962] 1 QB 237, [1961] 3 All ER 740, CA.

1 *O'Connor v Waldron* [1935] AC 76 at 81, [1934] All ER Rep 281 at 283. And see *Trapp v Mackie* [1979] 1 All ER 489, HL (a Scottish case on the privilege of a witness at an inquiry, but not one on defamation).

2 Per DEVLIN LJ, in *Lincoln v Daniels* [1962] 1 QB 237 at 255–6, [1961] 3 All ER 740, CA.

3 *Lincoln v Daniels* supra.

4 *Addis v Crocker* [1961] 1 QB 11, [1960] 2 All ER 629, CA.

5 *Dawkins v Lord Rokeby* (1873) LR 8 QB 225, affirmed on appeal (1875) LR 7 HL 744.

6 On principle, these would seem to have been more properly within the 'legislative' privilege, but this is not the basis of *Goffin v Donnelly* (1881) 6 QBD 307.

7 *O'Connor v Waldron* supra.

8 *Attwood v Chapman* [1914] 3 KB 275.

9 *Royal Aquarium and Summer and Winter Garden Society v Parkinson* [1892] 1 QB 431, CA.

10 *Tadd v Eastwood* [1985] ICR 132, [1985] IRLR 119, CA.

11 *Hasselblad (GB) Ltd v Orbinson* [1985] QB 475, [1985] 1 All ER 173, CA.

12 *Seaman v Netherclift* (1876) 2 CPD 53, CA.

13 *Munster v Lamb* (1883) 11 QBD 588.

icitors,[14] and presumably jurors. Judges are protected although their statements are malicious or irrelevant.[15] The extent to which the others engaged in the proceedings are privileged is doubtful,[16] but they are not protected where the statement is so irrelevant that it is no longer made by a person in the character of participant in the proceedings.[17] It is usually stated that the privilege is lost when the court has no jurisdiction.[18]

The privilege extends to documents initiating,[19] or made in the course of, the proceedings, eg pleadings, affidavits.[20]

C. SOLICITOR-CLIENT COMMUNICATIONS

Closely related to the privilege last discussed is the question of how far statements to solicitors by clients, or by witnesses before trial, are protected. If the purpose of not restricting the prosecution of judicial proceedings is to be attained, it would be unrealistic to deny to a witness privilege in respect of a proof of his evidence made immediately before trial. The House of Lords has therefore held in *Watson v M'Ewan* that a witness making a proof after the issue of a writ before trial is absolutely privileged.[1] This extension by the House of Lords of the privilege surrounding judicial proceedings is restricted to matters outside the proceedings which are practically necessary for the administration of justice; it does not extend to a complaint to the Bar Council even though that is a recognised channel for complaints by the public about members of the Bar.[2]

Whether *all* communications between solicitor and client should be so privileged is clearly a different matter. Yet in *More v Weaver*:[3]

In a discussion between solicitor and client having no relation to litigation, actual or prospective, on whether a loan should be called in, the plaintiff was defamed. The statement was held absolutely privileged.

The House of Lords in *Minter v Priest* expressly left open whether *More v Weaver* was rightly decided.[4] It is submitted that *More v Weaver* was wrongly

14 *MacKay v Ford* (1860) 5 H & N 792.
15 *Scott v Stansfield* (1868) LR 3 Exch 220.
16 The doubt arises because judicial immunity may derive from the separate defence of judicial act (see p 95, ante) not from privilege in defamation—see *Hamilton v Anderson* (1858) 3 Macq 363 at 375; contra, *Law v Llewellyn* [1906] 1 KB 487.
17 In answer to the question: 'Were you at York on a certain day?', a statement by a witness: 'Yes, and AB picked my pocket there', would not be made in the character of witness (per COCKBURN CJ, in *Seaman v Netherclift* supra at 57) if the proceedings were entirely unconnected with AB.
18 Eg *Gatley* § 391.
19 But not if the initiating document is wrongly sent to the Bar Council, instead of to an Inn of Court: *Lincoln v Daniels* [1962] 1 QB 237, [1961] 3 All ER 740, CA.
20 See *Lilley v Roney* (1892) 61 LJQB 727; *Revis v Smith* (1856) 18 CB 126; *Veal v Heard* (1930) 46 TLR 448, Div Ct (which held that a notice of objection to the renewal by a judicial body of a licence is not privileged), is wrongly decided on this point. For the pre-trial statements of witnesses, see infra. What of a false oath leading to a warrant of arrest? The privilege confers a general defence to all torts, e g conspiracy, and not merely to defamation: *Marrinan v Vibart* [1963] 1 QB 528, [1962] 3 All ER 380, CA, and see p 133, ante.
1 [1905] AC 480, HL.
2 *Lincoln v Daniels* supra.
3 [1928] 2 KB 520, CA.
4 [1930] AC 558 at 579, [1930] All ER Rep 431 at 439 (per LORD ATKIN), HL.

decided, that, in the cases which it purported to follow,[5] solicitor-client communications were only held to be absolutely privileged because they referred to judicial proceedings actually pending, and that there is no such absolute privilege other than that derived from the privilege of parties in relation to judicial proceedings.

D. REPORTS OF JUDICIAL PROCEEDINGS

A fair and accurate report (not being blasphemous or indecent) in any newspaper or in a wireless broadcast,[6] of proceedings publicly heard before any court exercising judicial authority within the United Kingdom shall, if published contemporaneously with such proceedings, be privileged.[7] Although the statutory wording is imprecise, it is generally assumed that an absolute privilege is conferred.

A newspaper is 'any paper containing public news, intelligence or occurrences, or any remarks or observations therein printed for sale' or 'any paper ... containing only or principally advertisements' and published in England or Ireland periodically, or in parts or numbers at intervals not exceeding 26 days.[8] Whether specialist periodicals, eg of the medical profession, or even such periodicals as the *Radio Times*, are newspapers is undecided.[9]

Reports of such interruptions to judicial proceedings as may be regarded as taking place in the course of the proceedings (although they may be applications with which the judge has no power to deal) are protected.[10] The jury decides whether the report is fair and accurate.[11]

Once any absolute privilege is established, it extends to consequential communications in the ordinary course of things to clerks, typists and the like.[12]

SECTION 5.   QUALIFIED PRIVILEGE

In certain circumstances, it is thought desirable that reflections on the reputation of another, although untrue, should not give rise to tortious liability, provided that they were not published with 'malice': these are occasions of qualified privilege. 'Malice' is here a formula subsuming several matters,

---

5 Eg *Browne v Dunn* (1893) 6 R 67, HL.
6 See p 382, ante, for the definition of wireless telegraphy.
7 Law of Libel Amendment Act 1888, s 3, as amended by Defamation Act 1952, ss 8 and 9(2) and Contempt of Court Act 1981, s 4(3). Section 8 of the Rehabilitation of Offenders Act 1974 enacts that if in the course of judicial proceedings an unsuccessful attempt is made to introduce evidence of a spent conviction (see p 406, ante) a report of that attempt will not enjoy the privilege otherwise attaching to such reports, unless it is confined to a *bona fide* series of law reports or made for *bona fide* educational, scientific or professional purposes.
8 See the Newspaper Libel and Registration Act 1881, s 1.
9 A different definition of newspaper applies to the cases of qualified privilege contained in the Defamation Act 1952; see p 417, post.
10 *Farmer v Hyde* [1937] 1 KB 728 at 743 (per SLESSER LJ), [1937] 1 All ER 773, CA. (Spectator in court: 'May I make an application?' Report privileged.)
11 Although legal precision is not required, a report of a conviction for stealing a car was held not a fair report of a conviction for taking it without the owner's consent. *Mitchell v Hirst, Kidd and Rennie Ltd* [1936] 3 All ER 872.
12 *M Isaacs & Sons Ltd v Cook* [1925] 2 KB 391.

proof of any one of which by the plaintiff will defeat the privilege.[13] 'Malice' will be discussed before the occasions of qualified privilege are set out.

A. MALICE: HOW IT MAY BE ESTABLISHED

Qualified privilege is defeated if the plaintiff proves 'malice' in any of the following ways:[14]

(1) THE DEFENDANT DOES NOT BELIEVE IN THE TRUTH OF HIS STATEMENT

By far the most important way of rebutting the privilege is to show that the defendant did not believe in the truth of his statement or was recklessly careless whether the statement be true or false. 'If a man is proved to have stated that which he knew to be false, no one need inquire further.'[15] Thus, a solicitor who writes that his client has admitted his negligence when he knows that he has not admitted it has abused the privilege.[16] Many cases cited on other aspects of 'malice' will be found, on closer examination, to have been based on the defendant's not believing what he says.[17] In so many of the leading cases the judges are sifting the evidence in order to see whether any statement made by the defendant was, to his knowledge, false.[18] The mere proof that the defendant had no reasonable grounds for believing his statement to be true is not enough to rebut the qualified privilege.[19] In the leading case of *Horrocks v Lowe* the House of Lords held that if the defendant honestly believed his statement to be true his privilege is not lost merely because his conclusion that his statement was true resulted from unreasoning prejudice or was irrational with regard to the subject matter.[20]

There is probably one exception to the rule that a person who does not believe in the truth of a statement forfeits the privilege. LORD BRAMWELL stated this exception as follows:[1]

> A person may honestly make on a particular occasion a defamatory statement without believing it to be true; because the statement may be of such a character that on that occasion it may be proper to communicate it to a particular person who ought to be informed of it.

---

13 Malice is used in another sense in pleading in defamation. The plaintiff normally sets out in his statement of claim that the defendant published 'maliciously' but, as Winfield has said, the word is a 'pleader's adverb' of no substantive importance.

14 By RSC O 82, r 3(3), the plaintiff who is seeking to defeat a plea of privilege or fair comment by proof of malice must give particulars in his reply of the facts and matters from which malice is to be inferred.

15 *Clark v Molyneux* (1877) 3 QBD 237 at 247 (per BRETT LJ), CA.

16 *Groom v Crocker* [1939] 1 KB 194, [1938] 2 All ER 394, CA.

17 Eg *Royal Aquarium and Summer and Winter Garden Society v Parkinson* [1892] 1 QB 431, CA, where the defendant had stated that a male and a female had performed in an indecent manner at a place of entertainment. It was proved that he knew or at least was reckless in not knowing that the figures were dressed as two males, 'so that all this story of gross indecency was nothing but the defendant's own imagination' (per LORD ESHER, at p 422): the defence of privilege was therefore rebutted.

18 The approach of LORD PORTER in *Turner v Metro-Goldwyn-Mayer Pictures Ltd*, is a typical example: [1950] 1 All ER 449, HL.

19 *Clark v Molyneux* (1877) 3 QBD 237; cf *Pitt v Donovan* (1813) 1 M & S 639.

20 [1975] AC 135, [1974] 1 All ER 662, HL.

 1 *Clark v Molyneux* (1877) 3 QBD 237 at 244; cf *Botterill v Whytehead* (1879) 41 LT 588 at 590 (per KELLY CB).

Although authority is scanty it is submitted that this exception is sound law. There may well be circumstances where the obligation to communicate the defamatory matter is so pressing that the defendant should be free to do so: this is particularly true where such information as the defendant has is properly requested by another, or where an important interest is subjected to a serious risk of harm if the defendant does not publish the information.

(2) ABUSE OF THE PURPOSE OF THE PRIVILEGE

If the defendant does not act for the purpose of protecting that interest for which the privilege is given, then he loses it.[2] Even though the defendant did believe his statement to be true, if the court is satisfied that his dominant motive was an improper purpose the privilege is lost.[3] He must use the occasion in accordance with the purpose for which the occasion arose.[4] Thus, the House of Lords was prepared to hold 'malicious' a letter sent to the BBC by a film company about a radio film critic if its purpose were proved to be to stifle criticism.[5]

The courts normally use, with reference to this class of malice, such expressions as 'wrong motive', 'personal spite' or 'ill-will': if the defendant is actuated by such a motive, then he abuses the privilege. Where the defendant honestly believed in the truth of his statement the court should be very slow to draw the inference that he was activated by improper motives.[6] The language used occasionally by the courts, and more often by writers, might seem to suggest that whenever, on a privileged occasion, the defendant has exhibited an improper motive, the privilege is rebutted. This is not quite correct: not only must there be an improper motive, but that motive must have been a causative factor in the publishing of the defamation. The courts usually express it as follows: 'the defendant was *actuated* by motives of personal spite or ill-will'.[7] Thus, in *Winstanley v Bampton*, a creditor who wrote a defamatory letter to the commanding officer of the plaintiff debtor, and believed what he wrote, forfeited his privilege because his indignation and anger had led him to defame the plaintiff.[8] If, however, the defendant was using the occasion for its proper purpose, but incidentally happened to have feelings of resentment or wrath towards the plaintiff, this would not deprive him of the privilege. It seems that the privilege is not lost if the ill-will is not the primary purpose, but is nevertheless one purpose, of the defendant.[9]

In deciding whether there is the requisite ill-will, it is relevant to consider the violence of the language of the communication. Yet judges have firmly

---

2 Ibid at 246 (per BRETT LJ), CA.
3 *Horrocks v Lowe* [1975] AC 135 at 149, [1974] 1 All ER 662 at 669 (per LORD DIPLOCK), HL.
4 Per LOPES LJ, in *Royal Aquarium and Summer and Winter Garden Society v Parkinson* [1892] 1 QB 431, CA.
5 *Turner v Metro-Goldwyn-Mayer Pictures Ltd* [1950] 1 All ER 449 at 457–8 (per LORD PORTER), HL.
6 Per LORD DIPLOCK, *Horrocks v Lowe* [1975] AC at 149–50.
7 *Wright v Woodgate* (1835) 2 Cr M & R 573, approved by LORD SHAW in *Adam v Ward* [1917] AC 309 at 349, HL.
8 [1943] KB 319, [1943] 1 All ER 661.
9 Per LORD DIPLOCK, *Horrocks v Lowe* [1975] AC 135 at 149, [1974] 1 All ER 662 at 669, HL. Should the court have made a psychological inquiry and considered whether the defendant's unreasoning prejudice was mainly the product of an improper motive?

laid down the rule that the courts must be very reluctant to infer malice from such evidence alone. LORD ATKINSON said in *Adam v Ward*:[10]

> ... a person making a communication on a privileged occasion is not restricted to the use of such language merely as is reasonably necessary to protect the interest or discharge the duty which is the foundation of his privilege; but that, on the contrary, he will be protected, even though his language should be violent or excessively strong, if, having regard to all the circumstances of the case, he might have honestly and on reasonable grounds believed that what he wrote or said was true ...

(3) EXTRANEOUS MATTER

The introduction of extraneous matter in a communication may afford evidence of malice which will take away that privilege which would otherwise attach to the communication.[11]

(4) UNREASONABLE PUBLICATION TO PERSONS OUTSIDE THE SCOPE OF THE PRIVILEGE

Where a defendant deliberately slanders the plaintiff in the presence of persons to whom he has no privilege to communicate the matter (although he may have a privilege to inform some of those present), or, for example, publishes in the Press when he could have protected his interest by a private communication, this is evidence of 'malice' which may rebut the privilege.[12]

(5) JUDGE AND JURY AND BURDEN OF PROOF IN RESPECT OF MALICE

The respective functions of judge and jury were summarised by LORD FINLAY as follows:[13]

> It is for the judge, and the judge alone, to determine as a matter of law whether the occasion is privileged, unless the circumstances attending it are in dispute, in which case the facts necessary to raise the question of law should be found by the jury. It is further for the judge to decide whether there is any evidence of express malice fit to be left to the jury—that is, whether there is any evidence on which a reasonable man could find malice.

The burden of proving to the jury that, as a matter of fact, the defendant was 'malicious' is on the plaintiff. He discharges this burden if he proves the defendant malicious in any one operative factor: thus, if he proves any one material statement to have been made without belief in its truth, the plaintiff discharges his burden.[14] His task is made heavier by reason of RSCO 82, r 6 which prohibits the use of interrogatories about the sources of information or grounds of belief of a defendant who pleads either fair comment or qualified privilege.

---

10 [1917] AC 309 at 339, HL; cf *Spill v Maule* (1869) LR 4 Exch 232 for a good illustration of judicial refusal to deprive the defendant of his privilege on the ground that he used extravagant language.
11 *Adam v Ward* [1917] AC 309 at 318 (per LORD FINLAY LC).
12 *Oddy v Lord Paulet* (1865) 4 F & F 1009.
13 *Adam v Ward* [1917] AC 309 at 318, HL.
14 *Turner v Metro-Goldwyn-Mayer Pictures Ltd* [1950] 1 All ER 449 at 455, HL (per LORD PORTER).

B. EXCESS OF PRIVILEGE

It might perhaps have been sufficient to consider, as we have already done,[15] excess of privilege in relation to 'malice'. The House of Lords has, however, decided in *Adam v Ward* that there are two separate questions, whether the privilege has been exceeded, and whether there is evidence of malice.[16] Proof of excess of privilege has the same effect as proof of malice, viz, to deprive the defendant of his defence of privilege. The importance of the distinction lies in the fact that the judge decides whether the privilege is exceeded, but the jury decide whether there is 'malice'. 'And observations made by judges in directing juries on what is evidence of malice are not necessarily applicable when they have to rule as to excess of privilege.'[17]

There may be such an excess where statements quite unconnected with the main statement are introduced.[18] In *Tuson v Evans*, for example:[19]

In a letter to the plaintiff's agent setting out the basis of his claim against the plaintiff for arrears of rent, the defendant added: 'This attempt to defraud me of the produce of land is as mean as it is dishonest.' This 'wholly unnecessary' addition deprived him of his qualified privilege.

The privilege is lost by publishing to more persons than is necessary. It was exceeded, for example, when the minutes of a *preliminary* inquiry by a committee of a local authority into alleged petrol thefts by employees were placed in the public library: at that stage the body of ratepayers had not the necessary common interest.[20]

An occasion does not cease to be privileged because the defendant publishes to clerks or others in the reasonable and ordinary course of business practice.[1] The fact that persons are present other than those to whom there is a duty to make the statement will not end the privilege if the ordinary 'business of life could not well be carried on' were such restrictions to be imposed.[2] The presence of reporters at a meeting of poor-law guardians did not take away that privilege attaching to statements made there.[3] Nor does a company forfeit its protection if, in order to have circulated a copy of the auditor's report, it sends it to printers, for that is 'reasonable and necessary'.[4]

---

15 See p 413, ante.
16 [1917] AC 309 at 318 (per LORD FINLAY), 320–1 (per EARL LOREBURN), 327 (per LORD DUNEDIN), 348 (per LORD SHAW).
17 Per EARL·LOREBURN at 321.
18 If the statement though not in strict logic relevant to the privileged occasion is reasonably germane to the subject matter, then it is material only as evidence of malice to take the case out of the privilege: per LORD DIPLOCK in *Horrocks v Lowe* [1975] AC at 151, HL.
19 (1840) 12 Ad & El 733.
20 *De Buse v McCarthy* [1942] 1 KB 156, [1942] 1 All ER 19, CA; cf *Williamson v Freer* (1874) LR 9 CP 393 (privilege to publish by letter lost when sent by telegram).
 1 *Boxsius v Goblet Frères* [1894] 1 QB 842, CA; *Edmondson v Birch & Co Ltd and Horner* [1907] 1 KB 371, CA; *Bryanston Finance Co Ltd v De Vries* [1975] 2 All ER 609, CA. The last cited case, following *Toogood v Spyring* (1834) 1 Cr M & R 181, decides that where the publication is made only to the plaintiff, and not to third parties, there is then a qualified privilege for the publication to clerks if it is fairly warranted by any reasonable occasion (not, as in that case, for a threatening improper letter). And see also *White v Stone (Lighting and Radio) Ltd* [1939] 2 KB 827, [1939] 3 All ER 507, CA.
 2 Per PARKE B in *Toogood v Spyring* supra at 194.
 3 *Pittard v Oliver* [1891] 1 QB 474, CA.
 4 Per MELLOR J in *Lawless v Anglo-Egyptian Cotton Co* (1869) LR 4 QB 262.

C. JOINT PUBLISHERS AND MALICE

Some difficult problems relating to the abuse of privilege are raised when there is a publication by joint tortfeasors or the employees of the defendant.

An agent through whom a person publishes a privileged communication enjoys the same privilege as his principal; for instance, a solicitor has the defence of qualified privilege when he publishes on behalf of his client some matter which his client had a privilege to publish.[5] If a servant in the course of his employment publishes with malice, the fact that his master was not personally malicious will not exempt the master from vicarious liability: the servant has forfeited the privilege because of his malice and has therefore committed a tort in the course of his employment.[6] Where each party responsible for a joint publication has an individual right to publish the statement, for example, trustees or members of a committee, each has an independent privilege which is not affected by the malice of one or more of the other joint publishers. If committee man A is malicious and B and C are not, A loses his defence of qualified privilege, but B and C are not liable. These rules were established by the 1964 Court of Appeal decision in *Egger v Chelmsford*.[7] Sometimes, one of the persons sued for the publication is a mere ancillary, for example, a printer or a typist. The law probably now is that such an ancillary publisher may still plead qualified privilege even though all his principals published maliciously, provided that he himself was not actuated by malice.[8]

D. INSTANCES OF QUALIFIED PRIVILEGE

(1) GENERAL PRINCIPLE

All the instances of qualified privilege now to be considered can be subsumed within the one general principle: they exist for 'the common convenience and welfare of society';[9] 'originally and in principle there are not many different kinds of privilege, but rather for all privilege there is the same foundation of the public interest'.[10] The classic statement on the matter is that of PARKE B:[11]

> [The defendant is liable for a defamatory publication] 'unless it is fairly made by a person in the discharge of some public or private duty, whether legal or moral, or in the conduct of his own affairs, in matters where his interest is concerned ...
> If fairly warranted by any reasonable occasion or exigency, and honestly made, such communications are protected for the common convenience and welfare of

---

5 *Baker v Carrick* [1894] 1 QB 838, CA.
6 *Citizens' Life Assurance Co v Brown* [1904] AC 423, HL; *Riddick v Thames Board Mills Ltd* [1977] QB 881, [1977] 3 All ER 677, CA.
7 [1965] 1 QB 248, [1964] 3 All ER 406, which followed *Longdon-Griffiths v Smith* [1951] 1 KB 295, [1950] 2 All ER 662 and *Meekins v Henson* [1964] 1 QB 472, [1962] 1 All ER 899, and overruled *Smith v Streatfeild* [1913] 3 KB 764.
8 This was the view of the majority of the Court of Appeal in *Egger v Chelmsford* who took the bold step of disregarding statements to the contrary of the House of Lords in *Adam v Ward* [1917] AC 309, because their lordships had not heard argument on the point.
9 Per LORD UTHWATT in *Perera v Peiris* [1949] AC 1 at 20, PC.
10 Per PEARSON J in *Webb v Times Publishing Co Ltd* [1960] 2 QB 535 at 563, [1960] 2 All ER 789 at 800.
11 *Toogood v Spyring* (1834) 1 Cr M & R 181 at 193, approved by LORD SHAW in *Adam v Ward* [1917] AC 309 at 349.

society; and the law has not restricted the right to make them within any narrow limits.'

It is convenient to group the examples (and they are examples merely, and not necessarily exhaustive, for the general principle just mentioned is dominant) of qualified privilege as follows: those relating to matters of public interest, those protecting the interest of the publisher, those protecting the person to whom they are published, and those relating to matters of common interest.

(2) PUBLIC INTEREST

It must be made clear that there is no general defence of publication of 'fair information on a matter of public interest'. Legitimate interest in the subject matter of a report is insufficient to create qualified privilege.[12] A newspaper must establish a *duty* to publish to the general public.[13] So no defence of privilege at common law was available when a story was published speculating that the plaintiff was responsible for losses of public money on grants wrongly paid out to North Sea oil companies. A duty to publish matters of speculation and suspicion to the public at large could arise only in exceptional cases, for example, where public safety was endangered.[14]

(a) Reports

(i) *Parliamentary*

Fair and accurate reports of proceedings in Parliament or in committees thereof or a fair summary or sketch of that part of those proceedings which is of special interest,[15] are privileged at common law.[16] *Bona fide* reports of single speeches out of many delivered in a debate will be protected. The printing or broadcasting[17] of copies of, or extracts from, reports,[18] papers, votes or proceedings published by authority of either House of Parliament is privileged.[19]

(ii) *Judicial*

Common Law   The reason for the privilege in respect of judicial reports has been expressed as follows:[20]

> ... as everyone could not be in court, it was for the public benefit that they should be informed of what took place substantially as if they were present.

---

12 The 'public interest' of qualified privilege is narrower in scope than the 'public interest' of fair comment (p 422, post); *Chapman v Ellesmere* [1932] 2 KB 431, CA, points its strictness, which is no doubt explained by the fact that in qualified privilege, unlike fair comment, the defence will succeed although the facts are untrue.
13 *Blackshaw v Lord* [1984] QB 1, [1983] 2 All ER 311, CA.
14 See *Camporese v Parton* (1983) 150 DLR (3d) 208.
15 *Cook v Alexander* [1974] QB 279, [1973] 3 All ER 1037, CA.
16 *Wason v Walter* (1868) LR 4 QB 73.
17 Defamation Act 1952, s 9(1) extends this privilege to those forms of broadcasting to which the Act applies; p 378, ante.
18 Parliamentary Papers Act 1840, s 2.
19 Including blue books and reports of Royal Commissions presented to Parliament: *Mangena v (Edward) Lloyd Ltd* (1908) 98 LT 640, on appeal (1909) 99 LT 824, CA.
20 Per SIR GORELL BARNES P in *Furniss v Cambridge Daily News Ltd* (1907) 23 TLR 705 at 706, CA.

Fair and accurate reports, wherever and whenever published, are privileged. Whether they are fair and accurate is a question for the jury. As would be expected in view of the different reason for this privilege, the 'judicial proceedings' to which the privilege extends are not the same as those 'judicial proceedings', acts done in the course of which are absolutely privileged.[1] Although the tribunal does not perform 'judicial functions' in that narrow sense of the term, reports of its proceedings may be privileged, provided that the public are admitted, and the tribunal is not a mere domestic tribunal such as the Jockey Club.[2] The privilege still applies where the tribunal is merely considering the case in order to discover whether it has jurisdiction even though, in fact, the tribunal has no jurisdiction.[3]

Defamation Act 1952   Section 7 extends qualified privilege to those reports, whether published in a newspaper or broadcast,[4] set out in the Schedule to the Act, but the Act does not protect 'the publication of any matter the publication of which is prohibited by law, or of any matter which is not of public concern and the publication of which is not for the public benefit'. This provision, which does not apply to other qualified privileges, is the same as that contained in the now repealed section 4 of the Law of Libel Amendment Act 1888. There is authority under that Act for the view that both public concern and public benefit must be shown, and that the burden of proof is on the defendant.[5] The *ratio decidendi* of SLESSER LJ, in *Chapman v Ellesmere*[6] was that matters of interest only to a section of the public, eg racing men, are not of public interest: if the expression is so interpreted here, it will seriously restrict some of the scheduled cases. The definition of 'newspaper' is not the same as that for the statutory privilege in respect of newspaper reports of judicial proceedings under the Act of 1888. It is defined, for the present purpose, as 'any paper containing public news or observations thereon, or consisting wholly or mainly of advertisements, which is printed for sale and is published in the United Kingdom either periodically or in parts or numbers at intervals not exceeding 36 days'.[7] This definition raises the same doubts as the other one: whether technical and specialist periodicals or even the *Radio Times* are included. Because of these differences between the common law of qualified privilege and this statutory one, it is the more important to note that any existing common-law privilege is expressly saved by section 7(4).

Statements protected by the Act fall into two groups (a) those privileged without any explanation or contradiction, (b) those privileged subject to explanation or contradiction.

1 See pp 406–7, ante.
2 *Chapman v Ellesmere* [1932] 2 KB 431, [1932] All ER Rep 221, CA. Cf *Allbutt v General Council of Medical Education and Registration* (1889) 23 QBD 400, CA, and see especially LOPES LJ at 410. The privilege applied to foreign courts where the subject-matter was of legitimate interest to the English newspaper-reading public (eg where it was closely connected with the administration of justice in England, as in *Webb v Times Publishing Co* [1960] 2 QB 535, [1960] 2 All ER 789), but not otherwise. And see p 418, post, for a statutory privilege.
3 *Usill v Hales* (1878) 3 CPD 319; it will be obvious that this case is not an authority on absolute privilege for judicial acts done without jurisdiction.
4 This has the same meaning as elsewhere in the Act, p 378, ante.
5 *Kelly v O'Malley* (1889) 6 TLR 62 at 64 (per HUDDLESTON B); *Sharman v Merritt and Hatcher Ltd* (1916) 32 TLR 360.
6 [1932] 2 KB 431 at 469; [1932] All ER Rep 221 at 236, CA.
7 Section 7(5).

Fair and accurate reports privileged without explanation or contradiction

1 Of public legislative proceedings in any part of Her Majesty's Dominions.[8]
2 Of proceedings in public of an international organisation of which the United Kingdom or Her Majesty's Government is a member, or of any international conference to which that government sends a representative.
3 Of proceedings in public of the International Court of Justice or any other judicial or arbitral tribunal deciding matters in dispute between states.
4 Of proceedings before a court exercising jurisdiction throughout any part of Her Majesty's dominions outside the United Kingdom,[9] or of any proceedings before a court-martial held outside the United Kingdom under the Naval Discipline Act, the Army Act or the Air Force Act.
5 Of proceedings in public of a body or person appointed to hold a public inquiry by the government or legislature of any part of Her Majesty's Dominions outside the United Kingdom.[10]

Fair and accurate reports privileged subject to explanation or contradiction   Reports of the following proceedings cease to be privileged if the defendant has unreasonably refused a request[11] by the plaintiff that he should publish in the same newspaper in which (or, in the case of a broadcast, in the manner in which) the original communication was made, a reasonable statement by way of explanation or contradiction.

1 The findings (relating to members or other persons subject to their control) of any associations or committees or governing bodies thereof formed in the United Kingdom for the following purposes and empowered by their constitution to exercise jurisdiction over matters concerning the associations or the conduct of the members or other aforesaid persons:
    a To promote or encourage the exercise of, or interest in, any art, science, religion or learning,
    b To promote or safeguard the interests of any trade, business, industry, or profession or of persons engaged therein,
    c To promote or safeguard the interests of any game, sport or pastime carried on in public.
2 Proceedings at any meeting *bona fide* held in the United Kingdom for a lawful purpose and for the furtherance or discussion of any matter of public concern, whether the admission to the meeting is general or restricted.
3 Proceedings in the United Kingdom of
    a any local authority or committee thereof,[12]
    b any justice or justices of the peace acting otherwise than as a court exercising judicial authority,

---

8 'Dominions' in this Act includes India, Republic of Ireland, and any protected territory, protectorates or trust territory within the meaning of the British Nationality Act 1948; Defamation Act 1952, Schedule, Part III, para 14.
9 Presumably, whether the public is admitted or not, subject, of course, to proof of public interest or concern, p 416, ante.
10 Notices or advertisements published by or on the authority of any court within the United Kingdom or officer of such a court are similarly privileged by the section.
11 An aggressive letter from the plaintiff's solicitor that unless an apology is made a writ will be issued is not a sufficiently 'special request' for this purpose: *Khan v Ahmed* [1957] 2 QB 149, [1957] 2 All ER 385.
12 By the Public Bodies (Admission to Meetings) Act 1960, s 1(5), copies of the agenda of meetings of local authorities which are supplied to the press or members of the public attending the meeting, are also the subject of qualified privilege.

c any commission, tribunal, committee or person appointed for the purposes of any inquiry by statute or by the Administration,

d any person appointed by a local authority to hold a local inquiry in pursuance of a statute,

e any other tribunal exercising statutory functions,

provided that the admission of press and public to the particular meeting or sitting is not denied.

4 Proceedings at a general meeting of a public company.

5 A copy of a fair and accurate report or summary of any notice or other matter issued for the information of the public by or on behalf of any government department[13] officer of state, local authority, or chief of police.[14]

(b) Registers

The publication of a fair and accurate copy of, or extract from, any register kept pursuant to statute, and which the public are entitled to inspect, is privileged at common law.[15] The Defamation Act 1952 subject to the same conditions as those already dealt with, gives the same protection without need for explanation or contradiction.[16] Thus, trade protection societies may publish in their periodicals extracts from the registers of judgment debtors in the County Courts, and from other like registers giving information about the financial status of persons.

(c) Misconduct of public officers

The duty of a member of the public to bring to the notice of the proper authority any misconduct or neglect of duty on the part of public officers is recognised by according to such complaints a qualified privilege.[17] When the defendant *bona fide* complains to the wrong official he is not privileged.[18] A defendant who first addresses his complaint about misconduct to his member of Parliament will almost certainly be privileged.[19] It may also be assumed that the public officers will for the present purpose include the personnel of nationalised industries. But will it embrace the staff of privatised public services?

13 *Blackshaw v Lord* [1984] QB 1, [1983] 2 All ER 311 (covers oral as well as written information preferably given on the initiative of the department rather than elicited by a journalist's interrogation. Assumptions and speculation by the journalist clearly fell beyond the subsection).

14 *Boston v W S Bagshaw & Sons* [1966] 2 All ER 906, CA (police arranged television broadcast regarding theft of pigs; held to be privileged within the Act).

15 *Fleming v Newton* (1848) 1 HL Cas 363.

16 Schedule, Part 1, para 6. Why this statutory protection is needed is not clear.

17 E g *Harrison v Bush* (1856) 5 E & B 344 (to Home Secretary about county magistrate). But see *Blackshaw v Lord* (supra) (complaint concerning suspicions must be made to the proper authority and not the public at large unless public safety is at risk).

18 *Hebditch v MacIlwaine* [1894] 2 QB 54, CA; *Beach v Freeson* [1971] 2 All ER 854. This harsh rule may be compared with the *dictum* of LORD ATKINSON in *London Association for Protection of Trade v Greenland* [1916] 2 AC 15 at 34, HL that one who answers an inquiry in the mistaken *bona fide* belief that the inquirer had a legitimate interest, is privileged.

19 *R v Rule* [1937] 2 KB 375, [1937] 2 All ER 772.

(d) Statements by way of help in discovering criminals

Information given to the police[20] in order to detect crime is privileged.[1] Statements made by policemen in the course of their inquiries into suspected crimes are presumably also privileged.

(3) INTEREST OF THE PUBLISHER

Just as self-defence and protection of property are defences in torts affecting the person and property, so also is a statement made to protect or advance the defendant's interests a matter of qualified privilege in defamation.[2] For instance, a creditor may write to an auctioneer to protect his security.[3] A man who replied to a letter demanding payment of fees for medical services to his wife (who died from scarlet fever contracted in her confinement): 'I shall never pay him unless the law compels me, and that I do not fancy it can, as I could more easily indict Dr S for manslaughter' was held to be privileged.[4] He may take reasonable steps to collect money owing to him,[5] warn his servants of the bad character of their associates,[6] and reply to attacks on his reputation.[7]

(4) INTEREST OF OTHERS

The analogy here is with the defence of the person of others (in respect of torts to the person and property), which is recognised as a defence in certain cases. There is a privilege to publish in order to protect the interests of another, where the publication is needed for the protection of that other. As with defence of the person of another, the defendant must show that he ought in the circumstances to have endeavoured to protect that other—or, as it is styled, that he has a legal, social or moral duty to publish. If the duty is imposed by statute, he has, of course, the general defence of statutory authority.[8] In other cases, however, there is usually no such legally enforceable duty: the question is, in effect, whether in the circumstances it was reasonable that the defendant should interfere by making the statement complained of.

The situations of fact under this head are endless, and no list will be attempted. Answers to confidential inquiries about servants,[9] supplying information about credit,[10] protection by a solicitor of his client's interests,[11] a

20 But not to the wife of the accused; *Wenman v Ash* (1853) 13 CB 836.
1 *Padmore v Lawrence* (1840) 11 Ad & El 380.
2 *Toogood v Spyring* (1834) 1 Cr M & R 181 at 193 (per PARKE B).
3 *Blackmam v Pugh* (1846) 2 CB 611.
4 *Stevens v Kitchener* (1887) 4 TLR 159.
5 *Winstanley v Bampton* [1943] KB 319, [1943] 1 All ER 661.
6 *Somerville v Hawkins* (1851) 10 CB 583.
7 *Laughton v Bishop of Sodor & Man* (1872) LR 4 PC 495. But may a representative of the press, theatre, or other section of the community, create a privilege by replying to an attack on that section as a whole by the plaintiff? No, held DIXON J, in *Penton v Calwell* (1945) 70 CLR 219, but his decision was reversed by the High Court of Australia (full court) on the ground that the newspaper of the defendant newspaper proprietor had itself been attacked by the plaintiff.
8 Eg *Moore v Canadian Pacific SS Co* [1945] 1 All ER 128 (duty of captain under Merchant Shipping Act 1894 to record in the ship's log details of all desertions from ship).
9 *Kelly v Partington* (1833) 4 B & Ad 700.
10 *London Association for Protection of Trade v Greenlands Ltd* [1916] 2 AC 15, HL.
11 Cf *Baker v Carrick* [1894] 1 QB 838 at 841 (per LOPES LJ), CA.

host informing his guest of suspicions about the latter's servant,[12] are typical examples. A member of her family may warn a lady about the character of her fiancé,[13] but the privilege stops short of protecting idle gossip or officious intermeddling by strangers.[14] *Watt v Longsdon* is a much-cited case on this point:[15]

> A company director was held to be privileged in passing on to the chairman a report that an employee was associating with another woman and otherwise misconducting himself during his employment overseas, but he was not protected in informing the wife of the employee, although she undoubtedly had an interest in receiving it.

(5) COMMON INTEREST

There are cases of privilege based on interest where the public is not concerned, and where neither publisher nor a third party has a sufficiently protectible interest for the case to be brought within any of the preceding groups. These may be styled matters of 'common interest'.

There is, for instance, such a common interest between employer and employees in the misconduct of a particular employee, as *Hunt v Great Northern Ry Co* illustrates:[16]

> The defendants posted up a circular in such of their premises as would be frequented by their employees, stating (*inter alia*) that the plaintiff had been dismissed for neglect of duty. The privilege of common interest was held to extend to the defendants.

A bishop replying before an assembly of his clergy to an attack on him in the legislature,[17] communications within a family on matters affecting the welfare of a member of that family,[18] a letter by a parishioner to the bishop about an incumbent,[19] a report of a member of a trade protection society to its secretary about the trading conduct of another member,[20] speeches by a company shareholder at a shareholders' meeting,[1] or a trustee at a friendly society meeting,[2] a statement made by a creditor to another creditor about their debtor,[3] an invigilator informing the examinees of cheating by one of them:[4] these samples chosen at random show the range of matters privileged because they are of common interest.

In one respect the scope of this privilege has been curtailed by the Defamation Act 1952, section 10 of which provides that publications, even to a qualified voter, by or on behalf of a candidate at a parliamentary or local

---

12 *Stuart v Bell* [1891] 2 QB 341, CA.
13 *Todd v Hawkins* (1837) 8 C & P 88.
14 *Coxhead v Richards* (1846) 2 CB 569.
15 [1930] 1 KB 130, CA.
16 [1891] 2 QB 189, CA.
17 *Laughton v Bishop of Sodor and Man* (1872) LR 4 PC 495.
18 *Todd v Hawkins* (1837) 8 C & P 88.
19 *James v Boston* (1845) 5 LTOS 152.
20 *White v Batey & Co Ltd* (1892) 8 TLR 698.
 1 *Parsons v Surgey* (1864) 4 F & F 247.
 2 *Longdon-Griffiths v Smith* [1951] 1 KB 295, [1950] 2 All ER 662.
 3 *Spill v Maule* (1869) LR 4 Exch 232.
 4 *Bridgman v Stockdale* [1953] 1 All ER 1166.

government election are not privileged on the ground that they are material to a question in issue in the election.[5]

SECTION 6.   FAIR COMMENT

This defence may be defined as follows:

criticism of matters of public interest, in the form of comment upon true or privileged statements of fact, such comment being made honestly by a person who did not believe the statements to be untrue and who was not otherwise actuated by malice.

A. MATTERS OF PUBLIC INTEREST

The defence covers the public conduct of people in public offices,[6] but not their private conduct except in so far as it throws light on whether they possess those qualities, such as integrity and honesty, essential to a man in public life.[7] Matters of government and public administration,[8] including local government, are[9] within its scope. The management of institutions of substantial public concern, such as religious institutions, is also a matter for fair comment.[10]

Anything submitted to the public for its appraisal is of public interest. Books,[11] articles in periodicals and newspapers,[12] plays,[13] radio broadcasts (even themselves being film criticisms),[14] are examples. The work of an architect,[15] the performance of actors in public entertainments,[16] are also within the defence.

Any other circumstances which may fairly be said to invite comment is also within its scope. Traders who publish handbills,[17] or those who issue public advertisements, invite comment on them. How far the quality of goods offered for sale to the public is *ipso facto* the object of fair comment, important though the question is, remains undecided: it would be artificially restrictive if the answer depended on the extent of the manufacturer's advertising campaign.

---

5 *Braddock v Bevins* [1948] 1 KB 580, [1948] 1 All ER 450, CA, must now be read in the light of this section. And see *Plummer v Charman* [1962] 3 All ER 823, CA.

6 *Seymour v Butterworth* (1862) 3 F & F 372 (Recorder and MP).

7 At 382 (per COCKBURN CJ).

8 Eg *Henwood v Harrison* (1872) LR 7 CP 606 (the method by which defendant converted a naval vessel).

9 *Purcell v Sowler* (1887) 2 CPD 215.

10 *Kelly v Tinling* (1865) LR 1 QB 699.

11 *Thomas v Bradbury, Agnew & Co Ltd* [1906] 2 KB 627, CA.

12 *Kemsley v Foot* [1952] AC 345, [1952] 1 All ER 501, HL.

13 *Merivale v Carson* (1887) 20 QBD 275, CA.

14 *Turner v Metro-Goldyn-Mayer Pictures Ltd* [1950] 1 All ER 449, HL.

15 *Soane v Knight* (1827) Mood & M 74.

16 *Dibdin v Swan* (1793) 1 Esp 27; *Cooney v Edeveain* (1897) 14 TLR 34, CA; *London Artists Ltd v Littler* [1969] 2 QB 375, [1969] 2 All ER 193, CA. *Cornwell v Myskow* [1987] 2 All ER 504, [1987] 1 WLR 630, CA.

17 *Paris v Levy* (1860) 9 CBNS 342.

B. COMMENT ON TRUE FACTS

The rules relating to this part of the defence are, in particular, unnecessarily complicated by many technical rules. It is important to distinguish this defence from that of justification. Fair comment is available only in respect of expressions of opinion: justification is available in respect of both facts and opinion—a defendant may be unable to plead fair comment because it is not a matter of public interest. In fair comment, it is not necessary to prove the truth of the comment, but that the opinion was honestly held; if justification is pleaded in respect of matters of opinion, the defendant must prove not merely that he honestly held the views expressed, but that they were correct views. Thus, if the statement complained of was: 'X's speech last night was inconsistent with his professions of Socialism', then, on a plea of justification, the defendant would have to prove that it was inconsistent; in fair comment, merely that the defendant honestly held this opinion on X's speech.

Obviously, in many statements, it will be very difficult to unravel fact from comment. Yet they must be separated in due course by the court, for the defence of fair comment only lies on facts which are proved true, and on statements of fact not proved true but which were made on a privileged occasion.[18] If the facts are untrue, the defendant will not succeed in fair comment merely by proving that his comment is honestly made. Thus, a defendant who implied that a play was adulterous could not rely on this as comment where the court found as a fact that adultery was not dealt with in the play.[19] The words 'X is a disgrace' lead the hearer to believe that they are based on unstated facts. Therefore the defendant cannot plead fair comment in respect of those words alone. If, however, he had added 'he has deserted his wife and family' then the original words would probably be regarded as a comment on the stated facts.

The procedural complexities are best understood by considering how the defendant may plead. He has always been reluctant to tackle the difficult task of separating fact from comment in the defamatory statement. He used to try to avoid that by a 'rolled-up' plea; in so far as the words are fact they are true, and in so far as they are comment they are fair and on a matter of public interest. But now if he makes a 'rolled-up' plea he is required to give particulars of which matters complained of by the plaintiff are facts.[20] This new requirement applies only to a 'rolled-up' plea, so that that plea is no longer used extensively.[1] Instead he pleads simply fair comment. That plea carries the implication that the comment is based on facts which are true. Those facts need not be in the statement itself, but the plaintiff can insist on the defendant giving particulars of those facts.[2] The House of Lords in

---

18 *Mangena v Wright* [1909] 2 KB 958; *Grech v Odhams Press Ltd* [1958] 1 QB 310, [1957] 3 All ER 556, on appeal, [1958] 2 QB 275, [1958] 2 All ER 462, CA. Until this case it had seemed that one might limit the rule to conclusions in a privileged report, but this case decides that any untrue facts contained in a privileged statement (however false and whether they are antecedent facts or the findings of a report) can be the subject of fair comment. The facts must exist at the time of the comment: *Cohen v Daily Telegraph Ltd* [1968] 2 All ER 407, CA.

19 *Merivale v Carson* (1887) 20 QBD 275, CA.

20 RSC O 82, r 3(2).

 1 *Lord v Sunday Telegraph Ltd* [1971] 1 QB 235, [1970] 3 All ER 504, CA; and holding that the rule did not apply to a plea of fair comment.

 2 *Cunningham-Howie v F W Dimbleby & Sons Ltd* [1951] 1 KB 360, [1950] 2 All ER 882, CA; but under this plea he cannot insist on defendant identifying the facts in the allegation complained of: *Lord v Sunday Telegraph Ltd* supra.

Kemsley v Foot decided that if the facts on which the comment is based, though not mentioned in the alleged defamatory statement, are adequately pointed to or, as in the case of a book review, accessible to the recipient of the statement, the defendant may set out those facts in his pleadings and base a defence of fair comment on them.[3] The facts were:

> The defendants attacked a newspaper by publishing an article headed 'Lower than Kemsley'. Kemsley, a newspaper proprietor not connected with the newspaper attacked, sued the defendants. The House of Lords held that the substratum of fact, viz, that Kemsley was responsible for the Kemsley Press was sufficiently clear, and that a defence of fair comment would succeed if an honest man would have complained that the Kemsley Press was low.

This case also established that 'where the facts relied on to justify the comment are contained only in the particulars it is not incumbent on the defendant to prove the truth of every fact so stated in order to establish his plea of fair comment, but ... he must establish sufficient facts to support the comment to the satisfaction of the jury.'[4]

The need to extend this last rule to cases where the facts are contained in the defamatory statement itself was recognised in section 6 of the Defamation Act 1952 which provides:

> ... a defence of fair comment shall not fail by reason only that the truth of every allegation of fact is not proved if the expression of opinion is fair comment having regard to such of the facts alleged or referred to in the words complained of as are proved.[5]

This provision has been held not to afford a defence where facts on which the comment is based materially add to the harm to reputation—in that event the defendant will still have to justify those facts; the defence of fair comment will not extend to them.[6]

An imputation of corrupt or dishonourable motives will render the comment unfair, unless such imputation is an inference which a fair-minded man might reasonably draw from such facts, and also represents the honest opinion of the writer.[7]

---

3 [1952] AC 345, [1952] 1 All ER 501, HL.
4 At 362 (per LORD TUCKER).
5 The Faulks Report, para 172, takes the view that where a plaintiff relies only on part of the defendant's statement, the defendant cannot support his defence of fair comment by justifying other facts in his statement. It is possible, however, that the courts could pray in aid *Kemsley v Foot* supra, to avoid that undesirable conclusion. Where separate allegations have a common 'sting' O'CONNOR LJ has suggested that it is permissible in fair comment, as it is in justification, to rely on other uncomplained of parts of the relevant statement, *Polly Peck (Holding) plc v Trelford* [1986] 2 All ER 84 at 102.
6 So held in *Truth (NZ) Ltd v Avery* [1959] NZLR 274, on an identical New Zealand statute; and approved *obiter* in *Broadway Approvals Ltd v Odhams Press Ltd* [1965] 2 All ER 523, CA.
7 *Campbell v Spottiswoode* (1863) 3 B & S 769, where COCKBURN CJ, variously uses the expressions 'well-founded', 'not without cause', and 'not without foundation'; *Walker v Hodgson* [1909] 1 KB 239 at 253, per BUCKLEY LJ, approved in *Harris v Lubbock* (1971) Times, 21 October, CA; and see [1971], CA Transcript 346A.

C. COMMENT MUST BE HONEST AND NOT ACTUATED BY MALICE

There is a *prima facie* case of fair comment only when the comment is shown to be one which the defendant made honestly.[8] The matter has been lucidly put by LORD ESHER as follows:[9]

> Every latitude must be given to opinion and to prejudice, and then an ordinary set of men with ordinary judgment must say whether any fair[10] man would have made such a comment on the work. .... Mere exaggeration, or even gross exaggeration, would not make the comment unfair. However wrong the opinion expressed may be in point of truth, or however prejudiced the writer, it may still be within the prescribed limit. The question which the jury must consider is this—would any fair man, however prejudiced he may be, however exaggerated or obstinate his views, have said that which this criticism has said of the work which is criticised?'

When assessing whether the comment could honestly have been made by a fair-minded man, evidence of the plaintiff's standing and reputation among his fellows at the time of publication is clearly relevant. Evidence of enhanced reputation by the time of the trial is not. The vital issue is whether at the time of publication the comment could be considered fair.[11]

Even if the defendant survives this objective test of 'fair comment' his defence will still fail if he is shown to have been actuated by malice in the making of the comment.[12] As with qualified privilege, there is 'malice' if the defendant had no genuine belief in the truth of his comment.[13] If the purpose of the maker of the fair comment is not to give the public the benefit of his comment but to injure the plaintiff, then the defence does not lie.[14] The defendant 'is the person in whose motives the plaintiff in the libel action is concerned, and if he, the person sued, is proved to have allowed his view to be distorted by malice, it is quite immaterial that somebody else might without malice have written an equally damnatory criticism.'[15] 'It is of course, possible for a person to have a spite against another and yet to bring a perfectly dispassionate judgment to bear upon his literary merits, but, given the existence of malice, it must be for the jury to say whether it has warped his judgment'.[16]

If a servant is malicious so as to lose his defence of fair comment then in

---

8 Per FLETCHER MOULTON LJ, in *Plymouth Mutual Co-operative and Industrial Society Ltd v Traders' Publishing Association Ltd* [1906] 1 KB 403 at 418, CA. In *Cherneskey v Armadale Publishers* [1979] 1 SCR 1067, the Supreme Court of Canada held that when a newspaper published a letter containing a comment with which it disagreed, even though the correspondent might have the defence of fair comment, the newspaper did not. *Gatley* 730 disagrees, maintaining that if the maker of the statement believed the comment other participants in the publication have the defence.

9 *Merivale v Carson* (1887) 20 QBD 275, at pp 280–1, CA; a comment may be unfair because a material fact was omitted from the defamatory statement: *Dowling v Time Inc* (1954) Times, 25 June, CA.

10 This *dictum* was approved by LORD PORTER in *Turner v Metro-Goldwyn-Mayer Pictures Ltd* [1950] 1 All ER 449, except for the substitution of 'honest' for 'fair'.

11 *Cornwell v Myskow* [1987] 2 All ER 504, [1987] 1 WLR 630.

12 The separateness of these two matters was emphasised in *McQuire v Western Morning News Co* [1908] 2 KB 100, CA.

13 RSC O 82, r 6 prohibits interrogatories as to the defendant's source of information or grounds of belief where qualified privilege or fair comment is pleaded.

14 *Merivale v Carson* (1887) 20 QBD 275 at 281–2 (per LORD ESHER).

15 *Thomas v Bradbury, Agnew & Co Ltd* [1906] 2 KB 627, CA at 638 (per COLLINS MR).

16 At 642.

accordance with the ordinary principles of vicarious liability, his employer will also be deprived of the defence. It will be seen later that in defamation vicarious liability may extend to a principal-agent relationship.[17] Therefore the publisher of a periodical could not establish fair comment when the writer of a book review was himself malicious—the court found that the writer was an agent.[18] On the other hand, the publisher's defence of fair comment is not affected when the writer of a letter in the correspondence column of his newspaper is malicious.[19] Probably a joint publisher does not lose his defence of fair comment because of the malice of another joint publisher unless he is vicariously liable for that other.[20]

D. BURDEN OF PROOF AND THE FUNCTIONS OF JUDGE AND JURY

The defendant has the onus of proving that the matter is of public concern, that the facts on which the comment is based are true, and that the comment is such as an honest man might make. The plaintiff must then prove that the defendant was actuated by malice in publishing the matter. It is for the judge to decide whether the matter commented on is one of public interest.[1] LORD PORTER has said:[2]

> It is for the jury in a proper case to determine what is comment and what is fact; but a prerequisite to their right is that the words are capable of being a statement of a fact or facts. It is for the judge alone to decide whether they are so capable, and whether his ruling is right or wrong is a matter of law for the decision of an appellate tribunal.

The defence of fair comment resembles that of qualified privilege. In each case, the defendant, in order to raise a *prima facie* defence, must establish certain facts, and each defence fails if it is shown that the defendant was 'actuated by malice' in publishing the statement.

SECTION 7.   APOLOGY

The offer or the making of an apology is not at common law a defence, although it may be given in evidence in mitigation of damages. Section 2 of the Libel Act 1843, however, enacts:

> In an action for a libel contained in any public newspaper or other periodical publication, it shall be competent to the defendant to plead that such libel was inserted in such newspaper or other periodical publication without actual malice, and without gross negligence, and that before the commencement of the action, or at the earliest opportunity afterwards, he inserted in such newspaper or other

17 P 449, post.
18 *Gros v Crook* (1969) 113 Sol Jo 408, doubted by Faulks Report, para 272(a).
19 *Lyon v Daily Telegraph Ltd* [1943] 1 KB 746, [1943] 2 All ER 316, CA. Contra *Gatley*, § 730.
20 In *Gros v Crook*, supra the court held that it would not have found the defendant liable for the writer's malice had he not been vicariously liable. To the same effect LORD DENNING in *Egger v Chelmsford* [1965] 1 QB 248 at 265; contra DAVIES LJ at 269, and *Gatley* § 787.
 1 *South Hetton Coal Co v North-Eastern News Association* [1894] 1 QB 133 at 141 (per LOPES LJ), CA.
 2 *Turner v Metro-Goldwyn-Mayer Pictures Ltd* [1950] 1 All ER 449 at 461, HL.

periodical publication a full apology for the said libel, or, if the newspaper or periodical publication ... should be ordinarily published at intervals exceeding one week, had offered to publish the said apology in any newspaper or periodical publication to be selected by the plaintiff in such action.

Every such defence must be accompanied by a payment of money into court by way of amends.[3] The issues of malice, gross negligence, and the adequacy of the apology are to be decided separately by the jury.

This defence is very little used, for two reasons. If the defendant fails in his plea, the jury must assess the damages without regard to the payment into court, and the plaintiff is entitled to a judgment for the sum awarded by the jury and costs even though the sum awarded does not exceed the sum paid into court. Secondly, it is better for a defendant to pay into court under the general provisions of O 22, for, by virtue of that rule, if the award of the jury does not exceed the amount paid into court, judgment will be given for the defendant together with (unless the judge in the exercise of his discretion otherwise orders) his costs since the date of the payment into court.

SECTION 8. DAMAGES

The main function of the tort of defamation is to compensate the plaintiff for his loss of reputation: ie the extent to which he is held in less esteem and respect and suffers loss of goodwill and association.[4]

Damages for this loss of reputation are at large in respect of libel and slander actionable *per se*, and the principles ordinarily applicable to damages at large apply.[5] Accordingly, by way of parasitic damages compensation may be given for insult or injury to feelings.[6] Likewise, circumstances of aggravation and mitigation are important. Damages may be aggravated by such matters as the mode, circumstances and extent of publication and the conduct of the defendant from publication to verdict.[7] The defendant's belief in the truth of his statements,[8] the fairness of his reports,[9] his being provoked by the plaintiff;[10] all these may mitigate damages. Where partial justification is proved while the defendant may be unable to prove sufficient facts to establish justification at common law or to bring himself within section 5 of the Defamation Act, the defendant may be able to rely on the facts proved to reduce damages,[11] in an exceptional case almost to vanishing point.[12] Persistence in an unsubstantiated plea of justification will lead to a higher award of damages. Exemplary damages may be awarded in one circumstance,

---

3 Libel Act 1845, s 2.
4 The best judicial survey is in the judgment of DEVLIN LJ, in *Dingle v Associated Newspapers Ltd* [1961] 2 QB 162, [1961] 1 All ER 897, CA, affirmed [1964] AC 371, [1962] 2 All ER 737, HL.
5 See p 464, post.
6 *Goslin v Corry* (1844) 7 Man & G 342; *Ley v Hamilton* (1935) 153 LT 384, HL per LORD ATKIN at 386. Are damages recoverable for injuries to the plaintiff's feelings caused by publishing the libel to him? *Hayward v Thompson* [1982] QB 47.
7 *Praed v Graham* (1889) 24 QBD 53.
8 *Bryce v Rusden* (1868) 2 TLR 435; *Forsdike v Stone* (1868) LR 3 CP 607 (*bona fide* mistake of identity).
9 *Smith v Scott* (1847) 2 Car & Kir 580; *East v Chapman* (1827) Mood & M 46.
10 *Moore v Oastler* (1836) 1 Mood & R 451 n.
11 *Atkinson v Fitzwalter* [1987] 1 All ER 483, [1987] 1 WLR 201.
12 *Pamplin v Express Newspapers* (1985) 129 Sol Jo 190 ($\frac{1}{2}$p!).

namely, when the defendant calculated that the money to be made out of his wrongdoing would probably exceed the compensation payable for the defamation, and did so knowing that his conduct was illegal or recklessly disregarding the illegality.[13] Where several plaintiffs are libelled the amount of exemplary damages may properly take account of the fact that the defendant has libelled more than one person, but the total should not exceed the total representing a proper sum by way of punishment for the defendant.[14]

Sometimes the loss of reputation will occasion pecuniary loss, eg loss of business, and that loss, in addition to general damages, will be recoverable.

Actual damage must be proved in the case of slanders not actionable per se. It is doubtful whether any damages other than actual damages are recoverable for those slanders:[15] if the damages are so restricted, the rules of the preceding paragraph do not apply.

Evidence of the bad reputation of the plaintiff will be a ground for mitigation of damages—a reputation already lost is of less value. The rules governing the evidence of reputation are complex, and, in practice, a trial often resolves itself into a tactical battle over this issue. The governing principle is that general evidence only (and this after prior notice and particulars have been given)[16] is permitted; evidence of specific facts to show the disposition of the plaintiff is not admissible.[17] The court is concerned with the esteem in which the plaintiff is in fact held, with his established reputation,[18] not with his actual character nor with the reputation which he deserves. Where a newspaper published on a privileged occasion extracts from a parliamentary report and then embellished this report with details not found in the report, it could not mitigate its damage by asserting that the plaintiff's reputation was already tarnished by the privileged publication of the parliamentary report.[19] In assessing damage to reputation it is the plaintiff's reputation at the time of the trial which is in issue where the defendant has persisted in a plea of justification.[20] Of course, the ordinary rule of evidence applies: that if the plaintiff gives evidence he may be cross-examined as to credit, although evidence to rebut his answers is forbidden. The jury should be directed to disregard this cross-examination when fixing damages.[1]

---

13 *Cassell & Co Ltd v Broome* [1972] AC 1027, [1972] 1 All ER 801, HL.
14 *Riches v News Group Newspapers Ltd* [1986] QB 256, [1985] 2 All ER 845, CA.
15 Spencer Bower *Actionable Defamation* (1st edn) p 174, states that no other damages may be given; there is an *obiter dictum* by WILLIAMS J, in *Brown v Smith* (1853) 13 CB 596 to the same effect. In *Dixon v Smith* (1860) 5 H & N 450 the plaintiff doctor claimed a guinea, being the loss of a particular patient in consequence of the slander, together with damages for general decline in business, and deterioration of goodwill. After denying on the grounds of remoteness such general damages as resulted from repetition of the slander, the court held the damages not to be limited to the guinea. Whether the further damages were at large, or some non-remote business loss other than the loss of the patient is not clear, but an observation by MARTIN B at 452 (*arguendo*), supports the latter interpretation.
16 O 82, r 7.
17 *Scott v Sampson* (1882) 8 QBD 491, Div Ct; *Hobbs v Tinling* [1929] 2 KB 1, CA.
18 *Plato Films Ltd v Speidel* [1961] AC 1090, [1961] 1 All ER 876, HL, approving *Scott v Sampson* and *Hobbs v Tinling* supra.
19 *Associated Newspapers Ltd v Dingle* [1964] AC 371, [1962] 2 All ER 737, HL.
20 *Cornwell v Myskow* [1987] 2 All ER 504 at 508, CA.
 1 *Hobbs v Tinling* supra.

SECTION 9. INJUNCTION

Plaintiffs in defamation actions often seek interlocutory injunctions as soon as they have served the writ so as to prevent further publication. The courts, conscious of the need not to interfere unduly with press freedom, normally do not grant such interim injunctions when the case is contested and the plaintiff is unable to show that a defence of justification, fair comment or privilege is most likely to fail at the eventual trial.[2] But where the Attorney-General sought an injunction to prevent further publication of an alleged contempt, it was said that in that instance the interest in the protection of justice (as perceived by the Attorney-General) prevailed over the interest in free speech.[3] The courts will readily grant injunctions to successful plaintiffs where further publication is apprehended.[4]

2 *Bonnard v Perryman* [1891] 2 Ch 269, CA. For recent illustrations see *Crest Homes Ltd v Ascott* [1980] FSR 396; and *Harakas v Baltic Mercantile and Shipping Exchange Ltd* [1982] 2 All ER 701, CA; *Al-Fayed v The Observer Ltd* (1986) Times, 14 July.
3 *A-G v News Group Newspapers Ltd* [1987] QB 1, [1986] 2 All ER 833, CA; and see *Gulf Oil (GB) Ltd v Page* [1987] Ch 327, [1987] 3 All ER 14 (rule in *Bonnard v Perryman* (supra) does not apply to an action for conspiracy).
4 *Monson v Tussauds Ltd* [1894] 1 QB 671, CA.

Part VII

Misuse of process

CONTENTS

Chapter 26

Misuse of process

The nature of the motive with which an act is done does not in general make that act unlawful and a tort.[1] The torts discussed in this chapter represent exceptions to that general rule. The essence of the wrongful conduct becomes the misuse of a right conferred on individuals for the public good. Abuse of that right for private benefit or other improper ends gives rise to tortious liability.

SECTION 1. MALICIOUS INSTITUTION OF PROCEEDINGS, ESPECIALLY MALICIOUS PROSECUTION

The torts considered in this section are concerned with protecting the interest in freedom from unjustifiable litigation. Obviously, this function comes very close to that of defamation, viz the protection of reputation. The difference is that institution of proceedings will sometimes cause pecuniary loss or loss of personal liberty without damaging reputation—when that happens, there may be malicious prosecution but there cannot be defamation.

It is also necessary to distinguish this branch of the law of the torts from false imprisonment. It is of the essence of false imprisonment that the initial act in itself is wrongful, for example, the wrongful use of a form of judicial process when an arrest is made upon a warrant which is in fact invalid. Malicious prosecution presupposes that the proper procedural formalities have been carried out, and is concerned with the purposes for which they were used. Obviously, false imprisonment does not cover all the ground traversed by malicious prosecution, because interference with freedom of movement is required in false imprisonment.

It is a tort maliciously and without reasonable and probable cause to initiate against another judicial proceedings which terminate in favour of that other and which result in damage to his reputation, person, freedom or property.

A. INSTITUTION OF PROCEEDINGS

The defendant must have been 'actively instrumental' in instigating the proceedings.[2] If he merely states the facts as he believes them to a policeman[3] or a magistrate,[4] he is not responsible for any proceedings which might ensue

1 *Bradford Corp v Pickles* [1895] AC 587; *Allen v Flood* [1898] AC 1.
2 *Danby v Beardsley* (1880) 43 LT 603 at 604 (per LOPES J). In *Evans v London Hospital Medical College* [1981] 1 All ER 715, it was held that a hospital which provided pathology reports for the police did not institute proceedings.
3 *Danby v Beardsley* (1880) 43 LT 603.
4 *Cohen v Morgan* (1825) 6 Dow & Ry KB 8.

433

as a result of action taken by such policeman or magistrate on his own initiative. It is enough if the defendant has set the prosecution in motion before a body which has jurisdiction to deal with it.[5] Charging the plaintiff will no doubt constitute setting the prosecution in motion. The legal adviser of a litigant may be deemed to be responsible for the prosecution where he does more than merely advise the litigant in good faith.[6] Although the defendant has properly commenced proceedings, if, during their continuance, he learns of facts which do not justify him in carrying on with them, he is liable if he proceeds with the suit.[7]

B. NATURE OF PROCEEDINGS

It might have been expected that the 'damage' requirement of this tort would be satisfied whenever the plaintiff proved that he suffered harm to his person or his reputation or suffered pecuniary loss as a non-remote consequence of the wrong. This is not so.

In 1698 HOLT CJ delivered a judgment in *Savile v Roberts*[8] which required that the proceedings must be such as to inflict one of the following: '1. The damage to a man's fame, as if the matter whereof he is accused be scandalous ... 2. ... such [damages] as are done to the person; as where a man is put in danger to lose his life, or limb, or liberty ... 3. Damage to a man's property, as where he is forced to expend his money in necessary charges, to acquit himself of the crime of which he is accused.' Since that time the courts have regarded this judgment as marking the outer limits of the tort.

The most scholarly survey of this judicial approach has been made by DIPLOCK J in *Berry v British Transport Commission*:[9]

> Quarter Sessions allowed an appeal by the plaintiff against her conviction for pulling the communication cord while travelling on a train and awarded her 15 guineas costs. After allowing for the 15 guineas she was £64 2s. out of pocket through defending these proceedings. She then sued the defendants who had prosecuted her unsuccessfully.

He showed that in HOLT CJ's judgment the damage to fame had to be a necessary and natural consequence of the charge itself, and that, as regards the second head, actual loss of liberty had to be proved; it was not enough that a charge exposed the plaintiff to imprisonment if he were convicted. Subsequently, the Court of Appeal[10] had mistakenly thought there would be damage under the second head if the crime charged were punishable by imprisonment even though the plaintiff had not in fact been imprisoned. DIPLOCK J held that to accuse the plaintiff of pulling a communication cord neither led to her imprisonment nor necessarily defamed her.

---

5 *Mohamed Amin v Jogendra Kumar Bannerjee* [1947] AC 322, PC, as explained in *Casey v Automatic Renault Canada Ltd* (1966) 54 DLR (2d) 600 Sup Ct Canada.
6 *Johnson v Emerson* (1871) LR 6 Exch 329.
7 Per LORD GODDARD CJ (*obiter*), in *Tims v John Lewis & Co Ltd* [1951] 2 KB 459 at 472, [1951] 1 All ER 814, CA; rvd sub nom *John Lewis & Co Ltd v Tims* [1952] AC 676, [1952] 1 All ER 1203, HL.
8 [1698] 1 Ld Raym 374.
9 [1961] 1 QB 149, [1960] 3 All ER 322; on appeal [1962] 1 QB 306, [1961] 3 All ER 65, CA.
10 *Rayson v South London Tramways Co* [1893] 2 QB 304; *Wiffen v Bailey and Romford UDC* [1915] 1 KB 600.

She further alleged that her £64 2s. legal expenses were sufficient damage. The Court of Appeal had previously held[11] that in a civil action (a winding-up petition) the difference between the actual costs incurred and the party and party costs awarded were not damages for the purpose of this tort, although it found for the plaintiff on the ground that a winding-up petition, like a bankruptcy petition, necessarily harms the reputation and credit of a trader. The Court of Appeal based its decision on costs on the flimsy ground that the court in the original action would have awarded the plaintiff all the costs which she deserved. DIPLOCK J had refused to distinguish criminal and civil costs, and consequently held that the plaintiff had failed to show damage under any of HOLT CJ's three heads. The Court of Appeal now reversed DIPLOCK J by holding that the plaintiff's costs amounted to sufficient damage. DEVLIN LJ demonstrated conclusively that the costs awarded to a plaintiff in a civil action were not a complete indemnity for his expenses of litigation, and had the matter been *res integra* he would have welcomed the abandonment of that fiction. Because there is no assumption that the successful defendant in criminal cases will be awarded costs, the Court of Appeal was able to distinguish criminal and civil costs, and thereby avoid extending the unsatisfactory rule of malicious prosecution in civil cases to criminal proceedings. It followed that the Court of Appeal did not find it necessary to consider the other two heads of damage. Whether the courts will accept the undoubtedly historically correct analysis of DIPLOCK J and restrict the tort to cases where damage to fair fame was a necessary consequence, or where imprisonment was actually suffered, or whether the more extended interpretation by the Court of Appeal of the older cases will be followed, is uncertain.

The tort is committed if arrest[12] or process against property, eg a search warrant,[13] is procured maliciously and without probable cause. A solicitor may be so liable even if his evidence in open court on applying for the warrant of arrest causes the arrest to be made;[14] the rule that actions may not be brought against a witness for what he says does not then apply.[15]

C. TERMINATION IN FAVOUR OF PLAINTIFF

The proceedings must have terminated in favour of the plaintiff.[16] Even though the plaintiff has been convicted of a lesser offence,[17] or has had his conviction quashed on appeal,[18] or has been acquitted on a technicality, eg a defect in the indictment,[19] this requirement is satisfied. If the conviction of the plaintiff stands, then even though there is no right of appeal from it and although he can satisfy the court in the instant proceedings that the conviction

11 *Quartz Hill Gold Mining Co v Eyre* (1883) 11 QBD 674 CA.
12 *Pike v Waldrum and Peninsular and Oriental Steam Navigation Co Ltd* [1952] 1 Lloyd's Rep 431.
13 *Reynolds v Metropolitan Police Comr* [1985] QB 881, [1984] 3 All ER 649, CA; *Churchill v Siggers* (1854) 3 E & B 929.
14 *Roy v Prior* [1971] AC 470, [1970] 2 All ER 729 HL.
15 Page 439, post.
16 This requirement is not imposed where, for example, an arrest or search warrant is procured, supra.
17 *Boaler v Holder* (1887) 51 JP 277 Div Ct.
18 *Reynolds v Kennedy* (1748) 1 Wils 232.
19 *Wicks v Fentham* (1791) 4 Term Rep 247.

was grossly unjust, there is no cause of action in this tort.[20] The plaintiff seems to satisfy the present requirement if he proves that the defendant has discontinued the proceedings;[1] the plaintiff cannot sue, it seems, while the proceedings are still pending.[2]

D. ABSENCE OF REASONABLE AND PROBABLE CAUSE

This tort is not regarded with favour by the courts, because it runs counter to the policy of freedom to prosecute suspected criminals and to the interest in bringing litigation to a close. This judicial attitude is reflected in the development of the requirement that there must be an absence of reasonable and probable cause.

It will be noted that the plaintiff has the difficult task of proving a negative— a burden which he does not discharge merely by proving malice on the part of the defendant,[3] and the court will not order the defendant to give particulars of the grounds on which he prosecuted.[4]

The House of Lords has approved the following definition of reasonable and probable cause:[5]

> an honest belief in the guilt of the accused based upon a full conviction, founded upon reasonable grounds, of the existence of a state of circumstances, which, assuming them to be true, would reasonably lead any ordinary prudent and cautious man, placed in the position of the accuser, to the conclusion that the person charged was probably guilty of the crime imputed.

The House of Lords has held that, in order that the plaintiff may succeed on the issue of reasonable and probable cause, he must prove one or other of the following.[6]

Either—

1 The defendant did not believe that the plaintiff was probably guilty of the offence.

Evidence should be given by the plaintiff of some fact or facts which, either inherently or coupled with other matters proved in evidence, would permit the inference that the defendant did not believe in the plaintiff's guilt. If such evidence is given, the question must be left to the jury, whether it has been proved to their satisfaction that the defendant did not believe in the plaintiff's guilt. But unless such evidence is given it is not proper to put a question to the jury as to the defendant's belief.[7] This question to the jury must be formulated precisely and should not refer to reasonable cause. It should be either: 'Did the defendant honestly believe in the

---

20 *Basébé v Matthews* (1867) LR 2 CP 684; nor can a plaintiff sue who is merely ordered to enter into recognizances to keep the peace; *Everett v Ribbands* [1952] 2 QB 198, [1952] 1 All ER 823 CA.
1 *Watkins v Lee* (1839) 5 M & W 270.
2 Per WILLES J (*obiter*) in *Gilding v Eyre* (1961) 10 CB (NS) 592 at 604.
3 *Johnstone v Sutton* (1786) 1 Term Rep 510.
4 *Stapley v Annetts* [1969] 3 All ER 1541, CA.
5 *Hicks v Faulkner* (1881) 8 QBD 167 at 171 (per HAWKINS J); affd (1882) 46 LT 130 CA, approved in *Herniman v Smith* [1938] AC 305.
6 *Glinski v McIver* [1962] AC 726, [1962] 1 All ER 696 HL. *Reynolds v Metropolitan Police Comr* (supra).
7 *Herniman v Smith* [1938] AC 305 at 317 (per LORD ATKIN).

plaintiff's guilt?' or 'Did he honestly believe in the charges he was preferring?' It must not be: 'Did he honestly believe that there were reasonable
grounds for the prosecution?' for that would cause the jury to pass on the
whole issue of reasonable and probable cause.[8] Merely to prove that the
defendant had before him information which might or might not have led
a reasonable man to form an opinion that the plaintiff was guilty is not
evidence that the defendant did not believe him to be guilty. If this ground
is relied on, the plaintiff must give some evidence from which an inference
may be drawn as to what the defendant's belief actually was: it is not
sufficient to give evidence from which a guess may be made as to what it
was. Nor is it sufficient merely to supply evidence of reasons for non-belief;
and if such evidence is relied on there must also be evidence that these
reasons were in fact operative.

Or—

2 That a man of ordinary prudence and caution would not conclude, in the
light of the facts in which he honestly believed, that the plaintiff was
probably guilty.

It is for the judge and not the jury to determine whether a man of
ordinary prudence would have so concluded. It is for the judge alone to
determine whether there is reasonable and probable cause.[9] The trouble
experienced in splitting the functions of judge and jury in consequence of
this rule accounts for most of the complexities of this tort. There is the
ever-present danger that the questions addressed to the jury will be so
general that the ultimate question left to the judge of reasonable cause is
instead improperly decided by the jury. In conducting the trial the judge
has two alternatives: he may direct the jury that, if they find certain facts,
or arrive at certain answers to specific questions which he puts to them,
there is reasonable and probable cause, leaving it to the jury to find a
general verdict on this hypothetical direction; his alternative—and this is
the better course—is to direct the jury to settle the facts in dispute, whereupon he decides, upon the whole case, whether there is reasonable and
probable cause.[10]

It is impossible to enumerate all the factors which may be relevant in
deciding whether there was reasonable and probable cause. Particularly
important points would be that the defendant acted in good faith on the
advice of counsel[11] (although that he did so act is not conclusive[12]), or on the
advice of the police,[13] where the defendant, however honest his act, had taken
reasonable care to inform himself of the true facts,[14] whether the defendant's
mistake was one of fact or law (obviously a plaintiff cannot treat a mistake
on a difficult legal point as evidence of lack of reasonable cause).[15]

---

8 *Tempest v Snowden* [1952] 1 KB 130, [1952] 1 All ER 1, CA.
9 *Lister v Perryman* (1870) LR 4 HL 521.
10 *Abrath v NE Ry Co* (1883) 11 QBD 440 at 458 (per BOWEN LJ), CA; affirmed (1886) 11 App
    Cas 247, HL. And see *Green v De Havilland* (1968) 112 Sol Jo 766.
11 *Ravenga v Mackintosh* (1824) 2 B & C 693; cf *Bradshaw v Waterlow & Sons Ltd* [1915] 3 KB
    527.
12 *Abbott v Refuge Assurance Co Ltd* [1962] 1 QB 432, [1961] 3 All ER 1074, CA.
13 *Malz v Rosen* [1966] 2 All ER 10.
14 *Abrath v NE Ry Co* (1883) 11 QBD 440 at 451 (per BRETT MR), CA.
15 *Philips v Naylor* (1859) 4 H & N 565. In *Riches v Director of Public Prosecutions* [1973] 2 All
    ER 935, CA, it was held that allegations of malice and want of reasonable cause in an action
    against the DPP stood no chance of success when the committing magistrate, the trial judge
    and the jury all shared the view of the evidence held by the DPP.

E. MALICE: IMPROPER PURPOSE

In addition, the plaintiff must prove malice on the part of the defendant,[16] ie 'any motive other than that of simply instituting a prosecution for the purpose of bringing a person to justice'.[17]

The judge decides whether there is any evidence of malice and the jury decides whether there is malice in fact.[18] There is, for instance, evidence of malice where the defendant landlord makes the charge in order to evict the plaintiff tenant from his house,[19] or where the defendant charges the plaintiff with being a rogue and vagabond in order that the wife of the plaintiff might obtain relief from the parish.[20] The question is not whether the defendant is angry or inspired by hatred,[1] but whether the defendant has a purpose other than bringing an offender to justice—there is malice, for instance, if he uses the prosecution as a means of blackmail or any other form of coercion. Where the motives of the defendant are mixed, the plaintiff will fail unless he establishes that the dominant purpose is something other than the vindication of the law.[2]

A plaintiff who proves malice but not want of reasonable and probable cause still fails. Should a tenant, therefore, establish that his landlord has instituted proceedings against him for stealing the landlord's fixtures, with the object of determining his tenancy, the tenant's action in this tort will still fail if absence of reasonable cause is not also proved by him.[3]

F. DEFENCES

No questions on defences call for special comment other than that of whether it is a defence to establish that the plaintiff was guilty of the offence for which he was prosecuted. Obviously, in the rare case where a defendant had no reasonable cause and was malicious, and the proceedings terminated in the plaintiff's favour, and yet, at the trial for malicious prosecution, the defendant is able to establish the guilt of the plaintiff, the plaintiff would recover at best a very small sum of damages; there is, indeed, some authority for the view that in such a case the action fails altogether.[4]

---

16 *Brown v Hawkes* [1891] 2 QB 718 CA. In *Wershof v Metropolitan Police Commissioners* [1978] 3 All ER 540, the plaintiff proved absence of reasonable cause, but failed because he could not prove malice.
17 Per ALDERSON B in *Stevens v Midland Counties Ry Co* (1854) 10 Exch 352.
18 *Brown v Hawkes* [1891] 2 QB 718.
19 *Turner v Ambler* (1847) 10 QB 252.
20 *Heath v Heape* (1856) 1 H & N 478.
1 *Brown v Hawkes* supra at 722 (per CAVE J).
2 Not malice when the defendants' motive was to recoup themselves in a civil action, so that they first prosecuted in order to conform to the rule that prosecution for felony must precede civil actions relating thereto: *Abbott v Refuge Assurance Co Ltd* p 437, ante.
3 *Turner v Ambler* supra.
4 *Heslop v Chapman* (1853) 23 LJ QB 49 at 52 (per JERVIS CJ and POLLOCK CB); cf *Shrosbery v Osmaston* (1877) 37 LT 792 at 794 (per LINDLEY J); contra WIGHTMAN J in *Williams v Banks* (1859) 1 F & F 557 at 559. In *White v Metropolitan Police Commissioner* (1982) *Times*, 24 April each of two plaintiffs were awarded £2,500 aggravated damages against the police for distress, anxiety and damage to reputation when the police prosecuted them for obstruction in the execution of duty, knowing that they were innocent, and in order to escape the consequences of the police's unlawful entry and arrest.

SECTION 2. ABUSE OF PROCESS

It is a tort to use legal process in its proper form in order to accomplish a purpose other than that for which it was designed and thereby cause damage.

The leading case is *Grainger v Hill*:[5]

The defendant was held liable when he had the plaintiff arrested, ostensibly for non-payment of a debt, but in fact in order illegally to compel him to surrender the register of a vessel, without which the plaintiff could not take the vessel to sea.

The case decided that in the tort the plaintiff need not prove want of reasonable and probable cause; nor need the proceedings have terminated in his favour.[6] The plaintiff must show that the defendant has used the process for some improper purpose;[7] thus, a defendant who issued by mistake a plaint note for a debt which had already been paid was held not liable.[8] In contrast with malicious prosecution, damage to fame, person or property need not be proved; any special damage is enough.[9]

SECTION 3. ABUSE OF PROCESS BY JUDICIAL OFFICERS

It was once a tort derived from the former action on the case for a justice of the peace[10] maliciously and within his jurisdiction to exercise his judicial functions,[11] for example, imposing excessive detention,[12] or refusing bail.[13] The continued existence of such a tort was doubted by their Lordships in *Re McC*.[14]

SECTION 4. EVIDENCE IN COURT

If a plaintiff's claim is based directly and substantially on the defendant's evidence in court, no action lies. This is a general principle[15] of which the

---

5 (1838) 4 Bing NC 212; *Gibbs v Pike* (1842) 9 M & W 351 (maliciously registering a court order). *Speed Seal Products Ltd v Paddington* [1986] 1 All ER 91, [1985] 1 WLR 1327; and see W Wells 'The Abuse of Process' (1985) 102 LQR 9.
6 *Speed Seal Products Ltd v Paddington* (supra).
7 *Clissold v Cratchley* [1910] 2 KB 244.
8 *Corbett v Burge, Warren and Ridgley Ltd* (1932) 48 TLR 626. It was also said in this case that loss.of business profits is not a recoverable head of damage, *sed quaere*.
9 Eg if a suit in deceit was instituted for the purpose of damaging the plaintiff's credit. In *Smith v East Elloe Rural District Council* [1956] AC 736, [1956] 1 All ER 855 HL, the House of Lords held there to be jurisdiction to hear a claim that a clerk to a council knowingly and in bad faith wrongfully procured a compulsory purchase order to be made and confirmed by a Minister, even though a statute precluded the courts from challenging the validity of the order itself on the grounds of bad faith.
10 Though no case has been traced, the tort probably extends to all persons (not being courts of record) who exercise judicial functions, eg if an administrative tribunal maliciously exercised its power of issuing a subpoena.
11 Justice of the Peace Act 1979 s 44. *O'Connor v Isaacs* [1956] 2 QB 288, [1956] 2 All ER 417.
12 *Davis v Capper* (1829) 10 B & C 28.
13 *Salmon v Percival* (1630) Cro Car 196.
14 [1985] AC 528, [1984] 3 WLR 1227 HL.
15 *Roy v Prior* [1971] AC 470, [1970] 1 All ER 729, HL.

following are examples. No action lies in defamation for words spoken as a witness in court,[16] nor will conspiracy lie against policemen who conspire to defame the plaintiff at a criminal trial.[17] A plaintiff who is imprisoned in consequence of the defendant's giving false evidence on oath at the plaintiff's trial has no cause of action,[18] perjury is a crime but not a tort. On the other hand, in proceedings for malicious arrest the plaintiff can rely on statements made by the defendant in court when seeking the warrant: the wrong is the arrest with malice, of which the statement in court provides evidential support.[19]

SECTION 5. MISUSE OF ADMINISTRATIVE PROCESS

A successful application for judicial review of administrative action which results in an administrative process being quashed as invalid or unlawful does not[20] of itself create any liability in tort for loss or damage suffered by the applicant. There is, however, an ill-defined and, in England, embryonic tort of misfeasance in public office.[1] Where an individual suffers loss or damage consequent upon administrative action which the relevant officer knows to be unlawful that loss or damage is recoverable in tort.[2] The plaintiff in *Roncarelli v Duplessis*[3] lost his liquor licence after the defendant, the then Prime Minister of Quebec, ordered the Quebec Licensing Commission to revoke the licence. Duplessis acted against the plaintiff as part of his campaign against Jehovah's Witnesses. He recovered damages in tort for the malicious abuse of the licensing process.

In *Bourgoin SA v Ministry of Agriculture*[4] the plaintiffs were French turkey producers who had been banned by the defendants from exporting turkeys to England. The reason given was risk of disease but, for the purposes of the preliminary point of law, the Ministry admitted that the true grounds were protection of British turkey producers and that they acted accordingly in breach of Article 30 of the EEC Treaty[5] in imposing unjustifiable import restrictions. They contended that they were nevertheless not liable for misfeasance in public office because there was no intent to injure the plaintiffs but, rather, to protect British interests. Mann J held, and the Court of Appeal

---

16 Chapter 25 ante.
17 *Marrinan v Vibart* [1963] 1 QB 528, [1962] 3 All ER 380, CA.
18 *Hargreaves v Bretherton* [1958] 1 QB 45, [1958] 3 All ER 122, approved *obiter* in *Roy v Prior* supra at 477 (per Lord Morris of Borth-y-Gest). In *Evans v London Hospital Medical College* [1981] 1 All ER 715, it was held that this immunity extends to statements made before the issue of a writ or the institution of a prosecution, distinguishing *Saif Ali v Sydney Mitchell & Co* [1980] AC 198, [1978] 3 All ER 1033. This case threatens to restrict liability for professional negligence (see p 188 et seq ante), for it raises doubts whether it also applies to doctors, automobile engineers, valuers and others preparing reports which are connected with possible future litigation.
19 *Roy v Prior* and p 435 ante.
20 *Dunlop v Woollahra Municipal Council* [1982] AC 158, [1981] 1 All ER 1202, PC.
 1 See Wade *Administrative Law* (5th edn, 1982) p 669.
 2 *David v Abdul Cader* [1963] 3 All ER 579, [1963] 1 WLR 834; *Davis v Bromley Corpn* [1908] 1 KB 170.
 3 (1959) 16 DLR (2d) 689.
 4 [1986] QB 716, [1985] 3 All ER 585.
 5 On tortious liability for breach of Article 30 see ante at p 367.

confirmed, that proof of malice is not essential to the tort. It is sufficient that the plaintiff prove that the defendant knew that he acted unlawfully and that his act would injure the plaintiff. Malice is a possible but not essential ingredient of the tort.

Part VIII

Remedies and parties

CONTENTS

Chapter 27

Servants and independent contractors: the circumstances in which an employer may be liable where harm is caused by an act or omission of someone doing work for him[1]

SECTION 1. IMPORTANCE OF THE DISTINCTION BETWEEN SERVANTS AND INDEPENDENT CONTRACTORS

For the present purpose the law divides persons into two groups:

1 Those employed to perform services in connection with the affairs of the employer, and over whom the employer has control in the performance of those services. In tort, these persons are commonly and conveniently styled 'servants'.

2 Those who do work for another, but who are not controlled by that other in their conduct in the performance of that work. Normally such work will be carried out in pursuance of a contract, and the persons doing it are therefore called 'independent contractors'.

The distinction is important for the following reason. If a servant commits a tort in the course of his employment, then the employer is liable regardless of whether he himself has committed a tort: 'every act which is done by a servant in the course of his duty is regarded as done by his master's orders, and consequently is the same as if it were the master's own act. . . .'[2] This is, of course, the clearest case of a strict tortious liability, and may be regarded as a judicial decision of policy that the employer is to bear the financial responsibility for those torts committed by his servants in the course of his enterprise—both because he is better able to stand the loss (or he can insure against it) and pass it on to the public in the form of increased prices, and because he will be encouraged to maintain higher standards of conduct in the running of his business.[3]

If the act complained of is not that of a servant, then the employer is not, without more, liable: he can then be sued only if he himself has, in the circumstances, committed a tort. An employer may be vicariously liable for the torts of his servants, but he is not liable for the torts of those who are his independent contractors. Clearly, the criteria for distinguishing the two classes of persons must now be looked for.

---

1 On this chapter generally see Atiyah *Vicarious Liability in the Law of Torts.*
2 *Bartonshill Coal Co v McGuire* (1858) 3 Macq 300 at 306 (per LORD CHELMSFORD LC), HL.
3 Characteristically, the courts have often in the past taken refuge in some rather barren phrases in order to explain the doctrine, eg *respondent superior, qui facit per alium facit* per se. For the history of the doctrine, see *HEL*, viii, pp 472–82.

SECTION 2. CRITERIA FOR DISTINGUISHING SERVANTS AND INDEPENDENT CONTRACTORS

A. CONTROL

The formula, regularly used by the courts to mark the distinction, is 'control'. '... The final test ... lies in the nature and degree of detailed control over the person alleged to be a servant.'[4] A person is a servant where the employer 'retains the control of the actual performance' of the work.[5]

In a simple industrial society such as England was until this century, where work was done by agricultural labourers or craftsmen under the directions of employers who had the same or even greater technical skill than their workmen, it would ordinarily be enough to say that the employer could tell the man not merely what task he was to perform but also how he should perform it: if the employer could do both these things, the man was a servant. But now, when a new class of managers, as distinct from owners, has arisen in industry, and when so many employees have some technical skill or other which is often not possessed by any of their employers, the relationship has become more subtle and hardly capable of exact definition: the test formerly applied will not necessarily be adequate.[6] In short, 'control' has become a legal fiction rather than a technical reality.

In deciding whether enough 'control' is exercised over another to make him a 'servant' one must take into account several factors, no one of which is conclusive. That is a rule of law, but the application of those factors to the circumstances of the case is a question of fact. The criteria include the extent to which the employer can control the details of the work, whether the method of payment is on a time or a job basis, whose tools, equipment and premises are to be used,[7] the skill called for in the work, the intention of the parties, the freedom of selection of labour by the employer,[8] and the power to dismiss. All these matters, and many more, but especially and increasingly that mentioned in the quotation from DENNING LJ, immediately following, must be considered in order to decide whether this right of control can be inferred. DENNING LJ said:[9]

> It is often easy to recognise a contract of service when you see it, but difficult to say wherein the difference [between a contract of service and a contract for services] lies.[10] A ship's master, a chauffeur, and a reporter on the staff of a newspaper are all employed under a contract of service; but a ship's pilot, a taxi-man, and a

---

4 *Performing Right Society Ltd v Mitchell and Booker Ltd* [1924] 1 KB 762 at 767 (per McCARDIE J).

5 *Honeywill & Stein Ltd v Larkin Brothers Ltd* [1934] 1 KB 191 at 196, [1933] All ER Rep 77 at 81 (per SLESSER LJ), CA.

6 *Short v Henderson Ltd* (1946) 62 TLR 427 at 429 (per LORD THANKERTON), HL. The inadequacy of this test was expressly stated in *Cassidy v Ministry of Health* [1951] 2 KB 343 at 352 (per SOMMERVELL LJ), [1951] 1 All ER 574, CA.

7 *Quarman v Burnett* (1840), 6 M & W 499.

8 At common law the owner of a ship was not liable for the negligence of a compulsory pilot; *The Halley* (1868) LR 2 PC 193 (see now Pilotage Act 1913): but the statutory obligation that watermen on Thames barges shall be licensed does not prevent a waterman from being a servant since there are many from which to choose, and the barge-owner can dismiss; *Martin v Temperley* (1843) 4 QB 298.

9 *Stevenson, Jordan and Harrison Ltd v Macdonald and Evans* [1952] 1 TLR 101 at 111, CA. Cf somewhat similar observations by LORD WRIGHT in *Montreal v Montreal Locomotive Works* [1947] 1 DLR 161, PC, at 169.

10 Contract of service/contract for services are here merely synonomous with servant/independent contractor.

newspaper contributor are employed under a contract for services. *One feature which seems to run through the instances is that, under a contract of service, a man is employed as part of the business, and his work is done as an integral part of the business; whereas, under a contract for services, his work, although done for the business, is not integrated into it but is only accessory to it.*[11]

B. SOME PARTICULAR CASES EXAMINED

In the majority of cases, there is no difficulty in determining the status of the person.[12] Factory employees, official clerical staff, agricultural hands and the like are clearly servants; garage proprietors, house-builders, and dry-cleaners are the independent contractors of the members of the public who employ them. A typical instance where a man might fall into either group, depending on the circumstances, is that of a salesman.[13] Similarly, a chauffeur is a servant, but a taxi-driver is not.[14]

(1) HOSPITAL STAFFS

The courts have often been concerned to decide which members of hospital staffs are servants. After much uncertainty it is now settled that nurses, radiographers,[15] house-surgeons,[16] and assistant medical officers[17] in the full-time service of hospitals are servants. Part-time anaesthetists have also been held to be servants on the ground that they are members of the organisation of the hospital.[18] Surgeons and consultants under the National Health Service, even though only engaged part-time or occasionally, will for the same reason be servants of the hospital authority. It is only when the surgeon or consultant treats the patient by virtue of a contract between him and the patient that the hospital authority is not answerable for his torts.

(2) BORROWED SERVANTS

It is often difficult to decide whose servant a man is when he is lent by his employer to another. The authoritative decision is *Mersey Docks & Harbour Board v Coggins & Griffith (Liverpool) Ltd:*[19]

The board owned many mobile cranes, each handled by skilled workmen

---

11 Author's italics. Cf *Bank Voor Handel en Scheepvaart v Slatford* [1953] 1 QB 248 at 295 (per DENNING LJ), [1952] 2 All ER 956, CA: 'It depends on whether the person is part and parcel of the organisation'; reversed on other grounds [1954] AC 584, [1954] 1 All ER 969, HL, sub nom *Bank Voor Handel en Scheepvaart v Administrator of Hungarian Property.*

12 For the special statutory provisions defining when a trade union is vicariously liable for various torts involving industrial action, see the Employment Act 1982, s 15 and p 517, post.

13 Or the holder of a university research fellowship who is required also to act as part-time demonstrator.

14 When is a director a servant?

15 *Gold v Essex County Council* [1942] 2 KB 293, [1942] 2 All ER 237, CA.

16 *Collins v Hertfordshire County Council* [1947] KB 598, [1947] 1 All ER 633; *Cassidy v Ministry of Health* [1951] 2 KB 343, [1951] 1 All ER 574, CA.

17 *Cassidy v Ministry of Health,* supra.

18 *Roe v Minister of Health* [1954] 2 QB 66, [1954] 2 All ER 131, CA.

19 [1947] AC 1, [1946] 2 All ER 345, HL. *Karuppan Bhoomidas v Port of Singapore Authority* [1978] 1 All ER 956, PC (even though a byelaw provided that those loading and discharging vessels shall be under the superintendence of the ship's officers, stevedores were held to remain employees of the Port Authority, which was vicariously liable for their torts).

engaged and paid by it. In the ordinary course of its business, it hired out a crane to the respondents, a stevedoring company, for use in unloading a ship. The power to dismiss remained with the board, but the contract provided that the driver was to be the servant of the hirers. While loading the cargo, the driver was under the immediate control of the hirers in the sense that the hirers could tell him which boxes to load and where to place them, but they could not tell him how to manipulate the controls of the crane. Through the negligent handling of the crane by the driver while loading, a third party was injured. The House of Lords was called upon to decide from which of the two, the board or the hirers, the plaintiff was to recover his damages: ie whose servant was he at the time of the accident?

It was held that the board was solely liable. There is a very strong presumption indeed[20] that a man remains the servant of the general or permanent employer although another employer borrows his services. Where cranes or vehicles were let out on hire with a driver the owner was responsible for his servant's negligence unless he had divested himself of all possession and control.[1]

SECTION 3.   IS THERE A SEPARATE CATEGORY OF AGENTS?

We have seen that a person who does work for another may be either a servant or an independent contractor. Such a person may also, at the same time, be an agent; ie, the category of 'agent' partially overlaps the categories of both 'servant' and 'independent contractor'. It is submitted that this category of agents, although of great importance in other branches of the law, such as contract, has little relevance (subject to the exceptions discussed on the following page) in the present context. An agent may or may not be subject to that degree of control which will make him a servant: the law of torts is here concerned only to know in any particular case whether or not he is a 'servant'. A man employed on a weekly wage to sell vacuum cleaners and under orders as to his times and place of employment will be at once an agent (in contracting to sell cleaners) and a servant: on the other hand, no one would suggest that, if the defendant employed a chartered accountant to settle his liability for income tax, the defendant would be liable if the accountant negligently knocked down a pedestrian while driving to the tax office in order to discuss the matter. The accountant would be an agent and an independent contractor of the defendant, but not his servant.[2]

One tort, namely that of deceit, affords an important exception to this rule that the law of torts is not concerned with the separate category of agents.[3]

---

20 No English case on vicarious liability decided since 1947 holding that the original employer has shifted his liability for a driver hired out with a vehicle has been traced.

1 Per LORD DENNING, *John Young & Co (Kelvinhaugh), Ltd v O'Donnell* (1958) Times, 25 January, HL.

2 The *obiter dicta* of the House of Lords in *Heatons Transport (St Helens) Ltd v Transport and General Workers Union* [1973] AC 15 at 99 that the test to be applied in determining the responsibility of a master or principal for the act of a servant or an agent 'is the same: was the servant or agent acting on behalf of and within the scope of the authority conferred by the master or principal?' must not (it is submitted) be taken to apply in tort so as to refute the propositions advanced in this section. See also *Watkins v Birmingham City Council* (1975) Times, 1 August, CA, schoolboy distributing milk to classrooms in his school not servant of local education authority, although he might well have been an agent.

3 And see ch 8, ante.

Where a principal delegates authority to another person to negotiate a contract on his behalf, he may be liable for the fraud of his 'agent'. So, for example if an estate agent, in the course of negotiating the sale of a house of his principal, knowingly makes untrue statements about that house to a third party who acts on them to his detriment, in some circumstances the principal will be liable in deceit. And yet the estate agent is not the principal's servant. This liability exists only where the principal can be said to have held out this estate agent as one authorised to make such representations in the course of making the contract.[4] This affords the clue to the problem—such misrepresentations, though capable of giving rise to tortious liabilities, are so intimately associated with, and inseparable from, the contractual relation to which end the agency is directed that they partake of the quality of contract, where agency as such, of course, is important.[5] The concept of agency is applicable also to negligent statements made by an estate agent.[6] But it is an essential prerequisite of liability of the principal that the agent acted within the scope of the authority which the principal's acts led the plaintiff to believe the agent enjoyed. Where the agent is at the same time a servant of the principal the House of Lords has rejected contentions that the agent could act beyond the scope of his authority but still remains within the general course of his employment.[7]

The other area which demands special attention is the liability of the owner of a vehicle when it is driven by someone else. Of course the owner is liable if his servant drives it negligently in the course of his employment. The courts have not stopped there and the House of Lords in *Morgans v Launchbury*[8] has affirmed that if the vehicle is driven by the owner's agent and the user is as the owner's agent, the owner is again liable. The facts in *Morgans v Launchbury* were:

> The defendant wife owned the car and with her permission her husband took it on a pub crawl. When he was too drunk to drive, he asked his drinking companion to drive. The wife was held not liable for the companion's negligent driving.

The court held that the driver was not the agent of the owner, that a car owner is liable only if the driver is his servant acting in the course of his employment or is his authorised agent driving for and on behalf of the owner:

4 Cf *Uxbridge Permanent Benefit Building Society v Pickard* [1939] 2 KB 248 at 254–5 (per SIR WILFRID GREENE MR) [1939] 2 All ER 344, CA.

5 Whether this exception will be restricted to deceit because of the need for a contractual element or whether the parallel concept of 'holding out' will permit its extension to any tort where the defendant has held out a person to represent him in performing a transaction with others is doubtful. The High Court of Australia has held an insurance company liable when its agent (not a servant) defamed a rival company while soliciting business: *Colonial Mutual Life Assurance Society v Producers Assurance Co of Australia* (1931) 46 CLR 41; *dicta* in *Houldsworth v City of Glasgow Bank* (1880) 5 App Cas 317 at 326, HL (per LORD SELBOURNE) and *Lloyd v Grace, Smith & Co* [1912] AC 716 at 734–5, HL (per LORD MACNAGHTEN) lean towards the Australian position. But was BLAIN J right in *Gros v Crook* (1969) 113 Sol Jo 408 in holding in a libel action that a book reviewer in *The Times Literary Supplement* was an agent, and not an independent contractor?

6 *Kooragang Investments Pty Ltd v Richardson & Wrench Ltd* [1982] AC 462, [1981] 3 All ER 65, PC. In that case therefore the principal was held not liable for the agent's negligent statement because the agent was not authorised to make the valuations, the subject of the negligent statements.

7 *Armagas Ltd v Mundogas SA, 'The Ocean Frost'* [1986] AC 717, [1985] 3 All ER 795.

8 [1973] AC 127; approving *Hewitt v Bonvin* [1940] 1 KB 188, CA.

LORD WILBERFORCE added that 'agency' in such a context was merely a concept the meaning and purpose of which is that the owner ought to pay.[9] The House rejected the argument that it was so desirable to find someone liable who was covered by compulsory third-party insurance, that it should hold the owner liable for anyone who drove with his permission: only Parliament, not the courts, could make that extension of liability.[10] It is submitted that *Morgans v Launchbury* does not upset the general rule in vicarious liability that a principal is not liable merely because his agent commits a tort while acting as agent.[11]

The liability of the employer of independent contractors and of servants will now be examined.

SECTION 4.   LIABILITY IN RESPECT OF AN INDEPENDENT CONTRACTOR

The employer is not liable merely because an independent contractor commits a tort in the course of his employment: the employer is liable only if he himself is deemed to have committed a tort. This may happen in one of three ways.

A.   AUTHORISING HIM TO COMMIT A TORT

In many circumstances the law will attribute to a man the conduct of another being, whether human or animal, if he has instigated that conduct. If X sets his dog upon Y it is as much battery as if X had struck Y with his fist. He who instigates or procures another to commit a tort is deemed to have committed the tort himself;[12] it matters not whether that other was servant, independent contractor or agent, human or otherwise. In *Ellis v Sheffield Gas Consumers Co* the facts were:[13]

> Having no legal power to do so, the defendant gas undertaking employed an independent contractor to dig up a part of a street. The plaintiff fell over a heap of earth and stones made by the contractor in the course of digging, and the defendants were held liable on the ground that they had authorised this nuisance.

It is not always easy to decide whether the defendant can be said to have authorised the tortious act. Where a lessee was empowered to erect certain structures, but the lease reserved to the lessor the right to approve the plans for such structures (which right the lessor is not reported to have exercised),

---

9 At 135.
10 *Norwood v Navan* [1981] RTR 457, CA, a husband was held not liable for the negligence of his wife when driving his car for family shopping. In *Nelson v Raphael*, [1979] RTR 437, the seller of a car asked a friend to hand over the car to the buyer and collect his cheque. When the friend demonstrated the controls to the buyer, the seller was vicariously liable for the friend's negligence while doing so.
11 *Nottingham v Aldridge* [1971] 2 All ER 751.
12 Even if that other would have a defence, the principal may still be liable; *Barker v Braham* (1773) 3 Wils 368 (defendant authorised sheriff to arrest plaintiff on an illegal warrant: although the sheriff was protected from liability by reason of acting under the warrant, the defendant was still liable in false imprisonment).
13 (1853) 2 E & B 767.

this was not enough to make the lessor answerable for the lessee's negligence in the course of building the structure.[14] On the other hand, although a taxi-driver is not a servant, if his fare orders him to drive fast or to take other risks, he is jointly responsible for any ensuing tort.[15]

If a person commits a tort while purporting to act on behalf of another, but in fact without his authority, and that other later ratifies the act which amounted to a tort, he thereby becomes answerable for the tort in the same way as if he had given a precedent authority for its commission. The principal must know, at the time when he ratifies,[16] of the commission of the act which constitutes a tort, but he is not excused because he was unaware that the ratified act was a tort if he would have been liable in tort had he done the act himself. Thus, if he ratifies the purchase of goods which the vendor had no right to sell, he is liable in conversion, although he is unaware that the sale was unlawful.[17]

B. TORTS WHERE INTENTIONAL OR NEGLIGENT CONDUCT NEED NOT ALWAYS BE PROVED

The torts of 'strict liability' previously discussed are characterised not only by the fact that, in some instances, there is a liability where no intentional or negligent act has been committed, but also by the fact that one may be answerable for such torts when committed by one's independent contractors. Thus we have seen that in nuisance,[18] *Rylands v Fletcher*,[19] breach of statutory duty,[20] the employer may in some circumstances be liable for the conduct of his independent contractor.

C. NEGLIGENCE

An employer may be liable in negligence for damage caused by the acts of his independent contractors.

(1) PERSONAL NEGLIGENCE ON THE PART OF THE EMPLOYER

First, there may be such an element of personal negligence on the part of the employer as to make him liable for the acts of his independent contractor, and this may be so even though the duty of care owed by the employer in a particular case is not so extensive as to make the employer liable merely because his independent contractor has been negligent. Thus, the employer is liable where he carelessly appoints an incompetent contractor. Where the risk of harm, unless precautions are taken, is foreseeable, failure by the

---

14 *Hurlstone v London & Electric Ry Co* (1914) 30 TLR 398, CA.
15 Cf *M'Laughlin v Pryor* (1842) 4 Man & G 48. Mere failure to object or other passive acquiescence would not be enough.
16 *Freeman v Rosher* (1849) 13 QB 780.
17 *Hilbery v Hatton* (1864) 2 H & C 822.
18 Eg *Matania v National Provincial Bank Ltd* [1936] 2 All ER 633, CA; cf *Hole v Sittingbourne Ry Co* (1841) 6 H & N 488; *Dalton v Angus* (1881) 6 App Cas 740, HL (the right of support); *Bower v Peate* (1876) 1 QBD 321.
19 The case itself; (1868) LR 3 HL 330.
20 *Hosking v De Havilland Aircraft Co Ltd* [1949] 1 All ER 540.

employer to provide in the contract for those precautions is actionable negligence.[1] *Robinson v Beaconsfield Rural Council*[2] furnishes another example of personal negligence on the part of the employer:

> The defendants employed contractors to clean out cesspools in their district. No arrangements were made for the removal of the deposits of sewage upon their being taken from the cesspools by the contractors. The contractors deposited sewage on the plaintiff's land. The defendants were held liable for their failure to take proper precautions to dispose of the sewage.

Failure to inspect after a job has been completed may also constitute negligence.

(2) THOSE DUTY-SITUATIONS WHERE THE DUTY EXTENDS TO A RESPONSIBILITY FOR THE NEGLIGENT ACTS OF AN INDEPENDENT CONTRACTOR—NON-DELEGABLE DUTIES

In some categories of negligence the duty to take care is so wide that it is not discharged by properly instructing and supervising a competent contractor: there is a positive duty not to act, even by a contractor, without taking due care. Such duties are often termed non-delegable duties. It must be emphasised that this is not true of all duty-situations[3]—and it is, of course, a question of law whether such a wide duty is owed.

Where the activity is particularly hazardous, such as the lighting of open fires on bush land,[4] or the taking of flash-light photographs in a cinema,[5] the duty of care has been held not to be delegable. Where employers are carrying out inherently dangerous operations on or near a highway which may foreseeably harm highway users, and the negligence of their independent contractors does cause such harm, the employers are liable. Thus, in *Holliday v National Telephone Co*:[6]

> The defendants, in laying telephone wires along a street, employed an independent contractor to solder the tubes in which these wires were carried. In negligently using a benzolene lamp, he injured a passer-by. The defendants were held liable.

On the other hand removing a hawthorn tree from a garden adjoining a highway is not an inherently dangerous activity, so that its owner is not liable for harm caused to the plaintiff by his contractor removing it negligently.[7]

---

1 Cf *Hughes v Percival* (1883) 8 App Cas 443, HL.
2 [1911] 2 Ch 188.
3 This is the flaw in the valuable article by Chapman 'Liability for Negligence of Independent Contractors', (1934) 50 LQR 71. For the liability of occupiers of land to their visitors for the acts of independent contractors under the Occupiers' Liability Act 1957, see p 264, ante.
4 *Black v Christchurch Finance Co* [1894] AC 48, PC. And see *Balfour v Barty-King* [1957] 1 QB 496, [1957] 1 All ER 156, CA (owner liable for fire when independent contractor plumber used blowlamp in loft to thaw defendant's frozen pipes).
5 *Honeywill and Stein Ltd v Larkin Brothers Ltd* [1934] 1 KB 191, CA.
6 [1899] 2 QB 392, CA; cf *Hardaker v Idle District Council* [1896] 1 QB 335, CA (damaging gas-pipe while laying sewer under highway); *Penny v Wimbledon Urban District Council* [1899] 2 QB 72 (heap of soil left unlighted on highway). *Walsh v Holst & Co Ltd* [1958] 3 All ER 33, CA. In *Pickard v Smith* (1861) 10 CB(NS) 470, the same principle was applied to hold a railway refreshment-room proprietor liable to a passenger who fell down a hole which the servant of the defendant's independent contractor negligently left on the platform.
7 *Salsbury v Woodland* [1970] 1 QB 324, [1969] 3 All ER 863, CA.

Structural operations damaging neighbouring premises are also within the rule.[8] Similarly, a railway company owes a duty to passengers to see that bridges along its lines are carefully built.[9]

The categories of non-delegable duties are not closed. The courts seem poised to include N.H.S. hospitals in respect of the treatment of their patients. With the setting up of a nationalised health service, hospital treatment has imperceptibly assumed an impersonalised and institutional form. A patient whose success in an action for negligence depends on his establishing negligence on the part of a particular servant of a hospital often has an impossible burden of proof to discharge: he may, while anaesthetised, be the victim of negligence in the operating theatre and not be able to show whether the senior surgeon, his assistant or the theatre sister was responsible. One obvious solution would be to hold that hospital authorities have a duty to provide proper treatment at all stages, a duty which they do not throw off by entrusting it to competent staff. *Lindsey County Council v Marshall*,[10] *Gold v Essex County Council*[11] and *Collins v Hertfordshire County Council*[12] have pointed the way, and that there was such a non-delegable duty constituted the *ratio decidendi* of the judgment of DENNING LJ in *Cassidy v Ministry of Health*;[13] in 1969 it was held that a hospital authority which ran a casualty department had a duty to provide proper medical and nursing attention for those who presented themselves there, complaining of illness or injury.[14] In view of the nationalisation of the hospital service, the considerations of policy favouring this extension are obvious.

The Employer's Liability (Defective Equipment) Act 1969 applies when for the purposes of his business an employer provides equipment (which includes any plant and machinery, vehicle, aircraft and clothing) for his employee and the employee suffers personal injury in the course of his employment in consequence of a defect in that equipment. The injury is then deemed to be also attributable to the negligence of the employer, if the defect is attributable wholly or partly to the negligence or other tort by an independent contractor or other third party. This Act therefore imposes an extensive statutory duty on employers. It leaves unchanged the common-law duty of the employer to provide a safe system in respects other than the provision of equipment.[15]

In *McDermid v Nash Dredging and Reclamation Co Ltd*[16] the plaintiff was employed as a deckhand by the defendants. He was instructed to go and

---

8   *Hughes v Percival* (1883) 8 App Cas 443, HL (party wall negligently cut into while contractor was rebuilding part of adjoining premises).
9   *Grote v Chester and Holyhead Ry Co* (1848) 2 Exch 251.
10   [1937] AC 97, [1936] 2 All ER 1076, HL.
11   [1942] 2 KB 293 at 301 (per LORD GREENE MR), [1942] 2 All ER 237, CA.
12   [1947] KB 598, [1947] 1 All ER 633.
13   [1951] 2 KB 343 at 362–3, [1951] 1 All ER 574, CA (but probably not of the other two judges). And see *Wilsher v Essex Area Health Authority* [1987] QB 730, [1986] 3 All ER 801, CA cf *Jones v Manchester Corporation* [1952] 2 QB 852 at 869 (per DENNING LJ), [1952] 2 All ER 125, CA; *Razzel v Snowball* [1954] 3 All ER 429, CA; *Hayward v Board of Management* 1854 SLT (Notes of cases) 63; *MacDonald v Glasgow Western Hospitals Board of Management*, 1954 SLT 226.
14   *Barnett v Chelsea and Kensington Hospital Management Committee* [1969] 1 QB 428, [1968] 1 All ER 1068.
15   Page 281 et seq, ante. Note also the obligation to insure under the Employer's Liability (Compulsory Insurance) Act 1969, p 287, ante.
16   [1987] 2 All ER 878, [1987] 3 WLR 212, HL and see *Davie v New Merton Board Mills Ltd* [1959] AC 604 at 646 (per LORD REID).

work on another tug owned by a different company within the same group as the defendants. As a result of the negligence of that tug master, who was not a servant of the defendants, the plaintiff suffered severe injuries. The House of Lords held the defendants liable for failing to provide a safe system of work. The breach of their non-delegable duty in respect of their servant's, the plaintiff's safety, was not discharged by delegating that duty to the master of the tug. The duty to devise and to operate a safe system of work was finally held to be non-delegable.

The grounds of social policy for imposing non-delegable duties on employers and on health authorities may explain the development of such duties in those areas. But in one or two other instances the courts have also been prepared to extend the categories of non-delegable duties. In *Rogers v Night Riders*,[17] for example, the plaintiff's mother telephoned the defendants for a taxi to take her daughter to the station and the mother paid for the cab. On the journey a door flew open and the plaintiff was injured. The taxi driver was not an employee but an independent contractor for the defendants. Nevertheless the defendants were held to be in breach of their primary duty to the plaintiff. As far as she knew it was the defendants who undertook to convey her safely and carefully to her destination. What has to be considered now is whether the courts are moving towards the development of a principle that, where one person or organisation undertakes to provide a service for another, albeit independently of any contract, he has a duty not only to exercise care personally, but also to ensure that, whoever actually carries out the service, the service is performed carefully.

SECTION 5.   WHERE THE EMPLOYER IS NOT LIABLE FOR THE ACTS OF AN INDEPENDENT CONTRACTOR

A.   NO BREACH BY EMPLOYER OF ANY DUTY IMPOSED ON HIM BY THE LAW OF TORTS

An employer is liable for damage caused by tortious acts of his independent contractor only where there is a breach by the employer of a duty owed by him: the question always is what is the extent of the risk against which the employer has the duty to guard.[18] In the case of all other duty-situations (and they are very numerous), the employer discharges his duty by taking care in the appointment of an independent contractor. No catalogue of instances falling in this last-mentioned group will be attempted: one example must suffice. In *Phillips v Britannia Hygienic Laundry Co*[19] the owner of a lorry was held not liable when a third party's vehicle was damaged in consequence of the negligent repair of his lorry by a garage proprietor.

---

17 [1983] RTR 324 CA; and see *Cynat Products Ltd v Landbuild (Investment and Property) Ltd* [1984] 3 All ER 513.
18 *Dalton v Angus* (1881) 6 App Cas 740 at 831, HL (per LORD WATSON).
19 [1923] 1 KB 539, Div Ct, affirmed, [1923] 2 KB 832, CA, followed in *Stennett v Hancock and Peters* [1939] 2 All ER 578. But would the garage be liable for the negligent repair by its independent contractor? And see *Taylor v Rover Co Ltd* [1966] 2 All ER 181. A recent example is *Rivers v Cutting* [1982] 3 All ER 69, CA (a policeman arranged, under powers given by the Removal and Disposal of Vehicles Regulations 1968, for a garage to tow away a car broken down on the M1 motorway; he was not liable for the garage's negligent towing).

B. COLLATERAL NEGLIGENCE

Employers of independent contractors, unlike those employing servants, are never liable for, as it is commonly stated, the 'collateral negligence' of their contractors. *Padbury v Holliday & Greenwood Ltd*[20] at once furnishes facts which illustrate the principle and contains what, it is submitted, is the soundest statement of the principle:

A employed B to fit casement windows into certain premises. B's servant negligently put a tool on the sill of the window on which he was working at the time. The wind blew the casement open and the tool was knocked off the sill on to a passer-by.

Holding the employer not liable, FLETCHER MOULTON LJ said:[1]

... before a superior employer could be held liable for the negligent act of a servant of a sub-contractor it must be shown that the work which the sub-contractor was employed to do was work *the nature of which, and not merely the performance of which*, cast on the superior employer the duty of taking precautions.

In short, the employer is liable for those risks of harm created by the work itself which the employer is having done. 'Collateral' means collateral to the risk which marks the limit of the duty of the employer. If the employer is to be liable, the danger must be inherent in the work; it is not enough that the contractor chooses a negligent way of performing it where the normal manner of performance would create no reasonably foreseeable peril to the plaintiff.[2]

The negligence must be 'in the employer's department of duty';[3] a householder who employs a contractor to repair his lamp over the highway is liable if the contractor repairs it in such a way that it falls on to a passer-by, for that is the very risk in respect of which the duty of the householder is imposed on him, but he is not liable if the contractor, while repairing it, allows a hammer to drop on to the passer-by, for that act would be outside the *employer's* range of duty. *Wilson v Hodgson's Kingston Brewery Co*[4] also shows how liability for the acts of independent contractors falls short of vicarious liability for the torts of a servant:

The defendants employed X, an independent contractor, to deliver beer at a public house. X delivered it through a cellar flap on the highway which he negligently left open, causing the plaintiff, who was passing along the

---

20 (1912) 28 TLR 494, CA.
  1 At 495; cf *Hardaker v Idle District Council* [1896] 1 QB 335 at 342 (per LINDLEY LJ), CA. *Thompson v Anglo-Saxon Petroleum Co, Ltd* [1955] 2 Lloyd's Rep 363 is another example.
  2 Many of the old cases state the rule rather differently by saying that the employer is not liable where the contractor does something collateral to the *contract*, eg *Hole v Sittingbourne and Sheerness Ry Co* (1861) 6 H & N 488 at 497 (per POLLOCK CB); *Penny v Wimbledon Urban Council* [1899] 2 QB 72. The formulation in the text is preferred because the contract cannot affect the scope of the duty of the employer—the contractor may do an act within the area of the contract itself, and yet the employer may not be liable because it is outside the area of his duty in tort; conversely, the employer may be liable for acts or omissions collateral to the contract if they are within the scope of his duty; cf *Robinson v Beaconsfield Rural Council* [1911] 2 Ch 188.
  3 *Cassidy v Ministry of Health* [1951] 2 KB 343 at 365 (per DENNING LJ); [1951] 1 All ER 574, CA; this judgment contains a lucid statement of the nature of collateral negligence. For the difficulty in ascertaining exactly the defendant's duty for the purpose of this rule, see *Salsbury v Woodland* [1970] 1 QB 324 at 349 (per SACHS LJ).
  4 (1915) 85 LJ KB 270, Div Ct.

pavement, to be injured. Pointing out that X could have delivered it through the front door, the court held that the incident was not within the scope of any duty on the part of the defendant to take care.

SECTION 6.   LIABILITY IN RESPECT OF SERVANTS

A.   THE COMMISSION OF A TORT BY THE SERVANT

An employer is liable whenever his servant commits a tort in the course of his employment. All the elements of the particular tort[5] must subsist during the employer-servant relationship, except that the employer may be answerable even though the relationship has ceased when the damage occurs.[6]

Where a duty of care imposed on the employer has been broken, but the plaintiff cannot prove which servant of the employer is responsible for the breach, as would be expected, the employer is liable:[7] the burden of proving that due care was taken is shifted on to the employer.

In *Roe v Minister of Health* all three judges in the Court of Appeal stated (*obiter*) that where a plaintiff established negligence on the part of some one or more of several employees of the defendant hospital authority, the defendant authority was vicariously liable although the plaintiff could not prove which of those servants committed the negligent act.[8] Further, the *ratio decidendi* of *Cassidy v Ministry of Health* is that where the plaintiff has been injured as a result of some operation in the control of one or more servants of a hospital authority (and he cannot identify the particular servant who was in control) and in all other respects the requirements of the *res ipsa loquitur* rule in respect of the act are satisfied, the hospital authority is vicariously liable unless it proves that there has been no negligent treatment by any of its servants.[9] These two decisions were arrived at on the basis of vicarious liability,[10] not on breach of duty of employer: there seems no reason, therefore, why they should not be regarded as generally applicable to vicarious liability—there do not appear to be special rules relating to hospital authorities.

B.   THE COURSE OF EMPLOYMENT

Everything depends on whether the servant did the act 'in the course of his employment'.[11] This is an issue of law to the extent that judges have devised

---

5 A procedural bar against suing the servant will not prevent the master from being vicariously liable; and see *Staveley Iron and Chemicals Co Ltd v Jones* [1956] AC 627, [1956] 1 All ER 403, HL; *Broom v Morgan* [1953] 1 QB 597, [1953] 1 All ER 849, CA.

6 *Briess v Woolley* [1954] AC 333, [1954] 1 All ER 909, HL.

7 *Grant v Australian Knitting Mills Ltd* [1936] AC 85, at 101, PC; *Olley v Marlborough Court Ltd* [1949] 1 KB 532, [1949] 1 All ER 127, CA (guest left bedroom key at hotel office: upon the key being taken and the bedroom burgled, onus cast on defendant hotel to prove that they and their staff took reasonable care of the key).

8 [1954] 2 QB 66, [1954] 2 All ER 131, CA.

9 [1951] 2 KB 343, [1951] 1 All ER 574, CA.

10 Although DENNING LJ would have founded liability in *Cassidy*'s case on breach of duty, he agreed with his brethren, SOMERVELL LJ and SINGLETON LJ, in respect of the statement in the text.

11 Even though the act is outside the scope of employment the employer may still be liable for breach of his own duty to provide a safe system of work: in *Hudson v Ridge Manufacturing Co Ltd* [1957] 2 QB 348, [1957] 2 All ER 229, an employer was held liable to an employee for failure to prevent horseplay by another workman known to be likely to harm other workmen; it seems that a claim based on vicarious liability would have failed.

certain principles of law which must be applied, and even when a court has a power of appellate review only on matters of law and not of fact, eg an appeal to the Court of Appeal from the County Court, it will not hesitate to reverse the decision below if these principles are disregarded.[12] The applicability of these rules of law to a particular case is, of course, a matter of fact, and the diversity of employer-servant relationships is so great that it will not be surprising to discover that these issues of fact are frequently of exceptional difficulty. The legal element of which 'course of employment' is composed must now be examined.

C. RELEVANT FACTORS IN DETERMINING WHETHER THE ACT WAS COMMITTED IN THE COURSE OF EMPLOYMENT

(1) MODE OF DOING THE WORK THAT A SERVANT IS EMPLOYED TO DO

One must distinguish a servant's wrongful mode of doing authorised work—for which the employer is liable—from an act of the kind which the servant is not employed to perform.[13] The possible variations of fact here are endless, but one or two examples will explain the working of the rule.

In *Century Insurance Co Ltd v Northern Ireland Road Transport Board*:[14]

> The driver of a petrol lorry, while transferring petrol from the lorry to an underground tank at a garage, struck a match in order to light a cigarette and then threw it, still alight, on the floor. An explosion and a fire ensued.

His employers were held liable for the damage caused, for he did the act in the course of carrying out his task of delivering petrol: it was an unauthorised way of doing what he was employed to do. Similarly, in *Bayley v Manchester, Sheffield and Lincolnshire Ry Co*:[15]

> Erroneously thinking that the plaintiff was in the wrong train, a porter of the defendants forcibly removed him. The defendants were held liable.

And in *Harrison v Michelin Tyre Co Ltd*:[16]

> The plaintiff was injured when an employee of the defendants deliberately steered the truck which he was driving a few inches off the designated passageway and knocked the plaintiff over as he stood at his machine. The defendants were held liable. The momentary horseplay engaged in by the defendant's servant did not take him outside the course of his employment.

Cases of the class now being examined illustrate how much wider is the employer's vicarious liability for the torts of his servant than his personal liability for those of his independent contractor. The facts in very many instances, for example, those in the case last cited, would constitute mere 'collateral negligence' in the case of independent contractors, and yet are 'in the course of employment' for the purposes of the doctrine of vicarious liability. On the other hand, a transport company is not liable when the conductor, instead of the driver, in turning round, on his own initiative, an

---

12 Eg *London County Council v Cattermoles (Garages) Ltd* [1953] 2 All ER 582, CA.
13 *Goh Choon Seng v Lee Kim Soo* [1925] AC 550, PC.
14 [1942] AC 509, [1942] 1 All ER 491, HL.
15 (1873) LR 8 CP 148.
16 [1985] 1 All ER 918; and see *Duffy v Thanet District Council* (1984) 134 NLJ 680.

omnibus at the terminus, negligently injures a third party,[17] but is liable for the negligence of the *driver* who allows a conductor to drive the omnibus.[18]

(2) AUTHORISED LIMITS OF TIME AND SPACE

The conduct of a servant is within the scope of his employment only during his authorised period of service or a period which is not unreasonably disconnected from the authorised period. Thus, a man paid for working until 6 pm who stays on for a few minutes in order to finish a job will still be within the scope of his employment, but not a man who comes into his employer's premises without permission during his holiday. Perhaps the furthest extension to this rule that the courts have made is to be found in *Ruddiman & Co v Smith*:[19]

> The defendants provided a washroom for their clerks. After office hours had ended, and preparatory to going home, a clerk used the washroom, and left a tap running. His act was held to be within the scope of his employment so as to make the defendants liable for the ensuing flooding of adjoining premises.

The courts have often been called upon to decide whether a detour by a servant is within the scope of employment. The classical ruling is that of PARKE B in *Joel v Morrison*:[20]

> If he was going out of his way, against his master's implied commands when driving on his master's business, he will make his master liable; but if he was going on a frolic of his own, without being at all on his master's business, the master will not be liable.

Whether the detour by the servant is a 'frolic of his own' is clearly a matter of degree. Here are two cases, one on each side of the line.

> A carter was in charge of a horse and cart through the day. Without permission he drove them home, $\frac{1}{4}$-mile out of his way, for his midday dinner, and left the horse unattended outside his home. His employer was held liable for damage done by the horse when it ran away.[1]

> A carman, having delivered wine, was to bring back some empties directly to the shop of his employers. On the return journey, before reaching the shop, he deviated from his route in order to pick up a cask at the home of the clerk accompanying him and take it somewhere else for that clerk's private purposes. While on the way to the clerk's home he drove the cart negligently and injured the plaintiff. His employers were held not liable.[2]

A point of great difficulty is to determine when a man, who has gone on a frolic of his own, can be deemed to have re-entered his employer's service. An attempt to establish such a resumption failed in *Rayner v Mitchell*:[3]

---

17 *Beard v London General Omnibus Co* [1900] 2 QB 530; cf *Kay v ITW Ltd* [1967] 3 All ER 22, CA. *Iqbal v London Transport Executive* (1974) 16 KIR 329, CA.
18 *Ricketts v Thos Tilling Ltd* [1915] 1 KB 644, CA. And see *Ilkiw v Samuels* [1963] 2 All ER 879, CA.
19 (1889) 60 LT 708, Div Ct.
20 (1834) 6 C & P 501 at 503.
 1 *Whatman v Pearson* (1868) LR 3 CP 422.
 2 *Storey v Ashton* (1869) LR 4 QB 476.
 3 (1877) 2 CPD 357.

X was employed to deliver beer and pick up empties. He took out the cart on an unauthorised trip and on his return picked up some empties. This was held not enough to constitute a resumption of his employment, and his master was held not liable for his negligent driving while returning, with the empties on board, to the premises of his master.

(3) EXPRESS PROHIBITION

Often, of course, an employer expressly forbids his servant to do certain acts. But it does not follow from this that an act done in defiance of the prohibition is thereby placed outside the scope of employment. If it were so, the employer would only have to issue specific orders not to be negligent in order to escape liability for his servant's negligence. The House of Lords has laid down the rule as follows:[4]

> .. there are prohibitions which limit the sphere of employment, and prohibitions which only deal with conduct within the sphere of employment. A transgression of a prohibition of the latter class leaves the sphere of employment where it was, and consequently will not prevent recovery of compensation. A transgression of the former class carries with it the result that the man has gone outside the sphere.

Again, a few illustrative examples will be given. First, *Canadian Pacific Ry Co v Lockhart*:[5]

> The defendants prohibited their staff from driving uninsured cars on the company's business. In breach of this instruction S drove an uninsured car negligently, whilst engaged on the company's business, and injured the plaintiff.

Holding the defendants liable, the Judicial Committee advised:[6]

> ... it was not the acting as driver that was prohibited, but that non-insurance of the motor-car, if used as a means incidental to the execution of the work which he was employed to do. It follows that the prohibition merely limited the way in which, or by means of which, the servant was to execute the work which he was employed to do, and that breach of the prohibition did not exclude the liability of the master to third parties.

Likewise, a garage hand employed to move vehicles in a garage, but forbidden to drive them, was acting in the course of his employment when he drove a van out of the garage on to the highway in order to make room in the garage for another vehicle, and collided on the highway with the plaintiff's van.[7] These cases may be contrasted with *Rand v Craig*:[8]

> The defendant employed his servants to carry rubbish from X to Y. Instead they deposited some of this rubbish on the land of the plaintiff.

The defendant was held not liable for this trespass because they were

---

4 *Plumb v Cobden Flour Mills Co Ltd* [1914] AC 62 at 67 (per LORD DUNEDIN), HL; (a Workmen's Compensation case, but the principles are still the same).
5 [1942] AC 591, [1942] 2 All ER 464, PC.
6 At 601.
7 *London County Council v Cattermoles (Garages) Ltd* [1953] 2 All ER 582, CA; cf *Limpus v London General Omnibus Co* (1862) 1 H & C 526 (omnibus driver, contrary to instructions, raced a rival omnibus in order to get custom—a direction to jury that these instructions defined the scope of employment held wrong in law).
8 [1919] 1 Ch 1, CA.

employed, not to carry rubbish *generally* but only to carry it from X to Y: the act was therefore of a *kind* that they were impliedly forbidden to do.

If a driver gives a lift to a third party in breach of his employer's instructions and tortiously injures that passenger through careless driving, the courts approach the question of the employer's liability as follows. The issue does not turn on the fact that the passenger is a trespasser.[9] The employer is not liable if his prohibition has marked the limits of the scope of employment, so that giving the lift was outside that scope. On the other hand, if the prohibition affected only the mode in which the employee was to perform his duties, the employer may be vicariously liable. Two cases show the distinction.

In *Twine v Bean's Express Ltd*:[10]

> The employer has a contract to employ his vans on Post Office business. Contrary to his express instruction his driver gave a lift to a third party.

It was held that giving the lift was outside the scope of employment. In *Rose v Plenty*:[11]

> A milkman employed a 13-year-old to deliver and collect milk bottles on his milk round contrary to his employer's order that children were not to be employed by roundsmen in the performance of their duties. The driver negligently injured the boy.

The employer was held vicariously liable because the prohibition affected only the manner in which the roundsman was to perform his duties of delivering milk and did not limit the scope of those duties.

It may be assumed from *Alford v National Coal Board* that the same principles apply where the prohibition is statutory:[12]

> A miner who was acting in breach of statutory duty in acting as shot-firer was held to be acting outside the scope of his employment.

(4) CONNECTION WITH EMPLOYER'S WORK

Frequently, servants do acts which they have no express authority to do, but which are nevertheless calculated to further some proper objective of their employer. Unless the means of accomplishing this objective is so outrageous that no employer could reasonably be taken to have contemplated such an act as being within the scope of employment, the employer will be liable for torts thus committed, as the following cases show.

Poland v Parr is the leading case:[13]

> H, an employee of the defendants, while going home to dinner, reasonably believed that a boy was stealing sugar from a bag on a passing lorry of his employers. He struck the boy, who fell and, in consequence, had to have a leg amputated. Although his act in defence of his master's property was so unreasonable as to be tortious it was not sufficiently excessive to be outside the scope of his employment.

---

9 *Young v Box & Co* [1951] 1 TLR 798, CA; *Rose v Plenty* [1976] 1 All ER 97, [1976] 1 WLR 141, CA.
10 (1946) 175 LT 131, CA.
11 [1976] 1 All ER 97, [1976] 1 WLR 141, CA.
12 [1952] 1 All ER 754, HL (Workmen's Compensation case).
13 [1927] 1 KB 236, CA.

Holding that 'a servant has an implied authority upon an emergency to endeavour to protect his master's property if he sees it in danger or has reasonable ground for thinking that he sees it in danger',[14] the Court of Appeal found the defendants liable. ATKIN LJ, did, however, point out:[15]

> ... where the servant does more than the emergency requires, the excess may be so great as to take the act out of the class. For example, if H had fired a shot at the boy, the act might have been in the interest of his employers, but that is not the test.

With this may be contrasted *Warren v Henly's Ltd*:[16]

> A garage attendant employed by the defendants accused the plaintiff, in violent language, of leaving the garage without paying for his petrol. After paying, the plaintiff called the police and said that he would report him to his employers. At this the attendant assaulted the plaintiff.

It was held that there was no evidence to go to the jury that 'this assault ... was so connected with the acts which the servant was expressly or impliedly authorised to do as to be a mode of doing those acts'.[17]

(5) DELIBERATE CRIMINAL CONDUCT

Evidence that the servant's conduct was a criminal or otherwise wilful wrong-doing will not of itself take that conduct outside the scope of the servant's employment.[18] So an employer may be liable where an overenthusiastic defence of his interests results in an assault which is in the circumstances a crime as well as a tort.[19] A firm of cleaners to whom a furrier had entrusted the cleaning of the plaintiff's mink stole were liable for the theft of the stole by the very servant whose job it was to clean the stole.[20] A dishonest or criminal act is no bar to the employer's vicarious liability.[1] The crucial question is whether that act was committed in the course of employment. Thus the theft of the mink stole by the man entrusted with the job of cleaning it constituted an unlawful mode of doing his job.[2] The theft of the stole by a cook in the canteen at the firm's factory would be an act unrelated to his

14 Per BANKES LJ at 240.
15 At 245.
16 [1948] 2 All ER 935. In *Keppel Bus Co Ltd v Sa'ad Ahmad* [1974] 2 All ER 700 PC, a bus conductor struck a passenger after a quarrel. Given that conductor's duties extended to keeping order, his employer was not vicariously liable because there was no evidence of disorder.
17 Per HILBERY J, at 938.
18 *Barwick v English Joint Stock Bank* (1867) LR 2 Exch 259; *Lloyd v Grace Smith & Co* [1912] AC 716 HL.
19 *Poland v Parr* (supra).
20 *Morris v C W Martin & Sons Ltd* [1966] 1 QB 716, [1965] 2 All ER 725, CA. Even a gratuitous bailee has the burden of proving that he was not negligent if the bailed goods are lost; *Port Swettenham Authority v T W Wu & Co Sdn Bhd* [1979] AC 580, [1978] 3 All ER 337, PC. A bailee is also liable for the negligence of the servants of his independent contractor: *British Road Service Ltd v Arthur Crutchley & Co Ltd* [1967] 2 All ER 785. In *Fairline Shipping Corp v Adamson* [1975] QB 180, [1974] 2 All ER 967, a director who was not himself a bailee, assumed responsibility for refrigerated goods and was held liable for carelessly allowing them to defrost.
1 *Port Swettenham Authority v TW Wu & Co* (supra).
2 As did a burglary by a porter in a block of flats when the porter burgled the flat using keys entrusted to him by his employers, the management company who ran and maintained the flats; *Nahhas v Pier House (Cheyne Walk) Management Ltd* (1984) 270 Estates Gazette 328.

employment there. In the absence of personal negligence by the employer, for example in employing servants known to be dishonest, he will not be liable simply for supplying the opportunity to commit a crime.[3]

Fraud

In *Barwick v English Joint Stock Bank*[4] fraudulent misrepresentations by a bank manager were held to be in the course of employment. Before 1912 it had been thought that the employer would only be liable for wilful wrong-doing where, as in *Barwick*'s case, the act was done for his benefit. In that year *Lloyd v Grace, Smith & Co*[5] was decided by the House of Lords.

In an action to recover title deeds by the plaintiff, a client of the defendant firm of solicitors, the material point was whether the firm were liable for the act of their managing clerk, who, when the plaintiff consulted him about selling her property and realising a mortgage, fraudulently induced her to sign documents transferring these properties to him. The managing clerk was employed to carry out (*inter alia*) conveyancing transactions. Although the firm derived no benefit from these frauds, perpetrated by their servant for his own purposes, they were held liable for his acts.

But the issue of vicarious liability for fraud must be approached cautiously. The liability of an employer for a fraud perpetrated by his servant is not to be treated identically with liability for other forms of wrongdoing. LORD KEITH put it this way:[6]

> ... dishonest conduct[7] is of a different character from blundering attempts to promote the employer's business interests involving negligent ways of carrying out the employer's work or excessive zeal and errors of judgment in the performance of it. Dishonest conduct perpetrated with no intention of benefiting the employer but solely with that of procuring a personal gain or advantage to the employee is governed, in the field of vicarious liability, by a set of principles and a line of authority of particular application.

The key question where it is sought to make an employer liable for a fraud committed by the servant, for his own benefit, is whether the plaintiff relied on ostensible authority with which the employer had clothed the servant. Was it anything said or done by the employer which induced the plaintiff to trust the untrustworthy servant? In *Kooragang Investments Pty Ltd v Richardson & Wrench Ltd*,[8] the respondents had instructed their servant, a valuer, not to act for a particular group of companies in which the valuer had a financial interest. He did so act and submitted valuations to the appellants on the strength of which they lent money to the group. The valuer stamped the valuations with the respondents' corporate name. His own name did not appear on the paper. The Privy Council held that the appellants did not rely on any ostensible authority granted to the valuer by his employers and that he acted beyond the scope of his actual authority which was limited by the prohibition against acting for the group.

A rather different point was canvassed in *Armagas Ltd v Mundogas SA*

---

3 See *Clerk and Lindsell* para 3–28.
4 Supra.
5 Supra.
6 *Armagas Ltd v Mundogas SA ('The Ocean Frost')* [1986] AC 717, [1985] 3 All ER 795.
7 Will LORD KEITH's comments be equally applicable to theft by a servant?
8 [1982] AC 462, [1981] 3 All ER 65.

(*'The Ocean Frost'*).[9] The vice-president of the defendant company had negotiated via a broker a deal with the plaintiffs from which he received a secret
profit. He had no authority to arrange the deal nor did anything done by the
defendants induce the plaintiffs to believe that he had such authority. The
plaintiffs argued that even though the vice-president acted beyond the scope
of his authority as the defendants' agent, he remained within the course of
his employment as their servant. The House of Lords held that, at any rate as
far as the tort of deceit was concerned, the parameters of the servant's course
of employment were determined by his scope of authority.

D. STATUTORY DUTY AND VICARIOUS LIABILITY

It remains undecided to what extent an employer may be vicariously liable
for breach by a servant of a statutory duty imposed directly on him and not
on his employer. In *Stanbury v Exeter Corporation* the local authority which
appointed a sanitary inspector was held not liable for the negligence of that
inspector in carrying out public duties imposed on him by authority of
statute.[10] Both the House of Lords and Court of Appeal have considered
(obiter) whether employers are liable for breaches of statutory duty by miners
employed by them. The point was left open in *Harrison v National Coal
Board*[11] and *England v National Coal Board*,[12] although in the later case it
was held that the employer was vicariously liable for the breach (because it
was still open for the court to regard the act as negligent at common law
despite the fact that the statute covered the same ground[13]). It is thought that
the question is one of statutory interpretation: does the statute intend to
create not only a liability on the employee on whom the duty is expressly
imposed, but also on his employer.[14] So far as the Crown is concerned, it
seems that the rather obscurely worded section 2(3) of the Crown Proceedings
Act 1947 has the effect of making the Crown liable for breaches of statutory
duty by its servants.[15]

---

9 [1986] AC 717, [1985] 3 All ER 795.
10 [1905] 2 KB 838, Div Ct.
11 [1951] AC 639, [1951] 1 All ER 1102, HL.
12 [1953] 1 QB 724; [1953] 1 All ER 1194, CA; and [1954] AC 403, [1954] 1 All ER 546, HL,
   and in *Imperial Chemical Industries Ltd v Shatwell* [1965] AC 656, [1964] 2 All ER 999, HL.
13 See also the Mines and Quarries Act 1954, s 159.
14 *Darling Island Stevedoring Co Ltd v Long* (1956), 97 CLR 36 (H Ct Australia), especially the
   judgment of FULLAGAR J. It may well be that those statutes which impose some duties
   expressly on employers and other duties on employees do not impliedly make the employers
   liable in respect of those duties expressly imposed only on employees.
15 It reads: 'Where any functions are conferred or imposed upon an officer of the Crown as
   such either by any rule of the common law or by statute, and that officer commits a tort
   while performing or purporting to perform those functions, the liabilities of the Crown in
   respect of the tort shall be such as they would have been if those functions had been conferred
   or imposed solely by virtue of instructions lawfully given by the Crown.'
     Section 2(2) provides that the Crown can be liable only for those breaches of statutory
   duty which bind persons other than the Crown and its officers; but since s 2(3) makes the
   Crown liable, not as if for breach of its own statutory duty, but as if it had instructed its
   servant to perform the work, it seems that s 2(3) is unaffected by s 2(2). Contra, the relations
   of public officers with public authorities other than the Crown, on which *Stanbury v Exeter
   Corporation*, [1905] 2 KB 838, probably remains the law.

Chapter 28

Remedies

SECTION 1. EXTRA-JUDICIAL

The availability of a limited number of self-help, extra judicial, remedies has been touched on earlier.[1] The person invoking self-help should remember that he acts at his peril.

SECTION 2. JUDICIAL

A. DAMAGES[2]

(1) NOMINAL

Some interests, for example, one's freedom of movement, the exercise of a vote at an election, possession of one's property, are considered to be so important that any violation of them is a tort.[3] The damages are said to be at large in respect of all these torts, ie although the interest protected may not have a precise cash value the court is free on proof of the commission of the tort to award substantial damages: there is sufficient evidence to support an award of substantial damages.[4] Nominal damages will be awarded where the court decides in the light of all the facts that no damage has been sustained.[5] The function of nominal damages, then, is to mark the vindication, where no real damage has been suffered, of a right which is held to be so important that infringement of it is a tort actionable per se. Nominal damages are given only in respect of torts actionable per se[6] and are not to be confused with a small sum of substantial damages.

One case runs counter to these principles—*Constantine v Imperial Hotels Ltd*:[7]

> The plaintiff, a famous coloured cricketer, was improperly refused accommodation at the defendants' hotel. This was a tort derived from the former action on the case, and actionable per se. BIRKETT J held that he could not grant substantial damages.

The decision is wrong because damages were at large in accordance with the above principles and he found that the plaintiff suffered unjustifiable

---

1 See ante at p 79 (self-defence) and p 98 (recaption, abatement etc ...)
2 Ogus *Law of Damages* (1972); Burrows *Remedies for Torts and Breach of Contract* (1987).
3 For the difficulties involved in deciding whether an action on the case is actionable per se, see the judgment of VISCOUNT HALDANE in *Hammerton v Dysart (Earl)* [1916] 1 AC 57, HL.
4 Eg £5 damages were awarded to the plaintiff in *Ashby v White* (1703) 2 Ld Raym 938 (right to vote); £50 damages were treated as appropriate in *Nicholls v Ely Beet Sugar Factory, Ltd* [1936] Ch 343 (interference with fishery).
5 *The Mediana* [1900] AC 113 at 116 (per EARL OF HALSBURY LC), HL; *Neville v London Express Newspaper Ltd* [1919] AC 368 at 392 (per VISCOUNT HALDANE), HL.
6 Cf *Embrey v Owen* (1851) 6 Exch 353 at 368 (per PARKE B).
7 [1944] 1 KB 693, [1944] 2 All ER 171.

humiliation and distress; he should therefore have made an award of damages which reflected the injury to feelings.[8]

(2) CONTEMPTUOUS

These are derisory damages, marking the court's low opinion of the claim of the plaintiff or their disapproval of his conduct in the matter. They differ from nominal damages in that they may be awarded in respect of any tort, whether actionable per se or not, and in that the fact that they have been awarded might be material in deciding whether to allow costs to the plaintiff.

(3) GENERAL AND SPECIAL DAMAGES DISTINGUISHED

These expressions have various meanings. General damages are such damages as the law will presume to have resulted from the defendant's tort; special damages are such a loss as will not be presumed by the law. The expenses which the defendant has actually incurred up to the date of the hearing are also styled special damages; for instance, in personal injury cases, expenses for medical treatment. Damages which must be specially pleaded in order to give the defendant adequate notice are called special damages. The substantial damage capable of pecuniary assessment which must be proved in the case of all torts not actionable per se is called 'special damage'; all other heads of damage, eg mental distress, are sometimes called general damage.

(4) PERSONAL INJURIES

Detailed discussion of the principles governing compensation for personal injuries and their relationship to other compensation systems can be found in the subsequent chapter.

(5) DAMAGES AND TAX

If the award of damages is not subject to income tax and damages are calculated by reference to income which would be taxable, then tax must be deducted in calculating damages. Therefore tax must be deducted in calculating loss of earnings,[9] or in awarding damages in trespass for loss of rent[10] (rent is taxable but the damages are not). On the other hand tax is not deducted from damages for loss of use of a taxi, for the damages take the form of the income which they represent and are taxable.[11]

(6) 'PARASITIC' DAMAGES

There is no general rule that simply because a particular head of damage is recoverable in some tort then that head of damage is recoverable in any other tort: in that sense English law does not recognise any principle of 'parasitic'

---

8 And see p 466, post for general confirmation by the House of Lords of this approach; *Cassell & Co Ltd v Broome* [1972] AC 1027, [1972] 1 All ER 801.
9 *British Transport Commission v Gourley* [1956] AC 185, [1955] 3 All ER 796 HL. For an assessment of the *Gourley* principle see *Burrows* at pp 115–17.
10 *Hall & Co Ltd v Pearlberg* [1956] 1 All ER 297n. Gourley has also been applied to awards for libel; *Rubber Improvement Ltd v Daily Telegraph* [1964] AC 234.
11 *Morahan v Archer* [1957] NI 61.

damages.[12] At the same time pecuniary loss may be recovered even though the tort is not concerned to protect that pecuniary loss suffered and even though no other tort affords such protection; for example, loss of hospitality may be recovered in slander.[13] And in *Campbell v Paddington Corporation* the facts were:[14]

A nuisance on the highway (stands erected by the defendant for viewing a procession) obstructed the plaintiff's house. The plaintiff was deprived by this of a view from his windows, and suffered pecuniary loss through not being able to charge for the viewing of the procession from the windows. Although the right to view is not a tort-protected interest, this pecuniary loss was held to be recoverable in the tort derived from public nuisance.[15]

(7) AGGRAVATED AND EXEMPLARY DAMAGES

The object of an award of damages in tort is normally to compensate the plaintiff for what he has lost and/or suffered as a consequence of the tort. Yet it is well established that an award of compensatory damages may '... take into account the motives and conduct of the defendant where they aggravate the injury done to the plaintiff. There may be malevolence or spite or the manner of committing the wrong may be such as to injure the plaintiff's proper feelings of dignity and pride.'[16] Such damages are traditionally styled 'aggravated damages'. They are commonly awarded in actions for defamation and trespass. Their availability in other torts is much disputed.[17] Insofar as any award of aggravated damages properly reflects additional injury to the plaintiff, for example, mental distress occasioned by a particularly spiteful libel or humiliating trespass to his person, that award is accurately described as part and parcel of the plaintiff's compensation. The problem is that malice and ill-will may be proved without evidence of any correlative injury to the plaintiff. At that point the addition of any further sum to the compensatory damages becomes punitive in function. And despite LORD DEVLIN's efforts in *Rookes v Barnard,* distinguishing between aggravated (but still compensatory) damages and exemplary (punitive) damages is extremely difficult. Now that mental distress is available as a head of damage in a range of torts, where the availability of aggravated damages is dubious to say the least, is there any genuine need for aggravated damages as such?[18]

---

12 *Spartan Steel and Alloys Ltd v Martin & Co (Contractors) Ltd* [1973] QB 27 at 35 (per LORD DENNING MR), CA.

13 *Davies v Solomon* (1871) LR 7 QB 112.

14 [1911] 1 KB 869. And see especially the clear statement of the principle by LUSH J at 879. Followed in *Owen v O'Connor* [1964] NSWR 1312 (loss of sunlight). The pecuniary loss resulting from the public nuisance has to be foreseeable: *Overseas Tankship (UK) Ltd v The Miller Steamship Co Pty Ltd* [1967] 1 AC 617, [1966] 2 All ER 709, PC.

15 Damages for loss of reputation have been held recoverable in replevin (*Smith v Enright* (1893) 63 LJQB 220), and conversion (*Thurston v Charles* (1905) 21 TLR 659) and it seems that a wife can recover damages for loss of consortium in her action of negligence (*Lampert v Eastern National Omnibus Co Ltd* [1954] 2 All ER 719n) even though she has no action against a person whose negligent conduct in relation to her husband deprives her of consortium. This decision seems unaffected by section 2 of the Administration of Justice Act 1982, but that section prevents a husband from claiming damages for loss of his wife's consortium.

16 *Rookes v Barnard* [1964] AC 1129 at 1221.

17 In *Kralj v McGrath* [1986] 1 All ER 54 WOOLF J vigorously rebutted suggestions that aggravated damages could be awarded in all torts.

18 See A S Burrows *Remedies for Torts and Breach of Contract* pp 202–211.

Exemplary damages are an anomaly in the law of torts. Their object is to punish and deter. The preponderance of opinion is that exemplary damages should be abolished.[19] Their continued existence confuses the functions of the civil and criminal law. The defendant is 'punished' without being afforded the safeguards provided for accused persons in criminal proceedings. And the plaintiff who benefits from the award of exemplary damages receives an unwarranted windfall. Those who defend exemplary damages, notably Lord Wilberforce,[20] stress that the objects of the law of tort have never been exclusively compensatory. Tort retains a deterrent function and, most importantly, in relation to the categories in which exemplary damages remain available, a role in reinforcing the civil liberties of the individual.

It is perhaps the practical problems in applying the present rules on exemplary awards which may tip the balance towards abolition.[1] LORD DEVLIN in *Rookes v Barnard* limited exemplary awards to those categories of cases.

1 'Where the plaintiff has been the victim of oppressive, arbitrary or unconstitutional action by servants of government'. The latter term embraces central and local government and includes police officers.[2] Where unlawful conduct by a police officer is proved it is not additionally necessary to prove that it was arbitrary or oppressive as well.[3]
2 'Where the defendant's conduct has been calculated by him to make a profit for himself which may well exceed the compensation payable to the plaintiff'. Thus publishers who as in *Broome v Cassell & Co Ltd*[4] calculate that a libel may well sell so many copies that they will still profit despite having to pay compensatory damages to the victim may be taught that 'tort does not pay'.[5] So too awards of exemplary damages are commonly made against landlords committing torts against tenants to drive them out of their property in order to profit from selling the property or letting it to someone else at a higher rent.[6]
3 'Where authorised by statute.'[7]

What remained unclear from LORD DEVLIN's purported restriction of exemplary awards in *Rookes v Barnard* was whether the range of torts in which exemplary damages were available, if the defendant's conduct fell into one of the above three categories, was greater than that established by previous authority. Could exemplary damage be awarded say against a producer cynically disregarding the risk posed by a defective product? Are exemplary damages available in torts protecting against the exploitation of

---

19 See (*inter alia*) the proposals for abolition of exemplary damages in defamation in the *Faulks Report—Report of the Committee in Defamation* Cmnd 5609 (1975); A I Ogus *The Law of Damages* (1973) at pp 27–38; *McGregor on Damages* (14th edn) at para 309; A S Burrows op cit at pp 247–250.
20 See his forceful judgment in *Cassell & Co Ltd v Broome* [1972] AC 1027, [1972] 1 All ER 801, HL.
1 Consider the *cri de coeur* from STEPHENSON LJ in *Riches v News Group Newspapers Ltd* [1985] 2 All ER 845 at 850.
2 *Broome v Cassell & Ltd* (supra) at 1130.
3 *Holden v Chief Constable of Lancashire* [1987] QB 380, [1986] 3 All ER 836.
4 Supra.
5 But could an action for unjust enrichment achieve the same laudable aim? See *McGregor on Damages* (14th edn) paras 324–325.
6 *Drane v Evangelou* [1978] 2 All ER 437, [1978] 1 WLR 455.
7 See the Reserve and Auxiliary Forces (Protection of Civilian Interests) Act 1951; s 3(2).

intellectual property?[8] Can exemplary damages ever be awarded in contract? For if not how an evicted and harassed tenant frames his action may determine the availability of exemplary damages.

(8) MITIGATION OF DAMAGE[9]

This expression covers two separate rules in the law of torts:[10]

a There is the situation the converse of the circumstances in which aggravated damages may be awarded[11]—evidence may be given of circumstances which justify a lesser award of damages at large.[12] For example, damages in defamation will be reduced where the defendant has been provoked by the plaintiff.[13]

b The discussion of causation showed that it is the policy of the law not to allow a plaintiff to recover to the extent to which he has brought the loss on his shoulders by his own act.[14] Similarly, where the plaintiff is negligent *after* the commission of the tort against him, he cannot recover further damages caused by that carelessness. *The Flying Fish* illustrates:[15]

> The plaintiff's ship was damaged by the negligence of those in charge of the defendant's vessel. The plaintiff's captain showed want of nautical skill in that he refused aid after the collision; in consequence of this negligent refusal the ship was destroyed. The plaintiff was able to recover the damage caused by the collision but not that additional damage accruing when the ship was destroyed by this negligence of the captain.

In short, contributory negligence is concerned with negligence of the plaintiff before the cause of action has matured by the occurrence of some damage; after damage has occurred and an action in tort is vested in the plaintiff, he has a duty to take care to mitigate his loss. So an injured plaintiff should generally seek medical attention. Where a plaintiff refuses treatment or surgery which could have lessened the consequences of his injury, the onus lies on him to prove that his refusal was reasonable.[16]

This distinction is important, especially because the Law Reform (Contributory Negligence) Act 1945 does not extend to these avoidable consequences of a tort.[17]

---

8 *Morton Norwich Products v Intercen Ltd (No 2)* [1981] FSR 337 (yes); *Catnic Components v Hill* [1983] FSR 512 (no).

9 See Burrows op cit ch 5.

10 For another meaning, particularly in the law of contract, see Street *Damages* p 37 et seq.

11 See p 466, ante.

12 *Peruvian Guano Co Ltd v Dreyfus Brothers & Co Ltd* [1892] AC 166 at 174 (per LORD MACNAGHTEN), HL. *Drane v Evangelou* [1978] 2 All ER 437, CA.

13 *Moore v Oastler* (1836) 1 Mood & R 451n.

14 See ch 14 ante. In *Dodd Properties Ltd v Canterbury City Council* [1980] 1 All ER 928, CA the plaintiff's premises were damaged in 1970, but when he repaired them in 1978 the cost of repairs was much greater. He was allowed the 1978 repair costs on the ground that in deciding what it was reasonable for a plaintiff to do in mitigation it was relevant to ask whether he could afford to repair sooner; distinguishing *Liesbosch Dredger v Edison SS* [1933] AC 449, HL; *Perry v Sidney Phillips & Son* [1982] 3 All ER 705, CA also distinguished *Liesbosch Dredger v Edison SS* in the same way.

15 (1865) 3 Moo PCCNS 77.

16 *Selvanayagam v University of West Indies* [1983] 1 All ER 824, [1983] 1 WLR 585; for criticism see (1983) 46 MLR 754, 758.

17 The 1945 Act applies if the plaintiff's negligence before the accident increased the harm even though it did not contribute to the accident; *Froom v Butcher* [1976] QB 286, [1975] 3 All ER 520, CA (plaintiff passenger not wearing seat belt) and see p 246, ante.

Where the plaintiff does take reasonable steps to minimise the consequences of the defendant's tort he can recover for the harm sustained by him in consequence of his action[18] or expenses thereby incurred,[19] regardless of whether his total loss would have been less had he not acted at all.

(9) SUCCESSIVE ACTIONS ON SAME FACTS

The difficulties presented by this topic are of the same character as those arising from the undefined stand of English law with regard to parasitic damages.[20] The following principles may be spelt out of the decided cases.

The guiding rule can be shortly stated (the difficulty is in defining its terms): *if one and the same act produces two different heads of damage, but does not give rise to two separate causes of action, the plaintiff cannot bring successive actions but must recover in respect of all his damage in the first proceedings.* The policy is to avoid excessive litigation. The leading case is *Fitter v Veal*:[1]

> The plaintiff recovered £11 damages from the defendant for assault and battery. Some years later, he discovered that his injuries were much more serious than he had at first thought, and he underwent a surgical operation for removal of part of his skull. He was held to be unable to recover in a second action any damages for his additional injuries.

(a) Violation of two rights separately protected

If one and the same act violates two rights which are accorded separate protection by the law of torts, then there are two separate causes of action, the prosecution of one of which will not bar proceedings in respect of the other. Thus, in *Brunsden v Humphrey* the facts were:[2]

> A cab driven by the plaintiff collided with the defendant's van through the negligent driving of the defendant's servant. In County Court proceedings the plaintiff recovered compensation for damage to his cab. He then brought a second action in the High Court for personal injuries sustained by him in the same collision, and the Court of Appeal held that this action was not barred by the earlier one.

The interest in bodily security is separate from that in one's goods—hence there were two separate causes of action.[3] Likewise, the following interests are distinct for the present purpose, viz in land, in reputation, freedom of the person, freedom from excessive litigation (ie malicious prosecution).[4] Where one and the same act caused a shortened expectation of life and damaged

---

18 *The Oropesa* [1943] P 32, [1943] 1 All ER 211, CA.
19 *Kirkham v Boughey* [1958] 2 QB 338, [1957] 3 All ER 153.
20 See p 465 ante.
 1 (1701) 12 Mod Rep 542.
 2 (1884) 14 QBD 141, CA.
 3 But does a man have distinct interests in, say, a leg, and an arm? COLERIDGE CJ, dissenting in *Brunsden v Humphrey,* said that was the logical consequence of the decision in that case, but one of the judges who constituted the majority subsequently said that the case 'is no authority for holding that if there be an actionable injury to the person one action may be brought for injury to one part of the body and another action for injury to another part'; per Lord Esher MR in *Macdougall v Knight* (1890) 25 QBD 1 at 8.
 4 *Guest v Warren* (1854) 9 Exch 379. And see *Ash v Hutchinson & Co Ltd* [1936] Ch 489, [1936] 2 All ER 1496, CA, for a further addition to the list.

goods, two actions lay.[5] On the other hand, the interest in length of life and in freedom from pain are deemed to be subsumed under the one interest viz that in bodily security, and only one action may be brought.[6]

(b) Consequential damage where two torts protect the same interest

If the primary purpose of two different torts is to protect the same interest, merely consequential damage which could have been recovered in proceedings for the first tort cannot be claimed in an action on the second tort. *Gibbs v Cruikshank* decides this:[7]

> The defendant executed an illegal distress on the land of the plaintiff. In an action of replevin the plaintiff recovered the goods and the replevin expenses. This action did not preclude a subsequent suit in trespass to land, but it did preclude a later action in trespass to goods for consequential business loss, for both replevin and trespass to goods protect primarily one's interest in goods and, parasitically, business interests.

It would seem that if the chief purpose of the second tort is to protect an interest different from that primarily protected by the first, then damages for the violation of the main interest protected by the second tort can be recovered in proceedings for the second tort even though those damages could have been recovered consequentially in the first action. If, as is supposed, damages for interference with land are recoverable in replevin, *Gibbs v Cruikshank* would be authority for this.[8] Suppose, for instance, that X took from Z letters which were in Z's possession and which were defamatory of Z, and gave them to Y, that in proceedings in conversion against X, Z recovered damages for his loss of the letters *qua* goods, but did not claim or recover (as he could by way of consequential damages[9]) damages for loss of reputation—it is submitted that he would be able to bring a further action for defamation against X, because defamation protects mainly the interest in reputation which is a different interest from that covered by conversion, viz interest in goods.

(c) Successive acts

Successive actions are barred only in respect of *one and the same act*. If, then, A assaults B today and again tomorrow, two actions lie; should he, however, in one and the same fight break B's nose and knock out some of his teeth, then no doubt B has only one cause of action. In less straightforward cases, presumably one must look to the pleadings of the first action to discover whether the facts there relied on do or do not include those later complained of.

(d) One tortious act causing damage on different occasions

Sometimes, however, one and the same act may cause the same damage over and over again. If X digs a hole in Y's land, Y's cattle may fall into it and suffer injury both before and after Y has sued X for trespass to land. There

---

5 *The Oropesa* [1943] P 32, [1943] 1 All ER 211, CA.
6 *Derrick v Williams* [1939] 2 All ER 559, CA; cf *Chant v Read* [1939] 2 KB 346.
7 (1873) LR 8 CP 454.
8 See also *Guest v Warren* (1854) 9 Exch 379.
9 See *Thurston v Charles* (1905) 21 TLR 659.

is, however, only one act of a tortious nature, viz, digging the hole—it follows that only one suit in trespass to land can be brought. If, on the other hand, A throws an object on B's land and B recovers in trespass to land, and thereafter B's cattle stumble over it and are injured, B can bring a second action, for leaving an object on the land of another is an act of trespass in itself, separate from the earlier trespass constituted by throwing the object on to the land.[10]

B. ADVANTAGES OF PROCEEDINGS IN TORT OR CONTRACT

Often, and especially where the defendant's conduct is either negligent or fraudulent, the plaintiff has a choice of suing either in tort or contract. Ordinarily it will not matter which cause of action is relied on. The choice is, however, important in the following respects.

1 Causes of action may perhaps be assignable if in contract for liquidated damages,[11] but not if in tort.[12]
2 Although the plaintiff may not freely evade the contractual immunities of minors and mentally disordered persons by suing in tort, in some circumstances he can sue them for torts committed in the course of a contractual relationship.[13]
3 It is not finally settled to what extent the Law Reform (Contributory Negligence) Act 1945 permits reduction of damages in actions based on contract.[14]
4 There are circumstances in which an action in contract will give greater damages than one under the Fatal Accidents Acts.[15] Although the Fatal Accidents Acts may perhaps bind the Crown in tort proceedings, they do not bind the Crown in contract actions (to which they also extend).
5 The Crown is answerable in tort for the acts of a restricted class of 'servants':[16] that restricted definition does not apply to actions against the Crown for breaches of contracts made by servants of the Crown.
6 In contract time runs from the breach, in negligence it runs from the suffering of the harm or the date when the plaintiff had the necessary knowledge of the facts to sue, if that date is the later.[17]
7 Trade unions are partially immune from tortious liability but are liable for breach of contract.[18]
8 The right of a defendant to have actions in tort by impecunious plaintiffs

10 In principle the same rules should apply to torts not actionable per se. *Maberley v Peabody* [1946] 2 All ER 192, decides that where two separate torts are committed here also two successive actions may be brought. One judgment only (that of LORD BRAMWELL) in *Darley Main Colliery Co v Mitchell* (1886) 11 App Cas 127, HL, does, however, hold that two actions also lie where the one tortious act causes damage on two different occasions, but no support for this isolated judgment has been found in other decisions.
11 *County Hotel and Wine Co v London and North Western Ry Co* [1918] 2 KB 251 at 258 (per McCARDIE J), not considered on appeal when affirmed on other grounds, [1919] 2 KB 29, CA, [1921] 1 AC 85, HL.
12 See Marshall *Assignment of Choses in Action* p 59.
13 See p 521, post.
14 See ante at pp 246–8.
15 *Sellars v Best* [1954] 2 All ER 389; Street *Damages* p 165; Guest (1961) 3 U of Malaya LR 191 at pp 200–201.
16 Crown Proceedings Act 1947 s 2, and p 511 post.
17 See post at p 504.
18 See p 517, post.

transferred from the High Court to the County Court does not apply in contract.[19]

C. TORT AND QUASI-CONTRACT

(1) ELECTION OF REMEDIES

It sometimes happens that a plaintiff has the choice of suing either in tort or in quasi-contract for a wrong. For example, if the defendant wrongfully takes the plaintiff's goods and sells them the plaintiff has the choice of suing in conversion or bringing an action in quasi-contract for the price received by the defendant. It is not proposed to make that detailed examination of the law of quasi-contract which would be necessary if every possible circumstance which could give rise to an action both in tort and quasi-contract were to be considered.[20] The torts which will most commonly be an alternative to an action in quasi-contract are conversion,[1] trespass to goods,[2] trespass to land by removing minerals,[3] and deceit.[4] In principle, the rule is capable of applying to any tort, but of course where the defendant has merely damaged the plaintiff without benefiting himself, quasi-contract will not be an alternative remedy.[5]

This election by the plaintiff to sue in quasi-contract has sometimes been erroneously described as a 'waiver' of the tort. The plaintiff does not 'waive' the tort if he elects to sue in quasi-contract.[6] He is free at any time before he has signed judgment to abandon his suit in quasi-contract and pursue his alternative remedy in tort instead. And his suit in quasi-contract will not bar proceedings in tort on the same facts against another wrongdoer unless the plaintiff has not merely obtained judgment but has also had satisfaction of it. It is true that if he signs judgment in quasi-contract, his claim in tort against that defendant is barred,[7] but that is merely an illustration of the rule that where the plaintiff has succeeded in one cause of action he has no further cause of action in respect of that very violation of a particular interest for which the first cause of action lay.

These rules are clearly illustrated by the leading case of *United Australia Ltd v Barclays Bank Ltd*:[8]

A cheque payable to the plaintiffs was wrongfully endorsed by M & Co, presented by M & Co for payment to, and collected for it, by its bankers, the defendants. The plaintiffs discontinued an action against M & Co in

---

19 County Courts Act 1959, s 46(1); *Edwards v Mallan* [1908] 1 KB 1002, CA.
20 For this, see Jackson *History of Quasi-Contract in English Law* (1936).
1 *Lamine v Dorrell* (1705) 2 Ld Raym 1216; *Thomas v Whip* (1715) Bull NP 130.
2 *Oughton v Seppings* (1830) 1 B & Ad 241; *Rodgers v Maw* (1846) 15 M & W 444; *Neate v Harding* (1851) 6 Exch 349.
3 *Powell v Rees* (1837) 7 Ad & El 426.
4 *Hill v Perrott* (1810) 3 Taunt 274; *Mahesan S/O Thambiah v Malaysian Government Officers' Co-operative Housing Society* [1979] AC 374, [1978] 2 All ER 405, PC.
5 And see *Phillips v Homfray* (1883) 24 ChD 439, CA.
6 And see *Maheson S/O Thambiah v Malaysian Government Officers' Co-operative Housing Society* [1979] AC 374, [1978] 2 All ER 405, PC, where the court also held that a principal whose agent had received a bribe could either sue for deceit or recover the bribe in quasi-contract, but that he could not be compensated twice over.
7 *United Australia Ltd v Barclays Bank Ltd* [1941] AC 1 at 30 (per LORD ATKIN).
8 [1941] AC 1, [1940] 4 All ER 20, HL.

quasi-contract for money had and received without obtaining final judgment. The plaintiffs then sued the defendants for conversion of the cheque. The House of Lords held that the plaintiffs could not be said to have 'waived' their right to sue the defendants by having instituted proceedings against M & Co—nothing less than satisfaction of a judgment in the first proceedings would have barred this action in tort for the same damage. The plaintiffs, therefore, were not precluded from bringing the present action in tort.

(2) ADVANTAGES OF PROCEEDING IN TORT OR QUASI-CONTRACT

There used to be several reasons why the choice of remedy might be important, but, with the ironing out of procedural differences and statutory provision for survival of actions in tort, the choice is now less often an important matter. The main reason now is the different measure of damages.[9] For example, if A converts B's watch valued £10, then in a suit in conversion B will recover £10, but if A sells it to C for £15 B can recover £15 in quasi-contract as money had and received by A. Some of the differences between contract and tort mentioned in the previous section are also relevant here: for example, assignment of choses in action, the disabling effect of infancy or insanity[10] and the operation of the Crown Proceedings Act 1947. A specially indorsed writ is available for quasi-contract: this has certain procedural advantages for the plaintiff over an ordinary writ.

D. ACCOUNT

Sometimes it is more advantageous for the plaintiff to seek an account of the defendant's profits resulting from the tort rather than to claim damages. Frequently the victim of a tort such as passing off[11] will obtain an injunction and an account of the defendant's profits, but the remedy is not confined to these torts.[12]

E. INJUNCTIONS

(1) AS A REMEDY FOR TORTS OR ADDITIONAL REMEDY TO DAMAGES

There are two kinds of injunctions, viz, prohibitory and mandatory. A prohibitory injunction may, for example, be issued against someone who has committed a trespass or nuisance, ie he will be restrained from committing or repeating the act. A mandatory injunction requires the defendant to do a positive act in order to end a state of affairs which amounts to a tort—for example, a mandatory injunction may require him to pull down a wall which interferes with the plaintiff's right to light.

Where an injunction is granted before the trial of an action in order to prevent, pending that fuller investigation into the case which will take place

---

9 In *Universe Tankships Inc of Monrovia v International Transport Workers' Federation* [1982] 2 All ER 67, [1982] 2 WLR 803, the House of Lords held that by bringing an action in quasi-contract (instead of inducing breach of contract) against a trade union the immunity of trade unions under section 13 of the Trade Union and Labour Relations Act 1974, s 13 was evaded by the plaintiff.
10 See *Morriss v Marsden* [1952] 1 All ER 925 at 927 (per STABLE J).
11 See p 116 et seq, ante.
12 See Street *Damages* p 259 et seq.

at the trial, the commission or continuance of an act alleged to be tortious, it is called an interlocutory injunction. Such an injunction is commonly applied for in respect of alleged economic torts such as interference with contract, where the plaintiff contends that the state of affairs resulting from the defendant's act is so serious that the defendant ought not to be allowed to continue to create that state of affairs pending the hearing. A perpetual injunction is a final one, issued after the hearing of the action. A *quia timet* injunction may be issued to restrain a tort which has not yet been committed, but commission of which is threatened.

The jurisdiction of the High Court to grant injunctions is discretionary. An interlocutory injunction may be granted even though the plaintiff has not made out a prima facie case; provided there is a 'serious question', the court decides on the balance of convenience.[13] The courts exercise sparingly their discretion to grant mandatory injunctions, and will refuse unless very serious damage would otherwise occur.[14] A prohibitory injunction will be granted to a plaintiff on proof that the wrongful act is continuing, unless special circumstances exist.[15] An injunction will not be refused because it is against the public interest to restrain the activity; the courts are reluctant to leave the victim of a serious interference with merely a remedy in damages; the leading case is *Shelfer v London Electric Lighting Company*.[16] The most that the courts are willing to do to mitigate the consequences of their granting these injunctions as of course is occasionally to suspend the coming into force of the injunction for a short period,[17] or to impose time restrictions on the injunction.[18]

(2) INJUNCTION AND DECLARATORY JUDGMENT AS A REMEDY WHERE AN ACTION IN TORT DOES NOT LIE

This is a problem of great complexity and importance, which has not been investigated in England, and on which one can only write with diffidence in a work on torts.

---

13 *American Cyanamid Co v Ethicon Ltd* [1975] AC 396, [1975] 1 All ER 504, HL. Lord Diplock enumerated at length the factors to be weighed in deciding where the balance of convenience lay. See also *Garden Cottage Foods Ltd v Milk Marketing Board* [1984] AC 130, [1983] 2 All ER 770 and *Francome v Mirror Group Newspapers Ltd* [1984] 2 All ER 408, [1984] 1 WLR 892 where SIR JOHN DONALDSON MR preferred the phrase 'balance of justice' to balance of convenience (at 413).

14 *Redland Bricks Ltd v Morris* [1970] AC 652, [1969] 2 All ER 576, HL, where detailed rules governing the exercise of this discretion are set out.

15 *Pride of Derby & Derbyshire Angling Association Ltd v British Celanese Ltd* [1953] Ch 149, [1953] 1 All ER 179, CA.

16 [1895] 1 Ch 287, CA. There have been recent attempts to extend the situations where the plaintiff will be left to his remedy in damages, especially *Miller v Jackson* [1977] QB 966, [1977] 3 All ER 338, CA, but the later case of *Kennaway v Thompson* [1981] QB 88, [1980] 3 All ER 329, CA held the *Shelfer* case to be binding, applied its rules strictly, refused to consider the public interest, and held *Miller v Jackson* to be not binding.

17 In *Woollerton and Wilson Ltd v Richard Costain Ltd* [1970] 1 All ER 483, the defendant building contractors operated a crane in the plaintiffs' air space. The court suspended the injunction until the defendants completed the building, because the plaintiffs had refused reasonable compensation and the air space had become valuable only because of the defendants' activities. In *Charrington v Simons & Co Ltd* [1971] 2 All ER 588, CA, the soundness of that decision about the injunction was left open by the court and in *John Trenberth Ltd v National Westminster Bank Ltd* (1979) 253 Estates Gazette 151, the court held that the *Woollerton* case was wrongly decided and refused to follow it.

18 Eg *Dunton v Dover District Council* (1978) 76 LGR 87, CA (the use of a playground was confined to children under 12 and between 10 am and 6.30 pm).

It has been seen that many actions in tort are brought mainly to settle a dispute about title, not to obtain compensation. Suppose that some element of the tort is not satisfied, an element which is properly thought material for a damage-seeking action, but which is irrelevant to the dispute about title. Does the plaintiff lose his action altogether? This question was posed and answered in *Loudon v Ryder (No 2)*:[19]

> L complained that R interfered with her title to investments in certain bodies by representing to the officers of those bodies that he, R, and not L, was entitled to these investments. L's action in injurious falsehood failed because she could not establish malice on the part of the defendant. Yet, held the court, she had established her title to the investments, and she was given a declaratory judgment to that effect.

Approving this decision, the Court of Appeal has since stated that its effect is to permit a declaration 'even though such slander has not been proved, where the court may think it appropriate to state, in the form of a declaration, its conclusion upon the title of the plaintiff which the defendant has in good faith challenged and continues to challenge'.[20]

It is normally stated that the injunction is only a remedy for a cause of action which has, independently of the claim for an injunction, been established by the plaintiff, ie if the plaintiff fails to prove that the circumstances amount to a tort or breach of contract or trust or the like, no injunction can be granted.[1] But is this so? The courts have repeatedly stated that the function of an injunction is to prevent interferences with 'property'. 'Property' in this sense has a very extended meaning going far beyond land and chattels— sometimes it seems almost to mean 'any interest of a plaintiff which in Equity ought to be protected by injunction'. Where a Court of Equity has been confronted with a case outside the range of existing torts it has sometimes granted an injunction, in order to protect 'property'; that is to say, interference with 'property' for the purposes of granting an injunction has had a wider meaning than in torts.

Interferences with economic interests are one illustration of this use of the injunction to protect 'property'. In *Springhead Spinning Co v Riley*,[2] trade union officials exhibited placards in order to deter persons from offering their services to the plaintiff millowners with whom the defendants had a trade dispute. It is difficult to see what tort (at least according to the then state of the law) the defendants had committed, but the plaintiffs sought an injunction. The court neither held that, nor even considered whether, a tort had been committed, but granted an injunction on the ground that injunctions lay to restrain damage to property (the nature of the 'property' was not specified, but no doubt the damage to the plaintiffs' business was meant).[3]

---

19 [1953] Ch 423.
20 *R J Reuter Co Ltd v Mulhens* [1954] Ch 50 at 74–5, [1953] 2 All ER 1160 (per EVERSHED MR). And see *Davis v Carew-Pole* [1956] 2 All ER 524.
1 Eg *White v Mellin* [1895] AC 154 at 163–4 (per LORD HERSCHELL LC) HL.
2 (1868) LR 6 Eq 551; cf *National Sailors and Firemen's Union v Reed* [1926] Ch 536 (injunction granted in respect of general strike on ground that the strike was illegal).
3 Doubts were cast on this case by LORD CAIRNS LC in *Prudential Assurance Co v Knott* (1875) 10 Ch App 142 at 147 (denying that an injunction could be granted in defamation actions), but since that case the courts have left no doubt that injunctions lie in defamation; *Monson v Tussauds Ltd* [1894] 1 QB 671, CA.

Examples need not be confined to economic interests. In *Gee v Pritchard*[4] the plaintiff obtained an injunction to prevent the defendant from disclosing confidential and private material contained in letters (which had already been returned to the plaintiff but of which the defendant had kept copies) written by the plaintiff to the defendant—because, said the court, an injunction lies to protect the plaintiff's right of property in the letters. The English law of torts does not protect privacy, but it is significant that this English case has been the cornerstone of the development in the United States of the tort of infringement of privacy.

Until 1982 it seemed that the injunction was available to protect victims of criminal violations of statutes even though no action for breach of statutory duty lay. We have seen earlier how *RCA Corporation v Pollard*[5] has ruled against the availability of injunctions in such cases.[6]

The possibility of a remedy by way of injunction, even though no tort has been committed, is doubly important when it is noted that Lord Cairns' Act 1858 enables the court to grant damages in addition to, or in substitution for, an injunction.[7]

---

4 (1818) 2 Swan 402. In *Savoy Hotel Plc v British Broadcasting Corporation* (1982) Times 28 December the BBC filmed a barman in the Savoy bar allegedly giving short measure. Because this was without permission the court granted an interlocutory injunction forbidding the televising of the film.
5 [1982] 3 WLR 1007, CA and holding that *Ex parte Island Records Ltd* [1978] Ch 122, [1978] All ER 824, CA, was overruled by *Lonrho Ltd v Shell Petroleum Co Ltd (No 2)* [1982] AC 173, [1981] 2 All ER 456, HL.
6 Ch 22, ante.
7 Now section 50 of the Supreme Court Act 1981.

Chapter 29

Compensation for personal injuries

SECTION 1. INTRODUCTORY

The function and the anomalies of torts as a system of loss distribution in society are well illustrated when we consider the overall provision made for compensation of personal injuries today.[1] The victim's financial future turns on whether he is successful in establishing that his injuries are someone else's 'fault', that a tort was committed. Should he succeed he and his family will receive a level of compensation, which while its method of assessment may be criticised, will meet most of his material needs and will far exceed the total of social welfare benefits available to an equally severely injured person unable to prove 'fault'[2] on the part of another.

Consider this rough example. No liability is accepted for the accuracy of the figures! X, Y and Z all aged 25 suffer severe brain damage rendering them incapable of continuing paid employment. X's accident happens when he is swimming in a cold lake. He gets into difficulties and by the time he is rescued from drowning and resuscitated, the brain damage inflicted by lack of oxygen is irreversible. Y suffers brain damage in the course of surgery to remove his appendix. Proceedings are started on his behalf but allegations of negligence against the hospital are not substantiated. Z's injuries are inflicted in a road accident for which the driver of the other car accepts liability. All three victims before their misfortunes were earning £10,000 a year.

Providing X and Y are successful in obtaining the maximum available social security benefits they may hope for a weekly income of just under £100.[3] A further £23–75[4] may be paid to a relative caring for them. Help from the local authority in converting living accommodation may be forthcoming, and some financial help with invalid aids is feasible. Z the only victim to benefit from the torts system can realistically expect an award of damages of, at the most conservative estimate, £270,000[5] providing him with an approximate weekly income[6] once invested of about £260.[7]

---

1 For full treatment of the topics treated briefly here, see Atiyah *Accidents, Compensation and the Law* (4th edn).
2 For an indictment of the 'fault' principle see *Atiyah* ibid at pp 415–437.
3 At April 1987–88 rates (ie before the April 1988 changes in benefit regulations): Invalidity pension £39.50 (should X or Y have not been contributing to the National Insurance Fund prior to their accidents they would receive only severe disablement allowance at the lower rate of £23.75); mobility allowance £22.10; attendance allowance (high rate) £31.60.
4 Invalid care allowance.
5 Made up as follows: loss of earnings £99,400 (multiplicand £7,100: multiplier 14); pain suffering and loss of amenity £30,000; loss of future care £100,000; provision for holidays and mobility £20,000; alterations to house £20,000.
6 Invested at 5%; see *Auty v National Coal Board* [1985] 1 All ER 930, [1985] 1 WLR 784.
7 Of course not all the capital sum will be invested. A proportion will be used for immediate needs such as conversion of accommodation, special wheelchairs etc. However, where these are specific allowance their cost will generally be added to the total damages award; see the computations in *Housecroft v Burnett* [1986] 1 All ER 332 at 334.

How can the discrepancy be justified? In the case of X, is it that his accident was his own 'fault'? He took the risk on himself. What about Y? Anaesthesia is a dangerous enterprise. Risk cannot be entirely eliminated however careful doctors are. Does Y have to accept the risk to attain the benefit of the surgery? After all X and Y could have insured themselves against their respective injuries. But then so could Z and, as we shall see,[8] if he has so done he will receive his insurance monies in addition to his award of damages. They will not be set off against that award. Consideration of the discrepancies in compensation for personal injuries forces re-consideration of the operation of the 'fault' system and torts.[9] Is the deterrent function of the law of torts more fundamental to the continuance of torts than was first suggested?[10] After all, if there is no moral imperative justifying why Z should be so much better off than X and Y, are there good moral and/or economic[11] grounds, why the negligent tortfeasor who injured Z be made to pay for that injury?

We shall see that the debate on compensating for personal injuries has raged for well over two decades now. Proposals for replacing torts relating to personal injuries by a comprehensive social welfare system have so far gained little ground in the United Kingdom,[12] although they have been implemented in New Zealand[13] and partially implemented elsewhere in the Commonwealth.[14] The overall context of compensation for personal injuries must be borne in mind as we examine the intricacies of the rules for assessment of damages for victims who are (comparatively) lucky enough to be able to prove a tort.

SECTION 2.   AWARDS OF DAMAGES TO LIVING PLAINTIFFS

It must not be forgotten that the overwhelming majority of claims for damages for personal injuries never come to court.[15] And save for one very limited exception,[16] damages are awarded on a once and forever basis. This results in less than perfect rules on how damages should be assessed. Predictability is at a premium perhaps at the expense of individual justice. LORD DIPLOCK explained some of the basic problems affecting awards of damages for personal injuries in *Wright v British Railways Board*:[17]

> claims for damages in respect of personal injuries constitute a high proportion of
> civil actions that are started in the courts in this country. If all of them proceeded
> to trial the administration of civil justice would break down; what prevents this is

---

8 See post at p 484.
9 See *Atiyah* op cit chs 24 and 25.
10 See the 'Report of the Royal Commission on Civil Liability and Compensation for Personal Injury' (Pearson Report) paras 1716–7 (Cmnd 7054–1).
11 See Calabresi *The Cost of Accidents* (1970).
12 See the Pearson Report.
13 See *Atiyah* op cit at pp 564–6 and see *Palmer* (1973) 21 American Journal of Comparative Law 1.
14 Eg Australia.
15 See *Atiyah* ibid at ch 11, and see *Compensation and Support for Illness and Injury* Clarendon Press (1984).
16 Where a provisional award may be made enabling the plaintiff to re-apply for further damages if a risk of further damage eg epilepsy or asteoarthritis does in fact materialise; see s 32A of the Supreme Court Act 1981 post at p 487.
17 [1983] 2 AC 773 at 776–8.

that a high proportion of them are settled before they reach the expensive and time-consuming stage of trial, and an even higher proportion of claims, particularly the less serious ones, are settled before the stage is reached of issuing and serving a writ. This is only possible if there is some reasonable degree of predictability about the sum of money that would be likely to be recovered if the action proceeded to trial and the plaintiff succeeded in establishing liability. The principle characteristic of actions for personal injuries that militate against predictability as to the sum recoverable are, first, that the English legal system requires that any judgment for tort damages, not being a continuing tort, shall be for one lump sum to compensate for all loss sustained by the plaintiff in consequence of the defendant's tortious act whether such loss be economic or non-economic, and whether it has been sustained during the period prior to the judgment or is expected to be sustained thereafter. The second characteristic is that non-economic loss constitutes a major item in the damages. Such loss is not susceptible of measurement in money. Any figure at which the assessor of damages arrives cannot be other than artificial and, if the aim is that justice meted out to all litigants should be evenhanded instead of depending on idiosyncrasies of the assessor, whether jury or judge, the figure must be 'basically a conventional figure derived from experience and from awards in comparable cases'.

Awards of damages to living plaintiffs can be broken down into three main components:

1 pecuniary losses primarily but not exclusively those resulting from loss of earnings or earning capacity;
2 cost of further care such as medical and hospital expenses. The aim of compensation under both these preliminary heads will be to restore the plaintiff, as far as money alone ever can, to the position which he would have enjoyed had the tort never been committed;
3 non-pecuniary loss, pain and suffering and loss of amenity, forms the third head of damage.

The Court of Appeal exercises overall supervision over the level of awards and sets the 'tariff' for non-pecuniary losses.[18] Itemisation of awards is now encouraged to enable awards from individual High Court judges to be scrutinised properly.[19]

A. PECUNIARY LOSSES[20]

(1) LOSS OF EARNINGS

A number of years is likely to elapse between the infliction of the relevant injuries and the trial. Loss of earnings up to the date of the trial are part of the plaintiff's 'special damages'[1] and must be specifically pleaded.[2] All claims for loss of earnings are computed after taking into account deductions which

---

18 Ibid at pp 784–5.
19 For an example see *Housecroft v Burnett* [1986] 1 All ER 332 at 334, CA; and see *Practice Direction (personal injuries actions: particulars of claim)* [1984] 3 All ER 165, [1984] 1 WLR 1127.
20 See Burrows *Remedies for Torts and Breaches of Contract* at pp 168–81.
 1 And see p 465, ante.
 2 *Ikiw v Samuels* [1963] 2 All ER 879.

would have been made by way of tax.[3] Loss of perquisities, such as a 'company car', will also be taken into account.[4]

Prospective loss of earnings is also recoverable. The court estimates the plaintiff's future employment prospects, his future incapacity and the number of working years of which he has been deprived.[5] The traditional judicial method is to arrive at a multiplicand derived from the estimate of his net annual loss and multiply that by a multiplier, the starting point of which is his remaining years of working life. That multiplier is reduced to take account of contingencies such as unemployment and sickness and above all of the fact that he receives a capital sum which he is expected to invest in some interest-bearing securities. The award is calculated on the basis that he will spend the income and part of the capital annually so that the capital will be exhausted at the age which the court has assessed as the appropriate age having regard to all the contingencies. The court assumes a rate of interest which is net after tax. In practice the experience of the court has resulted in a multiplier which, for example, in the case of a thirty-year-old, would ordinarily be about fourteen to fifteen, reducing to about 12 in the case of a man of about 40.[6] Practitioners are familiar with current judicial trends and out of court settlements are negotiated on the basis of the current 'going rate'.[7]

Actuarial evidence is discouraged despite the fact that actuaries are accustomed to using statistical tables to work out expectancies and to 'discount' capital awards so as to reflect contingencies and the immediate receipt of the capital sum.[8]

Nor will the courts hear evidence from economists on future inflationary trends.[9] The House of Lords considers such evidence highly speculative[10] and takes the view that by prudent investment the plaintiff can offset the effects of inflation.[11] Only in those instances where the award is so high that any annuity produced by its investment would attract tax at a high rate will some allowance be made for future inflation.[12] And this will be done by adjusting the multiplier so that in *Thomas v Wignall*[13] where the plaintiff received a then record award of £679,204 the Court of Appeal endorsed the selection of a multiplier of 15 to provide for her 28 years' life expectancy.[14]

3 *British Transport Commission v Gourley* [1956] AC 185, [1955] 3 All ER 796, HL. The case sets out in detail how the notional tax liability is to be calculated.
4 *Clay v Pooler* [1982] 3 All ER 570. Where a director is able to show that his company suffered a loss of profits through his incapacity, so that his earnings fell, damages for this loss were awarded; *Lea v Sheard* [1956] 1 QB 192, [1955] 3 All ER 777.
5 This paragraph is based mainly on the speeches of the House of Lords in *Taylor v O'Connor* [1971] AC 115, [1970] 1 All ER 365; and *Cookson v Knowles* [1979] AC 556, [1978] 2 All ER 604.
6 See *Pritchard v J H Cobden Ltd* [1987] 1 All ER 300, [1987] 2 WLR 627, CA.
7 Relying heavily on publications such as *Kemp and Kemp*.
8 *Mitchell v Mulholland (No 2)* [1972] 1 QB 65, [1971] 2 All ER 1205, CA. In *Auty v National Coal Board* [1985] 1 All ER 930 at 939. OLIVER LJ commented '... the predictions of an actuary can only be a little more likely to be accurate (and will almost certainly be less entertaining) than those of an astrologer'.
9 *Mitchell v Mulholland* (supra).
10 See *Lim Poh Choo v Camden and Islington Area Health Authority* [1980] AC 174 at 193 per LORD SCARMAN.
11 *Cookson v Knowles* [1979] AC 556, [1978] 2 All ER 604, HL.
12 *Cookson v Knowles* [1979] AC 556 at 557–78 (assuming a return of 4·5%–5%; see also *Auty v National Coal Board* [1985] 1 All ER 930, [1985] 1 WLR 784; *Robertson v Lestrange* [1985] 1 All ER 950).
13 [1987] 1 All ER 1185, [1987] 2 WLR 930, CA.
14 But note now the award of just over £1 million in *Aboul-Hosn* (July 1987) (£1,032,000).

The courts continue to show touching faith in the efficacy of fine tuning the multiplicand and multiplier in order to provide an award which is both just and meets the plaintiff's needs. Considerable problems have been encountered recently. As we have noted, several years may elapse between the accident causing injury and the trial. The plaintiff receives his actual loss of earnings up to the trial. The defendants in *Pritchard v J H Cobden Ltd*[15] sought to argue that the multiplier, which is fixed by reference to the period likely to elapse between the date of the trial and the end of the plaintiff's working life, should be reduced to allow for the actual loss recovered as special damages and to discourage delay in bringing personal injuries actions to trial. Their contentions were rejected. The Court of Appeal stressed the need plaintiffs had for a certain and predictable sum in lost earnings to defray their immediate post-injury expenses.

A further difficulty is encountered in fixing a multiplier where the medical evidence suggests that the plaintiff will die early as a result of his injuries. Can he recover compensation for his 'lost years', when but for the eventually fatal injury, he would have continued to earn? Loss of income in the 'lost years' is now recoverable[16] subject to deduction of the plaintiff's own living expenses. For plaintiffs injured in the middle of their working life when they have families and dependants such income should clearly be recoverable. It will be needed to ensure that even after the plaintiff's premature death his family do not suffer and the plaintiff himself can enjoy some relative peace of mind in what remains of his life. Where the plaintiff is a small child the problem of the 'lost years' is just one of the difficulties which make the task of assessing 'loss of earnings' more difficult than usual.

It seems clear that the courts will now compensate loss of earning capacity[17] as readily as loss of earnings. So a married woman who at the time of her injuries is engrossed in child rearing will be compensated for any loss of earning capacity when she would be likely to return to work outside her home.[18] Children and young people who have not started earning will receive compensation for the damage to or destruction of their employment prospects. The older the child and the more evidence there is of her prospects of remunerative work the larger the award will be.[19] With a very young child the speculative nature of assessing his loss of earning capacity will not disentitle him from such an award but may mean a relatively small amount is received under this head of damage. In *Croke v Wiseman*[20] a twenty one month old boy was permanently incapacitated in a medical accident. He was 7 at the date of the trial and likely to survive until he was 40. To compensate him for loss of earnings a multiplicand of £5000 and a multiplier of 5 were set by the Court of Appeal. No award was made in respect of loss of earnings

---

15 [1987] 1 All ER 300, [1987] 2 WLR 627.
16 *Pickett v British Rail Engineering Ltd* [1980] AC 136, [1979] 1 All ER 774 overruling *Oliver v Ashman* [1962] 2 QB 210, [1961] 3 All ER 323, CA.
17 *Smith v Manchester Corpn* (1974) 17 KIR 1, CA; But what of the plaintiff who elects to paint unprofitably rather than do well paid commercial work see *Keating v Elvan Reinforced Concrete Co Ltd* [1967] 3 All ER 611.
18 *Daly v General Steam Navigation Co Ltd, 'The Dragon'* [1980] 3 All ER 696, [1981] 1 WLR 120, CA.
19 See *Housecroft v Burnett* [1986] 1 All ER 332, CA (award of £56,000 for loss of earnings capacity to intelligent 16-year-old girl).
20 [1981] 3 All ER 852, [1982] 1 WLR 71, CA.

in the 'lost years', and this now seems standard for children and young people.[1]

(2) MEDICAL, NURSING AND HOSPITAL EXPENSES

A plaintiff is entitled to recover as special damages, those medical, nursing and hospital expenses which he has reasonably incurred up to the date of trial. His predicted future expenses will then be estimated and awarded as general damages. Where the plaintiff has received private health care or plans to arrange future treatment privately the possibility that the plaintiff could have avoided these expenses by using the facilities of the National Health Service is to be disregarded.[2] In other respects the expenditure must be reasonable both in relation to the plaintiff's condition and to the amount paid. If he has to live in a special institution or in special accommodation, the additional expense is recoverable.[3] He cannot claim the capital cost of acquiring special accommodation, for he continues to own that accommodation.[4] Any saving to the plaintiff which is attributable to his maintenance at public expense in a hospital, nursing home or other institution is set off against any loss of earnings.[5]

The plaintiff is able to claim his nursing expenses. If the court finds, however, that at some future time he will be unable to obtain all the private nursing services required, and will have to enter a National Health Hospital, an appropriate deduction from future nursing expenses is made.[6]

Where the burden of caring for the plaintiff is largely shouldered by relatives or friends, the plaintiff's right to compensation to pay for such services is unaffected.[7] He is entitled to receive a sum sufficient to recompense his wife, mother or friend.[8] That the carer has given up gainful employment must be taken into account and generally her loss should be made good although the total cost of care should not exceed current commercial rates.[9] Recompense is available even though the relative is caring for the plaintiff voluntarily out of love. There is no need for the parties to enter into any contractual agreement and any agreement made for the purpose of increasing the award for care will be treated as a sham.[10] The need for additional help for the family by way of night sleepers to help a paralysed plaintiff and substitute help to give family members a holiday must not be overlooked.

1 See *Housecroft v Burnett* (supra) (girl of 16).
2 Section 2(4) Law Reform (Personal Injuries) Act 1948. If the plaintiff does make use of the National Health Service he cannot recover what he would have had to pay if he had had private treatment; *Cunningham v Harrison* [1973] QB 942, [1973] 3 All ER 463; *Lim Poh Choo v Camden and Islington Area Health Authority* [1980] AC 174, [1979] 2 All ER 910, HL.
3 *Shearman v Folland* [1950] 2 KB 43 [1950] 1 All ER 976; *George v Pinnock* [1973] 1 All ER 926, CA.
4 *Cunningham v Harrison* [1973] QB 942, [1973] 3 All ER 463, CA.
5 Section 5 of the Administration of Justice Act 1982.
6 *Cunningham v Harrison*, ante.
7 *Donnelly v Joyce* [1974] QB 454, [1973] 3 All ER 475 (mother gave up job to care for six-year-old plaintiff); *Cunningham v Harrison*, supra (wife gave up job to nurse husband).
8 In *Croke v Wiseman* [1981] 3 All ER 852, [1982] 1 WLR 71, CA the plaintiff had a life expectancy of 33 years, throughout which he would need continuous nursing by professional nurses and his parents. In awarding £119,000 for the future cost of nursing care the court took account of the mother's losing her teacher's pension rights valued at £7,000 on giving up her post.
9 *Housecroft v Burnett* (supra).
10 Ibid.

(3) ADDITIONAL PECUNIARY LOSSES AND EXPENSES

Loss of earnings or earning capacity, and medical and nursing expenses commonly form the bulk of the pecuniary loss resulting from personal injuries. But in general other losses and expenses which can be shown to flow from the plaintiff's injuries will be recoverable. These include obvious additional costs of coping with a life of disability, removal expenses to a specially adapted dwelling,[11] specially built invalid car or some other means of giving the plaintiff mobility,[12] a telephone for emergencies[13] and so on. Similarly losses resulting from no longer being able to pursue a profitable hobby will be recoverable. A married woman whose injuries impaired her capability to do housework received an award for that impairment based on the cost of obtaining household help.[14] Such an award should on principle be generally available. Housework is no longer the preserve of married women.

But certain 'losses' resulting from injury are more problematical. Traditionally young unmarried women have received an award for loss of marriage prospects where they have suffered disabling or disfiguring injuries. That award was generally regarded as part of the plaintiff's recompense for loss of amenity. But it was paid for by young female plaintiffs in that in assessing the multiplier for loss of future earnings account was taken of the likelihood of marriage and motherhood reducing the number of years in which the plaintiff was likely to be earning.[15] In *Hughes v McKeown*[16] the judge made no award for loss of marriage prospects and consequently then, correctly, declined to reduce the multiplier used to calculate the award for loss of earnings from that appropriate to a young man of similar age. The Court of Appeal has suggested that either approach is equally acceptable.[17] Bearing in mind the change in women's status and lifestyle the time would seem to have come for a young girl's award for loss of earnings to be unaffected by speculation that she will marry and become dependent on her husband. The personal tragedy of loss of marriage and parenthood should be reflected solely in the award for loss of amenity and be equally available to young men.

A second problematic 'loss' occurs where injuries lead to the breakdown of the plaintiff's marriage. Can he recover the additional expenditure involved in running two homes and maintaining his former wife? The Court of Appeal[18] have held that such expenses are irrecoverable. They are not 'losses' resulting from the injuries but rather redistribution of assets. And in any case such 'losses' should be excluded as a matter of policy. The spectre of abuse, of sham 'divorces' clearly haunted the courts.

---

11 *Moriarty v McCarthy* [1978] 2 All ER 213, [1978] 1 WLR 155 (paraplegic moving to a bungalow).
12 *Housecroft v Burnett* (supra).
13 *Moriarty v McCarthy* (supra).
14 The award was made regardless of whether it was actually used to obtain domestic help; *Daly v General Steam Navigation Co Ltd* [1980] 3 All ER 696, [1981] 1 WLR 120.
15 *Moriarty v McCarthy* (supra).
16 [1985] 3 All ER 284, [1985] 1 WLR 963.
17 *Housecroft v Burnett* (supra); but what of the twenty-year-old law student who already has articles at a London firm? Her prospective earnings may be higher than her speculative 'husband's' and she today may well never give up paid work. And what about the financial loss to a young man deprived of the chance of winning a high earning 'bride'?
18 *Pritchard v J H Cobden Ltd* [1987] 1 All ER 300, [1987] 2 WLR 627.

The exclusion of certain heads of potential damage on policy grounds[19] has concerned the courts in two other very different kinds of cases. Arguments that the unplanned birth of a healthy child should never be recoverable as a matter of policy were firmly rejected by the Court of Appeal.[20] An attempt by a rapist, who had earlier recovered damages for the change of personality he suffered after traumatic injury, to obtain indemnity for the damages which he was then ordered to pay to his victims unsurprisingly failed.[1]

Where a plaintiff is permanently incapacitated and in addition to loss of earnings there is a 'cost of care' claim the House of Lords sought to avoid any duplication of damages as follows:[2] A full award for loss of earnings is made in the usual way with no deduction for living expenses except in respect of the 'lost years'. In calculating the award for cost of care, however, a deduction is made for the living expenses which the plaintiff would have incurred in any event had she not been injured.

(4) DEDUCTION FOR BENEFITS RECEIVED

The pecuniary losses and expenses resulting from injury may on occasion be offset by benefits received whether from social security, insurance provision or charity. The Law Reform (Personal Injuries) Act 1948[3] provides that in assessing the damages for loss of earnings, actual or prospective, there is to be deducted one half of the value of any rights which have accrued or probably will accrue to the plaintiff in respect of sickness benefit, invalidity benefit, non-contributory invalidity pension or disablement benefit for five years[4] from the time when the cause of action accrued.[5]

Whether other social security benefits are deducted has to be resolved in the light of decisions at common law. Unemployment benefit[6] and supplementary benefit are deducted.[7] Attendance and mobility allowances are not deductible;[8] nor is a state retirement pension.[9]

Social security benefits are not the only collateral benefits which may result from the plaintiff's injury and disablement. What general principles can be deduced from the authorities on when such benefits should be deducted from the award of damages for loss of earnings and additional expenditure? Any

19 See generally ante at p 181.
20 *Emeh v Kensington and Chelsea and Westminster Area Health Authority* [1985] QB 1012, [1984] 3 All ER 1044.
1 *Meah v McCreamer (No 2)* [1986] 1 All ER 943.
2 *Lim Poh Choo v Camden and Islington Area Health Authority* [1980] AC 174, [1979] 2 All ER 910, HL.
3 Section 2 as amended by the Social Security (Consequential Provisions) Act 1975. Deductions apply to loss of earning capacity as well as loss of earnings, *Foster v Tyne and Wear County Council* [1986] 1 All ER 567, CA.
4 Section 2(1) is exhaustive of the extent to which the prescribed benefits may be set off against damages. No deductions may be made for receipts after the five year period; *Haste v Sandell Perkins Ltd* [1984] QB 735, [1984] 2 All ER 615; *Denman v Essex Area Health Authority* [1984] QB 735, [1984] 2 All ER 621.
5 For interpretation of this section, see *Flowers v George Wimpey & Co Ltd* [1956] 1 QB 73, [1955] 3 All ER 165; *Hultquist v Universal Pattern and Precision Engineering Co Ltd* [1960] 2 QB 467, [1960] 2 All ER 266, CA; and *Eley v Bedford* [1972] 1 QB 155, [1971] 3 All ER 285.
6 *Nabi v British Leyland (UK) Ltd* [1980] 1 All ER 667, CA.
7 *Mehmet v Perry* [1977] 2 All ER 529; *Plummer v P W Wilkins & Son Ltd* [1981] 1 All ER 91; *Lincoln v Hayman* [1982] 2 All ER 819, CA.
8 *Bowker v Rose* (1978) 122 Sol Jo 147, CA.
9 *Hewson v Downs* [1970] 1 QB 73, [1969] 1 All ER 193.

attempt to present a rational picture of the rules is likely to fail.[10] The courts make every effort to encourage benevolence so charitable payments made to the plaintiff, for example, from a disaster fund, will not be deducted,[11] nor generally will *ex gratia* payments by employers.[12] Proceeds of personal insurance policies provided for by the plaintiff or his family will not be deducted.[13] But where even despite his sickness or disability the plaintiff receives sick pay as part of his contract of employment he must account for those monies[14] unless the contract provides that sick pay must be refunded in the event of a successful tort claim.[15] In *Parry v Cleaver*[16] the House of Lords held that an occupational disability pension was not deductible whether it was contributory or discretionary. The test, their Lordships held, was two fold: was the money received of the same nature as what was lost, and if not, was it a benefit still intended to be paid even if the plaintiff were to be re-imbursed from another source. Thus statutory sick pay payable by the employer under the Social Security and Housing Benefits Act 1982 was later held deductible.[17] It was essentially the same as a contractual entitlement for sick pay.

In *Hussain v New Taplow Paper Mills Ltd*[18] the injured plaintiff received long-term sickness benefit provided for by a permanent health insurance scheme arranged by his employers and taken out for their (the employers') benefit. The monies received were held to be indistinguishable from con-tractual sick pay as opposed to analogous to a disabling pension or private insurance monies. The defendants in this case were the plaintiff's employers but the Appeal Court[19] tentatively expressed the view that the result would have been the same had the tortfeasor been a third party. They further suggested that at any rate as between plaintiff employees and their employers *ex gratia* benefits ought to be accounted for. It remains to be seen whether *Hussain v New Taplow Paper Mills Ltd* heralds a greater readiness by the courts to require plaintiffs to account for benefits received.

Two principles of compensatory damages are in conflict when deduction of collateral benefits is in issue:

1 the plaintiff should receive his actual estimated loss and not benefit by his injuries; and
2 the tortfeasor's liability should not be reduced by monies paid to benefit the plaintiff. The tortfeasor should not benefit from the plaintiff's good fortune or prudence in insuring against disability.

In Mr Hussain's case the crucial factor appears to be that it was his employers who were found to have been prudent and to have intended their prudence ultimately to benefit themselves.

10 See the discussion in Burrows *Remedies for Tort and Breach of Contract* ch 2.
11 *Redpath v Belfast and County Down Rly* [1947] NI 167 approved in *Parry v Cleaver* [1970] AC 1, [1969] 1 All ER 555, HL.
12 *Cunningham v Harrison* [1973] QB 942, [1973] 3 All ER 463; but see *Hussain v New Taplow Paper Mills Ltd* [1987] 1 All ER 417, [1987] 1 WLR 336 (where the employer is the defendant).
13 *Bradburn v Great Western Rly Co* (1874) LR 10 Exch 1 approved in *Parry v Cleaver* (supra).
14 *Turner v Ministry of Defence* (1969) 113 Sol Jo 585.
15 *Browning v War Office* [1963] 1 QB 750, [1962] 3 All ER 1089.
16 [1970] AC 1, [1969] 1 All ER 555, HL.
17 *Palfrey v Greater London Council* [1985] ICR 437. Redundancy payments will be deducted only if the plaintiff's injuries are the sole cause of his redundancy; *Wilson v National Coal Board* 1981 SLT 67; *Mills v Hassall* [1983] ICR 330.
18 [1988] 2 WLR 266, HL.
19 [1987] 1 All ER 417, [1987] 1 WLR 336, CA.

B. NON-PECUNIARY LOSSES

(1) PAIN AND SUFFERING

The plaintiff is entitled to compensation for the pain and suffering, both actual and prospective, which is caused by the injury or subsequent surgical operations.[20] If his expectation of life has been reduced by his injuries, an award of damages for pain and suffering shall take account of any suffering caused or likely to be caused to him by awareness that his expectation of life has been shortened.[21] A permanently unconscious plaintiff has no claim for pain and suffering.[1]

(2) LOSS OF AMENITIES

Compensation is also recoverable for loss of faculty. Even though the accident has converted the plaintiff into a human vegetable so that he is unaware of his injuries, he is still entitled to claim for any loss of bodily function.[2] Damages cannot be refused because the plaintiff will be unable to enjoy the damages in view of the severity of his injuries.[3] Damages are awarded for the fact of deprivation, a substantial loss. The award for loss of amenities must be made on the basis of amenities lost; it is irrelevant that the plaintiff is unaware of his deprivation. The court will take into account deprivation of sexual pleasures,[4] loss of a holiday,[5] inability to fish,[6] disfigurement,[7] as well as more obvious losses, such as inability to play games or to walk. In short, damages under this head may be increased by taking into account subjective factors, but they are not reduced because the plaintiff has been rendered unconscious or unable to appreciate his loss.

(3) ASSESSING THE QUANTUM

Non-pecuniary damages differ from pecuniary damages in that there is no scientific method of deciding what sum should be awarded. Damages for loss of amenity and pain and suffering are normally awarded as an aggregate lump sum. This is a conventional sum which is taken to be the sum which society deems fair, fairness being interpreted by the courts in the light of previous decisions. There has evolved a set of conventional principles providing a provisional guide to the comparative severity of different injuries,

---

20 *H West & Son Ltd v Shephard* [1964] AC 326, [1963] 2 All ER 625, HL; *Cutler v Vauxhall Motors Ltd* [1971] 1 QB 418, [1970] 2 All ER 56, CA. In *Sutton v Population Services Family Planning Programme Ltd* (1981) Times, 7 November; damages were awarded for the premature onset of the menopause. And in *Kralj v McGrath* [1986] 1 All ER 54 the plaintiff received damages for her trepidation concerning a further wanted pregnancy after an obstetric 'nightmare'.

21 Section 1(1)(b) Administration of Justice Act 1982. Damages for loss of expectation of life as such and as a separate head of damage were abolished by this Act.

1 *Wise v Kaye* [1962] 1 QB 638, [1962] 1 All ER 257, CA.

2 *H West & Son Ltd v Shephard*, supra, HL; *Lim Poh Choo v Camden and Islington Area Health Authority* [1980] AC 174, [1978] 2 All ER 910, HL.

3 *H West & Son Ltd v Shephard*, supra.

4 *Cook v J L Kier & Co Ltd* [1970] 2 All ER 513, CA.

5 *Ichard v Frangoulis* [1977] 2 All ER 461.

6 *Moeliker v A Reyrolle & Co Ltd* [1977] 1 All ER 9, CA.

7 Where a husband's disfigurement caused his wife to leave him and his children, £7,000 was awarded to him under that head in *Oakley v Walker* (1977) 121 Sol Jo 619. Financial losses resulting from divorce are generally irrecoverable see *Pritchard v J H Cobden Ltd* (supra).

and introducing a bracket of damages into which a particular injury will currently fall. The particular circumstances of the plaintiff, including his age and any unusual deprivation which he suffers, are taken into account.

The fall in the value of money leads to a continuing reassessment of these awards.[8] What happens in practice is that practitioners' books and periodicals[9] regularly publish judicial awards under all the relevant heads, such as blindness, loss of leg, loss of arm, paraplegia, with brief details of the plaintiff's circumstances. This enables plaintiff's lawyers and defendant's insurers to assess likely awards and judges to conform to the current levels of awards made by their brethren.

The intrinsic difficulty of awarding a sum of money as compensation for the loss of amenity resulting from catastrophic injury and the problem of updating awards to compensate for the fall in the value of money are well illustrated in *Housecroft v Burnett*.[10] The injuries sustained by the 16-year-old plaintiff resulted in tetraplegia. The life which she could have expected with its pleasures, career prospects and the hope of a family was replaced by complete dependance on her mother for every aspect of her care. The court recognised the imprecise nature of the task but stressed the need for uniformity where possible. The bracket of acceptable awards should be set by reference to recent decisions. No attempt to backtrack to, and then allow for inflation on, pre-1980 awards should be encouraged. £75,000 was set as the tariff for tetraplegia where the plaintiff was fully aware of her disability but not in pain. Physical pain, impairment of speech of hearing would justify an award of above the average. Lack of awareness of the disability might justify a lower award.

(4) PROVISIONAL AWARDS

Frequently the courts are called on to award prospective damages where the medical prognosis is imprecise. For example, the injury may have created a risk of epilepsy or osteoarthritis developing later in life. The courts used to estimate the percentage change of such a condition developing and award an equivalent proportion of damages for the results of that condition. Plaintiffs were consequently over compensated if the risk did not materialise and under-compensated if it did. The Administration of Justice Act 1982 accordingly has provided an alternative. Where there is a chance that the plaintiff at some definite or indefinite time in the future will as a result of the tortious act or omission develop some serious disease or suffer some serious deterioration in his physical or mental condition that Act provides as follows:[11] rules may be made, and have now been made, to enable the court to assess damages on the assumption that the development or deterioration will not occur and to award further damages at a future date if it does occur on an application by the plaintiff.[12]

---

8 *Birkett v Hayes* [1982] 2 All ER 710, CA.
9 Especially Kemp and Kemp *Quantum of Damages* and the monthly publication *Current Law*, under the heading of Damages.
10 [1986] 1 All ER 332, CA.
11 Section 6(1) introducing a new s 32A(i) to the Supreme Court Act 1981.
12 Section 6(2) and s 32(A)(ii) respectively. And see RSC Ord 37, rr 8–10.

(5) INTEREST

The courts have power to award interest on all or any part of an award of damages and should do so on awards for personal injuries or death unless there are 'special reasons' not to do so.[13] Detailed exposition of the rules on interest is beyond the scope of this work.[14] The general rule is that interest on pre-trial pecuniary loss will be payable at half the average rate on short-term investment accounts for that period.[15] Interest payable on non-pecuniary loss will be low—not more than 2% at present.[16]

C. DAMAGE OR DESTRUCTION OF GOODS

Claimants in personal injury actions often also have a claim for damage to goods, especially to their cars, so that it is convenient to outline here the relevant law for assessing compensation for that loss. Where the car or other goods are destroyed damages are made up of the cost of buying a replacement, together with compensation for loss of use pending replacement, with a deduction for the salvage value of the destroyed goods.[17] Where there is damage to goods, the measure is the diminution in value, normally based on the cost of repair.[18] Damages are also given for loss of use, even though the goods were non-profit earning and not replaced during repair. Thus a motorist who has a car for pleasure can claim repair costs and compensation for loss of use while it is off the road.[19] If a substitute has been hired then the cost can be claimed, provided that the goods hired and the price paid are reasonable.[20]

SECTION 3.   DEATH

It has been assumed so far that the tortious injuries have not proved fatal. When death ensues two issues arise. The deceased's estate may wish to proceed with the cause of action which the deceased himself would have had if he had not died. Secondly, others, especially relatives, may claim that they have suffered a loss in consequence of the death. In the main, two statutes will be examined: the Law Reform (Miscellaneous Provisions) Act 1934 which deals with survival of actions, and the Fatal Accidents Act 1976 with respect to death as giving rise to a cause of action.

13 Supreme Court Act s 34A inserted by the Administration of Justice Act 1982.
14 See *Burrows* (supra) at pp 224–8.
15 *Jefford v Gee* [1970] 2 QB 130, [1970] 1 All ER 1202.
16 *Birkett v Hayes* [1982] 2 All ER 710, [1982] 1 WLR 816, CA; *Wright v British Railways Board* [1983] 2 AC 773, [1983] 2 All ER 698, HL. The reasons are (1) damages should take into account inflation up to the time of judgment and (2) damages for nonpecuniary loss are often difficult to quantify until the plaintiff's condition has stabilised.
17 *Moore v DER Ltd* [1971] 3 All ER 517, CA; *Thatcher v Littlejohn* [1978] RTR 369, CA. And see *Liesbosch Dredger v Edison SS* [1933] AC 449.
18 *Dodd Properties (Kent) Ltd v Canterbury City Council* [1980] 1 All ER 928, CA.
19 *The Mediana* [1900] AC 113, HL; *H L Motorworks (Willesden) Ltd v Alwahbi* [1977] RTR 276, CA.
20 *H L Motorworks (Willesden) Ltd v Alwahbi*, supra (reasonable to hire a Rolls Royce till plaintiff's Rolls Royce repaired).

A. SURVIVAL OF CAUSES OF ACTION

The Law Reform (Miscellaneous Provisions) Act provides that, subject to three significant exceptions, on the death of any person all causes of action vested in him survive for the benefit of his estate.[1] Actions for defamation do not survive. The right of a person to claim under section 1A of the Fatal Accidents Act 1976 for bereavement[2] does not survive for the benefit of his estate.[3] Nor are exemplary damages available to an estate.[4] All are regarded as claims personal to the deceased.

The effect of the 1934 Act is that where the death of the deceased has been caused by the act or omission giving rise to the cause of action this Act enables his estate to bring proceedings in tort against the defendant.[5] His estate may claim damages according to the usual principles for the period between when the cause of action arises and the death. Thus damages may be awarded for pain and suffering[6] and loss of amenity[7] for that period during which the deceased actually suffered such deprivations. Damages may also be awarded for earnings lost[8] and medical expenses incurred[9] up to the time of death.

The damages awarded to his estate 'shall be calculated without reference to any loss or gain to his estate consequent on his death'.[10] For example, if the deceased loses an annuity to which he was entitled, or if insurance monies become payable upon his death, these losses and gains are disregarded in estimating the damages under the Act of 1934.

The rights conferred by the 1934 Act are in addition to and not in derogation of any rights conferred by the Fatal Accidents Act.[11] The award of damages under the 1934 Act is the same whether or not an award is also made under the Fatal Accidents Act 1976.

No damages may now be awarded to the estate in respect of loss of income in the deceased's 'lost years'.[12] The potential overlap between claims by dependants under the Fatal Accidents Act for loss of dependency and an estate's claims for lost income from the 'lost years' is thus avoided.[13]

The Act of 1934 applies even though death follows instantaneously upon the commission of the tort.[14] Since the Administration of Justice Act 1982

---

1 Section 1(1), as amended by the Law Reform (Miscellaneous Provisions) Act 1970.
2 P 492, post.
3 Section 4(1) of the Administration of Justice Act 1982.
4 Section 4(2) of the 1982 Act, replacing s 1(2)(a) of the 1934 Act.
5 For the limitation periods within which these proceedings must be brought, see s 11(5)(6)(7) of the Limitation Act 1980, and p 510, post.
6 *Andrews v Freeborough* [1967] 1 QB 1, [1966] 2 All ER 721, CA (£2,000 awarded to the estate of a child of 8 who remained unconscious for a year between the accident and death); *Murray v Shuter* [1976] QB 972, [1975] 3 All ER 375 (£11,000 awarded to the estate of a man of 36 in respect of pain and suffering and loss of amenity during the four years he survived the accident in a coma).
7 *Rose v Ford* [1937] AC 826, [1937] 3 All ER 359, HL (£2 awarded for loss of leg amputated 2 days before death).
8 *Murray v Shuter* [1976] QB 972, [1975] 3 All ER 375.
9 *Rose v Ford* [1937] AC 826, [1937] 3 All ER 359, HL.
10 Section 1(2).
11 Section 1(5) of the 1934 Act: *Yelland v Powell Duffryn Associated Collieries Ltd (No 2)* [1941] 1 KB 519, [1941] 1 All ER 278, CA.
12 Administration of Justice Act s 4(2)(a) amending s 1(2)(a) of the 1934 Act.
13 See *Gammell v Wilson* [1982] AC 27, [1980] 2 All ER 557.
14 *Morgan v Scoulding* [1938] 1 KB 786, [1938] 1 All ER 28.

came into force, however, there is only one circumstance in which a claim may be made under the 1934 Act where death is immediate, and even that is of restricted application. Whether the deceased dies immediately or not, a claim for funeral expenses may be made.[15] But if a dependant incurred funeral expenses in respect of the deceased, and even though he was unable to prove any loss of pecuniary advantage consequent on the death, those funeral expenses may be claimed under the Fatal Accidents Act 1976.[16]

B. DEATH AS A CAUSE OF ACTION

(1) HISTORICAL INTRODUCTION

At common law no action in tort could be brought by third parties who suffered loss through the killing of another.[17] It has been questioned whether the reasons, derived from legal history, which the courts have adduced in support of this rule, are sound,[18] but there is little point in discussing that: the rule has been authoritatively upheld by the House of Lords in *Admiralty Commissioners v SS Amerika*.[19]

Fatal accidents became so frequent with the development of railways that in 1846 Parliament had to pass the Fatal Accidents Act (commonly called Lord Campbell's Act), which made considerable inroads on the common-law rule. This Act, now the Fatal Accidents Act 1976 as amended, must now be looked at in detail. The Act only benefits certain dependants. Except as thereby provided, the law of torts still does not recognise the interest of one person in the life of another. An employee, therefore, never can sue if his employer is killed and he loses his job; a church may have the prospect of large financial support for many years from a wealthy member, but will have no action if he is killed; an insurance company has no cause of action because it has to discharge its obligations under a life policy sooner than it otherwise would: interests beyond those of the family have no recognition when death occurs.

Section 1(1) of the Fatal Accidents Act 1976 enacts:[20]

> If death is caused by any wrongful act, neglect or default which is such as would (if death had not ensued) have entitled the person injured to maintain an action and recover damages in respect thereof, the person who would have been liable if death had not ensued shall be liable to an action for damages, notwithstanding the death of the person injured.[1]

(2) WHO MAY SUE?

The action is brought in the name of the executor or administrator[2] of the deceased, and lies for the benefit of the following relatives:[3] wife, husband or

---

15 Section 1(2)(c).
16 Section 3(5) and *Stanton v Ewart F Youlden* [1960] 1 All ER 429.
17 *Baker v Bolton* (1808) 1 Camp 493.
18 See Holdsworth, HEL vol iii, pp 331–6, 676–7; cf *Rose v Ford* [1937] AC 826 at 834 (per LORD ATKIN).
19 [1917] AC 38, HL.
20 As amended by the Administration of Justice Act 1982.
 1 For railway accidents, see Carriage by Railway Act 1972 as amended by s 4(3) of the Fatal Accidents Act 1976 as amended by the 1982 Act.
 2 Section 2(1) of the 1976 Act.
 3 Section 1(2)(3)(4)(5) as amended by the 1982 Act.

former wife or husband,[4] children, grandchildren, father, mother, step-parents, grandparents, brothers, sisters, uncles, aunts and their issue, adopted and illegitimate dependants and step-children of the several categories.[5] If there is no executor or administrator, or if he fails to bring the action within six months after the death of the deceased any dependant may bring the action.[6] The Administration of Justice Act 1982 responded to social changes by including for the first time any person who was living with the deceased in the same household for at least two years before that date, and was living during the whole of that period as the husband or wife of the deceased.[7]

(3) NATURE OF THE ACT COMPLAINED OF

It must first be proved that the act caused the death.[8] An action lies only where there is a 'wrongful act, neglect or default' by the defendant; these words presumably embrace any tort.[9] Consequently, if the defendant's act was never tortious because he would have had a defence to any action brought by the deceased in his lifetime, no action will lie.[10] Where the deceased died as the result partly of his own fault and partly of the fault of any other person, damages are reduced to a proportionate extent[11] in the same way as under the Law Reform (Contributory Negligence) Act 1945.[12] If a dependant's contributory negligence is a cause of the deceased's death that dependant's damages are reduced, but the awards to other dependants are unaffected.[13]

At the time of his death the deceased must have been in a position to sue the defendant had he not died because of the wrongful act. If the limitation period expired between the injury and his death, the Limitation Act 1980 enacts that no Fatal Accidents Act claim can come into existence.[14] This ordinarily[15] means that if more than three years have elapsed between the injury and death, the claim is barred.[16] The 1980 Act also provides that if the

---

4 An addition by the 1982 Act to s 1(3)(a) of the 1976 Act. By section 1(4) of the 1976 Act a former spouse includes a person whose marriage has been annulled or declared void as well as a divorced person.

5 Section 1(5)(a) 'any relationship by affinity shall be treated as a relationship by consanguinity, any relationship of the half blood as a relationship of the whole blood, and the stepchild of any person as his child'. The defendant must be given particulars of the dependants for whom a claim is made and of the nature of this claim; s 2(4) of the 1976 act as amended by the 1982 Act.

6 Section 2(2) of the Fatal Accidents Act 1976, as amended by the Administration of Justice Act 1982.

7 Section 1(3)(b) of the 1976 Act as amended by the 1982 Act.

8 In *Pigney v Pointer's Transport Services Ltd* [1957] 2 All ER 807, the deceased committed suicide while in a depressive state induced by the defendant's negligent act; the death was held to have been caused by that act, so that an action under the Fatal Accidents Act was successful.

9 And a negligent breach of contract: *Grein v Imperial Airways Ltd* [1937] 1 KB 50, [1936] 2 All ER 1258, CA.

10 *Murphy v Culhane* [1977] QB 94, [1976] 3 All ER 533, CA (if the deceased would have failed because of the defence of *ex turpi causa*—see ch 6, ante—no action lay under the Act).

11 Fatal Accidents Act 1976, s 5, as amended by the Administration of Justice Act 1982, s 3(2).

12 See p 238, ante.

13 *Dodds v Dodds* [1978] QB 543 [1978] 2 All ER 539. The negligent dependant may also be required to make a contribution under the Civil Liability (Contribution) Act 1978 towards the damages which the defendant has to pay for the benefit of the dependants.

14 Section 12(1).

15 The three-year period can be extended if the deceased did not have 'relevant knowledge' of his cause of action; and see p 510 et seq post.

16 Section 11(1) and see ch 15, ante.

deceased had settled his own claim,[17] no action lies under the Fatal Accidents Act,[18] but an action still lies (and without any limit on the damages) if the plaintiff had merely agreed beforehand that no more than £x damages should be recoverable in the event of his being the victim of this tort.[19]

(4) THE NATURE OF THE INTERESTS PROTECTED

The Administration of Justice Act 1982 for the first time provides that in certain restricted circumstances an action under the Fatal Accidents Act may consist of or include a claim for damages for bereavement.[20] This claim may be brought for the benefit of the wife or husband of the deceased.[1] It is not available for former spouses or where the parties, though living together as husband and wife, were not married. The only other case in which a claim may be made is where the deceased was a minor (ie under the age of 18) who was never married and the claim is on behalf of his parents, if he was legitimate, or on behalf of his mother, if he was illegitimate.[2]

Apart from that claim for bereavement, a claim by a dependant lies only on proof of pecuniary loss.[3] The language ordinarily used by the courts is that there must be a loss of 'prospective pecuniary advantage' and that a 'speculative possibility' of pecuniary gain is not enough[4]—a parent therefore could recover when his 16-year-old daughter died, having almost completed her unpaid dressmaking apprenticeship;[5] but the parent of a three-year-old child has been held to have no cause of action.[16] Strict application of the *dicta* in these cases would lead to the conclusion that nothing is recoverable for loss of the investment in a deceased child's education or for loss by a child of his deceased father's advice and guidance—the courts appear to restrict the claim to loss of that direct financial contribution to the dependant which the deceased would have made had he lived. And although it is not essential that the dependant should have a legal right to that aid[7] (the loss of services gratuitously rendered is enough)[8] if the pecuniary benefit to the dependant would have accrued, not *qua* family relationship, but *qua* business

---

17 *Pickett v British Rail Engineering Ltd* [1980] AC 136 at 146–7 (per LORD WILBERFORCE) and 152 (per LORD SALMON), [1979] 1 All ER 774 at 780 and 787 respectively, HL.
18 Section 12(1).
19 *Nunan v Southern Rly Co* [1924] 1 KB 223, CA.
20 The Act adds a new section 1A(1) to the Fatal Accidents Act 1976.
 1 Section 1A(2)(a).
 2 Section 1A(2)(b).
 3 *Duckworth v Johnson* (1859) 4 H & N 653.
 4 *Davies v Taylor* [1974] AC 207, [1972] 3 All ER 836, HL, wife deserted husband five weeks before his death; shortly before his death he instructed solicitor to begin divorce proceedings. The deserting wife had no claim, for she had to show reasonable expectation of pecuniary benefit—there had to be significant prospect, not mere speculative possibility, of reconciliation with husband had he lived, and this she failed to prove. In *Kandalla v British European Airways Corporation* [1981] QB 158, [1980] 1 All ER 341, elderly parents of two young women doctors were awarded damages on proof that the doctors intended to flee from Iraq (where they had been working) to England where they would have supported their parents.
 5 *Taff Vale Rly Co v Jenkins* [1913] AC 1, HL.
 6 *Barnett v Cohen* [1921] 2 KB 461.
 7 *Stimpson v Wood & Son* (1888) 57 LJQB 484; the mere fact that a wife by her adultery had lost her legal right to maintenance did not bar her claim. No claim may be made by a widow who knew that her support came from the proceeds of her husband's crimes; *Burns v Edman* [1970] 2 QB 541, [1970] 1 All ER 886.
 8 *Berry v Humm & Co* [1915] 1 KB 627.

relationship, no action lies: thus, a father could not sue in respect of the loss of business contracts occasioned by the death of his son, who worked for the father's firm.[9] Yet, in *Pym v GN Ry Co*[10] it was held that younger children of the deceased had sustained loss of pecuniary advantage because most of the income from the settlement of which the deceased had been tenant for life passed on his death to his widow and eldest child.

(5) PERIOD OF LIMITATION

The action must be brought within three years from either the date of the death, or 'knowledge' of the person for whose benefit it is brought, whichever is the later.[11] Where there are several potential claimants, the limitation period runs separately against each; if one had the required knowledge more than three years before the action, the action is barred against him but not against the others.[12] Where the dependant's limitation period has run out before an action was brought on his behalf, the court has a further discretionary power to extend the period.[13]

(6) ASSESSMENT OF DAMAGES

The sum to be awarded as damages for bereavement is £3,500.[14] The intention is to relate the award to one-half of average annual earnings, so that the sum can be varied from time to time by statutory instrument.[15] Where both parents claim this sum it is divided equally between them.[16] Damages other than damages for bereavement are such as are proportioned to the injury[17] resulting from the death to the dependants respectively.[18] The actual pecuniary loss resulting to each dependant from the death is ascertained[19] and separately

---

9 *Sykes v NE Rly Co* (1875) 44 LJCP 191; *Winfield* 538 has a different explanation of this decision. The decision was followed in *Burgess v Florence Nightingale Hospital for Gentlewomen* [1955] 1 QB 349, [1955] 1 All ER 511 (husband could not recover for loss of services of wife as dancing partner). And see *Behrens v Bertram Mills Circus Ltd* [1957] 2 QB 1, [1957] 1 All ER 583; and *Malyon v Plummer* [1964] 1 QB 330, [1963] 2 All ER 344, CA.

10 (1863) 4 B & S 396.

11 Section 12(2) of the Limitation Act 1980. And see p 510 et seq, post, for a detailed examination of 'knowledge'.

12 Section 13(1) of the 1980 Act.

13 Section 33 of the 1980 Act. And see p 510, post.

14 Section 1A(3) of the Fatal Accidents Act 1976, as amended by the Administration of Justice Act 1982.

15 Section 1A(5) as amended by the 1982 Act.

16 Section 1A(4) as amended by the 1982 Act.

17 'Injury' includes any disease and any impairment of a person's physical or mental condition; s 1(6) of the 1976 Act.

18 Section 3(1).

19 *Davies v Powell Duffryn Associated Collieries Ltd* [1942] AC 601 at 612 (per LORD WRIGHT), [1942] 1 All ER 657, HL. A dependant's damages are not reduced because his mother was contributorily negligent; *Dodds v Dodds* [1978] QB 543, [1978] 2 All ER 539. When assessing a claim by a mother for the death of her son, the court must take account of the possibility of the son's marriage; *Dolbey v Goodwin* [1955] 2 All ER 166, CA. Where husband and wife with either separate incomes or a joint income share their living expenses the amount by which their joint living expenses are less than twice the expenses of each one living separately is a benefit arising from the relationship, and may be the subject of a claim under the Fatal Accidents Acts by the husband in respect of the death of his wife; *Burgess v Florence Nightingale Hospital for Gentlewomen* [1955] 1 QB 349, [1955] 1 All ER 511. The damages awarded to a widower for the loss of his wife are not restricted to the cost of providing a housekeeper; a further sum in respect of her constant attendance on young children is

assessed.[20] Where an award is made to a widow and her children it is suggested that the proportion awarded to the children should represent their genuine dependency,[1] and not follow the practice of awarding the bulk of the money to the widow on the assumption that she will provide for her children.[2] *Inter alia* the children need protection against the risk of their mother dying and the money passing into the hands of a stepfather.

LORD WRIGHT explains the method of measuring the damages:[3]

> The starting point is the amount of wages which the deceased was earning, the ascertainment of which to some extent may depend on the regularity of his employment. Then there is an estimate of how much was required or expended for his own personal and living expenses. The balance will give a datum or basic figure which will generally be turned into a lump sum by taking a certain number of years' purchase. That sum, however, has to be taxed down by having due regard to uncertainties ...

The House of Lords elaborated this in *Taylor v O'Connor* in 1970.[4] The damages to a widow must make available to her to spend each year a sum free of tax equal to the amount of the dependency—an award sufficient to buy an annuity of that amount is not enough because part of the annuity will be taxable. The multiplier must be calculated from the date of the victim's death[5] and should be such that the capital sum awarded, together with the income earned by its investment, will be exhausted by the end of the period intended to be covered. It is supposed that the dependants will spend each year a part of the capital as well as the whole of the income they receive from so much of the capital as remains.[6] The multiplier of the annual loss of dependency is seldom fixed at more than 16 times that annual figure; so if the dependants have lost £2,000 a year from the death the award will rarely exceed £32,000.

In assessing future earnings, probable deductions for income tax are to be made.[7] No account may be taken of the fact that the dependant is of independent means, except in so far as it shows what pecuniary aid to that dependant was made by the deceased.[8] In *Cookson v Knowles*[9] the House of Lords refined further the method of calculation. As a general rule damages up to the date of trial are to be assessed separately from those after that date. For the first part, the loss of dependency will be multiplied by the actual period between accident and trial; interest on that sum will be awarded at half the short term investment rate current during that period. For the second

---

appropriate: *Regan v Williamson* [1976] 2 All ER 241. In *Mehmet v Perry* [1977] 2 All ER 529 the widower gave up his job on medical advice that his sick children needed his services on their mother's death. His damages were assessed on the basis of his earning loss. But see *Spittle v Bunney* (1988) Times, 8 February, CA (children over 6 need less maternal care: award to orphan accordingly reduced)!

20 *Dietz v Lenning Chemicals Ltd* [1969] 1 AC 170 at 183 (per LORD MORRIS OF BORTH-Y-GEST). Court directs how the award be divided; s 3(2) of the 1976 Act as amended by the 1982 Act.

1 *Benson v Biggs Wall & Co Ltd* [1982] 3 All 300 at 303.

2 *Clay v Pooler* [1982] 3 All ER 570 at 578 (the children merely received pocket money).

3 *Davies v Powell Duffryn Associated Collieries Ltd*, supra at p 617.

4 [1971] AC 115, [1970] 1 All ER 365, HL.

5 *Graham v Dodds* [1983] 2 All ER 953, [1983] 1 WLR 808, HL.

6 *Young v Percival* [1974] 3 All ER 677, CA; and see *Taylor v O'Connor*, supra.

7 *Bishop v Cunard White Star Co Ltd* [1950] P 240 at 250 (per HODSON J), [1950] 2 All ER 22.

8 *Shiels v Cruikshank* [1953] 1 All ER 874, HL, a Scottish case, but presumably applicable to England also.

9 [1979] AC 556, [1978] 2 All ER 604.

part the court will arrive at the amount of dependency (the multiplicand) by estimating the probable rate of earnings of the deceased at the date of the trial. It will calculate the multiplier in the usual way. The multiplier will be fixed by reference to the date of the death and the number of years actually elapsing between the death and the trial will then be deducted.[10] Interest is not awarded on the second sum.[11] Inflation is disregarded except in estimating earnings at the date of trial.

If the dependants have incurred funeral expenses in respect of the deceased, damages may be awarded in respect of those expenses.[12]

In assessing damages payable to a widow in respect of the death of her husband, there shall not be taken into account the remarriage of the widow or her prospects of remarriage.[13] It will be recalled that subject to certain conditions persons living together as man and wife, though not married, are treated as 'dependants'.[14] In assessing their damages the court has to take into account the fact that the dependant had no enforceable right to financial support by the deceased as a result of their living together.[15]

To what extent can the courts take account of events occurring between the death and trial? If such an event enables the courts to fix more precisely that which they are otherwise called upon to estimate, they must have regard to that event. Thus they have taken into account that, before trial, the dependant has died,[16] or the outbreak of war would have reduced deceased's life expectancy,[17] or tax rates are reduced,[18] for each of these events enables the courts to quantify more precisely a dependant's loss of contribution from the deceased. Hypothetical events which would, but for the deceased's death, have increased the dependant's dependency will not be taken into account. So the plaintiff widow's greater prospective loss had she, as she would have so desired, given up work to have a family, was rightly disregarded in *Malone v Rowan*.[19] Before the Administration of Justice Act 1982 came into force the courts had to assess the gains to the dependant on the death (such as the inheritance of stocks and shares under the deceased's will), and there was much complex law on the topic.[20] Now the Act provides that in assessing damages benefits which have accrued or will or may accrue to any person from his estate or otherwise as a result of the death are to be disregarded.[1]

---

10 *Graham v Dodds* (supra).
11 For the award of interest generally on damages where the award exceeds £200 see s 35A of the Supreme Court Act 1981, as amended by section 15(1) and Part I of Schedule I to the Administration of Justice Act 1982.
12 Section 3(5) of the Fatal Accidents Act 1976, as amended by the Administration of Justice Act 1982.
13 Section 3(4) of the 1976 Act as amended by the 1982 Act. Her remarriage prospects might still affect awards to her children; *Thompson v Price* [1973] QB 838, [1973] 2 All ER 846.
14 P 491, ante. If an unmarried father is killed, even if the mother of his children has no claim, their children recover the loss of all the benefits which their father had provided for them, including such benefits given to the mother for the children's advantage; eg cost of her air fares for a family holiday, *K v JMP Co Ltd* [1975] 1 All ER 1030.
15 Section 3(4) of the 1976 Act as amended by the 1982 Act.
16 *Williamson v John Thorneycroft & Co Ltd* [1940] 2 KB 658, [1940] 4 All ER 61, CA.
17 *Hall v Wilson* [1939] 4 All ER 85.
18 *Daniels v Jones* [1961] 3 All ER 24, CA.
19 [1984] 3 All ER 402.
20 For details of the old law, see the 6th edition of this work.
 1 Section 4 of the Fatal Accidents Act as amended by the 1982 Act.

SECTION 4.   ALTERNATIVE COMPENSATION SYSTEMS

A. RESPONSIBILITY AND THE WELFARE STATE[2]

Public responsibility for the victims of personal injury is recognised in the existence of a safety net of benefits and provision made for accident victims in a number of ways. The plethora of systems created leads to confusion and inequality and can be explained here in outline only.

(1) The welfare state provides essential services for accident victims in two main respects. Medical advice and treatment for injury and disease are largely available free within the National Health Service. The victim of a tort, however, retains the option to elect for private treatment and to charge the cost of that treatment to the tortfeasor.[4] Where long-term care is required that advantage may be substantial in nature. The Chronically Sick and Disabled Persons Act 1970 empowers local authorities to provide benefits and services for the disabled. In theory that Act should ensure that all accident victims may be provided with home helps, holidays and assistance in adapting their homes. In practice pressure on local authority budgets means that only minimal benefits and services may now be available. The tort victim can, as we have seen, claim the total estimated cost of such services as part of his proper measure of damages.

(2) A wide range of social security benefits are available to persons incapable of work by reason of accident or disease. The level of payments made is at a subsistence rate, in general, and in no way equates with the loss of earnings suffered by the incapacitated victim. Those benefits which are non-means tested are available to tort victims over and above any award of damages, thus exacerbating the gap in the financial outcome of incapacity dependent on whether or not the victim can establish 'fault'.

Just a few examples of relevant social security benefits are given here. A person incapable of work because he is sick or disabled may claim sickness benefit for the first 28 weeks that he is incapacitated providing that he has previously been in work and paying national insurance contributions. In 1987–88 sickness benefit is paid at a rate of £30.05 per week plus £18.60 for an adult dependent. After 28 weeks, if he is still incapacitated, the accident victim may be able to claim invalidity benefit at a slightly higher rate of £39.50 per week plus £23.75 for adult dependants and £8.05 for children.

Should the accident victim need a great deal of care by others he may be able to claim an attendance allowance. He must establish that he is so severely disabled that he requires from another person either assistance with bodily functions or constant supervision. The higher rate of attendance allowance for 24 hour attention is £31.60 per week and the lower rate for persons needing only day or night time help is £21.90. A friend or relative spending at least 35 hours a week caring for a severely disabled person may be able to claim an invalid care allowance of £23.75. Other social security benefits for the disabled include mobility allowances and, where needed, supplementary benefit to top up other allowances to meet the basic requirements of life.[5]

---

2 See generally *Compensation and Support for Illness and Injury* (1984) Oxford Socio-Legal Studies, Clarendon.

3 See *Atiyah* op cit at ch 18.

4 Law Reform (Personal Injuries) Act 1948, s 2(4).

5 Additional benefits are available to persons injured at work or contracting an industrial disease via the industrial injuries scheme. On disability benefits generally see *The Disability Rights Handbook* (12th edn) produced by the Disability Rights Alliance.

Such a brief survey illustrates one issue with clarity. The better off you are to start with, the more you will suffer from an incapacity in respect of which you have no remedy in tort. The university professor who succumbs to an inherent risk of surgery stands to lose a great deal more than the single mother on social security benefits before she is incapacitated. However, if this state has limited resources to compensate for disability it might be argued that high earners have no special claim for special treatment. The professor could after all have taken out an insurance policy covering him against all forms of personal injury or disease.

(3) Certain groups of the disabled may in addition receive extra payments related to their disability. The Vaccine Damage Payments Act 1979 provides for payments of £20,000 to persons suffering 80% disablement consequent on vaccination. The Act resulted from one of the few proposals of the Pearson Report to be implemented. Vaccination of children against diseases such as whooping cough, measles and diphtheria benefits the community as a whole. The rationale of the Act is that it is unjust to leave one family to bear alone the burden of any damage resulting from vaccination. Haemophiliacs who have contracted AIDS from contaminated transfusion, sought similar special treatment. They successfully argued that they entrusted themselves to the National Health Service. They should not shoulder the total cost of the unknown danger lurking in the blood products which they relied on for continued life and health. But, while the D.H.S.S has agreed to set up a fund to compensate haemophiliacs contracting AIDS from blood products, other victims who contracted that disease from blood transfusions are excluded from the scheme. Why?

B. OTHER COMPENSATION SYSTEMS

(1) CRIMINAL INJURIES COMPENSATION SCHEME

The Criminal Injuries Compensation Board administers from Government funds a non-statutory scheme for compensating victims of crimes of violence.[6] If they suffer personal injury as a result of violent crime or while apprehending, or seeking to apprehend, a suspect the Board may award compensation assessed in the way in which claims in tort are assessed by the courts. The maximum compensation for loss of earnings is twice the national average of industrial earnings. Social security payments received are deducted in full. Claims may also be made by dependants of a person killed.

(2) OCCUPATIONAL SICK PAY

About two-thirds of those in employment are entitled to continued payments from their employer in replacement of loss of earnings at least in part, for a limited absence from work through sickness or injury.[7]

(3) OCCUPATIONAL PENSIONS

Many millions are members of pension schemes run by their employers, which entitle them to compensation beyond social security in the event of personal injury compelling their early retirement.[8]

6 For a full copy of the scheme, see Hepple and Matthews: *Tort—Cases and Materials* 3rd edn p 800 et seq.
7 Pearson Report, para 137.
8 For details, see Pearson Report, para 145 et seq.

(4) TRADE UNIONS

About 10 per cent of employees receive some payment from trade unions or friendly societies during absence from work owing to sickness or accident. Many charities also support the sick and disabled. Disaster funds are often set up for grave disasters.

(5) INSURANCE

In many cases the person killed or injured will have taken out an insurance policy providing for benefits in the event of his death or personal injury.[9] There are three main forms of this first-party insurance. The most common is a life policy providing a guaranteed minimum sum on death. Personal accident policies cover death, loss or disablement resulting from accidents for a prescribed period. Permanent health policies provide periodic payments if the insured person becomes unable to follow his usual occupation because of sickness or accident. Sometimes these forms of insurance are provided by employers for their staff. About 10 per cent of those injured in 1973 had insurance cover.[10]

The Pearson Report estimated that about one-half of the total compensation for personal injury and death comes from social security and a quarter from the tort system. The remaining quarter comes from the other sources listed above. These figures show how limited a view of accident compensation is obtained if one examines only tort, and ignores these other sources of compensation.

C. THE PEARSON REPORT

It was against all this background that in 1974 the Royal Commission on Civil Liability and Compensation for Personal Injury was set up under the chairmanship of Lord Pearson. It reported in 1978.

The fundamental issue confronting the Commission was the respective merits of a tort system and a social welfare system. New Zealand has, for instance, abandoned a system based on fault and replaced it by a social welfare scheme making compensation for injury by accident a state responsibility, like our existing social security schemes. The criticism made of the United Kingdom system is that, as we have seen, it is a blend of tort and social security. The two systems have been fashioned independently, and no attempt has been made by Parliament to harmonise them.

Advocates of a social welfare approach argue that there is no justification for singling out for special treatment areas like industrial accidents. They contend that the present divide between tort and social security is illogical. I spike my foot with a garden fork while working in my garden. I might claim sickness benefit, free treatment under the National Health Service, payment by my employer while off sick, perhaps a claim under a personal accident insurance policy or, if hospitalised, perhaps a claim on a medical protection policy. But I would have no tort claim. Alter the facts a little; I am hurt by a defect in my powered lawn mower. Now we add a claim against my retailer

---

9 Much more widespread is insurance against fire or damage to one's buildings, homes, furniture and to one's car, where the insured has a right of subrogation against tortfeasors.
10 Pearson Report, para 154.

in contract and possibly in tort, and conceivably a negligence and/or a strict liability claim against the manufacturer, whereupon all the problems of duplicating benefits, and issues of whether some or all must be offset against my tort damages arise. Does the distinction make any sense? They deplore, too, the emphasis on cause of the accident, rather than on the injuries to victims. They then demonstrate how costly to administer the tort system is. The Report showed that in the 1970s it cost £175 million per annum to collect and distribute tort payments of £202 million, so expensive are the judicial process and administering private insurance third party liability. For every £1 of insurance premium 45p went in costs and 55p to tort victims. In contrast, under the social security system it cost £47 million per annum to distribute £421 million to accident victims. They complain further that two-thirds of damage awards are for pain and suffering. They criticise, too, the long delays in obtaining tort compensation, and the forensic lottery that any system of fault liability must inevitably be.[11]

Nonetheless the Report rejected widespread adoption of a social welfare system, in part especially because it lacked data on the probable cost of a comprehensive accident and disease scheme and because it saw justice in having those at fault make reparation. Its basic proposal was to retain the mixed system of tort law and social security, with a gradual swing towards social security. It made 188 detailed proposals of which one of the most interesting was a proposal to bring road traffic accidents within social security schemes on the model of industrial injuries.

There is little prospect at present that the major proposals of the Report will be implemented. A wholesale change to a social welfare system which abandons 'fault' is unlikely in England in the immediate future. In particular categories of accident there is increasing pressure for limited 'no-fault' compensation systems. For example, the Pearson Report in its chapter[12] on medical injury recommended against immediate implementation of a 'no-fault' scheme for medical accidents, but expressly accepted that 'changing circumstances' might cause that decision to be reviewed. Ten years later proposals for such a scheme command increasing support notably from the BMA. But on what rational grounds should victims of medical accidents be singled out for special treatment? The damage done to good medical practice and doctor/patient relationships by the increasing pace of medical litigation are cited by proponents of a 'no fault' scheme for medical injuries. And the concept of 'fault' may seem especially unjust when applied to a junior doctor making an error after a 48 hour shift in an under-resourced hospital. The arguments convince me.[13] Nevertheless a cautious approach to piecemeal implementation of 'no fault' schemes must be adopted. Otherwise we simply add to the plethora of present compensation systems.

11 See *Compensation and Support for Illness and Injury* ch 3.
12 Chapter 24.
13 See Brazier *Medicine, Patients and the Law* ch 9.

Chapter 30

Extinction of remedies

SECTION 1. WAIVER

The circumstances in which waiver will extinguish liability in tort are neatly summarised by Lord Atkin:[1]

> ... if a man is entitled to one of two inconsistent rights it is fitting that when with full knowledge he has done an unequivocal act showing that he has chosen the one he cannot afterwards pursue the other, which after the first choice is by reason of the inconsistency no longer his to choose.

Thus, a lessor who has brought ejectment proceedings by way of forfeiture for breach of covenant cannot afterwards sue for rent.[2] Similarly, when an act is done professedly on behalf of a principal but in fact without his authority the election by the principal to ratify deprives him of a later action alleging breach of authority.[3]

'It is essential to bear in mind the distinction between choosing one of two alternative remedies,[4] and choosing one of two inconsistent rights.'[5] It has been seen that merely to choose one remedy is not inconsistent with the continued availability of another remedy.[6] For instance, misdelivery by a carrier gives alternative remedies for breach of contract and conversion; a buyer who has failed in an action for rescission may subsequently recover damages in deceit.[7] In many of these cases of alternative remedies 'the plaintiff has never the slightest intention of waiving, excusing or in any kind of way palliating the tort'.[8] Obviously, then, where there is no evidence of waiver, and no inconsistency, the plaintiff will not be deprived of his alternative remedy—if a man finds that a thief has stolen his jewellery, he does not, by maintaining an action in quasi-contract for the proceeds, thereby say in effect: 'It is my intention to abandon my claim against you for the tort of conversion.'

Nor will the intention to waive a tort be imputed to a plaintiff merely because he receives back part of what he has lost, and still less, because he demands from the defendant the price of goods of which he has been deprived.[9] *Burn v Morris* is illustrative:[10]

> The plaintiff lost a £20 note. X found it, and the defendant bought it from her for £18, knowing that it was a lost note. When it became known that

1 *United Australia Ltd v Barclays Bank Ltd* [1941] AC 1 at 30, [1940] 4 All ER 20, HL.
2 *Jones v Carter* (1846) 15 M & W 718.
3 *Verschures Creameries Ltd v Hull and Netherlands SS Co Ltd* [1921] 2 KB 608, CA.
4 See pp 472–3, ante.
5 Per Lord Atkin *United Australia Ltd v Barclays Bank Ltd* [1941] AC 1 at 29.
6 See pp. 472–3, ante.
7 *Clarke v Dickson* (1858) EB & E 148; *subsequent proceedings* (1859) 6 CB (NS) 343.
8 Per Lord Atkin [1941] AC 1 at 28–9.
9 *Valpy v Sanders* (1848) 5 CB 886.
10 (1834) 2 Cr & M 579.

X had merely found the note, she was brought before the Mayor of London's Court where she surrendered £7, being all of the £18 she then retained. Acceptance by the plaintiff of this sum of £7 did not prevent him from recovering the balance from the defendant.

Nor is it likely that the plaintiff will be held to have waived unless he has full knowledge of the material facts.[11]

Lastly, in those circumstances (which we have previously examined[12]) where more than one action can be brought on the same facts, suing in respect of one of those causes of action will not be waiver of the remainder.[13]

SECTION 2.   SATISFACTION

Where judgment for a sum of money has been given for the plaintiff against the defendant and the defendant has satisfied that judgment by payment in full of that money, this discharges the claim of the plaintiff arising out of the same facts, not merely against the defendant, but against any other tortfeasor. Thus, in *United Australia Ltd v Barclays Bank Ltd* VISCOUNT SIMON stated that if the plaintiffs had obtained judgment in quasi-contract against the converters of the cheque, and if the latter had then satisfied that judgment, the plaintiffs could not subsequently have sued the bank for the tort of conversion;[14] judgment, not followed by satisfaction, would not, however, have barred a claim against the bank.

SECTION 3.   JUDGMENT

Final judgment in a suit has two effects. First, the original cause of action is terminated by its merger in the judgment. Where, therefore, the plaintiff elects to sue in conversion rather than for money had and received, although, as has been seen, that election does not amount to a waiver of his alternative remedy, judgment in that suit of conversion, even if unsatisfied, will bar a further action against the same defendant in quasi-contract.[15] And, of course, in those cases where successive actions on the same facts may not be brought[16] one judgment bars any further proceedings.

By virtue of the rule known as *res judicata*, judgment also operates to terminate certain other claims by either of the parties against the other. Suppose that A sues B for trespass to land, and the court decides that A was in possession of the land and returns a verdict in his favour: if B later sues A for assault in ejecting him from the land on that occasion, and A raises the defence that he used reasonable force for the purpose of ejecting a

---

11 Per LORD ATKIN, [1941] AC 1 at 30, LORD PORTER at 54 left open this point.
12 See p 469, ante.
13 *Caxton Publishing Co Ltd v Sutherland Publishing Co* [1939] AC 178 at 199 (per LORD PORTER), [1938] 4 All ER 389, HL.
14 [1941] AC 1 at 21. Contra, if the parties merely arrive at a settlement, which, though embodied in a judge's order, is not a judgment; *Rice v Reed* [1900] 1 QB 54, CA.
15 *Buckland v Johnson* (1854) 15 CB 145; approved in *United Australia Ltd v Barclays Bank Ltd* [1941] AC 1 at 16–17 (per VISCOUNT SIMON LC).
16 See p 468 et seq, ante.

trespasser, B will be estopped by the earlier judgment from denying that he was a trespasser.

SECTION 4.   RELEASE

Any surrender of a cause of action may be styled a release, but the term is usually reserved for surrenders by deed: the latter type of release will, therefore, discharge the cause of action even though there is no consideration.[17] Release may discharge tortious liability, whether it is given before or after the commencement of the action.[18]

SECTION 5.   ACCORD AND SATISFACTION

The terminology used with reference to this method of discharge is confusing, but the law is clear. If the plaintiff enters into a valid contract with the defendant to settle a cause of action, and the defendant performs this contract, the defendant has a defence to any proceedings by the plaintiff based on that cause of action. The agreement is the 'accord'; satisfaction is used variously to mean the 'consideration' given for the plaintiff's promise or the 'performance' of the promise.

Whether the cause of action will be discharged by mere agreement and before that agreement has been performed is a matter of interpretation of the agreement. Probably, the burden is on the defendant to prove that the tort has been discharged even without performance of the contract.[19]

SECTION 6.   LIMITATION

A. PERIOD OF LIMITATION

At common law there was no time limit restricting the right to sue. Successive statutes from 1623 onwards introduced limitation periods after the expiry of which an action in tort is time barred. The victim of an alleged tort must serve his writ within a specified number of years or forfeit his remedy. The need for limitation periods is self-evident. Potential defendants would otherwise face years of uncertainty not knowing whether or not they will be sued. A fair trial becomes increasingly difficult as witnesses' memories fade and in some cases witnesses die or leave the country.

Very short and rigid time limits however also result in injustice, to the plaintiff. He may not discover for some years that he has been the victim of a tort. Consider the common examples of persons contracting industrial disease, and the owners of negligently constructed buildings. Damage to the body from working conditions is likely to be stealthy and progressive.

---

17 For an example of a release of an action in tort, see *Phillips v Clagett* (1843) 11 M & W 84.
18 *Apley Estates Co Ltd v De Bernales* [1946] 2 All ER 338, affirmed [1947] Ch 217, [1947] 1 All ER 213, CA, where the point was not discussed.
19 The judgment of GREER LJ, in *British Russian Gazette and Trade Outlook Ltd v Associated Newspapers Ltd* [1933] 2 KB 616, [1933] All ER Rep 320, CA, is a very clear judicial exposition of the law; cf LORD ATKINSON in *Morris v Baron & Co* [1918] AC 1 at 35 HL, and the alternative *ratio decidendi* of HOLROYD J in *Brewer v Sparrow* (1827) 7 B & C 310 at 313, *Lee v L & Y Ry Co* (1871) 6 Ch App 527, *Ellen v GN Ry Co* (1901) 17 TLR 453.

Definitive symptoms of disease may manifest themselves years after the disease was in fact well established.[20] When a building is erected on defective foundations cracks may begin to ruin the fabric of the building years before they become apparent to even the most prudent homeowner.[1] It would scarcely be fair to deny the worker suffering from disease or the unfortunate homeowner any remedy at all because a rigid limitation period had expired before they could have realised that they might have a right to compensation.

The relevant and complex law on limitation is now mainly contained in the Limitation Act 1980 as amended by the Latent Damage Act 1986. In the case of actions for damage for negligence, nuisance or breach of duty (whether the duty exists by virtue of a contract or of provision made by or under a statute or independently of any contract or any such provision) when the damages claimed by the plaintiff consist of or include damages in respect of personal injuries to the plaintiff or any other person the period of limitation is three years.[2] In cases of actions for negligence, except claims for personal injuries or death, the Latent Damage Act 1986[3] introduced a primary limitation period of six years, with provision in special circumstances for a further period of three years to run from the 'starting date' set by that Act, subject to a final 'long-stop' of fifteen years.

An action for libel and slander must be brought within three years.[4] Where the plaintiff sues invoking strict liability for defective products under the Consumer Protection Act 1987 he must normally bring his action within three years of suffering the relevant damage, or within three years of acquiring the necessary knowledge of the facts to sue if that date be later.[5] No action may be brought under the 1987 Act more than ten years after the product was first put into circulation.[6] The plaintiff may still have an action in negligence after that date where even by then he has not discovered his injury or damage or other relevant facts pertaining to his right of action in negligence. The limitation period for other tort actions remains six years.[7]

The three-year period of limitation for personal injuries applies only to 'any action for negligence, nuisance or breach of duty (whether the duty exists by virtue of a contract or of provision made by or under a statute or independently of any contract or any such provision)'.[8] The Court of Appeal has held that these words cover breach of any duty under the law of tort and not merely the torts of negligence and nuisance named in the section; therefore a plaintiff with a claim for personal injuries was not allowed to evade the three-year rule by relying on trespass rather than on negligence.[9]

'Personal injuries' includes any disease and any impairment of a person's

20 See *Cartledge v E Jopling & Sons Ltd* [1963] AC 758, [1963] 1 All ER 341 (pneumoconiosis from inhaling dust); *Thompson v Smith Shiprepairers (North Shields) Ltd* [1984] QB 405, [1984] 1 All ER 881 (industrial deafness); *Brooks v J & P Coates Ltd* [1984] 1 All ER 702.
1 See *Anns v Merton London Borough Council* [1978] AC 728, [1977] 2 All ER 492; *Pirelli General Cable Works Ltd v Oscar Faber & Partners* [1983] 2 AC 1, [1983] 1 All ER 65.
2 Section 11 (1); Limitation Act 1980.
3 By inserting a new section 14A into the 1980 Act.
4 Section 4A Limitation Act 1980 inserted by the Administration of Justice Act 1985 s 57 (2).
5 Consumer Protection Act 1987, s 5(5) and Sch I.
6 Ibid.
7 Section 2 Limitation Act 1980 (except in the case of proceedings for loss of postal packets under s 30 (1) of the Post Office 1969 where the period is twelve months).
8 Section 11.
9 *Letang v Cooper* [1965] 1 QB 232, [1964] 2 All ER 929, even where the trespass to the person is intentional: *Long v Hepworth* [1968] 3 All ER 248.

physical or mental condition.[10] This still leaves undecided whether injury to the feelings caused by torts such as assault, false imprisonment and defamation is an 'impairment of a mental condition' within the Act. It is thought that the Act contemplates illness and disease of the mind or body, and that injuries to feelings, if unaccompanied by illness, are not 'personal injuries' for the purpose of the Act.

B. WHEN DOES A CAUSE OF ACTION ACCRUE?

The period of limitation begins from the date on which the cause of action accrued. A cause of action accrues at that moment in time when a potential plaintiff is entitled to succeed in an action against a potential defendant.[11] There must then be in existence such a plaintiff and a defendant. If a tort is committed against the estate of a deceased person, for example, if his goods are taken away, the cause of action does not accrue until an executor or administrator is appointed.[12] A cause of action against an ambassador does not accrue until his diplomatic immunity ends.[13] On the other hand, a plaintiff whose car has been stolen by a thief whom he does not know and cannot trace, has a cause of action against that thief from the time of the theft.[14] When a cause of action arises without proof of damage, clearly time always runs from the wrongful act.

Whereas in negligence the cause of action accrues only when damage is suffered. And this is the case in all torts where damage is essential to the cause of action. Ascertaining when damage occurs may be difficult. The crucial date is the date of the damage not its discoverability.[15] So a claim in respect of negligent construction of a building prima facie accrues when cracking and subsidence begin[16] not when the physical damage becomes patent. Where the relevant negligence consists of negligent advice the question arises of whether the damage founding the cause of action is suffered when the plaintiff relies on that advice,[17] or when the subsequent financial loss is suffered.[18] The injustice to a plaintiff who would otherwise lose his right to a remedy before he could know of its existence explains why in the tort of negligence special provision is now made for all forms of latent damage with separate rules for personal injuries and other forms of damage.

---

10 Section 38 (1).
11 More than one cause of action may arise from one set of circumstances: in *Duke of Brunswick v Harmer* (1849) 14 QB 185, the defendant's newspaper had published a statement defamatory of the plaintiff. Seventeen years later an agent of the plaintiff purchased a copy at the defendant's office. The plaintiff's cause of action accrued upon the sale of this copy, not when the newspaper was first published. Was any other defence open to the defendant?
12 *Murray v East India Co* (1821) 5 B & Ald 204; *Pratt v Swaine* (1828) 8 B & C 285.
13 *Musurus Bey v Gadban* [1894] 2 QB 352, CA.
14 *R B Policies at Lloyd's v Butler* [1950] 1 KB 76, [1949] 2 All ER 226.
15 *Pirelli General Cable Works Ltd v Oscar Faber & Partners* [1983] 2 AC 1, [1983] 1 All ER 65.
16 The cause of action against the builders accrues when physical damage occurs. Any claim in negligence against the local authority in respect of negligent inspection accrues later when that damage poses a threat to health and safety; *Governors of the Peabody Donation Fund v Sir Lindsay Parkinson & Co Ltd* [1985] AC 210, [1984] 3 All ER 529.
17 *Forster v Outred* [1982] 2 All ER 753, [1982] 1 WLR 86, CA. *Secretary of State for the Environment v Essex Goodman & Suggitt* [1986] 2 All ER 69, [1986] 1 WLR 1432.
18 *UBAF Ltd v European American Banking Corpn* [1984] QB 713, [1984] 2 All ER 226.

C. SPECIAL RULES FOR PERSONAL INJURIES

Where the plaintiff contracts some form of pneumoconiosis such as silicosis from inhaling dust, his cause of action in negligence arises even though he is unaware of the onset of the disease. In *Cartledge v E Jopling & Sons Ltd*[19] the House of Lords held that at common law time started to run as soon as the damage was suffered; in this case, therefore, time ran once material scarring of the lung tissue has occurred, even though X-ray examination would not have revealed it. The Limitation Act 1980[20] seeks to avoid the injustice that might otherwise result when a cause of action for personal injuries became time-barred before the plaintiff knew of it. The limitation period ends only three years after the date of the plaintiff's knowledge of the cause of action if that date is after three years from the accrual of the cause of action. If the plaintiff dies before the expiration of the period, the period as respects the cause of action surviving for the benefit of the estate of the deceased by virtue of section 1 of the Law Reform (Miscellaneous Provisions) Act 1934 is three years from the date of death or the date of knowledge of the personal representative.[1]

The Act provides in section 14 a detailed definition of 'knowledge', the interpretation of which has given rise to complicated case law. When in a personal injuries case time runs from the date of a person's knowledge, the date is the date on which he first had knowledge of the following facts:[2]

1 That the injury in question was significant. Any injury is significant if the person whose date of knowledge is in question would reasonably have considered it sufficiently serious to justify his instituting proceedings for damages against a defendant who did not dispute liability and was able to satisfy a judgment.[3] It would appear that the particular plaintiff's intelligence should be considered,[4] but that his personal reasons for not suing are irrelevant.[5]

2 That the injury was attributable in whole or in part to the alleged wrongful act or omission.[6] This means that the plaintiff must know that the wrongful act was a cause in fact of his injury.[7] But it is not relevant that the plaintiff was unaware that as a matter of law he had a cause of action in respect of that injury.[8]

3 The identity of the defendant.[9]

4 If it is alleged that the act or omission was that of a person other than the

---

19 [1963] 1 All ER 341.
20 Section 11.
 1 Section 11 (5) (6). For the application of these provisions to claims under the Fatal Accidents Act see ss 12 (1) and 33.
 2 Section 14 (1).
 3 Section 14 (2).
 4 *McCafferty v Metropolitan Police District Receiver* [1977] 2 All ER 756 at 775, CA, per Geoffrey Lane L J.
 5 *Miller v London Electrical Manufacturing Co Ltd* [1976] 2 Lloyd's Rep 284 (not suing for dermatitis through fear of losing job); *Buck v English Electric Co Ltd* [1978] 1 All ER 271 (not suing for pneumoconiosis because he was receiving wages and did not wish to 'sponge').
 6 See *Wilkinson v Ancliff (BLT) Ltd* [1986] 3 All ER 427, [1986] 1 WLR 1352.
 7 And see *Pickles v National Coal Board* [1968] 2 All ER 598.
 8 *Brooks v J and P Coates (UK) Ltd* [1984] 1 All ER 702.
 9 The plaintiff may have been knocked down by a hit and run driver, or the defendant's firm may be a member of a group of interlocking companies—see *Simpson v Norwest Holst Southern Ltd* [1980] 2 All ER 471.

defendant, the identity of that person and the additional facts supporting the bringing of an action against the defendant. If, therefore, the plaintiff seeks to hold an employer vicariously liable time does not run until he identifies the employee and ascertains whether he was acting in the course of his employment.

Section 14 (1) expressly states that knowledge that any acts or omissions did, or did not, as a matter of law, involve negligence, nuisance or breach of duty is irrelevant. In effect he is deemed to know the legal significance of facts.[10]

And it is not the plaintiff's actual knowledge alone which is relevant. Section 14 (3) makes the following provision for constructive knowledge.

> For the purposes of this section a person's knowledge includes knowledge which he might reasonably have been expected to acquire
>
> a from facts observable or ascertainable by him; or
> b from facts ascertainable by him with the help of medical or other appropriate expert advice which it is reasonable for him to seek; but a person shall not be fixed under this subsection with knowledge of a fact ascertainable only with the help of expert advice so long as he has taken all reasonable steps to obtain (and, where appropriate, to act on) that advice.

If he consults the expert he is not prejudiced if the expert fails to find, or inform him of, the ascertainable facts.[11] The sub-section applies only to knowledge of a 'fact'—if the plaintiff delays suing because he has received wrong legal advice, time will run against a plaintiff who has not issued a writ.[12]

Nevertheless in exceptional cases the victim of personal injuries who fails to start his action in due time may with permission of the court still be able to proceed. Thus the plaintiff who had knowledge of all the relevant facts but was unaware of his legal rights or the plaintiff who has received duff legal advice has one last chance to seek a remedy.

By section 33 (1) the court may still allow an action to proceed notwithstanding the expiry of the limitation periods. The court has a discretion to extend the statutory time limits if it considers it equitable to do so having regard to the degree to which the ordinary limitation rules prejudice the plaintiff and any exercise of the power would prejudice the defendant. The court must have regard to all the circumstances, including

a the length of, and the reasons for, the delay on the part of the plaintiff[13]
b the effect of the delay on the cogency of the evidence in the case
c the conduct of the defendant after the cause of action arose, including his response to the plaintiff's request for information
d the duration of any disability of the plaintiff arising after the cause of action
e the extent to which the plaintiff acted promptly and reasonably once he knew of the facts which afforded him a cause of action
f the steps taken by the plaintiff to obtain medical, legal, or other expert advice and the nature of any such advice received.

10 See *Brookes v J & P Coates (UK) Ltd* (supra).
11 *Marston v British Railways Board* [1976] 1 CR 124.
12 If the solicitor's advice is wrong on the facts, as distinct from the law, time does not start to run.
13 *Thompson v Brown Construction (Ebbw Vale) Ltd* [1981] 2 All ER 296, HL.

A very wide discretion, and one not limited to the six named factors, is given to the court.[14] There is, however, one restriction: where the plaintiff has commenced proceedings and then discontinued them, only in the most exceptional case will discretion be exercised in his favour.[15]

D. LATENT DAMAGE OTHER THAN PERSONAL INJURIES

The special provision made by section 11 of the Limitation Act to assist plaintiffs who lacked the necessary knowledge to start an action was restricted to action for personal injuries. Yet the problems limitation periods pose for the victim of a latent defect can be just as acute in relation to damage to property. A series of Court of Appeal judgments sought to establish that the cause of action in such cases accrued only when the defect was discoverable.[16] The House of Lords in *Pirelli General Cable Works Ltd v Oscar Faber and Partners*[17] overruled those decisions as inconsistent with *Cartledge v E Jopling & Sons Ltd.*[18] The facts in *Pirelli* highlight the problems of latent damage.

In 1969 the plaintiff engaged the defendants to advise them in relation to building a new chimney. The defendants' design was negligent. Cracks occurred in the chimney which had to be replaced. The plaintiffs first discovered the cracks in 1977 but they must have occurred in 1970. The plaintiffs served their writ in 1978 contending that the (six year) limitation period did not begin to run until 1977 when they could first reasonably have discovered the defect.

The House of Lords held that the cause of action accrued in 1970, when the damage, the cracks, first occurred so that the claim was time barred. Two further acute difficulties for plaintiffs emerged from the judgment in *Pirelli*. Lord Fraser in an *obiter dicta*[19] suggested that where a defect was so gross that the building was 'doomed from the start'[20] time would begin to run even earlier, from the completion of the building. The result of such a doctrine that the worse the negligence the more favourable the limitation period would be to the defendant did not find favour in later judgments.[1] The second difficulty arising from the common law in relation to latent defects affected subsequent owners' of buildings. In *Pirelli* it was said time did not start to run again in favour of the subsequent owner once he acquired the property.[2] But subsequent owners' problems were in fact more acute than simply being entitled only to the tag end of their predecessors' limitation period. Had they

14 *Firman v Ellis* [1978] QB 886, [1978] 2 All ER 851, CA, and see *Birkett v James* [1978] AC 297, [1977] 2 All ER 801, HL, and *Liff v Peasley* [1980] 1 All ER 623, CA.
15 *Walkley v Precision Forgings Ltd* [1979] 2 All ER 548, HL. *Deerness v John R Keeble & Son (Brantham) Ltd* [1983] 2 Lloyd's Rep 260, HL.
16 See *Sparham-Souter v Town and Country Developments (Essex) Ltd* [1976] QB 858 [1976] 2 All ER 65; *Dennis v Charnwood Borough Council* [1983] QB 409, [1982] 3 All ER 486.
17 [1983] 2 AC 1, [1983] 1 All ER 65.
18 [1963] AC 758, [1963] 1 All ER 341; see above at p 505.
19 At 16.
20 See *Dove v Banhams Patent Locks Ltd* [1983] 2 All ER 833, [1983] 1 WLR 1436; *Jones v Stroud District Council* [1986] 1 WLR 1141.
1 In *Ketteman v Hansel Properties* the House of Lords adopted a severely restrictive view of 'doomed from the start'. The doctrine, if it existed, did not embrace any latent defect bound at some stage to result to damage to the property, [1987] AC 189, [1987] 2 WLR 312.
2 At 18.

any claim at all in respect of damage to property to which at the time damage occurred they had no title?[3]

The Law Reform Committee reported on these several problems concerning latent damage to property in 1984.[4] Their proposals are largely enacted by the Latent Damage Act 1986 which applies not solely to latent damage to property but to all negligence actions other than claims in respect of personal injury or death. The Act came into force on 18 September 1986.[5] The Act first inserts a new section 14 A and B into the Limitation Act 1980. The limitation period in actions to which section 14 A and B apply shall be either six years from the date on which the cause of action accrued or three years from the 'starting date' when the plaintiff had the necessary knowledge of the facts to bring an action. 'Knowledge' is defined in section 14A(6)–(8) in terms virtually identical to those used to define 'knowledge' in the original section 14 of the 1980 Act for the purpose of extending the three year period to bring an action in respect of personal injuries.[6] Section 14B imposes a 'long stop' of fifteen years from the date of the alleged negligence. Once fifteen years has elapsed no action may be brought albeit the plaintiff may not have discovered the relevant damage. Nor is there provision similar to section 33 of the 1980 Act for a judge to exercise his discretion to override this final limitation period in section 14B.[7]

The Latent Damage Act represents a worthy attempt at compromise between the rights of plaintiffs and defendants. It leaves some key questions unanswered. Sections 14A and B apply to actions for negligence. Will they be applied, for example, to actions for nuisance or breach of statutory duty where the essence of the wrong complained of is absence of reasonable care? No clear definition of damage is provided. Damage to buildings is often progressive. Will the cause of action accrue when the first slight crack is judged to have occurred?

Section 3 of the 1986 Act addresses the rights of successive owners of property. It provides that where a cause of action has accrued to A while he has an interest in that property 'then providing B acquires the property' ... after the date on which the original cause of action accrued,

'... but before the material facts about the damage have become known to any person who, at the time when he first had knowledge of the facts, has any interest in the property; a fresh cause of action in respect of that negligence shall accrue to that other person on the date on which he acquires his interest in the property'.

The limitation period as against the new owner is once again either six years from when his cause of action accrued (ie his acquisition of the property) or three years from when he acquires knowledge of the relevant facts subject once again to the fifteen year 'long stop' in section 14B. Two points must be noted about section 3. First, although drafted with defective buildings[8] in

---

3 In *Perry v Tendring District Council* (1984) 30 B LR 118 Judge Newey QC (the official Referee) held a subsequent owner had no cause of action. Consider the nature of his claim at common law. It is essentially for economic loss resulting from damage to property to which at the time of the relevant damage he had no title. On which see *Leigh and Sillivan Ltd v Aliakmon Shipping Co Ltd* [1986] AC 785, [1986] 2 All ER 145.

4 *Twenty-fourth report; Latent Damage* Cmnd 9390.

5 For transitional provisions see s 4 Actions barred before 18 September 1986 or commenced before that date still fail to be governed by the common law.

6 See ante at p 506.

7 But see s 2 of the 1986 Act re fraud, concealment or mistake.

8 To reverse *Perry v Tendring DC* (supra).

mind it applies to all property including goods. Second the new cause of action for the new owner arises only where his predecessor did not have any actual or constructive knowledge of the relevant defect.[9]

E. CONTINUING WRONGS

Where the act of the defendant is a continuing wrong, for example, if he erects a building on the plaintiff's land, there will be a continuing trespass;[10] so long as it remains there, any cause of action will lie, which is based on the continuance of that wrong during the six years (or three years in the case of personal injuries) immediately preceding the action.[11]

F. EFFECT OF DISABILITY OF THE PLAINTIFF

If, on the date when any right of action accrued, the person to whom it accrued was an infant[12] or a person of unsound mind,[13] the action may be brought at any time before the expiration of six years (or three years in the case of personal injuries) from the date when the person ceased to be under that disability, or died, whichever event first occurred.[14]

Where the cause of action has once vested in a person who is free from disability, and the period has therefore commenced to run, should that person or some other person to whom the cause of action has passed subsequently become disabled, the period will not on that account be further extended.[15] When a right of action which has accrued to a person under disability vests, on the death of that person while still under a disability, in another person also under a disability, there also no further extension of time shall be allowed by reason of the disability of the second person.[16] Where a person, in whom a cause of action has vested, was, at the moment of vesting, under one disability, for example, infancy, and, at or before the cessation of that disability, becomes insane, time does not begin to run until he has 'ceased to be under a disability',[17] ie until the last of his disabilities has ended.

G. POSTPONEMENT OF LIMITATION PERIOD IN CASE OF FRAUD OR CONCEALMENT

Where the action is based upon the fraud of the defendant or his agent, or

---

9 In what circumstances could the subsequent owner sue the vendor who Failed to disclose his knowledge of the relevant defects.
10 See ch 5, ante.
11 *Hardy v Ryle* (1829) 9 B & C 603; *Earl of Harrington v Derby Corporation* [1905] 1 Ch 205.
12 Now under the age of 18 years by section 1 (1) of the Family Law Reform Act 1969.
13 By section 38 (3) 'a person is of unsound mind if he is a person who, by reason of mental disorder within the meaning of the Mental Health Act 1983 is incapable of managing and administering his property and affairs'. And see section 38 (4). The court will not strike out an action by an infant plaintiff for negligence for mere inactivity on his part before his 21st birthday: *Tolley v Morris* [1979] 2 All ER 561, HL.
14 Sections 28 (1) 28A (inserted by the Latent Damage Act 1986) and 38 (1).
15 Section 28 (2).
16 Section 28 (3).
17 Section 28 (1).

of any person through whom he claims[18] or that person's agent, or where any fact relevant to the right of action is deliberately concealed by any such person, the period shall not begin to run until the plaintiff has, or with reasonable diligence could have, discovered the fraud or concealment.[19]

A tort is 'based upon fraud' only where fraud is a necessary allegation in order to constitute the cause of action;[20] presumably, deceit is the only tort based upon fraud in this sense. Deliberate commission of a breach of duty in circumstances in which it is unlikely to be discovered for some time amounts to deliberate concealment of the facts involved in that breach of duty.[1]

'Fraud' in the Act is to be interpreted very widely;[2] it appears to signify 'conscious wrongdoing'.[3]

SECTION 7.   DEATH

The Law Reform (Miscellaneous Provisions) Act 1934[4] provides that on the death of any person all causes of action subsisting against or vested in him shall survive against, or as the case may be, for the benefit of, his estate. But this does not apply to causes of action for defamation. If the plaintiff dies, the damages recoverable for the benefit of his estate shall not include exemplary damages.

The right of a person to claim under section 1A of the Fatal Accidents Act 1976 for bereavement[5] does not survive for the benefit of his estate.[6] No damages may be awarded for loss of income in respect of any period after the death of the injured person.[7]

If the plaintiff dies after the expiry of the limitation period, the claim does not survive in cases of personal injury. However, it is open to his personal representatives to ask the court, under the discretionary provisions of section 33 of the Limitation Act 1980,[8] to override the limitation period. If the plaintiff died before the limitation period expired, a new limitation period begins to run under the Limitation Act 1980.[9] This new period is three years from either the date of death, or from the date of the personal representative's knowledge, whichever is the later.

---

18 In *Eddis v Chichester Constable* [1969] 2 Ch 345, [1969] 2 All ER 912, CA, these words included the tenant for life where the plaintiffs were the trustees and owners of an heirloom fraudulently sold by the tenant for life.
19 Section 32 (1).
20 *Beaman v ARTS* [1949] 1 KB 550, [1949] 1 All ER 465, CA (conversion not an action based on fraud).
1 Section 32 (2). And see *Beaman v ARTS*, supra.
2 *Kitchen v Royal Air Force Association* [1958] 2 All ER 241, CA.
3 *Beaman v ARTS*, supra at p 572 (per SINGLETON L J).
4 Section 1 (1), as amended by the Law Reform (Miscellaneous Provisions) Act 1970.
5 P 492, ante.
6 Section 4 (1) of the Administration of Justice Act 1982, amending s 1 (2) (a) of the 1934 Act.
7 Section 4 (2) (b) of the Administration of Justice Act 1982, anending s 1 (2) (a) of the 1934 Act.
8 Section 33 (4) (5). And see p 502, ante.
9 Section 11 (5).

Chapter 31

Parties

SECTION 1. THE CROWN

A. VICARIOUS LIABILITY

By section 2(1) of the Crown Proceedings Act 1947:

> ... the Crown shall be subject to all those liabilities in tort to which, if it were a private person of full age and capacity, it would be subject in respect of torts committed by its servants or agents.

The servant must be directly or indirectly appointed by the Crown and paid wholly out of the Consolidated Fund or other specified national funds;[1] the Crown is not, therefore, vicariously liable for the torts of policemen,[2] or for the torts of borrowed servants.

The Act does not apply to the servants of those bodies which are not deemed to be agents of the Crown—in such cases the ordinary law affecting public bodies and public officers will apply. Many public bodies are therefore outside the Act: thus, the nationalised industries are not within the ambit of the Act.[3] In order to resolve this problem, which is often thorny, the nature of the functions of the body in question and the extent to which it is under Ministerial control, are especially relevant.[4]

B. NON-VICARIOUS LIABILITY

Section 2(1)(b) and (c) make the Crown liable for any breach of those duties owed at common law to servants or agents or independent contractors by an employer and for any breach of the duties attaching at common law to the ownership, occupation, possession or control of property. This subsection does not seem sufficiently wide to take account of all the cases where an employer is liable otherwise than vicariously: it has been shown that employers are frequently answerable for acts of independent contractors, not because the independent contractor has committed a tort in the course of his work, but because a duty is imposed on the employer. Section 2 may not be

---

1 Section 2(6); unless the tort complained of is infringement of copyright or any other tort within s 3 of the Act or, detinue or any other tort affecting property for which a petition of right formerly lay (s 1).
2 For the liability of the chief constable to pay damages out of public funds to those harmed by a policeman's torts, see the Police Act 1964, s 48.
3 *Tamlin v Hannaford* [1950] 1 KB 18; [1949] 2 All ER 327, CA.
4 *Bank voor Handel en Scheepvaart NV v Administrator of Hungarian Property* [1954] AC 584; [1954] 1 All ER 969, HL.

wide enough to cover, for example, the duties of hospital authorities to their patients.[5]

The Crown is liable in tort to the same extent as private persons for breaches of statutory duty imposed on it, provided that the duty is also imposed on persons other than the Crown and its officers.[6] If the duty is imposed, not on the Crown, but directly on its servants (and, presumably, even though that duty is not also imposed on persons other than servants of the Crown), and the servant commits a tort while performing or purporting to perform those functions, 'the liabilities of the Crown in respect of the tort shall be such as they would have been if those functions had been conferred or imposed solely by virtue of instructions lawfully given by the Crown'.[7] The Crown also has the same liability as other employers under the Employer's Liability (Defective Equipment) Act 1969.[8]

C. EXCEPTIONS

(1) JUDICIAL ERRORS

Section 2(5) provides that the Crown shall not be liable 'in respect of anything done or omitted to be done by any person while discharging or purporting to discharge any responsibilities of a judicial nature vested in him, or any responsibilities which he has in connection with the execution of the judicial process'.

The first part of the subsection would be otiose if it merely provided that the Crown shall not be liable wherever its servant has the defence of 'judicial act'. It seems, therefore, that whatever doubts there may be about the liability of inferior courts for malicious acts within the jurisdiction, or for acts done in excess of jurisdiction which purport to be in discharge of the judicial function, the Crown is exempted from liability.[9] Perhaps the first part of the subsection extends, not only to that limited class of bodies not being courts *stricto sensu* to which the defence of 'judicial acts' applies, but also to other administrative tribunals.[10]

(2) ARMED FORCES

The Crown Proceedings (Armed Forces) Act 1987 repeals section 10 of the 1947 Act which prevented members of the armed forces sueing the Crown in respect of injuries suffered in the course of their duties. The Act applies only to causes of action arising after its passing.[11]

---

5 See p. 453, ante. Yet in *Egerton v Home Office* [1978] Crim LR 494, the court held that a duty was owed to a sexual offender in prison to keep a protective watch to guard against his being attacked by fellow prisoners.

6 Section 2(2). Section 6 of the Occupiers' Liability Act 1957 provides that that Act (see p 257 et seq, ante) shall bind the Crown and that the common duty of care imposed by it shall apply as a statutory duty for the purpose of the Crown Proceedings Act 1947.

7 Section 2(3); and p 463, ante.

8 See p 453, ante.

9 See p 95, ante.

10 Is the Crown vicariously liable for a malicious prosecution by the Director of Public Prosecutions?

11 But the effect of s 10 had already been narrowed somewhat by judicial interpretation of that section. *Bell v Secretary of State for Defence* [1986] QB 322, [1985] 3 All ER 661; *Pearce v Secretary of State for Defence* [1987] 2 WLR 782, (1987) Times, 5 August, CA.

(3) CERTAIN STATUTES IMPOSING LIABILITY IN TORT

It is doubtful whether the Crown is bound by statutes imposing tortious liabilities unless the particular statute has clearly made the Crown liable. Most recent Acts making substantial changes in the law of torts have been made expressly applicable to the Crown: for example, the Law Reform (Contributory Negligence) Act 1945, the Congenital Disabilities (Civil Liberties) Act 1976, the Civil Liability (Contribution) Act 1978 and the Limitation Act 1980. Statutes about which the doubt persists include the Defamation Act 1952.[12]

SECTION 2. FOREIGN SOVEREIGNS

Foreign sovereigns cannot be sued in tort in the English courts except as provided in the State Immunity Act 1978.[13] Under that Act the State is no longer immune for (1) an act or omission causing death or personal injury or damage to or loss of property[14] (2) obligations arising out of the ownership, possession or use of property[15] and (3) actions for purely financial loss arising from a commercial transaction.[16]

SECTION 3. AMBASSADORS

The relevant law is contained in the Diplomatic Privileges Act 1964. Ambassadors and their staffs and families are exempt from the jurisdiction of English courts so long as they continue to exercise their diplomatic functions.[17] They are not immune from legal liability: consequently they can waive their procedural privilege and submit to the jurisdiction. Further, once their diplomatic immunity has ended, actions may be brought against them in respect of causes of action which accrued during their service.[18] Members of the administrative, technical and service staffs have no immunity for torts committed outside the course of their duties.

SECTION 4. POSTAL AUTHORITIES

By the Post Office Act 1969 the Post Office is now a public authority which is not an agent of the Crown.[19] It is liable subject to the financial limits and conditions prescribed by Post Office Regulations for loss of, or damage to,

---

12 Because the sea collision regulations did not bind the Crown, the Crown was held not liable for negligence based on such a breach in *Thomas Stone (Shipping) Ltd v Admiralty, 'The Albion'* [1952] 1 Lloyd's Rep 104—an important Crown immunity.
13 Section 1.
14 Section 5.
15 Section 6.
16 Section 3.
17 The immunity extends to such a reasonable period after an ambassador has presented his letters of recall as is necessary to enable him to wind up his official business and prepare for his return to his own country; *Musurus Bey v Gadban* [1894] 2 QB 352, CA.
18 Nor does the period of limitation commence to run until the privilege expires: *Musurus Bey v Gadban* [1894] 2 QB 352, CA.
19 Section 6(1) and (5).

inland registered postal packets.[20] Subject to that, neither the Post Office nor any of its servants, officers or sub-postmasters is liable for anything done or omitted to be done in relation to anything in the post[1] or for any omission to collect post.[2] Nobody engaged in the carriage of mail, or their servants, agents or sub-contractors is liable for loss or damage in relation to the post.[3]

SECTION 5.   HIGHWAY AUTHORITIES

Persons who suffer injuries caused by the defective state of a highway may have causes of action against highway authorities in negligence, in nuisance derived from public nuisance, or for breach of statutory duty: often they will have a choice of action.[4]

The liability of all highway authorities (including the Crown) for all these torts is regulated by the Highways Act 1980. The Act applies regardless of whether the plaintiff is suing in nuisance, negligence or for breach of statutory duty. The rule of law which used to exempt highway authorities from liability for non-repair of highways has been abrogated. Section 58(1) provides that:

> in an action against a highway authority in respect of damage resulting from their failure to maintain a highway maintainable at the public expense, it is a defence (without prejudice to any other defence or the application of the law relating to contributory negligence) to prove that the authority had taken such care as in all the circumstances was reasonably required to secure that the part of the highway to which the action relates was not dangerous for traffic.

Following the pattern of the Occupiers' Liability Act 1957 the section proceeds to define some of the criteria which will be relevant in deciding whether the highway authority has discharged its burden of proving that it took reasonable care. These criteria are:[5]

> (a) the character of the highway, and the traffic which was reasonably to be expected to use it; (b) the standard of maintenance appropriate for a highway of that character and used by such traffic; (c) the state of repair in which a reasonable person would have expected to find the highway; (d) whether the highway authority knew, or could reasonably have been expected to know, that the condition of the

---

20 Section 30. For an interpretation of the extent of liability for this statutory tort, see *Building and Civil Engineering Holidays Scheme Management Ltd v Post Office* [1966] 1 QB 247; [1965] 1 All ER 163, on s 9 of the Crown Proceedings Act 1947, now repealed by, but substantially re-enacted in, the Post Office Act 1969.

1 The addressee of a letter on the envelope of which the Post Office stamped 'Remember that Road Accidents are Caused by People Like You', could not recover damages in libel when the Postmaster-General pleaded s 9 of the Crown Proceedings Act, which was similar to s 29 of the 1969 Act. *Boakes v Postmaster-General* (1962) Times, 27 October. Nor is the Post Office liable in contract when its employee steals a postal packet for transmission overseas: *Triefus & Co Ltd v Post Office* [1957] 2 QB 352, [1957] 2 All ER 387, CA.

2 Section 29(1) and (2). In *Harold Stephen & Co Ltd v Post Office* [1978] 1 All ER 939, CA, the court left open whether the Post Office was liable for failing to sort mail during a strike. In *American Express Co v British Airways Board* [1983] 1 All ER 557, [1983] 1 WLR 701, it was held that this section exempted the Post Office and its sub-contractors from liability for breach of bailment and for breach of article 18 of the Warsaw Convention relating to liability for international carriage.

3 Section 29(3). Similar immunities afforded to British Telecom while in public ownership have now been repealed.

4 *Simon v Islington Borough Council* [1943] 1 KB 188, [1943] 1 All ER 41, CA.

5 Section 58(2).

part of the highway to which the action relates was likely to cause danger to users of the highway; (e) where the highway authority could not reasonably have been expected to repair that part of the highway before the cause of action arose, what warning notices of its condition had been displayed.

The Act has been interpreted in a series of cases. The plaintiff must prove that the highway is dangerous; a trifling defect such as one flagstone being an inch higher than the next will not avail the pedestrian who trips.[6] The plaintiff must further prove that the danger was caused by failure to maintain: an occasional flooding or an icy patch in winter is not evidence of failure to maintain,[7] but failure to drain a trunk road that was flooded in consequence made the Department of Environment liable.[8] Once the plaintiff has established these points the onus is on the defendant to prove that he did what was reasonably required.[9]

The section also enacts that:

> it is not relevant to prove that the highway authority had arranged for a competent person to carry out or supervise the maintenance of the part of the highway to which the action relates unless it is also proved that the authority had given him proper instructions with regard to the maintenance of the highway and that he had carried out the instructions.

Presumably the object is to make the highway authority liable whenever an independent contractor has negligently failed to maintain the highway, and despite some ambiguity in the language the courts may be expected to construe it in that way.

SECTION 6. CORPORATIONS

A. LIABILITY

Where the liability of an employer for the acts of his servants is in issue, there are normally four possible situations.

1 The act may be treated as the act of the employer himself so that no issue of vicarious liability arises.
2 The employer has authorised the servant to commit the tort.
3 The servant has committed the tort in the course of his employment.
4 The servant has committed the tort while acting outside the scope of his employment: the only one of the four cases where the employer is not liable.

---

6 *Meggs v Liverpool Corporation* [1968] 1 All ER 1137, CA; *Burnside v Emerson* [1968] 3 All ER 741. A hole 12" × 6" × 3" deep was held dangerous in *Bird v Tower Hamlets London Borough Council* (1969) 67 LGR 682.
7 *Burnside v Emerson* supra at 743 (per LORD DENNING MR).
8 *Tarrant v Rowlands* [1979] RTR 144. In *Bird v Pearce and Somerset County Council* (1979) 77 LGR 753, CA a local authority was held liable for a collision after it had obliterated white lines at a junction while resurfacing.
9 *Pridham v Hemel Hempstead Corporation* (1970) 69 LGR 523, CA (proof that it inspected the footpath of a minor residential road every three months and kept a complaints book, excluded it from liability). And see *Griffiths v Liverpool Corporation* [1967] 1 QB 374, [1966] 2 All ER 1015, CA. The duty to maintain a highway imposed by section 41 of the Highways Act 1980 includes a duty to remove snow and ice from footpaths, but a plaintiff who slipped on an icy footpath would have to prove that the authority had failed to take reasonable remedial measures in the circumstances: *Haydon v Kent County Council* [1978] QB 343, [1978] 2 All ER 97, CA.

It is submitted that where the employer is a corporation, there are exactly the same four possibilities.

In the House of Lords case, *Lennard's Carrying Co Ltd v Asiatic Petroleum Co Ltd*,[10] dealing with the defendant's plea that no act could be done with the 'fault of privity' of a corporation itself, as distinct from that of its servants, VISCOUNT HALDANE said:[11]

> [A corporation] 'has no mind of its own any more than it has a body of its own; its active and directing will must consequently be sought in the person of somebody who for some purposes may be called an agent, but who is really the directing mind and will of the corporation, the very ego and centre of the personality of the corporation. That person may be under the direction of the shareholders in general meeting; that person may be the board of directors itself . . .'

In order, then, to be the act of the company in this sense the act must be of 'somebody who is not merely a servant or agent for whom the company is liable on the footing *respondeat superior*, but somebody for whom the company is liable because his action is the very action of the company itself'.[12] If somebody of such authority in the company acts tortiously on behalf of the company the company is liable, not by way of vicarious liability, but because the tortious act is that of the company itself.[13]

Poulton v London & SW Ry Co[14] provides a clear example of the fourth case, an act outside the scope of employment:

> A stationmaster arrested the plaintiff for non-payment of the freight in respect of his horse. Because the defendant railway company, his employers, were empowered by statute to arrest passengers for non-payment of fares but for no other reasons, the court held that the stationmaster was acting outside the scope of his employment, and that the defendants were therefore not liable.

That is to say, in deciding what a servant is or is not impliedly authorised to do, one may be assisted by considering what his employers lawfully may do.

The reports abound, of course, with the commonplace event of a limited company's being vicariously held liable for torts committed by servants in the course of their employment—especially claims arising out of road accidents and claims by its workmen in respect of the negligence of their fellow-workmen.

Campbell v Paddington Corporation is a case where a corporation was held liable for the tortious act of its servants, when it had authorised the tort:[15]

> In pursuance of a resolution of the council of the defendant corporation, its employees erected a stand on the highway so that members of the

---

10 [1915] AC 705, HL.

11 At 713.

12 At 713. In *The Lady Gwendolen* [1965] P 294, [1965] 2 All ER 283, CA, the Guinness company were presumably liable for their managerial failure to detect and stop the habitual practice of their ship's captain in going full steam ahead in fog through reliance on the fact that his ship was fitted with radar.

13 The director may himself be liable as bailee when goods are stored with his company and he assumes personal responsibility for their storage: *Fairline Shipping Corporation v Adamson* [1975] QB 180, [1974] 2 All ER 967. On other circumstances in which a company director may be personally liable for a company servant's tort see *C Evans & Sons Ltd v Spritebrand Ltd* [1985] 2 All ER 415, [1985] 1 WLR 317, CA.

14 (1867) LR 2 QB 534.

15 [1911] 1 KB 869.

public could view a procession. This act was a public nuisance which the corporation, seemingly, had no authority to perform: the fact that the act was *ultra vires* did not prevent the corporation from being held liable in tort.

Lush J distinguished *Poulton v LSW Ry Co* as follows:[16]

> That case was only an illustration of the principle that where the wrongful act is done without the express authority of the corporation, an authority from the corporation to do it cannot be implied if the act is outside the statutory powers of the corporation. That principle has no application to a case where the corporation has resolved to do and has, in the only way in which it can do any act, actually done the thing which is unlawful and which causes the damage complained of.

This *Campbell* case (the only one on the point) seems to carry the proposition that a corporation can be liable for a tortious act arising from an activity beyond the powers of the corporation.[17]

B. POWER TO SUE

Corporations can sue for any tort other than those of which in the nature of things they could not be victims, eg assault.

SECTION 7. TRADE UNIONS

Trade unions are no longer immune from liability in tort generally for their own torts. As far as liability in negligence, nuisance or other non-economic torts is in issue, if the requisite elements of the tort are proved, the union is liable just as an individual would be.[18] Trade unions are further liable for acts of their members committing one of the various economic torts concerned with interference with economic and business interests other than in contemplation or furtherance of a trade dispute,[19] where the member's act has been authorised by a 'responsible person'[20] within the union. Financial limits related to the union's total membership restrict the amount of damage which may be awarded in such a case.[1] The remaining immunities afforded in respect of the commission of torts of interfering with contracts or business in the course of a trade dispute are made dependent on support for the action being enclosed in a ballot.[2]

---

16 [1911] 1 KB 869 at 878.
17 Contra *Atiyah* 386: '... there is nothing in the report to indicate that the erection was truly *ultra vires*, as distinguished from illegal ...' Section 9 of the European Communities Act 1972 provides that as regards companies it is deemed in favour of a person dealing in good faith with a company that any transaction decided on by directors is within the capacity of the company.
18 Regardless of whether the tort was committed in furtherance of a trade dispute; s 15(1) Employment Act 1982 repeals that earlier limitation on union liability in s 14 of the Trade Union and Labour Relations Act 1974.
19 On the now narrow definition of trade dispute see s 18 of the 1982 Act.
20 Section 15(3) Employment Act 1982.
 1 Section 16 Employment Act 1982.
 2 Section 10 Trade Union Act 1984.

Trade unions, which are not special register bodies, and few are, cannot sue for defamation.[3]

SECTION 8.   UNINCORPORATED ASSOCIATIONS[4]

This section is concerned with those bodies which apparently exist and carry on their activities as separate units, but which are not incorporated: members' clubs and friendly societies are important examples.[5]

A. LIABILITY

(1) SUBSTANTIVE

There are no special rules of the law of torts which determine whether a cause of action subsists against the members of an unincorporated association as such. If, according to ordinary principles, there is vicarious liability for the tort of a servant of the association, or if someone has been ordered to commit an act constituting a tort, or if there is a breach of the duties of an employer to an employee, then in any of those cases a cause of action would be established.

(2) PROCEDURAL

More difficult is the problem of who may be made defendant when such a cause of action is made out. Four possible solutions must be examined.

1 The body cannot ordinarily be sued in its group name.[6] In a few cases, statutes setting up certain bodies have been interpreted as imposing on them a liability to be sued in their collective names—besides trade unions, friendly societies are an example.[7]
2 There is no legal obstacle to joining all the members of the association as defendants in proceedings, but the practical inconveniences of doing this in the case of a large club with a possibly fluctuating membership are obvious.
3 RSC O 15, r 12 does, however, provide that where numerous persons have the same interest in any proceedings the proceedings may be begun and continued by or against any one or more of them as representing all of them.

It will often be impossible to make use of this rule in tort proceedings because not all the defendants will have the same common interest. Thus, in *Mercantile Marine Service Association v Toms* the facts were:[8]

---

3 *Electrical Electronic Telecommunication and Plumbing Union v Times Newspapers Ltd* [1980] QB 585, [1980] 1 All ER 1097; but see *Gatley* para 970.
4 And see Lloyd, 'Actions Instituted by or against Unincorporated Bodies', in (1949) 12 MLR 409.
5 See Section 7 supra and p 520 post, for trade unions and partnerships, which are other examples.
6 *London Association for Protection of Trade v Greenlands Ltd* [1916] 2 AC 15, HL.
7 Friendly Societies Act 1896; *London-Griffiths v Smith* [1950] 2 All ER 662, a fuller report on this point than [1951] 1 KB 295.
8 [1916] 2 KB 243, CA.

The plaintiffs wished to make three officers of a guild for the protection of seamen representative defendants in an action of libel. The Court of Appeal refused to allow this on the ground that all the general body of members had not the same interest in resisting the proceedings.

Obviously, this requirement that all the persons represented should have the same interest was not complied with, because not all members of the guild could have published, or authorised the publication of, the libel. And, no doubt, there are many circumstances where a representative action may be held inappropriate because different defences are available to the various defendants represented. It has been decided that O 15, r 12 can be invoked in tort actions.[9] The representative members chosen must fairly represent the members of the body.[10]

4 Actions may sometimes be brought against officers of clubs. There is no procedural problem here, but it must be stressed that such actions will fail unless, according to the ordinary substantive principles of the law of torts, those officials can be shown to have committed a tort. *Prole v Allen* illustrates this:[11]

The plaintiff was injured through falling down unlighted steps leading out from the premises of a club of which she was a member. Her action in negligence against the secretary and other committee members failed on the ground that they, as committee members, owed her no duty of care, any more than any other club member owed her a duty in respect of the steps. On the other hand, she was able to recover damages from the steward personally, because he had carelessly turned off the light which normally illuminated the steps.

B. AS PLAINTIFFS

The body cannot ordinarily sue in its own name, except, as in the case of friendly societies and trade unions, where an intention to permit this can be spelt out of a statute.

It will be recalled that O 15, r 12 provides for representation orders being made for plaintiffs in the same circumstances as those laid down for defendants. This raises the question to what extent English courts are prepared to follow practice in the United States and allow class actions by representatives of very large numbers alleging the infringement of similar rights. *Prudential Assurance Co Ltd v Newman Industries Ltd* shows that English courts are keeping such actions on a fairly tight rein.[12] A representative action may be brought by a plaintiff suing on behalf of himself and all other members of a class, where each member has a separate cause of action in tort, provided that the relief claimed could not have the effect of conferring a cause of action on a member who would not have had a separate cause of action, that all the members shared the same interest, and that the action benefited the class. The normal relief is a declaration, and sometimes an injunction. This action

9 *Campbell v Thompson* [1953] 1 QB 445, [1953] 1 All ER 831.
10 And cf LORD MACNAGHTEN in *Taff Vale Ry Co v Amalgamated Society of Railway Servants* [1901] AC 426 at 438, HL.
11 [1950] 1 All ER 476; cf *Shore v Ministry of Works* [1950] 2 All ER 228, CA.
12 [1981] Ch 229, [1979] 3 All ER 507.

is obviously useful where there are numerous small claims of a similar kind. Yet the court went on to say that damages could not be awarded in representative tort actions.[13] That statement goes too far, as was held in *EMI Records Ltd v Riley*.[14] The court directed an inquiry into damages in a representative action for infringement of copyright, as well as granting an injunction. Where the damage is to a property interest, in which the members of the body have a common interest, it is open to a court to award damages in a representative action. The courts may be expected to be grudging about awarding damages in other kinds of representative tort actions, especially where the harm alleged is not damage to property.

SECTION 9. PARTNERS

Partners are jointly and severally liable to any person not himself a partner[15] for torts committed by any one of them either while acting in the ordinary course of the business of the firm, or with the authority of his co-partners.[16] In addition to this vicarious liability statutorily imposed on partners, each partner may have a primary duty in tort, eg the occupier's duty of care to visitors is owed by each partner in a firm which occupies premises.[17]

SECTION 10. HUSBAND AND WIFE

The liability of one partner in a marriage for the torts of another is to be decided on the same principles as those applying where the parties are not married. There is no presumption that one is responsible for the other.[18]

Section 1(1) of the Law Reform (Husband and Wife) Act 1962 provides that 'each of the parties to a marriage shall have the like right of action in tort against the other as if they were not married'. In most cases where spouses wish to sue each other, the spouse is a nominal defendant, and the real defendant is an insurance company. The most important consequence of the Act is that where one spouse is injured in a car accident through the tortious driving of the other spouse, the victim can collect from the motor vehicle insurers. If another negligent driver is involved his insurers will be able to claim contribution[19] from the spouse's insurers.

At the same time Parliament was no doubt anxious to discourage the airing in tort actions of petty grievances between husband and wife, especially in defamation and battery. Section 1(2), therefore, allows the court to stay the action 'if it appears ... that no substantial benefit would accrue to either

---

13 See also *dicta* in *Markt & Co Ltd v Knight SS Co Ltd* [1910] 2 KB 1021.
14 [1981] 2 All ER 838.
15 *Mair v Wood* 1948 SC 83 (M, one of five partners of a trawler, injured through negligence of another partner. Held that neither under the Partnership Act nor under any common law rule unaffected by the Act could the other three partners be vicariously liable for the negligence of one partner to a fellow partner.)
16 Partnership Act 1890, ss 10 and 12; *Hamlyn v John Houston & Co* [1903] 1 KB 81, CA.
17 See *Meekins v Henson* [1964] 1 QB 472, [1962] 1 All ER 899.
18 Section 3 Law Reform (Married Women and Joint Tortfeasors) Act 1935. Husband and wife can be jointly liable in conspiracy: *Midland Bank Trust Co Ltd v Green (No 3)* [1982] Ch 529, [1981] 3 All ER 744, CA.
19 See p 530, post.

party from the continuation of the proceedings'. The expression 'substantial benefit' may give the courts some trouble. Does the court, when deciding whether to exercise its discretionary power to stay, have to balance its estimate of how much cash the plaintiff spouse is likely to collect in the form of damages against the chance of unhappiness or even disruption of the marriage resulting from the litigation? Will it inquire whether any damages awarded will be paid by the spouse's insurers?

It is true that spouses also embark on litigation with each other in order to settle disputes about property, particularly upon the break up of a marriage. Parliament long ago devised a useful remedy for this kind of dispute. Section 17 of the Married Women's Property Act 1882 provides that 'in any question between husband and wife as to the title or possession of property, either party ... may apply' to the court 'and the judge ... may make such order with respect to the property in dispute ... as he shall think fit'. The Act of 1962 has recognised the value of this enactment by providing that the court may stay any action between husband and wife if it appears that the machinery of section 17 is more convenient.[20] Moreover, instead of staying the proceedings for that purpose, the court can itself exercise any power conferred by section 17.

SECTION 11.   MENTALLY DISORDERED PERSONS

The problems here arise mainly from the incomplete analyses often made by the judges of the states of mind required in particular torts. The case most directly in point is *Morriss v Marsden*.[1]

> The defendant violently attacked the plaintiff, a complete stranger, while he was standing in the entrance hall of a hotel, and was sued for battery. The defence raised was insanity. The judge found that the defendant was not in a condition of automatism or trance at the time of the attack on the plaintiff, but that his mind directed the blows which he struck; he also found that at the material time, he was a certifiable lunatic who knew the nature and quality of his act, but, because of his lunacy, did not know that what he was doing was wrong. He nevertheless held that the defence of insanity failed.

This case is therefore authority for the proposition that if a mentally disordered person has that state of mind which is required for liability in the particular tort, then his insanity is no defence—all that is required in battery is that the defendant must intend to strike the blow at the plaintiff; the judge found as a fact that he did so intend; it therefore followed that he was liable. The case also decides that in tort, as distinct from criminal law, a defendant who intentionally invades the plaintiff's protected interest will not be excused because he was unaware that the invasion was a wrongful act.

These rules are definite and just. In every case one has to ask: what state of mind did the particular tort require? Did the defendant have that state of mind? It follows therefore, that in all torts, including those of 'strict' liability, if the defendant's conduct is, because of his insanity, involuntary and purely

20 Section 1(2)(b).
1 [1952] 1 All ER 925.

automatic, he has a valid defence. Thus, in *Morriss v Marsden,* STABLE J, said:[2]

> ... if a person in a condition of complete automatism inflicted grievous injury, that would not be actionable. In the same way, if a sleepwalker inadvertently, without intention or without carelessness, broke a valuable vase, that would not be actionable.

In short, one is never liable in tort for involuntary conduct—if the defendant is so insane that his conduct is involuntary, that insanity is a defence in proceedings against him for any tort. Further, where the tort requires improper purpose or malice, it is obvious that if his insanity is such that, although it does not render his act unintentional, it nevertheless prevents him from consciously forming such an improper purpose, that insanity will afford him a defence.[3]

If the defendant's insanity causes him to be under a delusion about the surrounding circumstances, then it seems that this will not afford him a defence provided that he did have that state of mind which the tort requires.[4]

SECTION 12.   MINORS

A. LIABILITY

A person ceases to be a minor when he attains the age of 18 years.[5] In the absence of authoritative decisions, it may be presumed that the rules are essentially the same as those for insanity.[6] Minority as such is not a defence: but like all other defendants, a minor is not liable for a specific tort if it is shown that he lacked the required state of mind. Should a one-year-old child pick up a letter defamatory of X, written by his father, and throw it through the window, whereupon Y picks it up and reads it, X will have no cause of action for libel against the baby. On the other hand, a fifteen-year-old youth who pushed a man into a swimming pool, was held liable in negligence and trespass.[7]

(1) WHERE THE ACT OF THE MINOR IS ALSO A BREACH OF CONTRACT

With certain exceptions a minor is not liable for breach of contract.[8] There-

---

2 At 927.

3 *Obiter dicta* in some old cases such as *Weaver v Ward* (1616) Hob 134, which might suggest that insanity is no defence in trespass, are easily explained: they were voiced at a time when the courts regarded trespass as a tort of strict liability, and merely inferred, therefore, that want of intention through insanity would be no defence. Given the premise, the conclusion is sound, but now that trespass is held not to be a tort of strict liability (see ch 2 ante), they are irrelevant. And see DENNING LJ (*obiter*), in *White v White* [1950] P 39 at 48, [1949] 2 All ER 339, CA, who would support the *dicta* in *Weaver v Ward*.

4 In *Buckley and Toronto Transportation Commission v Smith Transport Ltd* [1946] 4 DLR 721 (Ontario CA), the defendant driver had the delusion that his truck was under remote control from head office. This was a defence to negligence based on a road accident caused by his truck—not on the ground that delusion as such is a defence, but because by reason of the delusion 'he did not understand the duty which rested upon him to take care'.

5 Section 1(1) Family Law Reform Act 1969.

6 And see the discussion with regard to negligence, p 202 ante.

7 *Williams v Humphrey* (1975) Times 20 February cf *Wilson v Pringle* [1987] QB 237, [1986] 2 All ER 440 (13 year old schoolboy pulling bag off another) see ante at p 21.

8 See now Minors' Contracts Act 1987 which came into force on April 9, 1987.

fore, where the act of the minor is merely an improper performance of one of the acts contemplated by such a contract, it will not be open to the person aggrieved to sue him in tort so as to evade the contractual immunity. On the other hand, if the act complained of, though performed upon the occasion of a contract, is independent of it, the plaintiff may then sue in tort. Of course, this rule will be very difficult to apply in marginal cases, but its judicial recognition is beyond doubt. Thus a minor who had possession of goods under a hire-purchase agreement, and who wrongfully disposed of them to a third party was liable to the true owner for the independent tort of detinue which he committed by wrongfully disposing of them.[9] The hirer of a mare, hired for riding only, is liable in tort for doing an act of a nature not contemplated by the contract, viz jumping the mare, but if he were merely to ride her too far, this would not be an act of a different nature and no action in tort would lie.[10] The fact that the contract was, in both cases, void against the minor did not prevent him from being liable in tort.

The question of suing a minor in tort arises most often where he has obtained goods or a loan of money under contract by misrepresenting his real age. The courts have decided that no action in deceit then lies, because that would be tantamount to allowing the enforcement of a void contract.[11]

(2) LIABILITY OF THE PARENT

Although a plaintiff may have no cause of action against the minor he may sometimes be able to recover from its parent. The parent is liable only where he is accountable according to some other general principle of torts. He may be vicariously liable, eg if the minor is acting as his father's chauffeur and drives the car negligently. Similarly, the father will be liable if he instigates the son to commit a tort, and he will be liable if he himself has been personally negligent.[12] Accordingly, a father is not liable *merely* because his son has thrown a stone through his neighbour's window: unless the father ordered him to do so, or unless his negligent supervision is proved to have caused the act complained of, he will not be liable.

B. CAPACITY TO SUE

Except that he must sue by his next friend he is in the same position as any other plaintiff, when suing in tort. A child may sue either parent, and may wish to do so where the parent has an insurance policy (usually a comprehensive household insurance) which covers the particular liability, for example, if a loose tile from the family home is carelessly allowed to fall on the child while

---

9 *Ballett v Mingay* [1943] KB 281, [1943] 1 All ER 143, CA.
10 *Burnard v Haggis* (1863) 14 CB NS 45; *Jennings v Rundall* (1799) 8 Term Rep 335. See also *Walley v Holt* (1876), 35 LT 631, and *Fawcett v Smethurst* (1914) 84 LJ KB 473.
11 *R Leslie Ltd v Sheill* [1914] 3 KB 607 at 612 (per LORD SUMNER), CA.
12 *Donaldson v McNiven* [1952] 2 All ER 691, CA; *Newton v Edgerley* [1959] 3 All ER 337. The duty of school authorities is also to take the care which a reasonable parent would take, eg *Ricketts v Erith Borough Council* [1943] 2 All ER 629; *Rich v London County Council* [1953] 2 All ER 376, CA.

it is playing in the garden.[13] The capacity of children to sue for injuries sustained before birth has been considered earlier.[14]

SECTION 13.   BANKRUPTS

A. LIABILITY

Section 382 of the Insolvency Act 1986 provides that in respect of torts committed before the bankruptcy that liability is a bankruptcy debt and provable against the trustee in bankruptcy.[15] In respect of torts subsequently committed the bankrupt remains personally liable but may not be worth suing!

B. POWER TO SUE

Where the tort protects only a purely personal interest, for example, assault or slander,[16] the bankrupt retains the right to sue, and the claim does not pass to the trustee for the benefit of creditors. Where the purpose of the tort is to preserve property, for example, the action for recovery of land or where the damage is purely economic loss,[17] the cause of action passes to the trustee and any suit by the bankrupt personally may be met by the valid defence that the plaintiff is a bankrupt.

If there are two separate causes of action in the sense that two different actions may be brought in respect of them,[18] one of which is personal, eg in respect of loss of reputation, and the other of which is a tort to property, eg in respect of damage to business interests, the personal right remains with the bankrupt and the proprietary one vests in the trustee.[19] If the primary purpose of the only cause of action in tort is indisputably to protect property or to prevent pecuniary loss, then the cause of action passes to the trustee, and no portion remains with the bankrupt even though one head of damage is of a personal character—a split between trustee and bankrupt may only be made where there is more than one cause of action in the sense explained above. Thus, in *Hodgson v Sidney*:[20]

> The plaintiff claimed damages for both pecuniary loss and loss of reputation in consequence of the deceit of the defendant. The plaintiff having become bankrupt, the court held that the defendant had a valid defence to the suit

13   In *Ash v Lady Ash* (1696) Comb 357, a daughter sued her mother in false imprisonment and battery and succeeded subject to a new trial to fix damages. In a Scottish case, *Young v Rankin* 1934 SC 499, it was held that a child, who was injured by the negligent driving of his father, could sue his father.
14   See ante at pp 176–177.
15   S 382 repeals s 30(1) of the Bankruptcy Act 1914.
16   *Re Wilson Ex parte Vine* (1878) 8 ChD 364, CA.
17   In *Ramsey v Hartley* [1977] 2 All ER 673, CA it was held that a cause of action for negligent statement (p 185, ante) passed to the trustee; *Weddell v Pearce* [1987] 3 WLR 592.
18   See p 469 et seq ante.
19   *Wilson v United Counties Bank Ltd* [1920] AC 102 at 131 (per LORD ATKINSON), HL; cf *Re Kavanagh* (1950) 66 (Pt 1) TLR 65, CA (the fullest report).
20   (1866) LR 1 Exch 313, followed in *Wenlock v Moloney* (1967) 111 Sol Jo 437, CA; the bankrupt's conspiracy action was mainly for business and property damage, so that not even the consequential claim for injured feelings and loss of reputation could be pursued by him.

by the bankrupt in respect of both heads of damage, because the main element of the tort was pecuniary loss, and the personal claim was merely a separate head of damage, not a separate cause of action remaining available to the bankrupt plaintiff.[1]

The courts have made some surprising decisions in respect of actions of trespass to land. They have allowed a bankrupt to sue in trespass where he has maintained that his substantial damage was not to his property but for the interference with his personal enjoyment of the property.[2] The principle on which all these decisions have been based is summarised in the following *dictum*:[3]

> those rights of action are given in respect of the immediate and present violation of the possession of the bankrupt, independently of his rights of property, and are an extension of the protection given to his person, and the primary personal injury to the bankrupt is the principal and essential cause of action.

It is submitted that this is incorrect: that personal injury is not essential in an action in trespass to land so that these cases should have fallen under the previous rule, and that the cause of action was a proprietary one which passed to the trustee. It will be noted that in none of them did the defendant raise the defence that *part* of the damage was damage to property, but it was said (*obiter*) in *Brewer v Dew* that it might then be possible to apportion;[4] this *obiter dictum* also cannot be accepted because it conflicts with the principle set out above that separation of a single cause of action in tort is not allowed.[5]

SECTION 14.   ASSIGNEES

It seems settled that a right to sue in tort is not in general assignable.[6] Obviously, the law has an interest in preventing rights of action in tort from being a marketable commodity. There are, however, several glosses on this rule.

1 There is an *obiter dictum* in the Court of Appeal that 'an assignment of a mere right of litigation is bad ... but an assignment of property is valid, even although that property may be incapable of being recovered without litigation'.[7] This rule, if substantiated,[8] would be a sensible acknowledgement of the fact that the function of the torts of action for the recovery of land and of wrongful interference with goods is often to settle title to property.[9]

---

1 Especially BRAMWELL B at 315–16.
2 *Brewer v Dew* (1843) 11 M & W 625; *Rogers v Spence* (1844) 13 M & W 571; *Rose v Buckett* [1901] 2 KB 449, CA.
3 Per CRESSWELL J in *Beckham v Drake* (1849) 2 HL Cas 579 at 612.
4 (1843) 11 M & W 625.
5 Williams *Bankruptcy* p 321, also maintains that a cause of action can be split, but the cases on which he relies do not carry the point; on the contrary, the contract case of *Wilson v United Counties Bank Ltd* [1920] AC 102, HL, rests on the fact that there were two separate causes of action—see LORD ATKINSON at 131; cf *Re Kavanagh* (1950) 66 (Pt 1) TLR 65, CA (the fullest report).
6 Eg per FARWELL LJ in *Defries v Milne* [1913] 1 Ch 98 at 109, CA.
7 Per STIRLING LJ in *Dawson v G N Ry Co* [1905] 1 KB 260 at 271, CA.
8 *HEL* vol vii 533–4 n 7, deduces the same rule from *Prosser v Edmonds* (1835) 1 Y & C Ex 481, and *Dickinson v Burrell* (1866) LR 1 Eq 337, but these cases also do not carry the point.
9 At the same time it is not thought likely that the exception would extend to injuries to property, where title is not in dispute; eg damage to a ship.

2 A trustee in bankruptcy can assign any cause of action in tort vested in him to a third party or even to the bankrupt.[10]

3 The damages to be recovered in an action in tort, as distinct from the cause of action itself, can be assigned; ie the plaintiff may transfer to another the right to any damages recovered in a pending action, but of course must continue to bring the action in his own name.[11]

4 Where a plaintiff's insurers have paid a claim made by him in respect of circumstances which afford him a cause of action in tort against another, and, in consideration of the settlement of that claim on the insurance policy, have taken an assignment of the right to sue in tort, the insurers may maintain that suit.[12] This wise concession to commercial convenience applies even if subsequent investigation shows that the insured did not have in fact a valid claim on his policy, provided that the settlement by the insurers of his claim was a *bona fide* transaction.[13]

SECTION 15.   CONVICTED PERSONS

Those convicted of crimes, whether or not they be in prison, have the same tortious rights and liabilities as others.[14]

SECTION 16.   JOINT TORTS[15]

A. CATEGORIES

There are three broad categories of circumstances where one person may suffer damage as the result of torts committed by two or more defendants.

(1) JOINT TORTFEASORS

In this category are the following:[16]

a Master and servant in those cases where the master is vicariously liable for the tort of the servant.[17]

b Where one person instigates another to commit a tort.[18] Thus, a landlord who invited his lodger to help him detect an escape of gas on the premises by striking a match was a joint tortfeasor along with the lodger in respect of the damage caused by the ensuing explosion.[19]

c Where there is a breach of a duty imposed jointly on two or more persons,

---

10 *Ramsey v Hartley* [1977] 2 All ER 673, CA (where an action based on a negligent statement was validly assigned to the bankrupt, even though it was a term of the assignment that the bankrupt should retain only 65% of the net proceeds of the action). And see *Weddell v Pearce* ante at p 524.

11 *Glegg v Bromley* [1912] 3 KB 474, CA.

12 *King v Victoria Insurance Co* [1896] AC 250, PC; *Compania Colombiana de Seguros v Pacific Steam Navigation Co* [1965] 1 QB 101, [1964] 1 All ER 216.

13 *King v Victoria Insurance Co*, supra.

14 Criminal Justice Act 1948, section 70.

15 See Williams *Joint Torts.*

16 Cf SCRUTTON LJ in *The Koursk* [1924] P 140 at 155, CA.

17 See ch 27, ante.

18 And see pp 448–9, ante.

19 *Brooke v Bool* [1928] 2 KB 578, Div Ct; cf *Ash v Hutchinson & Co Ltd* [1936] Ch 489, [1936] 2 All ER 1496, CA.

e g two occupiers are joint tortfeasors if they are sued by a visitor for failure
to take reasonable care in respect of the premises jointly occupied by them.

d Where persons take 'concerted action to a common end'[20] and, in the
course of executing that joint purpose, any one of them commits a tort, all
of them are joint tortfeasors. The liability of partners for a tort committed
by one of them in connection with the firm's business, and the liability of
joint employers of a servant who commits a tort in the course of his
employment, are two examples; *Brooke v Bool* furnishes another:[1]

As has been mentioned above, the landlord and his lodger were looking
for an escape of gas, and an explosion occurred as a result of the careless
exposure by the lodger of a naked light to the escaping gas.

Besides holding that they were joint tortfeasors because the landlord had
authorised the lodger to do the act, the court held that they were joint
tortfeasors for the further reason that[2] 'the enterprise in which he [the land-
lord] and M [the lodger] were engaged was the joint enterprise of both, and
that the act which was the immediate cause of the explosion was their
joint act done in pursuance of a concerted purpose'. Similarly, where D1
imprisoned P, and D2 threatened to strike P if he resisted, they were joint
tortfeasors in respect of the false imprisonment even though D2's act was
also an assault.[3]

The Porter Committee summarised the position in defamation as follows:[4]

Where defamatory matter is contained in a book, periodical or newspaper, there
are normally a series of publications each of which constitutes a separate tort.
First, there is a publication by the author to the publisher for which the author is
solely liable. Secondly, there is the publication by the author and publisher jointly
to the printer, for which the author and publisher are jointly liable. Thirdly, there
is the publication of the printed work to the trade and the public, for which the
author, publisher and printer are jointly liable.

(2) SEVERAL CONCURRENT TORTFEASORS[5]

Several, or separate, or independent, tortfeasors are of two kinds; either those
whose tortious acts combine to produce the same damage, or those whose
acts cause different damage, to the same plaintiff. It is convenient to call the

---

20 Per BANKES LJ in *The Koursk* [1924] P 140 at 152, CA. Directors may be joint tortfeasors
with a limited company where they directed or procured the tortious act, or formed the
company for the express purpose of doing a wrongful act: *Rainham Chemical Works Ltd v
Belvedere Fish Guano Co* [1921] 2 AC 465, HL at 476 (per LORD BUCKMASTER); or if after
formation the company adopted a deliberate policy of wrongdoing: *Oertli A G v E J Bowman
Ltd* [1956] RPC 282 at 292.

1 [1928] 2 KB 578, Div Ct. Perhaps *Scarsbrook v Mason* [1961] 3 All ER 767, furnishes the
most remarkable recent example; *Held* where passengers and driver of a car combine on
equal terms for the enterprise of a specific journey by the car of another, each is jointly liable
for the driver's negligence.

2 At 585 per SALTER J.

3 *Boyce v Douglas* (1807) 1 Camp 60; see also the view of BANKES LJ at 149 in *The Koursk*
that if A, B and C conspired to attack P, and A and B carried out the attack, the fact that
A and B were sued in battery, and C was sued in conspiracy, would not prevent them from
being joint tortfeasors.

4 Cmd 7536 at p 29. If the plaintiff must prove malice in order to defeat a plea of qualified
privilege, only those defendants who are malicious are joint tortfeasors: *Gardiner v Moore*
[1969] 1 QB 55, [1966] 1 All ER 365.

5 This terminology has been borrowed from Williams, *Joint Torts*.

first group several concurrent tortfeasors, and they alone are being illustrated in the present subsection. This subsection is, then, concerned with acts which do not fit into any of the four sub-heads of joint torts already listed, but which result in the infliction of the same damage to the plaintiff. Thus in *Drinkwater v Kimber*,[6] where a passenger in a motor-car was injured in a collision between that car and another, MORRIS LJ said that the two drivers, both of whom were negligent, 'were separate tortfeasors whose concurrent acts caused injury to the female plaintiff'. *Thompson v London County Council* furnishes another example of tortfeasors who were not joint, but several, concurrent tortfeasors:[7]

> The plaintiff's house was damaged when its foundations subsided. This was caused by (1) negligent excavation by D1, (2) D2, a water company, negligently allowing water to escape from their main.

By way of further illustration, the facts in *The Koursk* were:[8]

> The *Koursk*, while sailing in convoy, negligently changed course so that it bore down on the *Clan Chisholm*, which was careless in failing to reverse its engines in order to avoid a collision. Immediately after the impact, the *Clan Chisholm* collided with the *Itria*. Having recovered damages of an amount less than the loss suffered (because of a special statutory provision) against the *Clan Chisholm*, the *Itria* sued the *Koursk*. The *Koursk* and *Clan Chisholm* were held not to be joint tortfeasors, but only several tortfeasors causing the same damage.

The feature common to all those illustrations is that there was only one unit of damage which it was impossible to divide between the various tortfeasors.

(3) SEVERAL TORTFEASORS CAUSING DIFFERENT DAMAGE

Where two or more persons not acting in concert cause different damage to the same plaintiff, they are treated differently in law from either joint or several concurrent tortfeasors.

In the straightforward kind of case the two defendants inflict quite separate harm on the plaintiff. For example, D1 gouges out P's eye, and D2 fractures his skull, whereupon D1 is answerable for the damage resulting from the loss of the eye and D2 for the damage following on the fracture of the skull. Similarly, suppose that a motorist carelessly knocked down a pedestrian, who sustained a fractured leg, and a surgeon treated the pedestrian's leg so carelessly that the pedestrian was crippled for life—because the motorist would not be answerable for the further damage occasioned to the pedestrian by the surgeon's negligence, the motorist and the surgeon would be several tortfeasors who had caused different damage to the same plaintiff.

In other cases it is much more difficult to decide whether there was an indivisible unit of damage, or whether the harm may be treated as capable of apportionment among the several defendants. The courts appear to have taken a sensible attitude, namely to avoid, if possible, saddling any one defendant with responsibility for more harm than he has caused. They will,

---

6 [1952] 2 QB 281 at 292, [1952] 1 All ER 701, CA. And see *Fitzgerald v Lane* [1987] QB 781, [1987] 2 All ER 455, CA.
7 [1899] 1 QB 840, CA; cf *Sadler v GW Ry Co* [1896] AC 450, HL.
8 [1924] P 140, CA.

therefore, be very ready to declare harm to be divisible. For example, in the common kinds of case of harm caused by the independent acts of various defendants, such as pollution of rivers, and nuisance by noise or smell, the courts will not hold each defendant liable for the entire damage; they will endeavour to ascertain the respective contributions to the harm made by each defendant, and, failing that, they will apportion the loss equally between them.[9] Flooding is a more difficult problem. If P's land is flooded for 30 days by the combined flood water of D1 and D2, and would have been flooded for 15 days by the flood water of either of them, each is liable for 15 days loss of farming activity; if however the flooding does not hinder P's work, but actually destroys his crops in circumstances where the flood water of either D1 or D2 alone would not have destroyed the crops, both D1 and D2 will be liable for the entire loss—the harm would then be indivisible. When the act of the defendant impinges on existing circumstances, eg D1 and D2 are already discharging water into a stream and not causing a flood, and D3, knowing of D1's and D2's acts, discharges such a further amount as causes P's lands to be flooded, then D3 is answerable for the entire flood damage.

B. THE IMPORTANCE OF THE DISTINCTION BETWEEN JOINT AND SEVERAL CONCURRENT TORTFEASORS, AND OTHER SEVERAL TORTFEASORS

1 Concurrent tortfeasors, whether joint or several, are each answerable in full for the whole damage caused to the plaintiff; other several tortfeasors are merely answerable for that damage which each has caused. It is therefore often of prime importance to decide whether the defendants were acting in concert. Suppose that A and B are engaged on a hunting expedition, that both of them simultaneously fire across a highway at game beyond the highway; that a shot injures a highway user, but it is not known which of A or B fired it; if they are joint tortfeasors acting in concert, the plaintiff, assuming that he establishes a tort, can recover full damages from either,[10] but if they are several tortfeasors they have not committed the same damage (for only one has caused damage at all) and the success of the action depends on proof of the commission of a tort by that one who is sued.[11] Questions of divisible harm do not arise where the defendants are joint tortfeasors; in any event, here also each joint tortfeasor is liable for all the harm sustained by the plaintiff.

2 Satisfaction[12] by any concurrent tortfeasor discharges the liability of all the others, whereas satisfaction by a several non-concurrent one does not.[13]

---

9 *Bank View Mills Ltd v Nelson Corporation* [1942] 2 All ER 477, especially STABLE J at p 483; reversed [1943] KB 337, [1943] 1 All ER 299, CA; *Pride of Derby and Derbyshire Angling Association Ltd v British Celanese Ltd* [1953] Ch 149, [1953] 1 All ER 179, CA. See also *Dingle v Associated Newspapers Ltd* [1961] 2 QB 162, [1961] 1 All ER 897 at 916 (per DEVLIN LJ), CA. The point was not discussed in the House of Lords [1964] AC 371. Sometimes the cumulative effect of D1's and D2's actions is greater than the sum of their respective contributions—this does not deter the courts from making them liable proportionately to the amount of harm which each would have caused in any event.
10 *Arneil v Paterson* [1931] AC 560, [1931] All ER Rep 90, HL.
11 Cf *Cook v Lewis* [1952] 1 DLR 1.
12 See p 501, ante.
13 And see *Bryanston Finance Ltd v de Vries* [1975] QB 703, [1975] 2 All ER 609, CA. For the effect of the plaintiff's accepting payment into court by one defendant on his right to sue others jointly liable, see *Townsend v Stone Toms and Partners* [1981] 2 All ER 690, CA.

3 The courts are less willing to exercise their discretion under RSC O 16, r 4 to allow joinder of defendants where the defendants concerned are not concurrent tortfeasors.

4 As will be seen shortly[14] there is in general a right to contribution in the case of concurrent tortfeasors, but not in respect of other tortfeasors.

C. THE DISTINCTION BETWEEN JOINT TORTFEASORS AND SEVERAL CONCURRENT TORTFEASORS

This distinction is of minor importance since the abolition by section 6(1) of the Law Reform (Married Woman and Tortfeasors) Act 1935[15] of the rule in *Brinsmead v Harrison*[16] that a judgment against one joint tortfeasor barred the action or the continuance of the action against the others.[17] One minor difference survives: a release under seal or a release by way of accord and satisfaction[18] (but not a mere covenant not to sue) in respect of one joint tortfeasor discharges the others, but does not have this effect in the case of several concurrent tortfeasors.[19]

The rules in this paragraph also now apply to both joint and several concurrent tortfeasors, and indeed, to all causes of action, and not merely torts. A plaintiff who has obtained judgment against one wrongdoer for any damage is free to obtain judgment later against anyone else jointly liable for that damage,[20] and the damages in the later actions can exceed the award in the first. The plaintiff is not entitled to costs in any such later action, unless the court is of the opinion that there was reasonable ground for bringing that action.[1]

D. CONTRIBUTION

(1) SCOPE

Section 1(1) of the Civil Liability (Contribution) Act 1978 enacts that 'any person liable in respect of any damage suffered by another person may recover contribution from any other person liable in respect of the same damage (whether jointly with him or otherwise).' The 1935 Act applied only to tortfeasors, but this section applies whatever the legal basis of liability, whether tort, breach of contract, breach of trust or otherwise.[2] If, therefore, a house owner had a cause of action in contract against his builder and one in tort against the local authority building inspector in respect of his defective structure, contribution could operate as between the two defendants.

---

14 See infra.
15 Section 6(1) has been repealed, and in this respect substantially re-enacted in section 1 of the Civil Liability (Contribution) Act 1978.
16 (1872) LR 7 CP 547.
17 If P had an unsatisfied judgment against D1 and a retrial is ordered of his action against D2 the judgment against D1 does not prevent P from recovering judgment against D2: *Wah Tat Bank Ltd v Chan Cheng Kum* [1975] 2 All ER 257, PC.
18 See p 501, ante.
19 *Duck v Mayeu* [1892] 2 QB 511, CA. *Cutler v McPhail* [1962] 2 QB 292, [1962] 2 All ER 474; *Gardiner v Moore* [1969] 1 QB 55, [1966] 1 All ER 365.
20 Civil Liability (Contribution) Act 1978 s 3.
1 Section 4 ibid.
2 Section 1(1).

(2) WHO MAY CLAIM CONTRIBUTION

The 1978 Act reaffirms the general principle that a person who is liable is entitled to claim contribution.[3] Frequently a person agrees to make a payment in settlement or compromise of a claim against him. If he can show that, assuming that the factual basis of the claim against him could be established, he would have been liable, he may claim contribution for a bona fide payment.[4] If he has settled because he was doubtful about his liability in law, even though the facts were established, he would obtain contribution only if he could prove that he was legally answerable, however bona fide and reasonable his decision to settle the claim. If he were liable at the time he made or was ordered, or agreed, to make the payment he is still entitled to recover contribution, even though he has since ceased to be liable either because of the expiry of a limitation period, or otherwise.[5] The right to claim contribution passes on the defendant's death to his personal representatives, whether or not his liability had before his death been established or admitted.[6]

(3) THOSE FROM WHOM CONTRIBUTION MAY BE CLAIMED

Contribution is recoverable from any one who is liable for the same damage.[7] If he were originally liable, but has ceased to be liable since the time when the damage occurred, he remains liable to make contribution.[8] Someone may have ceased to be liable because the plaintiff has waived his claim, or because he has settled with the plaintiff.[9] More commonly, the period of limitation for the plaintiff suing that defendant may have expired. Provided that contribution is sought within two years after his right to contribution arose[10] he may still seek contribution.[11]

(4) AMOUNT OF CONTRIBUTION RECOVERABLE

By section 2(1) of the Civil Liability (Contribution) Act:

Section 2(1) above

> ... in any proceedings for contribution under Section 1 above the amount of the contribution recoverable from any person shall be such as may be found by the court to be just and equitable having regard to the extent of that person's responsibility for the damage in question.

3 Section 1(1).
4 Section 1(4).
5 Section 1(2).
6 *Ronex Properties Ltd v John Laing Construction Ltd* [1983] QB 398, [1982] 3 All ER 961, CA.
7 Section 1(1).
8 Section 1(3).
9 *Logan v Uttlesford District Council* (1984) Times, 21 February.
10 The relevant date is the date of judgment or, where the case has been settled out of court, the date of the agreement to pay: s 10(3) (4) Limitation Act 1980. The period may be extended where the person seeking contribution is under a disability or is the victim of fraud, concealment or mistake: s 10(5).
11 Section 1(3). The subsection has a proviso that he is not liable if, on the expiry of the period of limitation or prescription, the right on which the claim against him was based, was extinguished. Because most tort actions are not extinguished by limitation—conversion is the important exception—this proviso is unimportant here.

Section 2(2) enacts

> The court shall have power in any such proceedings to exempt any person from liability to make contribution, or to direct that the contribution to be recovered from any person shall amount to a complete indemnity.

Neither causation nor culpability is the sole test to be applied in making the apportionment. It is not enough to discover merely who is guilty of moral blame, but, taking a commonsense view of the facts, the degree of 'responsibility' must be determined[12]—both the blameworthiness and the extent to which the act is directly connected with the damage are material in making this apportionment.[13] This view that moral blame is not the only criterion is supported by the cases which have authorised apportionment between a defendant liable for negligence at common law and one who was not negligent but who was in breach of statutory duty.[14]

If there is a limit on the amount for which a defendant could be liable to the plaintiff, by reason of an agreement between the plaintiff and the defendant, or if the amount would have been reduced by reason of the Law Reform (Contributory Negligence) Act 1945,[15] then the maximum amount of contribution is that amount so limited or reduced.[16]

It will be noted that the statute contemplates tortfeasors being entitled to a complete indemnity in some circumstances. Where, for example, a person who knows that he is not entitled to sell goods authorises an auctioneer to sell them, which he immediately does, the auctioneer, having been held liable in conversion, is entitled to an indemnity from his principal.[17]

Most important is the relation between master and servant. In *Lister v Romford Ice and Cold Storage Co Ltd*:[18]

> D, employed by P, took his father with him as mate. In backing his lorry he injured his father who, in an action against P, recovered damages in respect of D's negligent act. P brought an action against D claiming an indemnity in respect of the amount of the judgment and costs awarded against it.

---

12 *Weaver v Commercial Process Co Ltd* (1947) 63 TLR 466.

13 *The Miraflores and The Abadesa* [1967] AC 826 at 845 (per LORD PEARCE), HL: *Brown v Thompson* [1968] 2 All ER 708 at 709 (per WINN LJ) CA; *Cavanagh v London Passenger Transport Executive* (1956) Times, 23 October (DEVLIN J).

14 Eg *Jerred v Roddam Dent & Son Ltd* [1948] 2 All ER 104; *Dooley v Cammell Laird* [1951] 1 Lloyd's Rep 271.

15 Suppose that the plaintiff was injured by defective goods which he bought but he was also contributorily negligent. If contributory negligence is not a defence to actions for breach of contract the retailer will be liable in full to the plaintiff, but his claim for contribution against the negligent manufacturer will be reduced to the extent to which a claim by the plaintiff against the manufacturer would have been scaled down on account of the plaintiff's contributory negligence.

16 Section 2(3). The reduction to represent the plaintiff's degree of contributory negligence should be made separately against each tortfeasor's contribution; *Fitzgerald v Lane* [1987] QB 781, [1987] 2 All ER 455, CA.

17 *Adamson v Jarvis* (1827) 4 Bing 66. For an illustration of a statutory right of indemnity, see the Civil Aviation Act 1982, s 76(3).

18 [1957] AC 555, HL; distinguished in *Harvey v R G O'Dell Ltd* [1958] 2 QB 78 at 106, [1958] 1 All ER 657 at 666 (per MCNAIR J): 'I find it difficult to see on what grounds of justice and reason I should hold that by making his motor-cycle combination available for his employers' business on a particular occasion he should be held in law to have impliedly agreed to indemnify them if he committed a casual act of negligence'. And see *Vandyke v Fender* [1970] 2 QB 292 at 303 (per LORD DENNING MR), CA.

The House of Lords held that P was entitled to recover from D for breach of D's contractual obligation of care to his employer.[19] It follows that a master who has been made vicariously liable for the tort of his servant can claim an indemnity from the servant. It was clearly recognised before this decision that when the master himself was also at fault he would not obtain a complete indemnity but must suffer a reduction in respect of his own fault.[20] But these cases were based on section 6 of the Law Reform (Married Women and Tortfeasors) Act 1935.[1] What remains to be decided is whether and if so on what principles a reduction can be made in a claim by the master based on a breach by the servant of his contract of employment.[2]

---

19 The Report of the Inter-Departmental Committee (1959) set up by the Ministry of Labour and National Service, concluded that the decision raised no practical problem and that no legislative change was called for at present. Moreover, in *Morris v Ford Motor Co Ltd* [1973] QB 792, [1973] 2 All ER 1084, CA, it was held that the agreement in that case, being in an industrial setting so that subrogation against employees was unrealistic, contained an implied term excluding subrogation against them.
20 Eg *Jones v Manchester Corporation* [1952] 2 QB 852, [1952] 2 All ER 125, CA. Where the master's liability is purely vicarious, involving no personal fault, the master will obtain a 100 per cent contribution from the negligent servant, under the Act of 1978, as in *Harvey v R G O'Dell Ltd*, p 532 ante.
 1 *Lister v Romford Ice and Cold Storage Co Ltd* [1957] AC 555, left open whether an indemnity under the Act could also have been given.
 2 Whether the Law Reform (Contributory Negligence) Act 1945 applies to a suit in contract is obviously pertinent. See ante at p 246–7.

Index

Possession—*contd*
conversion, in 37. *See also* CONVERSION
land, of, kinds of 68
Post Office
exemption from liability 394–395, 513–514
mails, loss of, action for 61
officials of, publication of postal article to
401
public authority, as 513
Premises
activities on, care in respect of 260, 266,
271–272
architect's liability 278
articles—
falling from, presumption of negligence
217
found on, right of owner to 40–41
builder, duty to occupier 276–277
building inspectors 116–117, 185–186, 278–
279
business purposes, for 269
carrier, liability of 267
children, duty to 259, 270–271
contractor, liability of 264, 276–277
creation of dangerous conditions on 260,
266, 277
dangerous—
adjoining highway, as public nuisance 273
failure to remedy 273–275
dangerous installation—
landlord, liability of 279–280
defective—
damage caused to trespasser 270–271,
272, 280
injury to visitor 261–264. *See also* LICENCE
liability of non-occupier 275–280
local authority, liability of 278–279
persons entering under contract 266–267
demolition of, leaving in unsafe condition
278n
duty of care 261–264
education authorities' liability 260
employee of independent contractor, rights
of 280
employer's responsibility for adequacy of
261, 266, 284–285, 286–287
entrant—
contract affecting rights of 267–269
contributory negligence of 263–264
duty of care to 261–264
equipment, careless installation 276
exclusion of liability for 267–270
fixed or movable structures 264–265
flats or offices—
liability for safe access 268
highway, liability to users of 273
invitees and licensees compared with other
entrants 258
knowledge of risk, by visitor 263
landlord—
defect, liability for 279–280
exclusion of liability to visitors 268
landowners 277–278

Premises—*contd*
latent defect in, creating nuisance 276, 333
local authorities, liability of 257, 278–279
negligence as to—
person on adjoining premises, liability to
273–275
user of highway, liability to 273
negligent omissions 260
non-occupier, liability of 275–280
nuisance created by independent contractor
330
occupier—
damage, liability for 257–264
definition, 257
intended harm, liability for 271
owner's liability in negligence 277–278
persons outside premises, liability to 273–
275
professional advisers, liability of 278
property damage to 265–266
relation between tortious and contractual
liability 266–267
repair, failure of landlord to 279–280
repairs to, damage to adjoining property
273–275
requisitioned house, local authority occupier of 257
right of way, exercise of 258–259
risks afforded protection 259–260
safety of, implied condition as to 266
several occupants, joint liability of 527
statutory duty arising from occupation 258
structures, fixed and movable 264–265
surveyor's liability 278
unlawful use of 261
vendor, liability for defect 276–277
visitor—
contract affecting rights of 267–269
contributory negligence of 263–264
duty of care to 261–264
meaning 258
warning of dangerous 262–263
window cleaner, liability to 262
Prerogative
powers of Crown under 96
Prescription. *See also* LIMITATION OF ACTIONS
nuisance, as defence to action in 335
public nuisance, in relation to 342
Prisoners
battery alleged by 22–23
changes in conditions of custody 29–30
medical treatment of 22–23, 84
Privacy
right to, whether protected 153, 476
Privilege
absolute—
barrister, of 408
consequential communications 410
court-martial, in 408
Crown, matters of public policy 407
defamation, as defence in 406–410
executive matters 407
judge 408–409